MW00812912

SAGE
vantage

Course tools done right. Built to support your teaching. Designed to ignite learning.

SAGE vantage is an intuitive digital platform that blends trusted SAGE content with auto-graded assignments, all carefully designed to ignite student engagement and drive critical thinking. With evidence-based instructional design at the core, **SAGE vantage** creates more time for engaged learning and empowered teaching, keeping the classroom where it belongs—in your hands.

- **3-STEP COURSE SETUP** is so fast, you can complete it in minutes!

- Control over assignments, content selection, due dates, and grading **EMPOWERS** you to **TEACH YOUR WAY**.

- Dynamic content featuring applied-learning multimedia tools with built-in assessments, including video, knowledge checks, and chapter tests, helps **BUILD STUDENT CONFIDENCE**.

- eReading experience makes it easy to learn by presenting content in **EASY-TO-DIGEST** segments featuring note-taking, highlighting, definition look-up, and more.

- Quality content authored by the **EXPERTS YOU TRUST**.

Create   Watch   Log in   Join

⑤SAGE vantage™
engage. learn. soar.

sagepub.com/vantage

60,000 followers | 100,3...   Comments ∨   Follow

The
Hallmark
Features

Management Today: Best Practices for the Modern Workplace cuts through the noise by introducing students to the most effective evidence-based management theories, models, and strategies in a conversational writing style.

- A chapter on **MAKING DECISIONS AND USING ANALYTICS** explores how understanding data and developing analytical skills help managers make better decisions.

- **EXPERIENTIAL ACTIVITIES** and **SELF-ASSESSMENTS** provide hands-on learning opportunities for students as they apply chapter concepts.

- **CURRENT CASE STUDIES**, such as on Facebook/Cambridge Analytica and the college admissions scandal, engage students with topics they are familiar with and want to learn more about.

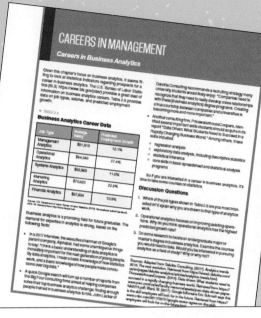

SAGE Publishing:
Our Story

At SAGE, we mean business. We believe in creating evidence-based, cutting-edge content that helps you prepare your students to succeed in today's ever-changing business world. We strive to provide you with the tools you need to develop the next generation of leaders, managers, and entrepreneurs.

- We invest in the right AUTHORS who distill research findings and industry ideas into practical applications.

- We keep our prices AFFORDABLE and provide multiple FORMAT OPTIONS for students.

- We remain permanently independent and fiercely committed to QUALITY CONTENT and INNOVATIVE RESOURCES.

Management Today

To T. K., for keeping it real.

—Terri

To the Gower family—who puts the fun into dysfunctional.
Dad, you would have been SO proud. Miss you every day.

—Kim

Sara Miller McCune founded SAGE Publishing in 1965 to support the dissemination of usable knowledge and educate a global community. SAGE publishes more than 1000 journals and over 800 new books each year, spanning a wide range of subject areas. Our growing selection of library products includes archives, data, case studies and video. SAGE remains majority owned by our founder and after her lifetime will become owned by a charitable trust that secures the company's continued independence.

Los Angeles | London | New Delhi | Singapore | Washington DC | Melbourne

Management Today

Best Practices for the Modern Workplace

Terri A. Scandura

University of Miami

Kim Gower

University of Mary Washington

Los Angeles | London | New Delhi
Singapore | Washington DC | Melbourne

FOR INFORMATION:

SAGE Publications, Inc.
2455 Teller Road
Thousand Oaks, California 91320
E-mail: order@sagepub.com

SAGE Publications Ltd.
1 Oliver's Yard
55 City Road
London, EC1Y 1SP
United Kingdom

SAGE Publications India Pvt. Ltd.
B 1/I 1 Mohan Cooperative Industrial Area
Mathura Road, New Delhi 110 044
India

SAGE Publications Asia-Pacific Pte. Ltd.
18 Cross Street #10-10/11/12
China Square Central
Singapore 048423

Printed in Canada

Library of Congress Cataloging-in-Publication Data

Names: Scandura, Terri A., author. | Gower, Kimberly S., author.

Title: Management today : best practices for the modern workplace / Terri Anne Scandura, University of Miami, Kimberly S. Gower, University of Mary Washington.

Description: First edition. | Los Angeles : SAGE, [2021] | Includes bibliographical references.

Identifiers: LCCN 2019030608 | ISBN 9781506385877 (paperback ; alk. paper) | ISBN 9781506385860 (epub) | ISBN 9781506385884 (epub) | ISBN 9781506385891 (ebook)

Subjects: LCSH: Management. | Executive ability.

Classification: LCC HD31.2 .S33 2021 | DDC 658—dc23

LC record available at https://lccn.loc.gov/2019030608

Acquisitions Editor: Maggie Stanley

Content Development Editor: Lauren Holmes

Editorial Assistant: Janeane Calderon

Typesetter: Hurix Digital

Proofreader: Alison Syring

Indexer: Sheila Hill

Cover Designer: Rose Storey

Marketing Manager: Sarah Panella

BRIEF CONTENTS

©fizkes/Shutterstock

DETAILED CONTENTS

©iStockphoto.com/Laurence Dutton

PART II: PLANNING

©iStockphoto.com/seb_ra

©iStockphoto.com/Jirapong Manustrong

PART III: ORGANIZING

©iStockphoto.com/pixelfit

©iStockphoto.com/Warchi

©iStockphoto.com/archideaphoto

PART IV: LEADING

©iStockphoto.com/Eoneren

PART V: CONTROLLING

©iStockphoto.com/anyaberkut

PREFACE

Management Today: Best Practices for the Modern Workplace is written to aid students in their learning and understanding of modern management. Rather than present a history of management, we decided to focus on the most effective management theories, models, and strategies students need to be successful when entering the workforce. We use contemporary business stories to help students apply what they have learned and see what job opportunities are available in the global economy. To keep up with the fast-paced, ever-evolving workplace, we wrote a book that will maintain student engagement through reflection questions, self-assessments, and experiential learning.

Between us, we have over 45 years of experience teaching management, leadership, ethics, strategy, organizational behavior, negotiation, and an array of business topics, and we have practical experience as consultants within and outside our universities. We have both worked with Fortune 500 organizations and small businesses going through organizational change as technology and the globalization of business caught many leaders and managers off guard. In addition, we both have an entrepreneurial side and have owned a series of businesses. This background helps prepare you for some of the anecdotes you read in the text, where we prove that truth is often stranger than fiction.

As you and your students read this book, we hope you agree that we achieved our goal: to write a modern textbook that you and your students actually enjoy reading and that provides information in every chapter that is tied to immediate application, professionally and personally. We worked hard to engage students with critical thinking questions throughout each chapter. The end of each chapter includes exercises and self-assessments that we use regularly in our classrooms, because our students say they enjoy exercises that "matter" and they love self-assessments because they understand the importance of knowing more about themselves from an objective perspective. We have found that the lessons learned through such experiential learning stay with students far longer than memorization of theories.

Target Audiences

This book is a great anthology of modern management, suitable for undergraduate students. Our goal was to write a book that would be appropriate for both business and nonbusiness majors. The examples and cases we use come from a variety of organizational settings and include both large corporations and small businesses. You will also find them helpful, as we already have, when you are leading seminars and consulting projects in management development, leadership development, organizational change, financial controls, strategic plan development, management control, and so much more.

Approach

As we considered ways to make this book stand out in the crowd of management books, we decided the top priority was to write it using much of the same language we use in class and to eliminate most of the timeline and historical content that other textbooks use so that the text could focus on exercises and critical thinking questions that support the learning objectives. The result is a textbook that addresses trends that managers of today and tomorrow will face. To that end, you and your students should find tremendous value in how we did things differently, such as:

- Relating real stories from our experiences and our students' experiences in management;
- Writing in a conversational tone to engage the reader;
- Providing modern stories of organizations, both good and bad;
- Weaving ethics through all parts of management: planning, leading, organizing, and controlling;
- Supporting the concepts with well-respected and new research studies that often complement each other in the modern management world;
- Focusing on the practical application of all things management, the right way and right now; and
- Supplying students with an array of critical thinking and self-assessment tools for their personal and professional knowledge and growth.

Evidence-Based Management

We include a significant amount of research to support the materials in the book, both to add relevance to concepts and to provide you with avenues for further exploration of specific topics that are of interest to your students. An evidence-based management approach is used throughout this book.

Hundreds of references to classic and current management research are used in this textbook to build a new way of looking at the research as the foundation for management development. The coverage of research is comprehensive, with a focus on the most important topics managers need to become effective leaders. This textbook offers a research-based approach that translates theory to practice, focusing on the contemporary approaches rather than the historical/classical approaches. Most students are less interested in historical development of theory and more interested in theories they can apply to be more effective managers.

Features

Chapter Learning Objectives

Each chapter begins with learning objectives that are tied to major sections of each chapter. These learning objectives are reinforced at the beginning of each section and summarized in the "managerial implications" section at the end of each chapter. These implications are the key takeaway points from each chapter.

Chapter-Opening Vignettes

To introduce each topic, each chapter presents an opening story to engage students. These stories highlight current trends such as the use of artificial intelligence for recruitment and how Amazon's Alexa is now learning to speak different languages as the product expands internationally.

Fact or Fiction?

Students are fascinated with management stories that are counterintuitive. We mentioned earlier that we used stories from our experience and stories our students have shared with us, and we have also worked hard to include the most up-to-date concepts and research available.

As part of that, the more we wrote, the more we understood how some of these things sounded like they could not be real—people would never behave this way when leading others or make decisions that were visibly wrong. Of course, they do!

You will find Fact or Fiction? features throughout the book, which were selected whenever we came across a story that just did not seem like it could be factual. These features include discussion questions that can be assigned prior to class or used to spark discussion on these stranger-than-fiction stories. Examples of the Fact or Fiction? features are Zappos's attempt to get rid of human managers (Chapter 4, "Organizational Culture and Change") and whether or not there are benefits to excessive video game playing (Chapter 10, "Motivation").

Careers in Management

Regardless of their college major, many students will become managers in organizations of all sizes. Another feature found in each chapter is a focus on management careers related to the content of the chapter. For examples, a discussion of careers in business analytics is included in Chapter 2 ("Making Decisions and Using Analytics"). Another example is a human resources specialist, ad discussed in Chapter 8 ("Human Resource Systems"). These features include discussion questions, which encourage students to conduct additional research on management careers and reflect on whether they would like to pursue the career option.

Critical Thinking Questions

Regardless of how you teach, having good critical thinking questions at your fingertips makes your job easier and keeps students' attention. To help with this, you will find several critical thinking question sections in each chapter. These can be assigned prior to class or used to have students reflect on the material and apply critical thinking skills to what they have read. For example, in Chapter 1, students are asked to reflect on the management process of planning, organizing, leading, and controlling: "Which of the four parts of the management process do you think is the most important? Why? Can you think of other processes that are part of management?" Rather than parroting back what they have read, these critical thinking questions ask students to evaluate the material and extend it.

Chapter Toolkits

In keeping with critical thinking and engagement, you will also find exercises at the end of the chapter that include great discussion questions that should keep you and your students interested in the topics at hand. The chapter toolkits include experiential learning activities, short case studies, and self-assessments.

The exercises themselves are ones we use in class regularly and ones we find keep students thinking. Some of them are modern scenarios of what is going on in the world of management, and others are things we actually developed for use and found to be huge hits with our students. For example, Chapter 11 ("Managing Teams") has a toolkit activity in which students develop a team charter. Another example is the global mindset self-assessment in Chapter 13 ("Managing in a Global Environment"). These exercises support and extend the material covered in the chapter and encourage students to apply what they have learned.

DIGITAL RESOURCES

A Complete Teaching & Learning Package

Engage, Learn, Soar with **SAGE vantage**, an intuitive digital platform that delivers *Management Today: Best Practices for the Modern Workplace* textbook content in a learning experience carefully designed to ignite student engagement and drive critical thinking. With evidence-based instructional design at the core, SAGE vantage creates more time for engaged learning and empowered teaching, keeping the classroom where it belongs—in your hands.

Easy-to-access across mobile, desktop, and tablet devices, SAGE vantage enables students to engage with the material you choose, learn by applying knowledge, and soar with confidence by performing better in your course.

Highlights Include:

- **eReading Experience.** Makes it easy for students to study wherever they are—students can take notes, highlight content, look up definitions, and more!
- **Pedagogical Scaffolding.** Builds on core concepts, moving students from basic understanding to mastery.
- **Confidence Builder.** Offers frequent knowledge checks, applied-learning multimedia tools, and chapter tests with focused feedback to assure students know key concepts.
- **Time-Saving Flexibility.** Feeds auto-graded assignments to your gradebook, with real-time insight into student and class performance.
- **Quality Content.** Written by expert authors and teachers, content is not sacrificed for technical features.
- **Honest Value.** Affordable access to easy-to-use, quality learning tools that students will appreciate.

Favorite SAGE Vantage Features:

- **3-step course setup** is so fast you can complete it in minutes!
- **Control over assignments,** content selection, due dates, and grading empowers you to teach your way.
- **Quality content** is authored by the experts you trust.
- **eReading experience** makes it easy to learn and study by presenting content in easy-to-digest segments featuring note-taking, highlighting, definition look-up, and more.
- **LMS integration provides single sign-on** with streamlined grading capabilities and course management tools.
- **Auto-graded assignments** include:
  - Formative **knowledge checks** for each major section of the text that quickly reinforce what students have read and ensure they stay on track;
  - Dynamic, hands-on **multimedia activities** that tie real world examples and motivate students to read, prepare for class;
  - Summative **chapter tests** that reinforce important themes; and
- **Helpful hints and feedback** (provided with all assignments) that offer context and explain why an answer is correct or incorrect, allowing students to study more effectively.
- **Compelling polling questions** bring concepts to life and drive meaningful comprehension and classroom discussion.
- **Short-answer questions** provide application and reflection opportunities connected to key concepts.
- **Instructor reports** track student activity and provide analytics so you can adapt instruction as needed.
- **A student dashboard** offers easy access to grades, so students know exactly where they stand in your course and where they might improve.
- **Honest value** gives students access to quality content and learning tools at a price they will appreciate.

⑤SAGE coursepacks

SAGE Coursepacks for Instructors

The **SAGE coursepack** for *Management Today: Best Practices for the Modern Workplace* makes it easy to import our quality instructor materials and student resources into your school's learning management system (LMS), such as Blackboard, Canvas, Brightspace by D2L, or Moodle. Intuitive and simple to use, **SAGE coursepack** allows you to integrate only the content you need, with minimal effort, and requires no access code. Don't use an LMS platform? You can still access many of the online resources for *Management Today: Best Practices for the Modern Workplace Edition* via the **SAGE edge** site.

Available SAGE content through the coursepack includes:

- Pedagogically robust **assessment tools** that foster review, practice, and critical thinking and offer a more complete way to measure student engagement, including:
  - Diagnostic **coursepack chapter quizzes** that identify opportunities for improvement, track student progress, and ensure mastery of key learning objectives.
  - **Test banks** built on Bloom's taxonomy that provide a diverse range of test items.
  - **Activity and quiz options** that allow you to choose only the assignments and tests you want.
- Editable, chapter-specific **PowerPoint®** slides that offer flexibility when creating multimedia lectures so you don't have to start from scratch but can customize to your exact needs.
- **Instructions** are provided on how to use and integrate the comprehensive assessments and resources.

⑤SAGE edge™

SAGE edge is a robust online environment featuring an impressive array of tools and resources for review, study, and further exploration, keeping both instructors and students on the cutting edge of teaching and learning. SAGE edge content is open access and available on demand. Learning and teaching has never been easier!

SAGE edge for Students at **https://edge.sagepub.com/scanduragower** provides a personalized approach to help students accomplish their coursework goals in an easy-to-use learning environment.

- **Learning objectives** reinforce the most important material.
- Mobile-friendly **eFlashcards** strengthen understanding of key terms and concepts, and make it easy to maximize your study time, anywhere, anytime.
- Mobile-friendly practice **quizzes** allow you to assess how much you've learned and where you need to focus your attention.

SAGE edge for Instructors at **https://edge.sagepub.com/scanduragower** supports teaching by making it easy to integrate quality content and create a rich learning environment for students.

- The **test bank**, built on Bloom's taxonomy (with Bloom's cognitive domain and difficulty level noted for each question), is created specifically for this text.

- **Sample course syllabi** provide suggested models for structuring your course.
- Editable, chapter-specific **PowerPoint® slides** offer complete flexibility for creating a multimedia presentation for the course, so you don't have to start from scratch but can customize to your exact needs.
- **Lecture notes** features chapter summaries and outlines, providing an essential reference and teaching tool for lectures.
- A set of all the **graphics from the text**, including all the maps, tables, and figures in PowerPoint® formats, are provided for class presentations.
- **Sample answers to questions in the text** help launch classroom interaction and reinforce important content.
- **Case notes** designed to help instructors expand questions to students or initiate class discussion include a brief summary of each case and sample answers to case questions.
- **Class activities and exercises** provide lively and stimulating ideas for use in and out of class reinforce active learning. The activities apply to individual or group projects.

$SAGE premium video

SAGE Premium Video

Management Today offers premium video, available exclusively in the **SAGE vantage** digital option, produced and curated specifically for this text to boost comprehension and bolster analysis.

SAGE Self-Assessments

Management Today features interactive Leadership Self-Assessments, available exclusively in the **SAGE vantage** digital option, to help students strengthen their leadership abilities by providing them with personalized feedback based on their responses to each questionnaire.

ACKNOWLEDGMENTS

When I, Kim, first began in my PhD program as an older scholar, I was told that when it was time to find a job, I should not emphasize all the teaching that I did or how much I loved it. By the time I went on the job market, it was a good thing to love to teach and my experience working in industry as a consultant and business owner became bonuses as well.

I am humbled and thrilled to work on any project with Terri Scandura and grateful to Maggie Stanley and Lauren Holmes at SAGE for remembering my name! Because of that, I had the opportunity to write the test bank for Terri's second edition of *Essentials of Organizational Behavior* and review the first few chapters of this book. Through that experience, I received a phone call from Terri one Saturday asking me to work on the book with her. Talk about the best weekend ever!

Any successes I have in the academic world come from the amazing mentors and friends who supported me in the doctoral program at Virginia Commonwealth University. Margaret Williams, Anson Seers, and Jeff Pollack introduced me to good people, like Terri, and supported me in ways I could never imagine I would need. You will always be my superheroes.

My students have always inspired me, and I was thrilled that Terri and SAGE allowed me to write a management book the way I teach a management class. When I told my students what I was working on, they were my biggest advocates and I think they will enjoy a book written for them, including some of their anecdotes!

I give special thanks to my mom and dad who had to listen to me incessantly talk about the book and working with Terri Scandura, and who took good care of me and my menagerie when I was working away. Also, Marcy, Lauren, and Dylan, thank you for food, beverage, and talk breaks, but only when I had time for them!

To the members of the Academy of Management–Management Education and Development Division, thank you for being the greatest colleagues and talented researchers and professors. I have learned so much from you that has impacted my teaching and students, and I continue to learn. Pat Hedberg, Barb Ritter, Nick Rhew, and Lucy Arendt, you are the best listeners and always there for me regardless of my question or predicament. I value your advice and friendship.

I also thank Ken Machande for hiring me at University of Mary Washington! I love it, and the College of Business is an outstanding place to find awesome students and supportive colleagues. I feel at home there, and you are a big reason why.

Finally, thanks Bennie Clark Allen at SAGE for your positive championing through the copy editing and printing process and for being an empathetic supporter when life happened!

Terri and I are grateful to the reviewers of this textbook who applied their own critical perspectives to the chapters. They made this textbook better in every way and we learned from their insightful comments and suggestions for additional research evidence to include. Thanks to the following reviewers for their participation in all stages of this book's development:

Angela M. Balog, Saint Francis University

S. Gayle Baugh, University of West Florida

Chip Baumgardner, Pennsylvania College of Technology

William Belcher, Troy University

Denie Burks, Georgia Highlands College

Travis Dalton, Columbia College

Dr. Robin R. Davis, Claflin University

Dr. Kellie Emrich, Cuyahoga Community College

Carla C. Flores, Ball State University

Justin Gandy, Dallas Baptist University

Susanne Hartl, Nyack College

Emmanuel Hernandez-Agosto, DBA, Gulf Coast State College

George Kelley, Erie Community College-City Campus

Dr. Debra D. Kuhl, EdD, Pensacola State College

Dr. Monica Law, Marywood University

Kayvan Miri Lavassani, PhD, Associate Professor, North Carolina
   Central University, School of Business

Lee W. Lee, Central Connecticut State University

Gil Logan, PhD, University of Hawai'i Maui College

M. Milena Loubeau, Miami Dade College

Martin Luytjes, Florida International University

Jeffrey B. Paul, PhD, Oral Roberts University

Beth Polin, Eastern Kentucky University

Scott A. Quatro, Covenant College

Jody L. Rebek, Lukenda School of Business, Lake Superior State University

Kerry Rempel, Okanagan College

Dr. Preston B. Rich, Richland College

Prof. Linda L. Ridley, City University of New York Hostos Community College

John Russo, Eastern Florida State College

Jenny Scott, Lewis-Clark State College

Dr. Andrea Smith-Hunter, Siena College

Mark S. Teachout, University of the Incarnate Word

Valerie Wallingford, PhD, Bemidji State University

Frankie J. Weinberg, PhD, Loyola University New Orleans

Ethlyn A. Williams, Florida Atlantic University

Juanita M. Woods, Augusta University

Qian Xiao, Eastern Kentucky University

Violet Zlatar-Christopher, California State University at Northridge,
   Antelope Valley College

ABOUT THE AUTHORS

Terri A. Scandura is currently the Warren C. Johnson Chaired Professor of Management in the Miami Business School at the University of Miami. From 2007 to 2012, she served as Dean of the Graduate School of the University of Miami. Her fields of interest include leadership, mentorship, and applied research methods. She has been a visiting scholar in Japan, Australia, Hong Kong, China, and the United Arab Emirates.

Dr. Scandura has authored or coauthored over 200 presentations, articles, and book chapters. Her research has been published in the *Academy of Management Journal*, the *Journal of Applied Psychology*, the *Journal of International Business Studies*, the *Journal of Vocational Behavior*, the *Journal of Organizational Behavior*, *Educational and Psychological Measurement*, *Industrial Relations*, *Research in Organizational Behavior*, *Research in Personnel and Human Resource Management*, and others. Her book, *Essentials of Organizational Behavior: An Evidence-Based Approach* (2nd edition), is published by SAGE.

She has presented Executive Education programs on Leadership, Mentoring, Leading Change, and High-Performance Teams to numerous organizations such as VISA International, Royal Caribbean Cruise Lines, Bacardi, Hewlett-Packard, and Baptist Health Systems.

Dr. Scandura is a Fellow of the American Psychological Association, the Society for Industrial and Organizational Psychology, and the Southern Management Association. She is a member of the invitation-only Society of Organizational Behavior (SOB) and the Academy of Management. She received the Distinguished Career Award from the Research Methods Division of the Academy of Management and the Jerry (J.G.) Hunt Sustained Service Award from the Southern Management Association. She is a past associate editor for *Group & Organization Management*, the *Journal of International Business Studies*, the *Journal of Management*, and *Organizational Research Methods*. She currently serves on editorial boards for major journals.

Kim Gower is an Assistant Professor of Management in the College of Business at the University of Mary Washington (UMW) in Fredericksburg, Virginia. She earned her PhD from Virginia Commonwealth University (VCU) in 2012, after spending 25 years in consulting and sales and as a business owner. Her concentration is leadership and organizational behavior, with a minor in entrepreneurship, and her dissertation research incorporated the use and misuse of 360 feedback in leadership assessment.

Dr. Gower taught many different business classes at VCU, Virginia State University, and the University of Richmond Jepson School of Leadership Studies before coming to UMW. There, she teaches Management, Leadership and Organizational Behavior, Leadership and Social Justice, and Leadership Theory and Application in the undergraduate and MBA programs. She enjoys engaging in service activities at the university to help promote programs for students and learning, and instilling a love for service in her students as they perform thousands of hours of community engagement each year.

She is the 2019–2020 Chair of the Management Education and Development (MED) Division of the Academy of Management. The MED membership consists of nearly 1,800 top-quality researchers and educators. Dr. Gower has extensive experience consulting with very large organizations and entrepreneurs in a full range of areas, including customer service, conflict management, organizational change, leadership development, team development, and process improvement, particularly in the rapidly changing global landscape.

In her spare time, Dr. Gower backpacks and is an active community advocate. She enjoys volunteering for local organizations in Richmond, Virginia (particularly Richmond Animal Care and Control), and excessively doting on her five rescue kids, Emma, Lilie, Buster, Teddy, and Izzy.

INTRODUCTION

Chapter 1
Becoming a Manager

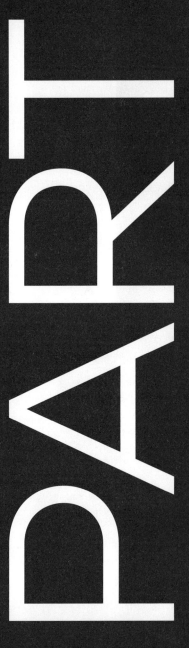

CHAPTER 1

BECOMING A MANAGER

After studying this chapter, you should be able to do the following:

1.1 Define the concept of management.

1.2 Explain the management process: planning, organizing, leading, and controlling.

1.3 Trace the development of management theory, noting key milestones for each decade.

1.4 Demonstrate understanding of managerial roles by providing examples.

1.5 Explain the three types of managerial behaviors.

1.6 Define the three skills managers need to be successful today.

Get the edge on your studies at **edge.sagepub.com/ scanduragower**

- Take the chapter quiz
- Review key terms with eFlashcards
- Explore multimedia resources, SAGE readings, and more!

What Managers Do

The work managers do may be a bit unclear to you at this point. A manager's job contains a wide variety of activities. Darko Butina, chief growth officer at the software company Netcetera, lists 10 important things managers do. He also offers best practices on how to execute them. Here is the list:

1. **Know your customers.** A manager must keep an eye toward the needs of their customers to meet organizational goals. Through knowledge of customer preferences, the manager changes products and services to better meet their needs, and this makes the organization successful.

   Best Practice 1: A manager must gain feedback from customers often. It is important to ask them about their customer experience and listen to their answers carefully. In other words, managers should resist the temptation to try to convince customers of the superiority of their organization's products or services; managers should simply listen. Managers should determine who their customers are and why they use the organization's products or services, then create an overview of customer demographics and preferences after listening to the customer experience.

2. **Know your products and services.** To be effective leaders, managers need to know what their organization does. This may be relatively simple for a small business with only one or two products or services. For a large conglomerate organization, however, there may be hundreds of products or services offered.

   Best Practice 2: A manager should purchase and use the services and products of their organization and play the role of a customer. By experiencing the entire process that customers go through, the manager will learn how customers see the organization and how they are treated by employees.

3. **Know your company and its processes.** Managers must be familiar with the organizational structure and procedures for making improvements. Most organizations have mission statements as well as policies-and-procedures manuals that the manager must review.

   Best Practice 3: A manager should read all the written policies and procedures of the organization—including its structure and operating procedures. Next, a manager should talk to employees and get to know how the policies and procedures are viewed and implemented (or not implemented). Some policies become outdated and are no longer useful. By talking to employees, a manager is now able to create successful changes to existing policies, because they understand them well enough to learn where improvements can be made.

4. **Prepare your business plan.** A manager needs to establish the organization's position at the current time as a starting point, then explain where the organization should be in the future (one month to three years). A manager must be able to describe how the organization will reach these business goals. This keeps employees' focus on the big picture and on actions that move the organization forward toward success.

   Best Practice 4: A manager should try not to use the term *business plan* with employees, since they do not require a long, complicated report that must be read and memorized. A manager should be able to explain where the organization is currently, where it is going in the future, and how the employees can help it get there. If the manager knows the organization's customers (Best Practice 1) and products and services (Best Practice 2), then putting together the business plan without the help of employees should be straightforward.

5. **Monitor and control.** Managers need to know where employees and the organization are in terms of meeting goals at all times. When a manager knows this, they can make the best decisions.

   Best Practice 5: Managers should be sure that checks and balances in the organization are in place to generate timely and relevant information. Managers should also be clear about the types of reports they need to read.

   For example, a manager may request marketing research reports on how well customers like products and services. Another example is a report on proposed budgets that includes actual costs. Also, the manager should tell the analysts how often they need each report. Be careful not to misuse analysts' time; focus on the reports you need. And don't fall prey to TMI ("too much information"), which will make it more difficult to see the big picture.

6. **Decide and act.** A manager's job is to make decisions. The higher a manager rises in the hierarchy of the organization, the more decisions they must make.

   Best Practice 6: Managers should not procrastinate and remain undecided for too long. Sometimes the decision to "do nothing" and stay in place is better than risking a bad decision. Decisions can always be reviewed again in the future. The decision to change or not change is a large one, and must be made carefully, without taking unnecessary chances.

7. **Inform.** Managers must always explain the reasons for their decisions to employees. Employees respond positively when they are "in the know" about organizational changes. When employees understand the reasons for change, they are more willing to support them.

   Best Practice 7: Managers should share information with employees. Employees need to know how the organization is performing, its standing in the industry, and changes that are going to happen. When employees know where they stand, they will likely respond with increased motivation and ideas on how to make improvements.

8. **Manage people.** A manager should keep in mind that organizations are created because a single person cannot produce a product or service by themselves. People must work together to achieve the organization's goals. The role of a manager is to coordinate the efforts of individuals and teams to ensure organizational success.

   Best Practice 8: A manager should be sure decisions are consistent and transparent and employees are informed. When a manager does this, employees are willing to follow the manager's leadership.

9. **Manage the relationship with the organization's owners/shareholders.** A manager must also look upward to address the owners (in a small business) or shareholders (in a corporation). Managers are often so involved with day-to-day operations that they forget that owners/shareholders have expectations, not only in terms of profit but also in terms of social responsibility. A manager must line up their goals with those of the owners of the company; the manager's plans must help the owners meet their goals.

   Best Practice 9: A manager should remember that owners are not the enemy. After all, they are the ones who will reward the manager for success. They are human beings too, and a manager should take the time to build positive relationships with them. This becomes more and more important as a manager is promoted to higher ranks in the organization.

10. **Keep focus.** Managers can't become overwhelmed with solving daily operations problems. They must keep their focus on the future and where they are taking the organization. This is a key to success.

    Best Practice 10: A manager should read their business plan every month. This will make it possible to adjust priorities in a timely way and maintain the focus on successful execution in the short term to ensure long-term success.

According to Butina, if managers execute these best practices, they are on their way to a successful career.

Source: Adapted from Butina, D. (2014). What managers do: 10 key activities you need to master as a manager. Retrieved from https://www.linkedin.com/pulse/20140428100850-921823-what-managers-do-10-key-activities-you-need-to-master-as-manager/.

As the list above suggests, the tasks of a manager are varied and challenging. This list is a great start to understanding what managers do, and this book will outline more best practices in every chapter. The goal of this book is to help you become an effective manager.

After reading this book, your approach to managing others will be grounded in the most important and current research conducted on organizations.

First, let's look at definitions of management and how the concept has evolved over time.

▼ FIGURE 1.0

Textbook Organization

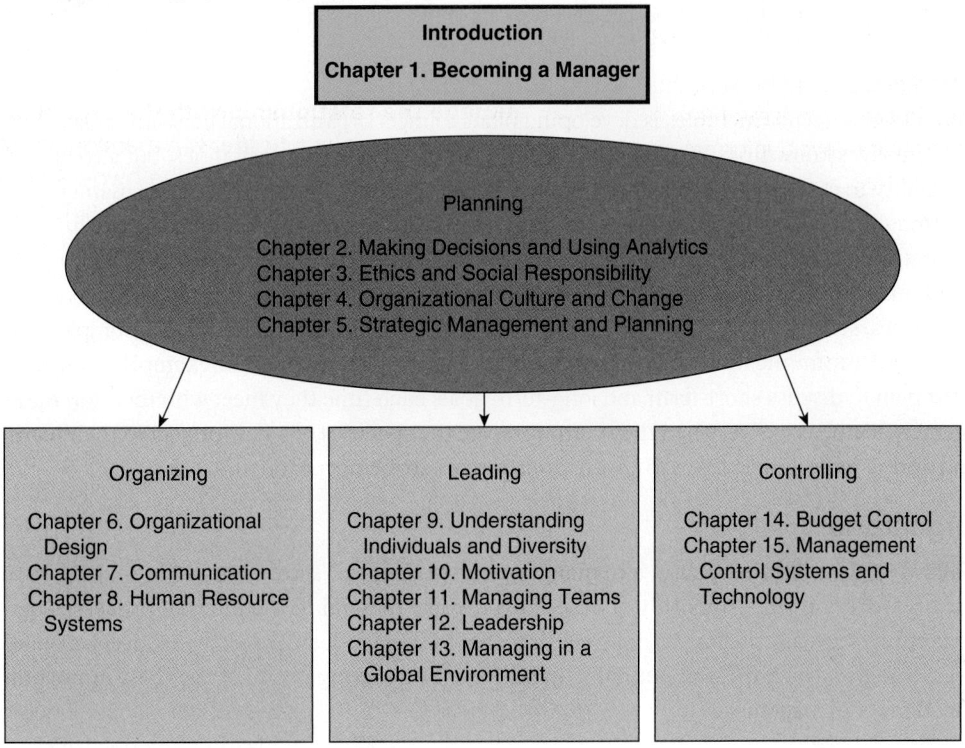

```
            ┌─────────────────────────────────┐
            │           Introduction          │
            │   Chapter 1. Becoming a Manager  │
            └─────────────────────────────────┘

                        Planning

            Chapter 2. Making Decisions and Using Analytics
            Chapter 3. Ethics and Social Responsibility
            Chapter 4. Organizational Culture and Change
            Chapter 5. Strategic Management and Planning
```

Organizing	Leading	Controlling
Chapter 6. Organizational Design Chapter 7. Communication Chapter 8. Human Resource Systems	Chapter 9. Understanding Individuals and Diversity Chapter 10. Motivation Chapter 11. Managing Teams Chapter 12. Leadership Chapter 13. Managing in a Global Environment	Chapter 14. Budget Control Chapter 15. Management Control Systems and Technology

What Is Management?

Learning Objective 1.1: Define the concept of management.

Management is defined as efficiently and effectively coordinating the planning, leading, organizing, and controlling of an organization department or function so that the outcome(s) contribute to meeting organizational goals and objectives. **Efficiency** can be thought of as "doing things right" with respect to maximum utilization of the organization's resources to attain its mission. To be efficient means to use resources (e.g., people, money, raw materials) wisely and cost-effectively. **Effectiveness** has to do with "doing the right things." To be effective means to achieve results, to make the right decisions, and to successfully carry them out so they achieve the organization's goals. In other words, the organization must have a **mission**, or overall goal, that fits its competitive environment and resources. For example, an organization could produce an obsolete product that no one wants to buy very efficiently and at low cost. However, this is not effective, because there is no longer a market for the product. Effectiveness is the concern of the top management team, and efficiency is typically the responsibility of operating managers on the front line.

The management process of planning, organizing, leading, and controlling is described next.

The Management Process

Originally identified by Henri Fayol as a five-part process comprising planning, organizing, command, coordination, and control,[1] management is now commonly viewed as encompassing four essential management functions: planning, organizing, leading, and controlling (*command* and *coordination* have been combined into *leading*). This process is summarized in Figure 1.1. Each of these aspects of the management process is described in the following sections. This textbook is organized around these four functions of management.

Planning

One of a manager's chief roles is developing plans to meet organizational goals and objectives. This involves knowing how to allocate resources and delegate responsibilities, but also having the ability to set realistic goals and timelines for completion. Planning requires managers to continually check on their team's progress and make adjustments when necessary while still maintaining a sense of the big picture (mission) of the organization's strategy. The **planning** function consists of working to determine which responsibilities must be given to which employees, setting priority levels for certain tasks, and creating timelines for task completion.[2] However, communication with others also plays an important role. For example, managers must plan to discuss short-term and long-term goals each time they meet with their top management team, as well as when they communicate the specifics of a new project to their team, and during periodic check-ins to ensure project goals are being met on time.

Organizing

Following the planning phase, a manager's **organizing** skills are essential in making sure the organization runs smoothly. These skills involve managing the internal processes and structures, such as assigning employees or teams to specific tasks and keeping everyone and everything on track throughout daily operations. Organizing is one of the most important functions of management.

▼ FIGURE 1.1

The Management Process

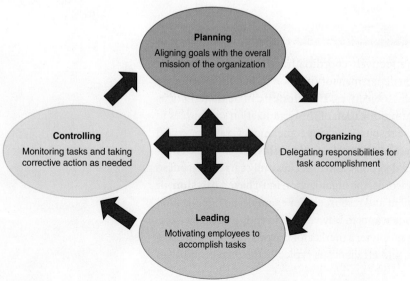

Source: Adapted from Fayol, H. (1948). Industrial and general administration. London, UK: Pitman. (Original work published 1916).

The organization function isn't just about making sure employees have what they need to accomplish their jobs. Managers also need to be able to reorganize in response to organizational change. This could come by slightly adjusting the timeline for a project or reallocating some tasks from one team to another, or it could mean significant reorganization in response to organizational change.

Leading

The **leading** process occurs when managers command their team, not only through daily tasks but also during periods of significant change. It involves projecting a strong sense of direction and leadership when setting goals. Managers must communicate to their followers about new processes, products, services, or policies. Leadership can manifest itself in a number of ways, from recognizing when employees need praise for good work and providing rewards to conflict resolution. Leading involves being fair and distributing praise and rewards equitably. While good leadership entails a focus on the big-picture mission and vision of the organization, it also includes providing one-on-one attention by supporting and encouraging each direct report.

Controlling

To ensure that the organization runs smoothly and that work is done optimally for the organization's success, managers must constantly monitor employee task performance, team performance, and operational process efficiency, assessing the quality of all. The **controlling** process relates to the efficiency part of management mentioned above. Quality control ensures that the goals of the organization are being met, and managers must take corrective action when they are not. Controlling involves comparing the team's work to standards and addressing any corrections that need to be made. The controlling function also includes monitoring the financial health of the organization through budgetary, management, and technical controls.

CRITICAL THINKING QUESTIONS

> Which of the four parts of the management process do you think is the most important? Why? Can you think of other processes that are part of management?

A Brief History of Management Theory

Learning Objective 1.3: Trace the development of management theory, noting key milestones for each decade.

Figure 1.2 shows a timeline indicating some of the big ideas that have radically changed management practice. While many other theories emerged during the time period shown, the figure highlights one key idea per decade to provide an idea of the shifts taking place in management thought. The timeline ends in the year 2010, because management historians need time to assess the influence of management theories on practice, a process which may take decades.

Early Management Theories

As shown in Figure 1.2, management theory began with an analytical approach known as **scientific management**. This approach was the study of how workers moved as they performed their work to improve productivity. In the 1880s, a mechanical engineer named Frederick Taylor began timing workers at the Midvale Steel company near Philadelphia, Pennsylvania, to assess their rate of output. Taylor became one of the first management consultants and focused on the efficiency of production. Taylor summed up his techniques in his 1914 book *The Principles of Scientific Management*,[3] which many management scholars consider to be the most influential management book of the 20th century.[4] During this period, managers were elevated in status, and the role of workers' individual responsibility was minimized. Other scientific management theorists followed and extended Taylor's work, including Frank and Lillian Gilbreth, who focused on time-and-motion studies of workers.

Management practices became known as "Taylorism," which continued to study how work could be designed to make production (particularly on assembly lines) more efficient.[5]

Mary Parker Follett was a key organizational theorist during the early development of management thought. She was educated at the University of Cambridge and Radcliffe, and her

▼ FIGURE 1.2

Milestones in Management Theory

1880	1932	1946	1954	1960	1978	1990	1995	2000	2010

Scientific Management	Hawthorne Studies	Organizational Development	Needs Hierarchy	Theory X and Y	Organizational Culture	Learning Organization	Ethics	Disruptive Change	Sustainability
Frederick Taylor	Elton Mayo	Kurt Lewin	Abraham Maslow	Douglas McGregor	Tom Peters	Peter Senge	Linda Treviño	Clayton Christensen	Tom Kuhlman & John Farrington

Sources: Adapted from A timeline of management and leadership. (2016). Retrieved from http://www.nwlink.com/~donclark/history_management/management.html; Kirby, J. (2010). The decade in management ideas. *Harvard Business Review*. Retrieved from https://hbr.org/2010/01/the-decade-in-management-ideas.

thesis was published in 1896. She later applied to Harvard but was denied admittance because she was a woman.[6] She was the first to write about integration across management functions in hierarchical organizations. This work later led to the development of matrix organizations, which you will learn about in Chapter 6. Instead of believing authority to be granted by bureaucracy, as advocated by the German theorist Max Weber, Follett considered authority to be based on expertise. In other words, she argued that a person can gain power in an organization by becoming an expert rather than being limited by their rank in the organization. You might notice this in places you work, or even in your student groups. Just because somebody has a title does not necessarily mean they are the "expert," or the person people go to for help

Mary Parker Follett, the mother of modern management.

and information. Follett is considered to be the "mother of modern management."[7] She promoted the idea of reciprocal relationships in understanding interactions between people in organizations. She believed in "integration," or noncoercive power-sharing, as her basis for the concept of "power with" rather than "power over."[8]

Following the work of early organization theorists such as Taylor and Follett, the human-relations movement[9] was ignited by studies conducted between 1927 and 1932. The human-relations approach led to a focus on the role of human behavior in organizations.

The Hawthorne studies were two studies conducted by Australian-born psychologist Elton Mayo at the Western Electric Company near Chicago.[10] Mayo spent most of his career at Harvard University and was interested in how to increase productivity in assembly lines. The first study was designed to examine the effects of lighting in the plants on worker productivity. Although quite simple by today's standards, the study produced some unexpected findings. Productivity increased rather than decreased even though the lights were being dimmed. Perplexed by this finding, the research team interviewed the workers and learned that the workers appreciated the attention of the research team and felt they were receiving special treatment. In another unexpected twist, productivity declined after the researchers left the plant. This has been called the **Hawthorne effect** and refers to positive responses in attitudes and performance by employees when researchers or other observers pay attention to them. Do you find that you perform better in class when the teacher pays attention to you or compliments you on a good answer?

The second Hawthorne study was designed to investigate a new incentive system. Once again, the results took the researchers by surprise. Instead of the incentive system increasing workers' production, social pressure from peers took over and had more impact on worker productivity than pay increases. Workers formed into small groups and set informal standards for production, requiring coworkers to reduce their production so pay was more equal among the group members.

Thus, the Hawthorne researchers concluded that the human element in organizations was more important than previously thought, and they learned that workers want attention. As a student in the 21st century, you might not be terribly impressed by these findings. Ironically, that understandable reaction can be viewed as evidence of the Hawthorne studies' impact on the working world. The importance of human factors in the workplace is now viewed as common sense, but this was not the case at the time of the studies. Employment as we know it today was in its relative infancy in 1924. In the centuries leading up to the Hawthorne studies, voluntary, organization-based employment competed with serfdom, slavery, indentured servitude, subsistence farming, and other labor systems that generally viewed workers in the way we now view machines. Even as these gave way to more humane employment arrangements, it took the Hawthorne studies to help society break its old habits.

The phrase "there is nothing as practical as a good theory" has been attributed to social psychologist Kurt Lewin. Lewin's work gave rise during the 1940s to the field of **organizational development (OD)**, in which theories from psychology are applied to the workplace to help managers solve problems. Lewin's work on **field theory** emerged as an important framework for the implementation of organizational change and remains in use today. Field theory examines the forces that are driving change and then compares them to the forces that are restraining change. For example, competition from another company for an organization's products might drive change. Customers may want new products that require an upgrade to factory equipment. This change will also reduce training time and maintenance costs. However, restraining forces may be the cost of overtime and employees' resistance to change due to fear of the new technology needed.

During the 1950s, an important idea was developed by Abraham Maslow known as the hierarchy of needs.[11] You will learn more about this theory of motivation in Chapter 10.

In the 1960s, as the field of management was developing, researchers began to examine the basic assumptions managers hold regarding their employees. This research resulted in two fundamental orientations managers may have toward their followers—Theory X and Theory Y. The next section provides an overview of this approach to understanding managers' underlying beliefs and what impact this has on their management style.

Theory X and Theory Y

Managers have a strong influence on employees. But some managers engage in behaviors that decrease employee performance. One of the reasons managers do this is that they hold subconscious assumptions regarding employees' willingness to work hard. An important theory on this topic emerged in the 1960s, suggesting that managers' assumptions regarding their followers' motivation affect the way they treat them. If managers assume followers are lazy and will perform poorly, they will treat them in ways that control their behavior and decrease creativity. In contrast, if managers assume followers are smart and motivated, they will allow them to participate in decisions and give them goals that stretch their talents. This theory describes two sets of leader behaviors related to these assumptions—Theory X and Theory Y.

One of the most influential books in management is *The Human Side of Enterprise* by Douglas McGregor.[12] This book is important because it presented the idea that leader behaviors are influenced by fundamental assumptions and beliefs about human nature. Most managers are not aware of their underlying assumptions; thus, their influence on behavior is pervasive, yet hard to detect. Have you ever entered a situation expecting certain behaviors from certain people, and did that influence how you behaved and treated those around you?

These assumptions are divided into pessimistic (Theory X) and optimistic (Theory Y) views of human nature. **Theory X** leaders assume that people are basically lazy, don't like to work, and avoid responsibility. Related manager behaviors include being directive, engaging in surveillance, and being coercive. In contrast, **Theory Y** leaders assume people are internally motivated, like to work, and will accept responsibility. Related manager behaviors include allowing discretion, inviting participation, and encouraging creativity on the job.

Although McGregor proposed Theory X and Y over 55 years ago, most quantitative research did not emerge until relatively recently. However, research findings on these managerial assumptions are interesting. For example, one study showed that Theory Y assumptions are more related to participative decision-making by leaders. In other words, if you believe your employees enjoy work and take responsibility, you will ask for their input in organizational decision-making.

Further, participative decision-making is actually perceived as a threat by Theory X managers because it reduces their power. Theory Y managers view participation differently and see it as a positive influence on their power and effectiveness.[13]

Another study of 50 military leaders and 150 of their followers found that the Theory Y management style was significantly and positively associated with subordinates' satisfaction with the leader, organizational commitment, and organizational citizenship behaviors. The Theory X management style had a significantly negative impact on subordinates' satisfaction with the leader, but no significant impact on commitment to the organization and organizational citizenship behaviors (that is, behaviors that employees engage in that go above and beyond their job descriptions).[14] The findings of this study in the military environment are interesting because they suggest that Theory Y relates to satisfaction but may not always relate to commitment and performance. The authors concluded that Theory X/Y assumptions provide unique insights into leadership behavior and outcomes.

In this textbook, you will be challenged to think critically about the theories and approaches presented. Theory X/Y is no exception. Over the years Theory X/Y has been criticized for being too simple and not considering the situation leaders and followers find themselves in.[15] For a long time, research was also hindered because good measures of Theory X/Y did not exist. However, Richard Kopelman and his associates have developed a measure of Theory X and Theory Y that shows promise for the valid assessment of these diverse management philosophies.[16] Their measure appears in the Toolkit at the end of this chapter (Self-Assessment 1.1), and you can learn about your own Theory X and Y assumptions by completing it. Despite its critics, McGregor's book *The Human Side of Enterprise* was voted the fourth most influential management book of the 20th century in a poll of top management scholars.[17] McGregor's theory continues to hold an important position in management theory due to the implication that it is important for leaders to understand their subconscious fundamental assumptions about how human beings relate to work.

CRITICAL THINKING QUESTIONS

> Give an example of how Theory X or Y assumptions influence how a manager treats an employee. Do you think most managers today are Theory X or Theory Y? Explain.

Behavioral Aspects of Management

The Hawthorne studies had a significant impact on the field of management and are considered the beginning of the application of psychology and social psychology to management problems. The 1970s saw continued growth of the human relations movement, and the field of organizational behavior emerged as a separate discipline in business schools. **Organizational behavior (OB)** is defined as the study of individuals and their behaviors at work. Behavioral aspects of management became an important focus of management research as OB scholars began to study employees' reactions to their work, such as job satisfaction. Many managers believed "a happy worker is a productive worker."

The field of organizational behavior is multilevel, drawing from applied psychology, cultural anthropology, communications studies, behavioral economics, and sociology. Some theories focus on the individual in the organization (e.g., in terms of diversity). Others focus on the group level (e.g., teams). Finally, there are theories that focus on the organization level (e.g., organizational design). This textbook will examine management from these various levels of analysis.

Organizational culture was brought to executives' attention with the publication of a 1978 book written by Tom Peters and Robert H. Waterman Jr.: *In Search of Excellence: Lessons From America's Best Run Companies.* This book is a best seller and considered a classic. To understand excellence, Peters and Waterman interviewed executives of excellent companies such as the Walt Disney Company and Procter & Gamble. They identified patterns these organizations had in common in terms of employees being loyal to particular core values. These values follow.

1. A bias for action—active decision-making and problem-solving
2. Closeness to the customer—learning from people served by the business
3. Autonomy and entrepreneurship—fostering innovation and nurturing ideas
4. Productivity through people—treating employees as a source of quality
5. A hands-on, value-driven management philosophy that guides everyday practice; management demonstrates commitment to this philosophy
6. "Sticking to the knitting"—staying with the business you know best
7. Simple form, lean staff; excellent companies have minimal headquarters staff
8. Simultaneous loose-tight properties—autonomy in shop-floor activities plus centralized values[18]

Tom Peters became one of the first "management gurus," a phenomenon that continues today. *In Search of Excellence* led to further study of organizational cultures and how they influence organizational performance through employee commitment to core values.

The Learning Organization

At the start of the 1990s, Peter Senge published a book titled *The Fifth Discipline*, which focused on systems thinking (using experience to help understand causes of problems, or wins, and their impact, or effect, on the whole system) and how it relates to an employee's ability to learn. In other words, if you see what the pizza looks like when it is finished and fresh from the oven, you can better visualize and learn what goes into making a successful pizza and what might need to change for the next time because you are viewing the finished product.

As the above example illustrates, organizations must be able to visualize the future and help employees execute change. By creating what is known as a **learning organization**, leaders can facilitate organizational change by having a workplace that is flexible and innovative.[19] Learning organizations are defined as "organizations where people continually expand their capacity to create the results they truly desire, where new and expansive patterns of thinking are nurtured, where collective aspiration is set free, and where people are continually learning to see the whole together."[20] A learning organization acquires and transfers knowledge and is adept at changing employees' behaviors when such knowledge creates new insights.[21]

The five disciplines in learning organizations are shown in Figure 1.3 and described here:

* **Personal mastery** is competence plus the discipline of continually clarifying and deepening our personal vision, of focusing our energies, of developing patience, and of seeing reality objectively.

▼ FIGURE 1.3

The Learning Organization

The Five Learning Disciplines

Personal Mastery · Mental Models · Building Shared Vision · Team Learning · Systems Thinking → Learning Organization

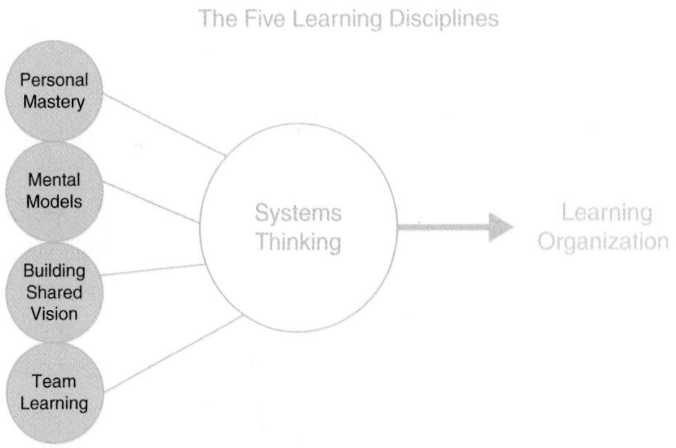

Source: Adapted from *Fifth Discipline* (Peter Senge). (2018). Retrieved from http://www.comindwork.com/weekly/2012-04-16/productivity/fifth-discipline-by-peter-senge-is-systems-thinking.

- **Mental models** are deeply ingrained assumptions, generalizations, or even pictures and images that influence how we understand the world and how we take action.
- **Building shared vision** is the sharing of a long-term view of the future that is uplifting and encourages experimentation and innovation.
- **Team learning** is aligning and developing teams to generate results they want. People on the team act and learn together. They grow rapidly from team interactions.
- **Systems thinking** is learning from experience, understanding cause and effect. This component integrates all the others and is the fifth discipline.

Learning organizations are adept at five major activities that facilitate the acquisition and transfer of knowledge and enable employees to change their behaviors based on new insights:

1. *Systematic problem-solving.* To find solutions to their problems, learning organizations employ the scientific method (see Appendix). This method relies on data—not guesses, assumptions, or hunches—to assess problems and determine adequate solutions. By employing simple statistical tools (correlations, histograms, etc.), a company can organize and display data to make logical inferences. Systematic problem-solving is an objective activity that relies on quantifiable, measurable data rather than subjective decision-making.

2. *Experimentation.* Experimentation is an activity guided by systematic inquiry; companies must seek and test new knowledge and opportunities. This activity requires risk-taking and the freedom to think beyond the status quo to expand an organization's horizons. There are two approaches to this activity: (1) ongoing programs that focus on incremental knowledge and (2) one-time demonstration projects that test out large-scale holistic changes.

   Ongoing programs are designed to prioritize continuous experimentation. These types of tests are commonly found in workshop environments. For example, a company that produces floor wax may regularly experiment with the chemical formula to improve the product. To ensure a successful ongoing experimentation program, organizations must:

   - Prioritize a steady stream of new ideas and innovations
   - Incentivize risk-taking to get buy-in from employees
   - Ensure that managers are trained in providing structure for experiments while simultaneously encouraging and rewarding creativity

   One-time demonstration projects typically pilot a dramatic change at one site with plans to later adopt it universally. For example, imagine that a social media platform decides to overhaul its process for reviewing posts that users have reported. A one-time demonstration project could test this large-scale change with one team in one location before implementing the new process company-wide.

   These types of projects are intended to set precedent and establish guidelines for later projects. However, these experiments also present opportunities for course-correction and trial and error. Without a clear plan for transferring knowledge or expanding the program, a one-time demonstration can fail to have an impact on the organization at large.

3. *Learning from past experience.* Learning organizations must critically reflect on past outcomes. What methods worked well? Which ones failed spectacularly? By systematically reviewing their successes and shortcomings, companies can document what they've learned and share these findings with employees. At the heart of this approach is the expectation that some ideas will fail and that employees should learn from failures. For example, case studies can be created from failures. Companies can also enlist the help of faculty and students at universities. Students' internships and case studies provide opportunities for them to gain experience and increase their own learning.

4. *Learning from others.* Sometimes the best ideas come from looking outside the organization. Smart managers know that examining the practices of successful organizations can provide good ideas. This seeking out and identifying of best practices is known as **benchmarking**. Other methods of learning from others include listening to customers and hiring consultants to provide new perspectives. Listening is a key element of learning organizations. Managers must be open to hearing criticism and bad news.

5. *Transferring knowledge.* Once knowledge is generated through problem-solving, experimentation, and learning from others, it must be shared throughout the organization. Reports are one of the most common ways knowledge is shared in organizations. Knowledge transfer is also achieved through education and training programs. Written reports are often supplemented by video communications. Learning organizations also employ training and education programs to share knowledge with employees.

You may have noticed that Senge's model reflects a focus on teams and systems thinking, and the learning organization has become a metaphor for organizations that are agile and respond to rapid change. By creating a learning organization, managers can prepare employees for the challenge of change.

Ethics

In the 1980s, trading on insider information, procurement scandals in the defense industry, and the savings and loan crisis began to focus the world's attention on unethical business activities. A business ethic based on social Darwinism, also known as "survival of the fittest," was pervasive in business culture. This gave business executives license to "win at all costs."[22]

The separation of the core values of business decision-makers from ethical principles resulted in risky activities that often resulted in corporate scandals. In response to continued corporate-ethics scandals, scholars began to examine the ethical practices of businesses. Linda Treviño's work on business ethics exemplifies this research.[23] Her work began with the publication of research articles on business ethics starting in 1986. In 1995, she published a book with Katherine Nelson, *Managing Business Ethics: Straight Talk About How to Do It Right*,[24] which became a key textbook for teaching undergraduates, MBAs, and business executives about ethical decision-making. In the introduction to the book, the authors write:

> This textbook examines ethical decision-making at all levels. It describes the influences on the ethical decisions of individuals, and then examines their decisions as managers. Finally, the organizational context is considered since some organizations have cultures that encourage unethical behavior. For example, organizational leaders may encourage managers to "cheat" by falsifying numbers on sales reports to make it look like the organization is reaching its targets.

Treviño and Nelson's book, now in its fifth edition, continues to help managers focus on what is important with respect to ethical decision-making and understand what may influence their ethical behavior. Dr. Treviño's work on business ethics and her textbook had a significant impact on top management teams, corporate legal counsels, human resource directors, and managers at all levels.

Dr. Treviño's work continued after the turn of the century with the development of a measure of and research on ethical leadership.[25] Her research in the 2000s also focused on cheating in academic institutions.[26] Her review of the research concluded that cheating is prevalent and has increased dramatically in the last 30 years. However, an institution's academic integrity programs and policies, such as honor codes, can have a significant influence on students' behavior.

Corporate-ethics scandals, of course, continued after the 1990s, one of the most prominent being the Enron scandal. Enron's former president and chief executive officer (CEO)

Jeffry Skilling encouraged an organizational culture that put employees under pressure to perform. "Do it right, do it now and do it better" was his motto. A *Harvard Business Review* case study on Enron contains employee quotations such as "you were expected to perform to a standard that was continually being raised," "the only thing that mattered was adding value," and "it was all about an atmosphere of deliberately breaking the rules."[27] The Enron culture rewarded unchecked ambition, which produced strong earnings, and Enron was admired on Wall Street. But over time it became more difficult to produce results, and employees engaged in more and more unethical conduct. Enron needed to keep borrowing money and pumping up its earnings reports to keep investors satisfied so they would not sell their stock and drive the stock price down. To avoid this, Enron entered into a deceiving web of partnerships and employed increasingly questionable accounting methods to maintain its high credit rating. The company was built on a house of cards that ultimately collapsed, and investors lost millions.[28] The Enron case highlights the continued importance of ethical decision-making for managers, and you will learn more about ethics and social responsibility in Chapter 3.

Disruptive Change

As the need for rapid organizational change has become the norm in many industries, organizations increasingly require visionary transformational leaders. Research on organizational change thus emerged as a central theme following the year 2000 and continues today. One of the best-known approaches discussed the need to go beyond rapid change and understand **disruptive change**. In an important book, *The Innovator's Dilemma*, Clayton Christensen describes disruptive change as change that alters the markets for an organization's products.[29] He provides the example of digital computers that dominated the market for minicomputers but missed the personal computing (PC) market, and failed.[30] He developed a framework for organizations to follow to meet the challenges of disruptive change by assessing and aligning an organization's resources, processes, and values.[31] Resources relate to *what* the company is able to do. Processes refer to *how* the organization does what it does (interaction, communication, coordination, and decision-making). Finally, values refer to the standards by which employees set priorities that enable them to judge and prioritize decisions. For example, values help guide an employee in deciding whether an employment offer is attractive or unattractive.

Disruptive change continues today. Researchers at Princeton University examined the disruptive change due to UberX on the taxi industry.[32] Their analysis found that UberX drivers have higher productivity compared to taxi drivers when the share of miles driven with a passenger in the car is used to measure capacity utilization. On average, the capacity utilization rate is 30% higher for UberX drivers than taxi drivers when measured by time, and 50% higher when measured by miles (the study was conducted using data from major cities that had utilization data available: Boston, Los Angeles, New York, San Francisco, and Seattle). The study found that four factors likely contributed to the higher capacity utilization rate of UberX drivers: (1) UberX's more efficient driver–passenger–matching technology, (2) the larger scale of UberX compared to taxi companies, (3) inefficient taxi regulations, and (4) UberX's flexible labor supply model and surge pricing more closely matching supply with demand throughout the day. The emergence of UberX and Lyft have created a crisis for the taxi industry from which they may not recover.

In response to organizational change, the late 20th century saw a rise in studies of visionary, or transformational, leadership. Given the rate of change, employees needed leaders who could articulate a new vision for the organization and enact organizational transformation. By the end of the

UberX created a disruptive change in the taxi industry.

decade, Bernard J. Bass's full-range model of leadership had emerged as the best-researched of these approaches (you will learn more about transformational leadership in Chapter 12 of this textbook).[33]

Actually, the idea of transformational leadership dates back to a groundbreaking 1978 book by James MacGregor Burns titled *Leadership*.[34] Bass's full-range model brought the idea of a transformational leader to prominence and sparked much research on transformational leadership. In essence, transformational leadership is about motivating followers through the influence created by their admiration as well as through inspirational motivation, intellectual stimulation, and consideration for followers as individuals.[35]

Sustainability

Al Gore's 2006 documentary *An Inconvenient Truth* advanced the hypothesis that human activity, particularly human activity organized on a large scale, can cause environmental damage on a global level. This sparked a widespread social discussion of how large corporations may be contributing to deterioration of the environment. The first 10 years of the 21st century will be remembered as the decade that businesses "went green."

The concept of **sustainability** became popular in the 2010s, but it is based on a 1987 report from the United Nations World Commission on Environment and Development that defined sustainable development as "development that meets the needs of the present without compromising the ability of future generations to meet their own needs."[36] In 2010, Tom Kuhlman and John Farrington published an article titled "What Is Sustainability?" which serves as a benchmark of the arrival of the concept in the mainstream. The authors write, "Sustainability is concerned with the well-being of future generations and in particular with irreplaceable natural resources—as opposed to the gratification of present needs which we call well-being."[37] Sustainability not only focuses on environmental impact but also consists of three dimensions—"environment," "economy," and "social well-being"—for which society needs to find balance.[38] Sustainability calls upon large corporations to have consciousness about the preservation of the planet in their decision-making.

Since 2010, major efforts have been made to induce organizations to reduce their carbon footprints and other environmental impacts. For example, many organizations have implemented recycling programs to collect paper and plastic trash and move it to local recycling centers. These efforts have been effective in terms of public relations, but it remains to be seen what impact they will have on the environment.

It is projected that the years 2010–2020 will be declared the decade of sustainability. The idea of preserving the environment existed prior to 2010, of course, but this was the decade it really took hold on organizational decision-makers and found a name in *sustainability*.[39] Many large corporations have created a top-management-team position of chief sustainability officer (CSO) to ensure that the organization is engaging in best practices with respect to the environment. According to Harvard Business School professor George Serafeim, "companies are monitoring the impact they're having environmentally and on society, and the appointment of the CSO reflects an underlying need for companies to not only monitor but also improve their performance."[40] Although the CSO role is typically related to environmental issues such as water and energy use, some companies are going further. Sustainability may now focus on improving working conditions in countries that supply raw materials and products and creating environmentally safe products.

Al Gore's documentary, *An Inconvenient Truth.*

©Moviestore Collection/Shutterstock

Of course, numerous other important management ideas have emerged throughout the decades, and they will be discussed in subsequent chapters of this textbook. The timeline outlined in this section serves to highlight some of the more important ideas that shifted thinking in management.

Managerial Roles

Learning Objective 1.4: Demonstrate understanding of managerial roles by providing examples.

An important framework for understanding the nature of managerial work emerged from the work of Henry Mintzberg,[41] who observed and analyzed the activities of the CEOs of five private and semipublic organizations in Canada. His goal was to focus on the day-to-day reality of what managers do. To describe the work of a CEO, Mintzberg first identified six characteristics of the job:

1. CEOs process large, open-ended workloads under tight time pressure—a manager's job is never done.
2. Managerial activities are relatively short in duration, varied, fragmented, and often self-initiated.
3. CEOs prefer action and action-driven activities and dislike paperwork.
4. CEOs prefer verbal communication through meetings and phone conversations.
5. CEOs maintain relationships primarily with their subordinates and external parties.
6. CEOs' involvement in the execution of the work is limited, although they initiate many of the decisions.

Based on his study, Mintzberg also identified 10 managerial roles, which are summarized in Table 1.1 and described in the following sections.

Interpersonal Roles

Interpersonal roles are managerial roles that involve providing information and ideas.

- **Figurehead**. Managers have social, ceremonial, and legal responsibilities. They're expected to be a source of inspiration. People look up to a manager as someone with

▼ TABLE 1.1

Mintzberg's Managerial Roles

Role category	Role type	Role nature
Interpersonal	Figurehead Leader Liaison	Representing an organization and performing ceremonial duties Motivating subordinates to achieve their goals and objectives Maintaining horizontal chains of communication
Informational	Monitor Disseminator Spokesperson	Collecting information concerning the organization and short-listing relevant information Sharing relevant information with subordinates Maintaining protocol and sharing information with outsiders
Decisional	Entrepreneur Disturbance handler Resource allocator Negotiator	Focusing on innovation and change within the organization Managing conflict by taking corrective action Optimizing resource allocation to different competing needs within the organization Representing an organization in all major negotiations

Source: Adapted from Mintzberg, H. (1973). *The Nature of Managerial Work.* New York, NY: Harper & Row, pp. 92–93.

authority and as a role model. For example, the CEO of a company may appear in a commercial for an organization's products.

- **Leader**. This is where managers provide leadership for their team, their department, or perhaps their entire organization, and it's where they manage the performance and responsibilities of everyone in the group. For example, a manager might provide performance appraisals to his direct reports.
- **Liaison**. Managers must communicate with internal and external contacts. They need to be able to network effectively on behalf of their organization. For example, a manager might attend a networking event at her alma mater to make business contacts.

Lei Jun, CEO and co-founder of Xiaomi, playing the spokesperson role as he experiences a self-balancing electric vehicle during a press conference announcing the Ninebot's acquisition of Segway in Beijing, China.

©Visual China Group /Getty Images

Informational Roles

Informational roles are managerial roles that involve processing information.

- **Monitor** (also known as the **nerve center**). Managers regularly seek out information related to their organization and industry, looking for relevant changes in the environment. They also monitor their team in terms of both their productivity and their well-being. For example, a manager might attend a trade show to learn about new and competing products in her organization's industry.
- **Disseminator**. Managers must communicate key information to their colleagues and their team. For example, after learning about innovation in a course, a manager might share best practices for brainstorming new ideas with his team.
- **Spokesperson**. Managers must often speak for their organization. In this role they are responsible for transmitting information about the organization and its goals to the people outside it. For example, a manager might organize a press conference to release a new product and demonstrate its benefits.

Decisional Roles

Decisional roles are managerial roles involving the use of information.

- **Entrepreneur**. Managers create and lead change within the organization. This means solving problems, generating new ideas, and implementing them. For example, a manager might make a presentation to her team about an upcoming company reorganization.
- **Disturbance handler**. Managers must take charge when an organization or team hits an unexpected roadblock. They also need to help mediate disputes within it. For example, a manager might meet with two employees who have been arguing to resolve the conflict.
- **Resource allocator**. Managers need to determine where organizational resources are best applied. This involves allocating funding as well as assigning staff and other organizational resources. For example, a manager might create and submit a yearly budget for approval to the finance office.
- **Negotiator**. Managers need to engage in important negotiations within their team, department, or organization. For example, a manager in an automobile company might negotiate a contract for car door handles with an overseas supplier.[42]

Throughout this textbook, you will have the opportunity to study the research on management and complete activities and self-assessments that will help you develop skills related to the entire management process. While some of the above functions of management can be learned through experience, you will be at an advantage by learning them before you become a manager. One of the most important frameworks for understanding management is knowing the roles managers must play. These roles are covered in the following section, and Toolkit Activity 1.1 provides you with the opportunity to learn the degree to which real-world managers play these roles in their work.

In a study of 225 managers at different hierarchical levels and in different functional areas,[43] the leader role emerged as the one universally required role for all managers. This makes sense; because managerial work consists of getting things done through other people, it is logical that this role would be required to a fairly high extent by all managers. The liaison role was the second highest required managerial role, since managers have to link their department's activities to those of others in the organization. The disturbance handler role was also highly ranked, as might have been expected due to the brevity, variety, and fragmentation that Mintzberg found inherent in managerial work.

A research study examined managerial roles 30 years after the publication of the original research and found that the main differences were a much larger workload, a contact pattern to a larger degree oriented toward subordinates in team settings, a greater emphasis on giving information, and less preoccupation with administrative work.[44] Another study found that the framework was useful in describing the work of entrepreneurs.[45] Mintzberg reflected on his own work some years later and commented that managers should be "well-rounded" and need to "think, link, lead, and do."[46] A manager who overthinks a situation may not be able to link it to others through leadership and may not get anything done. Since leading is central to being an effective manager, managerial leadership skills will be discussed next.

Managerial Behaviors

Learning Objective 1.5: Explain the three types of managerial behaviors.

A large-scale review of research[47] on management and leadership revealed that managerial behaviors can be grouped into three broad categories: **task behavior**, **relations behavior**, and **change behavior**. These skills are summarized in Table 1.2. Much research in leadership has demonstrated that managers must initiate structure by clarifying the activities their followers must perform. Managers also need to show consideration for their followers by supporting them and providing personal attention.[48] More recently, research in management has focused on the need for managers to address the disruptive change described in Christensen's research discussed above in the timeline of management theory. Managers must scan the environment for market disruptions and encourage followers to innovate and take risks to address the change.

Managerial leadership combines analytic skills and "soft skills." Analytic skills relate to the tasks that need to be performed to meet the organization's goals. Soft skills focus on the relationships managers develop with followers to motivate them to attain goals and provide for their satisfaction and well-being at work. Change skills are a combination of analytic and soft skills. The external environment of the organization must be monitored and analyzed, but managers must also inspire a shared vision and encourage innovation for the organization to change.

A study of 1,412 managers asked them to rate the relative importance of 57 managerial tasks to their jobs. Their choices included "Of utmost importance," "Of considerable importance," "Of moderate importance," "Of little importance," "Of no importance," and "I do not perform this task." Using these importance ratings, researchers statistically identified seven major factors or groups of management tasks: managing individual performance, instructing subordinates, planning and allocating resources, coordinating interdependent groups, managing group performance, monitoring the business environment, and representing staff.[49]

We all go to restaurants to enjoy a meal with friends or family. Have you ever wondered how your food is prepared and served? Who coordinates all of this? Behind the scenes is the important position of the restaurant manager. In a small business such as a café, this is often the owner of the restaurant. In larger restaurants and franchises like Shake Shack, the manager is hired by the organization to run the business. On a daily basis, restaurant managers do a lot of different things. Let's look at some of the things they do.

Hiring and Firing

Restaurant managers hire new staff for the kitchen and dining room. Of course, the manager must also provide performance evaluations and terminate employees who have low performance. It is very important that the servers who interact with customers have a high level of performance. In larger restaurants, kitchen positions may be filled by the head chef rather than the manager.

Ordering Inventory

A restaurant manager may order food for preparation. Inventory also includes dining room items, such as paper napkins, cleaning supplies, and restaurant dishware. Managers may also do the orders for liquor, beer, and wine for the restaurant. In larger restaurants, there is a bar manager or head bartender who covers this ordering. Also in larger restaurants, the head chef orders the food for the restaurant, since they create menus and supervise the cooks. No matter who does the ordering, however, the restaurant manager must oversee the orders and ensure they are within the budgets. Also, expiration dates on food must be watched carefully. No matter who is in charge of the food or liquor ordering, a restaurant manager signs off on the orders to maintain budget control.

Staff Scheduling

Most restaurants operate for breakfast, lunch, and dinner, which often lasts well into the night. Some restaurants are

A restaurant manager briefs his staff.

open 24 hours, such as the Waffle House. A restaurant manager arranges the weekly schedule to make sure all shifts are staffed. Managers put their best employees on the schedule during the busiest times. They may staff trainees during slow times. Managers also approve requests for days off and ensure there is fairness in how much time off employees receive.

Event Planning

Many restaurants also provide catering. A restaurant manager may be in charge of planning the schedule, finding rooms, and assigning waitstaff and kitchen staff to the event. Some restaurants deliver food, and the manager arranges for vans to deliver orders. If a catering operation is large, a restaurant may have a catering manager to cover these tasks.

Customer Service

As you know, poor service can break a restaurant. The restaurant manager ensures that customers receive excellent service. They are responsible for training the staff to provide a great experience before, during, and after the meal. A manager's job is to make sure customers leave happy. In many cases, managers collect information on survey cards or follow-up emails to learn about the customer experience. The manager shares survey results with employees during staff meetings. The manager may provide rewards such as cash or meals for outstanding customer service mentioned by customers on the surveys.

Marketing and Advertising

In many cases, restaurant managers create advertising. They manage the advertising budget, place ads in local periodicals, create mailings that may have coupons, and post about the restaurant on social media such as Instagram, Twitter, and Facebook (and encourage customers to do so). They may also implement promotions such as happy-hour specials, two-for-one deals, or holiday specials.

Bookkeeping

In a small business, the restaurant manager takes care of books and makes the bank deposits. Even in a small business, it is good practice to have a separate person track and reconcile bank accounts. One of the biggest problems for restaurant management is theft, so having checks and balances in place is important.

Qualifications required for restaurant managers include both people skills and business skills. Depending on the size of the restaurant and how formal it is, managers may need to have a business or hospitality management degree.

(Continued)

Managers are essential to the success of a restaurant. They run the daily functions of the kitchen and dining room. They sometimes work behind the scenes and sometimes greet customers or handle complaints. A restaurant manager must have excellent organizational, communication, and problem-solving skills.

Discussion Questions

1. What part of the restaurant manager's job do you feel is the most challenging? Why?

2. What specific "people and business" skills does a restaurant manager need to have? What managerial roles does the restaurant manager need to exhibit based on Mintzberg's managerial roles?

3. Give examples of the managerial leadership skills the restaurant manager must have (task, relations, and change behavior).

Source: Adapted from Mealey, L. (2017). What does a restaurant manager do? Retrieved from https://www.thebalance.com/what-does-a-restaurant-manager-do-2888854.

▼ TABLE 1.2

Managerial Behaviors

Task Behavior
• Plan short-term activities
• Clarify task objectives and role expectations
• Monitor operations and performance
Relations Behavior
• Provide support and encouragement
• Provide recognition for achievements and contributions
• Develop member skill and confidence
• Consult with members when making decisions
• Empower members to take initiative in problem-solving
Change Behavior
• Monitor the external environment
• Propose an innovative strategy or new vision
• Encourage innovative thinking
• Take risks to promote necessary changes

Source: Yukl, G., Gordon, A., & Taber, T. (2002). A hierarchical taxonomy of leadership behavior: Integrating a half century of behavior research. *Journal of Leadership and Organizational Studies, 9*(1), 15–32.

Skills Managers Need Today

Learning Objective 1.6: Define the three skills managers need to be successful today.

The manager's job has been evolving, and there are new sets of skills managers need to be effective. These skills involve the ability to solve problems using evidence, critical thinking, and analytics. These important skills will be discussed in the following sections as well as reinforced throughout this textbook. For example, the textbook is based on theories and research in the field of management (that is, evidence based). You will be encouraged to apply critical-thinking skills by answering the critical-thinking questions in the textbook. Finally, in the Appendix to this textbook, you will have the opportunity to learn analytic techniques, which you will apply to solve problems in the Toolkit exercises.

Evidence-Based Management

The ability to translate research to practice has been termed **evidence-based management (EBM).** The term *evidence-based* was originally employed in the field of medicine to guide how doctors make decisions regarding patient care. EBM improves a leader's decisions through disciplined application of the most relevant and current scientific evidence. Although many definitions of EBM are available, this is the most frequently quoted and widely used: "EBM means making decisions about the management of employees, teams, or organizations through the conscientious, explicit, and judicious use of four sources of information,"[50] shown in Figure 1.4 and listed here:

1. *Scientific literature empirical studies*—for example, research published in management journals
2. *Organization internal data*—for example, interviews or surveys completed by people in an organization
3. *Practitioners' professional expertise*—for example, the expert opinions of managers
4. *Stakeholders' values and concerns*—for example, groups that focus on whether the organization employs environmentally friendly practices[51]

▼ FIGURE 1.4

Sources of Information Used in EBM

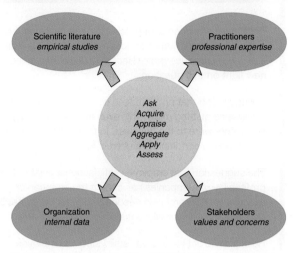

Source: Barends, E., Rousseau, D. M., & Briner, R. B. (2014). Evidence-Based Management: The basic principles. Retrieved from https://www.cebma.org/wp-content/uploads/Evidence-Based-Practice-The-Basic-Principles-vs-Dec-2015.pdf.

To use these sources of evidence to make better decisions and increase the likelihood of a favorable outcome, managers need to follow the process shown in the center of Figure 1.4. This process involves the following steps:

1. *Asking:* Translating a practical issue or problem into an answerable question
2. *Acquiring:* Systematically searching for and retrieving the evidence
3. *Appraising:* Critically judging the trustworthiness and relevance of the evidence
4. *Aggregating:* Weighing and pulling together the evidence
5. *Applying:* Incorporating the evidence into the decision-making process
6. *Assessing:* Evaluating the outcome of the decision taken[52]

To implement EBM, managers must have ability (basic skills and competencies), motivation (behavioral beliefs, behavioral control, and normative beliefs), and opportunity (support that overcomes organizational barriers).[53] For example, EBM was applied to an operational problem in a hospital. Researchers tracked the process through interviews. An EBM decision process was implemented by a physician manager. This research concluded that the "fit" between the decision-maker and the organizational context enables more effective, evidence-based processes.[54] Managerial involvement at all levels is essential for EBM to work in practice,[55] as well as in collaboration with researchers.[56] That said, managers should adopt a healthy skepticism about new management ideas.[57] Cynicism could be reduced by presenting ideas that have been able to "stand the test of time," such as the ones shown in the timeline presented earlier in this chapter. Some new ideas are not really new at all, and may be overstated.[58]

In making important organizational decisions, a manager may include information gathered from one or all of the four sources described previously in the definition of EBM. This can result in a lot of information. So how can a leader sort through it all and determine what is most relevant to the problem at hand? The answer lies in **critical thinking,** a process that has been

FACT OR FICTION?

Is a Happy Worker a Productive Worker?

There has been a long debate in the management field regarding whether or not employees who are happy at work produce more. Recent research has shed some new light on this question.

A study found that poor working conditions were related to employees quitting more. This even affected how loyal customers were to the business. In terms of the bottom line, poor working conditions resulted in lower revenue.

The suggestion that employee satisfaction is related to the profitability of companies has caught the attention of executives. Research has needed to dig deeper to better understand how and why satisfaction relates to revenue.

Researchers at Harvard University studied employee "perceptions, emotions, and motivations" that lead employees to form their understanding of what is happening in the workplace. Researchers asked 238 employees to write in an electronic journal every day describing how they felt about work and to describe the one thing that happened each day that stood out in their mind. The researchers ended up with mountain of data to analyze—12,000 diary entries were collected.

The results of the study uncovered some important findings about employee experiences at work. One-third of the employees said they were "unhappy, unmotivated, or both." Some of them were frustrated and disgusted by what was happening in their jobs. The researchers called these feelings the "inner work life." This inner work life predicted employees' productivity and loyalty to the organization. Employees who were frustrated were less creative and did not get along with others at work.

The study found that on days when employees were happy (expressing positive feelings in the diaries), they were more likely to have innovative ideas to improve work. This research found that employees do perform better when they are happy at work. The single most important aspect of work is an employee's feeling that they are making progress in meaningful work. When employees feel their work has meaning, they get excited about it. For example, one computer programmer in the study wrote this about finishing a challenging task: "This time it looks good! I feel more positive about this project and my work than I've felt in a long time." These feelings improve performance, since this is a positive inner work life experience.

Most managers have no idea that lack of support creates negative outcomes for employees. When researchers asked 669 managers to rank five employee motivators in terms of importance, they ranked "supporting progress" last. In other words, 95% of the managers did not realize that accomplishing meaningful work is the primary motivator, even though providing support doesn't cost as much as incentives like raises and bonuses. This failure reflects a common experience in organizations. Seven companies were studied, but only one had managers who consistently supported meaningful work by emphasizing learning. It is probably not a coincidence that this company was the only one in the study that had a major innovation while the study was being conducted.

In our lives, we spend more of our time awake at work than doing anything else. Think about that. As a manager, supporting a sense of meaning at work is the right thing to do. Employee well-being is ethical and also relates to bottom-line profit. It is a win-win. Managers can support positive inner lives that make work less frustrating and more satisfying.

Managers can increase worker satisfaction by engaging them at work. The experience of a positive inner work life seems to be a function of how well managers help employees experience a sense of accomplishment. For example, a manager can remove impediments to performance, help employees, and give positive feedback.

Discussion Questions

1. Describe other reasons a worker may be productive at work, besides experiencing meaningful work.

2. Provide an example of a job in which a worker would experience a high degree of meaningfulness. Then provide an example of a job in which a worker would experience a low degree of meaningfulness. How are the jobs different in terms of autonomy, resources, and learning?

3. Give examples of specific actions a manager can take to improve the inner work life of workers by increasing meaningfulness.

4. What do you think should be the next study in this line of evidence-based research on whether a happy worker is a productive worker? What do we need to know now?

Sources: Adapted from Amabile, T., & Kramer, S. (2011, September 3). Do happier people work harder? *New York Times*. Retrieved from https://www.nytimes.com/2011/09/04/opinion/sunday/do-happier-people-work-harder.html? ref=opinion; Harter, J. K., Schmidt, F. L., Asplund, J. W., Killham, E. A., & Agrawal, S. (2010). Causal impact of employee work perceptions on the bottom line of organizations. *Perspectives on Psychological Science, 5*(4), 378–389.

developed for over 2,500 years, beginning with the ancient Greeks and the Socratic method, which is the process of learning by questioning everything. Critical-thinking skills are applied to sort through all the information gathered and then prioritize it (and even discard evidence that appears to be invalid or irrelevant to the problem).

Critical Thinking

Critical thinking is defined as "persistent effort to examine any belief or supposed form of knowledge in the light of evidence that supports it and the further conclusions to which it tends."[59] Critical thinking is a mode of thinking about a problem we face where the problem-solver improves the quality of the process by taking control of it and applying rigorous standards. The process has been described as having three interrelated parts:

1. The elements of thought (reasoning)
2. The intellectual standards that are applied to the elements of reasoning
3. The intellectual traits associated with a cultivated critical thinker that result from the consistent and disciplined application of the intellectual standards to the elements of thought[60]

Critical thinking involves using justification; recognizing relationships; evaluating the credibility of sources; looking at reasons or evidence; drawing inferences; identifying alternatives, logical deductions, sequences, and order; and defending an idea. Critical thinking requires the decision-maker in an organization to apply a complex skill set to solve the problem at hand. A set of guidelines for critical thinking is shown in Table 1.3.[61] Critical thinking is, in short, self-directed, self-disciplined, self-monitored, and self-corrective thinking. It requires rigorous standards of problem-solving and a commitment to overcome the inclination to think that we have all of the answers.[62] A recent study demonstrated that students' attitudes toward and beliefs about critical-thinking skills are related to their GPA, due to their bearing on effective argumentation and reflective thinking.[63]

When it comes to asking questions, some of the best ideas come from a book by Ian Mitroff called *Smart Thinking for Crazy Times: The Art of Solving the Right Problems*.[64] Mitroff warns us about solving the wrong problems even though leaders solve them with great precision in organizations. This happens because they don't ask the right questions. Mitroff provides advice to managers who fall into the trap of solving the wrong problems by spelling out why managers do it in the first place. The five pathways to error are:

Students' critical thinking skills predict grade point average.

©Nomad_Soul/Shutterstock

- Picking the wrong stakeholders by not paying attention to who really cares about the problem.
- Selecting too narrow a set of options by overlooking better, more creative options.
- Phrasing a problem incorrectly by failing to consider at least one "technical" and one "human" variation in stating a problem.
- Setting the boundaries of a problem too narrow by ignoring the system the problem is embedded in.
- Failing to think systemically by ignoring the connection between parts of the problem and its whole.

Critical Thinking Skills

No one always acts purely objectively and rationally. We connive for selfish interests. We gossip, boast, exaggerate, and equivocate. It is "only human" to wish to validate our prior knowledge, to vindicate our prior decisions, or to sustain our earlier beliefs. In the process of satisfying our ego, however, we can often deny ourselves intellectual growth and opportunity. We may not always want to apply critical thinking skills, but we should have those skills available to be employed when needed.

Critical thinking includes a complex combination of skills. Among the main characteristics are the following:

Skills	We are thinking critically when we do the following:
Rationality	• Rely on reason rather than emotion • Require evidence, ignore no known evidence, and follow evidence where it leads • Are concerned more with finding the best explanation than being right, analyzing apparent confusion, and asking questions
Self-Awareness	• Weigh the influences of motives and bias • Recognize our own assumptions, prejudices, biases, or points of view
Honesty	• Recognize emotional impulses, selfish motives, nefarious purposes, or other modes of self-deception
Open-Mindedness	• Evaluate all reasonable inferences • Consider a variety of possible viewpoints or perspectives • Remain open to alternative interpretations • Accept a new explanation, model, or paradigm because it explains the evidence better, is simpler, or has fewer inconsistencies or covers more data • Accept new priorities in response to a reevaluation of the evidence or reassessment of our real interests • Do not reject unpopular views out of hand
Discipline	• Are precise, meticulous, comprehensive, and exhaustive • Resist manipulation and irrational appeals • Avoid snap judgments
Judgment	• Recognize the relevance and/or merit of alternative assumptions and perspectives • Recognize the extent and weight of evidence
In sum:	• Critical thinkers are by nature skeptical. They approach texts with the same skepticism and suspicion as they approach spoken remarks. • Critical thinkers are active, not passive. They ask questions and analyze. They consciously apply tactics and strategies to uncover meaning or assure their understanding. • Critical thinkers do not take an egotistical view of the world. They are open to new ideas and perspectives. They are willing to challenge their beliefs and investigate competing evidence.

Critical thinking enables us to recognize a wide range of subjective analyses of otherwise objective data and to evaluate how well each analysis might meet our needs. Facts may be facts, but how we interpret them may vary. By contrast, passive, noncritical thinkers take a simplistic view of the world. They see things in black and white, as either-or, rather than recognizing a variety of possible understanding. They see questions as yes or no with no subtleties, they fail to see linkages and complexities, and they fail to recognize related elements.

Source: Daniel Kurland, "What is Critical Thinking?" How the Language Really Works: The Fundamentals of Critical Reading and Effective Writing, http://www.criticalreading.com. Copyright © 2000 by Daniel J. Kurland. Reproduced with permission.

So what questions should a manager be asking? Mitroff provides the following list of basic questions facing all organizations (and ones we should be asking frequently if we expect to gain buy-in from employees for the implementation of their solutions):

- What businesses are we in?
- What businesses should we be in?
- What is our mission?
- What should our mission be?
- Who are our prime customers?
- Who should our customers be?
- How should we react to a major crisis, especially if we are, or are perceived to be, at fault?

- How will the outside world perceive our actions?
- Will others perceive the situation as we do?
- Are our products and services ethical?

CRITICAL THINKING QUESTIONS

> Give an example of how the answers to these questions will enable managers to think critically about their organization. How can they avoid the "pathways to error" described by Mitroff?

Analytics

The term **analytics** often conjures up images of powerful computers, complicated mathematics, and cryptic outputs only a scientist could love. Although somewhat outdated, those images are not entirely inaccurate. The types of analytics used by modern businesses do require powerful computers and complicated mathematics. Their outputs do take some training to interpret and use in the decision-making process.

Some interesting things have happened in recent years, however:

- The powerful computers needed to analyze all but the largest data sets have become quite common. You most likely have one on your desk, in the bag you carry around campus, even in your pocket.
- It is helpful to understand the mathematical logic that underlies analytic techniques, but there is no need to memorize formulas or crank through tedious calculations. Modern software does nearly all the heavy lifting for you and has become increasingly user-friendly.
- Analytics is no longer the realm of highly trained scientists. You can learn how to interpret the most commonly used analytic output even if you have had no previous training. In fact, this chapter will teach you to do just that.

In Chapter 2, you will learn the importance of decision-making in a manager's job. Analytics are used to facilitate and improve managers' decision-making processes in many ways. For example, managers use analytics to quantitatively assess employee motivation tactics, evaluate resource allocation decisions, test the security of their computing networks, and design customer-friendly websites. Because our topic is managers, we will primarily focus on the use of analytics in some of the most fundamental aspects of managerial decision-making. In later chapters you will read about the importance of analytics in the controlling aspects of management.

To fully understand how data analytics help managers make decisions, it is important to realize their connection to the notion of critical thinking, which is another key management skill. In fact, if used properly, analytics are simply mathematically assisted critical-thinking exercises. To see how this is true, recall that we defined critical thinking as a mode of thinking about a problem we face where the problem-solver improves the quality of the process by *taking control of it and applying rigorous standards*. Through analytics, a problem-solver takes control of the thought process by quantifying the variables at play and applying the rules of statistics. Standards do not get much more rigorous than that! More specifically, analytics facilitate critical thinking in two key ways:

1. They require that decision-makers apply scientific logic to the questions or problems they are trying to solve. This involves clearly identifying the problem, developing logical explanations and/or solutions, then testing those explanations and solutions. It is true

that the analytical element—the actual math, in other words—does not come into play until the testing phase. Translating an abstract problem (poor employee morale or performance, for example) into analytical terms, however, requires us to impose the rationality and discipline (recall these terms from Table 1.3) of logic on the problem. This helps us structure our thinking in a way that reduces the impact of perceptual bias and other detriments to critical thinking. More often than not, we can even structure analyses to quantify and remove these factors.

2. Beyond helping problem-solvers to think critically, analytics help us see if we have actually succeeded in doing so. It may be more accurate to say they provide evidence that we have or have not succeeded in thinking critically. For example, if a manager is absolutely convinced that younger employees learn faster than older employees but the data consistently tell a different story, it may be that some untested or irrational assumptions have found their way into the manager's thought process. This is, of course, not always true. No analytical technique is perfect, just as no decision-maker is perfect. When combined, however, critical thinking and analytics maximize the likelihood of an optimal solution by blending the knowledge and experience of individual decision-makers with the discipline and predictive value of statistics.

Plan For This Textbook

Numerous challenges face managers. Most organizations are experiencing rates of change unlike anything we have seen in the past.[65] External pressures have been created from mergers, downsizing, restructuring, and layoffs as organizations strive to remain competitive or even survive. Other external forces are global competition, product obsolescence, new technology, government mandates, and diversity in the workforce. The changes organizations have undergone have resulted in followers who are filled with cynicism and doubt about their leaders and organization.[66] Ethics scandals in business have fueled the perception that leaders are unable to lead their organizations in a principled way.

By now, you have realized that management is a problem-focused discipline aimed at making organizations more effective. Your ability as a manager will be enhanced through knowledge of the theory and applications from management research. Each chapter will review the essential and most current theory and research and relate it to how you can develop your leadership skills. At the end of each chapter, there are tools for your "toolkit," where you will directly apply the theories through cases, self-assessments, and exercises. To get on the path toward thinking about your career in management, complete Toolkit Activity 1.2 on defining success.

This textbook will cover the four aspects of the management process—planning, organizing, leading, and controlling. EBM, critical thinking, ethics, and analytics are themes that run throughout the textbook, each chapter concluding with activities, case studies, and self-assessments where you will apply what you have learned about management. This introductory chapter has provided an overview of management and what it means to be a manager. Next, Part II will examine the planning function of management. Decision-making and analytics will be covered in Chapter 2 to provide you with the skills you need to solve management problems. Ethics and social responsibility are part of every manager's job today, and these will be discussed in Chapter 3. The planning section will conclude with chapters on organizational culture and change (Chapter 4) and strategic management (Chapter 5), giving you a big-picture view of management planning.

Part II will address the organizing function of management and will cover organizational design (Chapter 6), communication systems (Chapter 7), and designing the human resource system (Chapter 8). Part III will discuss the leading function of management and will cover the manager's role in leading people in organizations. This section addresses understanding individual differences and diversity (Chapter 9), motivation (Chapter 10), teams (Chapter 11), and leadership (Chapter 12). Given the global nature of business today, Part III concludes with a discussion on leading globally (Chapter 13). The final section of the book, Part IV, looks at the controlling function of management, and includes information on budget control (Chapter 14) and management control technology in organizations (Chapter 15). Chapter 15 also provides an integrative view of the entire textbook, since control is now a major aspect of management and all the chapters address the issue.

As you read this book, refer back to the figure at the start of each chapter as a map of how to organize the vast amount of theory and research on management that has been generated for decades. It won't seem so overwhelming if you can place the material in the four broad groupings as shown in the figure—planning, organizing, leading, and controlling.

Managerial Implications

This chapter has provided an overview of management and traced the development of the concept over time. Here are key takeaway points:

- The concept of management has evolved over time, from engineering time-and-motion studies in the late 1800s to present-day thinking, which has added the behavioral aspect to management. This history helps you see how the field has progressed to being focused on people and how your behaviors and theirs play the biggest role in an organization's success.
- Management consists of planning, organizing, leading, and controlling functions (and this book is organized around these roles).
- It's important for managers to understand their underlying assumptions about people—Theory X versus Theory Y. These assumptions emerged as a key idea in the 1960s.
- By the 1980s, frameworks for understanding human behavior in organizations became prominent. Theories of psychology were applied to organizations. Also, organizational culture became an important area of study.
- Employees in organizations need to develop the ability to solve problems and learn from mistakes. The concept of a learning organization as a mechanism to creating more nimble organizations emerged in the 1990s with the work of Peter Senge.
- During the 1990s, the study of business ethics took a central role as a result of the ethics scandals of the two prior decades. Also, due to disruptive organizational change, it became important for managers to exhibit transformational leadership skills.
- Managers exhibit certain behaviors as they do their work, which fall into three categories: task, relations, and change behaviors.
- Managers today need three important skills. They need to understand evidence-based management (EBM) and apply critical thinking to solve problems in their organization. They also need a firm grasp of how to use analytics to make decisions.

Now that you have an understanding of what it takes to become a manager, we next turn to the planning phase with a discussion of decision-making and the use of analytics in the next chapter.

KEY TERMS

analytics 25

benchmarking 13

building shared vision 12

change behavior 18

controlling 7

critical thinking 21

decisional roles 17

disruptive change 14

disseminator 17

disturbance handler 17

effectiveness 5

efficiency 5

entrepreneur 17

evidence-based management (EBM) 21

field theory 9

figurehead 16

Hawthorne effect 8

informational roles 17

interpersonal roles 16

leader 17

leading 6

learning organization 11

liaison 17

management 5

mental models 12

mission 5

monitor or nerve center 17

negotiator 17

organizational behavior (OB) 10

organizational culture 11

organizational development (OD) 9

organizing 6

personal mastery 11

planning 6

relations behavior 18

resource allocator 17

scientific management 7

spokesperson 17

sustainability 15

systems thinking 12

task behavior 18

team learning 12

Theory X 9

Theory Y 10

TOOLKIT

Activity 1.1

Learning About Managerial Roles

For this activity, you will interview a manager (this can be a parent, a friend's parent, a university administrator—just be sure the person you interview manages other people as a key part of their job). The objective of this activity is to learn the degree to which Mintzberg's managerial roles are played by a specific manager on a weekly basis. Tell the manager you selected that this is for a class project and you don't need to report their name or the company they work for. Write down the industry (e.g., retail, accounting, manufacturing, education) and the size of the organization (number of employees) the manager works for.

Industry: _____

Organization size (number of employees): _____

Next, tell your chosen manager that "roles are defined as organized sets of behaviors belonging to identifiable offices or positions." Then ask your interviewee to rate the degree to which they engage in the roles shown in the table using the following scale:

0   1   2   3   4   5   6   7+ times/week

|--|

Never   Sometimes   Frequently   Daily or more

▼ TABLE 1.4

Nature of Mintzberg's Managerial Roles

Category	Role	Nature of Role
Interpersonal Roles	Figurehead	As a symbol of legal authority, performing certain ceremonial duties (e.g., signing documents and receiving visitors).
Interpersonal Roles	Leader	Motivating subordinates to get the job done properly.
Interpersonal Roles	Liaison	Serving as a link in a horizontal (as well as vertical) chain of communication.
Informational Roles	Nerve Center	Serving as a focal point for nonroutine information; receiving all types of information.
Informational Roles	Disseminator	Transmitting selected information to subordinates.
Informational Roles	Spokesperson	Transmitting selected information to outsiders.
Decisional Roles	Entrepreneur	Designing and initiating changes within the organization.

Decisional Roles	Disturbance Handler	Taking corrective action in nonroutine situations.
Decisional Roles	Resource Allocator	Deciding exactly who should get what resources.
Decisional Roles	Negotiator	Participating in negotiating sessions with other parties (e.g., vendors and unions) to make sure the organization's interests are adequately represented.

Source: Adapted from Dunphy, S. M., & Meyer, D. (2002). Entrepreneur or manager? A discriminant analysis based on Mintzberg's managerial roles. *Journal of Business and Entrepreneurship, 14*(2), 17–37.

Discussion Questions

1. What were the roles most frequently played by the manager you interviewed? Were you surprised by this result?
2. Were there any roles the manager you interviewed never or rarely played? If so, why do you think this was the case?
3. Do you think your results might be different if you interviewed a manager in a different industry? Why or why not? Compare your results with other members of the class who interviewed managers from different industries and organization sizes. Discuss the similarities and differences.

Activity 1.2

What Does It Mean to Be Successful?

Success is a loaded word. It can conjure up all sorts of associations, from opulent lifestyles to business empires.

How do you define success? Sometimes definitions of success can be too narrow and specific. For this activity, think about success as a concept rather than associating it with specific goals or sets of goals (e.g., "buy a home in a desirable neighborhood" or "become the top salesperson in the department"). Develop a definition of success that is applicable in a variety of scenarios, such as in the workplace, at home, and in social settings with friends or family.

1. Write your initial definition of success in the box below. Then mentally answer questions 2 through 6. Remember, do not simply set a goal or identify a task you can check off a list.

2. Why do you want to be successful?
3. What are some ways to achieve success?
4. What would people say about you if you were successful?
5. How would success enable you to contribute to or positively impact other people's lives?
6. Take a few moments to imagine yourself as successful. What does success feel like? What habits or behaviors have led to your success?
7. Reevaluate the definition of success you wrote to answer question 1. In the box below, revise it based on your answers to questions 2 through 6.

Discussion Questions

Now it is time to make use of your definition of success in your daily life. Does your definition make you feel motivated to try to achieve success? Does it feel complete? Is it something you can apply to your everyday life? Your definition of success should make you feel determined and give you clear guidance that you can apply whether you're working on a new project at work, spending time with friends and family, or simply trying to decide how to spend your day off. This is a lot to ask of a definition, so you may need to refine yours. Try living with it for a while. Write your working definition of success down in a place where you can look at it often—on a sticky note attached to your computer monitor, on a card in your wallet, or as a daily reminder in your calendar. Then use the questions below to help you test or revise your definition of what it means to be successful.

1. *Take inventory daily.* What do you want to have accomplished at the end of each day? What habits and traits do you want to embody in your daily life? Does your definition of success support your answers to these questions?
2. *Seek feedback from those who know you best.* Sit down with your family and friends. Ask them, "What does it mean to be successful?" Discuss their responses and share your own definition. Solicit their feedback, not so that you can change your idea to reach some kind of consensus but because they may provide input that helps you clarify your vision. What do those closest to you say about your definition? How does their feedback affect your thoughts about your definition?
3. *Look for concrete examples and role models.* Make a list of successful people you know, either in real life or as public figures. Why did you label them as successful? What behaviors or habits are they adopting in order to be successful? What do you think they would say it means to be successful?

Achieving your definition of success is an everyday work in progress. Success is not a heredity trait, an intrinsic value, or an innate skill — you have to work at it continually. As you strive for success daily, having your definition can keep you focused on progress. Success is not about having an epiphany or achieving one pivotal goal; rather, it is a long-term journey of implementing your definition of success each day. When you know what to do to be successful, you can make those actions and habits a sustained part of your daily life.

Source: Adapted from White, R. (2014). *Connecting happiness and success*. Retrieved from http://connectinghappinessandsuccess .com/wp-content/uploads/2013/09/Defining-Success-12_30_12 .pdf.

Case Study 1.1

Facebook.com: The Cambridge Analytica Scandal

What online community signs up 700,000 new members each day? The answer: Facebook.com. The Facebook community included 750 million followers by mid-2011. Facebook's founder, Mark Zuckerberg, was named *Time* magazine's "Person of the Year" in 2010.

The statistics associated with Facebook have taken on nearly epic proportions. If Facebook users in January 2011 were members of a country, that nation would have the third highest population in the world, with only China and India ahead. One out of every 12 people on the planet has a Facebook account. And, in the world of Internet hits, one out of every four page views in the United States occurs on the Facebook site. Facebook has caused dramatic shifts in everyday life, the core of which are new cultural patterns of interpersonal interactions. Marketing professionals have quickly moved into this realm, along with the companies they serve.

Many users around the world are familiar with the Facebook.com opening page. The screen prominently displays the Facebook logo, an important element of its international marketing presence. To maintain interest, the content of the opening photos rotates, giving the website an evolving visual presence. Also, by being user-friendly, the site encourages visitors to try the product. The effective use of the blue, light gray, and white background creates an appealing but simple opening page. The images fit well with the core selling points of the product.

The history of Facebook begins with a 19-year-old sophomore attending Harvard University early in the 21st century. Zuckerberg built a web service in his dorm to create a website that allowed students in college to connect with one another by networking. In less than a decade, the company grew to the size it now enjoys, dwarfing all other social media and making Zuckerberg a billionaire many times over along the way. In early 2011, Facebook was valued at nearly $50 billion. As *Time* noted, "we are now running our social lives through a for-profit network."

Enter Cambridge Analytica

Cambridge Analytica was a company that gathered information from social networking sites. For example, it used profile information to target voters with specific messages on Facebook and other online services during the presidential campaign during 2014–2016. These messages went beyond the messages based on party affiliation.

What did Cambridge Analytica do? It created profiles (or models) known as "psychographic" targeting. The company claimed it used "data to change audience behavior," both commercially and politically.

Here's where it gets interesting. In 2014, Cambridge Analytica hired a Soviet-born American researcher, Aleksandr Kogan, to profile Facebook users by analyzing the things they "liked" (the thumbs-up icon). He created an app called This Is Your Digital Life, which had a set of personality surveys. And 300,000 Facebook users downloaded the app. Because Facebook controls were not well understood, Kogan collected data not just on those users but on their Facebook friends—an estimated 87 million people. The app, in its terms of service, disclosed that it would collect data on users and their friends. But who actually reads the terms of service? People generally click the "I agree" box because they want to get on with personality surveys and learning about themselves, right?

Cambridge Analytica was hired to work for the 2016 campaigns of Donald Trump and other Republican party candidates. When the news broke on how Cambridge Analytica had gathered Facebook data, the company suspended its CEO, who had boasted on camera how the firm had been willing to offer bribes and use entrapment with prostitutes to ruin political candidates' reputations (all of this is illegal, of course). Cambridge Analytica flatly denied using data from Kogan's app or employing psychographic modeling in the 2016 election. But the Facebook data collected may have been used in other ways on certain voters.

In April 2018, Facebook CEO Mark Zuckerberg testified before Congress regarding how Facebook protects users' privacy. He was also questioned on whether social networks should be regulated.

Zuckerberg posted to his Facebook page, assuring users that additional steps were being taken to ensure user privacy. A feature was removed that had allowed users to enter phone numbers or email addresses into Facebook's search tool to find other people. The company also made it easier for users to adjust their privacy settings. However, Facebook shares dropped almost 18% in the 10 days after the news broke. An online "#DeleteFacebook" movement was started by angry users.

Exit Cambridge Analytica

Due to the scandal, Cambridge Analytica declared bankruptcy and shut down in May 2018. The London firm blamed "unfairly negative media coverage," saying that its practices are legal and that psychological profiles are widely used for online advertising. "The siege of media coverage has driven away virtually all of the company's customers and suppliers," Cambridge Analytica said in a statement. "As a result, it has been determined that it is no longer viable to continue operating the business."

Discussion Questions

1. How do you feel about Cambridge Analytica accessing the personal data of Facebook users without their specific knowledge? Is this ethical?
2. Do you think ads on social media influence the decisions of people who see them? Should social networking sites be used in this way? Explain your answers.
3. Was Facebook's response adequate? What specific actions should Facebook take now?
4. Do you feel that Facebook and other social media sites should be regulated by the government? Explain your position.

Sources: Adapted from Baack, D. W., Harris, E. G., & Baack, D. (2016). Facebook.com: Global marketing opportunities and connectivity. *SAGE Business Cases*. Retrieved from https://sk.sagepub.com/cases/facebook-global-marketing-opportunities-and-connectivity?fromsearch=true; Bloomberg. (2018, April 10). Facebook Cambridge Analytica scandal: 10 questions answered. Retrieved from http://fortune.com/2018/04/10/facebook-cambridge-analytica-what-happened/; Kang, C., Hsu, T.,

Roose, K., Singer, N., & Rosenberg, M. (2018, April 11). Mark Zuckerberg testimony: Day 2 brings tougher questioning. Retrieved from https://www.nytimes.com/2018/04/11/us/politics/zuckerberg-facebook-cambridge-analytica.html.

Self-Assessment 1.1

Are You Theory X or Theory Y?

This self-assessment exercise identifies whether your leadership philosophy is Theory X or Theory Y as determined by research. The goal of this assessment is for you to learn about your general assumptions about people and work and to understand how this may affect how you lead them. There are no right or wrong answers, and this is not a test. You don't have to share your results with others unless you wish to do so.

Part I. Taking the Assessment

Instructions: Circle the response that best describes your behavior.

Statements	Strongly Disagree	Disagree	Neutral	Agree	Strongly Agree
1. Most people will try to do as little work as possible.	1	2	3	4	5
2. Most people are industrious.	1	2	3	4	5
3. Most people are lazy and don't want to work.	1	2	3	4	5
4. People naturally like to work.	1	2	3	4	5
5. Most employees will slack off if left alone by managers.	1	2	3	4	5
6. Most employees are capable of providing ideas that are helpful to the organizations where they work.	1	2	3	4	5
7. Employees possess imagination and creativity.	1	2	3	4	5
8. Employees' ideas are generally not useful to organizations.	1	2	3	4	5
9. Most employees lack the ability to help the organizations where they work.	1	2	3	4	5
10. Most employees are trustworthy.	1	2	3	4	5

Part II. Scoring Instructions

In Part I, you rated yourself on 10 questions. Add the numbers you circled in each of the columns to derive your scores for Theory X and Theory Y. During class, we will discuss each approach, its strengths and weaknesses, and how this may affect your leadership style.

Theory X	Theory Y
1. _____	2. _____
3. _____	4. _____
5. _____	6. _____
7. _____	8. _____
9. _____	10. _____
Total _____	Total _____

Source: Adapted from Kopelman, R. E., Prottas, D. J. & Falk, D. W. (2012). Development of a measure of Theory X and Y assumptions. *Journal of Managerial Issues, 24*(4), 450–470.

Interpretation:

If your Theory X score is greater than 12, your assumptions are more in line with Theory X.

If your Theory Y score is greater than 12, your assumptions are more in line with Theory Y.

Discussion Questions

1. Were you surprised by your results? What does this tell you about how you view human nature?

2. Compare your scores with five other students in the class. Do you believe that most people are more Theory X or Theory Y?

3. How might your X/Y assumptions relate to how much you listen to the ideas of your followers and allow them to participate in decisions you are responsible for?

Get the tools you need to sharpen your study skills. SAGE edge offers a robust online environment featuring an impressive array of free tools and resources. Access practice quizzes, eFlashcards, video, and multimedia at **edge.sagepub.com/scanduragower**.

PLANNING

PART II

CHAPTER 2

MAKING DECISIONS AND USING ANALYTICS

CHAPTER LEARNING OBJECTIVES

After studying this chapter, you should be able to:

2.1 Explain why decision-making is important to a manager's effectiveness.

2.2 Describe the role of intuition in decision-making.

2.3 List and explain major decision traps and how to avoid them.

2.4 Define creativity and discuss the three components of creativity.

2.5 Give an example of business analytics.

2.6 Be familiar with the concept of big data and its use in business decision-making.

Get the edge on your studies at **edge.sagepub.com/scanduragower**

- Take the chapter quiz
- Review key terms with eFlashcards
- Explore multimedia resources, SAGE readings, and more!

Decisions: The Big Ones

It often seems that a manager's career is an endless succession of decisions. Managers make all kinds of decisions, ranging from routine daily decisions to long-term decisions on strategy. A solid record of good decisions leads an individual to the top of an organization. There are certain decisions a manager has to get right. We have all made decisions we regret. However, there are times when a bad decision can ruin not only a manager's career but the organization's success as well. What are the things a manager must get right? The following list provides examples of critical decisions that may make or break a manager's career. Smart managers pay close attention to these big decisions.

1. *Hiring.* One of the most important decisions a manager makes is who. Who will you choose to run your organization? If you select the right people, with the right skills, they will advance the organization's mission. If you do not have people working for you who are trustworthy,

you are in real trouble. When managers fail, it is often due to at least one poor decision regarding whom they hired. For example, suppose a manager hires a brilliant marketing manager from a top school. The marketing manager's big-picture perspective results in large cost overruns on an advertising campaign that fails. It reflects badly on the brand manager, since top management holds her responsible for the expensive and failed campaign.

Hiring decisions are tough. Managers have to make judgment calls about new employees based on limited résumé information and maybe one interview. Sometimes the process is rushed, and even when it is not, it is hard to assess potential from a résumé or even interviews. Skills are difficult to evaluate, and determining character is even more difficult. Nevertheless, managers know that great organizational performance is due to great people. Managers look everywhere to find the best talent and interview and assess potential employees. Keep this phrase in mind: "Hire slow." Hiring mistakes can be costly, and poor-performing employees can be difficult to terminate.

2. *Firing.* Effective managers remove the toxicity of poor-performing employees from their organization. This is tough. They recognize their responsibility for creating an effective workplace where everyone contributes. A negative employee poisons a working environment, and removing them is often the only choice. The negative employee should receive a lot of feedback, coaching, and opportunities to improve. However, sometimes this does not take, and the employee has to be let go. No one loves firing people, but firing a toxic employee leaves the manager feeling like they did the right thing for the team and the organization. For example, suppose an employee does not pull his weight on a team project. The project is ultimately successful, but the team members feel it was unfair that they had to do his work. Something has to be done about this situation to improve morale, and the employee is fired.

3. *Decisions with ethical implications.* Managers face ethical decisions that sometimes involve a gray area. It is not obvious what is right and what is wrong. However, the best decision-makers transform the gray zone into choices between right and wrong. This is not easy, since reward systems and the drive for short-term results make it tempting to take ethical shortcuts. A manager's reputation is on trial with these decisions. However, results are not worth sacrificing ethics.

For example, to do business in Latin America, an accounting manager might be asked by their boss to create a "slush fund" for tips to move products ahead when being loaded onto cargo ships. After all, this is a "cultural thing." The manager stands their ground and says no, but has to take responsibility for late shipments.

4. *"Fork-in-the-road" decisions.* There is a famous quote from leadership expert John C. Maxwell: "Every major difficulty you face in life is a fork in the road. You choose which track you will head down, toward breakdown or breakthrough."[1] Managers face challenging "moments of truth" that may result in success or failure. Their decisions will alter the future of the organization—and they know this. For example, a manager might have to choose among software packages to enhance data analytics. Another example is when managers make strategic calls regarding which markets to pursue. Operational decisions affect how efficiently employees can perform their work. The best managers think about these directional decisions carefully by diagnosing the situation and weighing options. They try to maximize success by asking for outside opinions and having others challenge their assumptions. They get the right data to learn the right direction. Then, they are decisive and turn the decision into action.

5. *Responding to mistakes.* Despite the best efforts, sometimes decisions result in unsuccessful outcomes. The competitive landscape may change, resulting in a prior decision not being effective. A manager must recognize this and "own" their decisions. They need to follow up and constantly monitor the results, and be ready to change course if needed. They are comfortable saying, "This was wrong, I was wrong, and we need to go in a different direction." A lack of this level of courage is too common, and perpetuates bad decisions and adversely affects organizations. For example, suppose a manager in a condiment company backs a new low-carb barbecue sauce, since the sales force says customers want lower-carb foods. However, it turns out that it has a regional flavor and will not sell outside the sales area. The manager changes course and limits production of the item.

Sources: Adapted from Azarello, P. (2013). The two most important decisions that an executive can make. Retrieved from https://www.tlnt.com/the-two-most-important-decisions-that-an-executive-can-make/; Myatt, M. (2012). 6 tips for making better decisions. Retrieved from https://www.forbes.com/sites/mikemyatt/2012/03/28/6-tips-for-making-better-decisions/#47294b8e34dc; Petty, A. (2017). 5 critical decisions that will make or break you as a leader. Retrieved from https://www.thebalance.com/decisions-that-make-or-break-you-as-a-leader-2275843.

▼ FIGURE 2.0

Textbook Organization

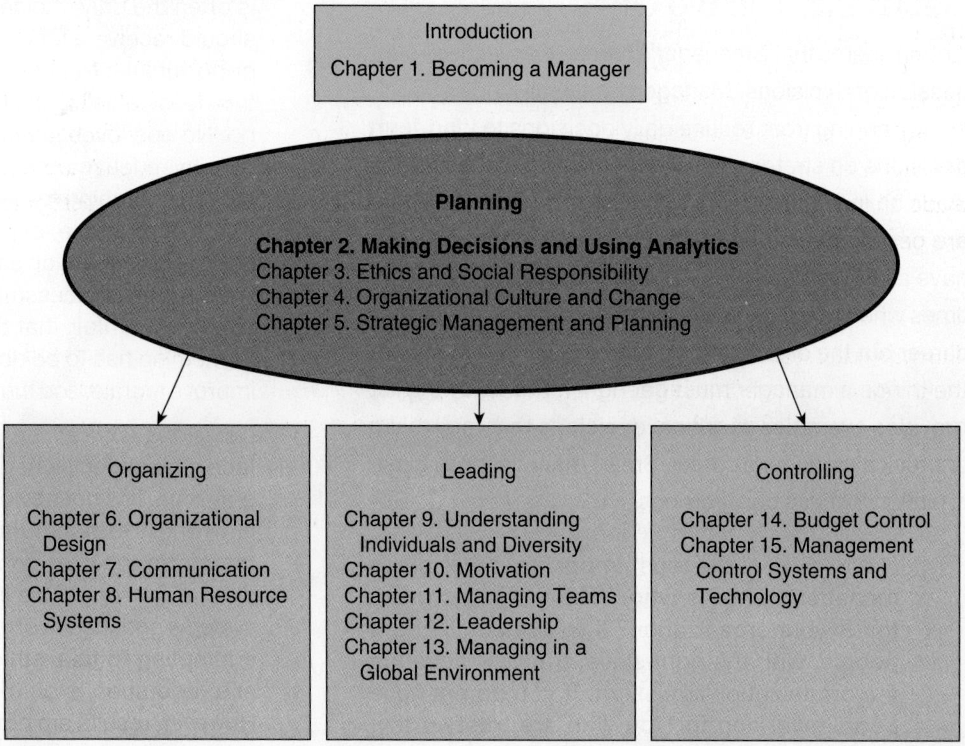

Introduction

Chapter 1. Becoming a Manager

Planning

Chapter 2. Making Decisions and Using Analytics
Chapter 3. Ethics and Social Responsibility
Chapter 4. Organizational Culture and Change
Chapter 5. Strategic Management and Planning

Organizing

Chapter 6. Organizational Design
Chapter 7. Communication
Chapter 8. Human Resource Systems

Leading

Chapter 9. Understanding Individuals and Diversity
Chapter 10. Motivation
Chapter 11. Managing Teams
Chapter 12. Leadership
Chapter 13. Managing in a Global Environment

Controlling

Chapter 14. Budget Control
Chapter 15. Management Control Systems and Technology

T hese big decisions illustrate the importance of effective decision-making for managers. Decisions and financial success are related. Rather than getting lost in the many decisions you face, pay particular attention to these five important ones. Top-performing managers get more of these decisions right than wrong.

From these examples of the five make-or-break decisions, it is clear that making the right decisions plays a large role in a manager's career success. This chapter will cover both classic and contemporary research on decision-making that every manager must know to make the right decisions, at the right time.

Decision-Making in Organizations

Learning Objective 2.1: Explain why decision-making is important to a manager's effectiveness.

Decision-making affects organizational performance. The right decisions ensure the success of strategies ranging from restructuring to the introduction of new products or processes. Researchers at Bain & Company Consulting surveyed executives worldwide from 760 companies, most with revenues exceeding $1 billion, to understand how effective those companies were at making and executing their critical decisions.[2] Executives were asked to assess their decision quality (whether decisions proved to be right more often than not), speed (whether decisions were made faster or slower than their competitors' were), yield (how well decisions were translated into action), and effort (the time, trouble, and expense required for each key decision). An overall score for each firm was created and then related to each firm's financial performance. The researchers found that decision effectiveness and financial results were highly related for all firms, regardless of the industry or country in which they were located. Firms that were more effective at decision-making and execution generated average total shareholder returns nearly six percentage points higher than those of other firms in the study. The researchers also found that many companies have room to improve their decision-making performance. The typical organization has the potential to double its decision effectiveness.

Managers who collect information and use analytical techniques make decisions that are more effective and profitable. As you learned in Chapter 1, decision-making is central in Mintzberg's classic analysis of the nature of managerial work.[3] Decision-making is a fundamental part of a manager's job. As a manager, you will likely be promoted based on your record of making solid decisions that improve your organization's efficiency and effectiveness. Managers must own the decisions they make, so it is important to know how they are best made. First, the rational approach to decision-making is discussed—this represents best practice in decision-making that every manager should strive to attain.

The Rational Decision-Making Process

The rational decision-making model presents a series of logical steps decision-makers follow to determine the optimal choice.[4] Examples of optimization include maximizing revenue and minimizing cost. The eight-step process for rational decision-making is shown in Figure 2.1. The steps follow.

1. Step 1: The problem (or opportunity) is defined, and then information is gathered and analyzed.
2. Step 2. Decision criteria are established.
3. Step 3. The decision criteria are weighted.
4. Step 4. Based on this information, a broad set of alternatives (or possible courses of action) are identified.
5. Step 5. These alternatives are evaluated in terms of the established decision criteria.

6. Step 6. Based on analysis of the alternative courses of action, a decision is made that is projected to achieve the best possible outcome for the organization. Sometimes the decision-maker has competing objectives and must balance the concerns and choose an optimal solution.
7. Step 7. Decision-makers develop action steps for implementation of the decision.
8. Step 8. The final step is to evaluate the decision, which provides feedback for the further identification of problems.

As you can see, the decision-making process is a cycle that generates new information that is fed back into the problem-solving process.

This model includes a number of assumptions. The rational model assumes that decision-makers have complete information, are able to develop an exhaustive list of alternatives, weight them, and then choose a decision with the highest value and/or lowest cost to the organization. At the operational level of management, some problems are routine and a procedure is used to solve them. In reality, however, most problems that managers must solve lack structure, and so it is impossible to program a response.[5] The level of problem structure decreases as one moves from the operational to the senior management level. The top management team faces the most unstructured problems, which have to do with the strategic direction of the organization.

CRITICAL THINKING QUESTIONS

Give an example of a decision you made that did not follow this eight-step rational process. Explain which steps in the model you did not follow and why.

▼ FIGURE 2.1

The Rational Decision-Making Process

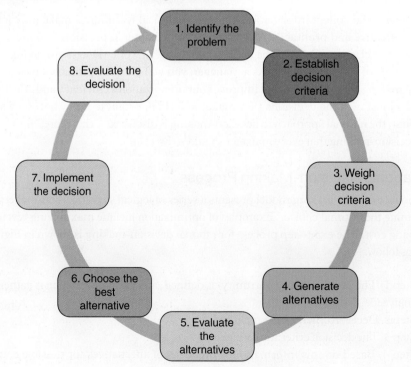

Source: Adapted from Nutt, P. (1984). Types of organizational decision processes. *Administrative Science Quarterly, 29,* 414–450.

Limits to Rational Decision-Making

Managers sometimes fail to identify the problem correctly at the start of the decision-making process. In addition, some managers consider only a few alternatives rather than a broad set of possible options. They may consider only the most obvious alternatives and not brainstorm creative solutions (creative problem-solving is discussed later in this chapter). Managers may choose a suboptimal course of action (resulting in a lose-lose scenario).[6]

Often, decisions are made without complete information. This happens because of the lack of available information relevant to the problem or time pressure. Sometimes the decision-maker does not have the time to follow the rational process. An experimental study found that under a time constraint, research subjects reverted to a familiar decision-making method rather than attempting to optimize.[7] A review of 89 samples with 17,704 subjects[8] found that time pressure weakens the effects of careful decision-making on performance. For example, a top management team confronted with a product defect might be under time pressure to make a decision on whether or not to recall the product from the market. Such decision constraints combine to jeopardize the ability of the team to implement the rational decision-making process and make a good decision. Decision-makers have limits on their ability to assimilate large amounts of information, and this is called **bounded rationality**.

Bounded Rationality

Decision-makers operate within bounded rationality rather than perfect rationality. What this means is that decision-makers simplify complex problems to limit the amount of information-processing needed.[9] Human beings have a limited capacity to process large amounts of information in the context of decision-making to make optimal decisions. In many instances, managers engage in **satisficing**—they make a decision that is satisfactory but not optimal. However, within the boundaries of this simplified model, they behave rationally.[10]

What do managers do when they satisfice? They limit the information analyzed, and they limit the number of alternatives considered. They choose the first acceptable alternative they see rather than continuing their information search and analysis until they find the best option. Bounded rationality in decision-making is the result of organizational factors (e.g., the top management team presses for their preferred course of action), individual limits on the ability to process information (e.g., limiting creative brainstorming), and perceptions (e.g., errors in interpretation of the data used to make a decision).[11]

Bounded rationality is also the result of two guesses the decision-maker must address: (1) a guess about uncertain future consequences and (2) a guess about uncertain future preferences.[12] This happens because at the time of a decision, managers cannot predict the future. At times, they do not even know what they want to see happen in the future. So the decision-making process may be influenced by other psychological processes, such as the need to justify prior decisions to others.[13] This perspective highlights the importance of uncertainty and risk in the decision-making process. The next section will describe **prospect theory**, which is one of the most important frameworks for explaining decision-making under risk and uncertainty.

Prospect Theory

Daniel Kahneman and Amos Tversky won the Nobel Prize in Economics in 2002, in part for their work on the prospect theory of decision-making.[14] Their work focused on risk perceptions in decisions people make. The authors conducted studies in which they asked research subjects to make decisions when given two monetary options that involved prospective losses and gains. The following set of choices is one they used in their classic studies.

Choosing B indicates that the person is more risk-averse than those choosing A. If you chose B for question 1, and then chose A for question 2, you are like the majority of people

You have $1,000 and you must pick one of the following choices:
Choice A: You have a 50% chance of gaining $1,000, and a 50% chance of gaining $0.
Choice B: You have a 100% chance of gaining $500.

You have $2,000 and you must pick one of the following choices:
Choice A: You have a 50% chance of losing $1,000, and a 50% chance of losing $0.
Choice B: You have a 100% chance of losing $500.

Source: Kahneman, D. & Tversky, A. (1979). Prospect Theory: An analysis of decision under risk. Econometrica, 47(2), 263-291.]

presented with this decision. If people made decisions according to rational decision-making norms, they would pick either A or B in both situations (that is, they should be indifferent because the expected value of both outcomes is the same). However, the results of this study showed that an overwhelming majority of people chose B for question 1 and A for question 2. Why? People are willing to settle for a reasonable gain (even if they have a reasonable chance of earning more), but are willing to engage in risk-seeking behaviors where they can limit their losses. In other words, losses weigh more heavily emotionally in decision-making than equivalent gains. Are you a risk-taker, or are you risk-averse? You will learn more about your attitudes toward risk by completing Self-Assessment 2.1.

Risk management is now a part of every manager's job.

©Den Rise/Shutterstock

Framing

Prospect theory explains that people put more emphasis on gains than losses—they make decisions that increase their gains and avoid loss. People treat the two types of risk (gain versus loss) in a completely different way to maximize their perceived outcome. However, this may result in irrational decisions that are not based on a correct calculation of expected utility. Prospect theory explains why decisions are sometimes irrational. This may be, in part, due to **framing**. Framing refers to whether questions are presented as gains or losses. Leaders must pay attention to how decisions are framed when they are presented. As the examples of monetary choices above illustrate, decisions may be affected by how options are presented (people are more risk-averse when decisions are framed in terms of loss). It is important to consider how information regarding risk and uncertainty is presented.

CRITICAL THINKING QUESTIONS

How could you use prospect theory to get a better deal on a used car you are buying? How could you frame options as gains or losses to get a lower price?

Kahneman's book *Thinking, Fast and Slow*[15] examines two modes of thinking that psychology has labeled System 1 and System 2 thinking (see Figure 2.2).[16] System 1 thinking represents automatic and effortless decision-making that is often involuntary. System 2 thinking is complex thinking that demands mental effort, including complex analytics. You will learn more about such analytics later in this chapter. That said, System 1 thinking represents **intuition**, which has received research attention as well as a great deal of interest in the popular press.

Two Decision-Making Routes

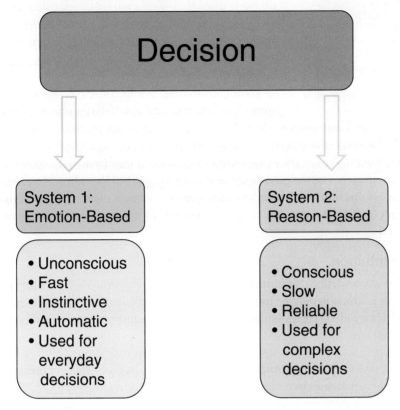

Source: Adapted from WebMarketingHub. (2018). B2B decision making process: The role of emotions. Retrieved from https://www.the-b2b-webmarketing-hub.com/index.php/2018/03/27/b2b-decision-making-process-the-role-of-emotions/.

Intuition

Learning Objective 2.2: Describe the role of intuition in decision-making.

"The essence of intuition or intuitive responses is that they are reached with little apparent effort, and typically without conscious awareness. They involve little or no conscious deliberation."[17] Four characteristics comprise intuition:

- a nonconscious process
- involving holistic associations
- that are produced rapidly,
- which result in affectively charged judgments.[18]

Intuition helps managers make fast and accurate decisions. While research on such unconscious thought processes is somewhat new, available evidence supports the idea that intuitive processes should be considered part of a manager's decision-making.

Malcom Gladwell's book *Blink: The Power of Thinking Without Thinking*[19] popularized the idea that intuition may play an important role in decision-making. Gladwell notes that people learn by their experiences and that they may not know why they know things but are certain they know them. He explains the influences of the unconscious mind on decisions and puts forth the premise that there can be value in a decision made in the "blink of an eye" rather than after months of analysis. Gladwell introduces the idea of "thin-slicing," in which the

Small business owners often rely on their intuition to predict which foods their customers will buy.

©iStockphoto.com/monkeybusinessimages

unconscious mind finds patterns in situations based on very brief experiences. However, he cautions that errors are made when thin-slicing is used to make decisions, due to the decision traps discussed later in this chapter.

Intuition is not the same thing as common sense. Intuition is perception without conscious thinking and can seem like common sense. However, intuition varies greatly, from basic gut feelings to complicated judgments like a physician's quick diagnosis. According to Simon, "intuition and judgment—at least good judgment—are simply analyses frozen into habit and into the capacity for rapid response through recognition."[20] In other words, intuition is the unconscious operation in the brain formed by freezing sensing and judgment. By contrast, common sense is not typically repetitive; it is a more simplified thought process. Another major difference is that intuition is individual and common sense is often social (i.e., what the majority of people think as a consensus).[21] A comparison of intuition and common sense is shown in Table 2.1.

Benefits of Intuition

Most managers acknowledge that intuition plays a role in their decisions. They often rely on "gut feelings" or instincts in making important decisions, particularly related to innovation.[22] In-depth interviews with 60 professionals across a variety of industries and occupations found that intuition has benefits:[23]

- *Expedited decision-making.* Intuition results in quicker decisions that get the job done, adapting to a changing environment.
- *Improvement of the decision.* Intuition provides a check and balance, allows for fairness, avoids having to rework the decision, and causes managers to pay more attention.
- *Facilitation of personal development.* Intuition gives a manager more power, develops instincts, helps the manager apply their experiences, and allows positive risk-taking.
- *Promotion of decisions compatible with company culture.* Intuition helps managers make decisions that correspond with the organization's values.

CRITICAL THINKING QUESTIONS

Give an example of when you made a decision based on your intuition. Why did you think you knew the right thing to do without analysis? Discuss the success or failure of this decision. Would you rely on your intuition for a similar decision in the future? Explain.

Another decision tool that is often used in organizations when decisions are routine is a heuristic. These useful decision rules are applied widely in organizations, and are discussed next.

▼ TABLE 2.1

Intuition Versus Common Sense

Intuition	Common Sense
• Perception without conscious thinking • Gut feelings • Individual (what an individual thinks)	• Perception with conscious thinking • Simplified thought process • Social (what the majority agrees)

Heuristics

The use of **heuristics** or decision rules is an effective way to manage information and make improved decisions. Heuristics rely on one or more of the following methods to reduce effort:[24]

1. Examining fewer cues—for example, by limiting information to only what's important.
2. Reducing the difficulty associated with retrieving and storing cue values—for example, by using *less than*, *equal to*, or *greater than* instead of actual values.
3. Simplifying the weighting principles for cues—for example, by weighing each piece of information equally.
4. Integrating less information—for example, by selecting threshold values and accepting what is "good enough."
5. Examining fewer alternatives—for example, by using pairwise comparisons and then selecting one alternative from each set.

Heuristics underlie both intuitive and deliberate decision-making.[25] The selection of decision rules is a two-step process in which the task and the individual's memory constrain the set of applicable rules. The individual's ability to process information and perception of what is rational guide the final decision. Deliberate judgments are less accurate than intuitive judgments. In both cases, accuracy depends on the match between the rule employed and the characteristics of the situation. For example, the use of a financial criterion to decide whether to enter an international market may miss opportunities that might only be realized if the national culture is considered. Table 2.2 shows 10 commonly used heuristics. For example, the **recognition heuristic** is commonly used in business decisions in which decision-makers select one of two alternatives because one has the higher value on a given criterion (such as return on investment, or ROI). Another possible heuristic is **fluency**, in which the quickest decision is selected (e.g., when there is a pressing need to bring a new product to market before competition enters). The **equality heuristic** prescribes that resources are allocated equally (e.g., through budgets allocated for entertainment expenses across sales units). **Imitating the majority** involves doing what most people do (e.g., creating an Instagram account because most others in your industry have one). **Imitating the successful** is what is commonly referred to as "best practices," in which successful practices are imitated. For example, college football teams may imitate the successful "turnover chain" implemented by Coach Manny Diaz at the University of Miami.[26] Whether decisions are based on intuition or analysis, using one of these 10 heuristics should reduce the effort expended in making decisions by simplifying them.

Imitating the successful: Defensive back Sheldrick Redwine (22) celebrates his interception with the University of Miami Turnover Chain during a game.

©Icon Sportswire/Getty Images

CRITICAL THINKING QUESTIONS

Provide an example of how heuristics are used in college admission decisions based on minimum SAT scores and grade point average. What specific cutoff scores are used to make college admission decisions? What are the limitations of using heuristics in this way?

Heuristics are useful because they aid in simplifying challenging problems so that the problem is then rapidly solved. However, there is a danger in simplification in that it may lead to biases and decision traps. Managers need to be mindful of these decision traps and know how to avoid them. The next sections review common decision errors.

Ten Heuristics for Managers

Heuristic	Definition
Recognition Heuristic	If one of two alternatives is recognized, infer that it has the higher value on the criterion
Fluency Heuristic	If both alternatives are recognized but one is recognized faster, infer that it has the higher value on the criterion
Take-the-Best	To infer which of two alternatives has the higher value, (a) search through cues in order of vality, (b) stop search as soon as a cue discriminates, and (c) choose the alternative this cue favors
Tallying: Unit-Weight	To estimate a criterion, do not estimate weights, but simply count
Linear Model	The number of positive cues
Satisficing	Search through alternatives, and choose the one that exceeds your aspiration level
Equality Heuristic: 1/N	Allocate resources equally to each of N alternatives
Default Heuristic	If there is a default, do nothing
Tit-for-tat	Cooperate first, and them imitate your partner's last behavior
Imitate the Majority	Consider the majority of people, and imitate their behavior
Imitate the Successful	Consider the most successful person/organization, and imitate the behavior

Source: Adapted from Kruglanski, A. W. & Gigerenzer, G. (2011). Intuitive and deliberate judgments are based on common principles. *Psychological Review,* 118(1), 97–109.

Decision Traps

Learning Objective 2.3: List and explain major decision traps and how to avoid them.

Hindsight Bias

Hindsight bias, also commonly referred to as the **I-knew-it-all-along effect,**[27] is well established as having far-reaching effects. Hindsight bias is defined as "the tendency for individuals with outcome knowledge (hindsight) to claim they would have estimated a probability of occurrence for the reported outcome that is higher than they would have estimated in foresight (without the outcome information)."[28]

Four processes underlie this belief.

- First, the person recalls the old event and responds consistently with the memory of it.
- Second, the person focuses on the outcome and adjusts their belief, pretending they did not know the outcome.
- Third, the belief is reconstructed based on what the person's judgment would have been prior to the outcome. Research shows people do this by first sampling evidence related to the judgment from their long-term memories and the external world. Once an outcome is known, people look for and retain evidence that fits the outcome rather than evidence that contradicts it.
- The fourth process is based on a person's motivation to present themselves favorably to others. People want to be seen as accurate, and they claim when something happens that they "knew it all along."

A review of 90 studies[29] of hindsight bias showed support for the existence of this bias in decision-making. Hindsight bias may influence how outcomes of decisions are interpreted after the fact and lead to poor decision-making, since a manager may ignore important information in the present and then reconstruct the past as if they had the knowledge. Thus, a manager's ability to learn from past mistakes is compromised by hindsight bias. This may be compounded if the manager is also overconfident in their decision-making ability and this is another decision trap.

CRITICAL THINKING QUESTIONS

Provide an example of a time when someone said "I knew it all along." Did you believe them? Why or why not?

Overconfidence

Overconfidence bias (sometimes referred to as **hubris**) is an inflated level of confidence in how accurate a person's knowledge or predictions are.[30] Hubris is foolish overconfidence. This implies a level of ignorance or arrogance that is likely to cause failures. The term *hubris* originates with ancient Greek mythology, where it was used to describe arrogance before the gods. The goddess Nemesis often doomed mortals with their own foolish overconfidence as punishment.[31]

The bankruptcy of the Schwinn bicycle company under the leadership of the fourth-generation CEO, Edward R. Schwinn Jr., offers a cautionary tale. The company was founded in 1895 by Schwinn's great-grandfather, a German-born bicycle maker. By the 1950s, Schwinn held 28% of the market and dominated the industry due to innovation. Schwinn was the best-recognized brand for low-cost, functional transportation for children and adults. However, when they were at the top, Schwinn began to take it easy. It lost the innovation edge. Schwinn dismissed three important new ideas: lighter bikes, sleeker bikes, and mountain bikes. They soon found they could not meet the challenges created by their competition.[32] Schwinn eventually declared bankruptcy and became part of a multinational conglomerate.[33]

Why does hubris occur? Due to bounded rationality, the ability to estimate probable outcomes is critical to a manager's ability to make sound decisions in organizations. Research has shown that accurate forecasting improves a manager's ability to create an effective vision for their organization.[34] To avoid overconfidence bias, managers may keep it in check by assigning a trusted follower to critique the decisions (i.e., play the "devil's advocate" role), by being open to different opinions, and by placing limits on their power by having someone else approve decisions (a peer, for example). Reminding oneself of past decision-making errors may also be an effective way to keep overconfidence in check.[35]

A bicycle zone sign sits outside the Schwinn/GT Corporation headquarters on July 17, 2001 in Boulder, CO, when it filed for bankruptcy protection for the second time.

©Michael Smith/Staff/Getty Images

Escalation of Commitment

Escalation of commitment occurs when individuals continue a failing course of action after receiving feedback that shows it is not working. In effect, they try to turn the situation around by increasing investment after a setback.[36] People continue to invest in failing courses of action to recoup their losses and to show that they have made the right decision all along. This is sometimes called the **sunk-costs fallacy**, as the continued commitment is made because a person has already invested in this course of action and does not recognize that what they invested initially is sunk (or gone).

An experimental study [37] found that decision-makers continued to invest in research and development (R&D) of a failing company when they had personal responsibility for the negative outcomes. The reason for this is self-justification, or the need to demonstrate to other people that one's actions are rational. In addition to self-justification, escalation may be caused by risk perceptions (recall prospect theory), group decision-making failures, or an organization's tendency to avoid change.[38]

Figure 2.3 shows the reasons why leaders may engage in escalation of commitment. It happens for a variety of organizational, social, and psychological reasons. Organizations may be rigid and resistant to change—decision-makers may be unable to change course. Instead of viewing the money already spent as sunk costs, decision-makers may focus on how much they have already spent.[39] Managers may let pride in their own decision-making ability (or the need to "save face") get in the way. The culture in the organization may reward decision-makers for being persistent, and this puts social pressure on them to continue to support a losing course of action. Managers hate to lose, and they want to be able to turn things around—they have the need to finish what they have started, and this may contribute to escalation.[40] Finally, continuing to invest in a decision justifies prior investments in the decision, even though it is "throwing good money after bad."

There are other examples of poor decisions due to escalation. Venture capitalists sometimes continue to invest in start-up companies even after results indicate the ideas are not working out in the marketplace.[41] Senior bank managers escalated commitment to loans they initiated

▼ FIGURE 2.3

Causes of Escalation of Commitment

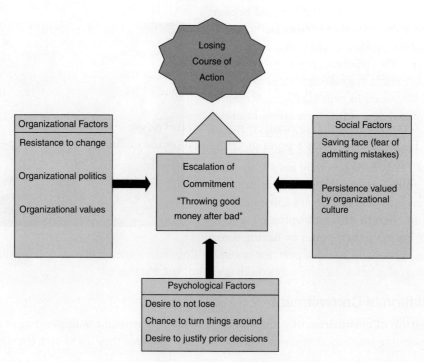

Source: Adapted from Staw, B. M. & Ross, J. (1989). Understanding behavior in escalation situations. *Science, 246,* 216–220.

by retaining them even after the loans were not being paid on time.[42] These examples illustrate that escalation is a serious decision trap leaders may fall into because they want to avoid regretting a bad decision.[43] Is it possible for a manager to avoid escalation of commitment? The following four antidotes to escalation have been proposed:[44]

1. Separate the initial decision-maker from the decision evaluator. In other words, remove the ego of the decision-maker from the evaluation of it.
2. Create accountability for decision processes only, not outcomes. Ask employees to explain or justify their decision processes (i.e., how they made the decision in the first place).
3. Shift attention away from the self. Make a balance assessment by considering the impact of the decision on other people.
4. Be careful about compliments. Try not to inflate the decision-maker's ego. Research has shown that positive feedback increases the risk of becoming overconfident about one's decisions.

Another important way that mangers can avoid falling into decision traps is through careful planning. As noted in Chapter 1, planning is the first step in the management process. Next, we will discuss how to avoid derailment of decisions by planning.

Avoiding Derailment Through Planning

Francesca Gino, in her book *Sidetracked: Why Our Decisions Get Derailed, and How We Can Stick to the Plan*,[45] describes how decision-makers often don't reach their goals due to their own decision-making traps, relationships with other people, and aspects of the situation. Her analysis suggests that things that may seem unimportant or even irrelevant to the decision may have a significant influence on sidetracking the decision-maker into following a different course of action than intended. She points out that acknowledgment of decision biases may not be enough to avoid being sidetracked into making the wrong decision. Her remedy is to start with a plan. In so doing, the leader is more prepared and better able to track progress toward goals. In the preparation of the plan, the following nine principles should be followed:

1. Raise your awareness. Become aware of your biases and keep them in check.
2. Take your emotional temperature. Examine how your emotions may cloud your decisions.
3. Zoom out. Keep the big picture in mind and other people's roles in your plan.
4. Take the other party's point of view. Analyze the decision from another person's viewpoint.
5. Question your bonds. Reflect on ties to the others and how they may affect your plan.
6. Check your reference points. Uncover the real motives behind your decisions, and whether or not you are trying to impress others.
7. Consider the source. Carefully examine the information, and consider the motives of the source as well as the situation.
8. Investigate and question the frame. Frame aspects of the decision in various ways—check whether you are too optimistic or pessimistic.
9. Make your standards shine. Reference your moral compass in making plans to be sure you do not get off course.

Managers can avoid decision traps through careful planning and analysis. Applying critical thinking (which you learned about in Chapter 1) can go a long way toward raising questions that will help avoid decision errors. Considering alternative possibilities will also help avoid decision errors such as escalation of commitment. It is important to ask "what if" during the course of the decision-making process. As you learned earlier in the description of the rational decision-making model, generating a broad set of alternative scenarios is one of the keys to decision-making. To do this, managers need to be creative. Next, the creative problem-solving process is described, as well as how a manager can become more creative in brainstorming solutions.

Creative Problem-Solving

Learning Objective 2.4: Define creativity and discuss the three components of creativity.

Creativity is defined as a process and/or a product, generally thought of as a useful solution to a problem, or novel and effective ideas.[46] However, an idea that is unique, but lacks usefulness to others, is not considered "creative."[47] This definition makes a lot of sense in the business context. For example, a team could brainstorm wild ideas for new products, and while this may be fun, they are not realistic or useful to the company in furthering its goals.

▼ FIGURE 2.4

Three-Component Model of Creativity

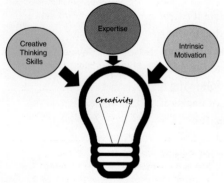

Source: Adapted from Amabile, T. M. (1998, September/October). How to kill creativity. *Harvard Business Review*, pp. 77–87.

Three-Component Model of Creativity

One of the most important models of creativity in organizations is the three-component model of creativity[48] developed by Teresa Amabile from Harvard University. As shown in Figure 2.4, creativity is a function of three contributing components: **expertise**, **creative-thinking skills**, and **intrinsic motivation**.

- *Expertise* refers to knowledge (technical, processes, and academic).
- *Creative-thinking skills* refers to how adaptable and imaginative individuals in the organization are.
- *Intrinsic motivation* refers to the urgent need to solve the problem faced, regardless of the monetary rewards expected.

Can creativity be learned? If a person has the expertise related to the problem, their creative-thinking skills can be enhanced through training.[49] In addition, managers can create the right procedures and workplace climates to enhance creativity. For example, managers can give followers challenging problems to work on and allow them the freedom to innovate. Support from the organization also matters. For creativity to thrive, Amabile believes people need resources, a positive work group climate, and encouragement.[50]

There are widespread myths about creativity. For example, some people believe that creativity is the result of a "lone genius" working in a laboratory. Quite the opposite is true; most innovative breakthroughs happen through teams that brainstorm new ideas. David Burkus's book *The Myths of Creativity: The Truth About How Innovative Companies and People Generate Ideas*[51] challenges commonly held "myths" about creative people and innovation processes. These myths and the reality demonstrated by Burkus's research are shown in Table 2.3.

CRITICAL THINKING QUESTIONS

Give an example of a time when you were creative. What was your motivation, your expertise, your creative thinking skill? How can you develop your creativity?

To implement creative ideas, managers must find the useful ones that have the best chance to be implemented. Such decisions must be based on good information. Fortunately, there is a field called business analytics that analyzes data to help mangers make good decisions.

Making Decisions Using Business Analytics

Learning Objective 2.5: Give an example of business analytics.

Business analytics is defined as "the use of data, information technology, statistical analysis, quantitative methods, and mathematical or computer-based models to help managers gain improved insight about their business operations and make better, fact-based decisions."[52]

Companies of all sizes increasingly value business analytics. According to an article in *Business Horizons*, "at its core, business analytics is about leveraging value from data."[53] Analytics is the number-one technology priority for top executives. Organizations get $10.66 of value for every $1 invested in analytics, and growth forecasts are stronger than expected, outpacing the growth in general information technology investment. Research has demonstrated that the use of analytics predicts corporate performance in terms of profitability, revenue, and shareholder return. Top-performing organizations (those that outperform their competitors) are three times as likely to be more sophisticated in their use of analytics than lower performers.[54]

Figure 2.5 depicts the relationships that are currently defining business analytics. Business analytics is considered a part of business intelligence. Statistics are the foundation for business analytics. Data mining is focused on better understanding patterns among variables in large databases using statistical and analytical tools. **Risk analysis** relies on spreadsheet models and statistical analysis to examine the impacts of uncertainty and is often supported with simulations. What-if analysis is facilitated by systematic approaches that optimize alternate scenarios through modeling. At the core of these techniques is visualization, which involves clearly communicating data at all levels of an organization, revealing patterns that aid management decision-making.

▼ TABLE 2.3

The Myths of Creativity

Myth	Reality (Evidence-Based Research Findings)
1. Eureka myth: New ideas are a flash of insight	New ideas are the result of hard work on a problem over time; the solution may come quickly after working on it
2. Breed myth: Creativity is genetic; some people are born more creative than others	Creative potential is in everyone; confidence and hard work lead to creative solutions
3. Originality myth: A new idea is one person's "intellectual property"	New ideas are actually combinations of old ideas; sharing ideas leads to more innovation
4. Expert myth: An expert or small team of experts come up with creative ideas in a company	An outsider may be better able to innovate because they are not limited by considering why something won't work
5. Incentive myth: Monetary incentives increase creativity and innovation	Incentives may help but may do more harm than good
6. Lone creator myth: Creative works come from one person working alone	Creativity is often a team effort; leadership makes a difference
7. Brainstorming myth: Generating "crazy" ideas produces creative ones	Just "throwing ideas around" alone does not result in innovation; there's a larger process
8. Cohesive myth: Everyone working on a problem should have fun together and like one another	The most creative organizations build constructive controversy and conflict into their innovation process
9. Constraints myth: Limitations hinder the process	Creativity thrives under constraints
10. Mousetrap myth: Once a new idea emerges, the creative process is finished	Great ideas are often rejected at first; finding the right marketing and the right customers is essential—new ideas must be communicated

Source: Burkus, D. (2013). The myths of creativity: The truth about how innovative companies and people generate great ideas. San Francisco, CA: Jossey Bass.

Managers rely on data to make business decisions.

©mrmohock/Shutterstock

Another useful way that managers think about analytics is to define it not as a concept but as a practice. Analytics comprises three distinct aspects:

- Descriptive analytics: statistical methods designed to explore "What happened?"
- Predictive analytics: machine-learning methods designed to predict "What will happen next?"
- Prescriptive analytics: uses optimization methods to identify best alternatives, and is designed to answer "What should the business do next?"[55]

Analytics are used throughout organizations for a variety of purposes. Some examples of business analytics are provided in Table 2.4.

Management Analytics

The term **management analytics** encompasses **behavioral analytics** and **operational analytics**. Behavioral analytics describes the collection and analysis of data on human behavior, its predictors, and its outcomes. One example of the application of behavioral analytics is the analysis of consumer behavior. Have you ever noticed that when you search for a product on Google, it begins showing up in your social media newsfeeds? E-commerce data analysis is now regarded as a "killer app" for the field of data mining. Large data sets are created by integrating click-stream records generated by searches and website activity with demographic

▼ FIGURE 2.5

Business Analytics

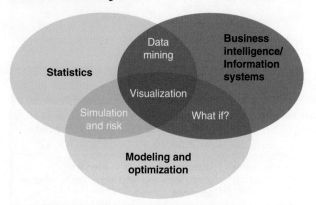

Source: Evans, J. R. (2012). Business analytics: The next frontier for decision sciences. *Decision Line*, 43(2), 4–6, p. 5.

▼ TABLE 2.4

Examples of Business Analytics

Function	Description	Exemplars
Supply chain	Simulate and optimize supply chain flows; reduce inventory and stock-outs.	Dell, Wal-Mart, Amazon
Customer selection, loyalty, and service	Identify customers with the greatest profit potential; increase likelihood that they will want the product or service offering; retain their loyalty.	Harrah's, Capital One, Barclays
Pricing	Identify the price that will maximize yield, or profit.	Progressive, Marriott
Human capital	Select the best employees for particular tasks or jobs, at particular compensation levels.	New England Patriots, Oakland A's, Boston Red Sox
Product and service quality	Detect quality problems early and minimize them.	Honda, Intel
Financial performance	Better understand the drivers of financial performance and the effects of nonfinancial factors.	MCI, Verizon
Research and development	Improve quality, efficacy, and, where applicable, safety of products and services.	Novartis, Amazon, Yahoo

Source: Davenport, T. H. (2006). Competing on analytics. *Harvard Business Review, 84*(1), 98–108, p. 103.

FACT OR FICTION?

Do Companies Know Your Secrets?

Andrew Pole was an analyst at Target. Two managers from the marketing department asked him if he had the ability to use statistics to figure out if a customer was pregnant—even if she did not want anyone to know. What a strange question! However, it turns out that new parents spend a lot of money in retail stores. Target sells a wide range of products, from housewares to clothing, and yes—items for a new baby. It is very difficult to change shopping habits, and marketers know this. People tend to visit the same stores for the same items, which they can find in the same places. The marketers knew that if a woman was pregnant and went to target for cleaning supplies, she would also start looking at baby items if she had received specialized mailings and coupons for baby items.

Research has shown that there are some short periods in a person's life where shopping habits are malleable. The biggest moment is just before the birth of a child. Expecting parents experience a lot of different emotions, and their loyalties for brands and stores are open as they anticipate buying for the new addition to their family. However, timing is important. Birth records are used to identify new parents, but usually, by the time they receive advertisements for baby products, they've already purchased most of them during pregnancy. The Target managers wanted to get to new parents before everyone else did—so could the analyst figure out when customers were expecting a child? Specifically in the first or second trimester of pregnancy, which corresponds with an explosion in spending on many new items such as lotions and maternity clothes. The marketers wanted a list of pregnant women, with their addresses.

This was important, because if women started shopping for a variety of items at Target during pregnancy, they would continue to be loyal to the store in the future due to changed shopping habits. New mothers are busy, and the idea that they can go to one store for diapers as well as groceries has a lot of appeal. In addition, they might see a nice pressure cooker and buy that as well to make meal preparation easier and faster for the family.

Retailers know what you buy based on ID numbers that are linked to your credit card number, and they save all the data on what you buy and when. The analyst went to work using data collected on the buying habits of women and built an analytical model by identifying women who had signed up for the baby registry—a solid indicator of pregnancy. He next compared the items bought by these women with those of all Target customers. There were 25 products that separated these women from the rest of the customers, such as unscented lotions, vitamins, scent-free soaps, large bags of cotton balls, hand sanitizers, and washcloths. Using the data on such purchases, the analyst was able to predict the chances that a woman was pregnant, and even her delivery date! For example, pregnant women buy hand sanitizers as they get close to their delivery date. Target used these predictions to identify which women should receive specific mailings with coupons. The 25 products were analyzed together to create a "pregnancy prediction" score for each shopper who visited a Target. He found that he could also estimate her due date to within a few days, so Target marketers would know exactly when to send coupons related to the stages of a pregnancy. Consider the following example:

> Take a fictional Target shopper named Jenny Ward, who is 23, lives in Atlanta and in March bought cocoa-butter lotion, a purse large enough to double as a diaper bag, zinc and magnesium supplements and a bright blue rug. There's, say, an 87 percent chance that she's pregnant and that her delivery date is sometime in late August.[57]

This all sounds like brilliant marketing, right?

Well, it turns out it was. Until the fallout hit the media.

A teenager in Minneapolis was one of the pregnant women identified by the analyst at Target, and she received coupons related to pregnancy (imagine her receiving a coupon for morning-sickness herbal-supplement pills). Her concerned father complained to a Target store manager that his daughter had been mailed pregnancy-related coupons. He felt that the coupons encouraged teens to become pregnant and were not acceptable. He later found out his daughter was pregnant and realized there were things going on under his roof he did not know about. Awkward. The *New York Times* wrote an article exposing how companies are learning our secrets. The story was picked up by Fox News and other major news programs. The public was shocked by Target's actions to delve into the private lives of their customers. Target learned that while this was legal, people were disturbed that the company knew about their pregnancies in advance. The company still uses analytics to determine if a woman is pregnant, but mixes other coupons with pregnancy-related ones so it's less obvious.

Discussion Questions

1. Explain the business reasons for Target wanting to be able to identify which of its customers were pregnant.

2. Why didn't marketers at Target anticipate the backlash that might occur if parents learned of their daughters' pregnancies through ads sent to the home? What could have been done to avoid this?

3. Do you feel that companies learning your secrets through your Google searches or purchase patterns is an invasion of privacy? Evaluate the ethics of this form of marketing.

Sources: Adapted from Duhigg, C. (2012). "How Companies Learn Your Secrets," *New York Times.* Retrieved from http://www.nytimes.com/2012/02/19/magazine/shopping-habits.html? pagewanted=all&_ r=0; Hill, K. (2014). How Target figured out a teen girl was pregnant before her father did. *Forbes.* Retrieved from https://www.forbes.com/sites/kashmirhill/2012/02/16/how-target-figured-out-a-teen-girl-was-pregnant-before-her-father-did/#3622196a6668.

and other behavioral data. The result is massive databases requiring a mix of automated analysis techniques and human effort that give marketing managers strategic insight about their customers.[56]

Another important application of behavioral analytics in management is employees. This has various names, including **people analytics**, **workforce analytics**, and **talent management**. These behavioral analytics help companies and managers improve employee selection, retention, motivation, training, and employee performance. People analytics applies the analysis of human behavior to such workforce challenges as:

- hiring the best employees
- assessing employees' training needs and the effectiveness of training programs
- learning the effectiveness of reward systems for motivating employees
- analyzing the reasons for employee turnover

Specific examples of people analytics described by organizations include:

- Performance analytics, which is a new class of business intelligence that ties human capital management to financial performance (Deloitte Consulting).
- Talent analytics, to gain understanding of staffing processes in order to analyze and optimize the whole system or improve individual aspects (Stepstone and Hire.com).
- Metrics and dashboards for various users, including recruiters, business executives, hiring managers, human resources, and more (Kenexa).[58]

As illustrated by the above three definitions, analytics is either an analytical technique, a process for gaining talent insights, or a set of measures. Allan Schweyer, a human resources and information technology consultant, points out that people analytics supports management decisions in important ways:

If you do proper workforce analytics and planning, then you know who to recruit, who to develop, who to redeploy and where to redeploy them, whether you should hire someone externally or promote someone from within, and whether you should look for a contingent worker, contractor, or full-time worker. Workforce-planning analytics can help you make the best talent-management decisions and align those with your corporate objectives.[59]

Operational analytics has been defined as "the application of advanced analytical methods to make better decisions."[60] Colin White, the founder of BI Research and president of DataBase Associates Inc., explains that analytics produced by traditional business intelligence applications and their underlying data warehouses help businesses understand what has happened in the past. There are three types of traditional analytics: strategic, tactical, and operational. Managers use strategic and tactical analytics for both long-term and short-term business decision-making and action-taking. A data warehouse can also be used in conjunction with advanced analytical and data-mining technologies to look for business trends and

CRITICAL THINKING QUESTIONS

Give examples of information (data) for selecting the best employees (list at least five different criteria that you believe relate to job performance). Next, rank your list in terms of the most important to the least important.

CAREERS IN MANAGEMENT

Careers in Business Analytics

Given this chapter's focus on business analytics, it seems fitting to look at statistical indicators regarding prospects for a career in business analytics. The U.S. Bureau of Labor Statistics (BLS; https://www.bls.gov/jobs/) provides a great deal of information on business analytics careers. Table 2.5 provides data on job types, salaries, and predicted employment growth.

▼ TABLE 2.5

Business Analytics Career Data

Job Type	Average Salary	Predicted Employment Growth
Management Analytics	$91,910	12.1%
Operational Analytics	$84,340	27.4%
Systems Analytics	$92,960	11.6%
Marketing Analytics	$70,620	22.8%
Financial Analytics	$97,604	10.8%

Source: U.S. Department of Labor, Bureau of Labor Statistics. (2016). *Occupational outlook handbook, 2015–16.* Retrieved from http://www.bls.gov/ooh.

Business analytics is a promising field for future graduates. The demand for expertise in analytics is strong, based on the following facts:

- In a 2017 interview, the executive chairman of Google's parent company, Alphabet, had some unambiguous things to say: "I think a basic understanding of data analytics is incredibly important for this next generation of young people. By data analytics, I mean a basic knowledge of how statistics work, and a basic knowledge of how people make conclusions over big data."

- A quick Google search will turn up a number of reports from the Big Four consulting firms aimed at helping companies solve their top business analytics challenge: finding enough people trained in business analytics to hire. John Lucker of

Deloitte Consulting recommends a recruiting strategy many university students would likely enjoy: "Companies need to recognize that they need to really develop close relationships with these [business analytics] degree programs. Creating a true courtship between companies and universities is becoming more and more important."

- Another consulting firm, PricewaterhouseCoopers, identified several important skills students should acquire in its report "Data Driven: What Students Need to Succeed in a Rapidly Changing Business World." Among others, these skills included:
  - regression analysis
  - exploratory data analysis, including descriptive statistics
  - statistical inference
  - core skills in basic spreadsheet and statistical analysis programs

So if you are interested in a career in business analytics, it's time to take some courses on statistics.

Discussion Questions

1. Which of the job types shown in Table 2.5 are you most interested in? Explain why you are drawn to that type of analytics work.

2. Operational analytics focuses on improving existing operations. Why do you think operational analytics has the highest predicted growth rate?

3. Do some research to locate an undergraduate major or master's degree in business analytics. Examine the courses you would need to take. Would you be interested in pursuing analytics as a field of study? Why or why not?

Sources: Adapted from Deloitte Consulting. (2017). Analytics trends 2016: The next evolution. Retrieved from https://www2.deloitte.com/us/en/pages/deloitte-analytics/articles/analytics-trends.html; PricewaterhouseCoopers. (2015). Data driven: What students need to succeed in a rapidly changing business world. Retrieved from https://www.pwc.com/us/en/faculty-resource/assets/pwc-data-driven-paper-feb2015.pdf; Ward, M. (2017). Google billionaire Eric Schmidt says this is the skill employers will look for in the future. Retrieved from https://www.cnbc.com/2017/03/31/google-execs-agree-on-the-skill-employers-will-look-for-in-the-future.html.

patterns in historical data, and the resulting predictive analytics are used to forecast what could happen in the future.[61] For example, spending patterns of credit-card holders detect fraud. If a cardholder typically uses their card to purchase groceries and gasoline, and then a charge comes through for an expensive hotel in France, the credit-card company flags it and sends an email to the cardholder to confirm the charge.

▼ FIGURE 2.6

Executives Struggle With Data Analytics

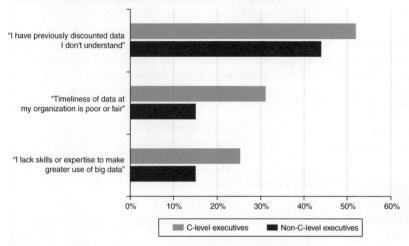

Source: PricewaterHouseCoopers. (2014). *Gut & gigabytes. SAGE Business Researcher.* Retrieved from http://businessresearcher .sagepub.com/sbr-1645-94783-2641913/20150209/big-data, p. 33.

Using big data requires summaries called dashboards.

©NicoElNino/Alamy Stock Photo

Overcoming the Fear of Data and Statistics

Many adults, especially in the United States think of themselves as being "bad at math" and, consequently, go out of their way to avoid it.[62] This belief often stems from memories of math and statistics courses being full of abstract symbols and formulas that had to be memorized. Some students are bored with math because they failed to see the usefulness of learning the formulas. However, math provides the foundations for statistical analyses, which managers rely on to make good decisions.

This discussion of analytics in a management course may come as a bit of a surprise to you. Despite its beginnings as a highly quantitative science (recall Taylorism discussed in Chapter 1), some managers overlook the value of statistical analysis. Managers are consumers of analytics. Yet some managers have not embraced the power of business analytics. As Figure 2.6 shows, many modern executives admit to being uncomfortable with quantitative data ("big data" in particular, which you will learn about next).

The situation is particularly troublesome for "C-level" executives (e.g., chief executive officer, chief financial officer) who represent leadership positions in corporations. A *SAGE Business Researcher* report sheds some interesting light on the issue. According to an individual quoted in the report, "the key is not actually understanding computing technologies so much as it is understanding how to interpret and evaluate the results of the analyses. This is really a problem dealing with mathematical and statistical sophistication."[63]

Do you fear mathematics and statistics used for analytics? Find out by completing Self-Assessment 2.2.

The Era of "Big Data"

Learning Objective 2.6: Be familiar with the concept of big data and its use in business decision-making.

Over the past few decades, the rapid development of computer hardware and software has resulted in the creation of mountains of data. In addition, advancements in sensor technology, the Internet, wireless sensor networks, and low-cost memory (e.g., "cloud storage") have resulted in the exponential growth of data in recent years.[64] You may feel intimidated by the daunting task of sorting through all the information now at your disposal. Organizations today hire analysts to create reports that interpret large amounts of data so that managers can make better decisions. You have probably heard the term **big data**. Big data involves collections of large amounts of data and has been defined in terms of high volume, high velocity, and high variety—the three Vs:

- High volume—the amount or quantity of data
- High velocity—the rate at which data is created
- High variety—the different types of data[65]

Big data is used by organizations to analyze patterns that improve decisions. Using publicly available data from Google and other websites combined with basic statistical analysis, author Seth Stephens-Davidowitz reached some interesting conclusions about human behavior. For example, data is being used to predict who will default on loans applied for in a peer-to-peer lending site. Applicants who mentioned the word *hospital* or *thank you* in their application were significantly more likely to default on that loan than borrowers who did not. Applicants who used words like *college graduate* or *lower interest rate* in their application were found to be safer-than-average borrowers.[66]

Recall the discussion of critical thinking from Chapter 1 of this textbook. Analytics are a powerful tool, but managers must use critical thinking to interpret data. When managers rely on analysis of big data, it is possible to draw the wrong conclusions. The aforementioned peer-to-peer lending example concluded that polite people (those who say *thank you*) are financially irresponsible. Even though this conclusion was supported by the analysis, many polite people will not default on loans. Thus, it is important to apply logic and critical thinking to the power of big-data analysis. Analytics are an aid in critical thinking, not a replacement for it.

Despite the caveat regarding the need for critical thinking, big data holds amazing potential for improving our business decisions. Analytics help solve the types of real-world problems that managers face every day. Not surprisingly, many corporations have increased their investment in big-data projects, as shown in Figure 2.7.

Examples of Big-Data Analytics

Hugh Watson, professor of management information systems at the University of Georgia, provides the following examples of applications of big data.[67]

A Starbucks Product Launch Goes Better With Big Data

Before companies had access to big data from social media platforms, obtaining consumer feedback was a lengthy and costly undertaking. Big data makes the process instant. For example, when Starbucks launched a new coffee flavor, they worried that customers would think it was too strong. The morning of the launch, they kept a close watch on social media to see what customers had to say about the product. Via blogs, Twitter, and discussion boards, they discovered something unexpected: customers enjoyed the new coffee, but they thought it was overpriced. Starbucks immediately adjusted the price point, and by the end of the day, the negative feedback had stopped.

Traditional methods like assessing sales figures and bringing in focus groups could have taken weeks, or even months, to yield results. Thanks to social media, Starbucks was able to respond to the market in a single day.

▼ FIGURE 2.7

Business Plans to Invest in or Deploy Big Data Projects

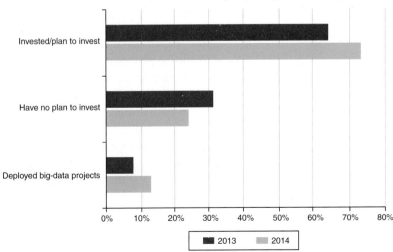

Source: Gartner Research. (2014). Press release, "Gartner Survey Reveals That 73 Percent of Organizations Have Invested or Plan to Invest in Big Data in the Next Two Years," Gartner Research, Sept. 17, 2014.

Starbucks monitors big data from social medium to set prices.

©iStockphoto.com/RichieChan

Analytics Helps Chevron Avoid Costly Drill Misses

Oil drilling is a risky business, and failure is expensive. Continuous improvement of data analysis capabilities helps Chevron avoid drill misses in the Gulf of Mexico. When the federal government suspended drilling after the BP Gulf spill in 2010, Chevron used the downtime to enhance its already advanced seismic data analysis. The company improved the odds of successful drilling by 13%. At first glance, that figure may not seem dramatic, but keep in mind, each drill miss can cost Chevron upwards of $100 million dollars.[68]

Monitoring Cab Data at U.S. Xpress Saves Times, Money, and Trouble

U.S. Xpress, a transportation company, is a prime example of how continuous data streaming increases efficiency. U.S. Express cabs stream more than 900 pieces of data to the cloud so it can be analyzed and delivered to users, from drivers to senior execs.[69] By keeping constant tabs on its vehicles' condition and location, the company can avoid common industry pitfalls. For instance, if a cab is low on fuel, a driver can be instantly directed to the nearest gas station with the lowest prices. Data streaming helps eliminate everything from running out of gas to breakdowns and traffic jams.

Managerial Implications

This chapter covered the important role that managers have in making decisions for their organizations. You should understand the following key takeaways:

- Decision-making is essential to managerial effectiveness. Making the right business decisions ensures the organization's success. Also, becoming an effective decision-maker will enhance your management career.
- The rational decision-making model represents best practice in decision-making. It is a cyclical process comprising eight steps: (1) define the problem (or opportunity), (2) establish decision criteria, (3) weight decision criteria, (4) generate alternatives, (5) evaluate alternatives, (6) make a decision, (7) develop action steps for implementation, and (8) evaluate the decision.
- Prospect theory provides insight into why managers sometimes are not rational in making decisions. The way decisions are framed will affect how a person will react in terms of the decisions they make. People are more likely to take risks when the decision is framed as a loss situation.
- Intuition plays a role in decision-making, and managers often rely on it. Intuition has both positive and negative effects on decisions that managers should be aware of. Heuristics support intuitive decision-making by setting forth decision rules that can be followed in advance of the decision.
- Managers fall into decision traps in decision-making: hindsight, hubris (overconfidence), and escalation of commitment. These traps can be avoided.
- Creativity is important to problem-solving, and three components must be present: expertise, creativity skills, and intrinsic task motivation.
- Business analytics are an essential part of critical thinking and effective decision-making.
- Whether your career takes you to small, traditional companies, big-data hubs, or anything in between, there are almost no management scenarios where analytic skills won't improve your decision-making skills and marketability.

- Management analytics include analysis of consumer behavior and people management. No matter what your interests, there is a high demand for analytic skills.
- You do not need to be a gifted mathematician to learn and apply analytical skills. You can begin by taking courses in statistics.

This chapter highlights the important process of decision-making, and it is clear that to make decisions effectively, managers need to be able to collect good data, analyze it, and summarize it. As you can see, the ability to interpret data is essential in making evidence-based management decisions that are successful.

KEY TERMS

behavioral analytics   50

big data   54

bounded rationality   39

business analytics   49

creative-thinking skills   48

creativity   48

equality heuristic   43

escalation of commitment   45

expertise   48

fluency   43

framing   40

heuristics   43

hindsight bias *or* I-knew-it-all-along effect   44

imitating the majority   43

imitating the successful   43

intrinsic motivation   48

intuition   40

management analytics   50

operational analytics   50

overconfidence bias *or* hubris   45

people analytics *or* workforce analytics *or* talent management   52

prospect theory   39

recognition heuristic   43

risk analysis   49

satisficing   39

sunk-costs fallacy   46

TOOLKIT

Activity 2.1

Exxel's New Product Development Decision

As a product development manager, you have the option of developing one of two potential new products. One product is an airbag sensor, and the other product is an antilock brake sensor. Both of the products are described below. You have already spent $3.175 million on preliminary marketing and technical assessment. To take either product to the next stage of development and testing, it would cost another $12 million. You have recently been promoted to your current position at Exxel Corporation, and you want to make a good impression on your new boss.

Product 1: Airbag sensor. The proposed new airbag sensor is highly innovative and will offer substantial advantages over the existing one. Unlike the current sensor, which is silicon based, the new sensor will incorporate a radically new diamond sensor technology that will make it resistant to all corrosive materials, elements, and weather conditions. While current sensors are reliable, the new sensor will be a vast improvement and will continue to work properly for decades. This is extremely important, since an airbag sensor must work perfectly; it cannot deploy an airbag in the absence of a collision, nor can it fail to deploy in a collision. Automakers face potentially huge lawsuits if an airbag system fails. In addition, with advances in industrial diamond fabrication, the new sensor will be substantially smaller (i.e., 75%).

Product 2: Antilock brake sensor. The proposed new antilock brake sensor will offer incremental advantages over the existing one, since it will be identical in form and function to Exxel's existing sensor. However, this new sensor is slightly more durable and will cost a little less to produce (i.e., 1.5%).

Discussion Questions

1. Which product did you decide to make the investment for further development? Explain why you chose this product.
2. Did you feel personally responsible for the decision you made? Explain the role personal responsibility played in your decision to invest. Did you consider the personal risks to your career? What were the risks?
3. What role did the innovativeness of the product play in your decision to invest? Did you consider the risks that the product would fail? What were the risks?

Source: Adapted from Schmidt, J. B., & Calantone, R. J. (2002). Escalation of commitment during new product development. *Journal of the Academy of Marketing Science, 30*(2), 103–118.

Case Study 2.1

A New Mission Statement for the MBC Corporation

The October 2011 board meeting of the MBC Corporation was two weeks away, and new CEO Dave Williams needed to decide whether to proceed with his plan to discuss changing the mission statement with the board. MBC's current mission statement read as follows:

> Our collective purpose is to achieve long-term profitable growth as a global supplier of high-quality metal-based chemicals. MBC is committed to excellence in customer service.

Williams found the current mission statement lacking; he thought it should articulate MBC's core values and inspire employees. When Williams raised the idea of changing the mission statement with the company's senior executives, however, he was met with disinterest at best. One vice president said, "I thought we were here to talk about important things." Williams was not sure if they were actually opposed to his idea or if he had failed to effectively communicate its importance. Although he was disappointed with his senior team's response, he had gotten support from one trusted board member, Larry Deer, and was still considering taking the idea to the full board.

MBC Corporation

Founded in 1946, the MBC Corporation was a manufacturer and marketer of metal-based chemicals with headquarters in Denver, Colorado, and plants in Colorado and Louisiana. Following a recent acquisition, MBC employed 200 people and generated $250 million in annual revenues. MBC's primary product, which helped reduce greenhouse gas emissions and strengthen building products, accounted for 80% of its sales. MBC was a family-owned company; the Williams and Giles families owned 98% of the company's stock. Dave Williams's grandfather had been a cofounder, and his father, Steve, had served as president and CEO for 34 years until his retirement in 2010. Steve Williams had guided the company through some rough spots and had grown annual revenue from $10 million to $250 million. He had also favored an "old-school" approach to management, creating a hierarchical structure and culture in which seniority and position were rewarded more than performance.

Dave Williams

Although MBC was his family's company, Dave Williams did not begin his career with the firm. After graduating from college, he first worked as an institutional broker for a large financial company and then in business development and trade execution for Harris Futures and Options. In 1998, Williams's father told him that if he wanted to come into the family business, "you need to do so sooner rather than later." Williams joined MBC later that year. Although he had not started his career with MBC, Williams had "paid his dues"; despite his work experience, he started at MBC in a clerical position so he could learn everything about the business. Later he assumed responsibility for developing markets for new products and selling existing products. In February 2010 he was promoted to executive vice president, and he was elected by the board as president and CEO five months later. Williams's election to the CEO role was not without controversy. The other two candidates for the job, brothers John and Jerry Giles, had been with the company longer than Williams, held senior leadership positions, and between them owned 49% of the shares in the company. Williams's father held his family's 49% ownership stake.

Approaching the Board

When he became CEO, Williams proceeded cautiously. He thought the company needed to create a culture that could attract top talent and adapt to impending changes in the market and regulatory environment, but he waited to turn his focus toward those strategic issues until he had succeeded in mending fences and gaining the support of the Giles brothers. Changing the mission statement would require approval from the board of directors. Two-day board meetings were held in March and October each year, one in Denver and the other in Montana or Louisiana. Of the nine board members, only four owned shares in MBC: chairman of the board Steve Williams, chair emeritus Larry Deer, and John and Jerry Giles. Before the full board acted on any issue, the four owners discussed it first; only if they could not reach consensus would the remaining directors be asked to make a decision. Williams was closer to Larry Deer than to any other board member except his father. Deer had formerly served as board chairman, was the son of one of the cofounders, and was the retired president of a regional automotive supply company. Over the years, he had been a mentor to Williams, and the two were good friends. When Williams discussed his proposal to change the mission statement, Deer supported the idea. The next day he sent Williams an email in which he suggested that the new mission statement should state that MBC "values results over effort" and that the goal of the company is "to maximize profits through sustained growth and continuous improvement."

Decision

Williams had just two weeks left to decide if he should discuss creating a new mission statement with the board, and if so, how to proceed. More immediately, he needed to respond to Deer and his suggestions.

Discussion Questions

1. What are the key concerns that Williams should consider in his decision to change the mission statement of MBC Corporation? Who are the key stakeholders in this decision?

2. Williams wants consensus from the board. What other decision-making approaches could he use?
3. What should Williams do if the board cannot reach a decision on the new mission statement?

Source: Feddersen, T. J. & Edwards, S. (2017). A new mission statement for the MBC Corporation. *SAGE Business Cases.* Thousand Oaks, CA: SAGE Publishing.

Case Study 2.2

"Effective . . . but Creepy" Employee Tracking and Data Collection

In Sara's past roles as managerial analyst and systems analyst, she had gotten used to thinking about the potentially far-reaching implications of her decisions. In her new job as a consultant, however, she was starting to realize that she had failed to appreciate just how much of the modern world was intertwined with the data corporations collected.

Controversy over companies collecting data—knowingly, unknowingly, and many places in between—from customers was nothing new. She had made those types of decisions in the past. When was it acceptable to collect customer data and when did it cross a line; how much responsibility did she and her employer have to keep the data private; were they allowed to sell it? All of this was old hat for Sara.

Somehow, she had never considered these decisions in the context of a company's own employees, though. Part of her felt that "what's good for the goose is good for the gander." If employees like her were willing to collect data from customers (who might or might not love the idea of her doing it), why couldn't the same logic be applied to employees? Heck, those people were paid to be there. If they could track the people who were paying the company (directly or indirectly, through advertising revenue and the like), why not the people doing the tracking? Even if it did involve things like tracking their Internet usage and . . . keystrokes. Was it that? Was it the invasiveness of her new client's proposal that made her feel queasy?

Even before she knew that literally everything employees typed would be logged (including work emails, reports, casual browsing, personal email, banking passwords—everything), she had some misgivings. Why did it seem so wrong? Companies had always tracked things like hours worked, efficiency and production levels, and sick days. That these forms of monitoring had evolved along with technology seemed like it should not be a surprise. It was certainly common enough. According to a 2014 research report Sara had recently read:

- 45% of companies tracked employees' keystrokes and time spent at the keyboard
- 43% of companies stored and reviewed computer files
- 43% of companies monitored employees' email

- 12% of companies monitored the blogosphere for comments about the company
- 10% of companies monitored social networking sites

Quite a bit of the proposed tracking could actually help employees. That guy who sat at his desk for 10 hours a day, 5 days a week, always complaining about how busy he was even though no one could put a finger on what exactly he did—he would be in big trouble, but everyone who had been picking up his slack might finally get recognition for their extra effort.

But still, she was having a hard time signing off on her client's proposal, even though her analyses left no doubt as to the financial benefits of expanded employee monitoring. It was some consolation that she wasn't the only one feeling this way. She recalled a recent incident that had benefited an employee, yet still evoked a sour response from the public:

The *New York Times* (NYT) last year highlighted a situation involving Jim Sullivan, a waiter at a Dallas restaurant whose actions came under scrutiny "not by the prying eyes of a human boss, but by intelligent software. The digital sentinel, he was told, tracked every waiter, every ticket, and every dish and drink, looking for patterns that might suggest employee theft. But that torrent of detailed information, parsed another way, cast a computer-generated spotlight on the most productive workers."

The monitoring worked out well for Sullivan, who was recognized as a stellar employee and promoted to manager. Although the surveillance was legal, the article provoked angry comments on the *NYT*'s website from readers complaining that it was overly intrusive.

The program monitoring Sullivan's workday was NCR's Restaurant Guard, a system that tracks restaurant transactions in real time, using artificial intelligence to detect patterns of fraud and to spot performance bottlenecks. Using software that detects specified keywords, many employers monitor telephone calls and network traffic, including even emails sent from an employee's private email account. Some companies also employ video cameras to watch employees and geolocation tools to track employees with company cars or cellphones.

Reflecting on the Restaurant Guard case, the phrase "effective . . . but creepy" came to mind, as it often did when she thought about these things.

The CEO who hired Sara was also worried by a rash of high-profile instances where employees had done an odd thing: using technology, they had broken laws in service of the company's goals. The CEO cited a report that summarized Volkswagen's notorious experience with this type of behavior in the summer of 2015:

Months after Volkswagen publicly admitted in August 2015 that it had installed software in 11 million diesel automobiles designed to deceive emissions tests, the public remains in the dark about just who was responsible.

Michael Horn, head of Volkswagen's American division, told Congress on Oct. 8 that neither Volkswagen's supervisory board nor its top executives ordered the installation of devices that could sense when they were being tested and then change the vehicles' performance to improve results. "This was not a corporate decision," Horn said. "This was something individuals did."

"Assuming their executives are telling the truth," the company president remarked, "we could be seeing a paradoxical situation where employees will break the law to do what they think they need to do to help the company succeed. We don't want that."

Sara reflected on the bigger picture. The same report went on to explain that because technology can make some deviant behaviors very easy and hard to detect, bending the rules has become more tempting for more people.

These situations illustrate how technology allows unethical and illegal actions to occur almost invisibly and "with comparatively few people being in the accountability line," says Ken Goodman, director of the University of Miami's Miller School of Medicine Institute for Bioethics and Health Policy and co-director of the University of Miami Ethics Programs. The situation puts an extra burden on companies—rather than lawmakers or regulators—to follow ethical practices in implementing new technologies, says Arthur Schwartz, general counsel of the National Society of Professional Engineers. "I don't think the laws and regulations ever keep up," Schwartz says.

That last sentence was the reason Sara had been hired, and she knew it. Because traditional behavioral controls had been losing ground in the battle to discourage unethical and illegal technology-assisted behaviors, companies were (somewhat ironically) turning to technology as a solution. More specifically, the use of high-tech employee monitoring and tracking technology had become an increasingly common technique for keeping employee behavior in check. This, of course, had sparked further debate. As someone familiar with both behavioral and systems analytics, Sara could see both sides. As her report stated:

"Sophisticated monitoring software and hardware allow businesses to conduct basic business transactions, avoid liability, conduct investigations and, ultimately, achieve success in a competitive global environment," according to Corey Ciocchetti, professor of business ethics at the University of Denver. At the same time, Ciocchetti wrote, "This trend is problematic because excessive and unreasonable monitoring can:

(1) invade an employee's reasonable expectation of privacy, (2) lead employees to sneak around to conduct personal activities on work time, (3) lower morale, (4) cause employees to complain and, potentially, quit and (5) cause employees to fear using equipment even for benign work purposes."

To be sure, there were plenty of well-informed people who believed the good outweighed the bad. Returning to her write-up of the Restaurant Guard case, Sara recalled a few strong arguments in favor of such monitoring tools:

The public's suspicions about Restaurant Guard's intrusiveness led Andrew McAfee, co-director of the Initiative on the Digital Economy at the Massachusetts Institute of Technology's Sloan School of Management, to write a *Harvard Business Review* column in defense of the software. He argued that it "doesn't engage in surveillance of employees' personal electronic communications, or any other activity they might reasonably consider private. Instead, it monitors their on-the-job performance, which is exactly one of the things that managers are supposed to do" to monitor employees.

"Most of this monitoring is perfectly legal and even prudent in today's employment arena," wrote Ciocchetti of the University of Denver. "While employee monitoring remains a contentious issue, employers have good reasons for checking in on their employees' activities. Sexual or pornographic e-mails and Web pages, containing pictures or merely sexually explicit language, can form the basis for a harassment lawsuit. Excessive personal use of company broadband capacity or e-mail accounts will lead to decreased productivity, storage shortages and slower network operations. Failing to monitor is also likely to allow rogue employees to steal trade secrets or send out confidential information in violation of various federal and state laws."

There was certainly some merit to the argument that these systems didn't seem to do much that managers weren't supposed to be doing anyway. But then, Sara thought, managers were people, just like employees. Computers had really changed that dynamic. This called to mind a final passage from her report that had stuck with her:

"Most employees know that their employer has the ability to conduct surveillance but they have no idea how much surveillance is really happening or the circumstances under which it happens," says Lewis Maltby, president of the National Workrights Institute, a worker advocacy group based in Princeton, N.J. For example, Maltby notes that many employees think that their boss looks at their email or Internet traffic only when there's a reason to do so. "But that's not how it works," he says. "It's an open secret that IT techs read other employees' emails for fun. And many employers don't even have a policy against this."

Decision

Sara was fairly certain that if she chose not to endorse this employee-monitoring proposal, she would likely be replaced by another consultant who would. By giving it her approval, however, she knew she would bear some responsibility for changing the employer–employee relationship at this company forever.

Discussion Questions

1. What benefits and drawbacks for employees might result from the sharp increase in employee monitoring and data collection being proposed here? What benefits and drawbacks might the company and its management experience?
2. From an ethical perspective, what arguments can be made in favor of the types of employee behavior and performance tracking discussed in this case? What arguments can be made against it?
3. If you were in Sara's position, would you endorse the tracking proposal or decline it, knowing it would likely cost you your current position?

4. If you were the CEO of this company and knew the pros and cons associated with employing these new forms of employee monitoring, do you think you would use it?

Source: Adapted from Marshall, P. (2016). Technology and business ethics. *SAGE Business Researcher.* Thousand Oaks, CA: SAGE.

Self-Assessment 2.1

What Is Your Attitude Toward Risk?

This self-assessment exercise identifies your attitudes toward taking risks as determined by research. The goal of this assessment is for you to learn about your propensity to take risks and how it may affect your decision-making. There are no right or wrong answers, and this is not a test. You don't have to share your results with others unless you wish to do so.

Part I. Taking the Assessment

Instructions: Circle the response that best describes your attitudes. How likely is it that you would engage in the behaviors shown in the questions?

Statement	Very Unlikely	Unlikely	Not Sure	Likely	Very Likely
1. Admitting your tastes are different than those of your friends.	1	2	3	4	5
2. Going camping in the wilderness, beyond the civilization of a campground.	1	2	3	4	5
3. Chasing a tornado or hurricane by car to take dramatic photos.	1	2	3	4	5
4. Disagreeing with your father on a major issue.	1	2	3	4	5
5. Going on a vacation in a developing country without prearranged travel and hotel accommodations.	1	2	3	4	5
6. Going down a ski run that is beyond your ability or closed.	1	2	3	4	5
7. Approaching your boss to ask for a raise.	1	2	3	4	5
8. Going whitewater rafting during rapid water flows in the spring.	1	2	3	4	5
9. Telling a friend their significant other made a pass at you.	1	2	3	4	5
10. Wearing provocative or unconventional clothing on occasion.	1	2	3	4	5
11. Periodically engaging in a dangerous sport (e.g., mountain climbing or skydiving).	1	2	3	4	5
12. Taking a job you enjoy over one that is prestigious but less enjoyable.	1	2	3	4	5
13. Defending an unpopular issue that you believe in at a social occasion.	1	2	3	4	5
14. Trying out bungee jumping at least once.	1	2	3	4	5

Part II. Scoring Instructions

In Part I, you rated yourself on 14 questions. Research has shown that risk depends on the situation. This assessment measured your attitudes toward risk in social and recreational settings. Add the numbers you circled in each of the columns to derive your score for social risk and recreational risk.

Social Risk	Recreational Risk
1. _____	2. _____
4. _____	3. _____
7. _____	5. _____
9. _____	6. _____
10. _____	8. _____
12. _____	11. _____
13. _____	14. _____
Total _____	Total _____

Scores can range from 7 (very low) to 35 (very high). In general, if your score is above 15, you have a propensity toward taking that type of risk (social or recreational).

Source: Adapted from Weber, E. U., Blais, A. R., & Betz, N. E. (2002). A domain-specific risk-attitude scale: Measuring risk perceptions and risk behaviors. *Journal of Behavioral Decision Making, 15*(4), 263–290.

Discussion Questions

1. Add your two scores together (social plus recreational risk). Is your score above 30? Do you feel you are a risk-taker in general?
2. Compare your scores for social and recreational risk. Is one higher than the other? Describe a situation in which you took a social or recreational risk. How did it turn out?

3. How will your attitudes toward risk affect your management career choice? How you will make decisions as a manager? Provide an example for each.

Self-Assessment 2.2

Are You Afraid of Statistics?

This chapter discussed the fact that many people reach adulthood with a firm belief that they are bad at math—many of those being convinced that they were "born that way." This sentiment is so common that researchers have actually investigated whether it is possible to inherit weak quantitative aptitude at birth.

An important step in overcoming the self-imposed barrier anxiety can cause is to recognize that it is there in the first place. Several math anxiety measures have been developed. This self-assessment uses one specifically designed to assess anxiety regarding the types of statistical analyses you will learn in this chapter.

We invite you to test your comfort level before you begin, and, as always, you do not need to share your score with others unless you choose to do so. The survey is a bit long (51 items), and some items may not seem applicable to you. Try to answer them all, even if you have to speculate about your response for some. After the assessment, we will provide descriptive statistics you can use to compare yourself to others who have completed all 51 items.

Part I. Taking the Assessment

Instructions: Circle the response that best describes your reactions to each of the following situations.

Statements	No Anxiety	Little Anxiety	Mild Anxiety	Moderate Anxiety	Strong Anxiety
1. Studying for an examination in a statistics course.	1	2	3	4	5
2. Interpreting the meaning of a table in a journal article.	1	2	3	4	5
3. Going to ask my statistics teacher for individual help with material I am having difficulty understanding.	1	2	3	4	5
4. Doing the coursework for a statistics course.	1	2	3	4	5
5. Making an objective decision based on empirical data.	1	2	3	4	5

6. Reading a journal article that includes some statistical analyses.	1	2	3	4	5
7. Trying to decide which analysis is appropriate for my research project.	1	2	3	4	5
8. Doing an examination in a statistics course.	1	2	3	4	5
9. Reading an advertisement for a car which includes figures on miles per gallon, depreciation, etc.	1	2	3	4	5
10. Walking into the room to take a statistics test.	1	2	3	4	5
11. Interpreting the meaning of a probability value once I have found it.	1	2	3	4	5
12. Arranging to have a body of data put into the computer.	1	2	3	4	5
13. Finding that another student in class got a different answer than I did to a statistical problem.	1	2	3	4	5
14. Determining whether to reject or retain the null hypothesis.	1	2	3	4	5
15. Waking up in the morning on the day of a statistics test.	1	2	3	4	5
16. Asking one of my teachers for help in understanding a printout.	1	2	3	4	5
17. Trying to understand the odds in a lottery.	1	2	3	4	5
18. Watching a student search through loads of computer printouts from his/her research.	1	2	3	4	5
19. Asking someone in the computer lab for help in understanding a printout.	1	2	3	4	5

(Continued)

(Continued)

		Strongly Disagree	Disagree	Neutral	Agree	Strongly Agree
20.	Trying to understand the statistical analyses described in the abstract of a journal article.	1	2	3	4	5
21.	Enrolling in a statistics course.	1	2	3	4	5
22.	Going over a final examination in statistics after it has been marked.	1	2	3	4	5
23.	Asking a fellow student for help in understanding a printout.	1	2	3	4	5

Instructions: Circle the response that best describes your reactions to each of the following situations.

Statements	Strongly Disagree	Disagree	Neutral	Agree	Strongly Agree
24. I am a subjective person, so the objectivity of statistics is inappropriate for me.	1	2	3	4	5
25. I have not done math for a long time. I know I'll have problems getting through statistics.	1	2	3	4	5
26. I wonder why I have to do all these things in statistics when in actual life I'll never use them.	1	2	3	4	5
27. Statistics is worthless to me, since it's empirical and my area of specialization is abstract.	1	2	3	4	5
28. Statistics takes more time than it's worth.	1	2	3	4	5
29. I feel statistics is a waste.	1	2	3	4	5
30. Statistics teachers are so abstract they seem inhuman.	1	2	3	4	5
31. I can't even understand secondary school math; how can I possibly do statistics?	1	2	3	4	5
32. Most statistics teachers are not human.	1	2	3	4	5
33. I lived this long without knowing statistics; why should I learn it now?	1	2	3	4	5

34. Since I've never enjoyed math, I don't see how I can enjoy statistics.	1	2	3	4	5
35. I don't want to learn to like statistics.	1	2	3	4	5
36. Statistics is for people who have a natural leaning toward math.	1	2	3	4	5
37. Statistics is a pain I could do without.	1	2	3	4	5
38. I don't have enough brains to get through statistics.	1	2	3	4	5
39. I could enjoy statistics if it weren't so mathematical.	1	2	3	4	5
40. I wish the statistics requirement were removed from my academic program.	1	2	3	4	5
41. I don't understand why someone in my field needs statistics.	1	2	3	4	5
42. I don't see why I have to fill my head with statistics. It will have no use in my career.	1	2	3	4	5
43. Statistics teachers speak a different language.	1	2	3	4	5
44. Statisticians are more number oriented than they are people oriented.	1	2	3	4	5
45. I can't tell you why, but I just don't like statistics.	1	2	3	4	5
46. Statistics teachers talk so fast you cannot logically follow them.	1	2	3	4	5
47. Statistical figures are not fit for human consumption.	1	2	3	4	5
48. Statistics isn't really bad. It's just too mathematical.	1	2	3	4	5
49. Affective skills are so important in my (future) profession that I don't want to clutter my thinking with something as cognitive as statistics.	1	2	3	4	5
50. I'm never going to use statistics, so why should I have to take it?	1	2	3	4	5
51. I'm too slow in my thinking to get through statistics.	1	2	3	4	5

Let's see what your responses tell you about your statistics anxiety level. Part of the reason this measure is so long is that it actually assesses six different dimensions of statistical anxiety. Use the table below to see your score for each. To compute the average for each dimension, total your ratings in each column and then divide by the number of items (for example, for the Testing dimension, divide by 8).

Testing	Interpretation	Asking for Help	Worth	Teacher	Self-Concept
1. _____	2. _____	3. _____	24. _____	30. _____	25. _____
4. _____	5. _____	16. _____	26. _____	32. _____	31. _____
8. _____	6. _____	19. _____	27. _____	43. _____	34. _____
10. _____	7. _____	23. _____	28. _____	44. _____	38. _____
13. _____	9. _____		29. _____	46. _____	39. _____
15. _____	11. _____		33. _____		48. _____
21. _____	12. _____		35. _____		51. _____
22. _____	14. _____		36. _____		
	17. _____		37. _____		
	18. _____		40. _____		
	20. _____		41. _____		
			42. _____		
			45. _____		
			47. _____		
			49. _____		
			50. _____		
Average _____	Average _____	Average _____	Average _____	Average _____	Average _____

Part III. Interpretation

As you may have deduced from the items in the survey, the first three dimensions in the scoring table assess specific types of anxiety: testing anxiety, interpretation anxiety, and anxiety related to seeking help. The next three dimensions assess your perceptions of the value (or "worth") of statistics, your fear of statistics teachers (yes, that is what they called it), and your "computation self-concept" (your belief in your ability to handle mathematical computations related to statistics).

A more detailed description is provided by a group of researchers who examined the effectiveness of this measure:

> Higher scores on an item or subscale indicate higher levels of that attitude or anxiety except for the "fear of statistics teachers" subscale where higher scores indicate lower levels of anxiety or more positive attitudes. The "worth of statistics" subscale attempts to measure the perceived usefulness of statistics. The "interpretation anxiety" subscale attempts to measure anxiety when interpreting statistical results. "Test and class anxiety" is designed to assess the anxiety experienced when taking a statistics test or attending a statistics class. The "computation self-concept" subscale is related to a person's self-belief in their ability to cope with the calculations and mathematics related to statistics. The "ask for help" subscale attempts to assess the anxiety experienced when an individual intends to ask for help on a statistical problem . . . "fear of statistics teachers" [measures] students' perceptions of their statistic teachers.

Because each dimension has a different number of items, there is no set "high" or "low" range. If you add your averages for all six dimensions, you should have a score somewhere between 51 and 306.

As promised, here are descriptive statistics for a group of 650 British college students who completed this same questionnaire.

	Testing	Interpretation	Asking for Help	Worth	Teacher	Self-Concept
Mean Score	27.07	30.26	10.39	56.98	18.20	23.91
Standard Deviation	6.69	8.42	3.87	14.13	4.72	6.60
Range of Scores	8–40	11–53	4–20	17–80	5–25	9–35

Age: Mean = 22, Standard Deviation = 5.44, Range = 18–56

Gender: 79% female, 21% male

Discussion Questions

1. How does your mean (average) score for each dimension of the statistical anxiety measure (Testing, Interpretation, Asking for Help, Worth, Teacher, and Self-Concept) compare to the average scores shown in the top line of the table above? What does this comparison tell you about yourself?

2. What do the results of this measure tell you about your overall statistical anxiety? For which of the six facets do you have the highest anxiety levels? What can you do to alleviate those types of anxiety?

3. Next, add to your interpretation of these descriptive statistics using the following steps:

   a. Calculate the total possible variation for each dimension by subtracting the lowest score from the highest score shown in the Range of Scores row.

   b. Now look at the Mean and Standard Deviation for each dimension.

   c. What do these three statistics tell you about the average person in this sample?

For example, the total possible variation for Self-Concept is 24 (35–39), the mean is 23.91, and the standard deviation is 6.60. This tells us that the 650 British students in this sample had very high confidence in their mathematical abilities (23.91/24), on average, but that there was some considerable variation. Since the maximum score is only 0.09 higher than the average, the standard deviation tells us that roughly 68% (see descriptive statistics table) of students scored between 24.00 and 17.40 and 95% scored between 24.00 and 10.89. (Can you see how the standard deviation was used to calculate those ranges?) Try this yourself with the Testing, Interpretation, or Asking for Help categories.

Source: Hanna, D., Shevlin, M., & Dempster, M. (2008). The structure of the statistics anxiety rating scale: A confirmatory factor analysis using UK psychology students. *Personality and Individual Differences, 45*, 68–74.

Get the tools you need to sharpen your study skills. SAGE edge offers a robust online environment featuring an impressive array of free tools and resources. Access practice quizzes, eFlashcards, video, and multimedia at **edge.sagepub.com/scanduragower**.

CHAPTER 3

ETHICS AND SOCIAL RESPONSIBILITY

CHAPTER **LEARNING OBJECTIVES**

After studying this chapter, you should be able to:

3.1 Explain the different ways managers view ethics as well as the basic components of ethical decision-making.

3.2 Develop an example for each stage of moral development.

3.3 Understand how managers influence an organization's ethical climate.

3.4 Explain the factors and challenges in making an ethical decision.

3.5 Understand the importance of social responsibility.

3.6 Discuss how the future of organizational social responsibility will be an important part of the management planning process.

Get the edge on your studies at **edge.sagepub.com/scanduragower**

- Take the chapter quiz
- Review key terms with eFlashcards
- Explore multimedia resources, SAGE readings, and more!

What Role Do Ethics and Social Responsibility Play in Effective Management?

This chapter will provide you and your class with a lot of things to think about in terms of decision-making and behaviors you choose individually, as a department, and as an organization. Ethics are often a consideration across all parts of an organization, including accounting, engineering, human resources, sales, marketing, management, leadership, and many more. Think about your role as a manager. If you know that rewarding employees with extra things like Free Lunch Friday will cause them to stay late on Thursday to finish a project that will make you look good, is that manipulation, or slightly unethical, or is it part of being a good manager? What about

having the opportunity to transfer a problem employee to another division because they know about the skills of the employee but not the large amount of time you spend making sure the employee puts in all their work hours, meets deadlines, is polite to other employees, or even, maybe, is respectful to you? Do you fist-bump your assistant manager, knowing this person will be gone, or do you go to the other manager and explain the problems, knowing there is a chance they will decide not to transfer the person into their department?

In fact, it can be argued that nearly every decision you make as a person or professional has some level of ethical dilemma attached to it, from getting extra change at the store (it's the clerk's fault) to giving overtime work and pay to your favorite employee (they need the money) to going out after work to hang with the team while your stay-at-home significant other is home juggling your kids' homework, dinner, and bedtimes (it was a long day; I deserve it). Just sit and think for a minute about some recent decisions you have made, large or small, and you will probably feel an ethical twinge or two about your final choice.

Therein lies the fickle part about ethics, though. Who is right? People weigh in on ethics philosophically and personally and from a purely business perspective.

Edward Hennessy, retired chairman and CEO of AlliedSignal Inc., says, "Ethics must begin at the top of an organization. It is a leadership issue and the chief executive must set the example."[1]

This means that in any type of leadership position, you are the person setting the tone for the team. While you might think that being ethical is not that difficult, now consider this quote from Aldo Leopold: "Ethical behavior is doing the right thing when no one else is watching—even when doing the wrong thing is legal."[2]

So to be clear, in the world of ethics, if something is the right thing to do and you know it, but even the wrong thing is legal, which do you choose? One that saves the company and/or saves your job and is perfectly legal, or the one that is the "right" thing to do?

Finally, think about this quote from a person who will be very familiar to most of you—Steve Jobs: "Great things in business are never done by one person. They're done by a team of people."

This is ironic, for many reasons, and if you want to read an enjoyable book that is full of ethical decision-making

Steve Jobs on teamwork.

©Justin Sullivan/Staff/Getty Images

choices, try *Steve Jobs*, by Walter Isaacson. In the quote above, Jobs attributes great things in business to teams, but in the book he is very clear that he is the brains behind all things Apple. He is also well-known for treating people poorly, stealing ideas from other companies (literally right off their desks), and his overall arrogance.

Hopefully the examples above provide you with a good starting perspective on the importance, and inconsistency, of ethics in the workplace and even the world. To assist you in developing your ethical standards and moral development, this chapter provides information on building these skills and on how you can help your organization have a strong ethical climate. It will also help you make ethical decisions by highlighting important points to consider when making them.

Another section of this chapter will talk about corporate social responsibility. History is lined with a path of organizations that have made poor ethical decisions that have resulted in the downfall of the organization and even the loss of life. Some organizations are working hard to avoid these catastrophes by putting their ethical standards in writing so there is a consistent message to members of their organization and transparency with their outside stakeholders.

CRITICAL THINKING QUESTIONS

How significant is the role of ethics in organizational decision-making? Explain your position. List some organizations you know of that have practiced substandard corporate social responsibility.

▼ FIGURE 3.0

Textbook Organization

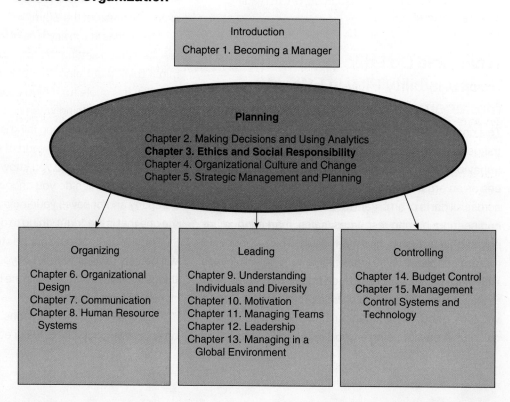

What Do People Think of When They Think of Ethics?

There were enough quotes in the beginning of this chapter to give you a good idea of what **ethics** means, but the definition is pretty simple: the rules or principles that define right and wrong. Now comes the challenging part, as discussed above: What is right and wrong?

Usually three fundamental ethical philosophies guide managers when they are trying to make ethical decisions. They are the **utilitarian view**, the **rights view**, and the **theory of justice** view. First, *utilitarianism* is the consideration of decisions that do the most good for the most people. A person who believes the "ends justify the means" is advocating the utilitarian approach. When using this approach, the decision-maker tries to maximize the satisfaction of the most people.[3]

Second, *individual rights* protect individuals. The Second World War marked a watershed in the history of rights. In the wake of the massive civilian suffering caused during the war—much of it knowingly and even intentionally inflicted—there was a resurgence of interest in individual rights in many areas. The United Nations General Assembly drafted the Universal Declaration of Human Rights, which contained 30 articles protecting individuals. These include the right to appeal a decision that affects you, the right to free consent, the right to privacy, the right to freedom of conscience (i.e., not having to do something that violates your moral standards), the right to free speech, and the right to due process.[4] For example, allowing employees to have a voice in decisions that affect them is a decision process that reflects individual rights.

Third, *justice* emphasizes social justice. In following this approach, decision-makers are guided by equity, fairness, and impartiality.[5] For example, rewards should be distributed fairly by compensating individuals based on their efforts and not on arbitrary factors.

The Social World Is Messy and Ethics Help Us Navigate It

The utilitarian view, the rights view, and the theory of justice are three contemporary approaches to ethics, but the study of ethics is an age-old project. From Plato in Ancient Greece to John Locke in 17th-century England, philosophers have contemplated ethics. There are three historical schools of ethics: **virtue ethics**, **consequentialist ethics**, and **deontological** or **duty-based ethics**.[6] Each of these approaches conceptualizes ethics differently when it comes to ethical behavior and decision-making. Since philosophers have devoted so much time to considering each of these schools of ethics, they have developed many divisions and subdivisions of each. Rather than reading an exhaustive analysis of each, you can find a broad overview in Table 3.1. It outlines the concerns and key questions that inform ethical decisions within each school, as well as a list of the philosophers who were instrumental in developing the approach.

Each school of ethics provides a different framework for understanding the concept, but none is all-encompassing. It can be a helpful analogy to compare ethics to health. For example, how can you achieve a healthy life? Through a good diet, exercise, and discipline. All of these elements are vital but inadequate by themselves. Now imagine someone asked, "How do you run a successful business?" You might name a variety of components for success: excellent management and training, strong human resources department, a high-quality product or service, a skilled sales team, and a commitment to bringing in new business. There is no singular component that works on its own; each is essential yet insufficient by itself. Bringing all of these components together, you can run a successful business. Behaving ethically, much like having a thriving business, requires a holistic mindset. In most cases, you will need to consider all three schools of ethics to make ethical decisions.

The Three Historical Schools of Ethics

Ethical School of Thought	Key Questions	Key Principles
Virtue Ethics	How would a virtuous person act in this situation? Would this action strengthen moral character?	Personal integrity Honesty Fairness
Consequentialist Ethics	Would this action make the world a better place? Will impact of this decision be more positive or negative?	Altruism Compassion Consider greatest good for the greatest number of people
Deontological Ethics	Does this action treat every stakeholder with respect and dignity in all situation? Is the action something that everyone should do?	Autonomy Rights Freedom

Source: Adapted from Dobrin, A. (2012). 3 Approaches to ethics: Principles, Outcomes and Integrity. Psychology Today. https://www.psychologytoday.com/us/blog/am-i-right/201205/3-approaches-ethics-principles-outcomes-and-integrity.

As a manager, you might find yourself gravitating toward one ethical approach, but remember that each has its limits. Instead of relying on one school exclusively, you have to mix and match the different ethical schools to exercise ethical judgment. For example, as a manager, sometimes you might face situations that require you to think critically about your personal integrity (virtue ethics). Other times, you may be in a scenario that requires you to focus on doing more good than harm (consequential ethics), or you might have to think about achieving the best outcome for the most people (duty-based ethics). Each manager has their own style and may be inclined to favor one school over the other, but each is an essential tool for making ethical choices.

In addition to the philosophies and questions and characteristics noted above, there is also an **ethics of care** component that focuses on the need to maintain relationships with others, and connections to others, to guide decisions.[7] For example, in following the ethics of care, a decision-maker considers the damage that might be done to a relationship if a decision is made that they feel is unfair.

Most individuals follow one or more of the philosophies discussed in making decisions, and consider the ethics of care, but the utilitarian approach is the most common among business leaders.[8] Despite the best of intentions, however, leaders do succumb to external forces such as economic conditions, scarce resources, and competition, and make decisions that are unethical.[9] Recent research has shown that excessively focusing on the desired outcome (i.e., career advancement and monetary gain) results in selfish and unethical behavior.[10]

Some unethical decisions may be unintended. Managers might have **bounded ethicality**: an unconscious psychological process that hinders the quality of decision-making. In other words, ethicality is limited in ways that are not visible. Bounded ethicality refers to systematic and predictable ethical errors due to the limited capacity to process information.[11] For example, a leader may not be able to articulate the ethical challenge in a decision to rate followers' performance lower because there is a limited salary pool. Research has shown that people may even lie to get more money while feeling honest about it.[12] Under conditions of bounded ethicality, people make unethical decisions they are unaware of and then engage in self-justification to explain their behavior. Leaders may lack awareness about ethical violations (bounded awareness), and they must also develop systems that uncover violations in their organization.[13]

Utilitarianism seems like a "fair" way to make decisions, but Wells Fargo provides us with an excellent example of the effects of utilitarianism in business. Employees were pressured to increase the sales of extra services offered by the bank. If they did not meet sales quotas, they were forced to work longer hours and even threatened with being fired from their jobs. What did they do to increase sales? After all, sales are good for business, so the ends justified the means, right? According to one account of the scandal, they engaged in a practice known as "pinning," in which

a Wells Fargo banker obtains a debit card number, and personally sets the PIN, often to 0000, without customer authorization. "Pinning" permits a banker to enroll a customer in online banking, for which the banker would receive a sales credit. To bypass computer prompts requiring customer contact information, bankers impersonated the customer online, and input false generic email addresses such as 1234@ wellsfargo.com, noname@wellsfargo.com, or none@wellsfargo.com to ensure that the transaction is completed, and that the customer remains unaware of the unauthorized activity.[14]

Wells Fargo employees were trying to meet their sales quotas and avoid being fired. But they were eventually caught, and over 5,000 were terminated. It all added up: Employees opened 1,534,280 deposit accounts that might not have been authorized and that might have been funded through simulated funding, or transferring funds from consumers' existing accounts without their knowledge or consent. Roughly 85,000 of those accounts incurred about $2 million in fees, which Wells Fargo refunded. Consumers were outraged when they learned they had been paying extra fees, and a congressional investigation followed.

To understand ethics a little better, it is helpful to find out how people develop their morals. There will be many times in your life that you will think somebody is unethical or making an unethical decision, so the next section explains how people acquire their moral compass. It will help you see that there are several levels and stages of moral development, and not all people fall in the same category.

CRITICAL THINKING QUESTIONS

In what different ways do managers view ethics? What are the basic components of ethical decision-making?

Kohlberg's Stages of Moral Development

Learning Objective 3.2: Develop an example for each stage of moral development.

Lawrence Kohlberg's stages of **moral development** are based on Jean Piaget's theory of the moral judgment for children (1932). Developed by Kohlberg in 1958, the theory focuses on the *thinking process* that occurs when somebody is deciding if a behavior is right or wrong. This is the follow-up to Learning Objective 3.1, which has to do with the ethical philosophies in how a manager makes a decision, as Kohlberg focuses on *how* they decide to respond to a moral dilemma, not what they actually decide or actually do.[15]

According to Kohlberg's theory of moral development, there are six stages of moral development, separated into three levels (see Figure 3.1):

Level 1: Pre-Conventional Level

At the **pre-conventional reasoning** level, morality is externally controlled. Children at this level conform to rules imposed by authority figures in order to avoid punishment or receive rewards. This perspective involves the idea that what is right is what one can get away with or what is personally satisfying. Level 1 has two stages: obedience/punishment and self-interest.

At this level of moral development, children are interested only in securing their own benefit. This is their idea of morality. They begin by avoiding punishment, and quickly learn that they may secure other benefits by pleasing others. No other ethical concepts are available to children at this young age. This Kohlberg's stage is parallel to Piaget's sensorimotor stage. For a child whose conceptual framework does not extend beyond their own senses and movements, the moral concepts of right and wrong are not yet able to develop.

Level 2: Conventional Level

At the **conventional reasoning** level, conformity to social rules remains important to the individual. However, the emphasis shifts from self-interest to relationships with other people and social systems. The individual strives to support rules that are set forth by others such as parents, peers, and the government in order to win their approval or to maintain social order.

According to Kohlberg, the conventional level is the stage at which children learn about rules and authority. They learn that there are certain "conventions" that govern how they should and should not behave, and learn to obey them. At this stage, no distinction is drawn between moral principles and legal principles. What is right is what is handed down by authority, and disobeying the rules is always by definition "bad."

This level is split into two stages:

- First stage: Children are interested in pleasing others and securing the favor of others.
- Second stage: Children extend the principle to cover the whole of their society, believing that morality is what keeps the social order intact.

▼ FIGURE 3.1

Kohlberg's Stages of Moral Development

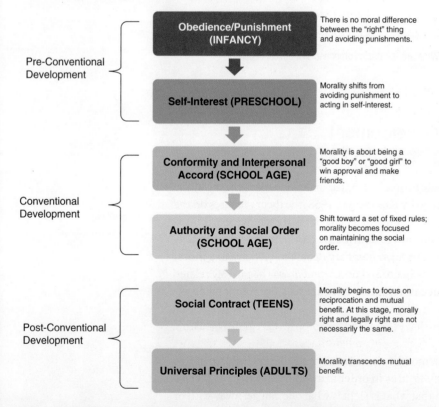

Source: Lawrence Kohlberg's Stages of Moral Development. Britannica.com. https://www.britannica.com/science/Lawrence-Kohlbergs-stages-of-moral-development.

Kohlberg believed that many people stay in this stage of moral reasoning for their whole lives, deriving moral principles from social or religious authority figures and never thinking about morality for themselves.

Level 3: Post-Conventional or Principled Level

Finally, at the **post-conventional reasoning** level, the individual moves beyond the perspective of their own society. Morality is defined in terms of abstract principles and values that apply to all situations and societies. The individual attempts to take the perspective of all individuals, and the two levels here are social contact and universal principles.

Age ranges of these levels are considerably more vague in Kohlberg's stages of moral development than in Piaget's stages, as children vary quite significantly in their rate of moral development.

At the post-conventional level, children have learned that there is a difference between what is right and wrong from a moral perspective and what is right and wrong according to the rules. Although they often overlap, there are still times when breaking a rule is the right thing to do. Post-conventional moral principles are either utilitarian principles or mutual benefit (closely related to the "social order" stage, but universal and nonauthoritarian in nature).[16]

The chart and description above provide a good snapshot of Kohlberg's work, but you might be wondering how these stages are assessed. Kohlberg developed an interview to determine the level of a person's moral reasoning by asking them what they would do in particular situations with ethical dilemmas. For example, a classic case was used in early research, in which a man's wife is in need of a drug that could save her life, but the only druggist who has the drug is charging a high price the man cannot afford. Should the man steal the drug to save his dying wife? What would you do? And what does your answer say about where you are in the levels and stages and how you arrived there, or how you can best advance to the next stage?

After Kohlberg's initial work, researchers developed business scenarios to determine the level of moral development of managers. Consider the following scenario:[17]

Evelyn worked for an automotive steel casting company. She was part of a small group asked to investigate the cause of an operating problem that had developed in the wheel castings of a new luxury automobile and to make recommendations for its improvement. The problem did not directly create an unsafe condition, but it did lead to irritating sounds. The Vice President of Engineering told the group that he was certain that the problem was due to tensile stress in the castings.

Evelyn and a lab technician conducted tests and found conclusive evidence that the problem was not tensile stress. As Evelyn began work on other possible explanations of the problem, she was told that the problem had been solved. A report prepared by Evelyn's boss strongly supported the tensile strength hypothesis. All of the data points from Evelyn's experiments had been changed to fit the curves, and some of the points which were far from where theory would predict had been omitted. The report "proved" that tensile stress was responsible for the problem.

CRITICAL THINKING QUESTIONS

Should Evelyn contradict her boss's report? Is it important that people do everything they can to make the truth known? The data in the boss's report are false. Would it be morally wrong for Evelyn to fail to contradict the report?

Research has shown that the stage of moral reasoning influences a manager's ethical decision-making.[18] A meta-analysis (research combining many past research findings) over 30 years with over 3,100 respondents[19] found that moral development was negatively related to unethical choices (that is, the higher your development, the more likely you are to make more ethical decisions).

This may explain why financial adviser Bernie Madoff ended up so egregiously stealing from his investors, since he started out by taking only a few thousand dollars. In the end, Madoff stole more than $18 billion.[20] It seems clear that Madoff was at the pre-conventional stage, making efforts to secure the greatest benefit for himself. He stopped stealing only when he got caught.

Criticisms of Kohlberg's Theory of Moral Development

While Kohlberg's theory is popular, cross-cultural psychologists (those who practice psychology in cultures other than America and Western Europe) have begun to assess it in recent years. Critics argue that Kohlberg may simply be presenting his own morals as psychological fact. They contend that his theory is problematic. They believe it aligns too closely with and may simply be another way to explain postmodern Western liberal ideas about justice and morality and implies that certain forms of moral reasoning are superior to others.

Some studies also poke holes in Kohlberg's theory. Some clinical data indicate that school-age children can begin to grasp concepts that, according to Kohlberg's theory, do not happen until adolescence or adulthood. For instance, kids as young as six can actually begin to understand the social contract (e.g., universal ethical principles like "no hitting"). These studies seem to suggest that, perhaps, "Kohlberg's stages of moral development describe not a one-way process of psychological growth for an individual, but a categorization of different types of moral values, which may be developed and prioritized differently for different individuals and moral cultures."[21]

CRITICAL THINKING QUESTIONS

What examples can you think of for each stage of moral development? How well do you think Kohlberg explains how we develop morality in levels and stages? At what points do you disagree with his theory? Do you feel that morality develops in the order he implies?

The previous discussion of moral development assumes that ethical behavior is due to the morality of individual decision-makers. Yet a major debate on what determines ethical or unethical behavior is known as "bad apples versus bad barrel."[22] Is ethical/unethical behavior a direct result of the personal traits of a person acting alone? Or, rather, is ethical/unethical behavior more heavily dependent on organizational climate and norms in a society,[23] or a combination of both? Next is a review of the influence of organizational climate on ethical behavior.

Ethical Climate

Learning Objective 3.3: Understand how managers influence an organization's ethical climate.

While Kohlberg outlined how all people are not at the same level of moral development, it is now important to remember that management and ethics are not separate issues, but rather intertwined.

There has been an increase in attention to ethics and morality in the study of organizations in the past 10 years, from specific companies like Enron (discussed in detail later in the chapter) and Wells Fargo to whole industries like mortgage, banking, and finance. Due to what seems to be an increase in unethical behaviors, researchers have responded by working on new theories that incorporate a moral component and place followers first.

These theories discuss the ethical role that managers and leaders can take, and how an ethical organization creates a positive ethical climate that works to serve all the stakeholders, not just the goals of the executives. These emerging theories are a good example of how research responds to current challenges organizations face, and how researchers generate new knowledge to guide managers and leaders.

Five Types of Ethical Climates

Wells Fargo's ethical image was destroyed after their account fraud scandal in 2016.

©iStockphoto.com/wdstock

The **ethical climate** within an organization reflects its orientation toward ethical decision-making. This climate has clear implications for encouraging ethical behavior in organizations. Since the late 1980s, there has been a stream of research on ethical climates—and organizations are showing great interest in improving ethical climates. Learning what the current climate is (organizations have five distinct types of ethical climates)[24] constitutes the first crucial step toward making the climate as appropriate and effective as it can be. These ethical climates are summarized in Table 3.2, and are reviewed below.

Employees perceiving an **instrumental ethical climate** see their organizational unit as having norms and expectations that encourage ethical decision-making from an egoistic perspective. In other words, self-interest guides behavior, even to the possible detriment of others. Decisions are made that serve the organization's interests or provide personal benefits.[25]

At the core of the **caring ethical climate** are altruism and compassion. Employees most frequently prefer to work in a caring climate[26] because they feel that empathy dominates decision-making. They know that ethical concern for others permeates the workplace environment, from the policies and best practices to the strategies the organization uses to do business.

The **independence ethical climate** prioritizes individualism. In this climate, one of the defining principles is that people should be able to act on their personal moral convictions in order to make ethical choices. It presumes that each person has arrived at their convictions through careful moral consideration.[27]

In a **law and code** ethical climate, decision-making is based on an external code of ethics—typically the law or an established professional code of conduct. Managers make choices based on whatever this code mandates. It is also presumed that individuals' ethics are mostly dictated by this code.[28]

In a **rules ethical climate**, company rules and regulations guide decision-making. This climate is similar to the law and code climate, but the rules are internally defined rather than externally defined.

A review of 42 studies[29] of ethical climate found that the instrumental climate is negatively related to job satisfaction and organization commitment, but the caring climate is positively related to these outcomes. The law and code climate is related to satisfaction, but not commitment. Thus, ethical climates strongly influence employee satisfaction and loyalty.

▼ TABLE 3.2

Ethical Climates

Ethical Climate	Employee Perceptions
Instrumental	"People are expected to do anything to further the company's interests."
Caring	"In this company, people look out for each other's good."
Independence	"In this company, people are expected to follow their own personal and moral beliefs."
Law and Code	"The first consideration is whether a decision violates any law."
Rules	"It is very important here to strictly follow the company's rules and procedures."

Source: Adapted from Cullen, J. B., Victor, B., & Stephens, C. (1989). An ethical weather report: Assessing the organization's ethical climate. *Organizational Dynamics, 18*(2), 50–62, p. 56.

Ethical Leadership

The study of ethics and morality in leadership will continue to be of interest to researchers as they continue to demonstrate relationships of ethical leadership with employee well-being and performance. Ethical decision-making is important to the practice of good management and leadership, and contemporary theories of ethical decision-making address morality as a key consideration.

Research on **ethical leadership** has found four moral components:

- Moral sensitivity involves recognizing that our behavior *impacts* others.
- Moral judgment involves determining the right decision.
- Moral motivation is having the need to do the right thing.
- Moral action is the result of principled reasoning, which leads to ethical behavior.[30]

Development of new approaches will continue to appear in textbooks, as they do in this one, for students and instructors. Additionally, you will probably be involved in corporate training programs designed to sensitize the next generation of managers, update you on the challenging ethical aspects of leadership, and, ideally, improve leadership practice.

FACT OR FICTION?

Misconceptions About Ethical Leadership

Business schools are encouraged to form ethical leaders through discussion of business ethics in the classroom. However, there are some misunderstandings about what constitutes ethical leadership. Ethics scholar Michael E. Brown dispels five common misunderstandings.

Misconception #1: Ethical leaders should not concern themselves with what others think as long as they are doing the right thing.

An old saying goes, "What is popular is not always right and what is right is not always popular." Conventional wisdom often suggests that external conceptions of ethics are not as valuable as one's inner moral compass. But is this good advice for ethical leaders? Should they really make ethical decisions based simply on the courage of their convictions? Studies indicate that this advice might not be so sound after all. It can be dangerous and unwise to ignore the external perceptions, or others' views, of your decision-making.

Misconception #2: Rules and policies are enough. Employees do not need ethical guidance.

Some leaders think that rules and regulations are enough to get their employees to behave ethically. Others presume that nothing they can do will change their employees' ethical mindset. In reality, employees do need guidance from ethical leaders. Studies routinely show that employee behavior is heavily influenced by the people around them. They consider other people's expectations in order to determine appropriate workplace conduct. Providing strong ethical guidance shows employees how to behave.

Misconception #3: There is no obligation to worry about ethics in business as long as no one breaks the law.

Some employers think legality and ethics are the same thing. They mistakenly think their responsibility ends with ensuring that employees obey the law, and therefore might ignore ethics. This is a problematic assumption. Business law should not be the sole focus; employees should also be required to consider business ethics.

Misconception #4: Business ethics is an oxymoron.

Due to the popularity of the "nice guys finish last" mentality, many people worry that behaving ethically is a liability for businesses. Recently, a popular business book even suggested that leaders act like Machiavelli, a historical figure known for being cutthroat and relentless. Despite the many depictions of ruthless businesspeople in popular culture, data demonstrate that ethical leadership is actually associated with positive business outcomes. When people associate your business with trust and integrity, it is an asset—not a liability.

Misconception #5: Leaders' personal conduct is irrelevant to their professional reputations.

Leaders should take care to keep their evaluation of employees focused on job-related performance, but what about *leaders'* private lives? Business ethics research shows that employees do, in fact, take leaders' personal lives into account when they judge ethical leadership. They believe that a leader's personal morality can be related to their professional integrity. Questionable ethical conduct in their personal lives can cast doubt on leaders' professional capabilities. Leaders should be mindful of their public visibility and take care to avoid scandals or poor choices that could reflect badly on their organizations.

Discussion Questions

1. Do you agree that employees need ethical guidance from leaders? Explain.

2. Explain the differences between ethical decision-making and obeying the law. Why is this distinction important?

3. In the business world, a lot of people believe that ethics compromises organizational effectiveness. Explain whether you agree or disagree with this position.

4. Should what a person does in their personal life matter in terms of how they are seen as an ethical leader? Provide an example of a leader who did something questionable in their personal life and how this affected their ability to lead.

Source: Adapted from Brown, M. E. (2007). Misconceptions of ethical leadership: How to avoid potential pitfalls. *Organizational Dynamics, 36*(2), 140–155.

Ethical leadership has been found to be positively related to work-group-level ethical behavior and negatively related to relationship conflict among coworkers.[31] A review of the research on ethical leadership concludes: "The research quite consistently shows that if employees indicate that their leaders are ethical and fair role models who communicate and reward ethical behavior, there is less deviance and more cooperative behavior, and employees perform better and are more willing to both expend effort and report problems to management."[32]

If leaders at the top of the organization are viewed as ethical by their followers, then ethics had a cascading effect throughout the organization; lower-level employees also view their manager as ethical.[33] Thus, ethical leadership at the top of an organization has a trickle-down effect to lower organizational levels. The moral component is emerging as a key aspect of contemporary leadership theories.

Based on both research and practical applications, you can see how managers can greatly influence ethics and decision-making processes within the organization through their actions and behaviors. They can also inspire others by following guidelines for creating awareness and encouraging ethical decisions:[34]

1. Talk "ethics"—make it a part of your workplace culture.
2. Publish your guiding principles.
3. Select, train, and retain employees who behave ethically.
4. Make ethical behavior part of business and performance reviews.
5. Work on increasing moral sensitivity from as many different perspectives as possible.
6. Attach consequences to desired behavior and measure its occurrence.
7. Ensure that structure and resources exist to monitor and enforce commitment to an ethical climate.
8. Invite external review by an ethics audit team.
9. Establish a set of criteria to evaluate your own actions and share those with others.
10. Encourage, model, and help others establish a method to discuss actions and increase alertness to the ethical issues in everyday decisions.

Following these guidelines should increase awareness of ethics in your organization and help avoid decision traps leading to compromised ethics. Many successful companies follow these standards. For example, consider number 2. If you Google *organizational ethics and corporate social responsibility*, you will find that a number of organizations publish their guiding principles. National Public Radio (NPR) is a prime example, spelling out its standards of journalism explicitly on its public website. The statement spells out ethical values, from transparency and accountability to accuracy in reporting.[35]

CRITICAL THINKING QUESTIONS

What are some ways managers influence an organization's climate?

Find the ethical statements or values of your university. Are they things you see in practice through the behaviors of your colleagues and professors? Try writing some additional or replacement ethical statements for your school, if you feel they are necessary. What should be added or deleted? How can the new ethical statements be modeled by you and your peers?

Ethical Decision-Making

The discussions in the beginning of the chapter about ethics and morals have probably seemed fairly calm, normal, and perhaps even just a good, commonsense way to approach things. What you know about dealing with people based on what you have learned so far, though, is that their responses are not always the same as yours, and that people have different morals and can be at different stages in moral development.

This section deals with how to make an ethical decision, but also the pushback you will receive from people based on their sense of justice, that is, their set of ethics and morals. You see, when people feel an event or decision is "unfair," their feelings come from their sense of what is ethical and moral. Just recently, the large automobile company General Motors (GM) announced several large rounds of employee layoffs as they significantly transitioned their business model to one they felt would best benefit the company and stockholders. This decision impacted many of their workers, who were no longer needed due to their skill set or geographic location.[36]

This sparked **moral outrage**, which is a severe reaction (including strong emotions such as anger and resentment) to a perceived injustice, such as losing one's job.[37] One study found that employees even engaged in sabotage when they perceived situations to be unfair,[38] so it will be interesting to see the final results of GM's announcements and changes.

The interesting takeaway, as a manager and leader, is that while the employees were outraged at the decision and announcement made by Mary Barra, CEO of GM, the day she made the largest announcement, stock prices rose. Many times managers are asked to make the "tough" decisions that will not make people happy, but the job is to run a successful organization.[39]

This is a good example of an ethical dilemma. Barra, as the CEO, purportedly has one job—to maximize shareholder wealth. That does not mean she is in favor of laying off employees, but it does show that accomplishing your job often comes at the cost of angering some, or many, others not in your position.

Barra's decisions and implementation also show a great deal of **moral courage**, or a personal fortitude to face ethical issues, challenges, or dilemmas and to pursue virtuous action. Another definition describes moral courage as an ability to consistently make decisions in light of what is good for others, despite the potential for personal risk.[40]

In this situation, Barra needed to make decisions to benefit many (utilitarianism), not just her employees, because the decision was made to set up the company (and the tens of thousands of other employees) for long-term success, avoid bankruptcy, and protect other stakeholders, such as the environment, as well. Her vision and decision-making also brought enormous pressure from outside entities, including threats from government officials.[41]

Now that you have an example of what is at stake when you are trying to make an ethical decision, you should also know that many ethical decision-making models have been developed over the years to illustrate the ethical decision-making process and the personal and situational characteristics involved. It should be noted that these models do not tell you what you ought to do when faced with an ethical dilemma, but rather are models of what the authors believe you should do when faced with an ethical dilemma.

Do you have moral courage? Find out by completing Self-Assessment 3.1.

One of the goals of this book is to provide you with contemporary solutions to the challenges of management, so you will be presented with several decision-making models to choose from. Some are focused on organizational decision-making

CEO of GM, Mary Barra.

©Rebecca Cook/REUTERS/Newscom

(covered later in the chapter), while some, like the PLUS decision-making model discussed below, are focused on individual management decision-making and take into account where you, as the decision-maker, might be a factor in the final decision based on your own personal characteristics. Also note that a decision-making guide is simply that, a guide, and that an ethical decision-making framework adds an ethical component to the decision. As such, these guides are descriptive ("here is how to test your decision") rather than prescriptive ("here is what you should do").[42]

The **PLUS decision-making model**[43] is from the Ethics Decision Making Center in Arlington, Virginia, and was designed to take into account the way many organizations do business today, such as by empowering employees to make their own decisions, keeping open lines of communication, and always keeping in mind the values of the organization.

The PLUS Decision-Making Model

Employee decision-making models must account for two essential truths:

1. Every employee makes decisions while doing their job, because organizations would fail if they were not empowered to do so.
2. For employees to be confident in their decision-making skills, they must test decisions against the organization's policies, values, and regulations as well as their own ideas about what is correct and fair.

The conventional model used in most ethics programs was failing employees. In fact, an estimated one in four employees could not implement it. Organizations needed a new decision-making process carefully constructed to be:

- aligned with current theories about decision-making and ethics
- clear and simple enough for all employees to incorporate into their decision-making process
- descriptive instead of prescriptive (i.e., to describe things as they occur naturally rather than telling people how they *should* make decisions)

The six-step decision-making process below combines decision-making models used in ethics training and problem-solving training.

Step 1: Find and define the problem. Why is the decision necessary, and what is the desired outcome? To figure out if there is a problem, compare the desired expectations to reality. A problem can be defined as the difference between what you want and what you get. How you define a problem determines how you identify its causes and search for solutions.

For example, imagine that your company owns an old office building downtown. Your tenants tell you their employees hate the elevator. Employees are constantly complaining and extremely frustrated about the long delay in getting an elevator at rush hour. Your tenants want to know how to solve this problem.

As with just about any problem, there are a number of ways to define the solution. When this question was posed to more than 200 focus groups during a training exercise, they identified the following solutions:

- Offer flexible hours so all of the employees aren't trying to use the elevator at once.
- Get faster elevators to shorten the travel time.
- Get bigger elevators so each can carry more people per trip.
- Install elevator banks so an elevator stops only at specified floors.
- Improve elevator controls.
- Install more elevators to increase capacity.
- Perform better maintenance so elevators work better.
- Discourage use of the elevators and instead recommend the stairs so that fewer people use the elevators.

Look closely at each solution. What was the definition of the problem? If you examine each alternative, you will see that several different definitions of the problem must have existed. If the solution is "flexible hours," the problem must be "too many people arrive at work at once." "Faster elevators" means that the problem is elevators that are too slow. "Bigger elevators" means the elevators don't hold enough people. "More elevators" means there aren't enough elevators.

The actual decision-makers in this case did something that none of the focus groups suggested. They defined the problem differently.

Problem: People have to wait, and that annoys them.

Solution: Make the wait less frustrating by playing music in the lobby.

It worked. Workers stopped complaining. This solution arose from the specific problem that the decision-makers defined.

Step 2: Identify available alternative solutions to the problem. Do not limit yourself. The most obvious solution or the solution that worked once before is not always the most effective. Be open to novel and more efficient ideas. Consider between three to five alternatives for every problem to avoid getting trapped in a false-binary choice between two options or having so many options that you become overwhelmed.

Step 3: Evaluate the identified alternatives. What are the pros and cons of each alternative you listed in Step 2? Usually, there is not one single solution that is markedly better than the others. Rather, there are typically small differences in value among all the choices, so you need to think critically about your choices. Try to distinguish between fact-based pros and cons and feelings-based pros and cons. Make an evaluation using evidence rather than hunches or gut feelings.

Step 4: Make the decision. If you are working independently, simply choose a solution. If you are working with a group, present Steps 1 to 3 to your team members and reach a consensus.

Step 5: Implement the decision. As Lou Gerstner (former CEO of IBM) said, "there are no more prizes for predicting rain. There are only prizes for building arks." Picking the best alternative is not the same as putting the solution into practice.

Step 6: Evaluate the decision. Did you fix the problem? Was the improvement miniscule or dramatic? Did you create any new problems?

Ethics Filters

The decision-making process above is generic. It does not account for ethics. Let's apply some "filters" to the above process. They will help you spot ethical concerns and give them proper consideration. By simplifying the ethical decision-making process, you dramatically increase the utility of the ethics-filters process.

To make it easy to remember, understand, and apply these ethics filters, use the mnemonic word PLUS.

- *P = Policies.* Does this approach fit into the company's established policies, procedures, and guidelines?
- *L = Legal.* Does this approach obey applicable laws and comply with relevant regulations?
- *U = Universal.* Does this approach align with the universal principles my company has in place?
- *S = Self.* Does this approach meet my own personal criteria for what is fair, correct, and acceptable?

The PLUS decision-making model requires effective communication to employees. They must understand the company's policies, applicable laws and regulations, and universal values. They should also be empowered to use their individual sense of ethics.

The PLUS filters should be applied to Steps 1, 3, and 6 of the decision process.

- **Step 1: Define the problem PLUS identify ethical issues.** Does the existing situation present any PLUS problems? Is there a problem with policy, law, the organization's values, or my own sense of ethics?
- **Step 2: Identify available alternative solutions to the problem.**
- **Step 3: Evaluate the identified alternatives PLUS assess their ethical impact.** Will the alternative I am considering resolve the PLUS problems? Will it cause any new PLUS problems? Am I making any ethical tradeoffs? Are they acceptable when I consider PLUS?
- **Step 4: Make the decision.**
- **Step 5: Implement the decision.**
- **Step 6: Evaluate the decision PLUS take inventory of any new ethical issues.** Does the solution fix the PLUS concerns I identified in Step 1?[44]

The PLUS filters enable you to consider decisions ethically and holistically. Applying the PLUS filters gives employees a simple, straightforward framework for making decisions that carefully consider policy, law, universal values set by the organization, and the employee's own individual sense of ethics. Good decision-making requires extensive questioning of the organization and the individual.[45] When applying the PLUS model, one must also consider ethical and moral intensity. Personal bias, beliefs, experiences, and character traits can influence how an employee uses the PLUS filters as well as the final outcome of the ethical decision.

CRITICAL THINKING QUESTIONS

How would you apply the PLUS framework to a current problem you need to solve? Is your decision different after you add the ethical framework to the standard decision-making model? Which moral intensity property do you think would alter your decision, and why?

Moral Intensity

Moral intensity, "the extent of issue-related moral imperative in a situation,"[46] has six factors:[47]

1. Magnitude of consequences is the total harm or benefit derived from an ethical decision.
2. Social consensus is agreement on whether behavior is bad or good.
3. Probability of effect is the chance that something will happen that results in harm to others.
4. Temporal immediacy is the time between an act and the consequences the act produces.
5. Proximity of effect is the social, psychological, cultural, or physical distance of a decision-maker from those affected by their decisions.
6. Concentration of effect is how much an act affects the average person.

So far we have concentrated on individuals and their moral development, tools to help them make the best ethical decisions they can, and some of the challenges that come along with that. The next section is going to discuss another very contemporary issue—that of organizational ethics in decision-making and corporate social responsibility.

The Importance of Corporate Social Responsibility

Learning Objective 3.5: Understand the importance of corporate social responsibility.

A question that often gets asked about ethics and morals at the organizational level is, "How could that happen?" Perhaps the best example of a complete meltdown from substandard, or no-standard, ethical behavior is a company called Enron. The intricate and nearly unbelievable story of Enron's leadership team bringing down their own company, as well as tens of thousands

The film *The Smartest Guys in the Room* traces the arrogance and lack of ethics of Enron and Arthur Anderson.

© RICHARD CARSON/REUTERS/Newscom

of employees and investors, makes for an interesting movie you can watch at http://watchdocumentaries.com/enron-the-smartest-guys-in-the-room/. Sarcastically titled *The Smartest Guys in the Room*, the movie traces the arrogance and complete lack of ethics of two companies: Enron and Arthur Andersen.

In 2001, while declaring unheard-of stock and profit margin increases, the leadership at Enron, and their auditors from Arthur Andersen, were frantically moving real and fake money around to hide the fact that they were a rapidly sinking ship. Even up until the last minute, Enron's CEO was convincingly encouraging his employees to purchase Enron stock for their entire retirement portfolios. You can imagine what happened to their investments.

Corporations provide many examples of unethical decisions. Volkswagen was long admired for ethical business practices and protecting the environment, but all of this ended in 2015 when the United States Environmental Protection Agency slapped Volkswagen with a notice of violation of the Clean Air Act. The auto manufacturer had been caught installing "defeat devices" in 482,000 of its diesel vehicles in the United States (11 million worldwide).

These cleverly engineered devices detected when a car was being driven under emissions test conditions and only at that point turned on emission controls. They switched off during normal driving, meaning that fuel performance improved, but up to 40 times more nitrous oxide was released.[48] A global scandal followed, and the company was seen as a villain by the media. Its reputation was ruined and its stock price tanked, losing almost a third of its market value in less than a week. A few days after the scandal, CEO Martin Winterkorn resigned under threat of a criminal investigation.[49]

Despite the severe consequences of this scandal, the fact that these types of decisions almost certainly *are* made in business tells us that leaders have probably been in unimaginable moral quandaries. Businesses want to improve profitability by touting high performance, but at the same time must comply with environmental laws.

These examples highlight the importance of **corporate social responsibility**. Corporate social responsibility (CSR) has been defined as entailing

four kinds of social responsibilities: Economic, legal, ethical and philanthropic. Furthermore, these four categories or components of CSR might be depicted as a pyramid. All of these kinds of responsibilities have always existed to some extent, but it has only been in recent years that ethical and philanthropic functions have taken a significant place.[50]

In other words, "the CSR firm should strive to make a profit, obey the law, be ethical, and be a good corporate citizen."[51]

A Change in Perspective

A hard-and-fast rule in business, and one that was mentioned earlier in the GM case, is that the CEO's only job is a fiduciary one—to maximize shareholder wealth.

Researchers at Michigan State University, while examining some of the organizational failures of the last two decades, decided that it would be better for CEOs to understand that "the heart of a good business is not profits or best-of-breed products and services. Those are results from what lies at the core of good business: good ethics."[52]

A long line of cases are mentioned in this chapter where unethical behavior has derailed companies across industries. "Few areas cause more harm in the business community than when businesses lack an ethical foundation," said Joseph Potchen, an attorney and visiting professor at Michigan State University's Eli Broad College of Business, where he teaches a graduate-level course on business ethics. "Most people would agree that having good ethics is important.

However, it's when people lose sight of proper ethical behavior that the problems and issues begin."[53]

As a result, there is a continued need for business leaders in the United States and around the world to uphold the highest ethical standards.

"Despite the negative headlines, the reality is that people still look to top executives and key managers in businesses for leadership and guidance," Potchen said.[54]

Two good ways for managers and leaders to heed Potchen's suggestions are to focus on **stakeholders** rather than **shareholders**, and to be concerned with the **triple bottom line (TBL)**, otherwise known as the **3Ps**—people, planet, and profit—rather than just being concerned about the monetary bottom line.

Stakeholders are people who can affect or be affected by the organization's actions, objectives, and policies. Some examples of key stakeholders are creditors, directors, employees, government (and its agencies), owners (shareholders), suppliers, unions, and the community from which the business draws its resources.[55]

The TBL is an accounting framework that incorporates three dimensions of performance: social, environmental, and financial. This differs from traditional reporting frameworks in that it includes ecological (or environmental) and social measures that can be difficult to assign appropriate means of measurement, hence people, planet, and profits. The trick to this method is how to measure the 3Ps. Profit is relatively easy, but how do you measure an organization's decision-making impact on people and planets?[56] Here is yet another challenge for the new batch of managers taking over organizations.

Figure 3.2 outlines the many stakeholders and considerations involved in making an ethical business decision, how they are connected by the impact, and the difficulty of measuring an organization's 3Ps in all of these areas.

For the final model of decision-making, here is Rushworth M. Kidder, author of *How Good People Make Tough Choices*. By now it is probably evident that ethical decision-making is really tough, especially now that you are also aware of the many stakeholders and the 3Ps.

▼ FIGURE 3.2

A Model of Business Ethics

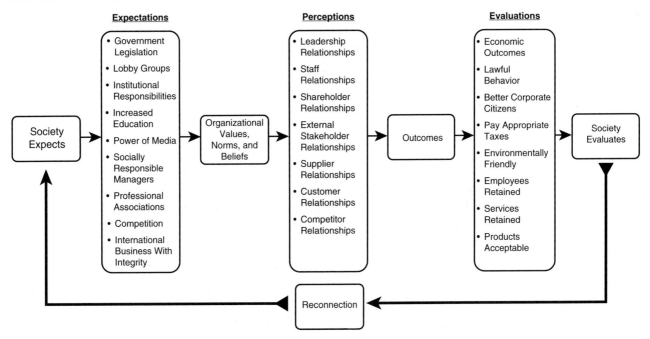

Source: Svensson, G., & Wood, G. (2008). A model of business ethics. *Journal of Business Ethics, 77*(3), 303–322.

Kidder provides a nine-step checklist a manager may use to determine if they are being ethical in their dealings with others.[57] It is important to note that this list is about managers being ethical in their dealings with others, not just managers making an ethical decision.

1. Recognize that there is a moral issue.
2. Determine the actor (and the players) in the issue.
3. Gather the facts.
4. Test for right versus wrong using four criteria:
    - Is it legal?
    - Does it feel right at the gut level?
    - Would you want to see this on the front page?
    - What would your mother/family think?
5. Test for right versus right (when both options seem moral, e.g., truth vs. loyalty; hard decisions).
6. Apply the appropriate ethical principles (e.g., utilitarian, rights, justice).
7. Ask, is there a third way through the dilemma?
8. Make the decision.
9. Revisit and reflect.

In addition to encouraging leaders to be ethical, organizations have implemented policies and programs that foster ethical behavior. These include ethics codes, policies, and training. In some cases these programs are required by law, but in other cases they result from top management's commitment to ethical behavior.[58] Laboratory and field studies support the idea that knowledge of what constitutes moral behavior results in ethical actions.[59] Education and training appear to be one of the keys to ensuring moral behavior in organizations. The goal is that these policies and training programs result in an organizational culture in which ethical behavior becomes the norm and employees behave in a manner consistent with moral values.

CRITICAL THINKING QUESTIONS

Think of a recent incident in where your decision hurt people. Did you ask yourself the types of questions recommended above? Would you make a different decision now? Explain how the decisions of managers and leaders can impact the whole organization.

The Future of Corporate Social Responsibility

Learning Objective 3.6: Discuss how the future of organizational social responsibility will be an important part of the management planning process.

In an increasingly competitive and complex marketplace—where the pressure to succeed is intense and ever present—how can organizations and individuals resist the urge to cut ethical corners? You have many, many ethical dilemmas ahead, and good ethical decision-making will be at a premium.

Forbes Magazine published an article in January 2018 asking about the future of ethics in technology as it pertains to human resource management. As a manager, if you knew you could track your employees at all times—would you? As the CEO, would you install software to track all the Internet sites your people go to each day?

New Scientist provides us with 10 equally tough ethical questions in their ethics issue, titled "The 10 Biggest Moral Dilemmas in Science."[60] While somewhat frightening, these questions are also fascinating to consider because they will be part of the not-too-distant future:

1. Should animals have the same moral rights as humans? Minimizing the suffering of other life forms is a laudable goal—but there's also human well-being to consider.

CAREERS IN MANAGEMENT

Corporate Social Responsibility (CSR) Director

Gregory Unruh, the Arison Group Endowed Professor at George Mason University, was curious about how CSR expert Alberto Andreu Pinillos saw the CSR director's role. Alberto found that he was often asked basic questions about his role—what he did and what his job was actually about. Alberto breaks his job into three core duties: foresight, nurturing, and evangelism.

1. Foresight

CSR directors act as a "radar," homing in on risks and opportunities—be they social or environmental. It is their job to think beyond the immediate into the medium and long term. They synthesize this information and put it in front of decision-makers so they can capitalize on opportunities and proactively address risks. Alberto points out that a decade ago, executives were not really thinking about social and environmental issues related to the supply chain, but innovative and dynamic CSR directors were. They helped prepare execs for a paradigm shift that was on the horizon. CSR directors have also predicted the increasing importance of diversity in the workplace and have helped HR directors implement changes in advance of regulations.

2. Nurturing

Alberto contends that CSR directors are also incubators for internal projects. They work with other departments to bring about social and environmental improvements.

For example, consider the issue of diversity. Imagine an organization operating in Europe. The CSR director might use their foresight to identify diversity as a key issue and take the lead, nurturing an initiative to achieve compliance. Once the project is kicked off, it can be handed over to HR.

CSR directors are like parents, Alberto argues. "The problem is that [managers] get confused in one of two ways: Either releasing projects before they're ready or holding on to them for too long. You can't make a mistake when it comes time to let your 'children' leave home . . . neither too soon, nor too late."

3. Evangelism

The long-term purpose of the CSR office is to educate the entire organization about sustainability. They must sell sustainability and a sustainable mindset throughout all levels of the organization and get buy-in. Alberto says, "The true test of a responsible company is when all functions and departments are capable of minimizing their own negative impacts and are thinking about making a positive impact on their community." The CSR department should be so adept at spreading the message of sustainability that sustainability becomes habit for all employees, without the CSR department's help.

Discussion Questions

1. Of the three principal activities and responsibilities, foresight, nurturing, and evangelism, which do you think is most important and why?

2. Explain the link between CSR and sustainability. Provide an example of how businesses address sustainability.

3. Do you agree or disagree that CSR is a part of everyone's job? Do you feel there is still a need for a CSR director in organizations? Explain your reasoning.

Source: Adapted from Unruh, G. (2015). What does a Corporate Responsibility Manager do? *MIT Sloan Management Review.* Retrieved from https://sloanreview.mit.edu/article/what-does-a-corporate-responsibility-manager-do/.

2. Should we edit our children's genomes? Tweaking genes to prevent your child dying early from a genetic disorder would be acceptable to most people, but we need to ask how far we should go.

3. Should we make everyone "normal"? If more people thought and acted in the same way, societies would probably be happier and safer. But at what cost?

4. Should we abandon privacy online? The battle between online privacy and national security is reaching fever pitch. Where we end up depends on which Faustian ("deals with the devil") bargains we are willing to strike.

5. Should we give robots the right to kill? Robot soldiers that follow orders, unclouded by human emotions, might reduce casualties in conflicts. But who will take responsibility for their actions? Should we let synthetic life forms loose?

6. Should we let new life forms loose? New forms of life could help tackle problems from famine to global warming, but releasing them into the wild raises biosafety concerns.

In the future, it will be possible for robots to perform military operations.

©Pavel Chagochkin/Shutterstock

7. Should we geoengineer the planet? We only have one Earth. How far should we go in our attempts to save it from ourselves?

8. Should we impose population controls? Future generations risk inheriting an overcrowded, suffocating planet. Taking action may mean what was taboo is now common sense.

9. Should we colonize other planets? As ever more potentially habitable exoplanets are discovered, it's time we asked ourselves: do we have the right to take over another world?

10. Should we stop doing science? Scientific research may lead to benefits and advances, but they seem to go hand-in-hand with death and destruction. Should we quit while we're ahead?[61]

CRITICAL THINKING QUESTIONS

From the list of 10 future questions, list your top three concerns. Explain why they concern you. What are your thoughts on how they should be answered? Which ethical standards would you apply to address them?

To provide an additional glimpse into the types of decisions you and other leaders will be making, here is the first ethical question posed in the Forbes list of "Tech Issues We Should All Be Thinking About in 2019":

For $25k–$50k, you can now clone your cat or dog. However, there are no guarantees you'll get a new pet that looks or acts like your old one, and the host animals used to gestate clones have a pretty miserable life. Is it right to invest in this technology when there are so many animals in need of homes already out there?[62]

Over the decades, much research has been devoted to the question of ethics as it applies to commerce, technology, academics, and medicine, among other fields. These studies have underpinned the development of numerous frameworks and theories designed to foster ethical behavior.

For the management decision-makers of the future, consider the ethical framework being used by Michigan State University in its Ethics Program. They propose a six-step model for ethical decision-making designed to prepare business managers and leaders and other professionals to face a range of organizational challenges and personal choices. The key is that this model is intended to prepare *you*, since the answers to these ethical questions of the future are going to made by you. Here are the six steps:

1. Know the Facts
Before you do anything else about an ethical issue, clearly define exactly what is challenging or problematic. Take the time to explore the issue in detail and from multiple perspectives so you can clearly define it.

2. Gather the Required Information
When you make a decision without all of the required information in front of you, you are asking for trouble. Go on an information-gathering mission and identify any assumptions you are making about the ethical problem.

3. Inventory the Concerns
Now explore the people, concerns, laws, rules, and professional standards that can influence your decision. Who is affected by or involved in the ethical issue? What are they concerned about? Are there any rules or laws or professional codes of conduct that relate to this issue?

4. Develop Possible Resolutions
Look closely at your possible solutions. Be creative and look beyond straightforward options. You might also seek advice from people who have applicable expertise.

WHERE DO WE DRAW THE LINE IN EMPLOYEE TECHNOLOGY PRIVACY?

The boundary is in constant flux.

Once upon a time, we held our privacy in the highest regard. We kept work at work and home at home. We held our personal data close to the vest. Times they are a-changing. Today's devices can track us from the subway to the office. Algorithms keep tabs on our preferences and behaviors. Our technology knows us well enough to predict where we'll go, what we'll want, and even whose company we'll enjoy.

Our brains are normalizing machines. We can get used to just about anything if we experience it long enough—even if we don't enjoy it. Even if we hate it. Social norms have evolved with alarming speed. Half a century ago, a teen would have instantly given up their seat on the train for an old woman with shopping bags. When people flew, they wore the kind of business attire you'd see in the boardroom. Today, these aspects of social etiquette have gone largely by the wayside. The new normal is faces glued to cell phones on public transit and yoga pants for the plane. Norms have changed dramatically.

The workplace is different, too. Many of the new norms are to employees' benefit. Jobs are safer and largely more flexible and stimulating; employees enjoy more collaboration. But working days last longer, and technology has eroded the once-sacred line between home and work. Our bosses expect us to be more available, more self-motivated, and, ultimately, more productive than ever before. And that's now. What about in the future and all the innovations it holds?

When your tablet or fitness watch or cell phone collects and disseminates an endless stream of data to your manager, how will you feel? What if, at the touch of a screen, your boss, your HR rep, and corporate have a pulse on not only your heartbeat but your mood, your habits, and your communications? Will you feel violated? What will happen when the cumulative pile of data about you is accessible to everyone? How will society change? What will the new social norms be?

HR and executives will have a dilemma before them. How will they use technology to unleash innovation while engaging workers without alienating them?

Source: Adapted from Vorhauser-Smith, S. (2018, January 14). HR: Can we please discuss ethics in the future of work? *Forbes.* Retrieved from https://www.forbes.com/sites/sylviavorhausersmith/2018/01/14/hr-can-we-please-discuss-ethics-in-the-future-of-work/#5d5380ca3dd5.

5. Evaluate the Resolutions

Do a careful inventory of the outcomes you predict. Consider the cost and impact as well as the compliance with laws and regulations. Think about the optics of your resolution. How will it look to the general public, to customers, and to corporate collaborators?

6. Recommend an Action

It's time to finalize your decision. Make sure to follow through on your recommended action with implementation. Determine what it will take to put your solution in place and identify key stakeholders who are instrumental in making your recommendation a reality.[63]

Managerial Implications

This chapter provided an overview of the different ways ethics can be viewed, the moral development process, and the complexities of ethical decision-making. Fortunately, we also provided you with several different frameworks to help you make decisions, test for their ethicality, and prepare for the even more complex ethical decisions you will be making as key managers and leaders and valuable organizational members.

The key takeaway points from this chapter are:

- Ethical decisions and behaviors can rarely be viewed in terms of "right" and "wrong." Ethics are inherently subjective, meaning that what one person views as ethical, another might view as unethical. Managers must be aware of this subjectivity and anticipate the views of their stakeholders. There are different perspectives that can be applied to ethical decision-making: the utilitarian view, the rights view, and the theory of justice. In addition, the ethics of care may be applied.
- As we learn, grow, and experience new situations, our own sense of ethics changes through a process called moral development. Kohlberg devised a model of the stages of moral development: pre-conventional, conventional, post-conventional.

- Managers are human beings and are subject to the same ethical weaknesses and challenges we all face. Their position often requires that they be held to higher moral standards than other employees, however. Learning to understand and manage one's own ethical decision-making process is therefore a key skill for effective management.

- The ethical decision-making process is deceptively complex, particularly for managers. Understanding the steps of this process is helpful for avoiding ethical mistakes in the eyes of employees, customers, and other stakeholders. The PLUS model is an excellent way to frame your future ethical decisions. In making decisions, managers should consider *policies*, *legal*, *universal*, and the *self*. This allows managers and employees to have a common language in the consideration of ethical questions.

- Not all ethical dilemmas are created equal. Moral issues vary in their moral intensity, and managers need to be aware of how factors such as the probability, magnitude, and proximity of consequences can influence their decision-making process—for better or for worse.

- Organizations can influence employee ethical decisions through the creation of caring ethical climates and the creation of clear rules for ethics. Also, managers should serve as role models through practicing ethical leadership.

- Social responsibility can improve a company's financial performance if its managers know how to harness its impact on innovation, recruitment, reputation, and culture. Two good ways are for managers and leaders to focus on stakeholders rather than shareholders, and to be concerned with the triple bottom line, or the 3Ps—people, planet, and profit—rather than just being concerned about the monetary bottom line.

- With respect to corporate social responsibility, the future will hold an increasing number of complex considerations, ranging from genomes to robotics. Managers must be prepared to address the ethical dilemmas on the horizon.

- Ethics may be a combination of individual moral development and shaping by the corporate climate and ethical leadership. Corporate social responsibility is good for business and the well-being of the stakeholders of the organization.

KEY TERMS

bounded ethicality 72

caring ethical
climate 77

consequentialist ethics 71

conventional reasoning 74

corporate social
responsibility 84

deontological ethics *or* duty-
based ethics 71

ethical climate 76

ethical leadership 77

ethics 71

ethics of care 72

independence ethical
climate 77

instrumental ethical
climate 77

law and code 77

moral courage 80

moral development 73

moral intensity 83

moral outrage 80

PLUS decision-making
model 81

post-conventional
reasoning 74

pre-conventional
reasoning 73

rights view 71

rules ethical climate 77

shareholders 85

stakeholders 85

theory of justice 71

triple bottom line (TBL) *or*
3Ps 85

utilitarian view 71

virtue ethics 71

TOOLKIT

Activity 3.1

Trolley Problem: Ethical Decision-Making Exercise

Instructions

1. Read the Trolley Problem Setup and Scenario 1 to a group of students.
2. Ask those who choose Option 1 to stand on one side of the room and those who choose Option 2 to stand on the other side of the room.
3. Ask for volunteers to share why they made their choice.
4. Discuss what personal value they used to help them make their choice. For example, did they choose Option 1 because they want the greatest good for the greatest number of people? Did they choose Option 2 because they don't want to be responsible for causing the death of someone?
5. Proceed through the other scenarios asking students to stand on sides of the room, asking why students made the decisions they did and which value(s) they used to guide their decisions.

Trolley Problem Setup

Suppose you are the driver of a trolley car. It is the first run of the day, and there is no one on the trolley besides you. As you start down a hill, you realize the brakes on the trolley car aren't working because the brake line has been cut.

SCENARIO 1:

- You are currently on Track A, but you can steer the trolley onto Track B if you choose to flip the switch.
- Five people are working on Track A, and one person is working on Track B.
- Anyone on the track along which your runaway trolley travels will be killed.

Discussion Questions

1. Would you change tracks and kill one person to spare five (Option 1), or would you do nothing and allow the trolley to continue on its path (Option 2)?
2. Why would you make this choice? What personal value is guiding this decision? Option 1 = greatest good for the greatest number (do what you can to save as many lives as possible) Option 2 = do no harm (don't be the cause of anyone getting killed).

SCENARIO 2:

- There is no Track B, just Track A with five people working on it.
- You are no longer the driver, but you are standing on a bridge and the runaway trolley will be going below you soon and will strike and kill five people.
- You can stop the trolley by dropping something heavy on the tracks below.

Discussion Questions

1. Would you push a very large man off the bridge and onto the tracks to stop the trolley, even if it meant the large man would die (Option 1)? Or do nothing and allow the trolley to continue on its path (Option 2)?
2. Why would you make this choice, and what personal values are you using?
3. Did you choose the same option as before?
4. Is pushing the large man onto the tracks the same as throwing the switch in Scenario 1?

Sources: Adapted from Edmonds, D. (2014). Would you kill the fat man? The trolley problem and what your answer tells us about right and wrong. Princeton, NJ: Princeton University Press; Foot, P. (1978). Virtues and vices and other essays in moral philosophy. Berkeley: University of California Press.

Follow Up: The Train Problem Has Been Tested in "Real Life" for the Very First Time

How far are you willing to go to save lives in an emergency? Are you willing to sacrifice a life?

The trolley problem is an ethical scenario meant to help you measure just that. Here it is in nutshell. Imagine that a runway carriage comes barreling down the tracks. It's headed straight for five people—and not just any five people, but five people who are tied to the tracks.

That's the bad news. The good news is that you have the power to save them.

All you have to do to save these poor folks tied to the track is pull on a lever. Sounds easy enough, right? Oh, but there's more bad news. If you pull the lever, the train diverts to another track where there's another person tied down and unable to escape the runway train.

There are all sorts of twists on this ethical dilemma, but the crux of the exercise is the same: Would you kill one person to save five? Or should you keep your hands clean and let the train take its course without your intervention? As if just thinking about this hypothetical catch-22 weren't enough to make you shudder, scientists have brought it to life—or at least partly.

In Belgium, scientists brought about 200 volunteer students into a lab and gave them a terrible choice to mimic the train scenario. They recreated the experiment with mice! In the lab, they hooked an electroshock machine to two cages. One cage housed five mice. The other had just one. Sound familiar?

Participants were told that, in 20 seconds, if they didn't intervene, all five mice in one cage would receive a survivable but extremely painful jolt of electricity. However, if they pushed the button before the 20 seconds was up, only one mouse in the other case would receive the shock.

In reality, the machine wasn't actually going to shock the mice, but the participants had no idea.

Eighty-four percent of the student volunteers pushed the button, sparing the five mice and shocking the one mouse.

In a separate experiment in which participants were simply told about the scenario, only 64% said they'd shock the single mouse.

Of course the experiment isn't exactly like the runway train scenario. We can't actually compare shocking a mouse to killing a person with a runway railcar, can we? But here's what the experiment suggests. In a real-life scenario, most people rely on a consequential version of ethics (considering the overall outcome) rather than deontological ethics (which says it would be unethical to decide to hurt anyone, regardless of the overall outcome).

Discussion Questions

1. What do you think you would do? Would you press the button and shock the single mouse? Explain why or why not.
2. Why do most people lean in the direction of consequentialism (do the most good for the most people) rather than deontological thought (harming one person is wrong)? How does this create ethical dilemmas in business decisions?
3. Develop a business example in which doing the most good for the most people would harm a single person. Does this change your perspective? Why or why not?

Sources: Adapted from Bostyn, D. H., Sevenhant, S., & Roets, A. (2018). Of mice, men, and trolleys: Hypothetical judgment versus real-life behavior in trolley-style moral dilemmas. *Psychological Science, 29*(7), 1084–1093; Dockrill, P. (2018, May 14). The trolley problem has been tested in "real life" for the very first time. Retrieved from https://www.sciencealert.com/the-trolley-problem-tested-in-real-life-first-time-consequentialism-deontologist.

Case Study 3.1

The College Admissions Scandal

Operation Varsity Blues. It sounds like a Netflix series, doesn't it? Bribes and cheats done by rich and famous parents to get their kids into top universities. So much drama.

The Justice Department calls this the biggest admissions scam in U.S. history. Operation Varsity Blues found that parents used connections with coaches and/or fake SAT/ACT scores to make sure the best universities accepted their children. The universities involved in the scandal were Yale University, Wake Forest University, the University of

San Diego, Stanford University, Georgetown University, the University of Texas, the University of Southern California, and the University of California, Los Angeles. Fifty people were charged in the investigation, including 33 parents. Some were TV stars, such as Felicity Huffman (*Desperate Housewives*) and Lori Loughlin (*Full House, Fuller House*). Also, some CEOs of top companies were indicted.

What They Did

According to the unsealed court documents, allegations included:

- bribing college entrance exam officials to facilitate cheating on college entrance exams
- bribing coaches and administrators to designate applicants as recruited athletes (when they were not athletes) to gain admission to colleges and universities
- using a charitable organization to conceal bribery payments
- having third parties take classes and exams in place of their children and submitting the earned grade as part of the students' college applications
- submitting falsified applications for admission that contained fraudulently obtained exam scores, grades, awards, and athletic activities

Who Was Behind All of This?

The mastermind behind all of this cheating to get into college seems to be William "Rick" Singer. He made sure these rich people got their children admitted to universities that have tough admissions standards. Singer created a counseling and admissions company called The Edge College & Career Network as well as a nonprofit called The Key World Foundation. The scheme used sports coaches and test administrators from the SAT and ACT examinations to fraudulently get students admitted to the universities. Singer would get another person to take the exams for students. He used a sneaky way of making the payments through "charitable contributions." For example, Felicity Huffman donated $15,000, and this was funneled to a person who created false college entrance exam scores for her daughter.

Another scheme was to bribe coaches to fake the athletic abilities of prospective students to get them admitted on scholarships. In the case of Lori Loughlin, she and her fashion designer husband Mossimo Giannulli allegedly bribed the rowing coach with $500,000 to have their two daughters designated as recruits to USC. And they had never participated in rowing! The scandal included photoshopping kids' heads onto athletes' bodies.

Follow the Money

Over $25 million dollars in bribes was paid to gain college admissions to the best universities. There were some very large payments. For example, a Chinese family paid $1.2 million in several installments to get their daughter admitted to Yale. The applicant's personal statement showed her interest in art—complete with links to her portfolio. However, it was altered by Singer to change her interest to soccer to get her admitted on an athletic scholarship. She was admitted and attended classes, but Yale rescinded her admission following the scandal.

The Consequences

It will be some time before all the outcomes of this large case, involving 750 families, will be known. Rick Singer has pled guilty to racketeering conspiracy, money laundering, tax conspiracy, and obstruction of justice. He faces up to 65 years in jail and a $1.25 million fine. In addition to the Yale student, other students had their admissions rescinded. Lori Loughlin pled not guilty and decided to fight the charges. She lost shows with the Hallmark Channel and Netflix. Felicity Huffman pled guilty and received a 4- to 10-month jail sentence besides paying $20,000 in fines and restitution. CEOs, top lawyers, and venture capitalists have lost their jobs due to the scandal.

Discussion Questions

1. Discuss the college admissions scandal from the perspectives of the utilitarian view, the rights view, and the theory of justice view. Which viewpoint(s) do you take on the situation? Explain why.
2. A class-action lawsuit has been filed by students and parents as a result of the scandal. Do you believe this lawsuit has merit? If you were denied entry to one of these universities, what would you do?
3. What are your thoughts on the SAT and ACT fraud in which third parties took or changed answers on student applicant exams? What issues of fairness does this raise?
4. The students of the parents who engaged in the bribery were apparently unaware of the actions of their parents. What do you think they should do now that they have learned what happened during their admissions decisions?

Sources: Adapted from Atkinson, K., & Sukin, G. (2019). Timeline: The major developments in the college admissions scandal. Retrieved from https://www.axios.com/everything-happened-college-admission-scandal-51e66764-23b2-4539-ba05-d55740939c46.html; Friedman, Z. (2019, March 12). Hollywood celebrities charged in major college admissions scandal. *Forbes.* Retrieved from https://www.forbes.com/sites/zackfriedman/2019/03/12/hollywood-celebrities-charged-in-major-college-admissions-scandal/#6f7cde531dc5; Kircher, M. M. (2019). College admissions scam fallout: What happened to everyone in the scandal. *New York Magazine.* Retrieved from http://nymag .com/intelligencer/2019/04/college-admissions-scandal-fallout.html; Levinson, E. (2019). Students and parents pursue class-action suit against universities linked to admissions scandal. *CNN.* Retrieved from https://www.cnn .com/2019/03/14/us/college-admissions-scheme-lawsuit-class-action/index.html; Taylor, K., & Medina, J. (2019). A mystery solved in the college admissions scandal: The family who paid $1.2 million. *New York Times.* Retrieved from https://www .nytimes.com/2019/04/26/us/college-admissions-scandal .html? rref=collection%2Fnewseventcollection%2Fcollege-admissions-scandal&action=click&contentCollection=us& region=rank&module=package&version=highlights&contentPlacement=1&pgtype=collection.

Case Study 3.2

Real Life Choices in Corporate Social Responsibility

A window-and-door-manufacturing plant decided to stop outsourcing the painting of its aluminum components and install its own paint facility. The paint used for this type of metal is known as a powder-coat finish, and the application process is simply blasting the color onto the raw aluminum.

The by-product of the powder finish, VOCs (volatile organic compounds), kept the large paint line filled with a constant mist of dust, and the rest of the VOCs left the room via air ducts and blowers installed in the ceiling and were released into the atmosphere.

After the first year of operation, the regional Environment Protection Agency (EPA) inspector came through and told the owner he did not have proper "scrubbers," or filters, in the air ducts and was causing harm to the environment around the plant. In fact, the plant was bordered on two sides by residential communities and on two other sides by wooded areas. The fine assessed was $100,000. The cost to fix the scrubbers was $1,000,000.

The following year the EPA inspector returned and once again fined the owner $100,000 because he had decided not to fix the air ducts. The process continued for the next decade.

As you read the discussion questions, keep in mind everything you have read in the chapter to help you assess and make recommendations for this case.

Discussion Questions

1. Why didn't the owner fix the problem?
2. What stakeholders were being harmed by the VOC emissions?
3. What would you do?
4. How would you justify your decision?

Self-Assessment 3.1

Moral Courage

Doing the right thing is not always easy; sometimes it takes courage. This self-assessment exercise measures your moral courage, defined as the willingness to engage in behaviors that you believe are ethical despite substantial risk to yourself. These types of behaviors are often asked of managers, and engaging in them is not always a safe career move. As such, there are no right or wrong answers to these questions. You don't have to share your results with others unless you wish to do so.

Part I. Taking the Assessment

Instructions: Circle the response that best describes your behavior.

Statements	Strongly Disagree	Disagree	Neutral	Agree	Strongly Agree
1. Although it may damage my friendship with a coworker, I would tell my supervisor when the coworker is doing something incorrectly.	1	2	3	4	5
2. Although my coworker may become offended, I would suggest to them better ways to do things.	1	2	3	4	5
3. If I didn't understand something at work but thought the question I'd need to ask was dumb, I would still ask it.	1	2	3	4	5
4. Even if my coworkers would think less of me, I'd lead a project with a chance of failure.	1	2	3	4	5
5. I would not tolerate a coworker's being rude to someone, even if I made the coworker upset.	1	2	3	4	5
6. Even if my subordinate disliked me for it, I would tell them if they were doing something against company policy.	1	2	3	4	5
7. I would let my coworkers know when I was concerned about something, even if they'd think I was too negative.	1	2	3	4	5
8. Even if it might damage our relationship, I would confront a subordinate who had been disrupting their workgroup.	1	2	3	4	5
9. Although it would make me look incompetent, I would tell my coworkers when I'd made a mistake.	1	2	3	4	5

10. Despite appearing dumb in front of an audience, I would volunteer to give a presentation at work.	1	2	3	4	5
11. Although it might completely ruin our friendship, I would give a coworker an honest performance appraisal.	1	2	3	4	5

Part II. Scoring Instructions

In Part I, you rated yourself on 11 questions. Add the numbers you circled in each of the columns to derive your score for moral courage.

Interpretation

In Part II, you calculated a score that should fall somewhere between 11 and 55. A higher score indicates a greater willingness to engage in a behavior that *probably* qualifies as "the right thing to do" even if doing so carries some kind of risk for you. These risks include damaging interpersonal relationships, looking foolish in front of your employees or peers, and offending others.

It is important to note that, as a manager, these risks could negatively impact your ability to do your job. It could be argued that offending your employees, for example, could create more ethical problems than it solves. As you can see, and as we have discussed a lot during the chapter, applying ethics and morals to your decision-making as a manager is difficult. It can be made even more difficult when you factor in your own personal characteristics—things like moral courage!

Discussion Questions

1. Are you satisfied with your moral courage outcome rating? Why or why not?
2. What problems could potentially arise for you, as the individual making the decisions, based on your score?
3. Think of a situation where high levels of moral courage would be helpful to you. Why? What impact would low moral courage have on you in the same situation?

Source: Adapted from Howard, M. C., Farr, J. L., Grandey, A. A., & Gutworth, M. B. (2017). The creation of the Workplace Social Courage Scale (WSCS): An investigation of internal consistency, psychometric properties, validity, and utility. *Journal of Business and Psychology, 32*(6), 673–690.

Get the tools you need to sharpen your study skills. SAGE edge offers a robust online environment featuring an impressive array of free tools and resources. Access practice quizzes, eFlashcards, video, and multimedia at **edge.sagepub.com/scanduragower.**

CHAPTER 4

ORGANIZATIONAL CULTURE AND CHANGE

CHAPTER **LEARNING OBJECTIVES**

After studying this chapter, you should be able to:

4.1 Define organizational culture and its characteristics.

4.2 Explain what a strong culture is and give examples.

4.3 Discuss how employees learn organizational culture through socialization.

4.4 Discuss four ways employees learn organizational culture.

4.5 Discuss the reasons for organizational culture change as well as its implications for an organization and its employees.

4.6 Outline the types of organizational change and how they can positively or negatively impact employees.

4.7 Discuss a manager's role in proactively overcoming resistance to change.

Get the edge on your studies at **edge.sagepub .com/scanduragower**

- Take the chapter quiz
- Review key terms with eFlashcards
- Explore multimedia resources, SAGE readings, and more!

A Small Business Implements Change

An organization's culture, much like the culture of your life, contains important elements that impact how people think, feel, and even what they do. Some of these elements are visible, like how you dress, while others are invisible, like your **values** and beliefs.

Culture drives an organization and its employees, sometimes without them even knowing it, and that can be a good or bad thing. In fact, some cultures can even be labeled "toxic," as a *Forbes Magazine* article outlined.[1] Therefore, creating and maintaining a healthy organization culture is a critical part of a manager's job as part of their planning role. Healthy cultures can create high performance by clearly communicating healthy organizational behaviors and norms and helping employees feel

a stronger sense of organizational connection, involvement, and support. The combination of these elements creates a strong sense of employee engagement and motivation,[2] which can lead to higher performance.

With the increasing pressure of global competition, the changes in technology that make communication, production, and customer service much more fluid, combined with the increasing demand from customers for better products at lower prices, many organizations find they need to modify the way they do business. Often these modifications are significant enough to require the organization to change its culture to keep up with the demands.

Even small, local organizations are finding that changing their business model to be more competitive causes a large culture change to occur. For example, a family-owned nursery business had for years set up annual Christmas tree sales at their locations so people could come look at and purchase their holiday trees. Recently, due to competition from companies like Amazon, who ship Christmas trees directly to people's homes, the organization began to offer free delivery and set up their own Amazon account to ship trees across the country. This means the people who normally just helped people pick out a tree and put it on top of their car are now in charge of choosing a tree that fits the needs of somebody they don't know, packaging the tree carefully to do well during transportation, and conducting an entire sale without ever seeing the customer. This is just a small example of a change in how an organization does business, but think about how this cash-and-carry business has now entered a national market that requires employees with different skills than before, thus creating a culture shift.

One of the owners, Robert, says:

This is just a small part of all the changes we know we need to make to remain in business, and we are finding that some of our employees are not all adapting well and moving on to other positions. Now we have to train the new employees, and the employees who have remained are not that comfortable either, so we are struggling with the culture change that comes from adjusting our 30-year-old ways of doing business. We, the leadership, want to change, but that does not translate well to the employees, at least the way we are doing it.

Robert's story is a common one. Many people do not like change, and a manager's job is to know that change is coming, plan for it, and help employees adapt as well as they can in order to reduce stress, turnover, and reduced performance. If you are a manager who does not like change, you might want to use the tips at the end of the chapter to get yourself ready. The only thing you can count on in organizations anymore is change, so this chapter on the importance of organization culture and managing change is one you will want to always have handy.

▼ FIGURE 4.0
Textbook Organization

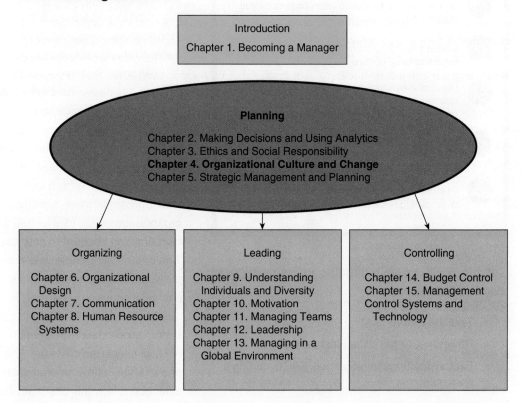

Organizational Culture and Its Characteristics

Learning Objective 4.1: Define organizational culture and its characteristics.

Organizational culture is the pattern of basic assumptions, that a given group has invented, discovered, or developed in learning to cope with its problems of external adaptation and internal integration, and that have worked well enough to be considered valid, and, therefore, to be taught to new members as the correct way to perceive, think, and feel in relation to those problems.[3]

This definition is pretty complex, but we discussed earlier how culture is the underlying foundation of an organization, so it is hard to get all the things that comprise that into a short definition. Perhaps you can just think about looking inside the building where an organization is headquartered, and taking in how it is set up, how the employees interact, the banners you might see on the walls, and even what time people come in and leave every

day. These are all part of the culture, or internal environment, in which people in organizations learn to be a part of that organization.

Another way to think of culture is as a set of shared meanings that people in organizations have with respect to how to adapt to the internal environment and cope with change. You experience the same thing with your roommates in how you adapt to each other's schedules in your dorms or apartments, such as shower and eating times, or how you handle cleanliness (or lack thereof), or how you act with your classmates in the classroom. Do you raise your hands, do you sit in rows, or do you all sit in the same seat every day? These shared behaviors are rules that you have developed as a part of your team of roommates or as part of the class group. They are informal rules that you might have talked about or that might just be understood or implicit between group members. They are known as norms.

Norms are defined as informal and interpersonal rules that team members are expected to follow.[4] These standards may be explicit and formally stated by the leader or members of the team. But norms may also be implicit. They are not written down, and communication of the norms to team members depends on the ability of the manager (or team members) to effectively convey the expected behaviors. Norms have a strong influence on behavior, and they are often difficult to change (hence one of the challenges of organizational change). If you research organizational norms, you might be surprised to find that the most research about them occurs in ethics journals. That is how strong the power of norms is in an organization.

Being expected to raise your hand before speaking in class is an example of a norm.

©iStockphoto.com/monkeybusinessimages

Levels of Organizational Culture

The strength of norms is evident in how much they influence the organization in forming its culture. Organizational culture norms have three distinct dimensions: (1) *content*, or what is deemed important (e.g., teamwork, accountability, innovation), (2) *consensus*, or how widely norms are shared across people in the organization, and (3) the *intensity* of feelings about the importance of the norm (e.g., are people willing to sanction others for violating cultural norms?).[5] In addition to these dimensions, culture operates at different levels, as shown in Figure 4.1 and described here:

1. **Artifacts and creations**—for example, the architecture of the buildings; the office decorations, including artwork; and the way that people dress. It all reflects the organization's culture. This can also include organization charts and new-employee orientation materials.
2. **Espoused beliefs and values**—the reasons people give for their behavior. Values can be stated (i.e., espoused), or they may be **enacted values** that people carry out unconsciously. For example, a person may state they believe in treating customers with respect—an espoused value. Treating customers with respect is an example of an enacted value.
3. **Assumptions**—underlying values that are often unconscious because people don't question them. To really understand an organization's culture, a person must go beyond what they can see and hear (artifacts and creations) and gain a deeper awareness of values first and then assumptions. What we can observe is an expression of values that are typically rooted in fundamental assumptions.[6]

▼ FIGURE 4.1

Schein's Levels of Culture

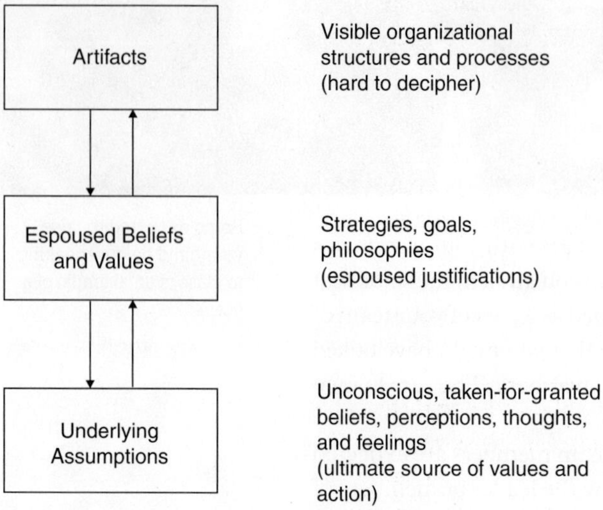

Artifacts
Visible organizational structures and processes (hard to decipher)
Espoused Beliefs and Values
Strategies, goals, philosophies (espoused justifications)
Underlying Assumptions
Unconscious, taken-for-granted beliefs, perceptions, thoughts, and feelings (ultimate source of values and action)

Source: Schein, E. H. (1984). Coming to a new awareness of organizational culture. *Sloan Management Review, 25*(2), 3–16, p. 4.

As shown in Figure 4.1, the levels of culture are related, and they reinforce one another.

CRITICAL THINKING QUESTIONS

Provide an example of an artifact found in an organization. Trace it to the underlying values and assumptions it represents.

Due to the importance of culture to organizations, it is no surprise that many studies have been done to see how different cultures appear in different industries. Below, some interesting results are described.

Seven Characteristics of Culture

A research study compared the organizational cultures of 15 organizations in four industries in the service sector (public accounting, consulting, the U.S. Postal Service, and transportation of household goods). Cultural values differed across these sectors and were related to the levels of industry technology and growth. Examples of findings regarding the seven characteristics of culture investigated in this research are given below.[7]

1. *Innovation and risk-taking.* Most cultures in the service industries studied were average on this dimension, with transportation showing the highest score. Why do you suppose transportation would be the most innovative out of the four industries? Perhaps the competitive nature and significant cost of transportation added to the price of finished goods?
2. *Attention to detail.* Consulting and accounting firms were highest on this dimension. This makes sense, since both of these industries are very focused on outcomes and dollar and cents.
3. *Outcome orientation.* All companies studied in the service industry were high on this dimension. Services are all about outcomes, since no product is being delivered. What are some services you have used recently that help you relate?
4. *People orientation.* All companies studied in the four industries were average on this dimension. This is an interesting outcome. The companies were only average *and* none was better than the others. This might be a cultural characteristic where you, as a manager, can make a huge difference.
5. *Team orientation.* All companies studied were average, but consulting firms were slightly higher on working in teams as part of their culture. If you go on to get an MBA, there is a good chance you will end up doing some internal or external consulting, or work for a consulting firm. These opportunities always involve a consulting team, so this result is to be expected.
6. *Aggressiveness (easygoingness reversed).* All industries were average; however, consulting firms were less easygoing than other companies. This might surprise you, but consulting is a competitive industry (there are a lot of consulting firms) because the stakes are very high, in terms of both what consultants charge and the outcomes that are expected.

7. *Stability.* Most industries were average on stability; however, the U.S. Postal Service was higher than other organizations on the need for stability as part of the organization's culture. This should not surprise you, since the postal service has been around for a long time and has reacted slowly, and not very well, to competitive entrants to the industry.

CRITICAL THINKING QUESTIONS

Do you agree with the findings of this study? Why or why not? Will there be changes to the characteristics of these industries based on the ongoing revolutions in organizations? What do you forecast, as a manager, they will be?

How Managers Shape Organizational Culture

Another important framework for understanding organizational culture and the roles managers play in shaping it is the **competing values framework** (CVF) summarized in Figure 4.2. This is a big name for a small but important distinction—people all have their own set of values, and sometimes their values compete with other peoples' values, and/or compete with the values of the company.

Values are set in terms of the degree of flexibility and the degree of external focus they have. This is why the CVF has been narrowed down to four key quadrants. The **open systems** quadrant deals with external forces and keeping the organization nimble during change. **Internal processes** focus on performance management and coordination to maximize control. The **rational goal-setting** quadrant fosters a productive work environment through planning and goal-setting. Finally, the **human relations** quadrant focuses on internal, flexible processes such as team-building communication.

Breaking it down even further, the manager's roles in these four areas are described as follows:[8] The top right quadrant, or open systems, includes the *innovator* and the *broker* manager. The innovator is creative, inventing new ideas and acting as an effective agent of change. The broker is politically savvy, collecting resources and legitimizing the unit by building its credibility and maintaining relationships with external contacts and collaborators.

These managers will show strength in open-systems thinking and adapting to external expectations. Open-systems thinking means being able to look at the entire system when making decisions or evaluations. The adaptation of external expectations means the manager in this quadrant is able to deal with change effectively, similar to what Robert in the opening story is doing.

The lower right quadrant, the rational goal-setting model, emphasizes the establishment and achievement of external goals, and includes two roles: the *producer* and the *director*. The producer motivates the group to finish tasks and produce work, while the director is devoted to goal-, objective-, and expectation-setting.[9] Managers who succeed in this type of work often find themselves working for an organization that places a premium on efficiency and measurable outcomes.[10]

The lower left quadrant is the internal process model. The roles in this quadrant focus on structure and stability. The two management roles here include the *coordinator*, who maintains structure, does the scheduling, coordinating, and problem-solving, and sees that rules and standards are met; and the *monitor*, who collects and distributes information, checks on performance, and provides a sense of continuity and stability.[11] As you can probably see, this quadrant contrasts with the rational goal-setting quadrant, since the process model is the degree to which the organization is oriented toward its own internal environment and processes, versus the external environment and relationships with outside entities, such as regulators, suppliers, competitors, partners, and customers, which the rational model addresses.[12]

▼ FIGURE 4.2

Competing Values Framework

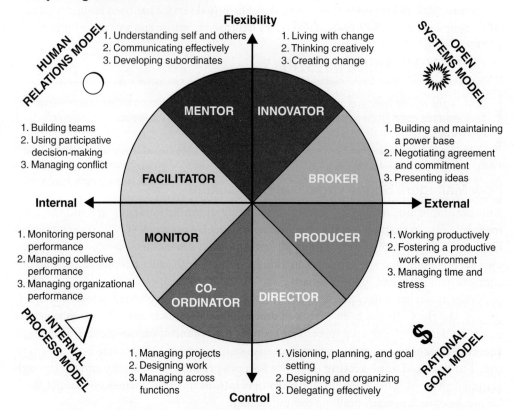

Flexibility

HUMAN RELATIONS MODEL

1. Understanding self and others
2. Communicating effectively
3. Developing subordinates

1. Living with change
2. Thinking creatively
3. Creating change

OPEN SYSTEMS MODEL

1. Building teams
2. Using participative decision-making
3. Managing conflict

MENTOR **INNOVATOR**

FACILITATOR **BROKER**

1. Building and maintaining a power base
2. Negotiating agreement and commitment
3. Presenting ideas

Internal ← → **External**

1. Monitoring personal performance
2. Managing collective performance
3. Managing organizational performance

MONITOR **PRODUCER**

CO-ORDINATOR **DIRECTOR**

1. Working productively
2. Fostering a productive work environment
3. Managing tlme and stress

INTERNAL PROCESS MODEL

RATIONAL GOAL MODEL

1. Managing projects
2. Designing work
3. Managing across functions

1. Visioning, planning, and goal setting
2. Designing and organizing
3. Delegating effectively

Control

Source: Adapted from Ng, T. (2014, February 21). Managing paradoxes in leadership with the competing values framework. *Everyone a leader.* Retrieved from https://titusng.com/2014/02/21/managing-paradoxes-in-leadership-with-competing-values-framework/; Quinn, R. E. (1984). Applying the competing values approach to leadership: Toward an integrative framework. In J. G. Hunt, D. Hostking, C. Schriesheim, & R. Stewart (Eds.), *Leaders and managers: International perspectives on managerial behavior and leadership.* Elmsford, NY: Pergamon Press.

Finally, the upper left quadrant is referred to in the framework as the human relations model, placing primary emphasis on human interaction and process. Managerial roles include the *facilitator*, who encourages the expression of opinions, seeks consensus, and negotiates compromise, and the *mentor*, who is aware of individual needs, listens actively, is fair, supports legitimate requests, and attempts to facilitate the development of individuals.[13] You will note that this quadrant is on the internal side of the model. Organizations with an internal and human relations focus emphasize flexibility, encourage broad participation by employees, emphasize teamwork and empowerment, and make human resource development a priority.[14]

The CVF model has been widely tested and studied for more than 25 years and has been named one of the 40 most important frameworks in the history of business.[15]

The manager's roles are influenced by the organization's needs for flexibility and external focus. Managers strive to create strong organizational cultures, and these are described next.

Strong Organizational Cultures

Learning Objective 4.2: Explain what a strong culture is and give examples.

Strong cultures are based on two characteristics: high levels of agreement among employees about what they value, and high intensity toward these values. If both are high, a strong culture exists. Some organizations are characterized by high levels of intensity but low agreement. In

Zappos CEO Tony Hsieh.
©dpa picture alliance/Alamy Stock Photo

this case, employees and/or groups are at war with one another over what is important for the organization to value.[16] For example, salespeople focus on customer-driven product features, while accountants focus on cost containment. Thus, while both groups intensely value what they do, they disagree on priorities.

Strong organizational cultures are critical to bottom-line performance in large organizations.[17] Employee agreement on cultural values is also related to lower turnover among newly hired employees.[18] A study[19] of firms in a variety of industries found that strong cultures affect organizational learning in response to internal and external change. In this research, firm performance was assessed by using yearly return on invested capital (ROI) and yearly operating cash flow. Strong-culture firms excelled at incremental change but encountered difficulties in more volatile economic environments. In other words, in relatively stable economic environments, strong-culture firms have more reliable performance.

The Perfect Culture

You have probably heard of Zappos, the online seller of shoes and clothing. By 2010, the CEO, Tony Hsieh (pronounced "Shay"), had developed a strong culture where employees very much agreed upon and were passionate about customer service. The original Zappos experience indicated that building a culture that resulted in a great place to work, exceptional customer service, and impressive organizational performance required specific drivers. The five drivers Zappos used to shape its culture were committed leaders, core values, customer-focused strategies, human resource practices, and management practices aligned with core values.[20] At Zappos, employees were encouraged to express their uniqueness in executing the mission of "delivering happiness." Zappos defined its culture in terms of these 10 core values:

1. Deliver wow through service.
2. Embrace and drive change.
3. Create fun and a little weirdness.
4. Be adventurous, creative, and open-minded.
5. Pursue growth and learning.
6. Build open and honest relationships with communication.
7. Build a positive team and family spirit.
8. Do more with less.
9. Be passionate and determined.
10. Be humble.[21]

To Hsieh, the Zappos culture is about more than money: "It's not me saying to our employees, this is where our culture is. It's more about giving employees the permission and encouraging them to just be themselves."[22] This sounds like a great culture in which to be a manager and a member of the gang.

CRITICAL THINKING QUESTIONS

Would you enjoy working at a company like Zappos? How do its core values match up with your core values as a professional?

FACT OR FICTION?

Zappos Part II: Do We Need Managers?

Let's fast-forward from Zappos, 2010, to Zappos, 2015. Over that time span, Hsieh decided it was time to experiment with the Zappos culture. He instituted a little-heard-of, old-fashioned management system known as a Holacracy.[22] In March 2012, Hsieh announced part of his culture change via an email to 1,443 employees. It was a lengthy email, which he encouraged employees to take 30 minutes to read, and in it he announced Zappos change from a management hierarchy to a system with no more human managers.

Hsieh went on to write:

> Zappos is moving from "Green" to "Teal," the next stage of its collective corporate evolution, and managers are no longer valued by the company. To make the transition easier, former managers will be permitted to keep their salaries, though not their responsibilities, through the end of 2015, if they choose to find new roles with the company, or they are welcome to leave.

Talk about culture change! Not only were the employees angry at what was arguably a 180-degree change in the company culture and the value placed on employees, but the email and subsequent announcements were ambiguous and gave no explanation as to why these changes were being implemented. Most of all, the employees wondered what in the world "Teal" meant in the corporate evolution cycle.

At the time he made the announcement, Hsieh and many of his employees lived or hung out in a trailer park called Airstream Park, where the CEO himself had a two-story Airstream trailer and several shipping containers as his home compound. It was a 24/7 party atmosphere, and it wasn't uncommon for Hsieh to call 10 p.m. corporate meetings. While this all seems like a great atmosphere, the "aggressively casual" nature of Hsieh and his announcement quickly took its toll on the employees. On the first deadline, over 200 employees left the company, and many others took advantage of the anonymity of the Internet to voice their concerns, most of them relating to their fear of now partaking in Core Value 6—open and honest communication. The year 2015 was particularly hard for the Zappos culture change, as 30% of employees left. Much of the attrition was blamed on confusion. For example, employees had no one to turn to when they needed questions answered. A 2016 follow-up said, "Zappos isn't at risk of closing shop." But the final departures represented another blow to Holacracy, and to Mr. Hsieh's vision of a harmonious, self-organizing company. Zappos declined to comment.

When employees leave, company culture goes with them. Assumptions, which are taken for granted and invisible, have no home other than within the employees. Values are also part of the invisible culture. Finally, artifacts often disappear, too, as they can be as simple as an organizational chart, which Zappos no longer had.

Zappos provides us with an excellent example of the importance of organizational culture, and the shock that a change in culture creates among employees and the repercussions that might follow.

Discussion Questions

1. Why did Tony Hsieh decide that Zappos needed to remove human managers? What were the forces driving the decision to change?

2. Why were the employees angry? How did the change to Holacracy affect perceptions of the organizational culture?

3. Do you agree or disagree that organizations need managers? Explain your position.

Sources: Adapted from Gelles, D. (2016, January 13). The Zappos exodus continues after a radical management experiment [Blog post]. *New York Times*. Retrieved from https://bits.blogs.nytimes.com/2016/01/13/after-a-radical-management-experiment-the-zappos-exodus-continues/? em_pos=large&emc=edit_nn_20160114&nl=morning-briefing&nlid=66141956; Hodge, R. (2015, October 4). First, let's get rid of all the bosses. *New Republic*. Retrieved from https://newrepublic.com/article/122965/can-billion-dollar-corporation-zappos-be-self-organized; Lam, B. (2016, January 15). Why are so many Zappos employees leaving? *The Atlantic*. Retrieved from https://www.theatlantic.com/business/archive/2016/01/zappos-holacracy-hierarchy/424173/; Robinson, M. (2016, September 3). Inside the Las Vegas trailer park that Zappos' multimillionaire CEO calls home. *Business Insider*. Retrieved from https://www.businessinsider.com/llamapolis-las-vegas-trailer-park-2016-8.

Subcultures

In addition to understanding the strong overall culture in an organization, it is important to recognize that organizations have **subcultures**.[24] For example, the marketing department of an organization may have a risk-taking orientation, whereas the accounting department may not because they value stability. You can see how this strong culture of stability in one department might regularly be at odds with the strong culture of risk-taking in the other. Organizations can increase flexibility without losing their strong overall culture by encouraging subcultures.[25] In this way, organizations reap the benefits of a strong culture while remaining responsive to change. For example, Procter & Gamble has a strong culture of data-driven attention to detail, but they foster a subculture of innovation and trial-and-error experimentation in their research and development.[26]

One challenge you will have as a manager is to be able to work between these subcultures. If you are managing the marketing department for a toy company where employees regularly throw stress balls at each other and passersby, and you have to head over to accounting to submit your budget, they will probably not appreciate you lobbing stress balls at them. They might, however, be grateful if you bring over samples from your latest toy conference to distribute among the employees to use themselves or to take home to their kids. This establishes a collegial environment and propels the friendly subculture you have developed in marketing by sharing it with other departments.

With all of the different subcultures, how can managers increase consensus on what the overall organization culture is? The next sections discuss how employees learn organizational culture. First, the process of **socialization** is discussed, followed by ways that employees learn culture through **stories**, **rituals**, **symbols**, and **language**.

Socialization

Organizational socialization is defined as the process an organization utilizes to ensure that new members acquire necessary attitudes, behaviors, knowledge, and skills to become productive organizational members.[27] When a new hire joins a company, the first six months on the job is characterized as a series of reality "shocks" as they are exposed to the unwritten rules defining the organizational culture.[28] For example, the job may be considered an eight-hour workday, but the new hire notices that everyone works at least 10 hours a day. The process of socialization follows the following steps: anticipatory socialization, entry and assimilation, and metamorphosis.[29] This process is diagrammed in Figure 4.3, and these steps are discussed in the following sections.

Anticipatory Socialization

Anticipatory socialization is the process an individual goes through as they attempt to find an organization to join. Organizational anticipatory socialization has two basic processes: recruiting and selection.[30] For example, as a student nears graduation, they visit the placement center at the university to learn about job opportunities and meet recruiters. The student then determines which jobs are the best fit with their college major, their skills, and the type of organization they want to work for. For example, the student may want to work for a large organization instead of a small one. During the organizational anticipatory socialization stage, both the applicant and the organization are looking for evidence of a good fit. The recruitment process may involve psychological testing and interviews to determine how well a person will fit with the culture. Sample culture-fit interview questions are shown in Table 4.1.

CRITICAL THINKING QUESTIONS

Take a minute to think about what organizational culture components are important to you. Are the answers to the questions that follow important, or are there other things that would make you feel like a part of the team you are ready to join? Make a list, like in Table 4.2, and keep it with you on your interviews. Culture fit is a two-way street.

Interview Questions to Determine an Employee's Fit With a Strong Culture

Question	Purpose
1. If you could be doing anything, what would you do?	This question assesses passions and interests for culture fit.
2. What are your top three values?	This question helps you figure out if the candidate's values match those for the position, department, or team.
3. Have the candidate read the company's mission and value statements, and discuss how they fit with their personal values.	This question reveals how closely a candidate's personal values align with the company's values.
4. If hired, what would you accomplish in your first week on the job?	This question shows a candidate's expectations and organizational skills.

Source: Greenberg, A. (2014). Start asking unique interview questions. Retrieved from http://www.recruitingdivision.com/start-asking-unique-interview-questions-2.

▼ FIGURE 4.3

The Socialization Process

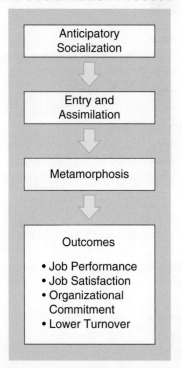

Source: Jablin, F. M. (1987). Organizational entry, assimilation, and exit. In L. L. Putnam, K. H. Roberts, & L. W. Porter (Eds.), *Handbook of organizational communication: An interdisciplinary perspective* (pp. 679–740). Beverly Hills, CA: SAGE.

It is also important for you, as a potential employee, to make sure you are comfortable with the culture, or vibe, you get from the organization. Is the building a pleasant place to be? Do the employees look up and smile at you when you are moving from interview to interview? Do you see the latest technology on everybody's desk? Do you feel respected by those interviewing you?

Organizational Entry and Assimilation

The **preentry** step occurs from the time someone is offered the job to when they actually start working. There are three important issues that arise during the preentry stage. First, the types of messages a new employee receives from the organization prior to starting work could include realistic job previews in which the members of the organization attempt to clarify what the job will be like. These might be different from what was discussed in the hiring process (and may be either positive or negative surprises). Second, new employees are typically concerned about how they are seen by existing organizational members and engage in **impression management**, the process (either conscious or unconscious) where an individual deliberately attempts to influence the perceptions and opinions of others. For example, the new hire might mention the rankings of their university to enhance perceptions of their qualifications for the job. Third, current organizational members form perceptions of the new hire and consider how well they will fit in. These perceptions may result in unrealistic expectations, so it's important to seek feedback in a new job to correct misconceptions.

A longitudinal study of 273 new software engineers in an Indian company[31] found that when both new employees and their managers were proactive, they adjusted well to the culture, performed better, and mastered their tasks better. They were also less likely to be thinking of quitting. The results suggest that newcomers who proactively seek information from their coworkers are at an advantage, because they are viewed as more committed to learning about the organization and fitting in. This in turn motivates their managers and peers to share more information with them. The takeaway for a new employee is clear—be proactive in learning the organization's culture during the first weeks of employment.

Next, the **entry** phase occurs, which happens when the new member starts work and begins to **assimilate** within the organizational culture. Often referred to as **onboarding**, it is the process of welcoming and orienting new members to facilitate their adjustment to the organization, its culture, and its practices. It refers to the process of facilitating new members' adjustment to the organization

and its culture.[32] During the entry period, new employees begin to understand the organization's culture and work expectations. This may include a formal orientation program to help the new employee learn the rules and expectations of the organization—the explicit information that dictates and governs employee behavior within the organization. For example, an orientation program may include a session on the ethical codes of the organization.

Organizations obviously have high expectations of you, since they are paying you for your knowledge, skills, and abilities. Employees, however, also have expectations of the organization, and the individual's expectations of what they will contribute and what the organization will provide in return are known as a psychological contract. It is really more *your* individual **psychological contract**, because everybody has different expectations. The psychological contract refers to the unwritten set of expectations of the employment relationship as distinct from the formal, codified employment contract. Taken together, the psychological contract and the employment contract define the employer–employee relationship.[33] For example, a coworker might be very interested in or expect high-quality day care, while you might be more interested in the potential to earn bonuses quarterly. Employers lay out many of their expectations in writing, but employees rarely get to do the same, and that is why it is something you have psychologically developed. It is an important part of your onboarding process, though, as it influences the degree to which you view the organization's processes (such as an orientation training program) as valuable.

A longitudinal study of 144 recruits from a European army[34] found that when new employees had a psychological contract that involved a higher sense of personal obligation at entry, they perceived the orientation training as more useful. They also developed better relationships with their supervisors and peers, which in turn facilitated their adjustment to their work. In addition to orientation and new-hire training, the organization may assign a formal mentor or "buddy" during this phase to help the new employee learn the norms of the organization. The informal expectations about how new employees should behave within the organization are "unwritten rules" that govern how new employees should act. For example, employees may be expected to eat lunch at their desk while working, but this is not specifically written down anywhere.

Metamorphosis

The final stage of organizational entry and assimilation is the **metamorphosis** stage. During this stage, a person transforms from a new employee to an established contributor who is valued and trusted by other members of the organization. Metamorphosis completes the socialization process—the new employee is comfortable with the organization, their boss, and their work group. They have internalized the organizational culture and understand their job, as well as the rules, procedures, and norms. Expectations are clear regarding what good performance means in the organization. Successful metamorphosis positively affects job performance, job satisfaction, and commitment to the organization. Also, there is a lower chance that the person will look for another job or quit.[35] Most often, this transition occurs over a long time period. However, the process may start over again (preentry to assimilation to metamorphosis) if a person gets a promotion to a new role in the organization or a transfer to a different department, which might have a different subculture.

Formal orientations within organizations often include a code of ethics which sets the standard expectations of the organization.

©iStockphoto.com/cnythzl

CRITICAL THINKING QUESTIONS

How can you make your socialization process smoother when you enter a new organization? What can you do now to prepare for the preentry and entry phases?

How Employees Learn Culture

Stories

Storytelling is now recognized as an important way to understand how employees make sense of what happens at work.[36] Storytelling is the sharing of knowledge and experiences through narrative and anecdotes to communicate lessons, complex ideas, concepts, and causal connections.[37] It is also important because it is the only type of communication that every culture in the world shares,[38] and in our diverse workforces where both verbal and nonverbal communication norms differ, the globally shared power of storytelling is just as important as in geographic cultures.

People try to understand complex events in the order they have occurred and mentally integrate their many components. Stories are important because they aid comprehension and suggest a causal order for events. They convey shared meanings and values representing the organizational culture and guide behavior.[39] For example, stories told by charitable organizations are typically designed to evoke a series of emotions.[40] First, the potential donor feels negative emotions when they hear a story told about animals in need of rescue. Next, a story is told about animals being helped by the generosity of others, evoking a positive emotion and desire to help.

An example of an organizational story that is told at FedEx follows.

FedEx—the overnight delivery service started by Fred Smith back in 1971 in Memphis, TN—was trying to make a name for itself by guaranteeing that any package could be delivered just about anywhere overnight.

One of the company's drivers was out late one snowy night to check a drop-off box. When he got to the box the lock was frozen and the key broke off. After failing to reach the packages inside, the driver drove to a nearby auto garage where he borrowed a torch and used it to cut the legs off the box. The driver then put the box into his truck and delivered it to the airport where a maintenance team drilled it open, removed the packages, and put them on the plane to their destination.

No corporate slogan could be more powerful than this simple FedEx story.[41]

This is an excellent representation of how stories serve a persuasive communication function for organizations by representing personal, interpersonal, and corporate perspectives.[42] The story depicts a determined employee going the extra mile and showing creativity to ensure that packages are delivered on time. As organizations continue to become more global and employees change jobs more often, the culture will require myriad interpersonal and social exchanges to survive, and previous research has positioned storytelling as a successful means of accomplishing these exchanges.[43] A research study found that participatory storytelling in organizational learning helped stimulate empathy among organizational members, allowing them to imagine their own position and the positions of their diverse counterparts.[44]

CRITICAL THINKING QUESTIONS

What have you learned about the organizational culture of FedEx from this story? What did you learn about employee commitment to the organization's goals?

Rituals

Rituals are defined as "a form of social action in which a group's values and identity are publicly demonstrated or enacted in a stylized manner, within the context of a specific occasion or event."[45] An example of a ritual is a graduation ceremony at a university. Rituals reinforce the cultural values of the organization by providing a tangible way for employees to see the values espoused. An inter-

Award ceremonies like the Grammys and Oscars are examples of rituals.

©iStockphoto.com/vzphotos

view study of restaurant workers found that a small pizza restaurant had a ritual linked with family values, and their emphasis on relationships was created at work but extended to interactions outside work. Restaurant staff and managers engaged in social activities such as going to a regular "movie night" as a group. When employees were probed as to why this was important, the consistent response was "friendship."[46]

Meetings are often ritualistic. Former CEO John Sculley described meetings at Pepsi where executives never removed their jackets no matter how stressful the meeting was. The way the attendees entered the meeting followed the same pattern each time. Executives entered in reverse order based on their rank in the company. Market analysts entered first, followed by junior managers, senior managers, the vice president, and lastly the president. When everyone was assembled and waiting, the VP went to get the chairman.[47] Another example is the Grammy Awards, which is a ritual that reinforces cultural values of the National Academy of Recording Arts and Sciences through performances, emotionally charged awards, legitimizing artists, and creating links among the members.[48] Many organizations hold similar ceremonies and corporate dinners where top employees are rewarded for their contributions.

Symbols

Symbols represent the sharing of knowledge through access and exposure to images, diagrams, or objects, which illustrate a culture value or an idea. Examples include a map of a city, the alien emoji, or a corporate logo.[49] Symbols are important to organizations—they are not accidental, but planned to communicate what the organizational culture represents.[50] Organizations make use of symbols in a variety of ways. Material symbols include office size and whether or not the office has a window.[51] The C-suite offices may be located on the top floor of the building to reinforce the idea that these individuals have attained the highest level in the organization. Symbols include how a leader is expected to dress at work.[52] For example, while it may not be written down as a policy, new managers may be expected to wear navy-blue or gray suits. Another example of the power of symbols comes from the CEO of a hospital who wanted to reinforce the value of transparency in the organization. He had an open-door policy where literally anyone in the organization could come in and talk to him about their concerns. He created a symbol by having the doors of his office removed from their hinges and then hung up inside the lobby of the hospital so that everyone in the organization would see them and be reminded of his message every single day they walked in and out of the building. This symbol of his transparency was more effective than sending out an email to communicate his open-door policy.[53]

Language

Employees may communicate using culture-specific language, jargon, or acronyms that can be confusing to a new employee. These terms and usage may be unique to the organization and represent the organizational culture and how it is transmitted to newcomers. The language used to refer to employees reflects underlying values. For example, some organizations have stopped using the term *employees* in favor of *team members*. Another example is the manner in which employees at Disneyland are trained to refer to customers as "guests." Rides are referred to as "attractions." Disneyland is divided into "backstage," "on-stage," and "staging" regions.[54] The language used by Disneyland employees demonstrates its core values of valuing guests and providing a "magical experience" for them as part of its strong organizational culture.

Slogans are another example of how language communicates cultural values. For example, a computer consulting company had the slogan "fun and profit," which communicated that results were equally important to having a positive work environment in which employees enjoyed their work.[55]

The use of organizational language reinforces who is in the culture and who is outside it. Think about the extensive language developed by J. K. Rowling in the Harry Potter books that only the wizards and witches know. For example, a "muggle" is a person totally without magical powers—muggles live in ignorance of the world of wizards and witches. And "quidditch" is the wizarding national sport played on broomsticks by seven players. Those who know the language are in and those who don't are lost in translation.

Organizational culture influences employee behaviors, as the previous examples demonstrate. Organizational culture creates organizational climates under which nearly all employees operate. For a number of reasons, though, such as Robert's story at the beginning of the chapter, these cultures and climates change, which puts managers in charge of one of the hardest situations they will ever face: organizational culture change.

CRITICAL THINKING QUESTIONS

> Provide an example of storytelling, a ritual, a symbol, or language that you encountered when you learned an organizational culture based on your experience (this can be from an experience in a fraternity/sorority, on a sports team, or at work). Explain how this helped you understand what the expected behaviors were in the organization.

Forces Driving Organizational Change

Learning Objective 4.5: Discuss the reasons for organizational culture change as well as its implications for an organization and its employees.

There are numerous forces for change in organizations (as depicted in Table 4.2)—for example, increased workforce diversity due to workers of different genders, of different races or ethnicities, or from different generations. Changes in the workforce as well as cultural differences will continue to be a force for organizational change.

The economy represents a significant source for change. For example, economic recessions result in major changes, such as downsizing and restructuring. Technology changes are rapid, and organizations must keep up with these advances. Technology advances have resulted in major changes in how people communicate inside and outside organizations. Globalization represents a significant source of change for organizations with the rise of the multinational corporation. Increased globalization of markets has also given rise to competition from abroad in addition to the competition between firms within a given country. As consumers, we enjoy a broader array of product options, lower prices, and increased attention to customer service. However, intense competition may lead to industry shakeouts, and we have seen some giants falter, such as AOL, which didn't see the decline in dial-up Internet until it was too late.[56] New competitors like Google were already using new technology to take advantage of faster Internet speed.

Forces Driving Organizational Change

Force for Change	Examples
Workforce Diversity	Sex, Race/Ethnicity, Cultural Differences, LGBTQ, Age/Generation
The Economy	Recession, Government Policy, Rising Health Care Costs
Technology	Mobile Devices, Social Media, Internet Security, Robotics
Globalization	Multinational Corporations, Political Instability, Fair Trade, Sustainability, Outsourcing, Emerging Markets
Competition	Global Competition, Mergers and Acquisitions, Customer Standards, Time to Market

Source: Scandura, *Essentials of Organization Behavior,* 2nd Ed., p.389. Thousand Oaks, CA: Sage.

▼ FIGURE 4.4

The New Organizational Model

The Workplace Today	The Workplace of the Future
Hierarchical structure	Project-based, more flexible structure
Teams form slowly and stay together for a long time	Teams assemble and disband quickly
Jobs based on titles, levels, descriptions	Jobs based on assignments and expert roles
Managers own teams	Managers sponspor teams and projects
Careers are owned by the manager and not shared	Careers are open in transpartent marketplace
Managers assign jobs	Employees seek out work based on skills
Employees work on single project	Employees work on multiple projects
Employee rewarded by level, tenure, and experience	Employees rewarded by outcomes, reputation, and sponsorship
Culture defined by diversity, inclusion, ethics, and sustainability	Culture defined by citizenship, collective thinking, shared values

Source: Bersin, J. (2017). The future of work: The people imperative. Retrieved from https://www2.deloitte.com/content/dam/Deloitte/il/Documents/human-capital/HR_and_Business_Perspectives_on_The%20Future_of_Work.pdf.

The forces for change have resulted in a new model for organizations, according to a report from Deloitte Consulting, shown in Figure 4.4. Organizations are moving from hierarchies to teams that mobilize quickly to responds to challenges. Rigid job descriptions are being replaced by assignments and expertise. Managers serve as mentors to others, and careers are more flexible. Reward systems will be based on outputs rather than hierarchical level or years of experience. Finally, organizational cultures will evolve to focus on the degree to which employees embrace shared values.

These changes are powerful forces that affect organizations, and leaders must help employees cope with them. The next section will offer more detail on the types of organizational change that occur, and what their impact is on employees.

Types of Organizational Change

Learning Objective 4.6: Outline the types of organizational change and how they can positively or negatively impact employees.

The forces for organizational change, from Table 4.2, create different types of change, and the best change, for all those involved, is to be **proactive** and plan rather than being forced to be **reactive** by neglecting to read the environment one operates in.

Types of Planned Organizational Change

	Reactive	Proactive
Incremental	**Put out small fires!** Solve problems on a day-to-day basis. Quick fixes to short-term concerns.	**Tweaking.** Anticipate and plan. Improve current ways of doing things. Fine-tune. Guided evolution.
Radical	**Stop the bleeding!** Crisis management. Industry shake-ups, economic turmoil, financial shocks.	**Transformation.** Do things fundamentally differently. Change basic assumptions. Revolution.

Source: Scandura, Essentials of Organization Behaviors, 2nd Ed., p.391.

Planned organizational change can have a number of targets, including structure, technology, processes, teams, and people.[57] The idea of being proactive when it comes to change is not new and dates to the classic management book *Overcoming Organizational Defenses*.[58] Yet most organizations still are in reactive mode (i.e., "putting out fires") when it comes to change. Change may also be incremental (e.g., adding blue dots to a detergent) or radical (e.g., a major restructuring).[59] Incremental change is evolutionary, and radical change is revolutionary. Revolutionary and evolutionary change are different in terms of the size and rate of upheaval. Revolutionary change occurs quickly and affects virtually all parts of the organization at the same time, whereas evolutionary change occurs slowly and gradually and may involve only one area of the organization at a time.[60] Putting these concepts together (reactive/proactive and incremental/radical) results in a useful framework for classifying the types of organizational change (see Figure 4.5). As shown in the figure, the most intense form of change is proactive and radical. The types of organizational change and the effect they have on the subsequent organizational subsystems are discussed next.

Organizational Subsystems Involved in Planned Change

Organizational change can seem like an overwhelming undertaking—and it is! It is helpful if you can think of change in terms of various dimensions involved, like the four organizational subsystems:

1. *Formal organization.* This provides the coordination and control necessary for organized activity, such as formal organizational charts and reward systems.
2. *Social factors.* These factors include individual differences, team interactions, and the organizational culture.
3. *Technology.* This is how raw materials and inputs transform into outputs, such as workflow design and job design.
4. *Physical setting.* These are the characteristics of the physical space and how it is arranged.[61]

CRITICAL THINKING QUESTIONS

Provide an example of a change for each of the four types of subsystems. Of the four examples you came up with, which one do you believe will be at the most risk of failure due to employee resistance? Explain your choice.

Why Organizational Change Efforts Fail

A *Harvard Business Review* article titled "The Hard Side of Change Management" points out that 66% of all change management efforts fail to meet their business objectives. Why? Figure 4.6 explains the major reasons why organizational change efforts fail. The number-one reason, mentioned 76% of the time in a survey of executives, is staff resistance to change. Almost as important is the lack of effective communication about the change. Other key factors are training, turnover during the change, and costs that exceed the budget. Overcoming resistance to change is critical, and we will discuss this next.

Resistance to Change

When faced with an organizational change, employee reactions vary from **resistance to change** to **compliance with change** to **commitment to change.** *Resistance* means employees fight the change and try to undermine it.[62] With *compliance*, they simply go along with the change but secretly hope it will come to an end soon. *Commitment* to change is the most desirable reaction, in which employees support change and help the organization implement it.[63]

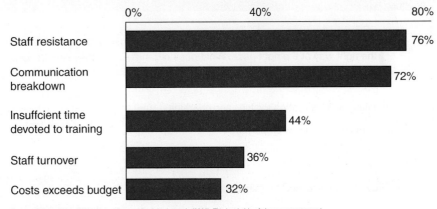

▼ FIGURE 4.6

Why Organizational Change Efforts Fail

Staff resistance	76%
Communication breakdown	72%
Insuffcient time devoted to training	44%
Staff turnover	36%
Costs exceeds budget	32%

Source: Adapted from Sirkin, H. L., Keenan, P., & Jackson, A. (2005). The hard side of change management. *Harvard Business Review, 83*(10), 108–121.

Since resistance is the most difficult reaction for the leader to deal with, this section will focus on understanding and overcoming resistance to change. Research on resistance to change dates back to a classic study of participative decision-making.[64] Employees were transferred to new jobs in which they encountered significant changes to their work. Interviews revealed that employees resisted changes in their work methods due to resentment, frustration, and a loss of hope of regaining their formal levels of proficiency. A second experiment was then conducted in which employees were transferred to new jobs, but they were allowed to participate in the changes through chosen representatives. This group recovered rapidly from the changes and reached a higher level of productivity compared to the group that was not allowed to participate in the change. This study showed that employee participation positively impacts resistance to change. A recent review of 70 years of research on resistance to change concluded that the findings of this classic study have held up over time and in subsequent research studies.[65]

There are a number of additional reasons why people resist change, including both personal reasons and organizational reasons.[66] Personal reasons include habit, security, economic concerns, and fear of the unknown. Organizational reasons for resistance are structural inertia (the structure is too rigid to support the change), group inertia, threats to expertise, and threats to established power relationships.

Resistance to change also has a negative impact on employee health. It has been related to insomnia and lower employee well-being.[67] Using a longitudinal research design, a study[68] of 709 participants in 30 work units revealed that resistance to change predicted emotional exhaustion a year later. Organizations should offer coaching and training to cope with organizational change for employees who are highly change resistant.

Resistance to change can lead to health problems such as insomnia and exhaustion.

©iStockphoto.com/yanyong

Organizational development keeps companies moving the right way at the right pace. What does organizational development entail? Here are some common functions that fall under OD:

- Evaluating an organization's values and priorities
- Assessing potential new employees
- Assisting with the implementation of new policies and procedures
- Improving organizational practices when problems arise

What Is Human Resources Organizational Development?

OD's primary function is to help people work efficiently within an organizational framework. The consulting firm Decision Wise contends that, above all, operational development is a method of "applying behavioral science to help organizations improve individuals and systems."[69] While there are some distinctions between HR and OD (e.g., one can earn a bachelor's degree in HR but not in OD), there is some overlap. Some jobs merge the functions of HR and OD. For instance, organizations are beginning to require HR departments to actively strategize for business success. In those types of strategic HR departments, experience with OD would be beneficial for job-seekers.

What Is the Primary Function of Organizational Development?

Organizational development entails "continuous diagnosis, action planning, implementation, and evaluation" with the ultimate objective of helping organizations solve problems and effectively create change.[70]

The OD professional must carefully observe and assess an organization's climate and culture to develop and present a strategy that includes elements such as:

- Diagnosis of potential problems
- Planning and implementation
- Intervention
- Assessment

The Organizational Development Network highlights the need for OD professionals to focus "on developing organization capability through alignment of strategy, structure, management processes, people, and rewards and metrics."[71] Does a career in OD appeal to your interests and goals? Explore these job descriptions.

Organizational development specialist. This role consists of assessing and strategizing. OD specialists look for opportunities to help employees work independently and as teams more effectively. They strive to help employees grow professionally and in turn make the organization more successful.[72]

Organizational development practitioner. Also referred to as an organizational development consultant, this role focuses primarily on the practice of OD. Practitioners work closely with organizations to plan and implement large-scale changes and improvements.

Organizational development manager. The OD manager is, first and foremost, a liaison. As an adviser to the organization's leader, the OD manager implements the organization's goals across departments and divisions, planning, developing, and serving as the admin for HR programs. This role is dedicated to creating and implementing initiatives that achieve business goals and objectives. If you Google this title, you will find an ample number of positions available, particularly in the human resources discipline, like you would find in the Society of Human Resource Managers (SHRM).[73]

Organizational development consultant. OD consultants do not typically work long-term at one organization. They are generally brought in when an organization is experiencing difficulties meeting business goals and objectives. They help these companies by applying OD theories and practices to develop improvement strategies.

Director of organizational development. The director of organizational development works diligently to help all employees thrive. They plan, create, and facilitate policies, processes, and procedures to develop an inclusive environment where employees can be successful. The role requires the following skills and functions: assessing employees' needs to develop programming, implementing the programming, and measuring the success of the programming.

How to Start a Career in Organizational Development

There is no one-size-fits-all path to a career in OD. With time, hard work, and careful planning, you can become an organizational development professional. While colleges generally do not offer OD degrees, positions in the field do typically require a candidate to hold a degree in a related field. Here is a high-level map of the steps you can take to set out on the OD career path:

(Continued)

(Continued)

1. *Get your education.* To become a training and development manager, you will likely need a bachelor's degree and, in some cases, a master's degree.

2. *Seek relevant work experience.* Relevant work experience is imperative for training and development managers to be successful.

3. *Obtain the necessary credentials.* Depending on the position, being a training and development manager may require licensure, certification, or registration.

4. *Practice.* At work, implement your knowledge and skills. Look for chances to evaluate and improve organizational concerns.

5. *Continuing education.* Keep pursuing formal and informal education opportunities to stay abreast of technology, business, and OD trends.

6. *Grow your network.* Build and maintain relationships with other professionals in your field.

Discussion Questions

1. Explain why research and data are an important aspect of OD. What types of data should an OD practitioner collect?

2. Of the types of positions in OD, what one do you find most interesting and why?

3. Do some Internet research to locate an internship experience in OD. How could you leverage such an internship to gain skills in OD?

Sources: Adapted from Gilbert, N. (n.d.). Everything you need to know to succeed in organizational development. Retrieved from https://www.noodle.com/articles/organizational-development-careers; Organization Development Network. (n.d.). What is organization development? Retrieved from https://www.odnetwork.org/page/WhatIsOD; Wride, M. (2018, February 15). What's the difference between human resources and organizational development? Retrieved from https://www.decision-wise.com/difference-between-human-resources-and-organization-development/.

Strong management is necessary to effectively implement organizational change. A study[74] of 40 health care clinics undergoing a three-year period of significant organizational change found that resistance to change had increasingly negative relationships over time with two important consequences: employees' organizational commitment and perceptions of organizational effectiveness. These relationships became stronger over time, suggesting that resistance to change festers. However, this study also found that supportive leadership was increasingly impactful in reducing change resistance over time. The most effective tactics for overcoming resistance and gaining support are communication and building relationships that support the change. The next section discusses the models for leading change that have been shown to produce the best results.

Overcoming Resistance To Change

Learning Objective 4.7: Discuss a manager's role in proactively overcoming resistance to change.

Change is a messy, collaborative, inspiring, difficult, and ongoing process—like everything meaningful that leads to human progress.
—Beth Comstock, *Imagine It Forward: Courage, Creativity, and the Power of Change*

We read in the last section that every manager's hope is that their employees will simply commit to the change. Truth be told, though, most people, probably even including you, at the very least approach change with some nervousness, and at the very most approach change with a hearty "Heck no!" The quote at the beginning of this section, however, comes from Beth Comstock, an agent of change who understands that the only thing that is constant is change—in yourself, in your career, and in your organization—and although it is hard and messy, pretty much anything worth doing is.

In her book *Imagine It Forward*, Comstock offers many proactive tips for managers, who understand that positive organizational change starts with positive change initiatives in

Tips for Successful, Proactive Change-Makers

• The pace of change is never going to be SLOWER than it is today. Think about that—both frightening and empowering at the same time!
• Who are you waiting for to tell you it's okay? Grab your own permission. You are probably empowered to do it, so don't wait!
• Invite outsiders in. Asking others to see the "forest for the trees" helps when you are embedded in the day-to-day and might not be able to see the big picture.
• Look at what isn't happening and imagine what could. What is your best vision of how this should work?
• To be a change-maker, think mindshare before market share. Talk it out with stakeholders.
• Most of us are adverse to conflict. But conflict is the primary engine of creativity and innovation. Learn to do it well, from beginning to end!
• In change, people have to find their own path. You can't mandate how that happens. But you can create the right conditions, with open and authentic communication.

Source: Comstock, B. (2018). *Imagine it forward: Courage, creativity, and the power of change.* New York, NY: Penguin.

themselves and that their attitude carries through to their employees and organization. Some of those great tips for successful, proactive change-makers appear in Table 4.3.

You might notice that Comstock has several recurring themes in her tips for change success: being proactive, being positive, and not being afraid to make mistakes. Managers sometimes believe they do not have the power to be a leader, but you already are leading your team, and you can take those skills to help make organizational change more successful for all of those involved.

Organizations typically approach change in different ways, but for your purposes as a manager, let's take a look at a three-step model that make logical sense when it comes to change and is supported by research as well. It will also help you understand the steps where employees might need your biggest assistance in overcoming their concerns.

To determine your organization's readiness for organizational change, complete Self-Assessment 4.1.

Lewin's Three-Step Model

The three-step model is the starting point for understanding the fundamental process of leading change. As shown in Figure 4.7, there are three steps in the change process: *unfreezing*, *changing*, and *refreezing*. First, **unfreezing** challenges the status quo by shaking up assumptions (see Comstock's suggestions above); next, **changing** represents movement toward a new desired state. Finally, **refreezing** the changes by reinforcing and restructuring to make the changes permanent is the third phase.

Think about an ice pack that you use when you have a sports injury. When you take it out of the freezer, it is hard and can't be changed much. As you use it, it becomes soft and malleable (this is the changing phase). After 20 minutes, you put it back in the freezer, and it becomes solid again. Change is like this: When people and systems are in the frozen stage, you can't change them. You have to literally "heat things up" to soften the attitudes and assumptions about change so that the system is malleable, like a defrosted ice pack. Once you have the changes you want in place, you can reinforce the new behaviors with rewards or change the structure to support the change (refreezing).

Employees will tend toward the status quo or equilibrium, so there needs to be constant attention to refreezing the new system and behaviors after a change is implemented. For example, an organization that wants to implement teams must first challenge old assumptions regarding working alone and getting rewarded for individual effort. A new organizational chart can be presented to employees, showing teams the new way work will be organized. Some employees may resist the team concept and even leave the organization as the change is implemented. There may be storms and team conflict (things are heating up). Once there are successful teams in place, then the new approach can be refrozen by offering team rewards and reinforcing the new organizational chart.

A study of a planned organizational

▼ FIGURE 4.7

Lewin's Three-Step Model of Organizational Change

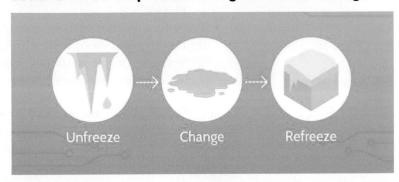

Source: Adapted from Lewin, K. (1951). *Field theory in social science: Selected theoretical papers* (1st ed.). New York, NY: Harper; Mulholland, B. (2017). 8 critical change management models to evolve and survive. Retrieved from https://www.process.st/change-management-models/.

change in a hospital system found that authentic leadership influenced the processes of unfreezing, change, and refreezing.[75] An interview study of 15 top executives who had been involved in significant organizational change found that it is necessary to balance the use of power with the autonomy of employees during change. One executive commented, "Leading change involves building social relationships to mobilize resources to create the power I need to make changes."[76] Change leaders should concentrate their resources on a few positively or negatively influential individuals and take advantage of communication networks to persuade and inform others to help with their change adoption. By partnering with opinion leaders in the organization, leaders can facilitate each player's proper role in the change effort.[77]

Practical Steps for Applying the Three-Step Model

Unfreeze

- Assess the organization and determine what needs to change.
  - Why is this change necessary?
- Get buy-in from senior management and win the support of integral stakeholders.
  - Who are the key players who need to support the change?
- Develop a compelling message about the change, emphasizing why it is necessary and providing evidence.
  - What are the benefits of the change?
- Be open to feedback from employees so that you can manage their worries or skepticism.
  - Listen objectively to learn about employees' concerns.[78]

It is interesting to note that unfreezing in some institutions follows a rather voluntary approach, while in others, people are more forcibly pushed into unfreezing. Voluntary change is usually the reaction of a company that is paying attention to its internal and external environments, while the forced change is usually the result of a sudden, episodic event. Regardless, unfreezing creates an opportunity for managers to investigate and engage in some conceptual thinking about the main driving forces of change, and how to best go about them.[79]

Change

- As you plan and implement change, communicate clearly and often.
  - Keep describing the benefits of the change.
  - Be precise and clear about how the change will affect employees

- Create a culture of transparency by honestly answering questions and dealing with concerns immediately.
  - This will help dispel rumors.
- Empower employees to be part of the change and involve them in the process.
  - Task managers with providing day-to-day instruction.
  - Get buy-in from organizational stakeholders, such as employee organizations.
  - Focus on short-term goals to boost morale and enthusiasm.

Most often, successful change initiatives use change theory or a planned approach to implement organizational shifts.[80] That is why you will find communication and paying attention to processes to be critical in achieving successful organizational change.

Refreeze

- Connect the change to organizational culture.
  - What supports the change?
  - What might stall, hinder, or undermine the change?
- Look for ways to sustain the change and implement them.
  - Get leadership's commitment to continue supporting the change.
  - Implement a system of positive reinforcement, such as rewards.
- Ensure that the team has the support and training needed to keep up the change in the long term.
- Celebrate the success of the change.[81]

Lewin's three-step model is pretty amazing. It dates back to the 1950s, but it is still relevant today. A review of research evidence on organizational change over the past several decades concluded that "rather than being outdated or redundant, Lewin's approach is still relevant to the modern world."[82] It is also a cross-cultural tool; one research study explored Eastern versus Western assumptions concerning organizational change based on speculation about culturally based differences in Eastern and Western learning styles. It also revealed that the primary model of change involved in most OD theory and practice is the three-stage change processes of unfreezing, change, and refreezing formulated by Kurt Lewin.[83]

Lewin's approach is based on field theory and the analysis of forces for and against organizational change, all of which are explained below.

Force-Field Analysis

To implement organizational change using the three-step model, a **force-field analysis** of the forces for and against an organizational change should be conducted. The steps in force-field analysis follow:

1. Define the problem (current state) and the target situation (target state).
2. List forces working for and against the desired changes.
3. Rate the strength of each force.
4. Draw a diagram (the length of the line denotes strength of the force).
5. Indicate how important each force is.
6. List how to strengthen each important supporting force.
7. List how to weaken each important resisting force.
8. Identify resources needed to support forces for change and reduce forces against change.
9. Make an action plan: timing, milestones, and responsibilities.[84]

Example of Force-Field Analysis

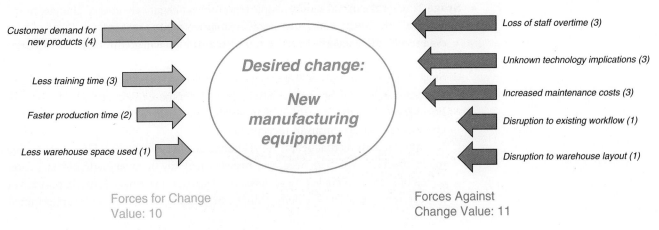

Force Field Analysis for Desired Change

Desired change:

New manufacturing equipment

Customer demand for new products (4)

Less training time (3)

Faster production time (2)

Less warehouse space used (1)

Loss of staff overtime (3)

Unknown technology implications (3)

Increased maintenance costs (3)

Disruption to existing workflow (1)

Disruption to warehouse layout (1)

Forces for Change Value: 10

Forces Against Change Value: 11

Source: Adapted from Mindtools. (n.d.). Force-field analysis: Analyzing the pressures for and against change. Retrieved from https://www.mindtools.com/pages/article/newTED_06.htm.

An example of a force-field analysis for a company that is upgrading a factory with new equipment is shown in Figure 4.8. The analysis shown in the figures suggests that change may fail because the forces against the change are greater than the forces for change. The forces for change will have to increase. For example, the company could provide a marketing analysis presentation to employees to help them understand that the change is needed due to customers wanting new products that the upgraded factory can produce. Alternately, the forces against the change could be reduced by communicating to the staff that they will not lose overtime due to the change.

The Change Curve

Lewin's basic model has been extended in a variety of ways over the years. An interesting approach is known as the **change curve**,[85] which is based on the stages of death and dying by Elizabeth Kübler-Ross,[86] now also related to any type of loss. When faced with a loss, people go through a range of emotions, beginning with shock and denial, then anger, and ending with acceptance and commitment. Based on this theory, a curve for understanding employee resistance to organizational change was developed, and is shown in Figure 4.9. People prefer to maintain the status quo, in which their work is predictable. Change is disruption and has a negative impact. People become angry and fearful and must overcome these strong emotions to move into exploration of what the change means and acceptance of the new ways of doing things. Finally, during the rebuilding phase, they commit to the change.[87]

▼ FIGURE 4.9

The Change Curve

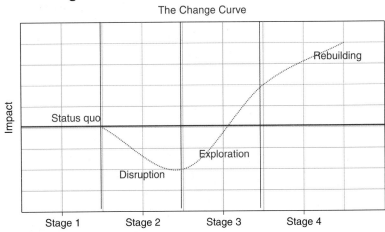

The Change Curve

Impact

Status quo

Rebuilding

Exploration

Disruption

Stage 1   Stage 2   Stage 3   Stage 4

Source: From *On Death and Dying* by Dr. Elisabeth Kubler-Ross. Copyright © 1969 by Elisabeth Kubler-Ross; copyright renewed © 1997 by Elisabeth Kubler-Ross. Reprinted with the permission of Scribner, a division of Simon & Schuster, Inc. All rights reserved.

The stages are described as follows:[88]

- **Stage 1.** People's initial reaction when a change is introduced may be shock or denial as they process the disruption to the existing condition.
- **Stage 2.** After the initial shock, people tend to react negatively toward change. Some may actively protest the changes while others may feel angry or scared.
  - As a result of the negative reactions, the organization will go through a disturbance which could quickly turn into chaos.
  - Stage 2 can be stressful and unpleasant. If people resist the change and remain in this stage, the change will be unsuccessful, especially for those resisting.
  - For everyone, it is much healthier to move to Stage 3, where pessimism and resistance give way to some optimism and acceptance.
  - It's easy just to think that people resist change due to lack of vision. However, change might affect some of them negatively in a very real way that you might not have foreseen. For example, people who've developed expertise in (or have earned a position of respect from) the old way of doing things can see their positions severely undermined by change.

The steps that have been reviewed so far are based on a research stream that has raised doubts regarding the manageability of culture. A number of theorists have contended that organizational culture is deeply embedded in the subconscious and cannot be susceptible to conscious manipulation by management.[89] However, a more positive outlook on the ability to manage change leads to the rest of the steps:[90]

- **Stage 3.** People stop focusing on what they have lost. They start to let go and accept the changes. They begin testing and exploring what the changes mean, learning the reality of what's good and not so good and how they must adapt.
- **Stage 4.** People not only accept the changes but also start to embrace them; they rebuild their ways of working.
  - Only when people get to this stage can the organization really start to reap the benefits of change.

While a structured and long-term program of incremental change may prove more efficient in guiding the culture of an organization to realize a more positive response,[91] with knowledge of the change curve, managers can plan how to minimize the negative impact of the change and help people adapt more quickly to it. Your aim is to make the curve shallower and narrower. Managers can use their knowledge of the change curve to give individuals the information and help they need, depending on where they are on the curve. This will help you accelerate change and increase its likelihood of success.[92]

Now it is easy to see why culture and culture change are included in the *planning* part of a manager's job. One quick piece of advice about planning—while it seems like a lot of effort to put forth when you could just dive in, planning saves you and your employees a lot of time and stress in the long run. In fact, planning in life often does the same thing. By planning what you are going to do, communicating this with the others involved, taking feedback on the plan, adjusting as necessary, and then moving forward, you will find that life as a manager is a much easier than it could be otherwise.

Now that you've acquired some knowledge of how culture is established and shared, what forces cause cultural changes in an organization, and at what points in the change employees might experience resistance—and now that you know that as a manager, *your* approach and attitude might well be the keys to making the transition easier and more successful for all those involved—let's give you some tried-and-true hacks on how to make you the agent leading the change.

Nine Tips for Managing Organizational Change

People can be resistant to or nervous about change, but the bottom line is this: Organizations simply must change in order to remain competitive in a dynamic marketplace. Successful implementation of new strategies requires a new mindset. By reframing the conversations we have about change, the behaviors we model when trying to make change, and the processes we use to implement it, we make change seamlessly and successfully.

1. Develop and stick to a process

Figure out where you are, then figure out where you want to go, and make a clear-cut plan of action to get there. The organizations that are most successful in changing are intentional and diligent about process. When you communicate about the change, make sure you are persuasively describing its efficacy and value. Maintaining positive, persuasive communication, encouraging active participation, and providing clear information can all help prepare stakeholders for making major organizational change.[93]

2. Start at the top

If you don't have total buy-in from the executives, the uncertainty and lack of commitment will creep down the hierarchy to operational-level employees. If employees sense that leadership doesn't accept the change, they won't accept it either. In order for change to be successful, high-level leadership must be:

- Agents of change
- Fully committed to adopting and implementing the change
- Transparent about how they will participate in the change

According to one Booz and Co. survey, 36% of all respondents admitted that their innovation strategy is not well aligned to their company's overall strategy, and 47 percent said their company's culture does not support their innovation strategy. Not surprisingly, companies saddled with both poor alignment and poor cultural support perform at a much lower level than well-aligned companies. In fact, companies with both highly aligned cultures and highly aligned innovation strategies have 30% higher enterprise value growth and 17% higher profit growth than companies with low degrees of alignment.[94]

In order to avoid this kind of discord from the top, it must be clear to execs exactly why the organization needs to change, and how they will make that change doable.[95]

3. Consider how the change will affect all stakeholders' needs and perceptions of all stakeholders in the change process

Carefully consider and plan for how the change will affect all stakeholders and assess their needs and perceptions. A great way to do this is through focus groups, or casual conversations with the stakeholders (employees, customers, managers, and leadership), or even a well-prepared survey.

Once you have the information, explore how you can help each level better deal with the change ahead, and how you can ensure they are part of the process to help with ownership of the change.

4. Pay attention to the individual change process

In times of transition, stakeholders go through an individual change process. First, they must *let go* of the old ways of doing things. People often experience a sense of loss during change.[96] Next, they go through a period of *exploring* the future, existing between the old way and the new way. This time can be confusing and frustrating for employees because everything is in flux. Finally, employees begin to accept the change, adopting it as part of their new normal.

When executives are personally impacted by a change, they can experience this same transition. While leaders may be uncomfortable talking about their personal experience in navigating change, it can be a powerful model for employees.

If you drink Coke products, a great example of this type of loss can be found in *The Real Story of New Coke*. On April 23, 1985, the company dropped a surprise change on their customers in the form of "new Coke." You need to read it to believe it, but it will confirm both the idea of grief over organizational change and how the individual change process is truly different for each individual.[97]

5. Focus on managers

Managers play a pivotal role in keeping employees engaged and productive. Because of this, they are essential in helping effect change. Unfortunately, managers are often neglected when it comes to preparing them for change. Equip them with the tools they need to truly understand the change, why it's necessary, and how it will drive organizational success so that they can help their employees do the same.

6. Effectively handle resistance

Resistance to change is a normal part of the change process. Establish a culture of transparency around struggle and resistance by creating forums for discussing challenges and providing workable solutions. Be curious about employees' feedback, even if they are hesitant and resistant. This will help you honor their feelings and create better strategies for implementing change.

7. Celebrate early wins

Celebrate every success and communicate it organization-wide. Tell the stories of each early success to help empower others to imagine that change is possible. These stories reinforce that everyone has an active role to play in change, no matter how small.[98]

8. Sustain the dialogue

Keep talking about the organizational change. Often, a failed change is the result of poor communication or lack of acceptance from employees. By sustaining a long-term conversation about the change, employees feel heard and there is a forum for discussing and addressing challenges. Ongoing conversations can happen through manager meetings or company-wide town halls.

9. Be clear on the metrics for success

How will you measure success? Giving employees a clear, concrete metric will help motivate them to achieve success. When everyone can visualize exactly how success will look, they can work together to achieve it. Clearly define targets and check in regularly to assess progress.[99]

The importance of these nine steps became abundantly clear at a recent change seminar conducted by one of the authors. Each employee in the room cited major concerns over one or more of these steps, and when each person's concerns were anonymously shared, it created not only a sense of camaraderie among the stakeholders that they were not alone, but also an increasing sense of concern about what lay ahead with major change initiatives on the horizon.

You will also notice the nine tips above cover almost everything we have discussed in the chapter as well as the critical role you, as the manager and leader, play in making this all happen. In fact, these things also refer to you being in charge of how the executives manage the change, and how your employees will emotionally react. Each "how" includes a helpful and practical "what" to do so that, once again, you have the tools you need to foster successful organizational change.

Managerial Implications

Any organization you work for, or any business you start, will undergo change, either by choice or by force. The key takeaway points from this chapter are:

- Organizational culture is the foundation upon which organizations are built.
- Organizational culture is made of spoken and unspoken stories, artifacts, values, and assumptions. Strong organization cultures are those in which employees agree on values and have intense feelings about them.
- Most employees learn an organization's culture through socialization processes. Culture is communicated to employees through rituals, stories, symbols, and language.
- Part of a manager's planning involves working with the culture that is in place while scanning the external environment for changes that might create a need for internal changes in the organization.
- The most successful organizational culture changes are those that are planned, proactive, and incremental.
- Managers must be able to embrace change themselves so they are able to model it for their employees. Resistance to change is the number-one reason that change efforts fail. Therefore, overcoming resistance to change is a major part of a manager's job. The change curve is a useful way to analyze resistance and overcome it.
- Guiding employees through organizational change can be a multi-step process that involves the manager doing as much planning as possible to help employees understand why the change is occurring, how it will occur, and then implementing processes to help the team get through it as positively and successfully as possible.

In our opening story, Robert shared the struggles his company was going through as they were thrust into forced change. In the past they had been able to see the outside environment change and translate that into a smooth, well-planned change internally. Now, thanks to technology and, arguably, physical space changes that technology brings by creating virtual business space, Robert's company had been forced into a major change in how they serviced their customers and had not had the time to plan it out the way they wanted or understand the repercussions it would have on their employees. As an aside, Robert also shared that the executive team was fine with all the changes—a classic example of how an executive team might fail to consider the rest of the organization's stakeholders, and how important managers are to making sure the people doing the real work on the ground feel they have a part in open communication, can actively participate in the change, and have the support of their managers.

Planning is a critical part of life and work. Great managers, whether in organizations, volunteer groups, or little league, plan, listen, and understand that members of each will experience different emotions when change is beginning, freezing, or unfreezing. Think about a recent situation where something changed and it caused an emotional response from you. That is why managers who work on their self-awareness and responses are the best leaders for others when change occurs. They will recognize that each employee might react differently but will be ready for the challenges those changes bring.

KEY TERMS

anticipatory socialization   105

artifacts and creations   99

assimilate   106

assumptions   99

change curve   119

changing   116

commitment to change   113

competing values
framework   101

compliance with change   113

enacted values   99

entry   106

espoused beliefs and
values   99

force-field analysis   118

human relations   101

impression management   106

internal processes   101

language   105

metamorphosis   107

norms   99

onboarding   106

open systems   101

organizational culture   98

organizational
socialization   105

preentry   106

proactive   111

psychological contract   107

rational goal-setting   101

reactive   111

refreezing   116

resistance to change   113

rituals   105

socialization   105

stories   105

strong cultures   102

subcultures   104

symbols   105

unfreezing   116

values   97

TOOLKIT

Activity 4.1

Comparing Organizational Cultures in the Gaming Industry

Tencent and Activision Blizzard Entertainment are both successful companies in the gaming industry. Tencent, headquartered in Shenzhen, China (Arena of Valor), is number one in gaming revenues, and Activision Blizzard, headquartered in Irvine, California (World of Warcraft), is ranked fifth. Use the template to compare and contrast their organizational cultures. The information can be searched on the Internet using Google or some other search engine. Try to find the most recent and specific information you can. For example, for organizational culture, don't just state "campus atmosphere." Describe what the offices look like and what is in them.

	Tencent	Activision Blizzard
Size (number of employees)		
Organizational vision and mission		
Employee development and activities		
Organizational culture		
Office design (artifacts)		
Values of employees		
Assumptions about work		
How was the company started, and what was the date of founding?		
Management philosophy		
Impact: Employee satisfaction and turnover (read reviews from employees from glassdoor.com/indeed.com)		
Impact: Organization performance (provide an update on gaming revenues and profitability)		

Discussion Questions

1. Discuss the similarities and differences between Tencent and Blizzard. Which organization has a stronger culture? Or are they the same?

2. How are Tencent and Blizzard different in their size and mission statements?

3. Describe reactions from employees in terms of job satisfaction. Which company would you rather work for and why?

Source: Newzoo. (n.d.). Top 25 public companies by gaming revenues. Retrieved from https://newzoo.com/insights/rankings/top-25-companies-game-revenues/.

Activity 4.2

Understanding Organizational Culture

As a manager who runs a company or leads a team, you will understand the importance of an organization's culture. But culture is challenging because it often creates obstacles to allowing employees to do their best work. Perhaps an organization's current culture is preventing employees from being as productive and purposeful as they can be. Maybe people seem disengaged and apathetic. Individuals and teams don't collaborate. Employees fail to generate new ideas—and any potential innovation is getting stuck before it can be launched.

Before you can decide how to improve or change your culture, you need to determine its current state on four levels: yourself, the individuals on your team, the team, and the organization. For this activity, conduct a one-on-one interview with an employed person you know who intensely explores how they experience culture. (If you don't think employees will speak candidly to someone inside the company, assure them of complete anonymity for themselves and their organization.)

Here are 13 probing questions to ask:

Self-Assessment for Individuals

Assess how the company's values and purpose intersect with each employee's professions goals and mission.

1. What part of your role makes you feel inspired and productive? Which of your daily activities leave you feeling useful and contribute to your job satisfaction, even if you aren't rewarded or praised?
2. Think about your daily behaviors and activities. Which habits do you need to adopt in order to align with the company's goals? Which habits do you need to adapt or eliminate?

Teamwork Assessment

Explore how company culture influences and affects teamwork:

3. Does company culture positively influence how your team works together to achieve goals and fulfill duties? How about the opposite? Does culture ever impede your ability to work together effectively?
4. Think about the company's values and how they affect teamwork. Do any values ever have unintended effects on teamwork?

Organizational Assessment

Explore an employee's perceptions of company culture:

5. What actions are needed to improve the current culture?
6. Describe the current culture. What aspects of the culture have room for improvement?

7. What is distinctive about the company's mission and values?
8. What formal and informal practices do managers use to establish their authority?
9. How does the organization support and reinforce success?
10. What happens when someone fails? How does leadership address it immediately? How is failure addressed in the long term?
11. Does leadership uphold the company's values in their actions and decisions?
12. What motivates leaders to be successful?
13. What should the organization prioritize as its first step in improving company culture?

Once you've gathered all the perspectives, analyze responses to extract the most important insights about the organizational culture. Pay particular attention to what employees care about most, what motivates them, and what they perceive the organization's strengths and weaknesses to be. Also pay close attention to what matters most to you as you listen to their responses.

These insights will form the foundation for developing both immediate and long-term action steps for taking an organizational culture from where it is today to where it needs to be—collaborative, supportive, participative, and productive.

Discussion Questions

1. Based on what you learned in the chapter and the answers to these questions, how well equipped would you feel if you were leading change in the organization?
2. How does a survey at every level help managers plan, promote, and implement change for employees?
3. Why do you think there are so many questions on the organizational level? How would you use these answers in your role as a change agent?

Source: Adapted from Davis, A. (2018). These 15 questions will assess your company's culture and help you decide how to improve it. Retrieved from https://www.inc.com/alison-davis/these-15-questions-will-assess-your-companys-culture-and-help-you-decide-how-to-improve-it.html.

Case Study 4.1

How It All Went Wrong at JCPenney

The American economy is thriving. People are eager to drop disposable income on the latest fashions, home furnishings and décor, toys, and electronics—but not at JCPenney. The retailer is deeply in debt (to the tune of $4 billion), and stock prices have plummeted below $2, leaving the company's future uncertain.

Mark Cohen, the director of retail studies at Columbia Business School, calls the company a "leaky ship." Former CEOs had muddled brand identity and fled, leaving JCPenney in a continued downward spiral.

The leak sprung in the late 1990s. Sales and profits began dropping under CEO Myron Ullman, who was unable to keep shoppers when the recession hit. As the economy rebounded, it seemed that JCPenney's once-loyal shoppers were gone for good.

Ron Johnson Takes the Helm of a Sinking Ship

Ron Johnson, former director of Apple's retail division, took the helm in 2011. Johnson, who had once achieved success at Apple, was no match for the dismal scenario at JCPenney. His attempts to overhaul strategy were poorly researched and badly executed. Less than 18 months after he was hired, Johnson was fired.

Johnson's Faulty Assumptions

What could possibly go wrong with a CEO, experienced at high-end technological retail success, being brought in to run a value-priced, coupon-driven department store? Let's start with Johnson's strength at making bad assumptions. In late 2011, he promised to make JCPenney "America's favorite store," but he started by ignoring the long-standing customer stakeholder base and implemented plans tied to misguided goals.

Johnson overhauled the retailer's advertising, logo, store layout, and pricing, all without testing shoppers' reactions. In an attempt to target wealthy shoppers, Johnson dropped reliable brands and replaced them with brands that didn't appeal to the low- and middle-income shoppers who formed Penney's base. He ended coupons and clearance sales, a mainstay of the Penney's experience. These moves were out of touch with Penney's core shoppers, and alienated them. According to Cohen, Johnson ditched his old audience and "assumed a new one would appear instantly from out of the blue."

In moving from a company that prided itself on telling customers what they needed, Johnson had crossed over into a culture where sales were driven by what the customers said they needed. In 2012, the company hemorrhaged more than $4 billion in sales, a quarter of its sales from 2011. The numbers made it clear: Johnson had to go.

Mediocre and Stuck

Desperate to stop the losses, Penney went back to Ullman, the former CEO, in 2013. He immediately reinstated coupons and old-standby brands, which stabilized sales and paused stock declines. Still, it was difficult for JCPenney to right the ship.

While rival retailers launched digital strategies and overhauled their shopping experiences, due to its financial struggles, Penney couldn't compete. In an effort to once again plug the hole in the sinking ship, in 2015 JCPenney brought in Marvin Ellison from Home Depot. Although clothing sales had always been Penney's bread and butter, the board of directors thought hiring Ellison would help them enter the appliance market to bolster sales. It didn't work, and stock continued to drop. Despite this, Ellison, partnering with Ullman as board chair, led JCPenney to $2.81 billion in revenue in 2015, narrowing the net loss to $68 million in the company's second-quarter earnings.

Soon, however, Ellison abandoned JCPenney to run the show at Lowe's. Ellison left the fashion unit directionless, desperately needing brands to satisfy moms and millennials. Penney's, which had dramatically shifted its target from older shoppers to younger ones, is now moving back toward middle-aged shoppers.

Does JCPenney Have a Future?

To remain solvent, JCPenney needs the tide to turn—and fast. The company must escape its massive debt and recoup a large chunk of its sales volume at a profit. A company spokesperson points to same-store sales growth in 2017 as proof that Penney's is still in the game. The company once bought as much merchandise as it needed to fill stores, but now it is forced to limit itself to proven sales trends. Still, in 2018, CFO Jeffrey Davis believed that JCPenney "can and will be a clear winner in the retail environment."[100]

Perhaps the final word on JCPenney will be left to current CEO Jill Soltau, who took over in January 2019. Note how many concepts in her announcement tie in to what you have learned so far in management:

> I am pleased with the strides we've made in setting key objectives, building our senior leadership team, executing significant changes in our assortment, such as eliminating major appliances, and mobilizing the entire organization around our priorities. We have made good progress on each of our immediate action steps highlighted last quarter, including our continued efforts to reduce and enhance our inventory position, which resulted in a 16% reduction in our inventory and a meaningful improvement in our free cash flow this quarter. As our inventory rationalization effort continues, we are testing a number of strategies around optimal inventory levels and assortment choice counts with a goal of delivering an improved experience for our customers and maximizing our return on investment.

Discussion Questions

1. As a client at JCPenney, how would feel throughout the change process as outlined in this article?
2. If you had been working as a department manager at JCPenney for 20 years, what would your responses, intellectually and emotionally, have been to this cycle of changes as you personally processed them?
3. What parts of JCPenney's culture do you think were impacted most by the actions in this article?

4. As a department manager, what would your reaction have been to each of the changes as they came about?

5. What would an effective manager do to help their employees through these changes?

Sources: Adapted from Executive Leadership. (2017, July 26). Was JC Penney's CEO doomed to fail? *Business Management Daily.* Retrieved from https://www.businessmanagementdaily .com/49264/was-jc-penneys-ceo-doomed-to-fail; Halkias, M. (2018, May). J.C. Penney CEO Marvin Ellison quits for top job at Lowe's and tells staff it was a once-in-a-lifetime opportunity. *Dallas News.* Retrieved from https://www.dallasnews .com/business/retail/2018/05/22/jc-penney-ceo-marvin-ellison-exits-top-job-lowes; JCPenney. (2019, May 21). JCPenney reports first quarter 2019 financial results [Press release]. Retrieved from https://ir.jcpenney.com/news-events/ press-releases/detail/578/jcpenney-reports-first-quarter-2019-financial-results; Kezar, K. (2016, July 21). Mike Ullman passing last role at J.C. Penney to CEO Marvin Ellison. *Dallas Business Journal.* Retrieved from https://www.bizjournals.com/ dallas/news/2016/07/21/mike-ullman-passing-last-role-at-j-c-penney-to-ceo.html; Meyersohn, N. (2018, September 27). How it all went wrong at JC Penney. *CNN Business.* Retrieved from https://www.cnn.com/2018/09/27/business/jcpenney-history/ index.html; O'Toole, J. (2013, April 8). J.C. Penney CEO Ron Johnson out after troubled tenure. *CNN Business.* Retrieved from https://money.cnn.com/2013/04/08/investing/ron-johnson-jc-penney/index.html.

Self-Assessment 4.1

Organizational Readiness for Implementing Change (ORIC)

Part I. Taking the Assessment

Instructions: Circle the response that best describes your organization's readiness for implementing change. This is not a test, and there are no right or wrong answers. You do not have to share your results with others unless you wish to do so.

Statements	Strongly Disagree	Disagree	Neutral	Agree	Strongly Agree
1. People who work here feel confident that the organization can get people invested in implementing this change.	1	2	3	4	5
2. People who work here are committed to implementing this change.	1	2	3	4	5
3. People who work here feel confident that they can keep track of progress in implementing this change.	1	2	3	4	5
4. People who work here will do whatever it takes to implement this change.	1	2	3	4	5
5. People who work here feel confident that the organization can support people as they adjust to this change.	1	2	3	4	5
6. People who work here want to implement this change.	1	2	3	4	5
7. People who work here feel confident that they can keep the momentum going in implementing this change.	1	2	3	4	5
8. People who work here feel confident that they can handle the challenges that might arise in implementing this change.	1	2	3	4	5
9. People who work here are determined to implement this change.	1	2	3	4	5
10. People who work here feel confident that they can coordinate tasks so that implementation goes smoothly.	1	2	3	4	5
11. People who work here are motivated to implement this change.	1	2	3	4	5
12. People who work here feel confident that they can manage the politics of implementing this change.	1	2	3	4	5

Part II: Scoring and Interpretation

In Part I, you rated yourself on 12 questions. Add the numbers you circled in each of the columns to derive your score for Change Commitment and Change Efficacy (defined below). During class, we will discuss each aspect of commitment to organizational change.

Change Commitment	Change Efficacy
2. _____	1. _____
4. _____	3. _____
6. _____	5. _____
9. _____	7. _____
11. _____	8. _____
	10. _____
	12. _____
Total_____	Total_____
÷ 5	÷ 7

Overall Commitment to Change: Change Commitment _____ + Change Efficacy _____ = _____

Change commitment (CC) reflects organizational members' shared resolve to implement a change. A hypothesized determinant of change commitment is change valence. Organization members may value an organizational change for any number of reasons; why they value it may be less important than how much they value it. The second facet of readiness, change efficacy, reflects organization members' shared belief in their collective capability to implement a change. Determinants of change efficacy include task knowledge, resource availability, and situational factors.

Change efficacy (CE) is expected to be high when organizational members know what to do and how to do it, when they perceive they have the resources they need to implement the change, and when they perceive situational factors such as timing to be favorable.

Discussion Questions

1. Which of the two dimensions are higher? In other words, are people in your organization more committed to change or are they more confident in their ability to implement change? Which do you think is more important and why?

2. Compare your results to three others. Explain any differences you see between your commitment to change and theirs.

3. Copy or take a photo of this assessment and send it to three people you know who are currently employed in different organizations. Explain any differences you see between their commitment to change by following up and asking them about their commitment to and efficacy for implementing change.

Source: Adapted from Shea, C. M., Jacobs, S. R., Esserman, D. A., Bruce, K., & Weiner, B. J. (2014). Organizational readiness for implementing change: A psychometric assessment of a new measure. *Implementation Science, 9*(1), 7.

$ SAGE edge™

Get the tools you need to sharpen your study skills. SAGE edge offers a robust online environment featuring an impressive array of free tools and resources. Access practice quizzes, eFlashcards, video, and multimedia at **edge.sagepub.com/scanduragower**.

Introducing...

 SAGE vantage™

Course tools done right.

Built to support teaching. Designed to ignite learning.

SAGE vantage is an intuitive digital platform that blends trusted SAGE content with auto-graded assignments, all carefully designed to ignite student engagement and drive critical thinking. Built with you and your students in mind, it offers easy course set-up and enables students to better prepare for class.

SAGE vantage enables students to **engage** with the material you choose, **learn** by applying knowledge, and **soar** with confidence by performing better in your course.

PEDAGOGICAL SCAFFOLDING

Builds on core concepts, moving students from basic understanding to mastery.

CONFIDENCE BUILDER

Offers frequent knowledge checks, applied-learning multimedia tools, and chapter tests with focused feedback.

TIME-SAVING FLEXIBILITY

Feeds auto-graded assignments to your gradebook, with real-time insight into student and class performance.

QUALITY CONTENT

Written by expert authors and teachers, content is not sacrificed for technical features.

HONEST VALUE

Affordable access to easy-to-use, quality learning tools students will appreciate.

 To learn more about **SAGE vantage,** hover over this QR code with your smartphone camera or visit **sagepub.com/vantage**

 SAGE Publishing

CHAPTER 5

STRATEGIC MANAGEMENT AND PLANNING

CHAPTER **LEARNING OBJECTIVES**

After studying this chapter, you should be able to:

5.1 Understand effective ways of developing a strategic plan.

5.2 Compare and contrast effective and ineffective mission statements.

5.3 Recognize the importance of competitive advantage and organizational values in a strategic plan.

5.4 Perform a five-forces analysis and SWOT analysis.

5.5 Set feasible goals and objectives for your strategic plan.

5.6 Understand planning for profit versus the 3Ps in strategic-planning outcomes.

Get the edge on your studies at **edge.sagepub.com/ scanduragower**

- Take the chapter quiz
- Review key terms with eFlashcards
- Explore multimedia resources, SAGE readings, and more!

How Important Is Strategic Management?

Monday is a holiday, so you and a couple of your college roommates are packing up for a long weekend trip. Where are you going? How will you get there? What should you pack? Let's choose the beach as your mission. Which beach? Whose car is in the best condition? Can it hold all of you comfortably? You're going to need to dig out all your beach clothes, most likely tucked far back in your closet—because, in college, who has time to go to the beach?

Now, how will you get from the university to the beach? You have GPS, so that's a piece of cake. Of course there might be traffic, and construction, and what if an energy-drink delivery truck jackknifes, blocking all the lanes? Depending on which GPS app you are using, some of these things might show up and some might not. And, believe it or not, sometimes the GPS satellite doesn't work correctly. Then let's think more about what you want to take, because just clothes doesn't cut it. Will you pack a cooler? What items will be in the cooler, and what items can you just take in bags? Will you bring towels, beach chairs, and boogie boards? Will your folks know where you are? Will you all have enough money for gas and other food? Is the spare tire ready for action in case of a flat? When you take all of this into consideration, suddenly the beach seems more like a lot of planning, preparation, critical thinking, and execution than a fun trip.

This is why strategic planning is so critical to an organization. They are not just going to the beach; they are planning for the short term and long term, preparing for roadblocks to come up along the way, and making sure they have enough resources on hand and the means to acquire more resources, or perhaps looking for ways to use fewer resources. They need to watch out for competitors, changes in the industry, changes within the company, and opportunities that might arise, looking ahead the whole time to make sure their decisions are keeping them on track to fulfill their mission. Not exactly a day at the beach, is it?

Strategic planning is a vital part of the planning process, but putting together a complete and feasible plan also relies on all facets of organizing, leading, and controlling. Strategic plans start with a vision and mission, decisions about competitive advantages and organizational values, and research into the environment inside and outside the company, then move on to goals and objectives that will direct the entire team on how to fulfill the mission and continue with the vision. Within these decisions are hundreds of others, and a whole lot of people (hopefully) weighing in on them. Many business majors will discover that a strategy course is their "capstone," or final, business course. This is because it takes into account everything learned along the way to earning any type of degree in business.

While this sounds daunting, this chapter will take you through the entire strategic-planning process, and you will find it is just as valuable to you personally as it is for you as a manager and leader. We all need to have visions and missions and ways for us to achieve them. Reading this chapter right now is part of your strategic plan to finish your degree, learn more about management, and gain understanding of the many choices before you and the amount of planning you need to do to make the right decisions when challenges and opportunities arise.

▼ FIGURE 5.0

Textbook Organization

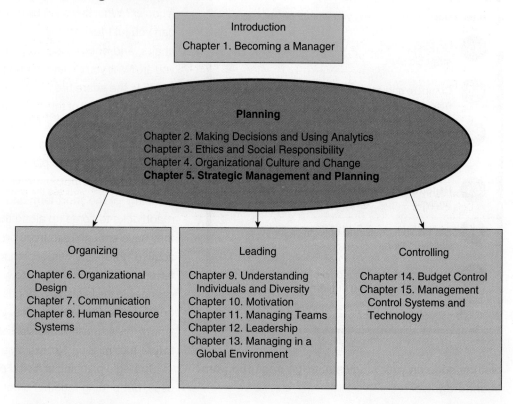

Introduction

Chapter 1. Becoming a Manager

Planning

Chapter 2. Making Decisions and Using Analytics
Chapter 3. Ethics and Social Responsibility
Chapter 4. Organizational Culture and Change
Chapter 5. Strategic Management and Planning

Organizing

Chapter 6. Organizational
Design
Chapter 7. Communication
Chapter 8. Human Resource
Systems

Leading

Chapter 9. Understanding
Individuals and Diversity
Chapter 10. Motivation
Chapter 11. Managing Teams
Chapter 12. Leadership
Chapter 13. Managing in a
Global Environment

Controlling

Chapter 14. Budget Control
Chapter 15. Management
Control Systems and
Technology

Strategic Plans

Learning Objective 5.1: Understand effective ways of developing a strategic plan.

As noted above, there are many components to consider when developing an effective **strategic plan**. The importance of your organization's strategic plan cannot be overstated, because at the heart of the answer to the question of why some firms succeed and others fail lies **strategic management**.[1] So, what exactly is a strategic plan? One definition is "a systematic process of envisioning a desired future, and translating this vision into broadly defined goals or objectives, and sequence of steps to achieve them."[2]

You might notice that strategic planning starts with the end in mind—the desired future—and then works backward. Therefore, you need to start by coming up with questions and answers about your organization. Table 5.1 offers you some ideas.

These five steps will help you get started, and the rest of the chapter will guide you through all the steps and challenges to formulating an effective strategic plan. You might still wonder, from a research perspective, how important a strategic plan is to an organization. Research says plenty, whether you are a small, medium, or large organization. In small and medium organizations, perceived profitability and success in achieving organizational objectives have been positively associated with planning detail, suggesting that strategic planning is a key component to improving performance. Planning detail has also been associated with a significantly higher level of perceived change in the business environment.[3]

Due to the rate of organizational change, time and strategic planning are tightly related.[4] Research has shown that the way CEOs think and feel about time may have a big influence on their firms' strategies. CEOs' attitudes toward time—time urgency (the feeling of being

132 ■ PART II • PLANNING

▼ FIGURE 5.0

Textbook Organization

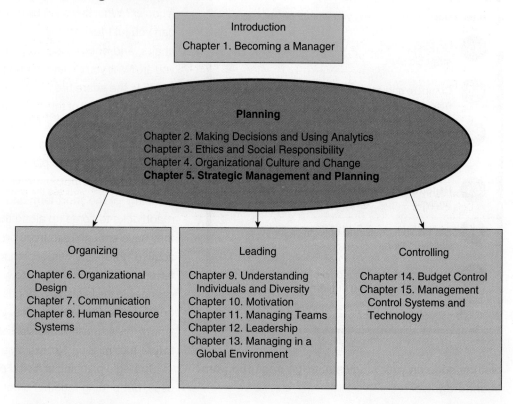

Introduction

Chapter 1. Becoming a Manager

Planning

Chapter 2. Making Decisions and Using Analytics
Chapter 3. Ethics and Social Responsibility
Chapter 4. Organizational Culture and Change
Chapter 5. Strategic Management and Planning

Organizing

Chapter 6. Organizational
Design
Chapter 7. Communication
Chapter 8. Human Resource
Systems

Leading

Chapter 9. Understanding
Individuals and Diversity
Chapter 10. Motivation
Chapter 11. Managing Teams
Chapter 12. Leadership
Chapter 13. Managing in a
Global Environment

Controlling

Chapter 14. Budget Control
Chapter 15. Management
Control Systems and
Technology

Strategic Plans

Learning Objective 5.1: Understand effective ways of developing a strategic plan.

As noted above, there are many components to consider when developing an effective **strategic plan**. The importance of your organization's strategic plan cannot be overstated, because at the heart of the answer to the question of why some firms succeed and others fail lies **strategic management**.[1] So, what exactly is a strategic plan? One definition is "a systematic process of envisioning a desired future, and translating this vision into broadly defined goals or objectives, and sequence of steps to achieve them."[2]

You might notice that strategic planning starts with the end in mind—the desired future—and then works backward. Therefore, you need to start by coming up with questions and answers about your organization. Table 5.1 offers you some ideas.

These five steps will help you get started, and the rest of the chapter will guide you through all the steps and challenges to formulating an effective strategic plan. You might still wonder, from a research perspective, how important a strategic plan is to an organization. Research says plenty, whether you are a small, medium, or large organization. In small and medium organizations, perceived profitability and success in achieving organizational objectives have been positively associated with planning detail, suggesting that strategic planning is a key component to improving performance. Planning detail has also been associated with a significantly higher level of perceived change in the business environment.[3]

Due to the rate of organizational change, time and strategic planning are tightly related.[4] Research has shown that the way CEOs think and feel about time may have a big influence on their firms' strategies. CEOs' attitudes toward time—time urgency (the feeling of being

y

▼ FIGURE 5.0

Textbook Organization

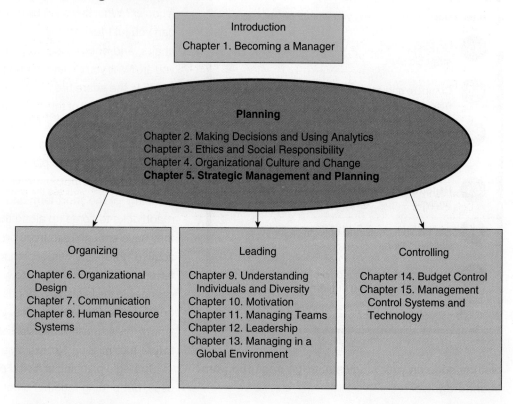

Strategic Plans

Learning Objective 5.1: Understand effective ways of developing a strategic plan.

As noted above, there are many components to consider when developing an effective **strategic plan**. The importance of your organization's strategic plan cannot be overstated, because at the heart of the answer to the question of why some firms succeed and others fail lies **strategic management**.[1] So, what exactly is a strategic plan? One definition is "a systematic process of envisioning a desired future, and translating this vision into broadly defined goals or objectives, and sequence of steps to achieve them."[2]

You might notice that strategic planning starts with the end in mind—the desired future—and then works backward. Therefore, you need to start by coming up with questions and answers about your organization. Table 5.1 offers you some ideas.

These five steps will help you get started, and the rest of the chapter will guide you through all the steps and challenges to formulating an effective strategic plan. You might still wonder, from a research perspective, how important a strategic plan is to an organization. Research says plenty, whether you are a small, medium, or large organization. In small and medium organizations, perceived profitability and success in achieving organizational objectives have been positively associated with planning detail, suggesting that strategic planning is a key component to improving performance. Planning detail has also been associated with a significantly higher level of perceived change in the business environment.[3]

Due to the rate of organizational change, time and strategic planning are tightly related.[4] Research has shown that the way CEOs think and feel about time may have a big influence on their firms' strategies. CEOs' attitudes toward time—time urgency (the feeling of being

132 ■ PART II • PLANNING

Strategic-Planning Questions to Get You Started

1. **Where are you?** While this may seem like a basic question, an honest assessment of the status quo can prove challenging. Organizations tend to see what they *want* to see rather than objectively assessing themselves the way others may perceive them. For an accurate picture of where you are, conduct external and internal audits to get a clear understanding of the marketplace, the competitive environment, and your organization's competencies (your real—not perceived—competencies). Going back to the chapter introduction, you are on campus, a known quantity, but you *want* to go to the beach. Do you have what you need, and is the path clear, for you to get there?
2. **Analyze your priorities.** Where do you want to take your organization over time? By answering these questions, you can figure out what's most important for your organization: • What is your mission? • What issues are most significant to the overall well-being and success of your organization? • What issues need your immediate and sustained attention?
3. **Establish your objectives.** What does your organization need to achieve in order to address the priorities you described in Step 2? Define a clear, actionable objective for each priority you identified.
4. **Create an accountability plan.** You've identified your starting point and your desired destination. You've set your priorities and established clear objectives. Now it's time to spell out exactly how you will achieve these objectives. Your plan should detail exactly who will be accountable for what. How will you allocate the following resources? • Time • Money Who is in charge of which objective(s)?
5. **Review. Review. Review.** It's not enough to make a plan. You have to implement it. Implementation requires constant assessment and the willingness to refine as needed. Schedule regular reviews of your process, whether formal or informal. You should review your plan quarterly, at minimum.

Source: Adapted from Aileron (2011). Five steps to a strategic plan. *Forbes.* Retrieved from https://www.forbes.com/sites/aileron/2011/10/25/five-steps-to-a-strategic-plan/#1508fb155464.

chronically hurried) and pacing style (one's pattern of effort over time in working toward deadlines)—influence entrepreneurship within firms, a key strategic behavior.[5] In strategic planning, a future perspective on time appears to be most prevalent, but it is also important to understand the past, "where we have been," to make plans for the future. Therefore, strategic planning in high-velocity-change environments depends less on the past and more on consideration of current factors important in the near term.[6] To understand your own time perspective, complete Self-Assessment 5.1 to learn if you are past, present, or future oriented.

In a large study of big firms, using a sample of 115 large manufacturing companies, the findings showed general support for the proposition that, to be effective, a strategic-planning system should be created in such a way that the specific situational setting of the firm is reflected in the design. The analysis also indicates that firms that adopt a more flexible planning system as the level of environmental complexity increases, including flexibility in the length of planning time and the frequency of plan reviews, are more successful.[7] This research will continue to be a factor throughout the chapter as the need to be flexible and attentive to your strategic plan becomes more and more evident to you.

CRITICAL THINKING QUESTIONS

Explain why the length of time the plan incorporates and the frequency of plan reviews are so important to strategic planning in complex environments. Provide an example of how one of these processes relates to the development process for a new video game.

Mission and Vision Statements

Effective vision and mission statements truly reflect where the organization is going. A **vision statement** describes what a company desires to achieve in the long run. The "long run" used to be five to ten years or even longer, but our current global business model requires organizations to regularly review their visions to be sure they are still feasible and truly depict what the company will look like in the future.[8]

A **mission statement** defines what line of business a company is in, why it exists, and what purpose it serves. Every company should have a precise statement of purpose that gets people excited about what the company does and motivates them to become part of the organization. A mission statement should also declare the company's corporate strategy and thus is generally a couple of sentences in length.[9]

One key to creating effective vision and mission statements is to make sure they are easy to remember and state the true future and purpose for all internal and external stakeholders. For example, Google's vision statement is "to provide access to the world's information in one click,"[10] and its mission statement is "to organize the world's information and make it universally accessible and useful."[11] You may Google these statements if you would like to confirm them, but they are easy to understand and remember for all stakeholders.

Even with the brevity of Google's statements, a lot of thought went into them, as the article in the following box outlines. Considerable thought goes into developing any vision or mission statement that truly represents what the organization is looking toward and what its purpose is.

On the other hand, at look at Stanford University's website reveals:

At this pivotal time of immense opportunity and profound societal change, our vision is grounded in both the founding purpose of the University "to promote the public welfare by exercising an influence in behalf of humanity and civilization" and in the following expression of our mission and values.

Starbucks' mission statement.

©John Trax/Alamy Stock Photo

- **Research:** Extend the frontiers of knowledge, stimulate creativity, and solve real-world problems
- **Education:** Prepare students to think broadly, deeply and critically, and to contribute to the world
- **Service:** Deploy Stanford's strengths to benefit our region, country and world[14]

It is pretty obvious that Google's statements are easier to remember. To be fair to Stanford, however, this is one of the better university mission statements. If you apply the same framework to Stanford's vision and mission as the one applied to Google's, though, you can see the differences. For example, "Deploy Stanford's strengths" means ... what? What

HOW GOOGLE BUILT AN EFFECTIVE VISION AND MISSION STATEMENT

If you set out to make a list of instantly recognizable global brands, Google would likely rise to the top. A quick glance at the stock market on any given day reveals that the Internet giant, founded in 1998, is one of the most valuable brands in the world. With competition like Facebook, Amazon, and Apple, it is essential for Google to stay mission focused and committed to embodying its vision.

Let's explore how an effective vision and mission statement play an integral role in Google's success and day-to-day operations.

The Four Components of Google's Mission Statement

Google's mission statement is straightforward and utilitarian: "to organize the world's information and make it universally accessible and useful."[12] Let's unpack it.

1. *World's information.* The company fulfills this obligation using website crawlers, or the automated gathering of websites that can be indexed on the Google search engine.

2. *Organization.* Google organizes Internet content using proprietary algorithms, which it is continuously refining and improving.

3. *Universal accessibility.* Google is laser focused on ensuring users' access to the information they need. Users can access Google products such as YouTube worldwide.

4. *Usefulness.* Since its inception, Google has focused on helping users seamlessly search and sort online content. The company has been so successful at achieving usefulness that, in many languages, "Google it" has become the go-to verb for conducting a web search.

Providing Access in One Click: Google's Corporate Vision Statement

Google's corporate vision is "to provide access to the world's information in one click."[13] Let's unpack this vision statement.

1. *World's information.* Again, Google's web crawlers and extensive search index enable the company to provide a massive repository of content.

2. *Access.* Google achieves its "accessibility" vision by offering products throughout the global.

3. *One click.* Google's "one click" vision is succinct and concrete. It propels the company to continuously strive for improving the ease of access to information.

Source: Thompson, A. (2019). Google's mission statement and vision statement (an analysis). Retrieved from http://panmore.com/google-vision-statement-mission-statement. See also Google Search. (n.d.). Our mission. Retrieved from https://www.google.com/search/howsearchworks/mission/.

---

strengths? This is a generic statement that sounds good but doesn't give specifics like Google's analysis does.

Many organizations try to do too much with their mission statement and forget the importance it has to employees and other stakeholders. Sometimes they get too caught up in attempting to get across the entire history and operations of the organization, or even in trying to sound good versus making sure the statement fulfills its purpose. For a look at some memorable and not-so-memorable current mission statements, and how to process the difference between the two, read the Fact or Fiction? box on page 136 (you might think it's fiction, but some large organizations have poor mission statements—and that is a fact).

As an interesting aside, organizations that struggle to come up with effective vision and mission statements might benefit from some tips from former Apple executive Guy Kawasaki. He has rebranded himself as an entrepreneurial guru and suggests that rather than making up vision and mission statements, organizations should consider creating a **mantra**. A mantra is three or four words that sums up what your organization is all about. One reason supporting the use of a mantra instead of vision and mission statements, or as a way to get your organization members to think of missions and visions in a different light, is that they are easy for all stakeholders to remember.

FACT OR FICTION?

Real Mission Statement Wins and Kefuffles

Walking through the halls of a typical office building, I asked one of the employees what they believed the mission of the organization was. He cocked his head a bit as he sputtered out something about serving clients with excellence and working hard. It was clear he was stringing the words together as they came out of his mouth. But when he was done, I could tell he felt somewhat pleased with himself and his creativity. I smiled, thanked him, and kept walking.

Three cubicles down I asked a young woman the same question. "What's the mission of your company?"

Her response was much more to the point: "We do public accounting."

So which is it?

A clear vision statement and compelling mission statement are the foundation of a culture that tends to keep employees longer. Mission and vision statements are important because they draw people in. But mission and vision statements will never retain employees until each person on your team understands their role in achieving the collective goal.

So how do some of America's top companies do when it comes to meeting the criteria of a great mission statement?

Some powerful mission statements:

To become the number 1 fashion destination for 20-somethings globally.

—Asos

To improve its customers' financial lives so profoundly, they couldn't imagine going back to the old way.

—Intuit

Our deepest purpose as an organization is helping support the health, well-being, and healing of both people—customers, Team Members, and business organizations in general—and the planet.

—Whole Foods

We save people money so they can live better.

—Walmart

To prevent and alleviate human suffering in the face of emergencies by mobilizing the power of volunteers and the generosity of donors.

—American Red Cross

To provide authentic hospitality by making a difference in the lives of the people we touch every day.

—Southwest

A mission statement should be unique enough to be memorable and short enough to remember. Unfortunately, some top brands just don't get it. Here are some profoundly disappointing mission statements from major brands:

To be one of the world's leading producers and providers of entertainment and information, using its portfolio of brands to differentiate its content, services and consumer products.

—Disney

To be a company that inspires and fulfills your curiosity.

—Sony

The Home Depot is in the home improvement business and our goal is to provide the highest level of service, the broadest selection of products and the most competitive prices.

—Home Depot

If you are part of your organization's vision and mission statement development or revision team, below are a few simple tips.

Good vision statements:

- Are forward looking
- Are motivating and inspirational
- Reflect a company's culture and core values
- Are aimed at bringing benefits and improvements to the organization in the future
- Define a company's reason for existence and where it is heading

Good mission statements will:

- Motivate employees
- Inspire customers
- Drive strategic planning
- Set values
- Explain *why* a business exists

Discussion Questions

1. Do you agree that the "good" mission statements do a good job of describing the organization's purpose? Why or why not?

2. Are there any of the "bad" mission statements that you think do a good job of describing the organization's purpose?

3. Remember, many consulting companies make millions of dollars working with organizations to come up with mission and vision statements. What is the problem with this approach? Which organizations listed above should ask for a refund?

(Continued)

(Continued)

4. Research your favorite clothing manufacturer. Where does their mission statement fall in comparison with the ones above, and with what you think it should be?

5. Rewrite the mission statements for any of the organizations you recognize on the list above where you think you could do a better job of describing the purpose of the organization. If you are on a team in class, choose one of the statements to rewrite individually, then compare your thoughts with those of your team members to collectively come up with the best statement.

Sources: Adapted from Bosché, G. (2019, 2). The 7 best and 5 worst mission statements of America's top brands. Retrieved from https://www.linkedin.com/pulse/7-best-5-worst-mission-statements-americas-top-brands-bosch%C3%A9/; Corporate Finance Institute. (n.d.). What is a mission statement? Retrieved from https://corporatefinanceinstitute.com/resources/knowledge/strategy/mission-statement/.

Many mission statements are long, often paragraphs, and virtually impossible for employees—the people who are working each day toward fulfilling the mission—to understand. Take a look at what Kawasaki is talking about in the YouTube clip "Don't Write a Mission Statement, Write a Mantra."[15] In it, he takes long mission statements and breaks them down into three or four powerful words, or "mantras," that describe the purpose of the organization in easy-to-remember and impactful ways so that all stakeholders understand. This is often helpful in focusing organization members on their commitment to their stakeholders, and can lead to more effective and powerful mission statements.

One way to get you into the mantra state of mind is to think of yourself in three or four words. This is usually a challenge that stumps students for a while, so to make it easier on you—how would your friends describe you? Thoughtful, kind, compassionate? Motivated, hardworking, and honest? What is your mantra? What words would you choose to have tattooed on you as a permanent symbol of who you are, once you receive your parents' permission? Well, maybe not tattooed, but what are some words it is important for everybody who knows you to use to describe you because those words drive everything you do? This will also help you answer that pesky interview question: "What sets you apart from all the other candidates we are interviewing?"

At this point you might wonder—if mission statements are so hard to develop, are they really important? Research and practical experiences agree that they are. In fact, written customer service mission statements in manufacturers, industrial service firms, and consumer service firms have all been found to have an impact on customer service performance. A survey of customer service managers revealed that firms with a customer service mission statement are more likely to survey customers and more likely to keep specific quantitative measures of customer service performance. In addition, the *total* number of customer service performance–related activities that are monitored is greater for firms having a customer service mission statement, regardless of whether the firm is a manufacturer, industrial service firm, or consumer service firm.[16]

There is also evidence that mission statements can affect financial performance. For instance, "commitment to the mission" and the "degree to which an organization aligns its internal structure, policies and procedures with its mission" were both found to be positively associated with "employee behavior." Employee behavior, then, was observed to have the greatest direct relationship with financial performance.[17]

CRITICAL THINKING QUESTIONS

Choose a company that you admire and research their mission statement online. If you worked for this company, would the mission statement inspire you to work harder? Why or why not?

While there has been a significant amount of information presented to you so far about the importance of an organization mission and vision statement, it was stated earlier that these start with the end in mind. It is impossible to come up with mission and vision statements if you do not know what the company stands for, how it does business, and how perhaps it should do business. The section below introduces you to the critical importance of organizations' choosing how they are going to do business based on their perceived competitive advantage and values.

Competitive Advantage

Learning Objective 5.3: Recognize the importance of competitive advantage and organizational values in a strategic plan.

In 1980, Michael Porter, a name synonymous with strategy, published *Competitive Strategy: How to Analyze Industries and Competitors*.[18] Porter's thesis was that there were only two ways to compete successfully, that is, to have a competitive advantage over others in your industry: cost leadership and differentiation.

Cost leadership means just that: achieving the lowest cost of goods or services sold in the firm's competitive domain (industry or industry segment). An example of a cost leader in discount retailing is Walmart, which uses the company's massive scale, the efficiency of its distribution system, and effective advertising to maintain its position. The challenge for any cost leader in any domain is not to be so cost focused that it fails to spot innovations that change the domain.

In contrast, **differentiation** is being different than your competitors. Porter's phrase is "perceived uniqueness." Successful differentiators set themselves apart from the competition by offering something—perhaps features, options, customer service, or images—for which customers are willing to pay more,[19] and that sets them apart from their competitors. It is easy enough to watch cell phone manufacturer commercials today and see them all compete for part of that differentiation—better cameras, better screens, more functionality, and so forth.

In an interview with *Fast Company* magazine, Porter admitted to being "consumed" by the idea of **competitive advantage** and what it could mean to a company in the process of developing an effective strategy.[20] This is what led him to follow up his initial strategy book with one that focused only on developing a competitive strategy based on one of the two pathways—differentiation and cost leadership. He argued that an organization was capable of delivering superior performance only through an appropriate configuration and coordination of its activities based on one of these methods.[21]

There are those who disagree with Porter's rather simplistic view of an organization's choice between the two. Some argue that price, together with image, after sales support, quality, and design, can be used as the basis of product differentiation.[22] Yet another research stream has fundamentally questioned the view and suggests that organizations must develop unique, firm-specific core competencies that will allow them to outperform competitors by doing things differently and better.[23] This uniqueness precludes general recipes for competitive advantage, such as those implied in the generic

Google headquarters in Mountain View, California.

Shutterstock.com

strategy framework. Nevertheless, differentiation of products and services remains fundamental to the means by which organizations seek to gain competitive advantage.

In the strategic-planning funnel in Figure 5.1, there is another component that some organizations consider the foundation of their firm, while others do not include it in the planning or operational process. It has to do with **organizational values**.

Values are enduring, passionate, and distinctive core beliefs. They're guiding principles that never change. Values are deeply held convictions, priorities, and underlying assumptions that influence attitudes and behaviors. Your organizational values guide your organization's thinking and actions. You can think of your organizational values in terms of dimensions: prosocial, market, financial, achievement, and artistic.[24]

It's important to recognize that while a well-articulated set of core values is critical to an organization's success, the creation of a values statement can, and often is, a separate process by itself. However, a strategic plan is not complete without a declaration of the underlying beliefs in your organization.[25]

The Strategic-Planning Funnel

Vision
Mission/Mantra/Purpose
Competitive Advantage
Organization Values
SWOT Analysis
Five Forces Analysis
Stakeholder Goals
Objectives to Reach
Each Goal
Bottom Line/3Ps
Values

It will probably not surprise you to find that defining your organization's values is one of the hardest steps in the whole strategic-planning process. This is because values mean different things to different people in the organization, and they need to be meaningful to your external stakeholders as well. That means your organizational values play a significant role in your organizational culture (as discussed in Chapter 4), and the better they are, the stronger your organizational foundation will be.

Values can be developed before or after the strategic plan, but to have the most effective impact on your organization, you ideally want to have your values firmly in place for strategic plan development. Due to the challenge of developing a set of organizational values that are meaningful to all and contribute to your organizational strategy, below are six steps to help you identify your values as they pertain to your culture.

Identifying Values in Six Steps

1. **Assess Your Current Organizational Culture**

   Assess your current culture by seeking internal and external feedback. Benchmark your culture by interviewing your stakeholders, such as employees, managers, clients, and vendors. Ask questions such as:

   - What are the words you associate with our organization's brand?
   - In your opinion, what are our organization's core values?
   - How effective is our integration of those values?[26]

2. **Assess Your Strategic Business Plan**

   Now that you've taken stock of the present, it's time to think about the future of your company. Where do you see yourself in the short term, the long term, and the time in between? Gather internal stakeholders to develop strategy for successfully integrating your values into your plans for revenue, development, production, and expansion.

3. **Determine the Culture Needed to Achieve Your Plan**

   Steps 1 and 2 should clearly reveal your organization's values. Take another look at your strategic plan and assess the kinds of changes you need to make to your culture to achieve your goals. Ask yourself what kinds of personalities, backgrounds, skill sets, and experience you need to add to your organizational culture.[27]

4. **Decide If Your Values Need to Shift**

   Culture, values, and profit are inextricably linked.[28] Now that you've taken a closer look at your culture and talent to identify goals, return to your values. Do they need to shift based on your assessments of your culture and strategic plan?

5. **Define What Your Chosen Values Really Mean**

   Values aren't just a catchy slogan or words to fill the bulleted list on your website. You must have a crystal-clear vision for how employees at every level will honor your organizational values. For instance, imagine that your organization values *diversity* and *inclusion*. What is "diversity"? Is it related to culture? To experience and ideas? How does the company strive to achieve "inclusion"? What do those concepts mean in practice? Everyone in your organization should know exactly how to incorporate each value into their daily operations and job functions. An organizational value is not just a word painted on the wall. It must be clear what specific behaviors and processes the employee is supposed to do at work to honor this value.[29]

6. **Incorporate These Values Into the Organization**

   It is isn't enough to simply know your values; you have to live them. It is essential for your newly defined values to permeate your organization. Integrate them into all operational areas of your business, especially talent acquisition. As you recruit and hire new talent, clearly communicate your organizational values and ask candidates about their personal values. Seek out mutual values. When you onboard and offer professional development for employees, make sure you are implementing your organizational values. As you review performance and benchmark compensation, ensure that your values are informing your processes.

   Staying true to your core values will help you hire the best people and build a culture of engagement, authenticity, and success.[30]

   There is even research to show that grounding strategic-planning processes in core organizational values helps define an organization's purpose in an integrated manner that allows for differentiation,[31] thereby enhancing the importance of values in determining differentiation, and differentiation is a key to defining your competitive advantage and therefore to effective strategic planning.

   Not only does identifying values help in defining differentiation and in hiring the right people, but a recent study showed that ethical values in an organization's culture promoted organizational citizenship behaviors among its employees.[32] **Organizational citizenship behavior (OCB)** is a complex phenomenon characterized by altruism, conscientiousness, sportsmanship, and courtesy. Another study showed that although any one instance of OCB may not appear to be significant, in the aggregate these behaviors have a major beneficial impact on organizational operations and effectiveness.[33] In all, values promote OCBs, and OCBs have major impacts on the organization's work and effectiveness, so their benefit to all involved is fairly evident in practice and in theory.

   What are your core values? Find out by completing Toolkit Activity 5.2.

   So far we have built the case for the importance of vision, mission, competitive advantage, and values in your organization's strategic plan and success, but regardless of these internally developed key components, as a manager and leader in the organization, you need to understand that your planning work is never done. You must constantly be scanning your internal and external environments for changes that might require you to change your plan.

   These scanning processes are often twofold: **Porter's five forces** and a **SWOT analysis**, or an examination of strengths, weaknesses, opportunities, and threats. Sometimes you will be combining your competitive advantage decision with what you learn from your SWOT analysis; other times your decision about your competitive advantage will drive your SWOT analysis. Needless to say, keeping constant vigil over your internal and external environments is a perpetual process, and the next section will help you make sure your team is ready to take on these challenges.

Porter's Five Forces and SWOT Analysis

Porter's position in the strategy field casts a much wider net than just his work in how to decide and establish a competitive advantage. He is also known just as famously, or perhaps even more famously, for the Porter's five-forces model. This innovative model spells out five forces that define an industry. **Five-forces analysis** also enables users to break down an industry's weaknesses and strengths. The ultimate goal of the model is to assess (a) the competitive intensity and (b) the "attractiveness" of an industry.

The beauty of Porter's five-forces model is that it is universally accessible. Whether you work in finance or tech, you can apply Porter's model.[34]

Using Porter's Five Forces for Analysis

Figure 5.2 illustrates the five forces that determine an industry's competitive intensity and attractiveness.[35]

1. *Competition in the industry.* How intense is the competition in the marketplace? To assess competitive intensity, determine the number of competitors and assess what each can do. A high level of competitive rivalry can result in advertising and price wars. Ultimately, that can hurt a business's profitability.[36]
2. *Potential of new entrants into the industry.* How difficult is it for new competitors to enter the marketplace? The easier it is for new competitors to enter, the harder it is for a single business to maintain an adequate share of the market. When assessing new entrants, think about how much it costs and how long it takes for a new entrant to get into the market.[37]
3. *Power of suppliers.* A large, diverse pool of suppliers makes it more difficult for a business to maintain its bargaining power. When assessing the bargaining power of suppliers, consider (a) how many suppliers make the same product or provide the same service and (b) the uniqueness of the product or service.[38]
4. *Power of customers.* Customers hold the power to lower an organization's prices. When considering how much power they have, think about the return on investment that customers get from a product or service, how many customers control an organization's sales, and customers' demand for the product or service.
5. *Threat of substitutes.* When customers can easily substitute an organization's product or service, sales and profits will decrease. To assess the threat of substitutes, consider what differentiates the product or service from competitors' versions and how many substitutes there are in the marketplace.

Look back at Walmart's mission statement on page 136—they compete based on low prices, so organizations with higher prices do not pose a threat, but perhaps a company that competes based on a competitive advantage, like a large selection of gluten-free items at reasonable prices, might.

▼ FIGURE 5.2

Porter's Five Forces

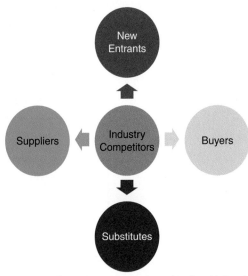

Source: Business Strategy planning and goal deployment. https://www.iwise2.com/library/business-strategy-planning-and-goal-deployment/strategy/porters-5-forces.

Assessing Porter's five forces will help a company to tweak strategy and, ultimately, generate higher earnings for its investors.

According to Porter, the potential for a firm to be profitable is negatively associated with increased competition, lower barriers to entry, a large number of substitutes, and increased bargaining power of customers and suppliers. The analysis of these forces is how Porter argues that an organization can develop a generic competitive strategy of differentiation or cost leadership.[39]

CRITICAL THINKING QUESTIONS

Which of Porter's five forces do you feel are most critical for an organization to be profitable? Explain your choice(s). Explain how these forces relate to differentiation of products and cost leadership.

SWOT Analysis

Some organizations use a SWOT analysis[40] (see Figure 5.3) instead of, or along with, Porter's five forces, as an analysis tool for their environmental scans.

Conducting a SWOT Analysis

Who should participate in a SWOT analysis?

Initially, the SWOT analysis was developed for execs. That said, it is important to involve other stakeholders in the process, particularly employees who have direct contact with customers. Often, these employees are intimately familiar with the company's strengths and weaknesses.

▼ FIGURE 5.3

SWOT Analysis Template

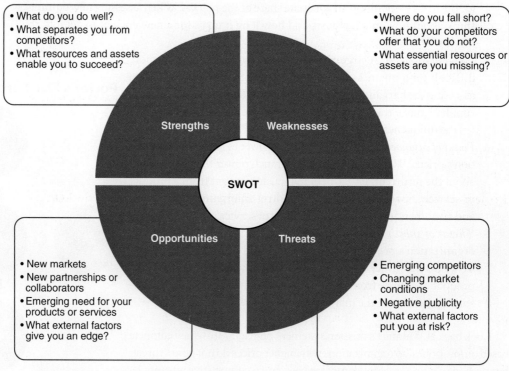

• What do you do well?
• What separates you from competitors?
• What resources and assets enable you to succeed?

• Where do you fall short?
• What do your competitors offer that you do not?
• What essential resources or assets are you missing?

Strengths **Weaknesses**

SWOT

Opportunities **Threats**

• New markets
• New partnerships or collaborators
• Emerging need for your products or services
• What external factors give you an edge?

• Emerging competitors
• Changing market conditions
• Negative publicity
• What external factors put you at risk?

Source: Adapted from Creately. (2019, June 17). SWOT analysis templates to download, print or modify online [Blog post]. Retrieved from https://creately.com/blog/examples/swot-analysis-templates-creately/.

Employees who have been with the organization for a significant amount of time can contribute their expertise, but new employees can be effective participants, too, bringing a fresh perspective to the assessment.

While internal stakeholders can bring valuable insight to the SWOT analysis, it is sometimes necessary to look outside the organization for additional perspectives. Vendors, suppliers, finance professionals, and even friends or business associates can be sources of valuable information for conducting your SWOT analysis.[41]

How often should an organization conduct a SWOT analysis?

Markets and industries are dynamic and ever changing. Employees leave, sales decline, and new competitors emerge. Reassess your SWOT analysis often and do a new one from scratch every 6 to 12 months. For start-up companies, a SWOT analysis is implemented during the business-planning process to help solidify the direction they plan on going in.[42]

How do I conduct an effective SWOT analysis?

It can be deceptively difficult to decide if a trait is a strength or a weakness. For example, an organization's flexible structure might be a strength, enabling it to move quickly and respond to the market. On the flip side, this same structure might be a weakness if it slows the decision-making process. For this reason, it's important to clearly define each segment of your SWOT template before you begin. It is much easier to classify strengths and weaknesses when you start with an unambiguous definition.[43]

How can I make sure my SWOT analysis is successful?

Use these guidelines to obtain valuable insights from your SWOT analysis and successfully navigate some of the model's limitations.

- *Keep competitors in mind.* Think about your strengths, weaknesses, opportunities, and threats as relative to your competition.
- *Stay focused.* In each quadrant, list at least three items, but do not list more than five.
- *Be concise, clear, and specific.* Ensure that each item you list is as concrete as possible. For example, avoid vague terms like "brand image" or "flexibility." Instead, try "brand image valued at $8 million" or "flexible organizational structure that enables innovation."
- *Stick to objective, measurable information.* Take care not to rely on gut instincts or guesswork. Instead, try to point to data and unbiased assessments.[44]

How to Evaluate Strengths and Weaknesses

Evaluating Internal Factors

Strengths are internal positive traits that give you an edge in the market. Strengths include:

- What you do well
- What separates you from competitors
- What resources and assets enable you to succeed

Weaknesses are external negative traits that detract from your strengths and/or jeopardize your ability to compete. Weaknesses include:

- Where you fall short
- What your competitors offer that you do not
- What essential resources or assets you are missing[45]

When evaluating strengths and weaknesses, use the following metrics:

- *Importance.* How important is the strength or weakness? Evaluate each on a scale of 1 (not important) to 10 (critical).
- *Rating.* Is the strength or weakness major or minor? Assign a score between 1 and 3, with 1 being minor and 3 being major.
- *Score.* To derive the score, multiply the importance by the rating. When developing strategic plans based on your SWOT, rely on your most important strengths and make it a priority to address your most pressing weaknesses.[46]

Evaluating External Factors

Opportunities are external factors that will likely make you more successful. Opportunities include:

- Emerging competitors
- Changing market conditions
- Negative publicity

Threats are potentially harmful external factors that you cannot control. Threats include:

- Emerging competitors
- Changing market conditions
- Negative publicity[47]

When evaluating threats and opportunities, use the following metrics.

- *Importance.* To what extent will it impact business? Assign a ranking from 1 (no impact) to 10 (very high impact).
- *Probability.* How likely is it that the opportunity or threat will have any impact on business? Rate each threat and opportunity from 1 (low probability) to 3 (high probability).
- *Score.* Importance multiplied by probability will enable you to assign a priority to each opportunity and threat when completing your strategic plan.[48]

What are your strengths, weaknesses, opportunities, and threats? You will have an opportunity to perform a SWOT analysis on yourself in Toolkit Activity 5.1.

Comparing Five Forces and SWOT

Both Porter's five forces and SWOT analyses are useful tools for strategic planning, and both help in assessing your company's strengths and weaknesses relative to industry opportunities and challenges. The primary difference is that SWOT focuses more on company-specific elements, while five forces involves a look at five industry-important competitive factors when making a strategic decision.

Another major distinction between the two is that a SWOT analysis is a general, overall assessment, while five forces is typically focused on a single growth decision. You might start with SWOT to paint the picture of your company's current position in the marketplace and then look ahead to future strategic options. Then, five forces provides a tool to assess the viability of expansion of a particular product, service, or industry. You can weigh diversification into a product category using five forces, for instance.

In short, SWOT is about your business and its position, and five forces is a tool you use to analyze competitors and how they could inhibit you. Generally, the best opportunities for a business lie in situations where a company's strengths relative to the competition align with its opportunities and less inhibiting competitive factors. Time orientation is also slightly different with SWOT and five forces. With SWOT, you assess your current position and future endeavors. Five forces is centered mostly on future decisions.

When your organization chooses the five-forces model or SWOT, the most important thing is to support strategic planning with regular **environmental scans**. Constant measurement and assessment will help you develop robust strategic plans. Here are some ways to take stock of your organization and the marketplace, both internally and externally:

- Interview stakeholders both within the company and outside it
- Conduct surveys and focus groups
- Assess internal programs regularly
- Use industry standards and trends to benchmark your organization's performance[49]

CRITICAL THINKING QUESTIONS

Compare five-forces and SWOT analysis. What are the similarities and differences? Would you use one of them or combine them? Explain your strategy.

Once the five-forces and/or SWOT analysis is completed, internally and externally, and the competitive advantage is solidified, it is time for the organization to set up goals and objectives based on this information. These are the **prescriptive**, or how-to-get-the-job-done, parts of a strategic plan. The next learning objective will help you understand the importance of applying critical thinking to these elements, since they are the road map, or GPS app, that get you to your mission and purpose.

Goals and Objectives

Learning Objective 5.5: Set feasible goals and objectives for your strategic plan.

Goals, in strategic planning, are broad accomplishments you hope to hit. If you have ever watched or participated in archery, you can think of goals as the whole target—a big round circle you want to hit. **Objectives**, on the other hand, are what you want to get done, with specific terms attached. Typically you think of yourself as being "goal-oriented," but in strategic planning the objectives are what you aim for—the bull's-eyes.

Table 5.2 shows an easy way to remember the difference when you are planning.[50]

For example, one goal for this textbook might be that it makes it easy to understand how to write an effective strategic plan. Our objective tied to that is that it will increase the number of college students who can write an effective strategic plan by 20,000 students at the end of 2021.

The challenge to writing your goals and objectives is that you need to make sure each piece follows the road map, like the one you set up for your beach trip, and will lead you to your mission and vision. That means you need to consider all your environment analyses and your competitive advantage, put them into goals, and beneath the goals write specific objectives to reach those goals. Additionally, it is imperative on managers and leaders to make sure all the organization's employees understand the objectives and have the resources they need to fulfill them, thus leading to accomplishment of your mission. It is a beautiful thing when a plan comes together.

▼ TABLE 5.2

Goals Versus Objectives

Goals are broad	Objectives are narrow
Goals are general intentions	Objectives are precise
Goals are intangible	Objectives are tangible
Goals are abstract	Objectives are concrete
Goals are generally difficult to measure	Objectives are measurable

Source: Tips for writing goals and objectives. (n.d.). Retrieved from https://www.google.com/search?q=Tips-for-writing-goals-and-objectives.pdf.&oq=Tips-for-writing-goals-and-objectives.pdf.&aqs=chrome..69i57j69i60.9813j0j4&sourceid=chrome&ie=UTF-8.

SWOT stands for strength, weakness, opportunity, and threat.

Shutterstock.com

Objectives

Objectives are based on SMART goals (goals that are clear and attainable), like the acronym spells out below:

- **S**pecific (simple, sensible, significant)
- **M**easurable (meaningful, motivating)
- **A**chievable (agreed, attainable)
- **R**elevant (reasonable, realistic and resourced, results based)
- **T**ime bound (time based, time limited, time/cost limited, timely, time sensitive) [51]

However, in strategic planning, these criteria are applied to your objectives rather than your goals. For example, you may want "to earn five A's by the end of the semester." All objectives in this plan are **s**pecific, **m**easurable, **a**chievable (if you're not starting with D's), and **r**elevant (A's are pretty good) and have a **t**arget date. You will learn more about SMART goals in Chapter 10 of this textbook.

Management by Objectives (MBO)

There is a popular theory often used to aid in the development of strategic objectives and goals, called management by objectives (MBO). It was developed by management writer Peter Drucker as a **performance management** approach in which a balance is sought between the objectives of employees and the objectives of an organization. [52] The basic principle involves determining joint objectives between members of the organization and providing feedback on the results. Setting challenging but attainable objectives promotes the motivation and empowerment of employees. By increasing commitment, managers are given the opportunity to focus on new ideas and innovation that contribute to the development and objectives of organizations. The MBO process cycle is shown in Figure 5.4.

A student whose company used MBO in their strategic planning recently shared this story in management class:

My company executives sat down and came up with the entire strategic plan for our organization. When they shared the plan, particularly the goals and objectives, with those of us who had to meet them, we just laughed. Even if we ran our production floor 24 hours a day, seven days a week, every day of the year, with no maintenance needed, the capacity of our machines to meet those objectives was impossible. We tried to explain that to them and showed them the numbers, and calculated how many new machines we would need to reach the objectives and goals. They did not believe us and said we just need to work harder. It was the perfect case of management not communicating with the other departments they needed in order to reach their objectives.

The big challenge—and often the fatal flaw—in the MBO system, then, is neglecting what Drucker sets as the conditions that must be met to successfully use MBO as a planning tool:

▼ FIGURE 5.4

Management by Objectives Process

- Set organizational objectives
- Set employee objectives and align to organizational objectives
- Monitor performance
- Assess performance
- Reward satisfactory performance

Source: (2018). Management by objectives. Retrieved from http://tierrasalto.com/management-by-objectives/.

- Objectives that are determined with the employees
- Objectives that are formulated at both the quantitative and qualitative level
- Objectives that are challenging and motivating
- Daily feedback on the state of affairs at the level of coaching and development instead of static management reports
- Rewards (recognition, appreciation, and/or performance-related pay) for achieving the intended objectives
- A basic principle of growth and development, not punishments[53]

As you scrolled down Drucker's guidelines, you probably quickly recognized that your management colleague's company used none of Drucker's conditions in setting their employees' and organization's objectives.

While this is just one example, MBO has been poorly implemented since as early as 1977, when a survey of Fortune 500 companies showed that only 120 had ever tried MBO; that of these, only 30% discussed their objectives as often as once a month; and that only 10 felt they had highly successful applications![54] Other researchers citing the failure of MBO are numerous,[55] but some organizations continue using and citing MBO as their objective generator, despite the evidence against its successful implementation.

Why does MBO, a practical tool in theory but mishap in application, fail so often? Researcher J. W. Leonard cites communication as the key factor in determining the success or failure of MBO programs. Successful MBO systems are participative, and it is suggested that all phases of MBO should be objectives oriented, have a problem-solving focus, and be conducted with effective communication and feedback. The discernible stages of successful MBO processes should be identified, emphasizing the importance of friendly, helpful supervisors and mature, honest subordinates and a climate of high mutual trust.[56] Think about Leonard's theory, and then the research results cited before that about MBO failure. It sounds as if communication and participation are things organizations like to think they do well, but the final results of MBO plans do not seem to bear that out.

Now that you have a good understanding of the components, development, application, and best and worst practices of strategic planning, let's focus on the strategic-planning end game.

Long-Term Objective Formulation

There are really two types of long-term objectives you will need to consider: **long-term financial** objectives and **long-term growth-related objectives**.[57] Common long-term financial objectives include increasing revenue, increasing profit margins, retrenching in times of hardship, and earning a return on investment.[58] Long-term growth-related objectives usually include specific improvements in the organization's competitive position, technology leadership, profitability, return on investment, employee relations and productivity, and corporate image.[59]

To help short-term and long-term planning, the strategic-planning research literature identifies knowledge management as a critical part of the process. **Knowledge management** (the process, cycle, and discipline of knowledge acquisition, knowledge creation, knowledge sharing, and knowledge application) determines organizational performance,[60] and financial performance is determined by organizational performance.[61] This implies that an organization has to convert its desired financial performance into organizational performance to know how much strategic knowledge and intelligence are needed. You will learn more about knowledge management throughout this textbook.

W hat's the first step for a CIO (chief information officer) contemplating the hire of a knowledge management (KM) professional? A lot of executives incorrectly position knowledge management within the information systems (IS) group, so perhaps the CIO should not be the one looking!

At most companies, high-ranking KM positions such as that of the chief knowledge officer, or CKO, should be on par with that of the CIO. Knowledge management is exactly that, a management function, and it impacts the entire organization. That said, there is a strong link between KM personnel and those in IS. Many CKOs came from the information technology (IT) arena, and technology remains a key enabler for most KM projects, such as resource databases and expert yellow pages.

And to be realistic, most companies don't have the deep pockets or organizational heft necessary to support a stand-alone KM department. For those who aren't interested in a full-blown KM strategy, a smaller investment can still prove worthwhile,[62] like the two different positions the organizations are seeking in the post listed below. After each title is the job description, then the minimum requirements.

Knowledge Management Engineer

Job Description:

Qualified candidates for the position of Knowledge Management Engineer will design and deploy Knowledge Management and Collaboration solutions to enhance productivity and operational effectiveness of the organization. This KM-focused role will be responsible for gathering requirements from each functional area within the organization and working with developers and key staff to develop and deploy a solution to meet those requirements. An effective solution could be an internally developed product a commercial solution with custom integrations or a combination of both.[63]

Knowledge Engineer, Junior

Job Description:

Assess a DoD organization's information environment and recommend improvements using IT and collaborative tools. Assess the usage of IT capabilities and recommend IT process improvement initiatives. Conduct technical analysis as directed by the government to enable data driven decisions to identify options or validate courses of action in the development and execution of enterprise level services. Provide data supported recommendations on directorate-proposed IT requirements, including utility, integration, and supportability of applications within the enterprise and the Joint Information Environment

(JIE). Develop SharePoint and Knowledge Management tools based in support of user requirements, review and provide recommendations. Support the development of a Knowledge Management strategy in which the organization will centralize data, standardize data elements, share database information, use common IT systems, and expose IT data or services for maximum information sharing. Create, maintain, archive, and present metrics in support of Knowledge Management transformation and process improvement efforts.[64]

Knowledge Management Engineer

Primary Responsibilities:

- Act as a technical SME (Subject Matter Expert) for all Knowledge Management and Collaboration systems within the organization

- Work closely with the program leadership team and developers to design and implement a custom Knowledge Management solution

- Design and Implement a Knowledge Management Solution for the organization using a commercial web-based collaboration platform (Confluence)

- Perform an analysis of alternatives (AoA) on commercially available KM and Collaboration products as needed to stay abreast of the capabilities in the space

- Play a key role in the creation of a DevOps toolset and supporting processes

- Provide database and web application support for existing KM tools[65]

Knowledge Engineer, Junior

Basic Qualifications:

- 2 years of experience in a Knowledge Management or engineering role

- Experience with Microsoft Certified Solutions Developer (MCSD) App Builder or previous MCSD SharePoint Applications

- Knowledge of Joint Staff business processes

- Ability to develop SharePoint and Knowledge Management tools

- Ability to develop point papers and presentations for senior government civilians and military leaders

- Top Secret clearance

- BA or BS degree in Engineering or CS

(Continued)

(Continued)

Additional Qualifications:

- Experience with Joint Staff or other major headquarters staff

- Experience with Joint Staff Directives and management system

- TS/SCI clearance preferred Clearance[66]

Knowledge Management Engineer

Basic Requirements:

- Bachelor's degree

- US citizenship is required and must be able to obtain security clearance.

- At least 3 years of experience designing and implementing Knowledge Management and Collaboration Systems with a focus on software development/deployment use cases.

- Experience designing, implementing, or maintaining workflows within a major KMCM solution (Archer, ServiceNow, JIRA, Demisto, or Phantom, etc.)

- Ability to write and verbally communicate effectively to both technical and non-technical audiences.

- Must have strong problem-solving and analytical skills and demonstrate poise and ability to act calmly and competently in high-pressure, high-stress situations.[67]

The most important step in deciding if you need an executive or a KM engineer, as in the two descriptions listed above, is to figure out how your company processes knowledge. That might sound obvious, but the role of the KM professional should be as important as the role of knowledge in any given organization. But that importance varies widely by company and industry.

Next, look for a broad set of skills. Typically you want big-picture people who have people skills, knowledge of taxonomy, library skills, technology know-how, etc. They don't have to be experts, but they need to be able to move between different areas of the organization effectively.[68]

Now that you can see the need for knowledgeable knowledge managers, you might want to see if your skill set fits. Don't be discouraged by the connections to IT in some cases, but rather be encouraged that the broad set of skills—moving between different areas of the organization, people skills, and so forth—fit a lot of management students and new college graduates.

Discussion Questions

1. What skills do you currently have that you think would fit into a knowledge management position?

2. Why are KM professionals going to keep increasing in value to organizations?

3. What types of organizations do you think need KM professionals the most?

Sources: Adapted from Booz, Allen, Hamilton. (2019). Knowledge management engineer [Job posting]. Retrieved April 19, 2019, from knowledge+management+engineer+job&oq=knowledge+managemen t+engineer+job&aqs=chrome..69i57j0.7777j1j4&sourceid=chrome&ie= UTF-8&ibp=htl;jobs&sa=X&ved=2ahUKEwilkr-TgqXiAhVqmeAKHdP_ B68Qp4wCMAJ6BAgJEB8#fpstate; Hildebrand, C. (n.d.). How to hire a knowledge management professional. Retrieved from https:// searchcio.techtarget.com/tip/How-to-hire-a-knowledge-management-professional; Leidos. (2019, May). Knowledge management engineer—US citizen required [Job posting]. Retrieved from https:// www.ziprecruiter.com/c/Leidos/Job/Knowledge-Management-Engineer-US-CITIZEN-REQUIRED/-in-Chantilly,VA?ojob=1b925b088c 68eda3ee68ce6e0490ee84.

The reason knowledge managers are important is that there is often a difference between the strategic knowledge and intelligence needed and what is available, known as the **intelligence gap**.[69] Another strategic-planning review of the literature contends that strategic intelligence gaps are of two types: macroeconomic and microeconomic.[70] **Strategic knowledge gaps** can be in areas of strategic knowledge management, such as the world of customers, resources, and competencies.[71] Identified strategic gaps in this stage of strategic planning must be filled out to achieve the long-term financial objectives and long-term strategic growth-related objectives.[72] It is impossible to have all the knowledge, but identifying those gaps adds a great deal of value to your strategic-planning process.

This early identification can result in the timely availability of knowledge and intelligence for the strategic management process, and the best way to identify strategic gaps early in order to fix them is by ensuring there is a thorough and extensive feedback loop built into your strategic plan.

Feedback Loop

One final element that was mentioned as a flaw in applying the MBO process, and that often sabotages a good strategic plan, is the lack of feedback. Every good communication system and planning system requires a **feedback loop**. That is, what you put into the system and what comes out as a result is analyzed to make sure it is performing as you intended. If not, you need to go back and find out where the disconnect exists and analyze the next output batch to make sure you fixed the problem.

Once again, technology plays a role here, as both the speed and quality of feedback in the management playbook emerging in the technology industry will have a lot to offer the management world, and at the heart of it is a continuous feedback cycle. This feedback will encourage and even force organizations to continually try new things in the market, testing and rapidly adjusting based on what they learn.[73]

Amazon, as no surprise, is already leading the way with a quantifiable feedback loop. They have set up a system where Amazon's management will have a quantifiable indicator (revenue, or lack thereof) that suggests when their internal tools are significantly lagging behind the competition. Amazon has replaced useless, time-intensive bureaucracy like internal surveys and audits with a feedback loop that generates cash when what they're doing is working—and quickly identifies problems when it isn't. They say money earned is a reasonable approximation of the value you're creating for the world, and Amazon has figured out a way to measure its own value in dozens of previously invisible areas.[74]

In short, managers and leaders will continue to be called on to gather many more data and personnel resources, including knowledge workers, big-data analysts, and strategic problem-solvers. Adding to these challenges of today and tomorrow are new ways to gather and analyze data, like the one Amazon is using, and new ways to view strategic-planning systems that will most likely impact you and your organization.

Chapters 15 will talk more about the ways technology is used in their discussion of the controlling aspect of the management function, but the next section will describe some of the more modern strategic-planning systems and challenges facing managers that differ from the strategic-planning-for-profit model we discussed earlier in this chapter.

Modern Strategic-Planning Considerations

As a manager, you will need to remember that you are walking into a global world connected by technology. That means you will have to be ready for types of strategic planning other than those serving straightforward, for-profit entities. You also need to have knowledge of not-for-profits, big data, wicked problems, emergent strategy formulation, blue-ocean strategy formulation, and corporate social responsibility. This adds even more to your strategic-planning knowledge, but at the same time complicates your work—and potentially the challenges your organization will face.

Not-for-Profit Strategic Planning

Many graduates will enter **not-for-profit organizations (NPOs)** for a variety of reasons, including passion for the mission, building management and leadership skills, and opportunities for advancement. *Not-for-profit* describes a type of organization that does not earn profits for its owners. All of the money earned by or donated to a not-for-profit organization is used in pursuing the organization's objectives and keeping it running.[75]

While these organizations are not in business to please shareholders, they should be in business to benefit stakeholders. While strategic planning and management have long been a part of corporate management practice, the social sector—both public-sector agencies and NPOs—has been slower to embrace those practices, for a variety of reasons. Unlike in the corporate private sector, managers organizing community-based strategic planning must consider different constraints: The process requires collective responses in a highly charged policy and political environment.[76] There is also the emotional aspect of NPOs, which can cloud the judgment of those managing the organization and otherwise participating in the strategic-planning process.

Wicked Strategic Management

Earlier in this chapter, some arguments were made regarding the potential weaknesses of Porter's competitive-advantage theory in today's environment. There are also some arguments to be made about the competency of today's standard strategic-planning models in dealing with what are known as **wicked problems**.

In a world of constant technological and global change, it is not too hard to think that there are some very large and multifaceted problems you are going to face as a manager and leader. The slang for these in strategic management is *wicked problems*. Current models presume reasonable stability in the task environment and in organizational design features. However, complex problems, or wicked problems, are prolific in a global world. They profoundly change the nature of strategic management as leaders face the challenges of an environment of unprecedented interdependence, yet unpredictable forces of chaos and volatility—a landscape of wicked problems.[77]

Researchers, though, rather than blaming undesired results on the failure of strategic management models to handle wicked problems, instead find that the fault often lies with the managers and leaders using them. They argue that regardless of results, executives pursue goals and objectives with a false sense of causation, use feedback filters that exaggerate good news and restrict bad news, and use only token measures to correct faulty design decisions and flawed decision processes. These are pretty strong condemnations of organizational leaders, but they challenge the culpability of the strategic management process.[78]

Big-Data Strategic Management

You were introduced to the concept of big data in Chapter 2 of this textbook. Another question has arisen over whether organizations are ready to handle "big data," and perhaps more importantly, whether big data is as helpful as it seems for organizations. Big data is a special, relatively new segment of business analytics,[79] which is the use of data, analysis, **predictive modeling**, and **fact-based management** to drive decisions and actions.[80] The business analytics domain originated at the same time as computers in the late 1940s. It is closely related to statistics and is classified into three main categories: descriptive analytics, **predictive analytics**, and prescriptive analytics. **Descriptive analytics** displays "What happened?" predictive analytics identifies "What will probably to happen?" and **prescriptive analytics** advises on "What should we do about it?"[81]

The importance of big data to the future of strategic planning cannot be stressed enough. In fact, there will more information about the amazing elements, and drawbacks, of Big Data in the control chapters of the book. Internal and external environmental scans will now often include quantifiable descriptive analytics, fed into a business model algorithm to produce the predictive and prescriptive decisions.[82] Strategic planning will also become even more of a time-sensitive, continual process, likely including modeling for every part of the operation, even personnel resources.

Emergent Strategy

Emergent strategy has taken hold, especially in not-for-profit and social justice organizations, because it applies a more creative and relationship-driven view of developing a strategic plan. In other words, it is people forward.

A book published in 1992, *Leadership and the New Science*,[83] came from the work of Margaret Wheatley and her strategic-planning work with organizational leaders through the lenses of quantum physics, biology, and chaos theory. Her key takeaways, despite the seemingly in-depth theoretical approaches they used, were that:

- Everything is about relationships and critical connections
- Chaos is an essential process we need to engage
- The sharing of information is fundamental for organizational success

Her final conclusion: Vision is an invisible field that binds us together, emerging from relationships and chaos and information. This is a rather simple and commonsense finding, but one that organizations shy away from, probably because relationships, chaos, and information-sharing tend to be human stressors, particularly in the workplace.

While this is certainly a sharp departure from the discussion of big data and quantitative analysis, you might have noticed throughout this chapter that regardless of which part of the strategic-planning process is being addressed, it always involves the importance of people, relationships, and feedback, just as Wheatley discovered—despite using a quantum-theory lens.

Adrienne Maree Brown used Wheatley's book as a basis for her own book, *Emergent Strategy: Shaping Change, Changing Worlds*. Brown discusses the principles she has seen emerge through her own experiences, as well as the continuing work of Wheatley and others:

- Small is good, small is all. (The large is a reflection of the small, break it down!)
- Change is constant. (Think flowing water.)
- There is always enough time for the right work. (Putting out fires or preventing them?)
- There is a conversation in the room that only these people at this moment can have. Find it.
- Never a failure, always a lesson. (The goal is not always the goal—find it as well.)
- Trust the people! Trust the people! Trust the people! (If you trust, they become trustworthy—this is the definition of trust!)
- Move at the speed of trust. Focus on critical connections more than critical mass—build the resilience by building the relationships.
- Less prep, more presence.
- What you pay attention to grows. (Gardens, relationships, skill building, etc.)[84]

Brown's emergent strategy might provide an excellent overlay to strategic planning in general, since regardless of how wicked or complex or quantifiable organizational problems and challenges get, it always comes back to the stakeholders involved.

Blue-Ocean Strategic Planning

Systematic strategic thinking about market-creating value propositions establishes a basis for conceiving and developing product or service innovations that will appeal to both current and new customers. **Blue-ocean strategy** aims to create products or services that enjoy little competition, precisely because they meet a need that is not being met—the so-called "blue oceans" of profitability.[85]

Market-creating value propositions involve a shift in thinking from the known to the unknown—from existing products to potential products, and from users to nonusers of the firm's products. This in turn means that organizations must redefine how needs are being met and, in the process, discover value for customers from offering something or doing something that the company or the industry currently doesn't provide.

This also means a shift from thinking of outputs of the organization to thinking of outcomes for the customer or end user. Customers are making fewer purchases to accumulate physical things and more purchases to achieve outcomes, convenience, and value.[86]

The final section talks about profit, but perhaps not in the way you have been taught to think about profit so far in your education.

CRITICAL THINKING QUESTIONS

> Why is the issue of trust so important in strategic planning? What are some of the big movements that will impact how you, as a manager and leader, prepare an effective strategic plan? Why is your attention drawn to these particular movements?

Understanding Profit and the 3Ps in Strategic Planning

Learning Objective 5.6: Understand planning for profit versus the 3Ps in strategic-planning outcomes.

At the end of the day, the completion of strategic planning is positively associated with a firm's profitability.[87] This makes strategic planning a crucial part of a manager's position, since of all the economic agents of a firm, corporate managers are the most likely targets for both internal and external pressure to create shareholder value, and they tend to adopt strategies in response to these pressures.[88] Therefore, whether looking at standard models, wicked-problem models, big data–driven models, emergent strategy models, or blue-ocean planning, it is important to keep in mind that the end result of all this planning is profit based.

Profit is a financial benefit that is realized when the amount of revenue gained from business activity exceeds the expenses, costs, and taxes needed to sustain the activity.[89] However, just like all the other parts of strategic planning, the concept of profit has become more complex in the last 20 years. At the turn of the millennium, the world's political leadership adopted **sustainable development** as a leading model for societal development,[90] which, of course, has a profound impact on strategic development. Unfortunately, this move to **corporate social responsibility** (CSR), the integration by companies of social and environmental concerns into their business operations and into their interaction with their stakeholders,[91] was proposed only as a voluntary move by each organization.

The original idea of the triple bottom line (social, environmental, and stakeholder concerns) is attributed to John Elkington.[92] It is now often referred to as the 3Ps—people, planet, and profit—highlighting the responsibility of a company toward stakeholders rather than shareholders.[93] This is a critical difference, as the term **shareholder** is typically used to describe people who own shares in publicly traded U.S. companies, which comprise less than 1% of overall U.S. companies.[94] **Stakeholders**, on the other hand, are present in all organizations, and as defined in Chapter 3, are the people inside and outside an organization who are impacted by the organization's behaviors and practices.

While Porter has been recognized as the contemporary founder and continuing developer of organizational strategy, he was also an early proponent of combining the economic and social issues facing an organization with the quest for profit. In *The Competitive Advantage of Nations*,[95] Porter theorizes that economic and social issues are inextricably connected. Attempting to separate the two is not only impossible but counterproductive. A successful economy depends on having a workforce that is healthy, has incentives to do better, and is employed in a safe environment where they feel valued. For the economy to thrive, the well-being of the workforce must be protected. A successful economy provides workers with safe working conditions, incentives to improve and compete, and respect that enables them to feel valued and motivated.

Often socialism and capitalism are pitted against one another and described as mutually exclusive. But what if they can be combined into a hybrid economic system? This question is at the heart of Porter's project. Porter set out to see if there was a way to protect both the environment and the economy. He discovered something incredible: If environmental standards are properly configured and adopted, they will incite innovation.

Consider, for example, a textile factory. Traditional mindsets would have you believe that there is a trade-off between the essential products made in the factory and its negative impact on the environment. If you accept this trade-off as a given, you either allow the production to continue unfettered and harm the environment, or you advocate regulations that will lessen that impact but add to the cost of production and reduce output. But what if you rejected the notion of a trade-off altogether? What if you pressured organizations to design their production processes with reduced pollution from the start? What if you incentivized innovation in this area? According to Porter, you would find that this approach saves the environment and saves money.[96]

Although the premise of incorporating the 3Ps into an organization's strategic plan has a fairly long history, as well as support from strategy theorists and empirical researchers, and has been adopted as the model for development by world governments for nearly 20 years, the CSR dimensions (3Ps) have not moved forward much, as viable accounting systems quantifying their impact are extremely complex, particularly in highly developed countries.

An excellent example of the complexities involved in 3Ps calculations are evident in a recent study in Nepal, which is currently completely rebuilding parts of its infrastructure after a massive earthquake in 2015.

All this rebuilding requires government and organization cooperation in developing strategic plans that protect people, places, and profits. Yet, a short excerpt from a recent article shows just how difficult this is:

> The level of understanding about CSR of our business community, socio-economic problems such as unemployment and poverty, religion and belief system certainly have a visible or invisible impact in analyzing and understanding CSR concept and dimensions. Moreover, the small number of business houses mostly family owned and their profit-making attitudes are the key factors to effect on CSR intention of Nepalese companies. In addition, perennial political instability, interrupted supply of electricity and power are also the reasons why our business community is more focused on making easy money. Of the 23.1 million people, 1.5 million of working age youths are totally unemployed. Almost 27 per cent of people are below the poverty line. The quality of governance at all level of government is still regarded as poor because of frequent changes of the government and weak reinforcement of rules and regulations.[97]

CRITICAL THINKING QUESTIONS

What approach would you use to tackle Nepal's challenges from a strategic-planning process? What are other dimensions of the 3Ps that might impact Nepal's rebuilding? How does strategic planning in Nepal differ from strategic planning in your country of origin?

Even this quick synopsis brings to mind the many, many dimensions and decisions that the developers, government officials, contractors, and people have to make when trying to incorporate all the stakeholders in planning and implementation, and the complications and intricacies involved with each decision.[98]

While the dimensions of the 3Ps and their role in CSR when it comes to definition and categorization will continue to evolve, research results confirm that CSR strategy is positively valued by investors and other stakeholders and lowers the cost of capital (i.e., the cost of borrowing money). Interestingly and sadly, however, the same study found that some organizations use CSR as a way to mask earnings management (EM); that is, they cover up lower or poor earnings by highlighting the positive aspects of CSR.[99]

Another study on employee impacts of a company practicing CSR showed a positive relation between CSR and employee performance, suggesting that employees in socially responsible companies generate better operating performance than their peers in less socially responsible companies. However, findings also revealed that socially responsible companies incur higher labor costs.[100]

Managerial Implications

This chapter provided an overview of the importance of good strategic management and how it is constantly evolving as both an academic discipline and as a reflection of management practice.[101] Throughout the chapter were many reminders about the never-ending process of reviewing your organization's vision, mission, competitive advantage, and values, all while constantly scanning the internal and external environments for changes and impending changes. There is also the tough question of whether you are managing for profit or managing for the 3Ps.

Your takeaways from this chapter should include:

- How to effectively develop a strategic plan for any organization
- How to determine where your competitive advantage and values lie
- What sources to use to develop goals and objectives to meet your organization's vision and mission (purpose), using your competitive advantage and values as a basis

There are many ways to develop a strategic plan, constant new challenges to consider, and numerous solutions that may be implemented. Job opportunities for knowledge managers, big-data analysts, and problem-solvers are vast. Through diligent attention to planning and change, your organization has a much better chance of remaining effective and sustainable in the fast-changing global environment—as do you.

KEY TERMS

blue-ocean strategy   152
competitive advantage   138
cost leadership   138
descriptive analytics   151
differentiation   138
emergent strategy   151
environmental scans   145

fact-based management   151
feedback loop   149
five-forces analysis   141
goals   145
intelligence gap   149

knowledge management   147
long-term financial objectives   147
long-term growth-related objectives   147
mantra   135
mission statement   134

TOOLKIT

Activity 5.1

SWOT Yourself

Take a large, blank sheet of paper and divide it into four quadrants. Now label each one just like you would for an organization—Strengths, Weaknesses, Opportunities, and Threats—and do your own SWOT analysis. Think about yourself. Who are you? What is your purpose? What is your competitive advantage over others? When you walk into a job interview and they say, "Why should we hire you over the other candidates?" what will you say?

Conducting a personal SWOT analysis helps you figure this out. Remember, before you start, you need:

1. Your vision:

_____

_____

_____

2. Your mission:

_____

_____

_____

3. Your competitive advantage:

_____

_____

_____

These answers will drive your SWOT analysis, but they are tough. To give you some inspiration for this project, watch this YouTube video of a speech given at a high school graduation that has gone viral: https://www.youtube.com/watch?v=_IfxYhtf8o4.[102] Listen carefully to the speaker, and compare notes with your classmates.

In addition, watch the Guy Kawasaki video mentioned earlier in the chapter: https://www.youtube.com/watch?v=2A2-7_nujtA.[103] Between the two videos, you should be able come up with the critical information you need to complete your SWOT analysis.

Discussion Questions

1. What is your mantra?
2. Why does knowing what makes you special give you a competitive advantage over others?
3. After completing the personal SWOT template, what categories do you have the most posts in?
4. Write out your goals and objectives in your SWOT to help you achieve and strengthen your current positions.
5. Now, using what you learned in the chapter, write out your three most important and timely goals below, as well as the objectives you will use to accomplish your goals (SMART).

   ○ Goal:
   ○ Objective:
   ○ Goal:
   ○ Objective:
   ○ Goal:
   ○ Objective:

Discussion Questions

1. What did you learn from assessing your SWOT?
2. How confident are you in addressing what you learned with the skills you have now?
3. How will having a personal SWOT analysis and objectives help you in the short term and long term?

Activity 5.2

How Much Do Your Core Values Matter to the Organization?

Part I. Completing the Activity

Instructions: Circle the response that best describes your behavior. This is not a test, and there are no right or wrong answers. You don't have to share your results with others unless you wish to do so.

Statements	Strongly Disagree	Disagree	Neutral	Agree	Strongly Agree
1. I never assume my employees know what is expected.	1	2	3	4	5
2. I encourage my staff to ask questions when in doubt.	1	2	3	4	5
3. I support my employees by offering help, resources, support, and information.	1	2	3	4	5
4. I make it a habit to support my employees even when they make mistakes.	1	2	3	4	5
5. I believe that for my team to exceed their current performance, I must assist the members to maximize their individual skills.	1	2	3	4	5
6. I believe in taking time to explain my vision and goals in detail to my employees.	1	2	3	4	5
7. I believe in taking time to get to know those who work for me (likes/dislikes, work preferences, and feelings about the job and company).	1	2	3	4	5
8. I support the notion that it is okay for my employees to fail as long as they learn from it.	1	2	3	4	5
9. I don't believe in "knee-jerk" responses when dealing with on-the-job surprises.	1	2	3	4	5
10. I believe in maintaining employee confidentiality.	1	2	3	4	5
11. I believe in encouraging my employees to question solutions to work-related problems they did not participate in resolving.	1	2	3	4	5
12. As a communicator, I make it a practice to listen more than I talk when working on employee-related issues.	1	2	3	4	5

Part II. Scoring Instructions

In this chapter we discussed the importance of values when developing an organization's strategic plan. Values, however, were also clearly noted as individual traits, meaning that individuals in an organization build the foundation on which the larger entity's values rest.

Research bears out that managers impact their employees' values. Results indicate that supervisors' business moral values are positively associated with subordinates' business moral values,[104] and that employees' perceptions of shared values in an organization affect customer-directed extra-role behaviors.[105] Extra-role behaviors are OCBs, and this research supports the earlier findings that ethical values in an organization's culture promote OCBs among its employees,[106] and additionally that in the aggregate, these behaviors have a major beneficial impact on organizational operations and effectiveness.[107]

Looking back over your answers to the core-values survey, mark your responses to each question in the blocks below by question number:

Strategic Planning Skills/Survey Questions	1	2	3	4	5
1. Clarity of expectations					
2. Questions					
3. Resources and information					
4. Support					
5. Skill building					
6. Vision and goals					
7. Relationships					
8. Innovation					
9. Stability					
10. Trust					
11. Challenges					
12. Communication					

Now when you read the survey questions, think about applying these core values to your team as their manager:

You will notice that many words used throughout this chapter are critical to effective strategic planning; communication, resources, values, knowledge management, information gaps, vision, goals, relationships, innovation, and listening are inherent in this self-assessment. You have also been presented with several sets of research findings that support the "value" of values in an organization.

Finally, there are very few things you can count on in life, but using values to drive successful strategic planning processes is probably a pretty good one,[108] and these values being a critical part of what you bring to the organization, are probably one of them.

Discussion Questions

In dealing with your strategic planning team:

1. What skills do you feel will be your strengths?
2. Which skills might be your weaknesses?
3. In what areas do you feel you have the most opportunities to grow?

In the box below, write an overall assessment of how you feel you will be as a team leader in strategic-plan development:

Sources: Adapted from Minter, R., & Thomas, E. (2000). Employee development through coaching, mentoring and counseling: A multidimensional approach. Review of Business, 21(1/2), 43–47; National Press Publications. (2001). The manager's role as coach: A coach guidebook. Shawnee Mission, KA: National Press.

Case Study 5.1

Did Transgenerational Response Cause Yahoo to Fail?

A lot can go wrong in business. Sometimes, products fail spectacularly. Even the most successful organizations are vulnerable to market disruption or bad publicity or ethical scandals that send customers scattering. Organizations that survive such traumatic reversals often attempt a comeback. Typically, they start over from scratch with new strategic plans and a leadership overhaul. But what happens when it doesn't work, when the fresh start flops or the new CEO fails, and the firm continues to underperform? This type of scenario could be caused by a "transgenerational response, a potentially crippling long-term condition stemming from the trauma that occurred in the past."[109]

The term *transgenerational response syndrome* is borrowed from a biological theory, but it can also apply to the business world. In biology, the syndrome occurs when a catastrophic environmental condition affects an organism. The catastrophe triggers a negative adaptive response. The adaptation is passed on to future generations, impacting their growth and health. For example, a grandparent's death (Generation 1) during childhood (Generation 2) can impact the birth of a child

(Generation 3) including low birth weight and premature birth. This shows that trauma has a way of reverberating through families, impacting the physical and mental wellbeing of descendants for generations.[110]

One study examined the babies of mothers who experienced post-traumatic stress disorder (PTSD) during pregnancy as a result of the World Trade Center attack in 2001.[111] This illuminating clinical research demonstrated that some of the effects of maternal PTSD were actually passed on to the babies. For example, the babies suffered low birth weight, increased response to stress, and a lasting increased risk for depression and other stress-induced conditions.

What About Organizations?

Businesses that survive chaos and seemingly rebuild only to be plagued by chronic performance problems may very well be demonstrating a transgenerational response to events that occurred years ago, too. When an organization struggles, it sometimes adapts by becoming risk averse. After a tragic failure, companies often seek out new C-suite execs to rescue them. Initially, they set out to get their heads above water and become profitable again through re-orgs and cost-cutting measures. Once they have come up for air, companies can start focusing not just on surviving but thriving. But if successive CEOs still can't manage sustainable success, it's possible that the trouble is, in fact, a transgenerational response.[112] When leadership is able to evaluate underperformance as a potential transgenerational response, they have data that will enable them to problem solve more effectively. By tracing the problem to its origins—the initial traumatic failure—they can potentially find a cure.

Going back to biology, humans that suffer trauma often do not recognize the full impact the trauma has on them. That creates an environment where either the people deal with the problem when the recognition is evident, or worse, do not deal with it at all. This is the same in organizations. Lingering effects of trauma can be detrimental to a company's ability to meet new challenges and, if CEOs don't address them swiftly, they can continue to hinder the management of the company for the foreseeable future.

Conventional crisis management wisdom prioritizes systematic problem solving through pre-planning, rehearsing, and swift reaction to high-priority problems. But this might not be practical for companies suffering from a transgenerational response to past trauma. In these situations, execs cannot simply solve the most immediate problems. Rather, they have to think long term and anticipate how their immediate actions will affect the organization's future.[113]

There are many variables that can cause an organization to experience a transgenerational response, such as terrorism, war, financial crisis, and corporate irresponsibility. These traumas become entrenched and draw on unconscious motives and work through unseen mechanisms. This helps explain why leaders, despite their best business attempts, might not be able to turn around an organization suffering this crisis.[114]

In order to try and overcome these types of embedded psychological impediments, however, leaders can try working through the same type of list a therapist would:

1. Identify a critical incident
These incidents are clearly identifiable and result in subsequent corporate effects and consequences that affect the viability and development of the firm. The initial review of corporate crisis situations ranges from scandals to disasters.

2. What is a corporate generation?
A corporate generation starts with a new CEO and ends when he or she leaves the organization. The average tenure of an American CEO is 9.9 years.[115] When a CEO's tenure is much shorter, it could be a sign of underperformance. An organization plagued by a traumatic failure that then hires and fires several CEOs in a short interval of time could be experiencing transgenerational response effects.[116]

3. Measuring the chronic problem
Chronic corporate underperformance has three hallmarks:

- Persistent declines in market share
- Dramatic reduction in operating include
- Decreasing share price in the stock market[117]

Yahoo Inc.

In 2008, Microsoft Corporation attempted to acquire Yahoo for $44.6 billion.[118] The maneuver was intended as a defense mechanism against Google's expanding empire and market dominance, but it fell apart rapidly. Microsoft and Yahoo could not reach an agreement about the valuation, and Yahoo has been underperforming since this Critical Corporate Incident.[119]

Since the Critical Corporate Incident, a whopping six CEOs have taken charge at Yahoo. The transgenerational fallout seems to have doomed them all.[120] While Google has been dominating the market and innovating with impressive results, Yahoo has remained trapped in a cycle of underperformance.

Since the Critical Corporate Incident in 2008, Yahoo's performance has been up and down. The long-term share price performance of Yahoo compared with Google (Alphabet Inc.) and the NASDAQ also reflects a mostly sluggish performance by Yahoo. There is one outlier, though. Yahoo's EBIT number has grown significantly since 2008, showing that the organization can generate earnings from operations.[121]

Discussion Questions

1. What good reasons does Yahoo have for blaming their failures on transgenerational impact?
2. Why do you think Yahoo's financial performance lags behind other tech companies the same age in most financial categories, but not EBIT (earnings before interest and taxes)?
3. What are your thoughts on transgenerational response impact, and what other world events could cause this phenomena?

Source: Oliver, J. (2017). Is "transgenerational response" a hidden cause of failed corporate turnarounds and chronic underperformance? *Strategy and Leadership*, 45(3), 23–29. Retrieved from https://umw.idm.oclc.org/login?url=https://search.proquest.com/docview/1908722411?accountid=12299.

Self-Assessment 5.1

Time Perspectives and Strategic Planning

This self-assessment exercise identifies how you perceive time. The way time is viewed predicts risk-taking, motivation, and goal attainment. The goal of this assessment is for you to learn about your general assumptions about time and to understand how this may affect your strategic planning. There are no right or wrong answers, and this is not a test. You don't have to share your results with others unless you wish to do so.

Part I. Taking the Assessment

Instructions: Circle the response that best describes you.

Statements	Very Uncharacteristic	Uncharacteristic	Neutral	Characteristic	Very Characteristic
1. I often think of what I should have done differently in my life.	1	2	3	4	5
2. I do things impulsively.	1	2	3	4	5
3. When I want to achieve something, I set goals and consider specific means for reaching those goals.	1	2	3	4	5
4. It gives me pleasure to think about my past.	1	2	3	4	5
5. Since whatever will be, will be, it doesn't really matter what I do.	1	2	3	4	5
6. Painful past experiences keep replaying in my mind.	1	2	3	4	5
7. I try to live my life as fully as possible, one day at a time.	1	2	3	4	5
8. Meeting tomorrow's deadlines and doing other necessary work comes before tonight's play.	1	2	3	4	5
9. Happy memories of good times spring readily to mind.	1	2	3	4	5
10. You can't really plan for the future because things change so much.	1	2	3	4	5
11. I've made mistakes in the past that I wish I could undo.	1	2	3	4	5
12. I make decisions on the spur of the moment.	1	2	3	4	5
13. I am able to resist temptations when I know there is work to be done.	1	2	3	4	5
14. I get nostalgic about my childhood.	1	2	3	4	5
15. It doesn't make sense to worry about the future, since there is nothing I can do about it anyway.	1	2	3	4	5

Part II. Scoring Instructions

In Part I, you rated yourself on 15 questions. Add the numbers you circled in each of the columns to derive your score for different time perspectives. We will discuss each approach and how it might affect your strategic planning.

Past-Negative	Present-Hedonistic	Future	Past-Positive	Present-Fatalistic
1. _____	2. _____	3. _____	4. _____	5. _____
6. _____	7. _____	8. _____	9. _____	10. _____
11. _____	12. _____	13. _____	14. _____	15. _____
Total _____	Total _____	Total _____	Total _____	Total _____

Interpretation:

Scores for each of the time perspectives can range from 3 to 15. If your score is above 7, that perspective may be characteristic of you.

Past-negative: Reflects a generally aversive view of the past. It suggests that a person thinks about bad things that have happened in the past, with regret. They may not be motivated to work for future rewards.

Present-hedonistic: Reflects a hedonistic, risk-taking, "devil-may-care" attitude toward time and life. It suggests an orientation toward present pleasure with little concern for future consequences. A person with this orientation tends to be highly energetic and engage in many activities.

Future: Suggests that behavior is dominated by striving for future goals and rewards. It reflects completing projects on time by making steady progress. People with this orientation are highly organized, ambitious goal-seekers who feel pressed for time. They stand out in terms of planning and efficiency.

Past-positive: Reflects an attitude toward the past that is warm and sentimental. It suggests that you enjoy stories about good times and like family rituals and traditions that are regularly repeated. People with this orientation may be somewhat introverted, yet they get involved in relationships with friends and tend to act in ways that their parents would consider to be "better safe than sorry."

Present-fatalistic: Reveals a fatalistic, helpless, and hopeless attitude toward the future and life. It suggests that a person feels that forces they cannot influence control their path in life. They are intelligent people living in a world that encourages personal self-efficacy. However, they do not believe that anything they do, or will do, is likely to make a difference in their lives.

Discussion Questions

1. What did you learn about how you view time? Are you more focused on the past, the present, or the future? Are you generally positive or negative?
2. Which time perspective(s) do you feel is/are most helpful for a manager who must do strategic planning? Explain your choice(s).
3. Provide an example of when your perspective on time affected your performance in school or work. Was this due to your ability to plan well in advance?

Source: Adapted from Zimbardo, P. G., & Boyd, J. N. (1999). Putting time in perspective: A valid, reliable individual-differences metric. *Journal of Personality and Social Psychology, 77*(6), 1271–1288.

⑤SAGE edge™

Get the tools you need to sharpen your study skills. SAGE edge offers a robust online environment featuring an impressive array of free tools and resources. Access practice quizzes, eFlashcards, video, and multimedia at **edge.sagepub.com/scanduragower**.

ORGANIZING

PART III

ORGANIZATIONAL DESIGN

CHAPTER LEARNING OBJECTIVES

After studying this chapter, you should be able to:

6.1 Articulate the meaning and importance of organizational structure.

6.2 Differentiate between high and low levels of organizational design dimensions.

6.3 Describe the five elements of organizational structure identified by Mintzberg.

6.4 Discuss the advantages and disadvantages of functional, product, geographic, and matrix organizational structures.

6.5 List the major objectives of the three levels of management and provide examples of typical job titles.

6.6 Describe the five properties of jobs in job characteristics theory.

Get the edge on your studies at **edge.sagepub.com/scanduragower.**

- Take the chapter quiz
- Review key terms with eFlashcards
- Explore multimedia resources, SAGE readings, and more!

Structure: Who Needs It?

Google's famous flexible organization structure is known as "heaven on earth" for youthful employees. To keep it nimble, a flat structure was designed to give high-technology employees autonomy and freedom. They can innovate and work on projects they choose during part of their work week. Google calls their colorful headquarters a "campus," and it has a cafeteria with meals and snacks, beanbag chairs, and dog-friendly policies—what more could a young person ask for?

Millennial and Gen Z Appeal

Google's organization was designed to appeal to so-called "Millennials," people born between 1980 and 2000. This is a relatively common range used to define Millennials (plus or minus a few years on either end of the range). Millennials have been characterized as people who want a lot of feedback (particularly positive praise). They are one with their smartphones and embrace technology. They are socially responsible and opinionated and want to be heard.[1]

The Z generation (also known as Gen Z) comprises individuals born between 1995 and 2010 (of course, this range overlaps with the Millennials). Generation Z is the "Net Generation" due to the highly developed digital era they were born into. Generation Z differs from the Millennials in interesting ways. They often use slang and expressions that seem strange to other generations, and this distances them from other groups. Since Generation Z was born into technology, they feel good in the digital world and surround themselves in the online environment. They are constantly online on a variety of devices, without interruptions. They look for new challenges continually, and they are not afraid of change. To solve problems, they search for solutions on the Internet.[2]

One disclaimer is that many of the conclusions drawn about these generational differences suffer from at least one major weakness: "the lack of a workable time machine," according to generational researcher Jeanne Twenge. Twenge explains, "Most studies on generational differences in work values are cross-sectional, with data on workers of different ages collected at one point in time. Thus, any differences could be due to age/career stage or to generation, and it is impossible to separate the two."[3] The interactions of different generations in the workplace will be discussed in greater detail in Chapter 9 of this textbook.

Given the generalizations about Millennials and Generation Z stated above, the assumption that these younger generations prefer the lack of structure and flexibility and

Interior view of Google Visitor Center Beta. The area is open to Google employees and their guests.

©JHVEPhoto/Shutterstock

freedom of Google's organizational design seems reasonable. But is it true?

Compared to previous generations, research is showing that Millennials (at least those born in the mid to late 1990s) are actually reporting a *stronger* desire for the rules, **hierarchy of authority**, clarity, and predictability that structure provides. Although this might be surprising, there is evidence that there has been a generational shift in attitudes toward structure for at least a decade. In a 2007 survey, 72% of Millennials indicated agreement with the statement "I prefer a structured [work] environment with clear rules." Conversely, 67% of respondents from the previous generation (Generation X) *disagreed* with this statement.

Do you prefer more or less structure in the classroom? Andrea Hershatter and Molly Epstein found that the shift in preference for structure among the younger generation appears in college classrooms now. They note: "A common complaint among college professors is the degree to which current students seek clarity and detail in course assignments. Any elements of ambiguity, or any project or exam that requires Millennials to work without guidelines, templates, or examples results in a great deal of angst."[4] Why? The researchers speculate that Millennials "have not had much practice producing without explicit instructions, well defined criteria for success, and specific deadlines set by others."[5]

Do you agree with this explanation? Perhaps the more important question is, what level of structure do *you*, as an individual—not based on whether you are a Millennial or Generation Z—prefer? Self-Assessment 6.1 can help you answer this question.

Sources: Adapted from Deal, J. J., Altman, D. G., & Rogelberg, S. G. (2010). Millennials at work: What we know and what we need to do (if anything). *Journal of Business and Psychology, 25*(2), 191–199; Hershatter, A., & Epstein, M. (2010). Millennials and the world of work: An organization and management perspective. *Journal of Business and Psychology, 25*(2), 211–223.

▼ FIGURE 6.0

Textbook Organization

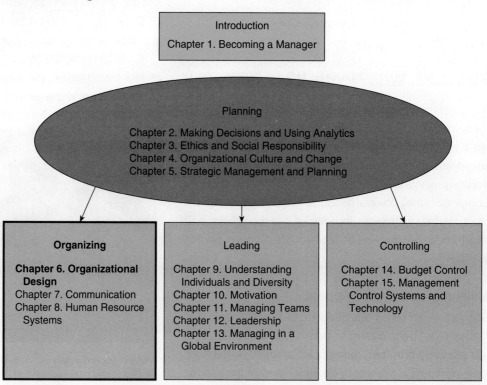

What Is Organizational Structure?

An effective analogy for understanding organizational structure is the blueprints architects use to design buildings.[6] The analogy works because blueprints provide both physical structure (they are used to build the structural frames that hold buildings up) and the intangible forms of structure we discuss in this chapter (they provide instructions, rules, and boundaries that builders must follow). You are probably more familiar with the first (physical) type of structure. Every time you stand up, you rely on your skeletal structure to keep you from falling back down again; every time you get into a car, bus, train, or airplane, you depend on the vehicle's structure to protect you from all the objects flying by at high speeds. Although we rarely think about it, the invisible structure that guides nearly all our behavior to at least some degree is an equally important presence in our lives. This structure is why you are safe driving on the correct side of the road (whichever side that might be in your country) but run a very high risk of collision if you cross the lane and drive on the other side. It is what enables populations to agree that slips of paper, disks of metal, or even just electronic representations of those things can be exchanged for any product or service.

The more you look for organizational structure, the more you will find it. Before reading this chapter, however, it is quite possible that you never gave it much thought. Why is that? One reason is that it is, as we mentioned, largely invisible. Organizations often codify key elements of their structure in writing, but you are unlikely to see drivers holding copies of their local driving laws in their laps or employees walking around with their employee handbooks. We generally commit the most important elements of structure to memory and go about our business. The ubiquity of organizational structure also plays a factor. There is very little about modern life that is not infused with structural rules and systems, to the point that we do not always give it much conscious thought. Think about this course you are enrolled in: Where do you see elements of structure? This book follows the structure laid out in the table of contents; your instructor probably uses a syllabus to structure the course; the course itself probably exists within a larger structure of course requirements and electives. We also become somewhat oblivious to structure due to our own human nature. While humans generally appreciate high levels of personal freedom, most of us also require a degree of structure to thrive in our work lives, as discussed in the opening vignette. Even if we are not aware of it, many of us will even impose structure in situations where it is not required. Here is an example that you might be able to relate to if you are taking this course in a traditional classroom format without assigned seating. Think about where you sat during your last class session. What part of the room? Which desk or chair? Now think back to where you sat during the previous class. How about the very first class of the term? Chances are good that, unless you made a conscious decision to relocate, you gravitate to the same part of the room—maybe even the exact same chair—every time.

CRITICAL THINKING QUESTIONS

What are some examples of structure that you have added to your life without consciously thinking about it? What are some potential pros and cons of doing this?

Why do we do this? Largely because structure provides a level of control and predictability that we would not have without it. With structure, instead of having to figure out the best course of action in every situation we encounter, we can take shortcuts and focus our attention more efficiently.[7] The same is true for organizations.[8] **Organizational structure** refers to the rules, relationships, communication channels, and duties that allow members to work toward their shared goals.[9] Organizational structure has a strong influence on strategic decision-making by the top management team.[10] The rules that guide employees' behaviors and decisions are typically summarized in written documents such as policy manuals, employee handbooks, and training guides. These guidelines reduce **uncertainty** for employees, which is the gap between the amount of information possessed and that required to perform a task.[11] To provide clarity for employees, organizations show the relationships, communication channels, and job duties within a structure in an **organizational chart**, such as the one shown in Figure 6.1 for Apple.

Although this chart was not developed by Apple, it is an accurate depiction of the company's upper-management structure in the last years of the Steve Jobs era (around 2010). The circles and squares identify the positions of each manager, which tell us which responsibilities are delegated to which employees. In this particular chart, the larger and more central shapes represent higher levels of authority. The lines connecting these positions to the smaller shapes farther from the center therefore represent power relationships. These lines typically depict lines of communication as well. For example, Apple's organizational chart indicates that under normal circumstances, the vice president (VP) of iPhone marketing would not report directly to the CEO. Instead, they would communicate directly with the senior vice president (SVP) of marketing, who would in turn report to the CEO. Individuals who are connected through the organizational structure in this way are often called **direct reports**, for this reason. The number of direct reports each person has is referred to as their **span of control**.

Although not included in Apple's chart, many organizations also employ dotted-line connections between two positions. These are used to indicate communication channels that exist without a direct power relationship. **Dotted-line relationships** often occur when an employee can provide useful information to a manager in a different part of an organization's structure.[12] For example, the manager of a company's marketing department might not have any direct authority over the company's engineers. Thus, if providing feedback on technical specifications used in the company's marketing materials is a formal part of the engineers' jobs, this would be represented as a dotted-line relationship.

Organizational structures change over time. Let's follow up on the example of Apple in Figure 6.1, in which the organizational structure was shown for 2010. Figure 6.2 shows Apple's structure in 2018 under the leadership of CEO Tim Cook. You can see that Apple has become more hierarchical as it has grown in size and the number of products it produces has increased. One advantage of this hierarchical organizational structure is tight control over all aspects of the business by the top management team. Also, promotion opportunities are clear and motivate Apple employees. The lines of authority and responsibility are now clearer compared to the structure in 2010. A disadvantage of this structure is that Apple may lose flexibility to respond to changes in the global marketplace. Communication across different departments may also be less effective.[13]

It will be interesting to see if Apple returns to a more decentralized structure in the future to keep pace with technological change and the global competition they face.

While most organizational structures outline these basic elements of rules, responsibilities, relationships, and communication lines, this is often where the similarity ends. This is particularly true in the case of more mature organizations. In their early stages, many start-up companies implement very simple hierarchical structures—often just a few employees led by a single supervisor.[14] As companies grow and evolve, however, so do their structures. There

Apple Computer's Organizational Structure, Circa 2010

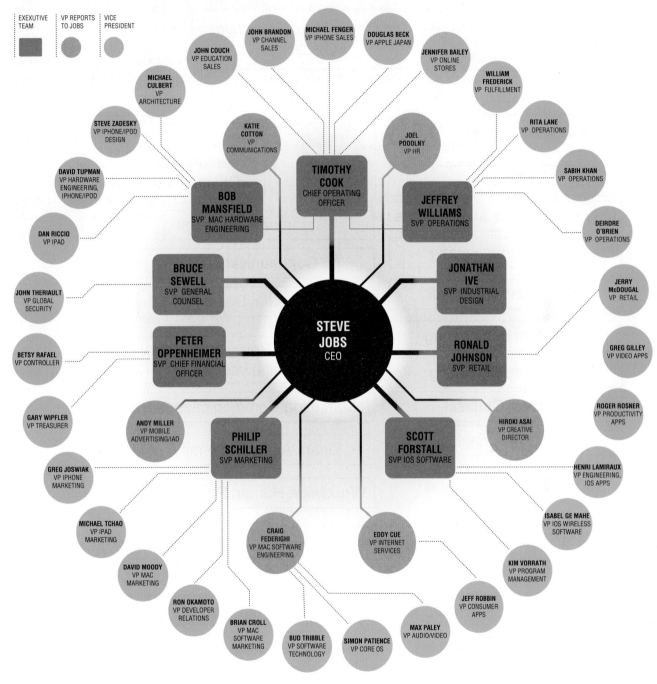

Source: Lashinsky, A. (2011). How Apple works: Inside the world's biggest startup. *Fortune.* Retrieved from http://fortune.com/2011/08/25/how-apple-works-inside-the-worlds-biggest-startup/.

are some common patterns that tend to emerge, as we discuss in the next section, but every organization must grow its structure in accordance with the unique challenges it faces.[15] This process of constructing and adjusting an organization's structure to achieve its goals is called **organizational design**.[16]

Apple's Organizational Structure, Circa 2018

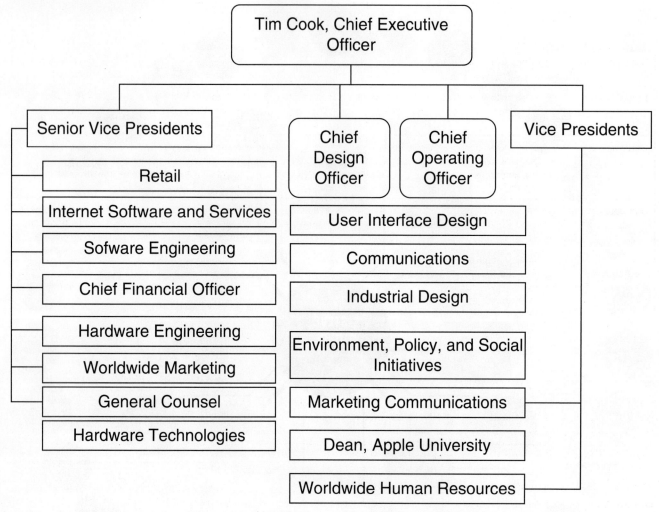

Dimensions of Organizational Design

Learning Objective 6.2: Differentiate between high and low levels of organizational design dimensions.

If you were to sit down and study the structures of several hundred modern companies, you might arrive at the conclusion that they share two traits: *complicated* and *arbitrary*. To some degree, you would be correct on both counts. The full organizational structure of a modern multinational company can be complex and often reflects hundreds or thousands of ad hoc, or as-needed, decisions rather than a carefully laid out plan for growth.

Despite this complex and often haphazard process, researchers have found that organizational design often proceeds in predictable ways. A loose analogy can be drawn between this process and human development. As you know from your own life, children grow into adults through a series of chaotic and unpredictable life experiences. No two childhoods are the same, yet, as we discuss in Chapter 9, the vast majority of people develop personalities that can be summed up with five or fewer traits (e.g., extraversion vs. introversion, Type A vs. Type B).

Dimensions of Organizational Design

	Examples	
	High Levels	Low Levels
Specialization	An automobile assembly plant: Each employee performs a specific task repeatedly.	A craft furniture workshop: Employees are involved in multiple phases of the production process.
Formalization	A bureaucratic government agency in which employees are bound by many rules and procedures.	Many universities: Professors are often given significant latitude in how they structure classes and deliver course material.
Centralization	Chain restaurants such as McDonald's and Burger King: Although franchise owners have some leeway, menu content, pricing, and appearance are largely dictated by central management.	Ride-sharing services such as Uber and Lyft: Drivers are self-employed and have little interaction with central management.
Standardization	Military organizations: Structure is well defined and strictly enforced. The automobile assembly plant example above also reflects a high degree of standardization.	Hair salon/barber shop: Because every customer's hair and style preferences are distinct, stylists and barbers rarely follow the exact same procedure from one customer to the next.
Complexity	Multinational conglomerates such as General Electric: Products include dishwashers, lightbulbs, locomotives, jet engines, windmills, mining equipment, MRI machines, and ultrasound scanners, among many others. Services include financing, consulting, and energy management systems, among others.	Mom-and-pop store or restaurant: Small companies that produce a small number of products/services.

Similarly, researchers have identified five "traits" or dimensions of organizational design that can be used to describe most modern companies.[17] These include specialization, formalization, centralization, standardization, and complexity.

Specialization occurs when jobs are narrowly defined and depend on unique expertise. **Formalization** refers to the amount of rules, regulations, and procedures an organization requires its employees to follow. **Centralization** occurs when most or all key decisions are made by an organization's top leadership rather than by the managers or employees of individual work units. **Standardization** occurs when work is performed in a routine manner, following the same steps each time. Finally, **complexity** describes the range of activities conducted within an organization. A highly complex organization might create hundreds of unique products and provide a range of services as well. Such an organization is likely to require a complex structure to support this wide range of activities, whereas a company producing only one or two products can often utilize a more basic structure. To help you understand these concepts, Table 6.1 provides an illustration of each of these dimensions at low levels of the dimension.

Specialization and standardization: In Shanghai Volkswagen's car factory, new cars are being produced on the assembly line.

©Jenson/Shutterstock

Forms of Organizational Structure

Learning Objective 6.3: Describe the five elements of organizational structure identified by Mintzberg.

Henry Mintzberg described organizations in terms of the various functions of different organizational units, as shown in Figure 6.3.[18] As indicated in the figure, the top management team is at the strategic apex of the organization. They are supported in their decision-making by the technostructure (e.g., operations research), and the support staff (e.g., legal counsel). The technostructure consists of analysts whose job is to standardize the work of others in the organization. The **support staff** provides advisement and guidance (e.g., public relations and legal counsel) and other support for the organization's employees (e.g., the cafeteria workers). The **strategic apex** (top management team) meets organizational goals by directing the **operating core** (i.e., the workers that create products or serve customers) through the **middle line** management. The technostructure and support staff may also provide guidance to middle managers (i.e., the middle line) in the execution of their job duties.

Mintzberg's organizational model also depicts an important principle of organization structure: the separation of overall strategic direction and the management of the operation. In other words, the people who create the strategic mission and general direction of the organization (senior managers in the strategic apex) are different from those who handle the implementation of plans and subsequent controlling of operations to ensure that the strategic mission is accomplished (the middle line managers). Thus, senior managers establish long-term organizational goals and directives. Middle managers (the middle line) are responsible for translating the general strategic plans into detailed action plans, and specifying managerial responsibilities for particular tasks and how resources are to be allocated.[19] Based on the general organizational model of structure described above, Mintzberg developed descriptions of five general types of organizational structures that may emerge.[20] These types are summarized in Table 6.2 and described in the following sections.

▼ FIGURE 6.3

Mintzberg's View of Organizational Structure

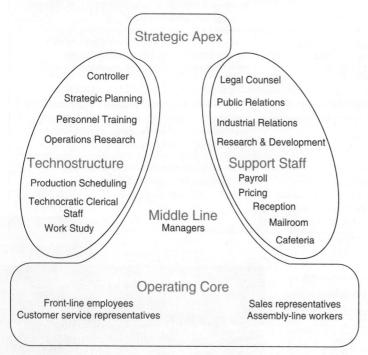

Source: Adapted from Mintzberg H. (1979). *The structuring of organizations: A synthesis of the research.* Englewood Cliffs, NJ: Prentice Hall; Mintzberg's five components of organization: Galbraith's and Mintzberg's technostructure. (n.d.). Retrieved from http://www.ebbemunk.dk/technostructure/technostructurep3.html.

Entrepreneurial Organization

An **entrepreneurial organization** has a simple and flat structure. It consists of one large unit with one or a few top managers. The organization is relatively unstructured and informal compared to other types of organizations, and the lack of standardized systems allows the organization to be flexible. For example, a family business that is carefully controlled by the owner is an example of this type of organization. However, a particularly strong leader may be able to sustain an entrepreneurial organization as it grows. When large companies face hostile conditions, they can revert to this structure to maintain strict control from the top. The entrepreneurial organization is fast, flexible, and lean, and it is a model that many companies want to copy. However, as organizations grow, this structure can be inadequate, as decision-makers can become so overwhelmed that they start making bad decisions. This is when they need to start sharing power and decision-making. Also, when a company's success depends on one or two individuals, there is significant risk if they sell the company, move on to new entrepreneurial ventures, or retire. The entrepreneurial organization, while effective in the founding and early years of the growth of an organization, is vulnerable. As the organization grows, it typically evolves

Research and Development: Employees are part of an organization's support staff.

©iStockphoto.com/poba

Forms of Organizational Structure

Structure Form	Key Features	Advantages	Disadvantages
Entrepreneurial organization	Simple, flat, few top managers	Fast, flexible, lean	Decision-makers overwhelmed, risky, vulnerable as organization grows
Machine bureaucracy	Standardization, formalization, routine procedures, centralized decision-making	Organizes work efficiently, economies of scale	Work feels monotonous, conflicting goals across departments, low intrinsic motivation, silo mentality
Professional organization	Highly trained professionals, high specialization, decentralized decision-making, complex rules and procedures	Efficiency, professionals have autonomy and power	Professionals may resent being "micromanaged"
Divisional organization ("M-form")	Organized according to specific products, product groups, services, markets, customers, or major programs; day-to-day decisions decentralized	Managers maintain control and accountability, top managers can focus on the "big picture"	Duplication of resources, conflict across divisions
Innovative organization	Loose rules, decisions decentralized, power delegated where needed, experts hired, use of consultants	Flexibility, central pool of talent, rapid response to environmental change	Conflict, ambiguity with respect to power and authority, stressful, high turnover

Source: Adapted from Mintzberg, H. (1979). *The structuring of organizations: A synthesis of the research.* Englewood Cliffs, NJ: Prentice Hall.

into another of the organizational types. We saw this with the example of Apple Computers—as the company grew, it became more hierarchical and divisionalized.

Machine Organization

The **machine organization** is defined by its standardization. Work is very formalized, there are many routines and procedures, decision-making is centralized, and tasks are grouped by functional departments. Jobs are clearly defined; there is a formal planning process in which budgets and audits and procedures are regularly analyzed by the technostructure employees for efficiency.

These characteristics contribute to high levels of bureaucracy in most machine organizations. Although this term has a negative meaning for many people today, bureaucracy can exist without the long lines, confusing forms, and general inefficiency we often associate with it. Believe it or not, bureaucracy was once viewed as the optimal form for organizing work efficiently.[21] It has fallen out of favor, partly due to poor implementation in highly visible organizations (in the United States, departments of motor vehicles and the postal service often come to mind). Changes in technology, societal norms, and the insights gained from management research have also led many organizations to shift away from the tight vertical structure of machine organizations toward flatter, more decentralized formations. The high degree of formalization and specialization can make work feel monotonous. When employees feel like "cogs in a machine," intrinsic motivation is very hard to come by.[22] Functional units can also form conflicting goals that can be inconsistent with overall corporate objectives. A **silo mentality** may emerge as organizational divisions begin to hoard information due to these divergent goals.[23]

That said, machine organizations can still be extremely efficient, relying heavily on **economies of scale** for their success. Economies of scale occur when more units of a good or a service are produced on a larger scale, yet with (on average) fewer input costs. This means that as a company grows and production volume increases, a company can decrease the cost per

Entrepreneurial organizations have a simple structure.

©iStockphoto.com/PeopleImages

unit. Large manufacturers are often machine organizations, as are government agencies and service firms that perform highly routine tasks. Despite the criticisms, there has been recent interest in reviving the positive aspects of bureaucracy because of its effects on operational efficiency and organizational performance.[24] If following procedures and meeting precise specifications are important, then the machine structure works well.

Professional Organization

Professional organizations are also very bureaucratic. The key difference between these and machine organizations is that professional organizations rely on highly trained professionals who demand control of their own work. So, while there's a high degree of specialization, decision-making is decentralized. This structure is typical when the organization contains a large number of knowledge workers, and this is why it is common in organizations such as schools and accounting and law firms. Another good example of a professional organization is a hospital, with its highly trained staff of surgeons, nurses, and other personnel who have a wide range of responsibilities for patient care and research.[25] The professional organization is complex, and there are lots of rules and procedures. This allows it to enjoy the efficiency benefits of a machine structure. The difference is that the output is generated by highly trained professionals who have autonomy and considerable power. However, such professionals may resist being supervised too closely.[26] Universities are examples of professional organizations. Your professors are highly trained, with advanced degrees. You may have noticed that they have autonomy over what happens in the classroom and give lectures without supervision and design projects for students to work on. They have the responsibility of grading papers and exams and assigning final grades.

Divisional (Diversified) Organization

"**M-form**" (short for *multidivisional form*) is the most common structure for organizations with a wide array of brands or products or divisions in different geographical locations.[27] For example, organizations like General Electric and General Motors are organized into a **divisional structure** by product, service, market, customers, or major programs.[28]

The primary benefit of this structure is that it enables division managers to take charge of day-to-day operations, production, and performance. This leaves top-level management free to focus on big-picture strategic decisions rather than getting bogged down with day-to-day decision-making. One major weakness, however, is that because divisions are often siloed, activities are often duplicated. Another drawback is that divisions are forced to compete for resources from headquarters.

M-form is the optimal structural choice for organizations in stable, established industries.

Innovative Organization ("Adhocracy")

Traditional organizational structures like those described above work best in stable, well-established industries. Emerging industries, however, rely on innovation and flexibility. In these industries, companies need to be able to reinvent themselves ad hoc.

The **innovative organization** structure enables companies to solve problems and function in a highly creative way because they are not boxed in by centralized decision-making. Power can be delegated and redelegated as needed, allowing such organizations to hire cutting-edge talent, bring in consultants to keep ideas fresh, and problem-solve quickly and efficiently.

One major drawback to this style is that conflict often arises in the absence of clear organizational hierarchy, and employee turnover is high.

This type of structure is common for tech start-ups and other businesses that depend on their ability to move quickly and make changes without bureaucracy.

Small businesses and start-ups can take a variety of forms. There are three entities that individuals or partners can form to do business.[29] Which form they select depends on three main considerations—taxation, liability, and record-keeping.

1. A **sole proprietorship** is the most common structure for small businesses.

   a. Advantages: Easy to create and gives the owner complete control.

   a. Disadvantages: The owner bears sole financial liability.

2. **Partnerships** are between two or more people who will assume responsibly for the business's profits and losses.

   a. Advantages: Tax burdens for profits and losses pass through to each partner to claim on their personal income taxes.

   b. Disadvantages: Each partner bears financial liability for the business.

3. **Corporations** are legal entities. They are separate from the people who form them.

   a. Advantages: There is no personal liability for the people who form the corporation. The entity bears financial responsibility for profits and losses. The entity can also be taxed and bears legal liability.

   b. Disadvantages: Operating as a corporation requires extensive record-keeping.

4. **Limited-liability corporations (LLCs)** are a hybrid of partnerships and corporations.

   a. Advantages: The profits and losses can be passed through to owners on their individual returns—the entity itself is not taxed. Liability is held by the entity, not the individual(s).

   b. Disadvantages: The LLC is popular because it enables partners to avoid the personal liability of sole proprietorships and partnerships and the record-keeping and tax liability of corporations.

CRITICAL THINKING QUESTIONS

> Consider an organization that you are familiar with (e.g., your university, a church group, or an organization you worked for). Which type of Mintzberg structure did it have? Explain why you believe it had this structure. What were the advantages and disadvantages of this structure?

There is no one-size-fits-all approach to organizational structure. Most companies incorporate tactics and elements of each and modify their structure over time to achieve a competitive advantage in their industry and meet customers' needs.[30]

When upper management sets out to choose an organizational structure, they should carefully evaluate the following:

- What are the organization's internal needs? Who has the capacity for meeting these needs?
- Who will have decision-making power?
- What are the organization's strategies and priorities?
- What type of industry and environment is the organization operating within?

In the next section, we will explore specific types of organizational structures and look closely at org charts.

Organizational Structure Types

Learning Objective 6.4: Discuss the advantages and disadvantages of functional, product, geographic, and matrix organizational structures.

Functional Organization

The **functional organization** structure, also known as the departmentalized structure, is the most common. This structure organizes work into different units (often called departments) based on business functions or expertise. For example, a functional organizational structure often organizes employees into accounting, marketing, production, and human resources departments. An advantage of functional organization is that work can be assigned to the units staffed by experts in the relevant field. For example, the marketing department would have market research analysts and creative individuals who develop advertisements based on analysis of the market research. Another advantage is that communication within departments is easier because everyone has similar training and speaks the same "language." For example, the accounting department would have people who are accounting majors, understand the meaning of accounting terms, and are up on the latest tax regulations.

Another challenge within functional organizations is that specialization can create a silo mentality, which makes **integration** across functional areas difficult. The managers of each unit may be more interested in furthering the goals of their area than in pursuing those of the entire organization. For example, the production department may drag its feet on implementing a change to the assembly line to create a new product that the marketing and sales team want to get to market quickly. Another disadvantage is that due to the difficulties in communication across departments, decision-making may be slower and become centralized at the top of the organization.

An example of a functional organization structure is that of Federal Express (FedEx), shown in Figure 6.4. The chief financial officer (finance), the chief information officer (information systems), and the general counsel (lawyers) all report to the CEO. In addition, the functional areas of human resources, as well as market and communications, report to the CEO. Departmental senior managers (DSMs) oversee the specific areas in each unit (for example, there is a DSM of human resources).

Product Organization

A **product organization** (also referred to as a service or brand organization) organizes the work into units that are responsible for producing specific products or services. In some

▼ FIGURE 6.4

Functional Organization Chart: FedEx

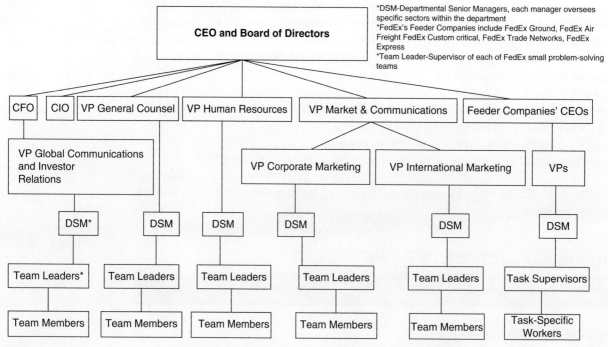

Source: Wikimedia Commons. (n.d.). File: FedEx organizational structure.jpg [Figure]. Retrieved from https://commons.wikimedia.org/wiki/File: FedEx_Organizational_Structure.jpg.

Product Organization Chart: Procter & Gamble

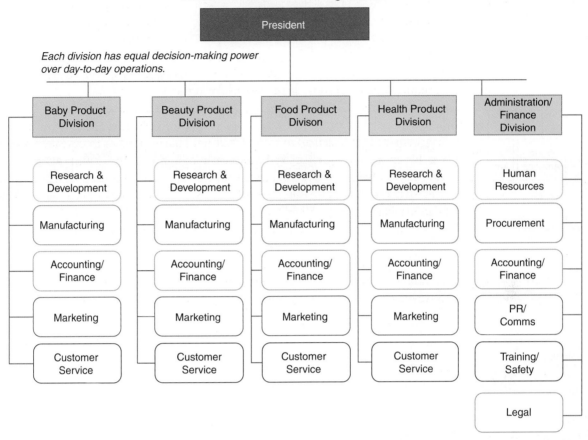

Procter & Gamble Divisional Organization

President

Each division has equal decision-making power over day-to-day operations.

Baby Product Division	Beauty Product Division	Food Product Divison	Health Product Division	Administration/ Finance Division
Research & Development	Research & Development	Research & Development	Research & Development	Human Resources
Manufacturing	Manufacturing	Manufacturing	Manufacturing	Procurement
Accounting/ Finance	Accounting/ Finance	Accounting/ Finance	Accounting/ Finance	Accounting/ Finance
Marketing	Marketing	Marketing	Marketing	PR/ Comms
Customer Service	Customer Service	Customer Service	Customer Service	Training/ Safety
				Legal

Source: Example of a product organizational chart [Figure]. (n.d.). Retrieved from https://pingboard.com/org-charts/evolution-org-charts

instances, the product organization is broken down even further into brands. This type of organization is often seen in consumer products companies such as Procter & Gamble (P&G), as shown in Figure 6.5. P&G organizes in terms of baby, health, beauty, and food. There is a separate division that provides oversight on functional areas such as human resources and accounting/finance. In this type of structure the managers and employees within a unit are specialists on a particular type of product (food products, for example). Managers develop broader expertise than they do in the functional organization because they work on all aspects related to a product. Performance evaluation in the product organization is more straightforward because the top management team can track the performance (e.g., sales) for each product line. Another advantage is that decision-making is faster because managers are dedicated to a particular product rather than being loyal to a department of specialists. The biggest disadvantage of the product organization is that there is typically a lot of duplication of effort. As shown in Figure 6.5, each product line has its own research and development, manufacturing, accounting/finance, marketing, and customer service. It may also be difficult for the administration and finance division to implement standardized policies across all departments.

Procter & Gamble offers distinctly different brands that are organized with a product organization.

©ROBERT SULLIVAN/Staff /Getty Images

Geographical Organization Chart: Anheuser-Busch InBev

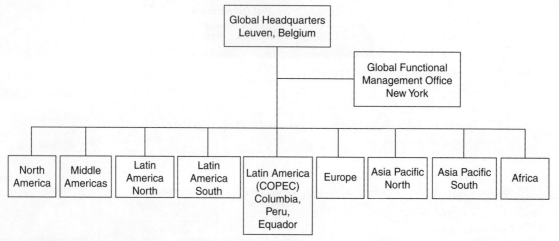

Source: Adapted from Anheuser-Busch InBev announces structure and leadership of combined group in recommended combination with SABMiller. (n.d.). Retrieved from http://www.ab-inbev.com/content/dam/universaltemplate/abinbev/pdf/investors/04August2016/ENGLISH.pdf.

A Budweiser beer delivery truck is parked on Columbus Avenue in Manhattan.

©iStockphoto.com/georgeclerk

Geographic Organization

An example of a **geographic organization** structure is shown in Figure 6.6. Organizations that use this type of organizational structure need to stay close to their customers because the delivery of fresh products is important. Anheuser-Busch InBev (AB InBev) is the largest brewery in the world, and its brands include Budweiser, Beck's, and Stella Artois. InBev was the result of a merger between the Belgium-based company Interbrew and the Brazilian brewer AmBev, which took place in 2004. AB InBev has over 500 brands sold in more than 150 countries and almost 173,000 employees.[31] They reorganized their divisions after their acquisition of SABMiller, based in London, a brewery that produced brands such as Foster's, Miller, and Pilsner Urquell.

You can see from the figure that they have a global headquarters in Belgium and functional management offices in New York. The North America region (headquartered in Saint Louis, where Budweiser was led prior to their acquisition by InBev) consists of the United States and Canada. The Middle Americas region is headquartered in Mexico City and includes Mexico, El Salvador, and Honduras. Latin America North, headquartered in São Paulo, includes Brazil, Guatemala, Panama, and the Caribbean. Latin America South, headquartered in Buenos Aires, includes Argentina, Uruguay, Chile, Paraguay, and Bolivia. As indicated in the figure, COPEC is headquartered in Bogotá, and includes Colombia, Peru, and Ecuador. Europe is headquartered in Leuven and includes European countries, Russia, and the Middle East. Asia Pacific North, headquartered in Shanghai, covers China, South Korea, and Japan. Asia Pacific South covers the regions of Australia, New Zealand, India, Vietnam, and other South Asian countries and is headquartered in Melbourne, Australia. Finally, the African region is headquartered in Johannesburg and covers all African countries.

As this example shows, AB InBev is a global brand that must have managers and employees located in every region to allow them the flexibility to deliver products and meet the unique tastes of each region. This is a primary advantage of the geographical structure. AB InBev has three brands that are marketed worldwide (Budweiser, Stella Artois, and Corona); however, most of its brands are local and serve the tastes of the particular region they are produced in. For example, Harbin Ice is brewed in China.

The geographical structure has some disadvantages. As in the product organization, a major challenge is the duplication of effort. Also, coordination across all business units and direction from the headquarters may be problematic. A research study of geographically distributed research-and-development projects[32] found that the sites were "out of sight, out of mind." Study respondents felt that employees were much less responsive to coworkers who resided at a different site. For example, they were much less likely to provide information quickly, to follow up on requests, and generally to consider concerns of the other site. Meeting face-to-face seemed to help; several respondents noticed a significant change for the better after they had actually met the person at the other site. Nevertheless, respondents at the geographically dispersed sites believed they still did not get the same level of attention they received from co-located coworkers.

Matrix Organization

In the matrix organization, the functions are combined with projects.[33] This organizational structure is well suited for organizations that are engaged in research and development (R&D), advertising, or management consulting.[34] For example, Novartis is an international pharmaceutical company known for working in the development of medicines for infectious diseases. The pharmaceutical strategy through the years has highly emphasized R&D. Most of their research has focused on cancer, cardiovascular diseases, diabetes, malaria, and meningitis. Novartis manages major projects such as the development of new vaccines, like H1N1. It is important for them to have centralized control with respect to the finance function and legal matters, for example. They are specialized in different functions, and this is reflected by divisions such as the Novartis Institute for Biomedical Research (NIBR), pharmaceuticals (Pharma), generic drugs (Sandoz), Vaccines and Diagnostics (V&D), and Novartis Consumer Health (NCH). NCH provides over-the-counter products such as antacids, cold and flu remedies, and contact lenses. Employees in each division report to their product/service line vice president as well as to the functional area vice presidents. Figure 6.7 shows the matrix structure for Novartis. A biomedical research team working on a project would report to the head of NIBR and also report to the heads of HR, the chief financial officer (CFO), general counsel, corporate communications, country management/external affairs, and quality assurance. The figure shows example projects in each of the divisions.

One advantage of a matrix organization structure is that there is less duplication of effort compared to the functional and geographical structures. Resources are shared between the units, allowing more open communication, which helps in knowledge sharing. When a matrix organization functions well, the organization is both efficient and effective.[35] Another advantage is that employees are exposed to both projects and functions, and this expands their skills and knowledge of the business. Employees develop broad-based skills, and this enhances the work done on project teams. This also enhances employees' career development and promotion potential.

The matrix organization is not without disadvantages, however. The main challenge of the matrix structure is conflict between the horizontal and vertical departments. Managers experience information overload and complain that there are too many meetings, and decision-making is slow.[36] Remember that employees have to report to two managers, which may cause conflict.[37] For example, a project manager may want to spend a lot to develop a new drug, but the finance (functional) manager may want to contain costs and review return on investment. Employees may be confused about priorities. In other words, employees working in matrix organizations may experience more stress because they have "two bosses." The matrix organization is complex, can be difficult to manage, and can be costly.[38] A research study of 86 R&D teams[39] in a matrix organization found that performance reached the highest level when organizational influence was centered on the project manager and influence over the

Matrix Organization: Novartis

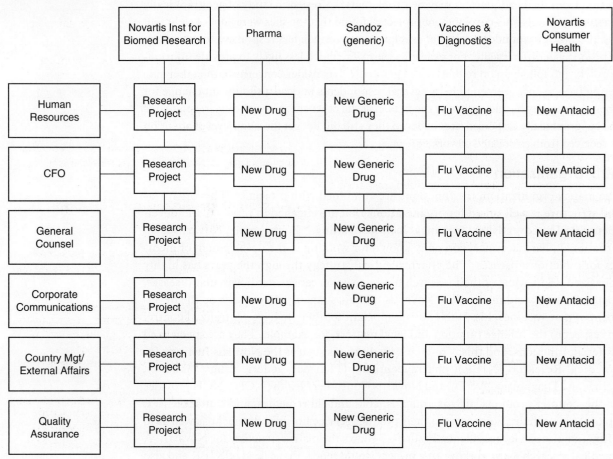

Source: Adapted from Isabella, N. (2010, December 7). Achieving results management in Novartis [Blog post]. Retrieved from http://natashaisabella4.blogspot.com/2010/12/achieving-resultsmanagement-in-novartis_07
.html.

technical details of the work was centered on the technical manager. Thus, balancing the power within the matrix organization is necessary.

Virtual Organization

The dot-com era gave rise to a new form of organization known as the **virtual organization**. A virtual organization is defined as "a temporary collection of enterprises that cooperate and share resources, knowledge, and competencies to better respond to business opportunities."[40] Yet some virtual organizations are not temporary, such as Wikipedia. Often the virtual organization is not tangible in terms of offices, facilities, and other types of infrastructure—it exists in people's minds. The sense of purpose and resources dedicated to achieving certain goals give meaning to the virtual organization. Virtual organizations are common in high-technology environments where there is intense global competition. For example, Symbian Limited was a virtual organization that developed mobile phones and consisted of a group of competitors, including Psion, Nokia AB, Sony Ericsson, Samsung Electronics, Panasonic, and Siemens AG. Its goal was to combine efforts to produce and market mobile phones and PDA devices (handheld devices with email and Internet access) to prevent Microsoft from extending its monopoly into the mobile phone market.[41] They didn't want to be tied to Microsoft's high licensing

CAREERS IN MANAGEMENT

Organizational Design Consultant

Many organizations develop their structures on an ad hoc basis to accommodate growth or other changes in the competitive environment. In other words, structure just evolves as departments and positions are added to cope with change. But we hear about large-scale organizational restructuring in the business news all the time. Who do companies rely on to perform such analyses and make these hugely important decisions? Organizational design consultants! Such consultants help clients design organizations to reduce costs, drive growth, and strengthen both short-term performance and long-term organizational health. Organizational design consultants are specialized professionals who meticulously define and organize the structure of an organization. They develop strategies for how the organizational chart will look after the organization is redesigned. They develop job titles and job descriptions. They create structures that organize employees to improve efficiency and increase productivity. In other words, these consultants figure out who should report to whom in the organization. They also figure out how large the accounting department should be relative to the marketing department. Organizational design consultants help managers make major decisions about the right structure of an organization. To do this, they study the business goals, strategies, processes, and operations. Recommended changes to the organization's design are aligned with the competitive environment of the organization.

Organizational design consultants engage in detailed research to develop their recommendations. For example, a consultant might learn that an organization has been experiencing an increase in lawsuit risk due to a product defect and recommend the addition of an extra lawyer in the legal counsel's office.

This isn't just about creating titles and job descriptions. Organizational design consultants design the structure of the organization and align policies and procedures with it. They ensure that the recommended changes result in improved efficiency. Let's look at organizational design in one of the top consulting firms, Deloitte, as an example.

At Deloitte, organizational design consultants use advanced analytical tools to work closely with clients on the following tasks:

- Developing and implementing organization strategies that support improved client future-state organizational design.

- Preparing organizational design alternatives, testing them against design criteria, and aligning leadership groups around design selection and implementation.

- Applying analytic and visualization tools to assess the impact of varying design and decision solutions.

- Supporting the process of identifying, assigning, and implementing decision-making authority and responsibility for both individuals and teams.

- Preparing workforce transition plans and programs, including strategies to transition talent at all levels.

- Designing jobs and roles, creating competency models and career paths to aid in the selection and transition of employees.

- Serving as a trusted adviser to clients through the organizational design process.

- Contributing to practice development initiatives, including culture building and internal community involvement.

Examples of Organizational Design Consultant Work

Another top consulting firm is McKinsey. Here are some examples of how the firm has helped organizations redesign their work.

1. For a power retailer seeking major revenue growth, a new organizational design supported by strategy transformed the sales model, eliminated non-value-added activities, and strengthened top management's role as "super coaches" to the sales team. Profits grew by 25 percent in a year.

2. In a global consumer goods company, a new CEO reduced the corporate center by 50 percent, redesigned key HR and finance processes for efficiency, and consolidated fragmented supply-chain functions. Savings totaled $500 million over three years.

3. A global consumer goods manufacturer eliminated complexity in several regions and functions, halving the time it needed to make decisions in critical processes. This helped it bring products to market faster in response to changing customer needs.

These examples show that organizational design consultants have a positive impact on profits, cost savings, and innovation. The work in these positions is meaningful, and the compensation tends to be quite impressive, so it is not a bad career in management to pursue.

Discussion Questions

1. Search online for organizational design consultant positions at other companies. How do they differ from the work of McKinsey consultants summarized above?

2. Looking at the description of what an organizational design consultant does, what elements of this chapter appear to be most relevant?

(Continued)

(Continued)

3. Think about a company you have worked for or one that you do business with regularly (a local restaurant, for example). What is one aspect of their organizational design you think they should change? Be sure to think through the potential downsides of your proposed change as well as the benefits—the ability to see nonobvious drawbacks in proposed structural changes is a key skill for those who work in organizational design.

Sources: Adapted from All About Careers (n.d.). Organizational design consultant. Retrieved from https://www.allaboutcareers.com/careers/job-profile/organisational-design-consultant; Mathews, T. (n.d.). Organization design consultant [Job posting]. Retrieved from https://www.reqcloud.com/jobs/826890/?k=x/SYgYYmOlUj5/0rNIC6S/3MI0xsnkil4NIlddyS/bk=&utm_source=twitter&utm_campaign=reqCloud_JobPost; McKinsey and Company. (n.d.). How we help clients: Organization design. Retrieved from https://www.mckinsey.com/business-functions/organization/how-we-help-clients/organization-design.

Steven Pruitt is the top Wikipedia editor in the entire world, with over 2,470,000 edits.

©The Washington Post/Getty Images

fees and coding. Often virtual organizations are temporary and set up to take advantage of a threat or market opportunity. The organization dissolves or is merged into a larger company after the opportunity is exploited. In the case of Symbian, it was acquired by Nokia in 2008.

The advantages of this type of organization are quick response and flexibility, with no long-term commitment to the project. Also, the combined strengths of different organizations can be leveraged. The disadvantages are communication difficulties (since they typically operate in a virtual environment), lack of trust among partners, and no real commitment to an organization and its mission. An example of a virtual organization that you will recognize is Wikipedia. It was started by Jimmy Wales and Larry Sanger in 2001; however, the concept and technological foundation of the site predated this. Wikipedia is self-defined as "a free encyclopedia, written collaboratively by the people who use it."[42] Today, Wikipedia is one of many "Wiki" sites owned and administered by the Wikimedia Foundation, a nonprofit organization that is supported through donations.

Levels of Management

Learning Objective 6.5: List the major objectives of the three levels of management and provide examples of typical job titles.

The levels of managers in an organization are shown in Figure 6.8. The **C-suite** refers to the CEO and other top management team members, such as the chief executive officer (CEO), who reports to the organization's board of directors, who is led by the chairman of the board. In some cases the CEO and chairman are the same person; however, in most cases, these roles are separated to best represent the interests of shareholders. Examples of other members of the top management team include the chief operating officer (COO), the chief financial officer (CFO), the chief marketing officer (CMO), and the chief diversity officer (CDO). C-suite executives are responsible for making key strategic decisions regarding the future directions of the organization. They take a long-term perspective on the goals and how the organization can best meet them. The CEO's symbolic actions have a positive impact on organizational performance. By being inspirational, they provide a vision and develop shared organizational values. Research has shown that the middle managers play an important role as "linking pins"[43] in that they then demonstrate similar leadership behaviors to their followers. Thus, leadership cascades through the organization to the middle managers to the operating level.[44]

The roles of managers are changing over time. Specific roles and activities for the three levels of management are shown in Table 6.3. Operating-level managers are often responsible for managing employees who interact directly with customers. Operating managers generate and allocate resources and identify new areas of growth for the organization. They focus on managing the performance of their followers and continually improving operations. Middle managers play the role of coaches and developers of people. They must be **boundary spanners** across the divisions of the organization to get things done. Boundary spanners are "individuals who are especially sensitive to and skilled in bridging interests, professions and organizations."[45] For example, middle managers may serve on cross-functional task forces to solve organizational problems. They are the people in the middle—they implement the vision of the top management team but temper it with what can be realistically achieved. Another example of a boundary spanner is the sales manager in the organization.[46] Top managers are the senior-level executives who are responsible for the overall strategy of the organization. Their role has shifted from allocating resources to becoming institutional leaders. The top execs represent the leadership of the organization and have broad responsibilities for its direction and financial stability. They must be visionary as they develop and maintain a strong organizational culture.

Given that the roles of all managers are shifting, all three levels must align the goals at their level with the overall goals of the organization so that the organization will succeed. For example, operational managers are now expected to be more entrepreneurial in looking for opportunities to help the company grow. Senior managers are no longer administrators but serve as supportive coaches who delegate to their followers. And top managers must now be visionary leaders who can shepherd the organization through disruptive change. At all levels of management, setting the right goals to be effective relies on solid analysis and decision-making, which

▼ FIGURE 6.8

Levels of Management

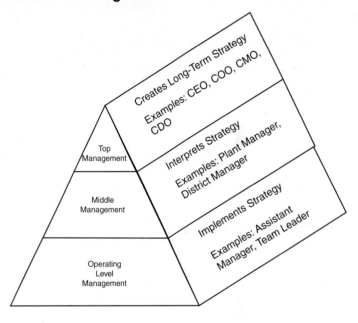

▼ TABLE 6.3

Levels of Management

	Operating-Level Management	Middle Management	Top Management
Changing Role	From operational implementers to aggressive entrepreneurs	From administrative controllers to supportive coaches	From resource allocators to institutional leaders
Primary Value Added	Driving business performance by focusing on productivity, innovation, and growth within front-line units	Providing the support and coordination to bring large company advantage to the independent front-line units	Creating and embedding a sense of direction, commitment, and challenge to people throughout the organization
Key Activities and Tasks	• Creating and pursuing new growth opportunities for the business • Attracting and developing resources and competencies • Managing continuous performance improvement within the unit	• Developing individuals and supporting their activities • Linking dispersed knowledge, skills, and best practices across units • Managing the tension between short-term performance and long-term ambition	• Challenging embedded assumptions while establishing a stretching opportunity horizon and performance standards • Institutionalizing a set of norms and values to support cooperation and trust • Creating an overarching corporate purpose and ambition

Source: Adapted from Bartlett, C., & Ghoshal, S. (1997). The myth of the generic manager: New personal competencies for new management roles. *California Management Review, 40*(1), 92–116, p. 96.

are two central themes in this textbook. As you learned in Chapter 2, analysis is also needed to ensure that the organization is running efficiently to meet its goals.

CRITICAL THINKING QUESTIONS

> Why do you think the roles of managers have been shifting? Provide an example of a manager's role at one of the three levels that you believe has changed in recent years.

In addition to understanding the overall structure of the organization, managers are responsible for ensuring clarity in the specific jobs that employees perform. The specific jobs employees perform are a result of the organization's structure, the technology used, and the way employees relate to their work socially. Next we turn to sociotechnical systems and job design.

Sociotechnical System and Job Design

Learning Objective 6.6: Describe the five properties of jobs in job characteristics theory.

Sociotechnical systems design is based on the premise that an organization comprises both the structure and social interactions among employees (i.e., the social and the technical).[47] Because the social and technical elements must work together to accomplish tasks, organizational structure can produce both physical products or services and social and psychological outcomes for employees. When both are optimized, the most positive outcomes are obtained (joint optimization). This method contrasts with traditional methods that first design the technical component and then fit people into it. The traditional approach often results in mediocre performance at high social costs. Some key questions a manager should ask regarding the organizational structure from the sociotechnical systems perspective are:[48]

A key activity of top management is creating an overarching corporate purpose and ambition. Founder and Chief Executive Officer of Spotify, Daniel Ek, speaks onstage during Spotify Investor Day in New York City.

©Ilya S. Savenok/Stringer/Getty Images

- Are the existing structures useful for the attainment of the goals and tasks?
- How do people adapt to or cope with these structures?
- Are the structures supportive of the needs and capabilities of the leadership (management) and the workforce?
- Do the structures encourage cooperation and collaboration?
- Do the structures facilitate a rational use of resources and technologies?
- What major strengths/weaknesses result from the structures interacting with other elements in the system?

The sociotechnical systems approach gave rise to an interest in the design of jobs for joint optimization. Research has shown that jobs have particular characteristics and that jobs can be designed to improve motivation. In addition to designing the organizational structure, managers must design the jobs that employees do on a day-to-day basis. A **job** is defined as "a set of task elements grouped together under one job title and designed to be performed by a single individual."[49] The job characteristics theory (JCT) outlines the different task elements of jobs. Consistent with sociotechnical systems theory, jobs can be designed so that people are more motivated, are more satisfied, and perform better. They are also less likely to quit their jobs when their work is designed properly.[50] Next, we turn to the design of jobs within organizations that can optimize performance and the social aspect of work, resulting in employee satisfaction.

Job Characteristics

JCT specifies five core job dimensions,[51] which are as follows:

1. **Skill variety**—the extent to which people use different skills and abilities at work. The employee is not doing the same repetitive tasks over and over.
2. **Task identity**—the task is one that people experience from beginning to end. In other words, they identify with an entire work product.
3. **Task significance**—the degree to which the job is seen as having an impact on others. The work does something good for society.
4. **Autonomy**—the employee has the freedom to plan and perform their own work. The employees have discretion about their work and are not intensely supervised.
5. **Feedback from the job**—the job provides information on how effective the employee's work is. Just doing the work itself provides performance feedback.

Skill variety, task identity, and task significance combine in the job characteristics model to produce a sense of meaningfulness in the work, as shown in Figure 6.9. For example, autonomy increases a person's responsibility for the work they perform. As in goal-setting, feedback provides knowledge of the actual results of a person's work. The states experienced from the nature of the work performed translate into high work motivation, work performance, satisfaction, and lower absenteeism and turnover. Research has demonstrated that the critical psychological states are an important explanatory factor in understanding how job characteristics translate into work outcomes.[52] Employees must experience these psychological reactions to their job so that their work has meaning. Also, the responsibility they feel for the outcomes is important to their taking ownership of their work. Finally, the feedback provided from the work allows for corrections and higher work effectiveness as well as satisfaction from a job well done.

Moderators affect the relationship between two variables (see Appendix). Of course, the knowledge and skills of workers matter. If they don't have the prerequisite skills, they will not be able to perform work that has high levels of autonomy, for example. Also, the growth needs of employees affect the degree to which a person experiences meaningfulness, responsibility, and knowledge of results from their work.

Growth-need strength refers to a person's need to learn new things, grow, and develop from working. People vary in this need; some people have a high desire to grow as a result of their work and others do not. This need also affects performance. In other words, people who don't really need to grow from the work may not have higher motivation and performance if their job is made more interesting. Employees who prefer challenging work experience have less stress after their work is redesigned.[53] Finally, **context satisfaction**, which is the degree to which employees are satisfied with various aspects of their job (such as their supervision and pay), will also affect their response to work that has high levels of variety, identity, and significance. For example, if employees are not paid well, they may resent having to learn more skills.

▼ FIGURE 6.9

Job Characteristics Model

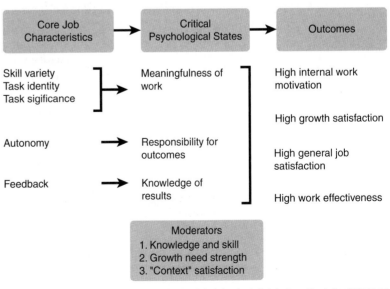

Source: Hackman, J. R., & Oldham, G. R. (1976). Motivation through the design of work: Test of a theory. *Organizational Behavior and Human Performance, 16*(2), 250–279.

How can a leader identify growth needs in followers? Provide an example of a job that has high levels of the five job characteristics.

Job Redesign

The options for designing (and redesigning) jobs are shown in Figure 6.10. Based on JCT research, organizations implement **job redesign** to enhance the motivating potential of work.[54] The basic idea is to load jobs with more of the core job characteristics that have been shown to motivate. This job loading may occur in the form of **horizontal loading** (e.g., **combining tasks**). **Job rotation** involves cross-training or allowing workers to do different jobs. In addition to job rotation, work may be designed to create natural work units by combining tasks. For example, a worker who drills holes for a door handle of a car would also learn to install the handle. Job rotation and combining tasks must be supported by adequate training and coaching for employees as they learn new skills on the job. Job rotation and combining tasks are examples of horizontal job loading. In forming natural work units, tasks are combined so that an employee completes an entire job. This helps employees feel a sense of task identity. This increases the skill variety, task identity, and task significance. For example, a person who works on an assembly line is rotated to a clerical position in which they learn the purchasing process for supplies needed on the line one day a week. This provides variety and also allows the worker to see more of the big picture of what is needed to perform the work.

Vertical loading is adding decision-making responsibility to the job. For example, jobs may also be loaded vertically by establishing client relationships in which workers can interact directly with clients to increase the meaningfulness of work. An example of vertical loading can be found in a study of callers requesting donations, which found that the callers were more persistent and motivated when they were in contact with undergraduate students funded by their efforts.[55] These strategies have been referred to as **job enrichment,** and some examples follow.[56] Toolkit Activity 6.2 will provide you with the opportunity to evaluate the motivating potential of different jobs and create suggestions for redesigning them.

Jobs may be redesigned so that employees have discretion in how they perform their work to increase the level of autonomy experienced. Finally, creating job feedback so that employees can learn more quickly about the results of their work may increase motivation. Research has shown that job enrichment does reduce turnover and increases employee motivation and satisfaction.[57]

Job-Crafting

In some cases, employees may redesign the work on their own. Recent research has examined **job-crafting**, or the extent to which individuals can demonstrate initiative in designing their own work. The term *job-crafting* is defined as "the actions employees take to shape, mold, and redefine their jobs."[58] Jobs vary in the degree of discretion they offer, but in many cases, employees may be able to design certain aspects of their own

Establishing client relationships: Call center employees at a university are motivated when they meet the undergraduate students funded by their efforts.

©iStockphoto.com/PeopleImages

▼ FIGURE 6.10

Job Redesign Strategies

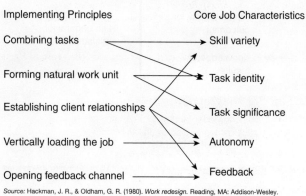

Implementing Principles	Core Job Characteristics
Combining tasks	Skill variety
Forming natural work unit	Task identity
Establishing client relationships	Task significance
Vertically loading the job	Autonomy
Opening feedback channel	Feedback

Source: Hackman, J. R., & Oldham, G. R. (1980). *Work redesign.* Reading, MA: Addison-Wesley.

FACT OR FICTION

Mean Companies? Lazy Employees? Why Telecommuting Is Off to a Rough Start

The idea of telecommuting–performing at least some of one's job duties from home–has followed a peculiar trajectory over the past 40 years or so. In the 1980s it was generally viewed as a futuristic idea, something that could conceivably become common in a far-off, technologically advanced future. In the 1990s, as ordinary people began hooking their computers up to phone lines, telecommuting began to seem realistic. By the first decade of the new century, much sooner than most would have expected, the last of the serious technological impediments to telecommuting had largely been resolved and major companies began experimenting with allowing employees to work from home.

Today, however, telecommuting has seemingly regressed to being an idea that sounds great in theory but does not seem to work well in practice. Arguably, the most significant blow to telecommuting came in 2013 when Yahoo, an early adopter and proponent of telecommuting, decided to end the practice. The announcement was met with anger among media analysts, academics, labor groups, and, of course, some of Yahoo's own employees. Some accused the company's leadership of greed and insensitivity. Others blamed its telecommunicating employees for taking advantage of the highly unstructured arrangements, allowing themselves to become distracted and unproductive.

While there may be elements of truth to these accusations, neither greed nor laziness appears to be the problem. It is becoming increasingly apparent that at least some of the declines in productivity and (believe it or not) job satisfaction companies like Yahoo have witnessed can be linked to the loss of organizational structure caused by telecommuting. More specifically, when an employee telecommutes, they become at least partially detached from the organization's structure. They no longer have unplanned discussions with coworkers in the hallways—discussions that often lead to new ideas and innovations. Their connections to other employees on the organizational chart remain the same, but their interpersonal connections may begin to deteriorate. The loss of (or detachment from) structure also has some more predicable consequences: The work life starts to invade the home life (since the workplace *is* the home), reducing job satisfaction, and home distractions start to invade the working day, reducing productivity.

This synopsis might lead you to wonder if maybe there is a balance to be struck somewhere between "no telecommuting"

and "100% telecommuting." Perhaps organizations can allow employees the flexibility of telecommuting when it is needed without going as far as Yahoo did by allowing almost full-time telecommuting. Two studies suggest that this may be the solution. Both studies found evidence of a "curvilinear" relationship between telecommuting and those two key outcomes: job satisfaction and productivity. Unlike linear positive and negative relationships typically seen in management research, a curvilinear relationship changes direction at different levels of the independent variable. Both studies found positive relationships at low to moderate levels of telecommuting (about 20% of working hours, or roughly one day out of a five-day work week). Telecommuting appears to make employees happy and productive at these levels but starts to drop off as it nears 50% of working hours. Anything over 50% telecommuting had increasingly negative impacts on employees' productivity and job satisfaction in both studies.

These studies suggest that hope for telecommuting is not lost. They also tell us that making it work is, like so much else in management, a matter of finding the right balance.

Discussion Questions

1. Have you or a family member ever telecommuted for a job? If so, what did you (or they) like and dislike about it?

2. What are some challenges managers are likely to face when their employees work from home? What can managers do to address them?

3. What are some challenges employees are likely to face when they work from home? What can employees do to address them?

Sources: Adapted from Gallup. (2013). State of the American workplace. Retrieved from http://news.gallup.com/reports/178514/state-american-workplace.aspx; Golden, T. D., Veiga, J. F., & Dino, R. N. (2008). The impact of professional isolation on teleworker job performance and turnover intentions: Does time spent teleworking, interacting face-to-face, or having access to communication-enhancing technology matter? *Journal of Applied Psychology, 93*(6), 1412–1421; Timestaff. (2014, June 5). Telecommuting: What Marissa Mayer got right—and wrong. Retrieved from http://time.com/money/2791618/telecommuting-what-marissa-mayer-got-right-and-wrong/.

work. This may include changes to the work itself as well as interactions with others that enhance the meaningfulness of the work performed.[59] An example of job-crafting would be a team member working on a marketing research project who is designing a set of team-building activities and implementing them to improve the way the team works together on the project. A review of the job-crafting literature notes that employees do sometimes create their own job design, and this is a relevant area for future research. However, managers should be aware that there may be dysfunctional consequences of employees designing their own work.[60] For example, an employee might redesign their work to include extraneous meetings with other department members that cause them to be away from the office, resulting in work disruptions to coworkers.

A research study[61] found that job-crafting had positive and linear effects on work-related attitudes (job satisfaction and affective commitment). However, moderate levels of job-crafting were associated with dysfunctional performance-related outcomes. The study also found that it is important to consider the features of work context (autonomy and ambiguity in the work), which made a difference in how dysfunctional job-crafting was. Another study found that the effectiveness of job-crafting depends on the nature of the job-crafting the employee engages in. **Approach job-crafting** includes role and social expansion, while **avoidance job-crafting** includes role reduction and withdrawal from work. Avoidance job-crafting positively relates to work withdrawal and tends to have fewer relationships with desired outcomes than approach job-crafting.[62]

CRITICAL THINKING QUESTIONS

Explain how an employee in a fast-food restaurant could engage in job-crafting. Provide an example of (1) approach job-crafting and (2) avoidance job-crafting for this type of work.

Managerial Implications

This chapter provided an overview of organizational design. The key takeaway points from this chapter are:

- People vary in the amount and type of structure they desire, just as organizations vary in the amount and type of structure they provide. When an employer's structure aligns with an employee's needs, job satisfaction and performance typically improve.
- We all rely on structure to navigate life's challenges inside and outside the workplace. Organizational structure is critical to efficiency and effectiveness.
- Most organizational designs contain five key elements: operating core, middle line, technostructure, support staff, and strategic apex. These areas have specific functions, with the strategic apex directing the organization's overall mission through the middle line managers.
- An organizational chart can provide important information about the power relationships and lines of communication built into an organization's structure. There are different types of organizational charts, including functional, product, geographical, and matrix charts. An emerging organizational form is the virtual organization, which is an "organization without walls." These organizations are sometimes temporary and are jointly formed by competitors to address a threat or opportunity.
- Small businesses have particular structures that have implications for how they are managed. A sole proprietorship is the most common form of business organization. It's easy to form and offers complete managerial control to the owner. However, the owner is also personally liable for all financial obligations of the business. A partnership involves two or more people who agree to share in the profits or losses of a business; a corporation is a legal entity created to conduct business; and the limited-liability corporation (LLC), a hybrid form, is gaining in popularity because it allows owners to take advantage of the benefits of both the corporation and partnership forms of business.
- Just as fit between an employee and an organization is important, so is fit between organizational structure and the competitive environment. Different organizational designs,

including machine bureaucracies and divisional structures, can be used to improve this fit. Thus, there is no "right" organizational structure, and organizations may need to adapt their structure to respond to competition.

- Sociotechnical systems design is based on the premise that an organization comprises both the structure and social interactions among employees (i.e., the social and technical).

- Job characteristics theory can be used to help understand the links between organizational structure and employee motivation. Jobs can be designed so that the motivating properties of skill variety, task identity, task significance, autonomy, and feedback are attained. Employees must experience meaning, have responsibility, and get feedback for the redesign of work to take effect. In some cases, employees design their own work through job-crafting.

This chapter reviewed the structural characteristics of organizations and the types of organizational charts that result. It is important for a manager to understand how the structure relates to employees' interactions with one another in the organization. Managers are also responsible for the design of work, considering both the social and technical requirements. They design jobs that get the work done—but also motivate employees to higher levels of satisfaction and job performance.

KEY TERMS

approach job-crafting   188

autonomy   185

avoidance job-crafting   188

boundary spanners   183

centralization   171

complexity   171

context satisfaction   185

corporation   175

C-suite   182

direct reports   168

divisional structure   174

dotted-line relationships   168

economies of scale   173

entrepreneurial organization   172

feedback from the job   185

formalization   171

functional organization   175

geographic organization   178

growth-need strength   185

hierarchy of authority   166

horizontal loading or combining tasks   186

innovative organization   174

integration   176

job   184

job-crafting   186

job enrichment   186

job redesign   186

job rotation   186

limited-liability corporation (LLC)   175

machine organization   173

M-form   174

middle line   172

operating core   172

organization chart   168

organizational design   169

organizational structure   168

partnership   175

product organization   176

professional organization   174

silo mentality   173

skill variety   185

sociotechnical system design   184

sole proprietorship   175

span of control   168

specialization   171

standardization   171

strategic apex   172

support staff   172

task identity   185

task significance   185

technostructure   172

uncertainty   168

vertical loading   186

virtual organization   180

TOOLKIT

Activity 6.1

Organization Chart

Darren is the manager of a branch of a well-known firm that produces tools for homebuilding projects such as hammers and screwdrivers. Anna is the assistant manager, and she reports to Darren. Anna delegates to the department managers—Jane (production), Tom (accounting), and Omar (marketing and sales). Felicity, Matt, and Ryan all report to Jane. Rachel, Sally, and Pete are accountable to Tom. Omar is responsible for Jon, Mark, Sam, and James. Draw the organization chart for the tool firm.

Discussion Questions

1. Who has the largest span of control, and how big is it?
2. How many layers are in this hierarchy?
3. Who does Tom delegate to?
4. Would you consider this to be a tall or flat structure? Why?

Source: Adapted from University of Salford, Manchester. (n.d.). Organization chart activity. In *The Times 100 Business Case Studies*. Retrieved from http://www.salford.ac.uk/library/access-to-e-resources/library-databases/the-times-0-business-case-studies.

Activity 6.2

Applying the Job Characteristics Model
Objectives

- To assess the motivating potential score (MPS) of several jobs.
- To determine which core job characteristics need to be changed for each job.
- To explore how you might redesign one of the jobs.

The first step in applying the job characteristics model is to diagnose the work environment to determine if a performance problem is due to demotivating job characteristics. This can be accomplished by observing an employee doing their work and then completing the job diagnostic survey (JDS). The JDS is a self-report instrument that assesses the extent to which a specific job possesses the five core job characteristics. With this instrument, it is also possible to calculate a motivating potential score for a job. The motivating potential score (MPS) is a summary index that represents the extent to which the job characteristics foster internal work motivation. Low scores indicate that an individual will not experience high intrinsic motivation from the job. Such a job is a prime candidate for job redesign. High scores reveal that a job is capable of stimulating intrinsic motivation and suggest that a performance problem is not due to demotivating job characteristics. The MPS is computed as follows:

MPS = Skill Variety + Task Identity + Task Significance + Autonomy + Feedback

Since the JDS is a long questionnaire, you will complete a subset of the instrument after observing a worker for five minutes. This will enable you to calculate the MPS and to identify the worker's job characteristics.

Instructions

Organize a group of four students. Each group member will first assess the MPS of one of the following jobs you can readily observe and then will identify which core job characteristics need to be changed. Once each group member completes these tasks, the group will identify the job with the lowest MPS and devise a plan for redesigning it.

Professional/Technical: manager in a grocery store, retail store, or fast-food restaurant or a professor

Clerical: secretary at a local business or the university

Sales: salesperson in a retail store or car dealership

Service: hairstylist, manicurist, or mechanic

Analytics

The following steps should be used. You should first complete the 12 items from the JDS for the job you observe. Write your response in the space provided next to each item. After completing the JDS, use the scoring key to compute a total score for each of the core job characteristics.

1 = very inaccurate
2 = mostly inaccurate
3 = slightly inaccurate
4 = uncertain
5 = slightly accurate
6 = mostly accurate
7 = very accurate]

_____1. Supervisors often let the person know how well they think they are performing the job.
_____2. The job requires the person to use a number of complex or high-level skills.
_____3. The job is arranged so that the person has the chance to do an entire piece of work from beginning to end.
_____ 4. Just doing the work required by the job provides many chances for the person to figure out how well they are doing.
_____5. The job is not simple and repetitive.

_____ 6. The job is one where a lot of other people can be affected by how well the work gets done.

_____ 7. The job does not deny the person the chance to use their personal initiative or judgment in carrying out the work.

_____ 8. The job provides the person the chance to completely finish the pieces of work they begin.

_____ 9. The job itself provides plenty of clues about whether or not the person is performing well.

_____ 10. The job gives the person considerable opportunity for independence and freedom in how they do the work.

_____ 11. The job itself is very significant or important in the broader scheme of things.

_____ 12. The supervisors and coworkers on this job almost always give the person feedback on how well they are doing in their work.

Scoring Key

Copy your answers below and add the job characteristics.

Skill variety (add scores from questions 2 and 5; divide by 2) _____
Task identity (add scores from questions 3 and 8; divide by 2) _____
Task significance (add scores from questions 6 and 11; divide by 2) _____
Autonomy (add scores from questions 7 and 10; divide by 2) _____
Feedback from job itself (add scores from questions 4 and 9; divide by 2) _____
Feedback from others (add scores from questions 1 and 12; divide by 2) _____
MPS (add all scores to calculate the total) _____

Finally, use the JDS norms provided to interpret the relative status of the MPS and each individual job characteristic.

Norms

Type of Job				
	Professional/ Technical	Clerical	Sales	Service
Skill variety	5.4	4.0	4.8	5.0
Task identity	5.1	4.7	4.4	4.7
Task significance	5.6	5.3	5.5	5.7
Autonomy	5.4	4.5	4.8	5.0
Feedback from job itself	5.1	4.6	5.4	5.1
Feedback from others	4.2	4.0	3.6	3.8
MPS	135	90	106	114

Discussion of Results

Once all group members have finished these activities, convene as a group to complete the exercise. Each group member should present their results and interpretations of the strengths and deficiencies of the job characteristics. Next, pick the job within the group that has the lowest MPS. Prior to redesigning this job, however, each group member needs more background information. The individual who works in the lowest-MPS job should thus provide a thorough description of the job, including its associated tasks, responsibilities, and reporting relationships. A brief overview of the general working environment is also useful. With this information in hand, the group should now devise a detailed plan for how it would redesign the job.

Discussion Questions

1. Using the norms, which job characteristics are high, average, or low for the job being redesigned?

2. Which job characteristics did you change? Why?

3. How would you specifically redesign the job under consideration?

4. What would be the difficulties in implementing the job characteristics model in a large organization?

Source: Adapted from Group exercise: Applying the job characteristics model. (n.d.). Retrieved from http://highered .mheducation.com/sites/dl/free/0077437632/946482/8_Group_ Exercise_Applying_the_Job_Characteristics.doc; Hackman, J. R., & Oldham, G. R. (1975). Development of the job diagnostic survey. *Journal of Applied Psychology, 60*(2), 159–170.

Case Study 6.1

Will Flat Management Fall Flat?

Bill Hunt initially thought "flat management" sounded like a pretty good deal. No bosses. The ability to set his own work priorities. What was not to like?

He found out soon enough. At one organization, Hunt, a Washington-based software engineer, was forced to stay up late drafting human resources plans and codes of conduct about which he knew nothing. At another, he wondered why the people who got stuck with the administrative work formerly done by managers were always women or minorities. In lieu of a formal hierarchy, cliques formed, making it tough for workers who were on the outside and creating what he viewed as a toxic culture.

"I have yet to work in [a flat organization] that was effective," he wrote in June in an article for *Medium*. "Although tech culture fetishizes rule breaking, disdain for authority and meritocracy . . . we could all do with a few more rules—and a few more managers."

Hunt is not alone in his skepticism. For a number of years, the key elements of flat management—trimming managerial layers and giving employees more control over decision-making—have become a go-to solution for lagging performance. In an era when the fastest-growing companies pride themselves on being lean, innovative, and poised to respond to an increasingly unpredictable global economy, this approach was supposed to make organizations more efficient. It is also millennial-friendly in its rejection of hierarchy and its goal of having all employees contribute to an overarching mission.

But as many companies struggle to make "flat" work, critics are pushing back over what some of them dismiss as just another management fad. Even executives who embrace the concept in the abstract often tell researchers they doubt its practicality, at least at their company.

"We've gone pretty far to the hype side," says Ethan Bernstein, a management professor at Harvard Business School. "It turned out that a flat structure opened up a whole new set of challenges. Some companies have the appetite to address these. Others don't."

Bernstein is referring to Holacracy, a self-management system used by Zappos, among other companies. The online shoe retailer's struggles to replace hierarchy with collaboration have been widely chronicled. Despite challenges, which included work time spent debating whether an employee should be allowed to bring her mini-pig to the office, Zappos has stayed with the program, but many companies are rethinking the no-bosses rule. Others are scaling back; limiting self-management to a single department, for example, or reintroducing some hierarchy as a way to regain control. Moving to flatter management, it turns out, is much harder than many bosses imagined it would be.

A pair of recent Stanford University studies found that many people actually like hierarchy and the incentive it provides for advancement. Despite today's cheaper communication technologies, social networking and crowd sourcing, Jeff Pfeffer, a professor of organizational behavior at Stanford, dismisses the idea that corporations are becoming more egalitarian as partly wishful thinking. Other business scholars worry that this view is shortsighted and that companies resistant to change are giving up too soon. "This is a trend that is not going away," says Joe Carella, assistant dean of executive education at the University of Arizona. "The world is changing at a pace it hasn't before, and we're moving at exponential speed. We need to redesign how management works."

Is the answer a flatter management structure? In a recent executive survey, Carella says he found that while 70 % of respondents admired flat management principles, half of them did not think they could make it happen at their company, primarily because of the capital outlay involved in shifting to a new system.

What Is a Flat Organization?

A flat organization is one with fewer layers of management. Variants include:

Lattice. Used by W.L. Gore & Associates, makers of Gore-Tex fabric, this structure is set up so that everyone in a company is connected to everyone else and can go directly to those they need to in order to get their jobs done.

Holacracy. Power is distributed across the organization in a series of teams or circles.

Network centric. Employees network inside the company with colleagues and outside the company with manufacturers.

"Flat management" is often used interchangeably with "self-management," the term consultants and academics generally prefer. "Just because you have no bureaucracy doesn't necessarily mean flat," says Harvard's Bernstein. "If you put a bunch of people in a room, they will find a way to order."

Bernstein pinpoints the advent of self-managed teams as occurring in British coal mines about 65 years ago. Until then, coal had been mined like an assembly line, with each team performing a single task and having to finish its shift before another team could begin. That is, until miners in South Yorkshire decided to organize their work differently. With minimal supervision, groups of workers interchanged roles and performed multiple tasks, which allowed the mine to function 24 hours a day without miners waiting for a previous shift to finish. Once self-managed teams proved successful, it was only a matter of time, Bernstein said, before people started thinking about self-managed organizations.

Discussion Questions

1. Discuss the advantages and disadvantages of flat management. Do you feel the advantages outweigh the risks?
2. List three things that you think are necessary for flat management to work. In other words, what are the characteristics of the employees, the work, and the organization that would support flat management?
3. Would you prefer to work in an organization that has flat management or a traditional organizational structure? Explain your answer.

Source: Adapted from Murray, K. (2017). Flat management. *SAGE Business Researcher.* Retrieved from http://businessresearcher .sagepub.com/sbr-1863-104388-2861221/20171023/flat-management.

Self-Assessment 6.1

How Much Structure Do You Need?

This self-assessment exercise identifies your personal need for structure. Although the items refer to structure in a general sense, they relate to the workplace also. There are no right or wrong answers, and this is not a test. You don't have to share your results with others unless you wish to do so. The goal of the assessment is to help you understand the level of structure at which you are most comfortable. This, in turn, can help you determine what type of organizational design (e.g., flat vs. hierarchical) might suit you best.

Statements	Strongly Agree	Agree	Neutral	Disagree	Strongly Disagree
1. It upsets me to go into a situation without knowing what I can expect from it.	1	2	3	4	5
2. I enjoy having a clear and structured mode of life.	1	2	3	4	5
3. I like a place for everything and everything in its place.	1	2	3	4	5
4. I don't like situations that are uncertain.	1	2	3	4	5
5. I hate to change my plans at the last minute.	1	2	3	4	5
6. I hate to be with people who are unpredictable.	1	2	3	4	5
7. I find that a constant routine enables me to enjoy life more.	1	2	3	4	5
8. I become uncomfortable when the rules in a situation are not clear.	1	2	3	4	5
9. I'm not bothered by things that upset my daily routine.	1	2	3	4	5
10. I like being spontaneous.	1	2	3	4	5
11. I find that a well-ordered job with regular hours makes my life tedious.	1	2	3	4	5
12. I enjoy the exhilaration of being put in unpredictable situations.	1	2	3	4	5

Part I. Taking the Assessment

Instructions: Circle the response that best describes your behavior.

Part II. Scoring Instructions

In Part I, you rated yourself on 12 questions. Add the numbers you circled in each of the columns to derive your personal need for structure score.

Personal need for structure: _____

Interpretation:

If you completed the assessment according to the instructions above, you should have a score somewhere between 12 and 60. The score can be generally interpreted as follows:

- 12–24: Low personal need for structure
- 25–45: Moderate personal need for structure
- 46–60: High personal need for structure

Discussion Questions

1. What is your level of personal need for structure? Provide examples from your life. For example, do you plan ahead, or do you tend to "wing it"? Do you keep your things organized or scattered around?
2. What types of jobs or industries might be a good fit for you, considering your need for structure? Which jobs or industries might not be?
3. Discuss the advantages and disadvantages of your personal need for structure.

Source: Thompson, M. M., Naccarato, M. E., Parker, K. C., & Moskowitz, G. B. (2001). The personal need for structure and personal fear of invalidity measures: Historical perspectives, current applications, and future directions. In *Cognitive social psychology: The Princeton symposium on the legacy and future of social cognition* (pp. 19–39).

Get the tools you need to sharpen your study skills. SAGE edge offers a robust online environment featuring an impressive array of free tools and resources. Access practice quizzes, eFlashcards, video, and multimedia at **edge.sagepub.com/scanduragower**.

COMMUNICATION

CHAPTER LEARNING OBJECTIVES

After studying this chapter, you should be able to:

7.1 Define communication and explain the significance of organizational communication.

7.2 Provide an example of how the use of language affects the communication process by creating noise.

7.3 Describe the areas in which organizations conduct training in communication skills.

7.4 Discuss the advantages and disadvantages of electronic communication.

7.5 Explain the strategies for communicating effectively across cultures.

7.6 Compare and contrast downward, upward, and horizontal communication.

Get the edge on your studies at **edge.sagepub .com/scanduragower.**

- Take the chapter quiz
- Review key terms with eFlashcards
- Explore multimedia resources, SAGE readings, and more!

Oprah Winfrey's Conversational Competence

Having good conversations with your boss or coworkers is invaluable to managers. But most people don't work on this very much. A popular TED Talk given by Celeste Headlee, "10 Ways to Have a Better Conversation," points out that "conversational competence is probably the most overlooked skill." But Headlee asks the question, "Is there any 21st-century skill more important than being able to sustain coherent, confident conversation?"

Oprah Winfrey knows the importance of conversation. This is how she got her start at deeply interviewing people on her legendary talk show. *Oprah Winfrey Show* ratings were higher than those of the three other competing programs on the air at the same time. Why? Her genuine concern for other people shone through in the conversations she had with people on her show. She was interested in people and wanted to learn from them.

According to *New York Times* best-selling author Cheryl Strayed, "the thing that makes [Oprah] get up and do that work that she does every day is that genuine desire to connect with people and be vulnerable and to be open to what is going to happen next. And that kind of curiosity has driven her to these great heights."

It certainly has. Oprah is one of the wealthiest and most powerful American women. Her net worth is estimated at over $3 billion. She is greatly admired and even loved by many. She is the chairwoman, CEO, and CCO (chief creative officer) of her own company, Oprah Winfrey Network. She is one of those rare celebrities who are recognized by their first name only.

Oprah is sincere and has a unique way of communicating without being boring—she often raised taboo topics but did so in a way that made audiences okay with it. She interviewed drugs addicts and people with all forms of alternative lifestyles. She asked questions that no one else would dare ask.

Oprah is also one of America's best storytellers. When she won the Cecil B. DeMille Award at the Golden Globes in 2018, she started her speech with a story: "In 1964, I was a little girl sitting on the linoleum floor of my mother's house in Milwaukee watching Anne Bancroft present the Oscars for the best actor at the 36th Academy Awards . . ." She went on to relate a touching story about her mother.

Oprah Winfrey accepts the 2018 Cecil B. DeMille Award during the 75th annual Golden Globe Awards.

©Handout/Handout/Getty Images

Maybe we can't all deliver the "Wow!" moments like Oprah does. But there are some things she does that we can all learn from.

- *Tell a story.* Stories are an important part of your communication competence. They make your conversations interesting. Oprah's rags-to-riches story is the American dream.
- *Seek opposites, and place them next to each other.* Talk about your greatest success, then pair it with a story about your greatest failure. This puts your success in context and makes the message of your success story even more forceful. Oprah did this with her Golden Globes speech by linking one of the pinnacles of her career with her humble beginnings.
- *Don't shy away from the pain.* Pain is where the depth of a story lives. Don't leave out the parts that are hard to talk about. Oprah has been open with her audience about the hard times in her life and career. She has openly discussed her experiences of poverty, neglect, and sexual abuse. People relate to her struggles, which makes her even more admirable.
- *Make it personal.* Don't hold back your own emotions; it gives others permission to feel. Oprah broke the mold in her television show by showing a range of emotions: laughing, gasping, and other nonverbal body language.
- *Use repeats.* Repeating a key phrase isn't boring, but it must be done carefully. It makes your message memorable. Repeating phrases works. Speaking is like singing; the chorus is repeated.

Oprah is the master of one of the most famous sound bites in TV history: "You get a car! And you get a car! And you get a car!"

Some people think Oprah's communication style is magic, but it might be more accurate to say she's a smart storyteller. She uses principles of effective communication to create moments we remember.

Oprah understands that effective communication is essential for success. This chapter will discuss organizational communications and how knowledge flows within (and outside) organizations. First, we will begin with the definition of organizational communication.

Sources: Adapted from Astrum People. (n.d.). Oprah Winfrey biography: Success story of American media mogul. Retrieved from https://astrumpeople.com/oprah-winfrey-biography/; Clifford, C. (2017). Oprah succeeded because of effective communication. Retrieved from https://finance.yahoo.com/news/oprah-succeeded-thanks-communication-skills-182532775.html; Coyle, D. J. (2018, January 12). The queen's method: How Oprah communicates so well. Retrieved from http://danielcoyle.com/2018/01/12/queens-method-oprah-communicates-well/; Headlee, C. (2015). 10 ways to have a better conversation [Video file]. Retrieved from https://www.ted.com/talks/celeste_headlee_10_ways_to_have_a_better_conversation?language=en; Rashidi, J. (2018). What can Oprah teach us about communication? Retrieved from https://seedx.us/what-can-oprah-teach-us-about-communication/.

▼ FIGURE 7.0

Textbook Organization

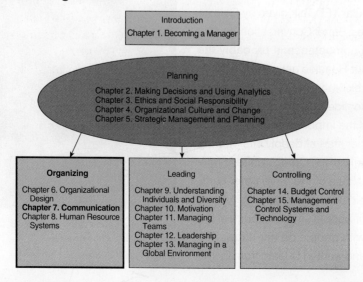

What Is Communication?

The Merriam-Webster dictionary defines **communication** as "a process by which information is exchanged between individuals through a common system of symbols, signs, or behavior."[1] The importance of communication by managers was first articulated in 1938 in the classic book *The Functions of the Executive*: "The first function of the executive is to develop and maintain a system of communication."[2] **Organizational communication** is "the process by which individuals stimulate meaning in the minds of other individuals by means of verbal or nonverbal messages in the context of a formal organization."[3] A manager's ability to communicate effectively is important, since it relates to both job performance and job satisfaction.[4] Organizational communication had emerged as a discipline by the 1960s and is an area of specialization in communication today.[5] Organizational communication has been referred to as "the social glue that ties organizations together."[6]

It is estimated that managers spend over 80% of their time communicating with other people.[7] In a study of 4,370 recent business administration graduates, 95% reported that the ability to communicate orally and in writing was considered important for success in their jobs.[8] The purpose of this chapter is to provide you with communication skills and an understanding of the management of knowledge flows in organizations. First, we will discuss research on why some people are afraid to communicate with another person, in a group, or when giving presentations.

Communication Apprehension

Some people are just uncomfortable communicating with others, and this may create problems for their success as managers. Communication researchers define **communication apprehension (CA)** as "an individual's level of fear or anxiety with either real or anticipated communication with another person or persons."[9] CA may affect communication between two parties, within teams, during meetings, or when giving presentations. A meta-analysis of 36 studies on CA found that it is negatively related to both the quality and quantity of communication.[10] CA may affect numerous aspects of communication in organizations. For example, people with high CA may seek jobs with lower communication requirements and then seek less advice from their boss.[11] A study of CA and leadership abilities of 263 students found that CA was detrimental to performance even though these students had high intellectual ability (i.e., their GPA was taken into account in the study).[12] The research showed CA to be negatively associated with students' perceptions of their adaptability, appreciation for a multicultural world, and willingness to take on leadership roles. The authors recommend self-awareness (being aware that you are high in CA) and assertiveness training to overcome this communication barrier. To learn whether or not you have CA, complete Self-Assessment 7.1.

You may have assumed that communication in organizations entails a manager giving directives to their employees. However, this is not the most effective mode of communication. The next section describes the difference between one-way and two-way communication.

One-Way Versus Two-Way Communication

In **one-way communication**, the manager sends a message (either verbal or written) and it is received by employees. There is no way for the manager to know if the message was received correctly, because there is no way to receive questions from the employees regarding whether the message was understood. For this reason, one-way communication is considered a flawed method of communicating in organizations. A better process is **two-way communication**, in which the manager sends a message to employees and allows for questions to be asked so that feedback is received by the manager regarding whether or not the message was understood.

You can learn the importance of two-way communication by completing Toolkit Activity 7.1. Research has demonstrated that two-way (bilateral) communication is more effective than one-way (unilateral) communication because receivers understand the information better and their ability to implement the information is improved.[13] Thus, we will begin our discussion of organizational communication by describing the two-way communication process.

The Communication Process

The **Shannon-Weaver model of communication** is a fundamental model of the dynamics of the two-party communication process.[14] The key elements of the communication process are shown in Figure 7.1. and described below.

1. **Sender.** This is the source of the message transmission who selects a desired message out of a set of possible messages. The message may consist of written or spoken words, pictures, music, or combinations of these. The message may also contain non-verbal behaviors such as gestures. For example, a manager prepares a new policy for her employees consisting of a written outline of the policy.

2. **Encoding.** This is the transformation of the message into the signal, which is sent over the communication channel from the transmitter to the receiver. For example, the manager transmits the new policy to all employees via email; the manager is the encoder.

3. **Channel.** The channel is the medium that transmits the message. The choice of communication channel (or medium) is influenced by institutional conditions (e.g., incentives, trust, and physical proximity) and situational conditions (e.g., urgency, task) and by the routine use of the media over time.[15] The choice of communication medium (e.g., email versus face-to-face) affects both attitudes and behaviors of the receiver.[16] In the example above, the channel is email.

4. **Decoding.** The receiver(s) then decode(s) the message sent through the selected channel or channels by translating what is seen and heard into an understanding of the message. This does not proceed perfectly, since there is **noise** in the communication process that affects the decoding process. Noise is any communication barrier that may affect how a person interprets a message. For example, perceptual biases, language choices, cultural differences, and/or a full email inbox may affect how a person decodes a message and result in errors. In the example above, the employees receive the manager's email regarding the new policy and consider how to implement it.

5. **Receiver.** The receiver is the person or persons who receive the message. There may be noise on the receiver's part as well. For example, the receiver may not be paying attention, or they may be distracted by receiving a pop-up on their computer with a new email. In the example above, the receivers are the employees included in the distribution list in the email sent from the manager.

The Importance of Feedback in the Communication Process

The Shannon-Weaver model was further developed by Melvin L. DeFleur in 1970 to factor in a feedback loop by which the success or failure of the messaging can be assessed, then addressed if necessary.[17] The arrow beginning at the base of the diagram in Figure 7.1 depicts the feedback loop that points from the receiver back to the sender. This arrow reflects a widely accepted contribution of the model, namely, that for a sender to know whether and how effectively a message has been communicated, feedback is needed from the intended receiver of the message. Feedback is therefore critical in the communication process. Feedback increases receivers' confidence that they have understood the message and improves the accuracy of

The Communication Process

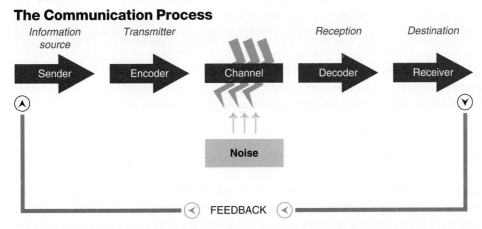

SHANNON-WEAVER'S MODEL OF COMMUNICATION

Sources: Communication Theory. (n.d.). Shannon-Weaver's model of communication [Figure]. In Shannon and Weaver model of communication. Retrieved from https://www.communicationtheory.org/shannon-and-weaver-model-of-communication/; Weaver, W. (1949). Recent contributions to the mathematical theory of communication. *The mathematical theory of communication, 1*, 1-12.

performance.[18] Thus, a manager must check to see that the message was understood by followers.

Example of the Shannon-Weaver Model

The following example illustrates how the communication process works, and how noise affects interpretation of the message. A manager sends a message via a mobile-phone text to his worker about a meeting happening about their brand promotion. The employee does not receive the full message because of noise.

> Manager: *We have a meeting at the office (at 8 a.m.*
>   *goes missing due to phone network*
>   *disruption—in other words, noise)*
> Employee (feedback): *At what time?*

This example has the following elements:
Sender: Manager
Encoder: Telephone network company
Channel: Mobile network
Noise: Missing text due to network disruption
Decoder: Mobile phone
Receiver: Employee

Phone network disruptions are a source of noise when using text messages to communicate.

©iStockphoto.com/Georgijevic

The transmission error is the noise in this case. The feedback loop lets the businessman know that the message reached the receiver incomplete. The receiver then gets the chance to comprehend the full message only after his feedback.[19] You will practice giving feedback to your teammates by completing the Toolkit Activity 7.2. Feedback reduces the noise in the communication process. Another important source of noise is the language that people use to communicate with one another. The next section discusses the additional language barriers to communication, including jargon and trigger words.

Language Barriers to Effective Communication

Communication in organizations may be affected by "noise" that results from the language managers and employees use to communicate. The next sections will discuss the use of jargon and trigger words and how they present barriers to effective communication.

Jargon

Words may have different meanings to different people, even if they are communicating in the same language. **Jargon** is defined as the language, especially the vocabulary, peculiar to a particular trade, profession, or group.[20] Jargon is frequently used in organizations and can be bewildering to new employees or those outside the organization. For example, a new employee may be told by her boss to "drill down" the data in her market analysis report. What does it mean to drill down? According to the Urban Dictionary, *drill down* is a term used by computer systems people to describe the act of clicking with a computer mouse down through several levels of folders or drop-down menus to reach a specific file, application, or folder.[21] But in information technology (IT), the word *drill down* means to move from summary information to detailed data by focusing in on something.[22] This example shows that beyond vocabulary, it is important to understand the context of business jargon and multiple meanings for the same phrase.

To make matters even more complicated, organizations develop their own jargon that is unique to their culture.[23] For example, employees who work at Disney theme parks know the meaning of *backstage* in their organization. Do you? Disney is careful to hide the more mundane features of its theme parks from guests, such as staff locker rooms, security offices, and utilities. Of course, the most famous (and extreme) example of Disney hiding things away from guests is the underground tunnels at Disney World's Magic Kingdom. These were based on Walt Disney's original ideas for the never-built Experimental Prototype Community of Tomorrow (now known as EPCOT), a futuristic city that would have seen its roads buried underground to avoid its residents having to deal with traffic and smog. The tunnels span an incredible 392,040 feet. This increased land preparation costs by some $5 million—a huge sum back in the late 1960s when work began.[24] The tunnels and other areas unseen to visitors are referred to as *backstage* by Disney employees.

Trigger Words

The words and phrases used by managers can evoke emotional responses and change the nature of communication.[25] The words used may not be actual insults but may have the same emotional impact on the receiver of the message. **Trigger words** (or "communication freezers") are phrases and words that result in communication breakdowns. These include such language as telling the other person what to do, delivering ultimatums, labeling the other person, and characterizing the other person's motives.[26] Examples of these emotional trigger words and phrases are shown in Table 7.1. Thus, the actual words that a manager uses to communicate may evoke unintended emotional reactions.

A research study[27] examined the effects of emotional trigger words during a conflict-laden negotiation situation. Results showed that trigger words that result in emotional responses are likely to increase the perception that the party using them is being unfair. However, the use of such words increases the optimism of observers that the conflict will be successfully resolved. Another interesting finding of this study is that trigger words affect women and men differently. Specifically, males are less likely to see emotional triggers as an aid to resolving

Examples of Emotional Trigger Words and Phrases

Emotional Interpretation	Phrases	Words
Being negatively labeled; being belittled	You are lying Don't be stupid You are being unfair It was your fault	Liar Silly Unfair Stupid
Being told what they can't do; being told what they ought to do	I can't do anything more You need to . . . Come on . . . No, that is impossible	Can't Must Ought to Never
Sender appealing to higher source (or an ideal); being blamed; sender abdicating responsibility	Why do you think that would be fair? You should have known that You are a better person than that	Fair Ethical Moral Better
Rude: sender not listening; sender giving insincere praise; sender using sarcasm; sender using absolutes; sender educating them	What do you mean? In all due respect . . . Who do you think you are? It is easy to see Why are you making this such a big deal? This is ridiculous	Why, why, why Whatever (interrupting) Truthfully, Obviously, You always You never
Sender labeling their own behavior as superior	I'm being reasonable I'm giving 110% to this project I deserve the most I should get more I know what I'm doing	Reasonable Deserve

Source: Adapted from Schroth, H. A., Bain-Chekal, J., & Caldwell, D. F. (2005). Sticks and stones may break bones and words can hurt me: Words and phrases that trigger emotions in negotiations and their effects. *International Journal of Conflict Management, 16*(2), 102–127.

a dispute. Men are more likely to see the absence of those triggers as indicative of fairness and problem-solving than women.

CRITICAL THINKING QUESTIONS

Describe a time when someone used one of the trigger phrases or words in communication with you. How did use of that language make you feel? Did you want to continue to engage in the conversation after this?

Improving Organizational Communication

Learning Objective 7.3: Describe the areas in which organizations conduct training in communication skills.

Organizations seek to improve organizational communication through training managers and employees. Next, we will discuss training (and active listening, which is a focus of training programs).

Training

Corporations spend over 13 million dollars a year in training, according to a study conducted by the Brandon Hall Group's Training Benchmarking Survey.[28] Millions of dollars of this training is in communication skills for managers and employees.[29] Employers look for applicants with good communications skills, and then continue to invest in communication skills training. Employers want managers who can express themselves both verbally and in writing. According to Anton Dvovin of Desktop Alerts, a communication company, communication training programs improve the communication skills of employees in the following areas.[30]

- *Public speaking:* This type of training focuses on speaking basics and practice. For example, the training may cover how to use changes in voice to capture attention.
- *Writing:* Managers often communicate through email messages and memos. Managers who write well are seen as more credible and capable. Poor writing is costly. Time spent fixing mistakes due to poor writing costs U.S. firms $3.1 billion every year.
- *Customer service:* Customer service employees listen and meet the needs of customers. Customer service training usually focuses on competencies like consistency (everyone is treated the same—no matter how nasty they are). Also, communications skills are taught (for example, positive phrases to say when customers are upset).
- *Interpersonal communication:* Employees interact with different communication styles. Role-play exercises are often used to help employees learn how to interact with different communication styles. This may include conflict resolution. Effective interpersonal communication helps prevent and resolve conflict.

Learn about your own communication style in comparison to others by completing Self-Assessment 7.2.

A key skill that is often taught in interpersonal communication training is active listening, which is needed in conflict resolution. Employees need to hear another person's point of view. Active listening is also needed by managers for gathering feedback from employees.

Active Listening

Active listening is a way of listening that is "a creative, active, sensitive, accurate, empathic, nonjudgmental listening."[31] People who are listened to feel they are understood better than participants who receive either advice or a simple acknowledgment. This increases the satisfaction people feel about the conversations they have. Active listening can increase job performance. For example, active listening is a tool used by effective salespeople—they do more listening than talking to their potential customers.[32] Active listening has three components:

1. It has moderate to high nonverbal involvement.
2. It reflects the speaker's message using verbal paraphrasing.
3. It asks questions that encourage speakers to elaborate on their experiences.[33]

Managers who are active listeners become more effective, since listening opens the feedback loop and they can verify their communications to clarify messages. It also encourages more two-way communication between managers and employees.[34] According to Kevin Sharer, former CEO of the biotechnology giant Amgen,

Customer service training is essential in a call center.

©iStockphoto.com/Kritchanut

Active Listening Guidelines

- Be compassionate and exercise empathy. Try to find solidarity with the other person. Imagine what it would be like to be in their position in order to understand how they feel and what they are saying.
- Pay attention. Eliminate distractions and listen carefully. Try not to let your mind wander and do not interrupt.
- Indicate your understanding and acceptance without speaking. Use nonverbal cues, including:

  o Changing the tone of your voice as appropriate
  o Using gestures and facial expressions
  o Making eye contact
  o Using body language and posture that indicate that you are receptive to the other person's ideas

- Reflect by restating what you have heard. Paraphrase the person's thoughts and feelings, asking for clarification if needed. Do not add judgment or assessment. For example, you could say, "I am hearing you say that . . . Do I have that right?" Avoid interjecting. Do not interrupt. Hold back on advice or suggestions unless they are specifically requested. Do not offer unsolicited stories about your personal experience or times when you had similar feelings. Refrain from expressing your feedback, such as emotions, disagreements, or opinions, unless it is requested.
- Stay impartial. It is not your job to take sides.
- When you ask questions, make them open-ended. If you need clarification, be polite and respectful—not defensive. For example, you might ask, "Can you tell me more about that?" or "Could you explain what you meant when you said . . .?"

Source: Stanford Graduate Center of Education, John W. Gardner Center for Youth and Their Communities. (2007). Youth Engaged in Leadership and Learning. Retrieved from http://gardnercenter.stanford.edu/docs/YELL.0712.Intro.final.pdf.

As you become a senior leader, it's a lot less about convincing people and more about benefiting from complex information and getting the best out of the people you work with. Listening for comprehension helps you get that information, of course, but it's more than that: it's also the greatest sign of respect you can give someone.[35]

Guidelines for active listening are provided in Table 7.2.

CRITICAL THINKING QUESTIONS

Provide an example of a meeting in which you will need to listen actively to another person (for example, you are trying to resolve a conflict with your roommate or a friend). Why is it important to listen to the other person's point of view? Using the guidelines in Table 7.2, outline your strategy for active listening in the meeting.

Communication Challenges

Learning Objective 7.4: Discuss the advantages and disadvantages of electronic communication.

The Impact of Technology on Communication

As the following sections will illustrate, technology has had a significant impact on communication in organizations. A review of how technology has impacted organizations highlights the role of information technology in particular. Information technology began with mainframe computers in the 1950s. Next came the emergence of personal computing in the mid-1970s, and this continues to have a strong influence on communications. The third stage was based on communication technology and began in the late 1990s.[36] During this time, the Internet emerged as a significant force through global networks of computers connected to create a single, large communication network.[37] In the future, information and communication technology will lead to a new stage in which computational technology permeates almost everything, thereby enabling people to access and control their environment at any time and from anywhere. Known as ubiquitous computing, this is creating a space that links people, computers, networks, and objects.

While having employees connected to work 24/7 seems like a good idea for productivity, such connectivity has resulted in more noise in the communication process. In the few minutes it takes to read this section of the textbook, chances are you'll check your phone for voice messages, answer a text, read email, or view an Instagram post. Distractions from work are not new, but as push notifications continually pop up on computer and cell phone screens, some managers believe the problem is getting worse and affecting productivity.

According to a *Wall Street Journal* article titled "Why You Won't Finish This Article,"[38] employees are interrupted—or self-interrupt—roughly every three minutes, with numerous distractions coming through in both digital and human forms. When thrown off track, it can take a worker some 23 minutes to return to the original task.

"It is an epidemic," according to Lacy Roberson, a director of learning and organizational development at eBay Inc. At most companies, it's a struggle "to get work done on a daily basis, with all these things coming at you."[39]

Given technology's impact on communication, it is important to understand the various forms of electronic communication in the workplace.

Electronic Communication

Email

Email has become a primary mode for communicating in organizations. Even employees who work in offices next to one another often communicate by email rather than face-to-face. A study of face-to-face and email communication in a Fortune 500 office equipment firm employing over 100,000 people used interviews, questionnaires, and actual emails. Researchers found that more information is conveyed in email than in other communication mediums. Also, people paid less attention to social cues that suppress information and were more uninhibited in emails.[40]

The Internet has evolved over time, and there are now rules for how to be polite in email. This is termed **netiquette** (email etiquette). Whether you are communicating with a prospective employer or to others you work with, it is sound advice to show good manners. Without knowing netiquette, you might annoy or even offend someone unintentionally. These rules have developed as norms (unwritten rules) over time, so everyone may not be aware of them. According to one communication expert, "netiquette rules are based on common sense and respect, but since email is so quick, we often forget that we are still using a form of written communication."[41] Research on email usage and performance is mixed. The amount of email sent and received is positively related to job performance.[42] Yet some research suggests that checking email frequently may result in interruptions that affect the flow of work.[43] Frequently checking email has been related to information overload and stress.[44] High levels of email use in the workplace relate to avoidant decisional styles, such as procrastination.[45] A study of knowledge workers found that employees adapt to email interruptions through new work strategies as they negotiate the constant connectivity of communication media. For example, employees find ways to leverage the importance of email for environmental monitoring by setting aside uninterrupted work time during which they shut off email alerts.[46]

The lack of visual cues may lead to difficulty in interpreting the meaning of email communications. Miscommunications of emotion occur in email messages more than in face-to-face communications, and this affects both the relationships and the information conveyed. These miscommunications affect both satisfaction and performance.[47]

Text Messages

With the ubiquitous use of smartphones and other mobile devices, employees can now check email and send text messages more frequently than ever—even during evenings and weekends. Text messages are far more likely to be sent from handheld mobile devices than from desktop or laptop computers. The Cellular Telecommunications & Internet Association (CTIA) reported that in 2018, 1.5 trillion text messages were sent in the United State every month.[48] For business communications, it is important to follow the rules of grammar and capitalization and avoid abbreviations (*brb* for *be right back*, for example). Due to their brevity, text messages will probably never replace email as the primary mode for electronic business communications. Also, there are concerns about the privacy of text messages. Finally, general business expectations dictate that sending text messages at work is not a good use of time or is undesirable behavior.[49] However, a recent study found that taking short breaks to use smartphones during working hours increased employee well-being. The authors believe that the use of smartphones may have benefits, but too much time using social media may harm productivity.[50]

When smartphones are used seems to be an important consideration. One interview study found mobile text and email usage patterns to be "dangerous, distracting, [and] anti-social and . . . [to] infringe on work-life boundaries."[51] This research also found that many employees check their email during their commutes to and from work.

CRITICAL THINKING QUESTIONS

> List the advantages and disadvantages of communicating about work using text messages. Explain whether or not you would use text messages to communicate with your boss.

Social Networking

You are probably familiar with **social networking** sites such as Instagram, Snapchat, Facebook, Twitter, and LinkedIn. But social networking has caveats. It is important to keep in mind that if your social media site, such as your Facebook page, is public, your current or prospective employers might check it. It's best to assume that what you post may become public, so discretion matters. For example, employees have been fired for writing about their employer in inappropriate ways in blogs (web logs).[52] The First Amendment does not protect employees by giving them the right to say whatever they want about their job or employer, and many employers, including Cisco, IBM, Intel, and Microsoft, now have specific blogging policies.[53]

On the other hand, blogs have become popular as a way for managers to promote their organization. Twitter is a microblog that limits messages to 140 characters called "tweets." A social media strategist noted that "smart brands use Twitter in meaningful ways, and most of them use their brand name as a way to make sure customers can find and recognize them."[54] She cited Chevrolet, Wachovia, The Home Depot, Zappos.com, and the Red Cross as some of the most successful Twitter brands. Social media outreach has become an integral part of a PR specialist's job in recent years. "With the onset of social infrastructure such as Facebook, LinkedIn, Twitter and Pinterest, combined with the versatility of web tools, the jobs of public relations specialists are growing at a fast clip," says Gerard Corbett, a chair of the Public Relations Society of America.[55] Today, social media influencers—"independent, third-party endorsers who shape attitudes through . . . social media"[56]—promote products and services. Social media influencers have large numbers of followers, who aspire to their luxurious lifestyle and purchase products shown in blog posts and videos. These influencers are often compensated and receive free products for discussing brands on social media.

Cyberslacking

Another challenge for organizations due to Internet use at work is **cyberslacking**. Research has documented an increase in the use of the Internet for personal reasons during working hours. This may include using social media, shopping, looking at pornography, and looking for another job while at work. "When employees use workplace PCs for personal reasons, the immediate effect is a loss of productivity. . . . Time is an asset and a misuse of that asset is just as wrong as the misuse of any other asset" (p. 56).[57] One study found that 60% of companies surveyed had disciplined employees for inappropriate use of the Internet during work.[58]

Despite the rise of email as the main communication mode for organizations, there still appears to be a need for face-to-face contact. Being able to see another person is important, since face-to-face contact is much richer due to the ability to read nonverbal messages that accompany the words. Thus, videoconferencing is now an important communication mode for organizations.

Videoconferencing

Videoconferencing (or conducting virtual meetings) has long been an important communication mode at the workplace. Virtual meetings may be done via telephone only (a conference call), or they may be face-to-face. Skype has made it possible to speak to one or more persons face-to-face nearly everywhere in the world. Videoconferencing is advantageous because you are able to discern emotions through the tone of voice and/or facial expressions. Most large organizations depend on videoconferencing to coordinate work among employees who are not located in the same place.

Accenture, a technology consulting firm, installed 35 videoconferencing rooms at its offices around the world. In one month alone, its consultants used virtual meetings to avoid 240 international trips and 120 domestic flights, for an annual savings of millions of dollars and countless hours of tiring travel for its workers.[59] Thus, there are cost savings plus reductions in employee travel stress that result from the use of videoconferencing.

Videoconferencing has not replaced face-to-face meetings at companies such as IBM but rather has reduced the number of travel days. For example, Darryl Draper, the national manager of customer service training for Subaru of America, used to travel four days a week for nine months of the year. Now, much of her training is done online.[60] However, the use of videoconferencing has often resulted in five types of communication problems.[61] Team members tend not to communicate local context to others, fail to distribute the same information to all team members, have difficulty understanding and communicating the relative importance of information, access information at different speeds, and have difficulty interpreting the meaning of silence. Virtual teams have higher levels of confusion and lower levels of satisfaction than their face-to-face counterparts, as well as less accuracy recording their decisions.[62] Despite its challenges, videoconferencing has made it possible for employees to communicate from anywhere in the world. Videoconferencing allows for participants to see one another, and this aids communication, since nonverbal communication is important. We will discuss the challenges of nonverbal communication in organizations next.

Nonverbal Communication

When it comes to face-to-face communication, approximately 7% of a person's understanding of others is attributed to words, whereas 38% is attributed to verbal tone and 55% is attributed to facial expressions.[63] **Nonverbal communication** includes the use of visual cues such as body language, posture, distance, eye contact, facial expressions, touch, and voice (paralanguage).[64] The meaning of a message can even be negated by a facial expression or a person rolling their eyes. For example, if a person says, "I love my management class" and rolls their eyes, it means the opposite of what they are saying. If a nonverbal message contradicts a verbal message, the nonverbal message will carry the meaning. On the other hand, nonverbal messages can reinforce a verbal message. For example, a leader can raise their voice slightly while speaking to emphasize a point they are making to the team. Leaders are observed constantly, and every action is analyzed by others.[65] So, it's important to pay attention to nonverbal as well as verbal communication.

Think of it this way: "Leaders are never *not* communicating. As a result, increasing their awareness of nonverbal communication may be a key factor in improving their communication skills and ultimately helping them to become better leaders."[66]

CRITICAL THINKING QUESTIONS

If a person tightly crosses their arms across their body while telling you about the grade they received on their midterm exam, what does the nonverbal communication indicate? Explain why you interpret the nonverbal behavior the way you do.

Cross-Cultural Communication

Learning Objective 7.5: Explain the strategies for communicating effectively across cultures.

An executive from India referred to women in the organization as "females," and U.S. women in the organization thought this was an odd way to refer to them and were offended. As this example illustrates, the ability to communicate effectively with those from other cultures is now an essential management skill.[67] **Cross-cultural communication** compares one culture to another.[68] For example, a cross-cultural communication study of 124 managers from the United States and Russia found that cultural values (respect for authority and group orientation) affected communication competence and performance in teams.[69] A study examined business meetings between British and Chinese managers and found that mismatches in expectations regarding silence during meetings resulted in feelings of "uncomfortable silence."[70] Some examples of miscommunication in intercultural communication follow (this may include literal translation of words as well as symbols):

- Some of IKEA's product names make their customers blush in Thailand. For example, the "Redalen" bed sounds like Thai slang for "getting to third base," while the "jatterbra" plant pot is a rather crude sexual word in Thai. As Thais can be quite conservative, IKEA has been forced to hire a team of local linguists to help them avoid committing any more translation mistakes.[71]
- Global Internet search engine Bing experienced a slight problem after they launched in China, because "Bing" in Mandarin Chinese sounds like "illness," or it could also mean "pancake," depending on what Chinese dialect is used. Therefore, the Internet giant changed the name to "Biying" in China, in reference to the longer Chinese expression "you qui bi ying," which roughly translates as "seek and ye shall find."[72]
- McDonald's inadvertently offended thousands of Muslims by printing a Koran scripture on its hamburger bags. The stir caused by the world's leading purveyor of fast food began with a World Cup promotion featuring the flags of the 24 nations competing in this summer's soccer championship. One of the flags was that of Saudi Arabia.

Bicultural employees understand the nuances of cultural meanings.

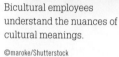

©maroke/Shutterstock

The green-and-white Saudi flag bears an Arabic passage that can be translated as "There is no God but Allah, and Mohammed is his Prophet." Offended Muslims complained that such sacred words should not be crumpled up and thrown in the trash. McDonald's printed 2 million of the bags, intended for takeout orders of children's Happy Meals at its 520 restaurants in Britain. McDonald's had to retreat on its use of the bags.[73]

As these examples show, it is important to have employees who are not only bilingual but bicultural so that they understand the nuances of the cultural meanings of words, as well as nonverbal behaviors. Bilingualism has been shown to improve communication efficiency, particularly when both parties are at least partially fluent with respect to the language of the person they are working with.[74] Differences in language are only part of the challenge of communication with a person from another culture. It has been noted that "language-related inefficiencies take numerous forms: loss of information, added work, loss of learning opportunities, and disruption of the collaborative process."[75] Misunderstandings often occur because of cultural value differences. For example, perceptions of time, individualism (being self-centered), risk, relationship orientation, and power distance (respect for authority) may affect intercultural communications.[76]

There are eight levels of differences where cross-cultural communication can falter: when to talk, what to say, pacing and pausing, listenership, intonation, prosody, formality, indirectness, and cohesion and coherence.[77] Preparation for cross-cultural communication challenges and active listening also improves communication with persons from a culture other than one's own.[78] Finally, training in cross-cultural communication is also effective.[79]

Guidelines for cross-cultural communication follow.[80]

- *The capacity to be nonjudgmental.* People want to explain themselves completely before being judged by another person. For example, when someone is interrupted before they have finished speaking or when they notice a nonverbal cue such as the listener shaking their head in disagreement, it creates a barrier to communication. In cross-cultural communication, people should try hard not to judge what the other person is saying until they have a complete understanding of the situation.
- *Tolerance for ambiguity.* People vary in their ability to deal with new situations they have not encountered before. Some people have a low tolerance for ambiguity and feel discomfort in a new environment. They may even appear hostile to the person from a different culture as they try to adjust. This is dysfunctional to the development of effective relationships. Learning to manage the feeling of frustration associated with ambiguity is important for being effective in communication with a person from a different culture.
- *The display of respect.* Knowing how to express respect for a person from another culture is an important part of effective cross-cultural communication and relationship development. The expression of respect varies by culture, and it is important to research how respect is shown in the culture of the person you will be interacting with. People love to feel respected by others. Using the right gestures, eye contact, smiles, and words to indicate that you are genuinely respectful of the other party goes a long way in starting

the relationship off on the right track. For example, when a businessperson hands you their business card in Japan, it is important to remember that the highest-ranking people exchange cards first and that one should give and receive cards using both hands, ensure that the card is turned toward the receiver, and keep the cards on display for the duration of the meeting.[81] Shoving another person's business card in your pocket or tossing it aside is considered disrespectful.

- *Personalizing knowledge and perception.* Different cultures interpret the world around them in different ways. Some cultures view their knowledge and perceptions as valid only within their culture. Others tend to assume that their beliefs, values, and perceptions are universal and hold for everyone. The more a person recognizes the extent to which knowledge is individual in nature, the more easily they will be able to adjust to other people in other cultures. Remember that cultural views of what is "true" or "right" are likely to be quite different across cultures.

- *Displaying empathy.* The capacity to "put oneself in another's shoes" is important for the development and maintenance of positive relationships between cultures. People differ in their ability to display empathy. Some people take a real interest in others and gain a complete and accurate sense of another's thoughts, feelings, and/or experiences. Others may lack interest—or fail to display interest—and may be unable to project even superficial understanding of another's situation.

- *Taking turns.* The interactions in which a person takes part must be managed carefully. Some people are skillful at withholding their own contributions until the needs and desires of others have been expressed. This plays a critical role in defining how information is exchanged, and is known as taking turns. This simple factor is important to how one is perceived in one's own culture as well as in other cultures, in which reciprocity in discussion can serve to indicate interest in and concern for the other person. Additionally, taking turns has value for gathering information that can lead to an improved understanding of the other person's communication style.

As the *Fact or Fiction?* box illustrates, differences in nonverbal communication across cultures matter. Gestures may not mean the same thing in different cultures. For example, in the United States not making eye contact may be associated with not telling the truth. However, in certain Arabic cultures, it may be viewed as rude and intrusive to look into another person's eyes. Another example is how close you should be to a person. In Japan, people are comfortable at about 30.2 inches apart; in Venezuela, it is 32.2 inches; and in the United States, it is 35.4.[82] For example, someone from Venezuela could make someone from the United States very uncomfortable by unknowingly invading their space. As these examples illustrate, knowledge of the meaning of nonverbal communication is essential in preparing for an expatriate assignment as well as in conversing at home.

CRITICAL THINKING QUESTIONS

Think of a time when you were communicating with a person from a culture other than your own and they could not understand your meaning. Explain why they didn't understand (for example, was it language or cultural differences?). What could you have done to improve your cross-cultural communication?

FACT OR FICTION?

Does Nonverbal Communication Have the Same Meaning Everywhere?

Nonverbal communication can take many forms, such as facial expressions and body language. If you think nonverbal communication means the same thing everywhere, think again—it's more fiction than fact. Effectiveness as a manager depends on knowing what nonverbal communication is and how meanings may differ between countries. Below are examples of seven forms of nonverbal communication, as well as some cultural differences.

Eye Contact

There is a lot of cultural variation in the acceptability of eye contact. There are also differences in how long you should look into another person's eyes. For example, in Asian cultures, not making eye contact is the respectful thing to do. However, in Latin and North America, eye contact sends the message that two people are equal to one another. Also, people who don't make eye contact in the United States and parts of Europe are presumed to be lying.

Touch

Culture is expressed by how people touch one another (or not). In the United States, for example, using a firm handshake is expected in business greetings. In France, however, people kiss on both cheeks to greet one another. In the Middle East, using the left hand to accept a gift or shake hands is considered very rude. Touching another person at all may be seen as rude in many parts of Asia, and should be avoided.

Gestures

Gestures—the movements you make with your hands or body—are not universal. They may be interpreted quite differently across cultures, so it is important to be aware and considerate of how you use gestures. For example, consider connecting the thumb and index finger in a circle while you relax your other digits. In the United States, this gesture can be understood to mean "okay." People may use it to indicate that something is complete. In Japan, the same symbol means "money." In other countries such as Argentina, France, and Portugal, the gesture can be used to mean "zero" or "nothing." If you make this gesture in an Eastern European country, people may interpret it as obscene.

Physical Space

Cultures vary in terms of how acceptable it is to get close and personal. People from Latin America and the Middle East feel it is fine to be much closer than people in the United States It's important to understand this, since some cultures don't want their physical space violated by others. But moving away from another person from Colombia, for example, might be seen as rude—*why is this person trying to run away from me?*

Facial Expressions

Facial expressions may have different meanings in different cultures. For example, winking is a facial expression particularly varied in meaning. In Latin America, the gesture is often considered a romantic or sexual invitation. The Chinese consider it rude. In Russia, smiling at people is considered rude.

Head Movements

In certain cultures, such as in the Middle East and Bulgaria, the head movement for yes is the opposite of what it is in most other parts of the world. In other words, shaking the head from left to right means yes and not no! If a manager didn't know this, they would think a negotiation had failed if they saw their negotiating partner shaking their head back and forth and smiling.

Posture

Posture can be loaded with meaning. It can be used to assert power, to convey a certain attitude, or even to demonstrate civility or lack thereof. In the United States, if you stand with your hands on your hips, it may be interpreted as a power posture, but someone in Argentina might think you are mad or being aggressive. In Taiwan, lazy, drooping posture is a sign of disrespect, yet people in other parts of the globe might not even notice. Some cultures take grave offense to showing the bottom of your shoe. In many Arabic countries, for instance, sitting with your legs crossed and the sole of your footwear showing would be perceived as an insult.

Paralanguage

It is not just what you say; it is also how you say it. "Paralanguage" refers to the ways you can alter your speech. It includes pitch, accents, volume, and the way you pronounce words. In Great Britain, people raise their voices when they're mad. In India, people get louder to get attention. Silence is yet another tool of paralanguage. In Greece, people use silence as a means of rejecting an idea. However, in Egypt, if someone goes silent in response to your comments, it may mean they agree with your point.

Learning cultural differences in nonverbal behavior is important when conducting international business. By researching the meaning of cross-cultural nonverbals, a manager can avoid embarrassment. Managers should take the time to find out what different gestures mean abroad. This will help them avoid being

(Continued)

(Continued)

seen as rude and decrease cross-cultural misunderstandings. This matters for negotiation, teamwork, and problem-solving.

Discussion Questions

1. Provide an example of a nonverbal communication used in your own culture. Then do an Internet search to determine whether this form of communication has the same meaning in every culture. Were you surprised at what you learned? Explain.

2. Select a country that you will be traveling to or would like to travel to in the future. Conduct an Internet search to learn how to show respect in that culture and describe your results.

3. Explain how understanding the differences in nonverbal communication across cultures will make you more effective in conducting international negotiations.

Sources: Adapted from Bernstein, R. (2017). 7 cultural differences in nonverbal communication. Retrieved from https://online.pointpark .edu/business/cultural-differences-in-nonverbal-communication/; Stoy, A. (n.d.). Nonverbal communication: Different cultures, different meanings for project teams. Retrieved from https://www.brighthubpm .com/monitoring-projects/85141-project-communication-tips-nonverbal-communication-in-different-cultures/.

One of the most important reasons why communication is important is its influence on how knowledge flows in the organization. Sharing knowledge is a key factor that relates to organizational effectiveness. Managers must be able to manage how knowledge flows, and this is discussed next.

Managing Knowledge in Organizations

Learning Objective 7.6: Compare and contrast downward, upward, and horizontal communication.

Knowledge management is "a systematic and integrative process of coordinating organization-wide in pursuit of major organizational goals."[83] It includes the generation, storing, and retrieval of information. Research has shown that knowledge management is related to organizational effectiveness (organization members' perceptions of the degree of overall success, market share, profitability, growth rate, and innovativeness of the organization in comparison with key competitors).[84] As you learned in Chapter 6, the organizational structure provides a general idea of how knowledge may flow in an organization. Based on the organization chart, communication channels in organizations flow in three distinct directions: downward, upward, and horizontally.[85] These communication flows within an organizational hierarchy are depicted in Figure 7.2. Examining these communication channels helps a manager better appreciate the advantages and disadvantages of the different ways knowledge flows in organizations.

▼ FIGURE 7.2

Upward, Downward, and Horizontal Communication

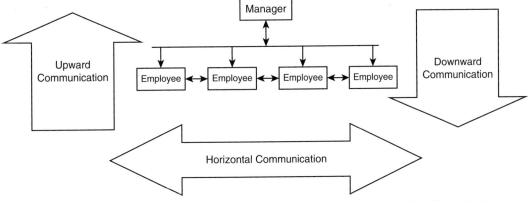

Source: Lunenburg, F. C. (2010). Formal communication channels: Upward, downward, horizontal, and external. *Focus on Colleges, Universities, and Schools, 4*(1), 1–7.

Downward Communication

As its name implies, **downward communication** flows through the chain of command from the C-suite execs to employees at the operating level. Whether communication goes from the highest to the lowest levels via a speech or an email, there are four categories of downward communication.[86]

- *Strategy.* High-level personnel communicate goals and objectives to low-level employees and explain how to achieve them. For example: "We must improve our relations with clients in order to increase retention rates."
- *Procedure.* These types of communications detail uniform procedural guidelines. They may include materials such as employee handbooks or instructional manuals. For example: "Please follow the attached guidelines for getting prior authorization to book overseas travel."
- *Feedback.* To work effectively toward achieving organizational goals and meeting expectations, high-level employees must provide lower-level employees with feedback. This type of feedback happens on two levels: individual and departmental. For instance, managers conduct periodic performance reviews to assess direct reports, and executives may communicate departmental progress at regular intervals. For example: "Juanita, your initiative on the Bauer account exceeded the department's expectations."
- *Socialization.* Social communications can be used to reinforce the organization's values, recognize exceptional performance, or build rapport among team members. Company picnics, awards receptions, and team-building activities are all examples of this type of communication. For example: "The organization would like to thank you for your hard work on the September release by providing a picnic lunch in the park next Monday."

While the downward flow of communication enables the organization's top tiers to set strategy, define procedures, provide feedback, and encourage socialization, it is not without pitfalls. Sometimes, information gets lost or becomes unclear as it makes its way down the chain. The more layers there are in the hierarchy, the more opportunity there is for a message to become distorted as it is passed on. It is essential for information to flow both ways. Upward communication allows managers to assess whether their downward communication was effective.

Upward Communication

While downward communication flows from the top down, **upward communication** flows from the bottom up. It is essential for both determining whether staff have understood downward communication and for enabling employees to share feedback with managers. These are the five types of communication that travel up the chain:

- *Problems.* Subordinate employees notify their supervisors and managers of problems, obstacles, or other difficulties that may affect performance or productivity.
- *Suggestions.* This type of upward communication focuses on improvements and solutions. Employees communicate their advice for maximizing efficiency, improving quality, or solving problems related to products or services.
- *Performance reports.* This information shows higher-level managers how well departments and employees are meeting objectives related to performance and production.
- *Grievances and disputes.* Employees direct their complaints or disputes to supervisors and managers in order to resolve them.
- *Financial and accounting reports.* Budget and expense reports travel from the operational and middle management level to the top tier of management.

Both downward and upward communication are integral to an organization's success. That said, communication from the bottom up does not always flow as readily as it does from the top down. Here are a few reasons for that:

- *Failure to respond.* Managers must work diligently to respond to staff's concerns, reports, and suggestions. Otherwise, upward communication will stall and ultimately shut down.
- *Defensiveness and negative attitudes.* When managers become defensive in response to feedback, employees will likely withhold their thoughts, suggestions, and complaints. When managers show willingness to hear concerns and feedback, it helps keeps the lines of upward communication open and functional.
- *Time and location.* When managers are physically separated from their employees, upward communication can prove difficult. Likewise, long lags in response time can make employees reluctant to speak up about suggestions or complaints.

The following methods can help to improve and foster the growth of healthy upward communication within an organization:

- *Implementing an open-door policy.* When a manager's door is either literally or figuratively open for communication, employees feel invited to share their concerns, feedback, and ideas.
- *Building surveys and exit interviews into the organization's culture.* When managers habitually seek the feedback of current employees and ask departing or retiring employees to share their thoughts, they can access valuable insights about employees' attitudes and the company's policies and practices.
- *Prioritizing participative management.* By enabling employees to participate in decision-making, managers can foster open upward communication. Managers can accomplish this goal by creating teams and task forces to develop policies and procedures.
- *Listening to the grapevine.* Managers may write the grapevine off as gossip, but it provides valuable information about employees' feelings and attitudes. Tuning in to what employees are saying among themselves can help managers problem-solve.

With careful fact-checking, the upward flow of communication in an organization can provide channels for the feedback of information up the organizational hierarchy. The upward flow of information can help solve problems, improve procedures, and build trust between the various levels of the hierarchy.

Horizontal Communication

Upward and downward communication flows follow the organization's formal chain of command. **Horizontal communication** occurs laterally across these chains. It focuses primarily on coordinating shared functions, activities, tasks, and projects within or across departments. Here are three common forms of horizontal communication:[87]

- *Intradepartmental problem-solving.* Members of the same department communicate to coordinate systems management and task completion.
- *Interdepartmental coordination.* Departments work together to manage joint projects or tasks within an organizational system.
- *Staff advice to line departments.* Specialists in functional areas (e.g., IT or finance) communicate with managers to offer support in these areas.

Horizontal communication does not have to follow the rigid hierarchy of top-down or bottom-up communication. It may happen in committees, task forces, or other structures designed explicitly to connect departments or divisions.

External Communication

External communication flows between employees inside the organization and with a variety of people outside the organization. These external communications may involve customers, suppliers, managers in other companies, governmental officials, and residents of the local community. Many large organizations have a public relations office to coordinate their external communications. The Public Relations Society of America (PRSA) defines **public relations** as "a strategic communication process that builds mutually beneficial relationships between organizations and their publics."[88] Public relations is about influencing, engaging, and building relationships with key stakeholders to shape and frame the public perception of an organization. More recently, public relations has been termed "reputation management,"[89] which reflects a recent emphasis on protecting the organization from reputational harm from the media and social media. The *Careers in Management* box describes the job of the public relations specialist in organizations. In addition to specialists, there are some employees, known as boundary spanners (which you learned about in Chapter 6), who communicate both internally and externally with suppliers, customers, or clients. For example, salespeople serve a boundary-spanning role and gather valuable information from customers that can be relayed to management decision-makers.

Communication Networks

In addition to moving through formal communications channels, knowledge may flow through organizations through informal networks. A **communication network** is a pattern of interaction that determines who communicates with whom. These networks can be centralized or decentralized. **Centralized networks** contain a person who is in the center of the communication channel; the information has to pass through them before going to any other member. These types of networks are known as the Y, the wheel, the chain, or the line (Figure 7.3). The line represents the downward communication from managers to employees described above. In the figure, the most central person is indicated in red. Note that the middle manager is most central in this network, and this is because middle managers have access to information from both above and below.

In **decentralized networks**, members of the organization can communicate with anyone. In other words, all the employees have equal communication access to all others. Decentralized networks are the all-channel, the open, and the circle (Figure 7.4). The all-channel network is the most decentralized, with all employees in the network communicating with all others. In the figure, no employees are indicated in red, because all have equal access to the information being shared in the network.

A public relations officer for a company holds a press conference.

©iStockphoto.com/microgen

CAREERS IN MANAGEMENT

Public Relations Specialist

Public relations (PR) specialists generate positive publicity for their organization and enhance the reputation of the organization. For example, the communication director for Amazon is a PR specialist. Another example of a PR specialist is a social media influencer who posts product videos on Instagram. One of the most visible public relations specialists is the press secretary for the president of the United States. A PR specialist may work within the organization in a staff position or be a PR consultant who has a variety of clients.

A PR specialist develops and maintains relationships with journalists, bloggers, and opinion leaders (e.g., a social media account with a large number of followers). They create communications materials such as press releases, interview questions, presentations, video scripts, and speeches. These materials are aimed at reinforcing the organization's positive image and mission. Should a crisis occur, the PR specialist may be the organization's spokesperson for media inquiries. During a crisis, they may also prepare managers for press conferences, interviews, and speeches.

Social media outreach has become an integral part of a PR specialist's job in recent years. "With the onset of social infrastructure such as Facebook, LinkedIn, Twitter and Pinterest, combined with the versatility of web tools, the jobs of public relations specialists are growing at a fast clip," says Gerard Corbett, a chair of the Public Relations Society of America.

The Bureau of Labor Statistics projects that employment for public relations specialists will grow 9% between 2016 and 2026. During that time period, 23,300 new jobs in PR will need to be filled.

What Does a Public Relations Specialist Do in a Typical Day?

To learn about some public relations specialists' duties, Dawn Rosenberg McKay at The Balance Careers looked at job announcements on Indeed.com. She discovered that on a typical day, a public relations specialist might perform some of the following tasks:

- Develop press kit materials, including press releases, pitch letters, case studies, feature articles, and trend stories

- Research, execute, and coordinate projects to advance the company's brand and public relations objectives

- Curate/produce a news web page, which includes building features, finding artwork, posting other stories as necessary, resolving technical problems, and maintaining the design of the pages/articles

- Assist in sharing PR results with internal communications

- Develop and attend trade-show press briefings, manage press-room accommodations, and conduct post-show follow-up

- Cultivate and maintain relationships with regional and media; fulfill media requests for photographs and facts

What Skills Does a Communication Specialist Need?

According to the Annenberg School for Communication and Journalism at the University of Southern California, a public relations specialist needs the following skills:

1. *Communication.* Of course, PR specialists communicate daily. They must be able to communicate ideas clearly and be good listeners. They need to be emotionally intelligent when communicating.

2. *Writing.* A PR specialist must write interesting content. Bring samples of your content to a job interview (e.g., blog posts, articles, press releases, or copy you have written).

3. *Social media use.* PR today is about using social media to manage the voice of the brand online. A PR specialist must know how to use various social media, such as Instagram, Twitter, and Facebook.

4. *Multimedia use.* A PR specialist must know how to use different media tools, such as Photoshop, YouTube, and SEO (search engine optimization).

5. *Creativity.* Whether by writing, rebranding a product or service, or finding ways to attract new customers, PR specialists need to innovate. Organizations are looking for content that catches on and spreads through social media.

Discussion Questions

1. Provide an example of an organization communicating through a social media platform to get the company's image across to followers. Do you think this was effective? Explain why or why not.

2. Why do you think the job prospects for PR specialists will grow in the next decade? Is this a job you would be interested in pursuing? Explain why or why not.

3. From recent events, give an example of a crisis situation that an organization had to handle in the media. Evaluate the effectiveness of the PR strategies employed.

Sources: Adapted from University of Southern California Annenberg, Annenberg School for Communication and Journalism. (n.d.). Five skills every public relations specialist needs [Blog post]. Retrieved from https://communicationmgmt.usc.edu/blog/five-skills-every-public-relations-specialist-needs/; McKay, D. R. (2017). Public relations specialist. Retrieved from https://www.thebalancecareers.com/public-relations-specialist-career-information-524873; U.S. Department of Labor, Bureau of Labor Statistics. (2019, April 12). Public relations specialist. In *Occupational outlook handbook*. Retrieved from https://www.bls.gov/ooh/media-and-communication/public-relations-specialists.htm; What is a public relations specialist? (n.d.). *U.S. News.* Retrieved from https://money.usnews.com/careers/best-jobs/public-relations-specialist.

Recall a situation you have been in where you worked with a team (this could be a class project or student organization). Describe the pattern of communication that occurred in the team. Which of the communication networks shown in Figures 7.3 and 7.4 best describe the communication pattern?

Information flow is faster and more accurate in centralized communication networks, and they work well when the task is simple because it improves efficiency. Centralized networks are generally more efficient when the task requires merely the collection of information in one place.[90] When the task is more complex and there is a greater need for more information, the centralized networks may be inefficient. The central person may become overloaded with information and unable to communicate it precisely down the line. Information may be lost or distorted. Decentralized networks are more efficient when further operations must be performed on the information before the task can be completed.[91]

▼ FIGURE 7.3

Centralized Communication Networks

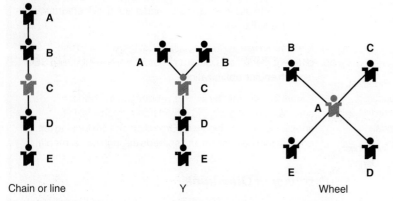

Chain or line   Y   Wheel

Source: Characteristics of groups: Group structure. (n.d.). Retrieved from https://www.tankonyvtar.hu/hu/tartalom/tamop412A/2011-0023_Psychology/070500.scorml; based on Leavitt, H. J. (1951). Some effects of certain communication patterns on group performance. *Journal of Abnormal and Social Psychology, 46*(1), 38–50.

A communication network in Japan.

©metamorworks/Shutterstock

Employees are more satisfied when they work in decentralized networks, as they feel more equal and more empowered. The efficiency of decentralized networks lies in the fact that when group members can freely share their ideas, better solutions can be generated to solve complex problems.[92] Clearly, networks are important to the transfer of knowledge within organizations, and we turn to this subject next.

Knowledge Transfer Within Organizations

Knowledge transfer among organizational units contributes to an organization's ability to innovate by providing opportunities for employees to learn from one another and develop new ideas.[93] Communication networks facilitate the creation of new knowledge within organizations through the various network linkages.[94] However, getting employees to share knowledge is sometimes difficult. A research study[95] of 24 business units in a petrochemical company and 26 business units in a food manufacturing company examined how organizational units gain knowledge from other units to enhance innovation and performance, which is known as **knowledge transfer**. The study found that organizational units produce more innovations and have better performance if they occupy central network positions that provide access to the new knowledge developed by other units. This effect, however, depends on units' **absorptive capacity**, or the capacity of an organizational unit to learn. This absorptive capacity is often reflected in the organization's investment in the unit's research and development.

Employees vary in their ability to transfer and acquire new knowledge because of their differences in access to knowledge and learning ability. Also, absorptive capacity relates to the employee's ability to do something with the knowledge required: to replicate the new knowledge and extend it. Groups that have more knowledge access and learning capacity have more impact on the innovation and performance of the entire organization.

Managerial Implications

This chapter provided an overview of communication and knowledge flows in organizations. The key takeaway points from this chapter are:

- Communication is about the exchange of information, which is essential in management. Organizational communication is the transfer of meaning from one person to another person or persons in the context of the formal organization structure. Managers must understand the communication process and the importance of receiving feedback from the person or persons receiving the message. Two-way communication is more effective than one-way communication.
- There are challenges in organizational communication that are called noise. Sources of noise include the use of jargon, trigger words, and language. Communication apprehension (CA) may also inhibit the communication process, since some people experience anxiety when communicating with another person or in groups.
- To meet the challenges of organizational communication, many organizations invest in training. This training may focus on public speaking skills, writing skills, cross-cultural communication skills, customer service skills, and/or interpersonal communication.
- In organizations, communication is downward (top-down from management to employees), upward (from employees to management), and horizontal (across organizational departments). Communication may also be external, and public

▼ FIGURE 7.4

Decentralized communication networks.

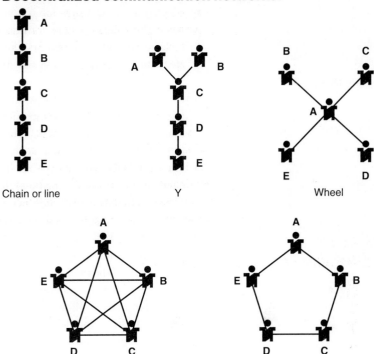

Chain or line   Y   Wheel

All-channel or open   Circle

Source: Characteristics of groups: Group structure. (n.d.). Retrieved from https://www.tankonyvtar.hu/hu/tartalom/tamop412A/2011-0023_Psychology/070500.scorml; based on Leavitt, H. J. (1951). Some effects of certain communication patterns on group performance. *Journal of Abnormal and Social Psychology, 46*(1), 38–50.

Knowledge transfer results in more innovations and better performance.

©ANDRANIK HAKOBYAN/Shutterstock

relations is an important function that protects the reputation of the organization. This is particularly important in a crisis situation.

- Electronic communication is now common in organizations, and email is used more often than face-to-face communication. Electronic communication has a lot of advantages, since managers can communicate from any location 24/7. However, electronic communication has disadvantages, since face-to-face communication is much richer and contains both verbal and nonverbal messages. Research has shown that nonverbal communication (e.g., facial expressions and gestures) carry much of the meaning in communication. Social media has changed the nature of external communication and public relations and exerts a powerful influence on people's perceptions of the reputation of organizations.

- Cultural differences may be a source of noise in communication, and language may be a barrier to understanding meaning. Guidelines for effective cross-cultural communication include being nonjudgmental, having tolerance for ambiguity, displaying respect for the other culture, personalizing knowledge and perception, showing empathy, and taking turns. It is also important to pay attention to nonverbal communication in interactions at home and abroad. Nonverbal behaviors such as gestures and facial expressions carry much of the meaning in communication.

- Managers must pay attention to how knowledge flows in organization and manage these flows. Knowledge flows through organizational networks, taking a variety of forms, both centralized and decentralized. Employees who are central in communication networks play an important role and have power—since knowledge is power. Research has shown that the knowledge transfer within organizational units is related to organizational innovation and performance.

This chapter reviewed practical guidelines for effective communication that every manager needs to know. Communication is interpersonal two-way exchanges between employees. But it is also a system that allows for knowledge transfer in organizational networks.

KEY TERMS

TOOLKIT

Activity 7.1

One-Way Communication

This activity demonstrates what can go wrong in communication: poor listening, lack of feedback, different perceptions.

Materials: 8½ × 11 sheet of paper for each person

Time: 25 minutes (10-minute discussion before, 5 minutes for paper folding, 10-minute discussion after)

Directions: Start this exercise with a discussion of what it means to be an effective communicator by asking the following questions:

1. *Do you think communication is easy or hard? Why?*
2. *What are the most effective ways to communicate meaning? Give some examples.*
3. *Do you think one-way versus two-way communication makes a difference? Why or why not?*
4. *I need a volunteer from the class who thinks they are a good communicator.* (Address the volunteer): *Explain why you are a good communicator.*

Then provide each student with a piece of paper and ask for the volunteer to read the following instructions to everyone:

This exercise requires listening to and following directions. As you hear the instructions, perform the task. You may not ask questions. You must close your eyes.

1. *Fold your sheet of paper in half.*
2. *Tear off the upper right corner.*
3. *Fold your paper in half again.*
4. *Tear off the lower right corner.*
5. *Fold your paper in half.*
6. *Tear off the upper left corner.*
7. *Fold in half a final time.*
8. *Tear off the lower left corner.*
9. *Unfold your paper and hold it up.*
10. *Open your eyes, look at your product, and compare it with the other students' origami.*

Discussion Questions

1. What happened? Does everyone's origami look the same?
2. If you were given the same directions, why are everyone's products different?
3. Why didn't everyone receive the message that was sent?
4. Would you have been able to perform better if you had been able to ask questions? What questions would you have asked?

Source: Adapted from New manufacturing alliance. (2015, August 19). Effective communication skills: Paper fold exercise. Retrieved from http://newmfgalliance.org/media/1472/effective-com-skills-paper-fold-activity-8-19-2015.pdf.

Activity 7.2

Giving and Receiving Effective Feedback

Nearly every organization has a formal system for giving and receiving feedback to employees, and as a manager you will most likely be in charge of providing feedback to your employees. To be clear, very few people like receiving feedback, but when it is done well, you are more likely to listen and implement what you hear. Also, you, too, will be on the receiving end of feedback from your supervisor, so understanding the feedback loop, and how to do it well, will give you a great advantage over many of your coworkers.

A large majority of Fortune 500 companies use what is called a multi-source or 360-degree feedback system. This is where feedback is gathered from the circle of people the employee works with. For example, if you are the manager, a 360-degree performance feedback for you would take into account feedback from your direct reports, your peers (other department managers), your direct supervisor, and you. These results would then be compared to see where agreements and disagreements exist, and most likely your direct supervisor or HR department will review these results with you.

Giving constructive feedback is a critical management skill. As a manager, if an employee is not performing the way you need them to, it is your job to deliver this information and offer ways in which the employee can improve. If you are not comfortable doing this or are not able to do it well, the employee will not know they are underperforming, and you will continue to be frustrated with their work. As you can see, it is not the employee's fault if you do not offer constructive feedback and ways to improve—it is yours.

As mentioned, hearing constructive feedback is hard. Very few of us eagerly seek out hearing what we are not doing well. Therefore, even while it might be difficult, learning how to effectively receive and implement constructive feedback is a critical part of our own self-improvement and self-awareness.

Giving Constructive Feedback

So, how do you learn to give constructive feedback? The first step is thinking of, and even writing down, the list of things the employee does well, and then the list of things they could do better in order to help the department and organization. The next step is thinking about how you would like to hear these things if you were in the employee's shoes. If you are a very blunt person, you will want to back off from that a little bit. Most people like hearing constructive feedback in what we sometimes call a feedback sandwich. Mention a good trait and how it helps, and then mention a constructive point, and follow it up with some suggestions on how to improve.

For example, let's say your employee Ben is often late for work, and as a result department meetings are often delayed, causing the other members to change their daily schedule. When you talk to Ben, start by mentioning that he is a well-liked member of the department (or another positive truth) and that this helps the team continue to work well as a group. Follow that up by saying he is often the last one to arrive at work and that perhaps being more punctual would help his teammates even more, since being late often disrupts the schedules of some of his coworkers. Now put the top on the sandwich and simply ask him why he is often late, and listen carefully to his answers. We often make assumptions about people's behaviors, and a good manager and leader makes sure they have context before taking action. Ben's reason could be any of a number of things, from important and more difficult to change (childcare does not open that early; he has an elderly parent who lives with him and always seems to have a last-minute need, etc.) to easily fixable (the Starbuck's line is long at that time of day). Based on Ben's answer, now ask him if there are any ways to fix this problem that he can think of, because it would really help the department if he arrived at work on time. Also, you should keep an open mind and be flexible based on what you hear. Another solution might be for you to change the meeting time.

Regardless, good constructive feedback is a conversation, not a lecture, and ends with commitments and solutions, which you add to the feedback form in writing (i.e., Ben understands the importance of being here at nine and has made a commitment to be punctual in the future), and both of you initial or sign the document. Always make sure to end the feedback session with positive comments that make you and the employee feel confident in your relationship as you move forward, knowing that you are both serving the best interests of the organization.

Receiving Constructive Feedback

Let's be honest—who wants to hear that they are doing something wrong, or not as well as others? Very few will say initially that they like it, but let's think about it for a minute through the lens of the toilet-paper-on-your-shoe story. Would you rather suffer the potential long-term trauma of finding out you dragged toilet paper around all day on your shoe, or the short-term pang of embarrassment from somebody pulling you aside and gently mentioning it to you so you could fix it right away? Most of us would choose being told right away, and that is the way you need to approach receiving feedback.

None of us is perfect, and if nobody tells us we need to improve or change how to do something, we may have no idea we are not doing it correctly. A good manager will give you frequent feedback to help you improve and not wait for an annual performance appraisal, but giving effective, constructive feedback, as we noted above, is nearly as hard as hearing it.

If you are in the position of receiving constructive feedback, hopefully your supervisor will have read the tips above. As the person receiving the feedback, you should be ready to take notes as you are given your feedback. If the feedback is not accompanied by solutions, a good employee will ask questions like, "What suggestions do you have that will help me improve?" or, "If you were in my position, what steps would you take to correct/improve this?" This gives you ideas directly from your boss, so chances are, if you incorporate the suggested solutions, they will be exactly what the boss is looking for.

Putting Feedback Into Practice

Practicing giving and receiving constructive feedback is easy to do, and just like in anything else, practice makes you better. Get together with your team in class, and come up with a list of personal characteristics you all agree are valuable to the group (one that always seems to pop up is being on time). Think of several others, based on either the performance of your group so far or based on problems you have had with groups in the past.

Once you have come to a group consensus, write up a performance evaluation for each group member using those criteria, and assign a grade of 1 to 5, 5 being the best (and the scale typically used in an organization). Each of your grades needs to be supported by a feedback sandwich, as described above.

After reviewing your performance appraisal and assigning grades for each member, add each person's scores together and divide by the number of criteria you rated to come up with an overall performance appraisal score. Now set up a meeting in a quiet place, or perhaps your instructor will provide time in class, to deliver your feedback to each other.

Don't be surprised if several members agree on your ratings of other members and their ratings of you. Our behaviors are usually obvious to others around us, but not always to ourselves. Also, listen carefully to the feedback others are receiving to make sure you do not develop bad habits, or to get tips on things your group members find to be valuable to the team.

By completing this exercise, your entire group can improve its performance, reduce team stress, and finish up your group project(s) more productively—and probably receive a higher grade. You will also now have a great skill set to take into the workplace to help you, your colleagues, and your organization be more successful.

Discussion Questions

1. How did you feel delivering feedback to your peers?
2. What will you do differently next time?
3. How did you feel receiving feedback from your peers?
4. How will the feedback help your performance?

Case Study 7.1

"Ask Dharmesh Anything" at HubSpot

HubSpot's organizational culture is unique. One of the strongest attributes of the company is the emphasis on open communication—transparency within and outside the organization. This digital marketing automation company redefined what it means to be transparent in business. One of the most notable examples was when HubSpot cofounder Dharmesh Shah published an article on his wiki page called "Ask Dharmesh Anything."

Dharmesh is an introvert, and he realized that while he might *think* he was transparent, many of his employees might not see him that way. Therefore, his wiki page encouraged HubSpotters to ask him anything. The questions could be about technology, strategy, product, marketing, start-ups, funding, or anything they wanted to know. Dharmesh agreed he would answer questions as long as no one was harmed by the response. This was his invitation:

> Ask me anything. Inbound marketing. Startups. Venture Capital. Angel Investment, Corporate Culture—or anything. If there are questions already ask that you're interested in, please upvote them. Feel free to answer questions others have asked! I welcome the discussion.

And that's exactly what "HubSpotters" did—engage in a lot of discussions directly with their chief technology officer.

What Did People Ask?

The communication experiment seemed to work well. Dozens of questions and comments between HubSpotters and Dharmesh appeared on the wiki, and there were some good conversations among the team members.

Wondering what HubSpotters asked Dharmesh? Questions were both serious and lighthearted, and here are some examples:

Question: *What are you naming the baby?* (Dharmesh and his wife were expecting at the time)

Dharmesh: *It's going to be a boy, but we have not yet kicked off the branding project.*

Question: *Why the name HubSpot?*

Dharmesh: *I was looking for a simple name that conveyed the "be at the center of your world" concept. I looked at a bunch of different variations. It turned out that the domain HubSpot.com was still freely available (nobody had registered it). Since I was still in my first year at MIT, and not quite sure where the business was going to head, it was nice to not have to pay thousands of dollars for a domain. The name HubSpot is by no means perfect (we had a couple of serious conversations in the early days about changing it). But, we (I think wisely) decided to stick with it—because we already had some brand equity, and none of the other options we looked at were better enough to warrant the change.*

Dharmesh answered other questions posted regarding HubSpot's culture code, which he posted on the wiki and the company's website. Here are some of the questions and answers:

Question: *There are more CEOs named John than there are female CEOs. How do you nurture women in leadership roles in your business?*

Dharmesh: *Great question. It's something we discuss all the time and have been working intensely on for many years.*

Here are some of the things we're doing:

- *We have a Women@HubSpot group led by the two female members of our leadership team focused on building global programs to empower women at every level of HubSpot*
- *Specifically on the senior leadership issue, we host events focused on increasing the percentage of women on boards that are open to the public and to all of our employees*
- *We also have a sponsorship program to help increase the promotion rate of senior middle managers to leadership positions in the company*
- *We have a Women in Sales group and a Women in Product group focused specifically on creating an amazing experience for women on teams that are historically male dominated*
- *Finally, we identify high value opportunities for rising stars who are women, including conferences, speaking opportunities, and leadership development opportunities*

We have (and are incredibly proud of) our two female board members, who in addition to the rest of our board are actively involved in mentoring and teaching our teams to get better, including targeted sessions for women on our team.

Having said that, we still have a lot of work to do (as does the tech industry generally).

Question: *I love the transparency on how the team at HubSpot has developed the culture and made it what it is today (and will continue to evolve).*

With that said . . .

1. *When you measure "all the things" how do you share that among the company itself?*

   o *Happiness brings about more happiness, so I can only imagine sharing the successes is equally, well Happy.*

2. *Do opportunities come up that you tend to keep internal vs looking for an outside candidate?*

   o *I ask because I've worked with many great customer success team members over the years because they keep getting promoted or offered a unique opportunity to expand themselves professionally. Better for me to get to pick another brain and better for them to continue to grow. But I rarely see those "positions" open up.*

Thanks for such an open and honest (even if everyone else doesn't agree with it) way of doing business, it truly does make it easy to love HubSpot.

Dharmesh: *Appreciate the kind words.*

> *All of the surveys/studies we do—especially the one on employee happiness, we share back with all the employees. That's part of our transparency thing.*
>
> *In most cases, we try to make opportunities available to internal candidates first, before going to the outside. We love internal mobility (people moving around across groups/divisions). Having said that, we also understand the importance of regularly bringing in outside people to ensure that we're not getting too set in our ways, and to learn from people's experience outside of HubSpot.*

Did Asking Dharmesh Anything Help?

When it comes to transparency, HubSpot employees particularly value the accessibility of its management team. In fact, HubSpot ranked number 10 on the 2018 *Boston Globe* Top Places to Work Awards "Management" Top Ten List based on employees' belief that senior managers at HubSpot understood what is going on within the organization.

Discussion Questions

1. What does Dharmesh's openness to answering questions indicate about the organizational culture at HubSpot? Explain.
2. View HubSpot's culture code at https://www.hubspot.com/jobs/culture. Give five words that describe HubSpot's culture.
3. Would you want to work for HubSpot? Explain.
4. Describe the communication strategy of the "Ask Dharmesh Anything" wiki. How does this promote the mission of the organization?

Sources: Adapted from HubSpot. (2016). Ask Dharmesh about the HubSpot culture code. Retrieved from https://inbound.org/blog/ask-dharmesh-about-the-hubspot-culture-code; Shah, D. (2013). I'm Dharmesh Shah, Founder/CTO of HubSpot. Ask me anything. Retrieved from https://growth.org/discuss/hi-i-m-dharmesh-shah-founder-cto-of-hubspot-ask-me-anything; TopWorkPlaces.com. (n.d.). Top work places 2018: HubSpot. Retrieved from https://topworkplaces.com/publication/boston/hubspot-inc/; Vaughan, P. (2011). HubSpotters can ask co-founder Dharmesh Shah anything. Retrieved from https://www.hubspot.com/blog/bid/8174/HubSpotters-Can-Ask-Co-Founder-Dharmesh-Shah-Anything.

Self-Assessment 7.1

Communication Apprehension

This self-assessment exercise identifies your attitudes toward communicating in various situations. The goal of this assessment is for you to learn about your general assumptions about people and work and to understand how this may affect how you lead them. There are no right or wrong answers, and this is not a test. You don't have to share your results with others unless you wish to do so.

Part I. Taking the Assessment

Instructions: Circle the response that best describes your behavior.

Statements	Strongly Disagree	Disagree	Neutral	Agree	Strongly Disagree
1. I dislike participating in group discussions.	1	2	3	4	5
2. Generally, I am comfortable while participating in a group discussion.	1	2	3	4	5
3. I am tense and nervous while participating in group discussions.	1	2	3	4	5
4. I like to get involved in group discussions.	1	2	3	4	5
5. Engaging in a group discussion with new people makes me tense and nervous.	1	2	3	4	5
6. I am calm and relaxed while participating in group discussions.	1	2	3	4	5
7. Generally, I am nervous when I have to participate in a meeting.	1	2	3	4	5
8. Usually I am calm and relaxed while participating in meetings.	1	2	3	4	5
9. I am very calm and relaxed when I am called upon to express an opinion at a meeting.	1	2	3	4	5

Statements	Strongly Disagree	Disagree	Neutral	Agree	Strongly Disagree
10. I am afraid to express myself at meetings.	1	2	3	4	5
11. Communicating at meetings usually makes me uncomfortable.	1	2	3	4	5
12. I am very relaxed when answering questions at a meeting.	1	2	3	4	5
13. While participating in a conversation with a new acquaintance, I feel very nervous.	1	2	3	4	5
14. I have no fear of speaking up in conversations.	1	2	3	4	5
15. Ordinarily I am very tense and nervous in conversations.	1	2	3	4	5
16. Ordinarily I am very calm and relaxed in conversations.	1	2	3	4	5
17. While conversing with a new acquaintance, I feel very relaxed.	1	2	3	4	5
18. I'm afraid to speak up in conversations.	1	2	3	4	5
19. I have no fear of giving a speech.	1	2	3	4	5
20. Certain parts of my body feel very tense and rigid while giving a speech.	1	2	3	4	5
21. I feel relaxed while giving a speech.	1	2	3	4	5
22. My thoughts become confused and jumbled when I am giving a speech.	1	2	3	4	5
23. I face the prospect of giving a speech with confidence.	1	2	3	4	5
24. While giving a speech, I get so nervous I forget facts I really know.	1	2	3	4	5

Part II. Scoring Instructions

In Part I, you rated yourself on 24 questions. Compute your score for four dimensions of communication apprehension (CA): group, meeting, dyadic (two-party), and public. Be sure to add or subtract based on the + or – sign before the score you write in below. Higher scores indicates higher levels of CA. Then, during class, we will discuss each dimension and how this may affect your communication as a manager.

Group	Meeting	Dyadic	Public
1. + _____	7. + _____	13. + _____	19. – _____
2. – _____	8. – _____	14. – _____	20. + _____
3. + _____	9. – _____	15. + _____	21. – _____
4. – _____	10. + _____	16. – _____	22. + _____
5. + _____	11. + _____	17. – _____	23. – _____
6. – _____	12. – _____	18. + _____	24. + _____
Total _____	Total _____	Total _____	Total _____

Overall CA = Group _____ + Meeting _____ + Dyadic _____ + Public _____

Source: Adapted from McCroskey, J. C., Beatty, M. J., Kearney, P., & Plax, T. G. (1985). The content validity of the PRCA-24 as a measure of communication apprehension across communication contexts. *Communication Quarterly, 33*(3), 165–173.

Interpretation

Developers of the CA instrument report that between 15% and 20% of the general population are highly apprehensive about communicating. Your scores on the overall CA will range between 24 and 120. National norms (based on 25,000 responses) reveal that scores below 51 indicate very low CA. Scores in the range of 51 to 80 are considered moderate. Scores of 81 points and higher are congruent with a high level of anxiety when communicating. You can compute your average score for each dimension by dividing by six and then comparing your dimension scores to the following norms.

Communication Apprehension	National Norms	25,000 People
	Mean	Standard Deviation
Group	15.4	4.8
Meeting	16.4	4.8
Dyad	14.5	4.2
Public	19.3	5.1
Overall	65.6	15.2

Source: Adapted from: Roby, D. E. (2009). Teacher leadership skills: An analysis of communication apprehension. *Education, 129*(4), 608–614, p. 612.

Discussion Questions

1. Which of the CA dimensions were you highest on? Which were you lowest on? If you have high levels of CA in one area (public speaking, for example), list some strategies you can implement to overcome it (for example, joining a speaking club).
2. How do your CA scores compare with national norms on CA? What did you learn about yourself and others from this assessment that you can use as a manager?
3. Compare your CA dimensions to those of another student in the class. Develop a plan to coach them based on your confidence in areas you are stronger in.
4. How would high CA affect a manager's ability to be effective in communicating with coworkers? How would it affect their ability to make a presentation for a new idea developed by their team?

Sources: Roby, D. E. (2009). Teacher leadership skills: An analysis of communication apprehension. *Education, 129*(4), 608–614, p. 612; Rosenfeld, L. B., Grant, C. H., III, & McCroskey, J. C. (1995). Communication apprehension and self-perceived communication competence of academically gifted students. *Communication Education, 44*(1), 79–89.

Self-Assessment 7.2

What Communication Style Are You?

Put a number 1 (one) by each statement you feel describes you.

____ 1. I am an aggressive person.
____ 2. I change my mind often. I zigzag through life rather than plodding down one monotonous path.
____ 3. I don't worry about the past or the future. I live for today.
____ 4. I am not very spontaneous or emotional. I believe the head should guide the heart.
____ 5. I have been called impractical.
____ 6. I don't like people who live for today without regard to the future. I look ahead and prepare for the rainy days.
____ 7. My work space looks very orderly and fairly stark.
____ 8. I rather like to be different: to dress differently from other people, to go to strange and exciting places, to do the unusual.
____ 9. I do not mind having people do sloppy work over as many times as necessary until they do it right.
____ 10. I sometimes go to extremes. My "highs" are very high, and my "lows" are very low.
____ 11. I am very sociable.
____ 12. I believe that the best technique for achieving results is through thorough, objective analysis.
____ 13. I like being in charge.
____ 14. I think I would succeed as an accountant.
____ 15. I am sensitive to the feelings of others.
____ 16. I believe the best technique for achieving results is through freedom and individual motivation.
____ 17. I value relationships. Getting along well with others is very important to me.
____ 18. My work space looks somewhat messy, but it does have a "homey" charm.
____ 19. It is important to me to feel that I "belong." I want very much to be accepted by the people with whom I work, my friends, my family.
____ 20. I like to compete.
____ 21. I believe the majority is right. I usually go along with the group. Whatever they think and do usually suits me.
____ 22. I am a dynamic, high-drive person.

_____ 23. When people begin to get upset, I try to calm them down. I don't like for people to be upset with each other.

_____ 24. I have a vivid imagination. I can see all sorts of possibilities that others can't see.

_____ 25. I love to be complimented and recognized.

_____ 26. I am neat. I'm bothered by messy people.

_____ 27. I play hard to win and I hate losing.

_____ 28. I enjoy meeting new people.

_____ 29. I am very practical. I believe in and value "what works."

_____ 30. My work space is a showcase for awards, plaques, posters.

_____ 31. Sometimes I overlook details in implementing my big ideas, and sometimes my ideas seem ahead of their time.

_____ 32. Sometimes people say I am a perfectionist. I guess I am, because I believe that anything that is worth doing is worth doing well.

_____ 33. I like to learn by experience, by actually doing it rather than reading books about it.

_____ 34. I think I could be a social worker.

_____ 35. I like people like Vince Lombardi, Clint Eastwood, and Oprah Winfrey.

_____ 36. I think through and try to do everything on a logical basis.

_____ 37. I have a "take charge" attitude.

_____ 38. I feel that I have great destiny. I know I am going to amount to something.

_____ 39. I am very goal or task oriented. I like to have specific goals or tasks to accomplish.

_____ 40. My favorite colors include black, white, and silver.

_____ 41. Sometimes people say I am visionary, that I am a dreamer, and maybe I am.

_____ 42. I believe in myself, particularly my physical strength and ability.

_____ 43. I believe in doing things because of principles—hard work, efficiency, morality, justice. I believe the world would be a much better place if everyone lived by the great principles of religion and justice.

_____ 44. My favorite color is red.

_____ 45. I am very orderly. I believe "there is a place for everything, and everything belongs in its place."

_____ 46. I am very excitable.

_____ 47. My work space is precisely organized and displays diplomas and other signs of achievement.

_____ 48. I believe the best technique for achieving results is through deadlines and managed schedules.

_____ 49. **My life is well organized. There is an appropriate time and place for everything, which is important.**

_____ 50. I like to deal with people and be dealt with in a very direct manner. I "tell it like it is," and I expect others to do the same.

_____ 51. I love to go to parties.

_____ 52. I am very creative.

_____ 53. I have many friends.

_____ 54. I admire people like judges and religious leaders who put principle above everything else.

_____ 55. Sometimes I am extravagant.

_____ 56. I believe in rules—in the home, at work, and in society. I am for law and order.

_____ 57. I like to read about great explorers and inventors. People who accomplished great feats against seemingly insurmountable odds.

_____ 58. I like people like Tina Fey, Ellen DeGeneres, and Jay Leno—friendly, nice people who laugh a lot.

_____ 59. I think I would enjoy being a creative designer.

_____ 60. My favorite colors are earth tones.

_____ 61. My favorite colors are vibrant/mixed combinations.

_____ 62. I am punctual. I get my work done on time. I am never late for appointments. I expect others to do the same.

_____ 63. In my work and social life, I try to be very cooperative. I like to get along.

_____ 64. I hate weakness in myself or others.

_____ 65. I believe the best technique for achieving results is through nonthreatening encouragement.

_____ 66. Things to me are right or wrong, "black or white," never gray.

_____ 67. I never spend time thinking of the past. I think very little about the present. My thoughts are on the future—the great things that are going to happen to me!

Scoring

Count one point for each of the items associated with the different communication styles as listed below, and enter the total for each style in the space provided.

_____ **DRIVER** (Items: 1, 3, 7, 13, 20, 22, 27, 29, 33, 35, 37, 39, 42, 44, 48, 50, 64)

_____ **AMIABLE** (Items: 11, 15, 17, 19, 21, 23, 25, 28, 30, 34, 43, 51, 53, 58, 60, 63, 65)

_____ **ANALYTICAL** (Items: 4, 6, 9, 12, 14, 26, 32, 36, 40, 43, 45, 47, 49, 54, 56, 62, 66)

_____ **EXPRESSIVE** (Items: 2, 5, 8, 10, 16, 18, 24, 31, 38, 41, 46, 52, 55, 57, 59, 61, 67)

Interpretation

Researchers have identified four categories of communication styles: *Analytical*, *Driver*, *Amiable*, and *Expressive*. Each of these styles is modified by the following dimensions: assertiveness, responsiveness, priority (task vs. relationship orientation), and pace (fast vs. slow). *Assertiveness* is behavior exhibited by those who feel the need to control a situation and are comfortable starting an interaction quickly. It is characterized by one talking more than listening and exists on a continuum of high to low assertiveness. *Responsiveness* is behavior exhibited by those who feel the need to express their emotions, feelings, and impressions. It is characterized by one listening more than talking and exists on a continuum of high to low responsiveness. *Priority* refers to a primary focus on people or on the task to be accomplished. *Pace* is a behavioral attribute that refers to speed of communication and exists on a continuum from fast to slow.

The four commonly used communication style descriptions and their attributes are described below.

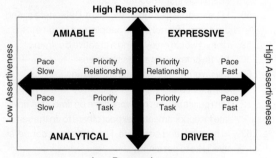

ANALYTICAL. An Analytical is a technical or systems specialist. This individual is not very assertive or responsive. The analytical prefers to remain in the background. Analyticals are industrious, persistent, serious, vigilant, and orderly, and at the same time can be uncommunicative, indecisive, stuffy, exacting, and impersonal. The Analytical's pace is slow, and their priorities are task-related. The Analytical asks "why" questions (e.g., "Why do you do it that way?" "Why didn't you use this process?"). The Analytical's goal is to work within the system. Analyticals tend to be comparatively low on responsiveness and not very assertive. When stressed, the Analytical retires to their comfort zone, which is dwelling on facts and figures.

DRIVER. A Driver is a control specialist. This individual is very assertive and not as responsive to differing viewpoints. Drivers are generally determined, demanding, thorough, decisive, and efficient but can also be seen as pushy, severe, tough-minded, dominating, and harsh. The Driver's pace is fast, and their priorities are task related. The Driver asks "what" questions (e.g., "What can I do for you?" or "What is the purpose of your plan?"). The Driver's goal is to obtain results. When stressed, the Driver dictates.

AMIABLE. An Amiable is a support specialist. They are very responsive and not very assertive. For the most part, Amiables are supportive, respectful, willing, dependable, and personable. They tend to be conforming, retiring, noncommittal, undisciplined, and emotional. The Amiable's pace is slow, and their priority is people. The Amiable asks "who" questions (e.g., "Who agrees with your plan?" or "Who have you considered when making this proposal?"). The Amiable's goal is to cooperate. When stressed, the Amiable conforms.

EXPRESSIVES. An Expressive is a social specialist. This individual is assertive and responsive. Expressives can be enthusiastic, dramatic, inspiring, stimulating, and personable, yet they can be opinionated, excitable, undisciplined, reacting, and promotional. The Expressive's pace is fast, and their priority is people. The Expressive asks "how" questions (e.g., "How can we work with other departments to achieve our goals?" or "How can we make this happen within our allotted time frame?"). The Expressive's goal is to create alliances. When stressed, the Expressive attacks.

Discussion Questions

1. Describe the advantages and disadvantages of your dominant communication style. Give an example of something you would like to change in how you communicate with others based on this assessment.
2. Compare your results to those of your team for this class (if you are not working in a team, create a team with four to five other classmates). What are the similarities and differences in your communication styles?
3. Based on the figure, which team members will you communicate best with? Explain why based on the proximity of your styles.
4. Based on the figure, which team members will you have difficulty communicating with? Explain why based on the distance in your styles.

Source: Adapted from Hartman, J. L., & McCambridge, J. (2011). Optimizing Millennials' communication styles. *Business Communication Quarterly, 74*(1), 22–44.

Introducing...

⑤SAGE vantage™

Course tools done right.

Built to support teaching. Designed to ignite learning.

SAGE vantage is an intuitive digital platform that blends trusted SAGE content with auto-graded assignments, all carefully designed to ignite student engagement and drive critical thinking. Built with you and your students in mind, it offers easy course set-up and enables students to better prepare for class.

SAGE vantage enables students to **engage** with the material you choose, **learn** by applying knowledge, and **soar** with confidence by performing better in your course.

PEDAGOGICAL SCAFFOLDING	CONFIDENCE BUILDER	TIME-SAVING FLEXIBILITY	QUALITY CONTENT	HONEST VALUE
Builds on core concepts, moving students from basic understanding to mastery.	Offers frequent knowledge checks, applied-learning multimedia tools, and chapter tests with focused feedback.	Feeds auto-graded assignments to your gradebook, with real-time insight into student and class performance.	Written by expert authors and teachers, content is not sacrificed for technical features.	Affordable access to easy-to-use, quality learning tools students will appreciate.

CHAPTER 8

HUMAN RESOURCE SYSTEMS

CHAPTER LEARNING OBJECTIVES

After studying this chapter, you should be able to:

8.1 Explain the role of human resource management in organizations.

8.2 Describe the core functions of human resource management.

8.3 Explain the relationship between recruitment and selection.

8.4 Discuss guidelines for using monetary rewards effectively in organizations.

8.5 Describe the steps in the training process.

8.6 Explain how strategic human resource management is used to achieve organizational goals.

Get the edge on your studies at **edge.sagepub.com/scanduragower**

- Take the chapter quiz
- Review key terms with eFlashcards
- Explore multimedia resources, SAGE readings, and more!

Will You Be Hired by a Chatbot?

Artificial intelligence (AI) is in the workplace, and it is here to stay. AI has now become a central part of human resources (HR)—it now does recruitment and can even have conversations with job applicants. These chatbots (also known as smartbots, conversational bots, chatterbots, and interactive agents) are conversational interfaces. A conversational artificial intelligence interface is a computer program that conducts a conversation through words or text. A recruitment chatbot simulates human conversational abilities during the recruiting process. Chatbots are like virtual personal assistants such as Alexa and Siri, which many people have used.

It's a brave new world. A report on artificial intelligence claims that AI is experiencing explosive growth. In 2017, 61% of businesses said they used AI, compared to 38% in 2016. Businesses said they used AI to communicate with employees.

Sahil Sahni is the cofounder of the computer software company AllyO, which uses an AI-enabled chatbot to speak to candidates and answer questions in the recruiting process. He claims that many people don't realize they are speaking with computer intelligence. AllyO studied its applicant pool and found that less than 30% of them caught on that they were talking to a chatbot. The other 70% didn't say or believed there was a real person operating the chatbot.

AllyO does not tell applicants they are not speaking to a human being. However, if someone asks directly, the system discloses that information. "The goal is not to trick anyone here. The goal is to have the best candidate experience. Lying about it is not the best candidate experience," Sahni said.

Candidates don't behave differently when speaking to an AI as opposed to a human, Sahni added.

"When you're a job seeker, it's not like you're calling customer service to complain about something. You're at your best behavior," he said. "You tend to be a lot more tolerant, you tend to be a lot more respectful, no matter what the process might be."

AI accumulates knowledge and learns from its interactions, much like people do. Although it matures and becomes more "human" over time, that still doesn't make it human, and there are certain questions a person might need to answer—for example, questions about company culture, according to Sahni. AI systems are set up to address this. For example, AllyO can recognize when a candidate asks a question that cannot be answered by a machine and puts on a person who can answer that question, Sahni said. This way, the candidate can have a positive experience and have all of their questions answered. A good AI system is complemented by human support.

Here are some examples of how chatbots are already being used for recruitment:

- U.S. Army: SGT STAR. The U.S. Army has a recruitment chatbot called SGT STAR. The chatbot answers basic questions about basic training, types of jobs available, and salary. Also, possible applicants message SGT STAR. SGT STAR has answered 11 million questions, which is the equivalent of 55 Army recruiters.

- Georgia State University: Pounce. Georgia State was the first U.S. university to use a chatbot named Pounce, after its panther mascot. Pounce communicates with admitted students using text messages. Students get reminders and can ask questions. Since Pounce, the university has experienced a 4% increase in enrollment and a 21% decrease in summer melt (the failure to actually complete the enrollment process).

- Sutherland: Tasha. Sutherland, an IT service provider, created a chatbot named Tasha to do applicant

Human resource systems now use chatbots to screen employees for jobs.
©iStockphoto.com/NicoElNino

screening. Applicants communicate with Tasha through text messages, email, or a dialogue box. Tasha fields questions, reminds applicants to complete applications, and schedules interviews. Tasha even collects data on why applicants leave the process—by asking them, and creating a report for the recruiters.

There is another side to AI recruiting, however. David Dalka, founder of the Chicago-based management consulting company Fearless Revival, believes that AI has limits. AI is simply a tool that analyzes content such as job titles and key words in résumés. He has a more traditional view of what recruiting should look like, arguing that companies should invest less in technology and more in human recruiters who work at the company long-term, know the company

culture, and know what kind of person would be a best fit for the job. "I'm not opposed to AI tools if someone built the full data library of all the factors and stopped focusing trivially on things like job titles," he said.

He suggested that companies should more carefully consider the attributes that matter in a candidate: What are their leadership roles? What is their attitude toward learning new things? What work values do they hold? "This idea that some wizard will magically create this black box that will hire the right people without you thinking of these things is a fallacy," Dalka said.

Sources: Adapted from Burjek, A. (2018, November 9). Meet your new colleague: Artificial intelligence. *Workforce*. Retrieved from https://www.workforce.com/2018/11/09/meet-new-colleague-artificial-intelligence/; Chatbot. (n.d.). *Wikipedia*. Retrieved from https://en.wikipedia.org/wiki/Chatbot; Ideal. (n.d.). A how-to guide for using a recruitment chatbot. Retrieved from https://ideal.com/recruitment-chatbot/.

CRITICAL THINKING QUESTIONS

What are the pros and cons of using AI to recruit employees? What possible biases could emerge when using AI to interview employees? Would you rather speak to a person or a chatbot about your future job?

▼ FIGURE 8.0

Textbook Organization

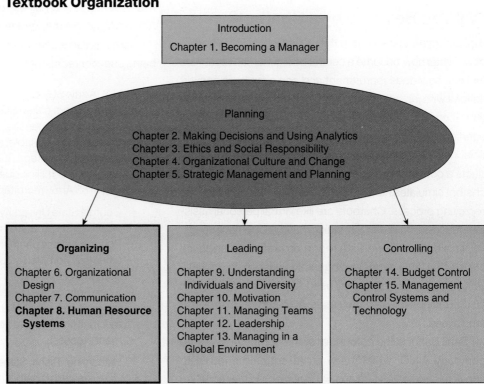

The use of chatbots for recruiting is a cutting-edge human resource system application. HR systems are now using AI to review and screen résumés. To see how well your résumé would fit with your ideal job in résumé screening, complete Toolkit Activity 8.1. In this chapter, we will explore classic and contemporary approaches to designing human resource management systems. First, we will define human resource management and discuss its role in the organization.

What Is Human Resource Management?

Learning Objective 8.1: Explain the role of human resource management in organizations.

Human resource management (HRM) is the use of employees to achieve organizational goals. Effective human resource managers translate the ideas presented throughout this text into actual policies and practices that fit the organization and its culture, goals, and employees. Shaping these policies to fit the organization's objectives is not always easy, particularly in small businesses that don't have the resources to employ human resource managers with specialized HR expertise. This is particularly true of young, rapidly growing companies such as high-tech start-ups. Given the tremendous pressure to generate revenue, small-business managers often feel they lack the resources needed for HRM. Attention to staffing, compensation, and training are especially critical during times of rapid growth.[1] In fact, not having an organized HRM function has been cited as a leading cause of failure among Silicon Valley start-ups.[2] But what, exactly, is HRM in organizations, and how does it differ from the broader concept of "management" discussed throughout this book? We turn to these two questions next.

HRM in Organizations

Human resource management ensures that the organization obtains and retains the skilled, committed, and motivated workforce it needs. This means taking steps to assess and satisfy current and future staffing needs and to enhance and develop the inherent capacities of people by providing continual development and learning opportunities. HRM involves the operation of recruitment and selection procedures, as well as employee development and training linked to organizational goals.[3] As with nonhuman resources such as machinery, computers, and financial assets, human resources (employees) cannot be thrust into an organization in some random way and then expected to contribute. If you have ever started a new job and found that no one guided you on your first day, you are familiar with this reality.

HRM aligns the **knowledge, skills, and abilities (KSAs)** of employees with the needs of the organization and, similarly, makes sure the needs of employees are met by the organization. This mutual fulfillment of needs is **person–job fit (P–J fit)**.[4] A broader form of employee "fit," known as **person–organization fit (P–O fit)**, involves the alignment of employees' personalities with the workplace culture of an organization.[5] While HRM plays a role in fit, particularly through employee screening and hiring processes, it has traditionally focused on P–J fit. This is because the KSAs needed for many jobs can often be systematically assessed as part of the employee selection process.[6] For example, a computer-programming job might require candidates to write a short program as part of the application process. P–O fit involves less tangible factors related to potential employees' personality, their creativity, charisma, and ability to think logically under pressure.[7] Although we are able to measure even these characteristics, it is often impractical to ask job candidates to fill out long personality assessments. There may also be legal issues in doing so.[8] More importantly, P–O fit is a distinctly "human" assessment that standardized measures cannot always assess effectively. So we need to consider the role of managers in day-to-day human resource decisions. In other words, all managers should play the role of human resource managers to some extent.[9]

Management Decisions Commonly Performed by HRM Systems

Category	Management Functions Commonly Performed by HRM Systems	Management Functions Commonly Performed by Managers
Staffing	• Assessing applicants' knowledge, skills, and abilities in light of job requirements	• Assessing compatibility between applicants' personality and the personalities of employees they would work with if hired
	• Procuring criminal background checks for finalists before a formal job offer is made	• Determining whether a public intoxication arrest revealed by the background check should prevent the applicant from being hired
Compensation	• Determining the number of paid vacation days employees receive based on the number of years they have worked at the organization	• Periodically reevaluating the number of paid vacation days employees receive based on employee feedback or the policies of competing organizations
	• Linking annual raise percentages to performance evaluation scores	• Determining if and when raises should be influenced by other factors, such as competing job offers
Training and Development	• Providing a standardized online orientation presentation for new employees	• Designing the content and format of the orientation and adjusting as needed
	• Providing an online management training program with predefined learning goals and assessments for employees being considered for promotion to their first management position	• Designing the management program and continually adjusting it based on employee feedback and changes in the challenges new managers are likely to encounter

HRM Versus "Management"

The use of HRM systems to assess P–J fit while relying on human deduction and intuition to assess P–O fit is an example of how HRM differs from management. HRM can be used to build systems that ensure that routine behaviors occur without requiring managers to provide the same instructions over and over. As in the vignette at the beginning of this chapter in which AI was applied to recruitment, these systems could include requiring all job candidates to submit qualifications for screening before they are forwarded to managers. In today's business world, job application systems often completely automate this process, and this saves time for both job applicants and hiring managers by preventing unqualified candidates from advancing beyond the initial screening stage. As you can see in Table 8.1 and in the sections that follow, this ability of HRM systems to build routine management decisions into automated systems is being implemented in a variety of ways.

Automated HRM systems are, however, limited in their capacity to apply human judgment to decisions. They may miss cues that are particular to a person or a situation. We can therefore think of HRM systems as a useful way to make routine and predictable management decisions so that managers can focus their attention on the nonroutine challenges where human judgement, experience, and intuition are necessary.[10]

The extent to which HRM automation can be, or needs to be, achieved depends partly on the size, financial resources, and growth rate of an organization. For example, a small automobile repair shop with five employees does not need a specialized HR manager designing and implementing routine procedures. A multinational company with thousands of employees located in different countries with different employment practices and laws, on the other hand, does. This is an important distinction to keep in mind as you read about the functions of HRM in this chapter. All organizations must perform HR functions, but there are more highly developed systems in larger organizations.

CAREERS IN MANAGEMENT

Human Resources Specialist

The area of human resources has a lot of interesting careers, and the job duties are varied. HR specialists are involved in recruiting, compensation, benefits, and training. In large organizations, HR specialists tend to focus on a single area, such as compensation. In a small business, there may be one person that covers all of the HR functions.

Typical daily tasks for an HR specialist include:

- Consulting with employers to identify employment needs
- Interviewing applicants about their experience, education, and skills
- Contacting references and performing background checks on job applicants
- Informing applicants about job details, such as duties, benefits, and working conditions
- Hiring or referring qualified candidates for employers
- Conducting or helping with new employee orientation
- Keeping employment records and processing paperwork

This infographic in Figure 8.1 shows some HR specialist jobs you might not know about.

What Skills and Abilities Are Important?

HR specialists need knowledge of human resource management and administrative functions. They must also have skill in computer applications and enterprise resource planning (ERP). Listening and social skills are also important. The ability to solve problems is essential. They need to be excellent communicators. HR specialists show a genuine concern for other people, and act with integrity.

What Is the Outlook for HR Specialist Positions?

Entering the field with a bachelor's degree in HRM may provide a number of options, including HR information systems, training and development, or analysis. The U.S. Bureau of Labor Statistics' current Occupational Outlook Handbook predicts employment of human resources managers to grow at a rate of 9% through 2026, a rate about as fast as that of other occupations. Human resources specialists are going to be necessary to navigate changes in employment laws and health care coverage. Most growth is projected to be in the employment services industry.

▼ FIGURE 8.1

Human Resources Specialist Jobs

Five Jobs in HR You Might Not Know About

Job Title	Job Skills
1. Training and Development Manager	✓ Presentation skills ✓ Problem-solving
2. Nonprofit HR Professional	✓ Project management ✓ Bootstrapping
3. HR IT Recruiting Specialist	✓ Communication ✓ Knowledge of technical roles and terms
4. Global HR Specialist	✓ Cross-cultural mindset ✓ Legal and financial savvy
5. Executive Recruiter	✓ Networking ✓ Negotiating

Discussion Questions

1. Were you surprised to learn about the variety of careers available in human resource management? Which ones did you expect and not expect to see listed?

2. What is the difference between an HR specialist and an HR generalist? Search on the Internet and find an example of each type of job in HR.

3. The U.S. Bureau of Labor Statistics estimates that jobs in HR will grow at a rate faster than the average occupation. Explain why this is the case.

Sources: Adapted from All Business Schools. (n.d.). An HR job description deals with a valuable resource: People. Retrieved from https://www.allbusinessschools.com/human-resources/job-description/; Bureau of Labor Statistics. (2019, April 12). Retrieved from https://www.bls.gov/ooh/management/human-resources-managers.htm. Human resource specialists. In *Occupational outlook handbook.* Retrieved from https://www.bls.gov/ooh/business-and-financial/human-resources-specialists.htm; My Next Move. (n.d.). Human resource specialist. Retrieved from https://www.mynextmove.org/profile/summary/13-1071.00.

The shift toward nonroutine and more strategic human resource management has broadened the appeal of HRM as a career option. An overview of what HR specialists do is provided in the Careers in Management box.

Human Resources and Human Capital

Before we cover the functions of HRM, it is important to note a new development known as *human capital*. Whereas the term *human resources* refers to an organization's employees as a finite resource, **human capital** is the economic value of employees' experience, knowledge, skills, and abilities.[11] For example, when an organization hires a new employee, it increases its human *resources*; when it puts that employee through a training program to learn new skills, it increases its human *capital*. **Human capital management (HCM)**, therefore, is the alignment of employees' experience, knowledge, skills, and abilities with the current needs and strategic goals of an organization.

Although the distinction between HRM and HCM seems clear based on that definition, practicing managers don't necessarily make the distinction. Sometimes the terms are even used interchangeably. However, HRM can be thought of as the administrative backbone of HCM.[12] For example, an organization with a strategic goal of increasing AI will develop a hiring strategy for AI specialists. The actual hiring process for AI specialists, including the drafting of a job posting, placement of advertisements, processing of applications, and ranking of the applicants, is the HRM domain.

HCM strategies are supported by the knowledge, change, strategic HRM, human resource development, and HR metrics that are provided by the HRM functions of the organization. For example, a firm that acquires another company to diversify its expertise (HCM) must implement change management programs to create the behaviors and attitudes needed to support the change (HRM) by developing knowledge, skills, and abilities (KSAs) that reduce resistance to organizational change. Another example is human resource development (HRD). By providing training and continual learning, HRM helps the organization maintain an up-to-date, flexible, and adaptable workforce. Finally, the metrics gathered and analyzed by HRM feed into the strategic plans for linking human capital to the value creation of the firm.[13]

HCM has resulted in an evolution of HR departments from simply compliance to strategic alignment of human resources with organizational goals. Some organizations have even added legal issues as an HR department function, so we must note its importance.[14] But trends indicate that the amount of time and effort HR departments spend keeping their organizations in legal compliance tends to be fairly small. As Figure 8.2 shows, this function constitutes about

▼ FIGURE 8.2

Percentage of Time Spent by HR Departments on Legal and Compliance Issues

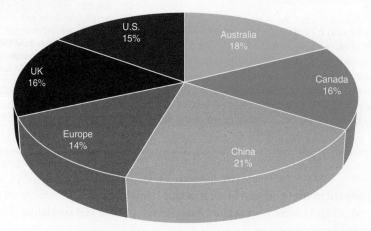

Source: Boudreau, J. W., & Lawler, E. E., III (2012). How HR spends its time: It is time for a change. Retrieved from https://ceo.usc.edu/files/2016/10/2012-04-G12-04-611-How_HR_Spends_Its_Time.pdf.

FACT OR FICTION?

Myths About Human Resource Management

As you have already seen in this chapter, public perceptions of HRM and reality are not always the same. In addition to confusion over what this field should even be called, there are several widespread misperceptions about its training, employee selection, and compensation practices.

Ray Riviera is director of solutions management, workforce planning, and analytics for SAP, a German company that produces management software used by millions of organizations. Here is a summary of his insights about HRM myths:

1. *All training is beneficial.*

This myth is pervasive. You may be surprised at how often more job training is proposed as the obvious solution to almost any problem. But training is not a magic pill that can cure all organizational ills. Riviera observes:

> A multibillion dollar business in its own right, training is universally recognized as a necessary component for remaining competitive. Ample, high quality training is no longer considered a perk, but rather a fundamental component of high performance work systems, and a key differentiator in developing an employer brand. It is so highly regarded by employees that it can be seen as a substitute for wage increases, particularly in the public sector.

Large organizations spend a lot money on training, and they are afraid to stop doing so and risk lower performance. After all, training can't hurt anyone, right? Riviera points out, however, that the costs associated with excessive training may be higher than you think. Time away from work, distractions, disruptions to the work flow, and expensive consultants are all costs of training. The lack of clear learning goals and evaluation of training may hide the benefits of training. And training may never get translated into real improvements in job performance.

2. *GPA predicts high performance.*

You are working hard to earn the highest grade-point average (GPA) possible. You believe that high grades are the key to your future success. After all, this is a quantification of your diligence and abilities. A review of recent research does show a small correlation between GPA and early job performance, but studies published in the 1960s probably better predicted this correlation because of the more recent issues with grade inflation, which of course cause a problem with the correlation comparisons. Today, seasoned HRM professionals know that hiring the right people is both art and science. This is especially true when hiring recent college graduates with limited work experience. So recruiters ask graduates to report their grade-point average when applying for jobs. But realize that after you are out of school for a year or two, no potential employer will ever ask about it again. Why is this?

The fact that many employers lose interest in your GPA so quickly probably tells you something about how well GPAs predict future performance (on average). So why bother asking current and recent students about it? Riviera provides some insights:

> Little of what would indicate superior talent is observable either during interviews or in most job situations. So we assume that past success predicts future success, and one of the most ready metrics is GPA. And why not? Many of the skills needed to achieve a high GPA are also those needed to succeed at work: diligence, intellectual insight, ability to learn abstract concepts and apply them to real situations, and the discipline to complete tasks.

That said, GPA predicts future performance *in school*. So keep up the hard work if you are thinking about applying to graduate school!

3. *Financial incentives are the only way to drive performance.*

You want your organization to "show you the money." But it is a myth to think money is everything. This belief is widely held. After all, people consider the salary to be one of the most important parts of negotiating a new job. But what about once a person is hired, and working on the job?

Research has shown that financial incentives relate to quantity of performance but not quality. Money does motivate, but it does not always produce the results organizations want (managers don't want only quantity in every job; quality matters too). In fact, compensation may even encourage cheating and other dysfunctional behaviors such as being overly competitive with peers. Some reward systems unknowingly incentivize "bad" behaviors at work. Monetary rewards work if the criteria for evaluating performance are crystal clear, and measurable. Also, they work if the work is independent and does not require contributions from coworkers. These criteria are difficult to meet for most jobs—especially jobs in management.

Discussion Questions

1. Which of these three myths surprises you the most? Explain why.

2. Mr. Riviera argues that GPA helps employers predict an applicant's job performance only in a narrow range of circumstances. Do you agree or disagree? Explain your position.

(Continued)

3. Mr. Riviera mentioned that "dysfunctional incentive systems" can cause dysfunctional behaviors. Briefly describe an example of this you have observed in your own life. It does not have to be a workplace example; the same logic applies to any situation where certain behaviors are encouraged or discouraged through rewards (for example, school, youth groups, or sports).

Sources: Adapted from Jenkins, G. D., Jr., Mitra, A., Gupta, N., & Shaw, J. D. (1998). Are financial incentives related to performance? A meta-analytic review of empirical research. *Journal of Applied Psychology, 83*(5), 777–787; Riviera, R. (2012, November 21). 5 myths of human resources management. *Forbes*. Retrieved from https://www.forbes.com/sites/sap/2012/11/21/5-myths-of-human-capital-management/#371224f424e2; Roth, P. L., BeVier, C. A., Switzer, F. S., III, & Schippmann, J. S. (1996). Meta-analyzing the relationship between grades and job performance. *Journal of Applied Psychology, 81*(5), 548–556.

15% of the time spent by HR in the United States, and it makes up about a fifth of the time spent by HR departments in one country, China. In fact, many of the compliance and routine functions of HR have been outsourced. Outsourcing compliance and other HR functions is a trend, which will be discussed next.

Outsourcing the HR Function

Many of the procedural and logistical functions of HRM are no longer handled internally by companies.[15] Instead, many organizations have outsourced the activities to firms who specialize in them.[16] Recall, however, that the procedures of personnel management are the basis of HRM. By contracting these functions out to other companies, many firms have essentially outsourced their HRM. Most of these organizations still have active HRM departments, however. Instead of compliance, an increasing number of HRM employees and managers are doing HCM strategy.[17] HR managers work with senior management to design and implement strategic HR goals rather than the routine work of processing background checks, printing paychecks, preparing compliance reports, or tracking employee benefit usage. The focus has shifted from viewing employees as an expense to be accounted for to an asset that can grow through investment and development, just like financial capital.[18]

HRM: What's in a Name?

Some time ago, HRM was known as personnel management.[19] The function evolved into HRM and, more recently, HCM as noted above. However, we rarely see an organization with a "Department of Human Capital Management." Instead, as the evolution from HRM to HCM happened, the familiar "Human Resource Management" term remained. HRM departments perform important functions within organizations (and if they do not, then the functions are outsourced, as noted above). We next turn to these functions.

CRITICAL THINKING QUESTIONS

Explain the difference between HRM and HCM. Provide an example of how HRM supports HCM (staffing, compensation, training, or labor relations). In other words, how do the HR functions support the development of human capital in an organization?

The Functions of HRM

Learning Objective 8.2: Describe the core functions of human resource management.

Human resource management comprises three major functions in organizations today. In this chapter, we will cover these functions:

- *Staffing*—recruitment and hiring practices
- *Compensation*—designing performance management and incentive systems
- *Training and development* (sometimes called *employee development*)—ensuring a skilled workforce

Labor relations, a fourth function of human resource management, has traditionally focused on relationships with labor unions, or at least viewed "labor" as an organized entity distinct from a company and its management. The labor-relations function of HRM is predominantly found in manufacturing plants. As participation in organized labor unions has diminished in parts of the world (particularly the United States), it is no longer clear that this is a primary function of many firms' HRM employees. It can be argued that employer–employee relationships are as important as ever, but much of what we might include in that category (ensuring that employees are motivated, for example) is addressed by other HR functions, such as compensation. We thus turn to the functions of HRM found in most organizations: staffing, compensation, and training.

Staffing

Staffing, employment, and recruitment is among the most critical HR function areas that contribute to an organization's business strategies, according to a Society for Human Resource Management (SHRM) report titled *HR's Evolving Role in Organizations and Its Impact on Business Strategy.*[20] **Staffing** is "broadly defined as attracting, selecting, and retaining competent individuals to achieve organizational goals."[21] To ensure that the organization has the best possible applicants, it engages in **recruitment**, which identifies the pool of potential employees. In addition to identifying applicants, recruitment efforts try to influence the applicant's decision to join the organization. A large-scale study[22] of recruitment summarizing 71 studies on recruitment practices found that applicants' perceptions of their P–O fit and characteristics of the job and organization were the best predictors of positive recruiting outcomes. The next strongest set of predictors tended to be perceptions of the recruitment process (e.g., fairness), followed by recruiter competencies and hiring expectancies. Thus, in recruitment, it is important to assess how well the applicant fits the organization and to have competent recruiters who are fair.

Another clear advantage that has emerged in research on recruiting is that the brand image of the organization matters.[23] The employer's image or reputation may draw applicants to the pool due to the visibility of the brand. For example, an applicant may want to work for Coca-Cola because of the strong brand image of the company. Another source of information on the reputation of organizations is lists such as the "Best Companies to Work For," as shown in Table 8.2. Glassdoor.com is a website that collects reviews of organizations and quotes from current employees. Every year it does a ranking of the top companies to work for based on a five-star rating system. You can see that getting on such a list of best employers can create interest among potential applicants.

Once the application pool has been generated, the organization engages in the process of **selection**. Selection has been researched for many years and consists of defining the

Staffing is among the most critical HR functions.

©iStockphoto.com/fizkes

Glassdoor.com: Best Companies to Work For

Ranking	Company	Quote From Employee
1	Bain & Company	"Bain really lives and breathes its values. I feel both challenged yet supported every single day, and truly feel that I am making an impact."
2	Zoom Video Communications	"Fantastic company culture of 'Happiness.' You feel it every day and you can't wait to come to work."
3	In-N-Out Burger	"You have great opportunities to advance both in store and corporate. They offer great training and have a great support structure."
4	Procore Technologies	"The BIGGEST pro of Procore, is the opportunity for career growth. Procore is all about making you better."
5	Boston Consulting Group	"Best work and life balance, amazing benefits, amazing people and most importantly a people-first focused company."
6	LinkedIn	"I love working for a company whose vision aligns with my personal beliefs."
7	Facebook	"I've never worked at a company that cares so much about its people."
8	Google	"Working at Google is truly amazing. The best people, perks, and awesome company culture with lots of opportunities for growth."
9	lululemon	"So fun and supportive! The company is phenomenal and really helps you towards your goals inside and outside the company!"
10	Southwest Airlines	"Profit sharing when applicable is wonderful. Salaries are competitive within Technology. Great culture and community give back events."

Source: Glassdoor. (n.d.). 2019 best places to work: Employees' choice. Retrieved from https://www.glassdoor.com/Award/Best-Places-to-Work-LST_KQ0,19.htm.

CRITICAL THINKING QUESTIONS

Describe the cultures of the "best places to work" based on the glassdoor.com rankings using five words. Would you like to work for one of these companies? Which one and why? If not, why not?

work to be done, identifying characteristics that predict performance with respect to the work to be done, and developing measures to assess the relative standing of job applicants on each of these.[24] Applicants are ranked based on their relative standing, and those with the best scores are selected for the job.[25] Examples of these characteristics are biographical data from application forms, background checks, tests of intellectual ability, and personality tests.

Tests of cognitive ability (e.g., IQ) are often used—and for good reasons. Research has demonstrated that they do a good job of predicting job performance.[26] You probably took the SAT as a college entrance examination, and this is an example of a test of general cognitive ability. In addition to testing, interviews are one of the most common methods for examining the relative standing of job applicants. Research has shown that structured interviews are better than unstructured interviews, and steps must be taken to address potential bias in the interviewing process.[27]

CRITICAL THINKING QUESTIONS

Describe potential sources of bias in the interview process. What can be done to reduce these biases?

For managerial and other high-level jobs, the assessments may include a **work sample test**, in which applicants must demonstrate specific knowledge and skills by performing a limited number of job-related tasks.[28] In recent years, **situational judgment tests (SJTs)** have gained popularity as a selection method. In an SJT, applicants are given realistic work-related situations. Respondents are then given several behavioral choices for addressing the situation and are then asked to indicate which options are most or least effective. SJTs have shown good levels of validity for selecting the best applicants and appear applicable at all levels. They may be particularly helpful in selecting the best managers for international assignments and are useful for training and development.[29] You can practice taking questions similar to those found on an SJT in Self-Assessment 8.1.

Confetti falls on Zoom employees as the company goes public on the NAS-DAQ. Zoom is one of the best companies to work for based on glassdoor.com surveys.

©Kena Betancur/Stringer/Getty Images

Another method that has been shown to predict job performance after a person is hired is an **assessment center**. Assessment centers present applicants with a variety of exercises (e.g., a presentation, or leaderless team discussion) designed to measure different management competencies. A review of research on assessment centers found that the average assessment center uses approximately five exercises, measuring interpersonal skills/social sensitivity, communication, motivation, persuasion/influence, organization/planning, and problem-solving.[30]

In recent years, organizations have also recognized the need to assess global management capabilities in the selection process for many jobs. These include adaptability, having a global mindset, cultural agility, and the ability to effectively manage relationships.[31] These attributes are often considered in promotion decisions. You will have the opportunity to decide whom to promote for a manager position in Toolkit Activity 8.2.

Once employees are selected and hired, they must be fairly compensated for the work they do in the organization. The next section describes different forms of compensation, and the importance of effective performance management as an input to compensation decisions.

Compensation

Learning Objective 8.4: Discuss guidelines for using monetary rewards effectively in organizations.

Compensation refers to pay and other rewards provided to employees for their efforts on the job. Compensation is defined as the total amount of the monetary and nonmonetary rewards provided to an employee by an employer in return for work performed as required.[32] Most organizations conduct salary surveys to benchmark and create **salary range structures**. A **salary range** is the span between the minimum and maximum base salary an organization will pay for a specific job or group of jobs. A salary range structure (or salary structure) is a hierarchal group of jobs and salary ranges within an organization. Salary structures are often expressed as pay grades or job grades that reflect the value of a job in the external market and/or the internal value to an organization.[33] There are also online database websites for salary information, where data is collected nationally and internationally. These sites, such as Payscale.com and Salary.com, provide recommended salary ranges, taking into consideration factors such as the job market, the location of the job, the size of the company offering the job, and job duties and responsibilities.[34]

As you learned from Table 8.2, real employees provide information about their jobs, including their salaries, on websites like Glassdoor.com. However, keep in mind that the data are not

Money is one of the major motivational tools in organizations.

©iStockphoto.com/guvendemir

as accurate as on salary surveys because they are self-reported by the employees. Also, they may not include all aspects of compensation packages (such as bonuses).

Money is one of the major motivational tools in organizations.[35] Organizations that appropriately tie pay to performance do have higher rates of return on investment.[36] For example, a study of hospitals showed that pay-level practices and pay structures combined to affect resource efficiency, patient care outcomes, and financial performance. For pay to be motivating, it is important to have an effective system for performance management in place in the organization.

The Relationship of Performance Management to Compensation

Performance management is essential for deciding pay raises. Most organizations use the performance management process for compensation decisions.[37] But other objectives are equally important. The performance management session is an opportunity to regularly discuss an employee's performance and results. The manager can identify the employee's strengths, weaknesses, and areas for improvement. Performance management provides essential feedback on job performance to employees. It can recognize exceptional performance and document weak performance. Also, it can lead to effective goal-setting for future performance and identify training that may be needed to improve skills.[38] Next, we discuss the sources and methods used by organizations to evaluate employee performance—who rates performance and how it is managed.

Sources of Performance Management Ratings

The immediate supervisor is often the only person conducting the review. The HR department typically reviews the performance management process. In some cases, the process is reviewed by a manager one level above the supervisor. However, recent trends in **360-degree feedback** include ratings from higher management, peers (coworkers), the employee's followers, and customers. Employees often provide self-ratings as a basis for discussion during the performance management review. However, self-ratings are used for development purposes and not for compensation or promotion decisions because they suffer from self-interest bias and usually don't agree with supervisor ratings.[39] Research on 360-degree feedback suggests it improves the input into the performance review process.[40] The challenge with 360-degree feedback is that organizations often don't provide necessary training for peers to provide constructive feedback. Peers, for example, tend to be more lenient than managers when rating their coworkers.[41] Despite these challenges, 360-degree feedback has been implemented successfully in numerous organizations.

An example of a successful implementation is Starwood Hotels and Resorts Worldwide. The executive team wanted to provide their managers with valuable feedback on their strengths and areas for development. The 360-degree feedback system produced the following individual and organizational benefits for the employees and the organization:[42]

Employee benefits:

- A simple, easy-to-use 360-degree feedback tool
- A "self-paced" 360-degree feedback report complete with targeted questions to guide the leader through the process of uncovering strengths and development areas

- Specific interpretive tables and graphs in the feedback report that helped leaders analyze their data
- A downloadable discussion guide for report recipients and their managers—what to focus on, how to lead and focus the discussion, and how to deal with emotions/defensiveness

Organization benefits:

- Competency/skill strengths and development areas across division and employee level
- Skill mix across the organization, enabling Starwood to more effectively leverage the leadership strengths and refocus efforts where developmental opportunities might exist
- Specific division data, allowing Starwood to target local training efforts, thereby saving precious resources
- Provision of division analysis results to each division leader so they could take specific actions on the data and have a better understanding of team strengths and development areas

One of the most important parts of a manager's job is providing feedback to employees.
©atipp/Shutterstock

Performance Management Methods

It is best to avoid rating emotional reactions, such as how much you like an employee, since this may not relate to job performance.[43] Most organizations use standard forms to evaluate employee performance. There may be an overall global rating for performance, but there are also specific dimensions that are rated. These ratings are typically made on a **graphic rating scale** having multiple points along a continuum. Here is an example:

Outstanding = Performance is consistently superior.
Exceeds expectations = Performance is routinely above job requirements.
Meets expectations = Performance is regularly competent and dependable.
Below expectations = Performance fails to meet job requirements on a frequent basis.
Unsatisfactory = Performance is consistently unacceptable.

Behaviorally anchored rating scales (BARS) provide specific examples of performance to managers. The creation and updating of BARS can be time-consuming, but they are more accurate because they focus on specific behaviors rather than general statements such as "knowledge of work." An example of a scale from a BARS for the performance of a store clerk on customer service performance is shown in Figure 8.3.

Some organizations use **forced ranking**, an assessment method in which all employees in the work group are ranked relative to one another. This approach, known as the "vitality curve," was made famous by Jack Welch at GE.[44] Those at the bottom of the rankings were let go. Even if the bottom 10% is not fired, forced-ranking systems make managers uncomfortable and create a culture of competition. Recently, such forced-ranking systems have been reconsidered. Microsoft, for example, has done away with their long-standing practice of forced rankings.[45]

Example of a Customer Service Scale From a BARS

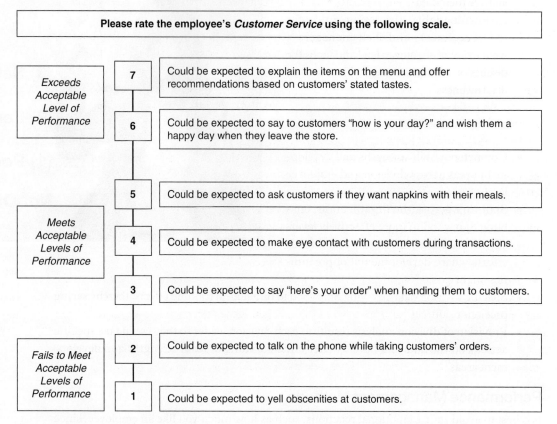

Please rate the employee's *Customer Service* using the following scale.

Exceeds Acceptable Level of Performance	7	Could be expected to explain the items on the menu and offer recommendations based on customers' stated tastes.
	6	Could be expected to say to customers "how is your day?" and wish them a happy day when they leave the store.
Meets Acceptable Levels of Performance	5	Could be expected to ask customers if they want napkins with their meals.
	4	Could be expected to make eye contact with customers during transactions.
	3	Could be expected to say "here's your order" when handing them to customers.
Fails to Meet Acceptable Levels of Performance	2	Could be expected to talk on the phone while taking customers' orders.
	1	Could be expected to yell obscenities at customers.

Source: Kell, H. J., Martin-Raugh, M. P. Carney, L. M., Inglese, P. A., Chen, L., & Feng, G. (2017). Exploring methods for developing behaviorally anchored rating scales for evaluating structured interview performance (Educational Testing Service Research Report No. ETS RR-17-28). Retrieved from https://files.eric.ed.gov/fulltext/EJ1168380.pdf, p. 7.

CRITICAL THINKING QUESTIONS

> Do you agree that forced rankings should be eliminated in evaluating performance? Why or why not? Discuss the positive side of having competition in the organization.

Challenges in Performance Management

There are complex issues related to performance appraisals that a manager should know. Some employees view the appraisal process as unfair and showing favoritism. Perceptual biases may affect the rater's ability to accurately assess follower performance. For example, **halo error** is the overall tendency to give an employee a high rating on all aspects of job performance. There may be a tendency toward leniency (or strictness) in performance ratings.[46] Ratings may fall prey to a **central tendency error** in which the manager rates all dimensions of performance as average (e.g., rating every dimension as 3 on a five-point scale). Training in how to avoid errors has been shown to be moderately effective in reducing these errors.[47]

Everyone dislikes receiving negative feedback—even people with a strong desire to learn.[48] Constant negative feedback does not help employees learn more from their jobs.[49]

Employees may begin to fear the appraisal process because they see it as punishing.[50] Based on a survey conducted by Deloitte, more than half the executives questioned (58%) believed that their current performance management approach drove neither employee engagement nor high performance.[51]

Some managers don't like to give negative feedback. They are not comfortable with face-to-face confrontation when an employee demonstrates low performance. There is a conflict between a supervisor's role as evaluator and their role as coach. In fact, research suggests that managers should primarily adopt a strengths-based approach, which focuses on what employees do well and encourages the continued and further use of these strengths.[52]

HR consultant Earl Silver agrees that ratings can be demotivating, so it is important for a manager to separate discussions of growth and development from salary increases. He reminds managers to make an investment in making their performance management process work effectively to motivate employees.[53]

Another challenge in performance management is that by focusing on individual achievement, teamwork is discouraged.[54] However, most employees prefer that their pay be based on individual merit rather than group output.[55] Of course, this preference is strongest among the most productive and achievement-oriented employees.[56] Thus, if pay is based on team performance, an organization's best performers may become frustrated and seek other jobs. To encourage teamwork, organizations should use mixed compensation systems, which include individual merit pay plus team incentives to leverage the advantages and disadvantages of both types of rewards.

McKinsey Consulting summarizes recent trends that reflect changes to traditional performance appraisals in organizations. These trends include the following:

CRITICAL THINKING QUESTIONS

> Explain how the management of individual performance may harm team performance. How can this be addressed?

- Some companies are rethinking what constitutes employee performance by focusing specifically on individuals who are a step function away from average—at either the high or low end of performance—rather than trying to differentiate among most of the employees that fall in the middle.
- Many companies are also collecting more objective performance data through systems that automate real-time analyses.
- Performance data are used less and less as a crude instrument for setting compensation. Indeed, some companies are severing the link between evaluation and compensation, at least for the majority of the workforce, while linking them ever more comprehensively at the high and low ends of performance.
- Organizations are developing better data back up as a shift in emphasis from backward-looking evaluations to fact-based performance and development discussions. Performance feedback is becoming more frequent and as-needed rather than annual events.[57]

What can a manager do to improve motivation, given these trends in performance management? Focus on what is important to the employee and what they learned from mistakes.

Performance management should be about employee growth and development. Leadership consultant Jose Luis Romero suggests that growth means two things:

1. To help employees possess the needed skill level to achieve desired performance; and
2. To help employees develop the ability to exceed desired performance and move to greater levels of more complex performance.[58]

Without a doubt, performance management is about providing feedback to employees. However, employees do expect their performance to be linked to monetary rewards.

What About the Money?

As noted, money is an important motivator for employees. But there are right ways and wrong ways to use money as a motivator. Table 8.3 provides best practices for using money as a motivator in organizations. It begins with the performance management process described above—defining and measuring performance accurately. Also, rewards should be contingent on performance, so compensation should include base pay plus bonuses. Rewards should be timely and fair. Finally, the compensation system should include both monetary and nonmonetary rewards. We will discuss other forms of compensation next.

▼ TABLE 8.3

Recommendations on How to Use Monetary Rewards Effectively

Principles	Implementation Guidelines
1. Define and measure performance accurately.	• Specify what employees are expected to do as well as what they should refrain from doing. • Align employees' performance with the strategic goals of the organization. • Measure both behaviors and results. But the more control there is over achievement of desired outcomes, the greater the emphasis should be on measuring results.
2. Make rewards contingent on performance.	• Ensure pay levels vary significantly based on performance levels. • Explicitly communicate that differences in pay levels are due to different levels of performance and not because of other reasons. • Take cultural norms into account. For example, consider individualism-collectivism when deciding how much emphasis to place on rewarding individual versus team performance.
3. Reward employees in a timely manner.	• Distribute fake currencies or reward points that can later be traded for cash, goods, or services. • Switch from a performance appraisal system to a performance management system, which encourages timely rewards through ongoing and regular evaluations, feedback, and developmental opportunities. • Provide a specific and accurate explanation regarding why the employee received the particular reward.
4. Maintain justice in the reward system.	• Promise only rewards that are available. • When increasing monetary rewards, increase employees' variable pay levels instead of their base pay. • Make all employees eligible to earn rewards from the incentive plan. • Communicate reasons for failure to provide promised rewards, changes in the payouts, or changes in the reward system.
5. Use monetary and nonmonetary rewards.	• Do not limit the provision of nonmonetary rewards to noneconomic rewards. Rather, use not only praise and recognition but also noncash awards consisting of various goods and services. • Provide nonmonetary rewards that satisfy needs for the recipient. • Use monetary rewards to encourage voluntary participation in nonmonetary reward programs that are more directly beneficial to employee or organizational performance.

Source: Adapted from Aguinis, H., Joo, H., & Gottfredson, R. K. (2013). What monetary rewards can and cannot do: How to show employees the money. *Business Horizons*, 56(2), 241–259.

Benefits of Telecommuting

Remote Work Benefits Business

☐ **35B miles** reduced annually in the United States when employees work remotely

☐ **60%** of employers identify cost savings as a benefit of having a work-from-home program

☐ **73%** of employees eat heathier when working from home

☐ **43%** of employees working remotely produce more business volume than their counterparts working in the office

☐ **$700B** per year savings in the United States with part-time remote working

Source: Bersin, J. (2017). The future of work: The people imperative. Retrieved from https://www2.deloitte.com/content/dam/Deloitte/il/Documents/human-capital/HR_and_Business_Perspectives_on_The%20Future_of_Work.pdf.

Other Forms of Compensation

Some of the issues with the use of pay as the only form of compensation may be avoided by rewarding for results rather than behaviors. For example, in **profit-sharing plans**, employee bonuses are based on reaching a financial target, such as return on assets or net income. **Stock options** are a variation of profit-sharing where employees are given stock options as part of their compensation package. **Gain-sharing plans** are another alternative, in which compensation is tied to unit-level performance (e.g., employees receive a percentage of the sales increase or cost savings for efficiency improvements). These plans tend to increase performance.[59] However, the pay may be too variable for employees to rely solely on these plans for their total compensation. Also, the focus on results may encourage engaging in unethical behaviors to reach the targets.[60]

Organizations typically provide packages of benefits to employees that may include health insurance, pension plans, and family leave. Other benefits that employees may value as rewards include **flexible working hours**, which research has shown relates to employee satisfaction and organizational commitment.[61] Flexible working hours may be formal (i.e., allowing employees to arrive later to work and stay later) or informal (i.e., a supervisor being flexible regarding an employee's need to pick up children from school). Another variation on flexible hours is **job sharing**, or splitting one full-time job into two jobs.[62]

Another noncompensation perk that many employees value is **remote working** (also known as **telecommuting**), or the ability to work from home—or anywhere. A study of 2,617 employees in four organizations[63] found that remote working and flexible hours were positively related to organizational commitment, which translated into higher job performance. The benefits of telecommunicating are shown in Figure 8.4. These benefits include cost savings to individuals and organizations.

Another reward that progressive organizations are offering is **sabbaticals** from work. A sabbatical is a leave taken from work to "recharge one's batteries" or take care of family responsibilities. In some cases, sabbaticals are paid, while others are unpaid. For example, Genentech, a San Francisco, California, breast cancer research firm, offers a six-week paid sabbatical after six years of continuous service with the company. In 2015, 1,100 employees took advantage of the program, in addition to their 18 paid vacation days.[64]

Training and Development

Learning Objective 8.5: Describe the steps in the training process.

Training and development in the United States began with the Industrial Revolution in the early 1900s. It then experienced a significant period of growth during and after World War II.[65] This happened because there was a significant increase in the demand for a skilled workforce due to the technological innovation needed for the defense industry. [66] After the war, training was provided to veterans under the Servicemen's Readjustment Act of 1944, commonly known as the GI Bill. Veterans were provided a number of benefits, including tuition reimbursement and job skills training. An estimated 5.5 million veterans received job skills training in the first decade after the bill was passed.[67]

Training is "a systematic approach to learning and development to improve individual, team, and organizational effectiveness."[68] **Development** can be thought of as "activities leading to the acquisition of new knowledge or skills for purposes of personal growth."[69] For example, mentoring in organizations can be considered part of employee development.[70] Mentoring enhances employee growth and development through coaching, networking, self-directed learning, and experiential learning, which are all considered types of informal learning that are less structured than classroom instruction. Development through mentoring provides authentic experiences and job challenges as the primary context for learning on the job.[71] Research conducted by Deloitte Consulting found that young people value training and development more than other job benefits, as shown in Figure 8.5. Flexible working hours was second.

The amount of money that organizations spend on training and development has been rising in recent years. A survey of U.S. corporations and educational institutions with more than 100 employees conducted by *Training* magazine found that total 2017 U.S. training expenditures—including payroll and spending on external products and services—had risen significantly, increasing 32.5% from 2016 to 2017, with an annual spending of $90.6 billion.[72] But what do organizations get for this significant investment? Research has demonstrated the benefits of training for organizations. These benefits include improved performance (e.g., employee productivity) as well as other outcomes that relate directly (e.g., reduced costs) or indirectly (e.g., employee turnover) to overall organizational performance.[73] For example, a study of 260 Korean companies[74] in diverse industries showed that corporate expenditures for internal training predicted interpersonal and organizational learning practices, which in turn increased the innovative performance of the organizations.

Eight separate reviews of research[75] on training have concluded that we know a great deal about how and why training works. We know that multiple training methods produce positive outcomes. Also, training works for managers as well as employees. Training is effective for both teams and individual performance. More recently, organizations have experimented with computer-based instruction, and we know that it works as well as face-to-face instruction.[76] However, computer-based and online learners need support during the training process. For example, learners can be provided with computer-generated tips on what to focus on and how much to practice based on their performance on tasks.[77]

Steps in the Training Process

The general process of developing a training program is shown in Figure 8.6. As shown in the figure, the evaluation process (Step 10) provides feedback for considering new needs and objectives and making changes to the training design for future training programs. These steps are described below.[78]

Training improves individual, team, and organizational effectiveness.

©iStockphoto.com/PeopleImages

Millennials Rate Development #1 Job Benefit

For Millennials,"Training and development" is the most coveted job benefit

Training and development	22%
Flexible working hours	19%
Cash bonuses	14%
Free private healthcare	8%
Retirement funding	6%
Greater vacation allowance	6%

0% 5% 10% 15% 20% 25%

Percent indicating job benefit in first place

Source: Telecommuting trends. (2017, April 24). *Facility Executive.* Retrieved from https://facilityexecutive.com/2017/04/infographic-telecommuting-trends/.

▼ FIGURE 8.6

Steps in the Training Process

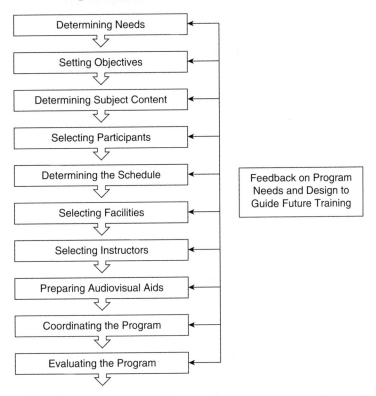

Determining Needs

Setting Objectives

Determining Subject Content

Selecting Participants

Determining the Schedule

Selecting Facilities

Selecting Instructors

Preparing Audiovisual Aids

Coordinating the Program

Evaluating the Program

Feedback on Program Needs and Design to Guide Future Training

Source: Adapted from Kirkpatrick, D., & Kirkpatrick, J. (2006). *Evaluating training programs: The four levels* (3rd ed.). New York, NY: Berrett-Koehler.

1. *Determining needs.* A training-needs assessment identifies the problems that the training needs to solve, the skills gaps to fill, the behaviors that need correction, and the learning needed. Current levels of employee skills, behaviors, and needed changes are assessed. For example, the social media skill levels of marketing staff are assessed to determine if the company is ready to launch a major campaign on several social media platforms.

2. *Setting objectives.* The learning goals of the training program should be stated. Specify what the program will accomplish (e.g., attitude change, quality, sales, or profits). Then spell out the skills and behaviors needed to attain these goals. For example, if the goal is to improve customer service, then training for call-center employees will focus on empathy and conversation skills.

3. *Determining subject content.* Steps 1 and 2—the needs assessment and objectives—determine the subject matter of the training. The topics that need to be addressed to achieve goals are selected. There may be constraints, such as the training budget, that must be taken into account. For example, a training program on managing stress may be deployed through online training rather than hiring a psychologist.

4. *Selecting participants.* When selecting participants for a program, managers need to consider who benefits, if programs are required by law, whether training is required or voluntary, and what groups of employees participate. For example, training in ethical accounting practices may be required as a matter of compliance with a new law.

5. *Determining the schedule.* Schedules need to consider the trainees, the needs of their managers, and the best conditions for learning. Another scheduling decision is whether to offer the program on a concentrated basis or to spread it out over weeks or months. For example, a team-building workshop might be presented over three days, followed by follow-up sessions for six months to see how the teams are doing.

6. *Selecting facilities.* A decision needs to be made on whether training will be conducted on-site or at a location away from the office. If away from the office, the facility should not create any travel inconvenience. That said, sometimes employees "get away" to another city as a longer-term retreat, which has benefits. Planning should include breaks with food and refreshments. For example, a manager might want to encourage creativity and thus arrange for the training to be conducted at a local university to remind engineers of their innovative college days.

7. *Selecting instructors.* The qualifications of instructors include knowledge of the subject being taught and presentation skills. They should understand the learning goals of the program. For example, an organization might hire a leadership expert from a top consulting firm to deliver a training program based on her new book.

8. *Preparing audiovisual aids.* An audiovisual aid has two purposes: to help the leader maintain interest and to communicate key points. For example, video content can be an effective addition to a training program to maintain interest and provide variety.

9. *Coordinating the program.* Sometimes the instructor coordinates as well as teaches. In other situations, the coordinator does not do the teaching. The coordinator is responsible for all aspects of the training process. For example, a coordinator might follow the step-by-step process outlined in Figure 8.6 to deliver a training program on understanding the Millennial generation, followed by feedback on improved relationships between the generations in an office.

10. *Evaluating the program.* Evaluation assesses the training program to determine if it has attained its goals. Evaluations focus on learning and performance. For example, following a training program, the trainer might collect surveys on satisfaction with the content and delivery of the training. This is the most basic level of evaluation. Refer to Table 8.4 for a description of the four levels of evaluation known as the Kirkpatrick model.[79]

Looks easy, right? You will have an opportunity to develop a training activity by completing Toolkit Activity 8.3.

An important consideration with evaluation of training is whether or not trainees are able to transfer the learning to the job afterward. This is covered next.

Assessing the Success of Training

Level 1	Reaction	Reaction measures how participants react to training, and is often referred to as satisfaction with the training.
Level 2	Learning	Learning is the assessment of improvement in knowledge, skills, and attitudes. For example, exams assess learning.
Level 3	Behavior	Behavior evaluation is the extent to which the trainees applied the learning and changed their behavior, and this can be assessed immediately and several months after the training, depending on the situation. For example, following a leadership training program, managers' followers are asked to rate their leader's transformational leadership behaviors.
Level 4	Results	Results evaluation is the effect on the business or work environment resulting from the improved performance of the trainee. For example, following a quality management training program, the organization measures the rate of errors made by employees.

Source: Kirkpatrick, D., & Kirkpatrick, J. (2006). *Evaluating training programs: The four levels* (3rd ed.). New York, NY: Berrett-Koehler.

Transfer of Training

As noted earlier in this chapter, organizations spend billions of dollars on training and development each year. Failing to apply the skills learned in training means a loss of time and money. **Transfer of training** is defined as "the application of knowledge, skills and attitudes learned from training on the job and subsequent maintenance of them over a certain period of time."[80] Trainees should be able to transfer their learning to their job by using the new skills and behaviors they learned in the training. Ensuring the transfer of training to the job is a coordinated effort; apart from the trainee, managers play a key role. Providing resources for trainees as well as supporting them through their mistakes and errors is key to the successful transfer of training, as is providing ongoing feedback on the changes in the trainee's performance. Trainees should also analyze and assess situations where they might apply the training.

CRITICAL THINKING QUESTIONS

What are the challenges of transferring training to the actual job? Give examples of factors that might limit the transfer of training based on individual differences, motivation, team norms, and organizational constraints.

The "New Finish Line"

It used to be that delivering a great training program was enough. But in today's workplace, there is more pressure to perform, and the finish line is more of a moving target. There is a new criterion for training success: improved job performance, known as the **new finish line**.[81] To reach the new finish line, managers must treat training as a process rather than an event. In other words, the final step in Figure 8.6 is just the beginning when it comes to supporting employees in the transfer of the training to their work.

Steps to the new finish line include the following:

1. *Treat training as a process.* In the past, training was treated as an isolated event. However, instruction is only one link in the chain that leads to performance improvement. As in any chain, instruction is only as strong as its weakest link. Therefore, even if the training is outstanding, weak managerial support can derail the transfer-of-training process and the goals not be met. For example, a study[82] of highly effective learning programs found that they were managed as end-to-end processes, beginning with clearly identifying the required business outcomes and ending with documenting the results.

2. *Follow through.* Following training, managers need to ensure that employees follow through with the application of training to their work. The new finish line means extending the period that trainers remain involved. Not only are they responsible for the planning and execution of training, but they must see training as one part of the overall learning experience. Follow-through can take a number of forms, from email reminders to teleconferences and perhaps even retraining. Elizabeth McDaid, agency education manager at Chubb Group of Insurance Companies, states, "Our philosophy is that training shouldn't be an event. It must be a process that goes beyond the classroom. Follow-through management is . . . perfect . . . for creating a network of people that we can repeatedly 'touch' long after the course ends."[83]

3. *Engage management.* The post-course period is the number-one place where training fails. The main reason for this appears to be lack of management support. Two recent studies[84] confirm this. At Pfizer, assessments were repeated several months after a leadership development program and compared to preprogram results. The program demonstrated clear improvement, but only if the participants' managers were actively engaged in the training. In contrast, participants who attended the same program but whose managers were not actively involved showed no performance improvement or made much smaller gains.

   A separate study at American Express also showed the managers' impact on training effectiveness. Participants who achieved significantly better results after the training were four times more likely to have conversations with their managers about how to apply the learning than those who produced little or no improvement.

At the technology and engineering firm Emerson, management support for the new finish line is clearly stated:

Development and learning is a lifelong activity—it never stops—so the idea of "The New Finish Line" means that employees continue to grow and learn in their roles on an ongoing basis. Our development process includes work experience, relationships and feedback, and focused training. Approaching training in phases rather than singular events allows employees to follow a path of ongoing development.[85]

CRITICAL THINKING QUESTIONS

Explain why management support helps employees reach the new finish line. Provide an example of how a manager can help an employee transfer team training to their daily work.

Best Practices for Cross-Cultural Training

Design	• Adjust the length of training based on the unique features of the assignment. • Determine according to organizational and expatriate needs whether cross-cultural training (CCT) should be culture-general or culture-specific. • Offer CCT to expatriates and accompanying family members. • Have the human resource department play a large role in planning and implementing the CCT intervention.
Delivery	• Use multiple delivery strategies within one training program. • Tailor the delivery strategy according to the goals of the training. • Provide expatriates with online real-time support materials. • Keep international staff members up-to-date on home organization issues by bringing them home for periodic meetings. • Provide expatriates with personalized coaches. • Offer CCT prior to departure, immediately following arrival in the host country, or at both times.
Evaluation	• Evaluate the CCT program each time it is implemented. • Use numerous criteria to evaluate success and/or failure. • Conduct surveys to assess the expatriate's satisfaction with the training and the overall assignment.

Source: Littrell, L. N., & Salas, E. (2005). A review of cross-cultural training: Best practices, guidelines, and research needs. *Human Resource Development Review*, 4(3), 305–334, p. 315.

Cross-Cultural Training

Cross-cultural training (CCT) has been defined as "an educative process focused on promoting intercultural learning through the acquisition of behavioral, cognitive, and affective competencies required for effective interactions across diverse cultures."[86] The goal of CCT is to improve the cross-cultural effectiveness of managers and increase the probability of success in an expatriate assignment. CCT differs from traditional training in that the focus is on attitudinal changes rather than on the acquisition of information.[87] CCT training typically focuses on cross-cultural adjustment as well as on how to interact with others from different cultures. A summary of best practices for CCT is shown in Table 8.5.

As this chapter has illustrated, HRM has evolved beyond legal compliance with respect to staffing, compensation, and training in many organizations. Following this transition, HR managers and employees have seen the role of "in-house" HRM develop in exciting ways. Rather than simply filling out paperwork and ensuring that proper procedures for hiring, firing, giving raises, and providing access to training are followed, HR is increasingly being given a "seat at the table" along with finance, marketing, manufacturing, and the other functional partners that guide organizations' goals and strategies. This has given rise to strategic human resource management (SHRM) as a field of study and practice.

Strategic Human Resource Management

Learning Objective 8.6: Explain how strategic human resource management is used to achieve organizational goals.

In the sections above, we covered the key functions associated with HRM. Most large organizations have a vice president for human resources, and this person is engaged in the overall HR strategies for the organization. This is **strategic HRM** and is defined as "the pattern of planned human resource deployments and activities intended to enable the firm to achieve its goals."[88] The Society for Human Resource Management (SHRM) points out that strategic HRM is a future-oriented process of developing and implementing HR programs that address and solve business problems and directly contribute to major long-term business objectives.[89]

Michigan: "Hard Strategic HRM"

A model for strategic HRM was developed at the University of Michigan and argues that there is a cycle affecting individual and organizational performance. This approach is shown in Figure 8.7 and is considered "hard HRM" because employees are viewed as a means of meeting the mission of the organization. This is due to political, economic, and cultural forces on the organization, forcing the organization to "match" the environment it is in. The need for matching the environment determines the structure of the organization. In addition, the way human resources are managed is the result of the mission and structure. The organizational mission or objectives involve consideration of the interconnected issues of structure and HRM. Performance is a function of all the human resource management components: *selecting* people who are best able to perform the jobs defined by the structure, *appraising* their performance to facilitate the equitable distribution of rewards, motivating employees by linking *rewards* to high levels of performance, and *developing* employees to enhance their current performance at work as well as to prepare them to perform in positions they may hold in the future.[90]

Harvard: "Soft Strategic HRM"

A competing model of strategic HRM was proposed by professors at Harvard, shown in Figure 8.8. This model is considered "soft HRM" because it concentrates attention on outcomes for employees, particularly their well-being and organizational commitment. This model does not put business performance (and the interests of shareholders) above other legitimate interests, such as those of the community or employees. In the Harvard model, organizational effectiveness is a long-term consequence of HR outcomes such as commitment and competence, but this is just as important as the well-being of employees and the society. An organization adopting this model would focus on making sure employees are involved in their work and participate in decision-making. HRM policies would be developed and implemented to meet employees' needs for influence, within the constraints of the overall business strategy and organizational culture.

CRITICAL THINKING QUESTIONS

Do you agree more with the Michigan model of strategic HRM ("hard HRM") or the Harvard model of strategic HRM ("soft HRM")? Explain why you find one more consistent with your own views than the other.

Strategic HRM plans human resource deployments that enable the firm to achieve its goals.

©iStockphoto.com/skynesher

Strategic HRM has shifted the focus away from the enforcement of HRM procedures and toward aligning them with an organization's goals. Seeing HR employees as performing the administrative and bureaucratic personnel function is increasingly a perception of the past.[91] The modern HRM professional is increasingly someone who spends their time reevaluating existing HR procedures rather than simply enforcing them. Strategic HRM is linked to firm

University of Michigan Model of Hard Strategic HRM

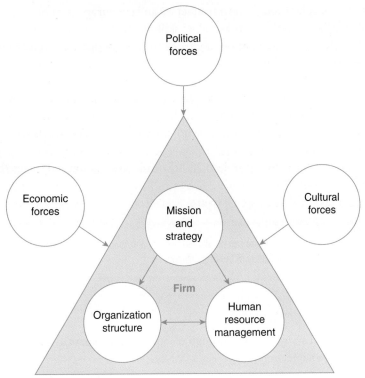

Source: Tichy, N., Fombrun, C. J., & Devanna, M. A. (1982). Strategic human resource management. *Sloan Management Review*, 23(2), 47–60, p. 48.

Harvard Model of Strategic Human Resource Management

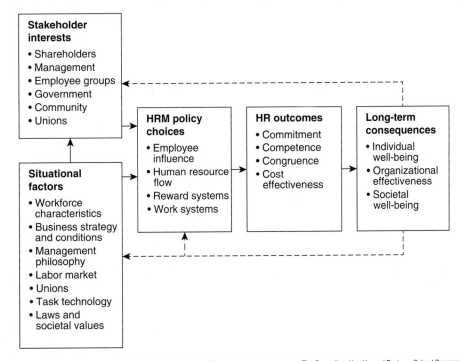

Source: Beer, M., Spector, B., Lawrence, P., Quinn Mills, D., & Walton, R. (1984). *Managing human assets: The Groundbreaking Harvard Business School Program*. New York, NY: Free Press, p. 16.

performance and sustained competitive advantage.[92] To be strategic, HRM needs to achieve the following goals to gain and sustain competitive advantage:

- to invest in people through the introduction and encouragement of learning processes designed to increase capability and align skills to organizational needs,
- to ensure that the organization identifies the knowledge required to meet its goals and satisfy its customers and takes steps to acquire and develop its intellectual capital,
- to define the behaviors required for organizational success and ensure that these behaviors are encouraged, valued, and rewarded,
- to encourage people to engage wholeheartedly in the work they do for the organization, and
- to gain the commitment of people to the organization's mission and values.[93]

CRITICAL THINKING QUESTIONS

Discuss how human resource practices can be aligned with organizational goals. Provide an example of how human resources supports the strategy of the organization.

Managerial Implications

This chapter provided an overview of human resource management systems. The key takeaway points from this chapter are:

- The role of human resource management in organizations is vast, having evolved from compliance with laws to the design of systems that enhance individual and organizational effectiveness. Further, the relationship between HRM and human capital management (HCM) is now a key element of the HRM process, as HCM works to ensure the alignment of employees' experience, knowledge, skills, and abilities with the current needs and strategic goals of an organization. It is the foundation for strategic human resource management (SHRM).
- The core functions of human resource management are staffing, compensation, and training. Staffing is the recruitment and hiring practices used by an organization. Compensation relates to the design of performance management and incentive systems that motivate employees to high performance levels. Finally, training and development ensure the presence of a skilled workforce that has opportunities for growth on the job.
- Compensation is based on solid practice in performance management. However, there are challenges in the performance management process, such as perceptions of unfairness and bias on the part of raters. Forms of compensation other than pay include profit-sharing and gain-sharing. These forms may be less susceptible to bias, but care must be taken that they do not motivate unethical behavior just to meet financial objectives. Ideally, compensation should be based on base pay plus incentives such as bonuses and stock options.
- There is a difference between employee training and development, and the importance of transfer of training to the job is critical. Also, due to the rise in the multinational

corporation and globalization, best practices in cross-cultural training (CCT) should be part of that training.

- Today, organizations engage in strategic human resource management to achieve organizational goals. People are a critical resource for organizations striving to compete effectively through the recruitment, selection, and development of talent. Additionally, strategic HRM requires the "hard" and "soft" aspects of how employees are viewed as resources for competitive advantage.

This chapter covered the important role of human resources in shaping the composition, motivation, and development of the workforce. People are unique individuals, and the next chapter will focus on these individual differences and diversity.

KEY TERMS

360-degree feedback   240

assessment center   239

behaviorally anchored rating scale (BARS)   241

central tendency error   242

compensation   239

cross-cultural training (CCT)   251

development   246

flexible working hours   245

forced ranking   241

gain-sharing plan   245

graphic rating scale   241

halo error   242

human capital   234

human capital management (HCM)   234

human resource management (HRM)   231

job sharing   245

knowledge, skills, and abilities (KSAs)   231

new finish line   249

performance management   240

person–job fit (P–J fit)   231

person–organization fit (P–O fit)   231

profit-sharing plan   245

recruitment   237

remote working *or* telecommuting   245

sabbatical   245

salary range   239

salary range structures   239

selection   237

situational judgment test (SJT)   239

staffing   237

strategic HRM   251

stock options   245

training   246

transfer of training   249

work sample test   239

TOOLKIT

Activity 8.1

Getting Past the AI Résumé Screening

Many organizations are now using artificial intelligence (AI) to screen résumés. To get an interview, you need to be able to pass the screening. Fortunately, there is help. Jobscan (www.jobscan.co) is a tool that gives job-seekers an instant analysis of how well their résumé is tailored to a particular job.

Here is what you do. Follow the tutorial at https://www.jobscan.co/jobscan-tutorial. Update your résumé and paste it in or upload it as a Word Document of PDF. Search for a job and then paste in the job description. The résumé match rate is a score (0% to 100%) based on how well your résumé

matches up with the job description you selected. Jobscan recommends aiming for a match rate of 80%. And it allows you to update your résumé to improve your match rate.

Your match rate is based on these priorities, in order:

1. Hard skills
2. Education level (only when an advanced degree is included in the job description)
3. Job title
4. Soft skills
5. Other key words

The Jobscan website has a lot of other résumé-writing and job-search tips (https://www.jobscan.co/learning).

Discussion Questions

1. What was your match rate? If less than 80%, work on improving your résumé to better fit the job you are interested in.
2. What did you learn about yourself from completing this activity? Discuss any skills you need to work on to better fit your ideal job.
3. Explain why you think this AI tool ranks the skills in the order it does. Would you rank them differently? Why?

Activity 8.2

Whom to Promote?

You are the HR manager for a retail chain of sporting goods stores. The district manager for your region oversees seven stores located in the southeast region and has asked for your input on whom to hire for an open management position in the store with the largest sales volume. The previous manager was very senior and decided to retire. He will stay on while you search for the best person to replace him.

Store managers are in charge of managing all the clerks and sales employees on two shifts. Because the job requires management skills as well as a detailed understanding of both retail and employee relations, the usual practice is to identify promising employees who exhibit management potential rather than hiring externally (from outside the company). Managers are hired externally 50% of the time. This is partly to bring fresh perspectives and experience into the company but also because very few sales employees have the background or training to be store managers. That said, to ensure motivation, any employees who show and interest and have potential are considered for open management positions. As the HR manager, you are interested in increasing promotion from within from 50% to 70% in the next five years.

Your district manager has prepared summaries of each eligible employee to help you identify candidates for future promotion to managerial positions. The district manager lacks HR background and may have included some information that legally should not or cannot be considered in promotion decisions. An important part of your job is to identify this information and point it out to the manager. The summaries are also a bit brief and uneven in the amount of relevant information. The district manager is leaving for a sales convention in two days and wants to wrap this up before she leaves. While it would be nice to have more information, you will need to make some recommendations based on what you have today.

There are six employees under consideration for the promotion to store manager. Your job is to rank the top three candidates and make recommendations. You may assume that if offered the position, any of these candidates will accept it, since they applied for the position.

The Candidates

John Martin—White male, age 32, inventory clerk. He has been with the store for eight years and had always received "excellent" performance evaluations until the last two years (the time of his divorce), when his ratings slipped to "average." He has an associate's degree in business from the local community college. He seems to like his present job but has had arguments over out-of-stock items with some of the salespeople.

Jimmy Cason—White male, age 50, salesperson. He has been with the store for four years, and his performance evaluations throughout that time have varied from "average" to "above average." He moved around from job to job prior to working for the store. He has a bachelor's degree in liberal arts from a good university. He is well liked by other employees and does a great job selling sporting goods. He has a great sense of humor. He is always the first person to leave when his shift is over, and he enjoys fishing. He talks about fishing as much as possible after retirement.

Thonya Jones—Black female, age 38, cash register clerk. She has been with the store since she dropped out of high school. Her ratings on her performance evaluations have decreased from "above average" to "average" in recent years. The district manager speculates that this drop reflects her frustration at being passed over for previous promotions due to her lack of a high school diploma. She participates in every technical training program the company offers, possibly to help offset the lack of a high school diploma.

Kimberly Sowers—White female, age 29, cashier. She has been with the store for four years and has received "above average" performance evaluations. She has a bachelor's degree in music from a local college but was unable to find a position related to her field. Overall, she is a good worker, but she's terribly shy and tends to work by herself and not socialize (either at work or outside work) with coworkers.

Geoff Evers—Black male, age 25, salesperson. He has worked for the company for four years and has always received "high" to "excellent" performance ratings. He played football in high school and loves to talk about sports. He constantly takes on new assignments, tries to learn everything about the job, and has no problem working overtime. In addition to working hard at the job, he is attending college classes in the evenings working on a bachelor's degree in business. He is liked by other employees, and customers find him helpful. His ultimate goal is to start and run his own business.

Maria Gonzalez—Hispanic female, age 25, accounting clerk. She has worked for the company since graduating from college with a bachelor's degree in accounting three years ago. She's a hard worker and has received "above average" to "high" performance ratings. She came to the United States from Guatemala a few months before she joined the store, and has a green card. She still has some difficulty with the English language. Though the store employees seem to like her, they don't really spend much time with her, since her language makes it difficult.

Discussion Questions

1. List the primary factors (at least three) that you considered in making your rankings. Which of these had the single biggest impact? What made it the most important factor?

2. Write down the names of your top three candidates and create a table like this:

Candidate Choice	Pros	Cons
First choice: Most important factors:	1. 2. 3.	1. 2. 3.
Second choice: Most important factors:	1. 2. 3.	1. 2. 3.
Third choice: Most important factors:	1. 2. 3.	1. 2. 3.

Note the most important factors in favor of and against promoting them to the store manager position. Try to come up with three factors in each list.

3. Review the pros and cons of the three potential employees. How close were your choices?

4. Based on what you learned in this chapter, what are the most important considerations when promoting from within an organization?

5. Discuss any ethical and legal issues you see with the information being used to evaluate these candidates for promotion.

Activity 8.3

Design a Communication Training Activity

Your boss has asked you to develop a training activity for improving communication between employees. You review the different approaches to communication from Chapter 7 of this textbook.

1. Decide the topic of your training activity (e.g., communication apprehension, one-way vs. two-way communication, feedback, cross-cultural communication, customer service, interpersonal communication, active listening).

2. State the learning objective of your training activity (e.g., to increase two-way communication).

3. Follow the guidelines for developing a training program discussed in this chapter. In designing the activity, keep in mind the following points provided by convergence training:

- Remember that it's important to design first.
- Focus primarily on the learning needs of the employees.
- Create training content and assessments that relate directly to learning objectives.
- Include as much hands-on practice or simulation as possible: People learn by doing.
- Put the employees in control of the learning process.
- Do everything possible to let the employees talk and interact with the trainer and with each other.
- Make sure there's plenty of opportunity for feedback.
- Break training materials up into small "chunks" that are easier to take in.
- Order "chunked" training materials in a logical manner—one step builds on top of another.
- Use at least two different formats (e.g., lectures, case studies, interactive activities, self-assessments, work sheets, role-plays).
- Integrate storytelling and scenarios.
- Appeal to a variety of your employees' senses during training. Sight is by far the most important sense for learning, but adding the others when possible does help.

4. Develop a measure for how you will evaluate the effectiveness of your training activity. This can be a brief survey of two to three questions.

Discussion Questions

1. What learning needs does your training activity address? Evaluate the importance of employees' knowing how to acquire this skill.

2. Adult learners:

- Are self-directed
- Come to training with a lifetime of existing knowledge, experience, and opinions
- Are goal-oriented
- Want training that is relevant
- Want training that is task-oriented
- Learn when they see "what's in it for them"
- Want to be and feel respected

Evaluate the effectiveness of your training activity in terms of the needs of adult learners.

3. Explain why you chose the learning formats you did. Why do you feel they were best matched to your learning objectives?

4. Have some friends or classmates complete your training activity and complete your evaluation measure. Did they learn what you had planned? Explain and discuss any changes you would make, based on the feedback.

Source: Adapted from Dalto, J. (2014, March 19). How to create an effective training program. Retrieved from https://www.convergencetraining.com/blog/how-to-create-an-effective-training-program-8-steps-to-success.

Case Study 8.1

Wearables and Employee Privacy

What are wearables? They are fitness bracelets that track employees' sleep and exercise habits. Some organizations are now even using badges that capture people's movements on the job. These wearable data-collection devices are now commonplace.

Employers are using wearables for HR tracking—and this is up 30% since 2014. Many organizations (55%) of companies are using the data from these devices to improve workforce productivity, according to a 2015 survey by HR technology consulting firm Sierra-Cedar Inc. Employees are bullish on the idea of wearables. According to the Kronos study Wearables at Work, nearly three-quarters of employees surveyed said that these types of tracking devices can help make workplaces better (e.g., safer or more efficient). According to the report, there is much more support for wearables among American students than in the general population. Seventy-two percent of student participants identified at least one positive outcome of using wearables. Therefore, support for use of these devices is expected to increase as new grads enter the workforce. For reference, just under half (48%) of the U.S. adult population supports companies using wearable devices to track employees.

Wearables at Work in the Workplace

How is wearable tracking technology already at work in the workplace? Examples can be found across industries. In the transportation and utilities industries, wearables are helping to ensure compliance with legal policies and increase workers' speed and efficiency. For example, wearables track truck drivers on the job and remind them to take legally mandated rest breaks. Utility engineers use the GPS data streamed from wearables so they can track crews' working time and send in backup or extra resources as needed.

Analysis of labor data collected by wearables is also used to make work more efficient. Wearables have made their way into call centers, where they can help employees boost collaboration and improve the lines of communication. For instance, when call center agents step away from their desk for scheduled or unscheduled breaks, wearables with an RFID chip can notify colleagues so that no calls go unanswered.

Some wearables—like the Apple Watch and its Android equivalents—can synchronize with other electronics. That means they can conveniently provide workers with access to email, texts, and calendar apps. By boosting connectivity among team members, wearables can make teamwork seamless.

Let's take a look at one practical application of wearable technology. Buffer, a social media start-up located in San Francisco, makes wearables part of the community culture from the moment an employee is hired. All new employees receive a fitness tracker called the Jawbone UP, enabling them to track various fitness data (e.g., steps, activity, and hours of sleep). Employees (and even their families) can voluntarily opt into the tracking process, which is intended to enhance Buffer's commitment to helping employees achieve their health and wellness goals. The data obtained via the Jawbone UP is collected by a smartphone app, which allows employees to discuss their data and have conversations about their health habits.

For another example of wearables in action, consider the HR analytics firm Humanyze. This Boston-based company supplies smart devices for its clients' employees. These badges, equipped with microphone technology, record employees' conversations and movements. Humanyze uses the data to help streamline communication, increase productivity, and even evaluate the success of changes to the office environment. In one instance, Humanyze used data collected by the smart badges at a Deloitte office in Canada to assess whether an office redesign had helped employees communicate more efficiently.

Recently, Fitbit, creator of a widely recognized fitness tracker, improved privacy protections by offering technology that complies with the Health Insurance Portability and Accountability Act (HIPAA). Making their devices HIPAA-compliant is likely to expand Fitbit's presence in the corporate wellness market.

Monitoring the Monitors

From security cameras in banks and retail storefronts, surveillance has been part of the workplace for decades. But, as wearable tracking devices becomes more mainstream, companies are entering a new frontier of digital monitoring. What does this mean for employee privacy? The rapid rise in implementation of these devices makes the conversation about their role in human resources management all the more urgent. Considerations like data security and employee confidentiality loom large. In fact, in the aforementioned Kronos study, data security was the top concern in regard to workplace wearables, cited by more than 40% of those surveyed. Companies that utilize "big data" could open themselves up to ethical criticism and even lawsuits. HR professionals are on the lookout for potential labor, privacy, and security concerns and are working to develop and enforce policies that keep both employers' interests and employees' data safe.

Stacey Harris, VP of research and analytics at Sierra-Cedar, says that wearables present a unique challenge because they make surveillance impossible to ignore. "The challenge is that [wearables] are a bit more invasive" than monitoring tools of the past. Ever innovative, technologists who design wearables are continuously expanding the types of data the devices can gather. Mike Morgan, a privacy and security lawyer at Jones Day in Los Angeles, warns that this data "can reveal quite a bit about someone."

That's exactly what concerns advocates who support employee confidentiality and privacy. The data collected by wearable technology may be opt-in—meaning that users don't *have* to share data such as heart rate or GPS location. But that does not necessarily mean that most people understand the quantity and data collected by these devices or the consequences of sharing it, Morgan cautions.

It is common for employers to avoid legal fallout by making wearables optional. Devices that collect data are typically part of corporate wellness programs implemented to decrease rising health care costs. The two primary federal regulations that protect employees' rights related to information privacy are the EEOC (Equal Employment Opportunity Commission) and the ADA (Americans with Disabilities Act). The EEOC protects workers' privacy by mandating that employers make participation in such wellness programs entirely voluntary. While the ADA limits employers' rights to access information about workers' health status, the law does allow for employees to voluntarily provide this information via optional wellness programs.

Although workers do have federal protections, simply making the use of wearable devices voluntary doesn't solve all the potential problems they present. Optional data sharing doesn't address the security risk of collecting data in the first place. Rather than being stored on the device itself, sensitive data may indeed make its way to the cloud or even the app provider, and it remains unclear what obligations the company has to protect employee data in these cases. Harris warns that the consequences of collecting data on the cloud or releasing it to the app provider could have catastrophic consequences for both employees and companies. Imagine, for instance, that a C-suite exec uses a wearable device that tracks information revealing a serious health problem. A hacker could breach security and release that information to the media and the public, presenting a whole host of problems for the company.

Pressure to Participate

Harris contends that wearable devices can offer employees "more ownership over their own decisions and give them more information to make their own choices about their health, working pace and break schedules." But that ownership can come at the expense of employee privacy. GPS-enabled apps and devices introduce the potential for constant surveillance of employees' whereabouts. Even if participation is optional, employees may feel obligated to give employers access to their data. "Companies are very aware from a cultural perspective that there's a creepy line," Harris says. The balance between obtaining useful data and protecting employees' confidentiality is tenuous.

Companies must stay abreast of the laws surrounding employee privacy and carefully consider ethical concerns. Programs that utilize data from wearables should be optional—never compulsory. After all, employees shouldn't have to tell their boss they skipped the gym, exceeded their daily calorie intake, or pulled an all-nighter.

The interest in using wearables at work is increasing. With new technology innovations every day, we can expect that organizations will want to use them. Wearables offer both opportunities and unique challenges, and we are at the start of the use of this technology for HR. It will be important for organizations to balance the usefulness of the technology for business purposes with employee privacy to mitigate potential risks.

Discussion Questions

1. Why do you think the HR managers see benefits in tracking employee movements through wearable technology? Give an example of how this can provide information useful to HR.
2. Discuss the benefits and risks of requiring employees to use wearables at work. What are HR's responsibilities?
3. If you were on a task force to examine whether to implement wearable technology in your organization, would you be in favor or against it? Explain your decision. Reflect on the ethical principles that may be involved in this decision.

Sources: Adapted from Brin, D. (2016, June 1). Does use of wearables increase HR's responsibility? Retrieved from https://www.shrm.org/hr-today/news/hr-magazine/0616/pages/0616-wearable-technology.aspx; Hernandez, P. (2014, October 28). Employees bullish about wearables at work. Retrieved from https://www.datamation.com/mobile-wireless/employees-bullish-about-wearables-at-work-survey.html; HR.com. (n.d.). Wearables in the workplace: The opportunities and challenges. Retrieved from https://www.replicon.com/blog/wearables-in-the-workplace-the-opportunities-and-challenges/.

Self-Assessment 8.1

Situational Judgment Test

Being able to quickly identify and come up with solutions for issues in the workplace is a highly sought-after skill for a variety of roles. Many employers use the SJT to ensure they are hiring individuals who are inclined to carry out effective problem-solving. The scenarios presented on this type of test rely on your intuition to resolve hypothetical conflicts. These conflicts will often be based on realistic workplace situations.

During a situational judgment test, you will be presented with between 25 and 50 different scenarios and given a time limit for completing the test. There will often be a set of instructions detailing how you should answer each question. To answer, you will need to either find the most (or least) suitable response to the scenario or rank the responses in the order of effectiveness. Many times the answers for a given scenario will not be completely straightforward. It is also very easy to be misled by an answer that seems to fit but may not be entirely appropriate for the situation at hand. To get an idea of the types of questions that might appear on an SJT, answer the following questions.

Scenario #1

You are a department manager and you have recently thought of a new procedure that you believe would improve the work process. Some of the employees in your department agree with the change and some do not. One of your employees openly criticizes the idea to your director. What would you do and why? Choose ONE option.

A. You decide not to respond to the critics in order to avoid unnecessary conflict.
B. You reprimand the employee for going over your head to the director and work to promote your idea with even more enthusiasm.
C. You meet the employee for a talk and explain that bypassing your authority is unacceptable.
D. Employees' trust in their manager is important, so you decide to implement only some of the changes to keep your employees satisfied.

The best answer is C.

Scenario #2

At a marketing meeting with your supervisor and the senior marketing manager, you find yourself in the middle of a conflict between them. You know that the two do not get along professionally and that they are in constant disagreement. They are now arguing about strategies for a new campaign and are asking you to pick a side. What would you do and why? Choose ONE option.

A. You accept the idea of the senior marketing manager. Since she is more senior, she has more influence on your status in the company, and therefore it is politically wiser to support her.
B. You accept the idea of your supervisor. Since he is directly above you, he has more influence on your daily routine in the company, and therefore it is politically wiser to support him.
C. You weigh the advantages and disadvantages of each side and decide accordingly without getting involved in their personal conflict.
D. You believe that getting involved in this dispute would be detrimental to you, as both sides are superior to you. Therefore, you refuse to pick a side, saying that both strategies are equally successful.

The best answer is C.

Scenario #3

After you have served two years as manager of the sales team, the director of your company appoints a new deputy manager. Although you have been able to work together, your impressions of her are negative—you find her arrogant and disloyal. The director has now considered sending her on a course that

would create an opportunity for her relocation to a different position within the company. However, it would also speed up her promotion. What would you do? RANK ALL responses from 1 (least effective) to 5 (most effective).

A. Since this course is likely to result in the relocation of the deputy manager, you approve her participation in the course.
B. You contact your director immediately and ask that she be relocated to a different position, more suited to her capabilities.
C. You veto her participation in the course and discuss it with her. You express your concerns and try to work out your differences. You update your director.
D. You approve her participation in the course, since it was offered by the director. However, you voice your concerns to the director.

The correct order is: C, D, B, A

Scenario #4

You have been working as a salesperson for the past year and have consistently achieved great sales numbers. For personal reasons, you have recently been unfocused at work, and as a result your work performance has declined. Additionally, due to changes in the market, the sales figures of your team have decreased as well. Your director does not seem to be taking the changes in the market into account and is blaming your poor performance on poor leadership on your part. What would you do and why? Choose the BEST and WORST options.

A. You explain your personal situation to the director and apologize for the decline in the performance of your team. You ask to take a few days off to recuperate.
B. You make a decision to put aside your personal situation and consult other sales directors regarding their ways of coping with a volatile market. You devote yourself entirely to your work.
C. You update the director on the changes in the market and explain that there is nothing that can be done at the moment to improve sales.
D. You scold your team members for their poor performance and set new, more attainable sales targets in line with the changes in the market.

The best response is B and the worst response is D.

Scenario #5

You've been working in the same place for the past three years and have managed to work your way up. Lately, you have been feeling that you have reached your potential in the company, so you start pursuing options for advancing your career in other companies. You are now in the midst of negotiations for a new position. Rumors that you are leaving have spread in your current workplace. What would you do and why? Choose ONE option.

A. Since the rumor is already out, you update all your acquaintances in the organization that you are in the midst of negotiations for a new position. This may even encourage your directors to promote you within the company.

B. Since it is only a rumor, you don't update anyone until you actually hand in your notice. Nothing has been decided yet.

C. Since the rumor is already out and you will probably leave, you invest a little less in your work and a bit more in attaining the new position.

D. Because the rumor is out, you update your manager and only him about your intention of leaving. Since you are still an employee there, you keep working normally.

The best response is D.

Discussion Questions

1. Typically, a person receives one point for each correct question on an SJT. How many questions did you answer correctly? What did you learn about effective judgement from answering these example questions?

2. Do you feel this is a fair way to assess a person's ability to perform well in a job? Explain your position.

3. Develop a scenario for an SJT for determining the best person to lead a volunteer or school organization that you are involved with. How could you use such scenarios to assess a person's judgment and decision-making for that specific job?

Source: Adapted from Job Test Prep. (n.d.). Free situational judgement test (SJT) practice questions. Retrieved from https://www.job testprep.co.uk/free-situational-judgement-test.

Get the tools you need to sharpen your study skills. SAGE edge offers a robust online environment featuring an impressive array of free tools and resources. Access practice quizzes, eFlashcards, video, and multimedia at **edge.sagepub.com/scanduragower.**

LEADING

PART IV

CHAPTER 9

UNDERSTANDING INDIVIDUALS AND DIVERSITY

CHAPTER LEARNING OBJECTIVES

After studying this chapter, you should be able to:

9.1 Provide the definition of personality.

9.2 Summarize the elements of psychological capital.

9.3 List the three aspects of emotional intelligence.

9.4 Describe different approaches to managing diversity.

9.5 Name the characteristics of four generations at work, and describe how Generation Z will affect organizations.

9.6 Explain the guidelines for managing diverse followers.

Get the edge on your studies at **edge.sagepub.com/scanduragower.**

- Take the chapter quiz
- Review key terms with eFlashcards
- Explore multimedia resources, SAGE readings, and more!

What Would You Do?

Consider the following two situations posed by researchers:

- The solutions manual, which has all the answers for the homework assignments as well as the exams, is sitting on the math professor's desk when Brenda walks in. The professor has stepped out for a minute. No one sees Brenda as she reaches down and puts the book in her backpack, then walks down the back stairwell.

- John has heard through the grapevine that someone is selling a copy of the final exam in his statistics class and *everyone* has bought it. Rumor has it that the final is impossible, so if John doesn't get a copy, he will fail while everyone else does well, eliminating the possibility of a curve. John decides to buy a copy of the final exam.[1]

What would you do in the situations described above? Do you think others would do something different?

These questions were part of a research study[2] that examined the effect of individual differences on ethical decision choices. Researchers gave scenarios like the ones above to 171 undergraduate students in management and organizational behavior classes. The study examined individual differences in personality as well as demographic variables (race and gender). Researchers wanted to know what individual characteristics explained the responses to these tough decisions.

One personality difference studied was **locus of control**. Locus of control reflects an individual's belief about the relationship between their behavior and its consequences. People who believe they control their own fate have an *internal* locus of control. In contrast, people who have an *external* locus of control think that what happens to them is due to fate or the actions of other people.[3] Researchers found that people with an internal locus of control were more likely to make ethical decisions in scenarios like the two shown above.

Another personality difference in the study was **delay of gratification**. Delay of gratification is a person's willingness to postpone immediate satisfaction of their needs to receive greater rewards later.[4] In the research study, students who were able to postpone gratification had higher personal ethical standards than individuals who wanted immediate gratification.

This chapter will also discuss diversity due to demographic differences, and this was included in the ethics study. Researchers learned that Black students were more likely to make ethical choices than Caucasian students were.[5] However, the study did not find differences between male and female students in terms of ethical decisions.

Another study looked at the personality trait of **Machiavellianism**.[6] This trait is based on Niccolo Machiavelli's book *The Prince*.[7] This book described the expected behavior of princes in the Middle Ages. People high in Machiavellianism (high Machs) use manipulation, lie, and have a cynical view of human nature. They tend not to trust other people. They want to win at all costs—and they believe "the ends justify the means." In leadership positions, high Machs are more likely to engage in unethical behavior.[8] Research has linked high Machiavellianism with maximization of profits and a greater likelihood to steal from others. High Machs are more likely to engage in questionable financial decisions.[9]

NICOLÒ MACCHIAVELLI

Niccolo Machiavelli, Italian Statesman, and author of The Prince.

An example of a questionable financial practice is insider trading, which was studied using the following situation:

At a family Thanksgiving dinner, Bob, the CEO of Visualogic, was asked by his brother-in-law Jim how his business was doing. "It is great. We are beating all of our expectations," Bob replied. The next morning Jim bought 1,000 shares of Visualogic. How ethical was Jim's decision to buy the shares?[10]

You will learn more about Machiavellian leadership traits in Chapter 12.

CRITICAL THINKING QUESTIONS

How would a high-Mach person respond to the insider-trading situation described above? How would they justify their behavior to themselves and others?

▼ FIGURE 9.0

Textbook Organization

Introduction
Chapter 1. Becoming a Manager

Planning
Chapter 2. Making Decisions and Using Analytics
Chapter 3. Ethics and Social Responsibility
Chapter 4. Organizational Culture and Change
Chapter 5. Strategic Management and Planning

Organizing

Chapter 6. Organizational Design
Chapter 7. Communication
Chapter 8. Human Resource Systems

Leading

Chapter 9. Understanding Individuals and Diversity
Chapter 10. Motivation
Chapter 11. Managing Teams
Chapter 12. Leadership
Chapter 13. Managing in a Global Environment

Controlling

Chapter 14. Budget Control
Chapter 15. Management Control Systems and Technology

Sources: Adapted from Clouse, M., Giacalone, R. A., Olsen, T. D., & Patelli, L. (2017). Individual ethical orientations and the perceived acceptability of questionable finance ethics decisions. *Journal of Business Ethics, 144*(3), 549–558; and McCuddy, M. K., & Peery, B. L. (1996). Selected individual differences and collegians' ethical beliefs. *Journal of Business Ethics, 15*(3), 261–272.

As the examples above show, individual differences matter for ethics and other employee behaviors in organizations. This chapter is designed to give you an overview of how both internal and external differences among individuals contribute to successes and challenges in an organization, and how they affect you as a manager and leader. This knowledge will help you understand (but not necessarily change) the behaviors of organizational members and use this knowledge to form stronger teams, make better decisions, and hopefully make your job a little easier. We begin with personality traits.

What Is Personality?

Learning Objective 9.1: Provide the definition of personality.

Personality is "regularities in feeling, thought, and action that are characteristic of an individual."[11] Managers need to have a good understanding of individual differences in personality—in terms of both understanding themselves and understanding others. Psychologists believe that personality traits are relatively stable over a person's lifetime. Personality matters to a manager because personality traits predict employee behavior in organizations. Personality affects a person's work habits. For example, some employees have a trait of being hardworking. Personality also affects how we behave in relationships at work. Another example is that a person may be shy and unwilling to speak out in a team meeting. That said, personality (and most individual differences) might be difficult to change even with training. For this reason, individual differences such as personality traits need to be *understood*, since managers must work with all different kinds of people in the workplace whom they cannot change. Let's face it—sometimes people just do not get along due to a "personality clash." Next we will discuss research that addresses the long-term nature of personality traits.

Heredity Influences Personality

Can an outgoing salesperson who is extraverted change their personality and become a deep-thinking introvert? In other words, are personality traits born or learned? This question was studied in the famous **Minnesota twin studies**. In this important and interesting research, twins born in Minnesota from 1936 through 1955 signed up to participate in the studies.[12] To qualify for the study, they had to be identical twins, either monozygotic (identical) or dizygotic (fraternal, nonidentical; MZAs and DZAs, respectively), brought up in different households. Researchers found 80% of the surviving, intact pairs and invited them to participate in a series of psychological studies. Some of the twins had been raised in different households for various reasons (e.g., adoption). This allowed researchers to look at the contribution of heredity versus the environment.

These twin studies tell us a great deal about the contribution of heredity compared to the child-rearing environment. One study showed that 50% of the difference in occupational choice (e.g., whether a person is an engineer or a nurse) is due to heredity.[13] Most people are surprised to learn this. Another study of MZA and DZA twins showed that 40% of the variance in work motivation is due to heredity, whereas 60% is due to the environment.[14]

We have learned a great deal about the influence of heredity on personality from the Minnesota twin studies.

© Lopolo/Shutterstock

What does this mean for a manager? While personality might change, most psychologists believe that it is a relatively stable individual difference. Instead of trying to change a coworker's personality, it is perhaps better to learn about personality differences, understand how different personalities relate at work, and then learn to work effectively with different types. Psychologists have developed inventories (personality tests) to assess personality differences. These tests are useful in training programs on conflict resolution and team-building. One of the most popular personality tests is the Myers-Briggs Type Indicator.

Myers-Briggs Type Indicator

Over 2 million people take the Myer-Briggs Type Indicator (MBTI) every year. The MBTI is the most often administered personality test to nonpsychiatric populations (i.e., the "well population").[15] Because it was developed and normed on "well people," it is popular with organizations, and many organizations (e.g., Hallmark, General Electric, the U.S. Armed Forces) use it in their leadership training and development programs. The MBTI was developed by a mother-and-daughter team, Katherine Briggs and Isabel Myers-Briggs, and is based on the personality theories of Carl Jung.[16] The MBTI measures four general personality preferences:

- **introversion (I)** vs. **extraversion (E)**: Extraverts tend to be outgoing; introverts tend to be shy.
- **sensing (S)** vs. **intuitive (N)**: Sensing types tend to be practical; intuitive people tend to be "idea people."
- **thinking (T)** vs. **feeling (F)**: Thinking types tend to use logic; feeling types tend to use emotion.
- **judging (J)** vs. **perceiving (P)**: Judging types tend to make quick decisions; perceiving types tend to be more flexible.

People who take the MBTI are grouped into 16 personality "types" based on these characteristics. For example, an ENTP would be extraverted, intuitive, thinking, and perceiving. This person might be attracted to starting their own business, for example. In contrast, an INTJ is introverted, intuitive, thinking, and judging and may be attracted to a scientific career. ISTJs are detail oriented and practical, whereas ESTJs are organizers and may be comfortable in managerial roles.

You may find the data interesting in Table 9.1, which shows the percentage of managers, administrators, and supervisors who fall into each of the MBTI Type categories. Most managers in this large sample were either ISTJ (introverted, sensing, thinking, judging) or ESTJ (extraverted, sensing, thinking, judging). The rarest MBTI Type in this managerial sample was the ISFP (introverted, sensing, feeling, perceiving).

Limitations of the MBTI

Despite its popularity, there has been limited research support for the reliability and validity of the MBTI. If you take the test again, you may not receive the same score, and the matter of whether people are actually classifiable into the

▼ TABLE 9.1

Myers-Briggs Types for Managers, Administrators, and Supervisors

Managers, Administrators, and Supervisors N = 4808					
Sensing		Intuition			
Thinking	Feeling	Feeling	Thinking		
ISTJ N = 935 % = 19.45 ■■■■■■■■ ■■■■■■■ ■■■■	**ISFJ** N = 261 % = 5.43 ■■■■■	**INFJ** N = 124 % = 2.58 ■■■	**INTJ** N = 392 % = 8.15 ■■■■■■■■	Judgment	Introversion
ISTP N = 175 % = 3.64 ■■■■	**ISFP** N = 80 % = 1.66 ■■	**INFP** N = 130 % = 2.70 ■■■	**INTP** N = 280 % = 5.82 ■■■■■■	Perception	
ESTP N = 158 % = 3.29 ■■■	**ESFP** N = 93 % = 1.93 ■■	**ENFP** N = 203 % = 4.22 ■■■■	**ENTP** N = 285 % = 5.93 ■■■■■■	Perception	Extroversion
ESTJ N = 786 % = 16.35 ■■■■■■■■ ■■■■■■■■	**ESFJ** N = 218 % = 4.53 ■■■■■	**ENFJ** N = 177 % = 3.68 ■■■■	**ENTJ** N = 511 % = 10.63 ■■■■■■■■ ■■■	Judgment	

Note: ■ = 1% of sample

Source: Gerald P. Macdaid, CAPT Data Bank, 1997. Center for Applications of Psychological Type, Inc.

16 categories is questionable.[17] However, the MBTI remains the most popular personality test in use for organizations, and there is an excellent chance you will take either the MBTI or a similar test when you apply for professional positions or be asked to analyze the personality test results of others in making your management decisions. Therefore, it is good for you to become familiar with personality testing. Also, it is important to note that the MBTI has not been validated for selection; in other words, its publisher makes it clear that you should not use the MBTI to hire people for particular jobs in an organization.[18] Yet some organizations do.[19]

CRITICAL THINKING QUESTIONS

Given the limited research support for the MBTI, what are the concerns regarding organizations continuing to use it for hiring purposes?

Applications of the MBTI in Organizations

The best uses for the MBTI appear to be for conflict resolution and team-building, and this is where it is most often used in management-training programs and classrooms. The value of the MBTI is in allowing people to discuss personality differences in their approach to work in a nonjudgmental way. All of the labels in the MBTI are neutral; it is not better or worse to be introverted or extraverted, for example. In fact, Briggs and Myers-Briggs titled their book *Gifts Differing*, and this captures the essence of their approach to understanding personality. In the workplace, everyone has something to offer, and it takes all types of people for teams and organizations to be successful. To contribute effectively, everyone needs to feel valued and engaged. For managers, this underscores the importance of understanding individual differences.

Of course, the MBTI is not the only personality assessment available; next we will discuss another personality theory that has had more research support (although it is currently not as well known as the MBTI to most practicing managers and the general population). This personality assessment is known as the "Big Five" personality test.

The Big Five

After much research examining various personality inventories, the developers of the Big-Five theory of personality concluded that personality could be summarized using five factors: openness, conscientiousness, extraversion, agreeableness, and neuroticism.[20] These factors and their definitions are listed in Table 9.2. Note that the table is organized such that the first letters of these personality traits spell the acronym "OCEAN," and this will help you to remember them.

Openness is a person's willingness to embrace new ideas and new situations. **Conscientiousness** represents the characteristic of being a person who follows through and gets things done. **Extraversion** is a trait of a person who is outgoing, talkative, and sociable and enjoys social situations. **Agreeableness** is being a nice person in general. Finally, **neuroticism** represents a tendency to be anxious or moody (this trait is often referred to by its opposite: emotional stability).

Can your personality traits affect your performance on final exams? One study examined this question in five samples, three universities, and two countries (875 students), and the results showed that conscientiousness and emotional stability were predictive of self-efficacy and performance (self-efficacy was the students' belief in their ability to do well on exams, and performance was the final exam score).[21] In addition, what about the time you spend in social networks online—do certain personality types post more, interact more, and have more online friends? An interesting study found that the personality traits of extraversion and openness were the strongest predictors of social networking.[22]

The Big-Five Personality Characteristics

Trait	Description
Openness	Being curious, original, intellectual, creative, and open to new ideas
Conscientiousness	Being organized, systematic, punctual, achievement oriented, and dependable
Extraversion	Being outgoing, talkative, sociable, and enjoying social situations
Agreeableness	Being affable, tolerant, sensitive, trusting, kind, and warm
Neuroticism	Being anxious, irritable, temperamental, and moody

Source: Adapted from Barrick, M. R., & Mount, M. K. (2005). Yes, personality matters: Moving on to more important matters. *Human Performance, 18,* 359–372.

There has been a good deal of research on whether these five traits predict job performance, and results indicate that the conscientiousness dimension strongly predicts performance on the job (it makes sense that people who are achievement oriented and dependable would be better employees and also better leaders).[23] Conscientiousness also translates into success in terms of job satisfaction, income, and higher occupational status (e.g., being an executive, business owner, or professional).[24] While conscientiousness is the best predictor of job performance, extraversion also has a moderate but significant relationship with performance, particularly in sales.[25]

Other Big-Five traits relate to other positive work outcomes. Research has also shown that emotional stability relates to the ability to cope with stress, and those with higher openness adjust better to organizational change.[26] Given the strong research support for the relationships between the Big-Five personality traits and performance and career outcomes, managers should understand that the big-five measures can be used successfully in making hiring decisions. For this reason, personality research has a great deal of practical applications for organizations. You can learn what your scores are on the Big-Five personality dimensions by taking Self-Assessment 9.1 at the end of this chapter.

CRITICAL THINKING QUESTIONS

What are the fairness issues involved in using personality tests for selection of new employees?

Personality Traits and Your Health

You may have heard the phrase "Stress kills," but is there any truth to this statement? Some years ago, cardiologists showed a link between a personality trait called Type A behavior and cardiovascular heart disease.[27] Their theory started by observing patients in their waiting room; some sat patiently reading a magazine, for example. Others sat on the edge of their seats and got up frequently (they literally wore out the edges of the chairs and armrests).[28] Friedman and Rosen conducted a study over a long period of time and asked questions such as the following:

▼ FIGURE 9.1

Personality Types A and B

Source: McLeod, S. (2017). Type A Personality. https://www.simplypsychology .org/personality-a.html.

Do you feel guilty if you use spare time to relax?
Do you need to win in order to derive enjoyment from games and sports?
Do you generally move, walk, and eat rapidly?
Do you often try to do more than one thing at a time?[29]

Study respondents were then put into one of two groups: **Type A** (competitive, aggressive), **Type B** (relaxed, easygoing) (see Figure 9.1.). By the end of this long-term study, 70% of the men who were classified as Type A had coronary heart disease. This study had several limitations, including that it was only conducted on men who were middle-aged, and the researchers did not take into account other factors such as the dietary habits of the study

FACT OR FICTION?

Should I Get a Trophy For Trying?

Stanford researcher Carol Dweck was interested in the reasons that some students diligently faced failures and were persistent while others avoided challenges. In her groundbreaking research, Dweck identified two traits that determine how people approach challenges: the **fixed mindset**, which is the belief that one's abilities are carved in stone and predetermined at birth, and the **growth mindset**, the belief that one's abilities can be developed through making a great deal of effort. She believes that people get smarter by sticking to something until they master it. For example, a student who has a fixed mindset will not work as hard to study for an exam if they believe their genes have determined their intelligence.

However, Dweck noticed that parents and educators did not completely understand her research. A "false growth mindset" emerged where the idea was oversimplified. Some educators thought that growth was only about trying—and everyone should get a trophy for participation. However, just telling students to try hard does not always produce results. For example, a teacher might praise a student for making an effort on a math test even if he has failed it, believing that doing so will promote a growth mindset in that student regardless of the outcome. Nevertheless, false praise actually creates more problems. We are now dealing with younger employees who cannot get through the day without receiving a medal for their efforts. According to Dweck,

> another misunderstanding [of growth mindset] that might apply to lower-achieving children is the oversimplification of growth mindset into just [being about] effort. Teachers were just praising effort that was not effective, saying, "Wow, you tried really hard!" But students know that if they didn't make progress and you're praising them, it's a consolation prize. They also know you think they cannot do any better. So this kind of growth-mindset idea was misappropriated to try to make kids feel good when they were not achieving.

The growth mindset is really about instilling the joy of learning new things. Training programs and workshops on the growth mindset have shown that when students learn a growth mindset, many of them regain their motivation to learn and achieve higher grades.

Dweck's research has important implications for teachers. Now corporations are interested in her ideas as well. Managers are using these concepts to assess the best ways to motivate diverse followers. It seems that organizational cultures may exhibit fixed or growth mindsets that send employees messages about how to fit into the culture and succeed.

In a *Harvard Business Review* article, Dweck states that when entire companies embrace a growth mindset, their employees report feeling more empowered and committed. They also receive far greater organizational support for collaboration and innovation. In contrast, people at fixed-mindset companies report more cheating and deception among employees, presumably to gain an advantage in the race to get ahead of others.

In a two-year study, several Fortune 1000 companies found that the growth mindset has positive impact on employees:

- *Trust:* Employees in companies with a growth-mindset culture of development expressed 47% higher agreement with statements demonstrating trust in their company.

- *Engagement:* Employees in companies with a growth-mindset culture of development were 34% likelier to feel a sense of ownership and commitment to the future of the company.

- *Innovation:* Those in growth-mindset companies showed 65% stronger agreement that their companies supported risk-taking and 49% stronger agreement that their organizations fostered innovation.

- *Ethics:* Those in companies with a growth-mindset culture of development disagreed 41% more strongly than those in fixed-mindset companies that their organizations were rife with unethical behavior.

For employees, it is important to praise not just effort but the learning process itself. The growth mindset has a lot of potential for improving both the motivation and well-being of employees. Employees need to stop working only for awards and become genuinely interested in learning and creating new ideas. Focusing on learning moves employees out of the fixed mindset and motivates them to learn on the job.

Discussion Questions

1. Do you believe you have a fixed or a growth mindset in your approach to learning? Explain.

2. Give an example of when you faced a challenge in learning something new. What did you do? How could you have adopted a growth mindset in addressing the challenge?

3. Do you believe that students/employees should be rewarded for making an effort even if their performance indicates failure? Why or why not?

Sources: Adapted from Dweck, C. (2015, September 23). Carol Dweck revisits the "growth mindset." *Education Week.* Retrieved from https://www.edweek.org/ew/articles/2015/09/23/carol-dweck-revisits-the-growth-mindset.html; Dweck, C. (2016, January 13). What having a "growth mindset" actually means. *Harvard Business Review.* Retrieved from http://thebusinessleadership.academy/wp-content/uploads/2017/03/What-Having-a-Growth-Mindset-Means.pdf; Dweck, C. (2017). *Mindset: Changing the way you think to fulfil your potential* (updated ed.). Hachette, UK: Robinson; Harding, J. (2017, June 8). Why all employees need to believe in the growth mindset [Blog post]. Retrieved from https://www.thepolyglotgroup.com.au/blog/why-all-employees-need-to-believe-in-the-growth-mindset/; Senn-Delany Leadership Consulting Group. (2014). Why fostering a growth mindset in organizations matters. Retrieved from http://knowledge.senndelaney.com/docs/thought_papers/pdf/stanford_agilitystudy_hart.pdf.

participants. However, this study generated media interest and led to additional research. A review of this research indicated that there is an association between Type A behavior (particularly hostility) and heart disease.[30] Examples of hostility-related questions are "Do you get irritated easily?" and "Are you bossy and domineering?"[31] Research has shown that the Type A behavior pattern (i.e., "stress energized") is exhibited in samples of women also.[32] To learn whether you exhibit the Type A behavior pattern, you may take Self-Assessment 9.2.

This may be scary news if you think you may have Type A personality characteristics. However, there is some good news. Being able to express your emotions may also reflect a "healthy" Type A pattern.[33] Second, having a "hardy" personality (e.g., letting stress roll off your back rather than ruminating on your problems) has been shown to reduce the potential for personality type to affect health.[34] Also, social support from family, friends, and coworkers can alleviate some of the detrimental effects of personality traits on health.[35]

CRITICAL THINKING QUESTIONS

How might knowledge of whether you have the Type A personality affect your decision about taking a job in a high-stress environment?

Given our discussion about the Type A behavior pattern, you may be wondering if there is any theory or research in management that suggests that personality traits can change. Some scholars believe that certain personality characteristics are **statelike** instead of **traitlike** (traits include personality traits and Type A). By *statelike*, we mean that the characteristics are relatively changeable and that a person can develop them through either awareness and/or training.

New research suggests that **psychological capital (PsyCap)** characteristics are more stable than fleeting states of mind but are open to change. This is an emerging area of study within the movement called positive psychology, and research is showing promising results.

Psychological Capital

Learning Objective 9.2: Summarize the elements of psychological capital.

Psychological capital (PsyCap) has four parts. In the same manner that people hold financial capital, these statelike qualities represent the *value of individual differences*. In other words, PsyCap is more than "what you know" or "who you know." The focus of PsyCap is on "who you are" and "who you are becoming."[36] These four characteristics are as follows:

Hope—the will to succeed and the ability to identify and pursue the path to success.
Efficacy—a person's belief that they have the ability to execute a specific task in a given context.
Resiliency—coping in the face of risk or adversity; the ability to "bounce back" after a setback.
Optimism—a positive outcome outlook or attribution of events, which includes positive emotions and motivation.[37]

▼ FIGURE 9.2
Dimensions of Positive Psychological Capital

HOPE	**EFFICACY**	**RESILIENCE**	**OPTIMISM**
A sense of energy to persevere toward your goals through proactive planning	A belief in your own ability to produce positive results and achieve self-defined goals	A positive way of coping even when it seems there are no solutions to negative situations	Being and remaining positive about the likelihood of personal success, now and in the future

Source: Positive Academy. (n.d.). Psychological capital. Retrieved from https://www.thepositiveacademy.net/en/kurzy/professional-development/230/psychological-capital.html.

The acronym HERO will help you remember these four characteristics. Research on Psy-Cap shows that the four elements predict job performance and satisfaction[38] and that training interventions may increase PsyCap.[39] Thus, PsyCap is important for human development, but it is also related to an organization's competitive advantage due to its impact on job performance.[40] Figure 9.2 summarizes the definitions of the four PsyCap dimensions.

Emotional Intelligence

Learning Objective 9.3: List the three aspects of emotional intelligence.

Another statelike individual difference is **emotional intelligence (EI)**. Research from the field of psychology shows that the ability to control emotions may be a form of intelligence.[41] This concept was first studied in children, but increasingly managers have found EI to be relevant to the workplace. EI may be more important for long-term success than IQ. EI is considered to have three aspects:

1. **Self-awareness**—recognizing your emotions when you experience them
2. **Other awareness**—being aware of emotions experienced by others
3. **Emotion regulation**—being able to recover from experienced emotions rapidly[42]

EI is related to job performance.[43] For example, EI becomes a stronger predictor of performance and helping behavior at work when cognitive intelligence (IQ) is lower.[44] In other words, employees with lower intelligence perform tasks correctly and engage in organizational citizenship behaviors frequently if they are also emotionally intelligent. In a study conducted with U.S. Air Force recruiters, EI predicted success in meeting recruiting quotas.[45] In a business setting, a study of more than 300 managers at Johnson & Johnson found that managers who scored higher on EI were rated as more effective by their followers.[46] Emotional intelligence also enables employees to work more effectively in teams.[47]

The consulting firm TalentSmart reports that EI has a lot of influence on professional success,[48] in part because it helps you focus your energy in one direction. TalentSmart tested emotional intelligence alongside 33 other important workplace skills and found that EI was the strongest predictor of performance, explaining a full 58% of success in all types of jobs. Of all the people the firm studied at work, 90% of top performers had high EI. They also reported that employees with a high degree of EI make more money—an average of $29,000 more per year than people with low EI. The link between emotional intelligence and earnings is so direct that every point increase in emotional intelligence adds $1,300 to an annual salary. These findings hold true for people in all industries, at all levels, in every region of the world. According to TalentSmart, there is not any job in which performance and pay are not tied closely to emotional intelligence.

Can Emotional Intelligence Be Learned?

Given the interest of managers in EI, there has been research to determine if the attributes of EI can be learned. In other words, can we send employees to a training program to increase their EI and improve their ability to get along with others? Research compared managers who received EI training to a group receiving no training. After the training, managers showed higher EI, and they also reported lower stress, higher morale, and treated one another in a more civil manner.[49]

Emotionally intelligent people accurately identify emotions. Can you name the emotions shown in this photo?

© TeodorLazarev/Shutterstock

A review of training interventions from diverse fields, including management, education, mental health, and sports, concluded that "it is possible to increase emotional intelligence and that such training has the potential to lead to other positive outcomes."[50]

The process through which people increase their EI (and sustain it) follows five stages of discovery:

1. The first discovery: Who do I want to be?
2. The second discovery: Who am I? What are my strengths and gaps?
3. The third discovery: How can I build on strengths and reduce the gaps?
4. The fourth discovery: Trying new behaviors, thoughts, and feelings
5. The fifth discovery: Developing trusting relationships that enable change[51]

Practice your EI with a partner in the Toolkit Activity 9.1 at the end of this chapter.

Limitations of Emotional Intelligence

Despite supporters of EI at work, there have also been criticisms that the concept is too vague and can't be measured.[52] There are many different measures of EI, and this has led to confusion regarding the best measure to use for assessment. A critical review of the literature on EI in the workplace concluded that initial claims of predictive value of EI may have been overstated.[53] Yet a review of 69 studies reported a modest but significant correlation between EI and performance.[54]

What We Know About EI

The EI concept has impacted the workplace through EI training programs, specialized EI consultants, and articles and blog posts.[55] This is what we can conclude about EI:

1. EI is distinct from but positively related to other intelligences (such as IQ).
2. EI is an individual difference, where some people are more endowed and others are less so.
3. EI develops over a person's life span and can be enhanced through training.
4. EI involves, at least in part, individuals' abilities to effectively identify and perceive emotion (in themselves and others), as well as possession of the skills to understand and manage those emotions successfully.[56]

CRITICAL THINKING QUESTIONS

What are the limits on the degree to which a person with low EI can change?

While we often use the term *diversity* to talk about differences among people, it has been used predominantly as a "surface-level" distinction—how somebody looks. After reviewing personality traits and states and EI and other "deep-level" personality differences (those you cannot see), you should now know that diversity is both unseen and seen and understand how very different people are in many, many ways. Not that you have knowledge of how deep-level differences impact your management decisions, we will review surface-level diversity in the same manner to see how knowledge of its many forms (gender, age, race, culture, etc.) provides additional help in managing all kinds of diversity in the workplace.

Diversity Approaches

Learning Objective 9.4: Describe different approaches to managing diversity.

The North American culture is deeply rooted in a sense of individuality. Employees want respect for their differences in gender, race or ethnicity, age, sexual orientation, and/or disability status (as examples). It is sometimes challenging to balance the needs of diverse employees with the needs of the organization. For example, some Latin American cultures are somewhat casual with respect to being on time. However, if managers allow some employees to show up late for work, members of cultures who tend to be prompt and on time may view it as unfair. Thus, managers in time-sensitive cultures might need to enforce organizational policies but do so in a respectful way. Keeping in mind that human beings are diverse but still want to have a sense of belonging, managers can integrate individual differences with the organization's goals and objectives. Managing diverse followers is one of the most challenging but rewarding parts of effective management as you work toward creating a high-performing group of talented and creative employees through a process of adjustment, consideration, and respect.

Surface-Level and Deep-Level Diversity

The demographic attributes that typically come to mind when we think of "diversity" are called **surface-level diversity** because they are visible to observers. Surface-level diversity is "differences among group members in overt, biological characteristics that are typically reflected in physical features."[57] A review of the research on surface-level diversity concluded that relationships of sex, race, and age had mixed results in the prediction of job performance and work attitude. Sometimes these demographic variables were related to performance and sometimes they were not. What this research demonstrated is that to completely understand diversity, we need to also consider **deep-level diversity**, which is "differences among members' attitudes, beliefs, and values."[58] When deep-level diversity is considered, diversity contributes in a positive way to work-group effectiveness. In other words, the underlying values and attitudes of employees matter more than surface demographic characteristics.

Discrimination and Fairness

Historically, the emphasis on diversity was rooted in the legal necessity to eliminate discrimination in the U.S. To address the past discrimination and to promote fairness, organizations introduced **affirmative action** programs that focused on making special efforts to recruit and hire qualified members of minority groups. Affirmative action is defined as "an active effort to improve the employment or educational opportunities of members of minority groups and women."[59] Law requires affirmative action for private employers with 15 or more employees. Affirmative action originated with Executive Order 11246 and is based on Title VII of the Civil Rights Act of 1964,[60] which prohibits discrimination in hiring and employment practices. Title VII prevents organizations from discriminating on the basis of race, color, religion, sex, or national origin. Title VII also created the Equal Employment Opportunity Commission, or EEOC (http://www.eeoc.gov), to administer the employment discrimination laws.[61] By taking initiatives like these, the government tries to increase opportunities provided to underprivileged citizens. These efforts had a strong impact on the composition of the U.S. workforce, resulting in more women, African Americans, and Hispanics being represented. Other laws enforced by the EEOC protect employees against discrimination on the basis of age and disability. Table 9.3 provides a list of the federal laws that prohibit employment discrimination.

What happens when an organization is found to be in violation of federal employment laws? According to the U.S. Equal Employment Opportunity Commission, the "relief" or remedies

CRITICAL THINKING QUESTIONS

Conduct an internet search and locate a court case for each of the employment laws in Table 9.3. Explain the outcome of the case. Do you agree or disagree with the verdict? Explain.

Federal Laws that Prohibit Employment Discrimination

Federal Law	Protections
Title VII of the Civil Rights Act of 1964 (Title VII)	Prohibits employment discrimination based on race, color, religion, sex, or national origin
The Equal Pay Act of 1963 (EPA)	Protects men and women who perform substantially equal work in the same establishment from sex-based wage discrimination
The Age Discrimination in Employment Act of 1967 (ADEA)	Protects individuals who are 40 years of age or older
Title I and Title V of the Americans with Disabilities Act of 1990, as amended (ADA)	Prohibits employment discrimination against qualified individuals with disabilities in the private sector, and in state and local governments
Sections 501 and 505 of the Rehabilitation Act of 1973	Prohibits discrimination against qualified individuals with disabilities who work in the federal government
Title II of the Genetic Information Nondiscrimination Act of 20013 (GINA)	Prohibits employment discrimination based on genetic information about an applicant, employee, or former employee
The Civil Rights Act of 1991	Among other things, provides monetary damages in cases of intentional employment discrimination

Source: U.S. Equal Employment Opportunity Commission. (2009, November 21). Federal laws prohibiting employment discrimination: Questions and answers. Retrieved from https://www.eeoc.gov/facts/qanda.html.

available for employment discrimination, whether caused by intentional acts or by practices that have a discriminatory effect, may include:

- back pay,
- hiring,
- promotion,
- reinstatement,
- front pay,
- reasonable accommodation, or
- other actions that will make an individual "whole" (in the condition s/he would have been but for the discrimination).

Remedies also may include payment of:

- attorneys' fees,
- expert witness fees, and
- court costs.[62]

You will have an opportunity to learn more about the experiences of diverse managers by completing Toolkit Activity 9.2.

Challenges to Affirmative Action

While great strides have been made under affirmative action, it is not without critics. Some courts have found that affirmative action results in preferential treatment of women and minorities at the expense of other qualified applicants.[63] In addition, those hired under affirmative action programs may be stigmatized due to the view that they were not qualified for the job. Experimental research studies found that female affirmative action hires were seen as less competent and that managers recommended smaller salary increases for them than for men and women not associated with affirmative action. This pattern held even when disconfirming performance information was provided to the managers.[64] In follow-up

research, the stigma effect on managers' perceptions of competence of affirmative action hires held for Black men and women as well.[65] One critical element that is missing from many affirmative action arguments, however, is that the opportunities for education for Blacks and women is hundreds of years behind that for White males. There is a reason that "first generation" college students are still a statistic at universities—to account for the late arrival of the acceptance of Blacks and women at colleges as a regular part of the student body.

The Americans with Disabilities Act protects the rights of qualified individuals with disabilities.

© Gerain0812/Shutterstock

Given the concerns above, other approaches to managing diversity include promoting diversity initiatives that focus on learning about others and understanding differences. These approaches are discussed in the next section.

Learning

Learning about diversity can have a positive impact on the culture of diversity in an organization. Diversity initiatives often involve training to increase both diversity awareness and skills. A survey study of 785 human resource managers was conducted to determine the factors associated with the success of diversity training. Researchers found that both training adoption and perceived training success were strongly associated with top management support for diversity. This study also found that training was more successful when attendance for all managers was required.[66] Although diversity training has many purposes, a primary one is to help integrate minority groups into the workforce, usually by attempting to confer on the entire workforce the skills, knowledge, and motivation to work productively alongside dissimilar others and/or to interact effectively with a diverse customer population. Training methods include a mixture of lectures and video presentations. In addition, interactive techniques such as discussions, role-playing, simulations, and exercises are employed.[67]

Mentoring is an important way to ensure that diverse employees have career opportunities in organizations. Seventy-one percent of Fortune 500 companies have formal mentoring programs.[68] In many cases, mentoring programs have been implemented with the goals of increasing the access of women and minorities to high-ranking executives.[69] Research has shown that both mentors and mentees learn from a program in which mentors are matched with diverse mentees.[70] A study of formal mentoring programs found that they do increase mentoring benefits if the mentees have input into the matching process and mentors receive high-quality training.[71]

In addition to ensuring that women and minorities have a mentor, organizations such as Ford have created support groups (sometimes called **affinity groups**) for women and minorities. Affinity groups are "communities within a corporation that are organized around the employees' similar circumstances and common goals."[72] Historically, affinity groups began with race, but today's groups include communities of people within a corporation who share ethnicity, gender, or sexual orientation, for example. Members of

Mentors provide career advice and social support.

© LightField Studios/Shutterstock

these groups tend to face similar challenges and come together for mutual support. For example, affinity groups within American Express include the following:

- AHORA: Hispanic network
- ASIA and EWEX Exchange: Asian employee network
- BEN: Black employee network
- CHAI: Jewish employee network
- DAN: disabilities awareness network
- PRIDE: lesbian, gay, bisexual, and transgender employee network
- Nation: Native American employee network
- Passages: employees over 40 network
- SALT: Christian employee network
- WIN: women's interest network[73]

Organizations provide learning opportunities for diverse members with respect to career development. Women and minorities are informed about career paths and the background needed for promotion to the next level. Cincinnati-based Proctor & Gamble (P&G) is a leader in this area, with a strong commitment to diversity and inclusion in its culture. With respect to career development, the company has created a comprehensive leadership development strategy featuring mentorship and programs to educate women and minorities about career opportunities. These efforts are working. Between 2008 and 2013, the representation of women among P&G managers grew from 40% to 44%, including 28% at or above the vice president level.

In addition to its attention to gender diversity, the company supports the career development of employees with disabilities. Funding for accommodations for persons with disabilities is allocated to ensure that all P&G facilities worldwide have the resources needed to accommodate all workers. For these initiatives, DiversityInc ranked P&G second among the top 10 companies for people with disabilities, seventh among its top 50 companies for diversity overall. DiversityInc credited P&G for highly valuing each employee's unique contributions and for the representation of women, African Americans, Latinos, and Asian Americans among management at rates higher than the U.S. average.[74]

Companies such as P&G believe that diversity is essential for their competitive advantage. This makes sense when you consider that women purchase many of P&G's consumer products. Having women represented in key decision-making roles can enhance the effectiveness of the organization by creating new products and marketing them to their consumer base. Next we examine the research that has demonstrated a link between diversity and organizational effectiveness.

Effectiveness

Embracing diversity is a competitive advantage, and organizations should include the following in their planning: cost, attraction of human resources, marketing success, creativity and innovation, problem-solving quality, and organizational flexibility.[75] The management of cultural diversity directly influences these six dimensions of business performance. Research evidence supports the argument that diversity increases performance and that organizations that embrace diversity build more inclusive work environments. In fact, ignoring individual differences may result in an apathetic workforce or one that is resistant to change. In addition, by not allowing individuals to express their differences, creativity may be suppressed. Organizations that have positive diversity cultures reap a number of benefits, including:

- Attracting and retaining the best employees
- Better perspective on diverse markets

- Leveraging creativity and innovation
- Organizational flexibility

But do these benefits translate into bottom-line profits? The consulting firm McKinsey studied the diversity of top management teams and financial performance. Their study of diversity in the workplace, Delivering Through Diversity, demonstrates a clear link between diversity (defined as a greater proportion of women and a more mixed ethnic and cultural composition in the leadership of large companies) and company financial outperformance. The new analysis expands a prior report published in 2015 by studying a larger data set of more than 1,000 companies and covering 12 countries. Researchers measured profitability (in terms of earnings before interest and taxes, or EBIT), longer-term value creation (or economic profit), and diversity at different levels of the organizations.

The findings of the study are summarized in Figure 9.3. In the original research, researchers found that companies in the top quartile for gender diversity on their executive teams were 15% more likely to experience above-average profitability than companies in the fourth quartile (lowest). In the expanded 2017 research, this number rose to 21% and continued to be statistically significant. For ethnic and cultural diversity, the 2014 finding was a 35% likelihood of outperformance, comparable to the 2017 finding of a 33% likelihood of outperformance on EBIT margin; both were also statistically significant. That said, the report also noted that women and minorities remained underrepresented in top management teams (14% women and 12% minorities in 2017).

So, what are the reasons that women remain underrepresented in top management? Is it due to their personal characteristics or to discrimination and structural factors in organizations? We turn to this question next.

▼ FIGURE 9.3

Diversity and Financial Performance

Likelihood of financial performance[1] above national industry median, %

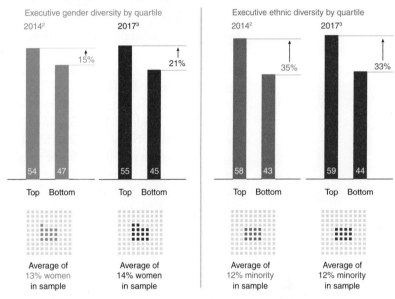

[1]Average earnings-before-interest-and-taxes (EBIT) margin, 2010–13 in Diversity Matters I and 2011–15 in Diversity Matters II.
[2]Results are statistically significant at p-value < 0.10.
[3]Results are statistically significant at p-value < 0.05.

Women and Men at Work

For years, it has been assumed that women's failure to be equal to men at work is because they negotiate poorly, lack managerial motivation, are too risk-averse, or do not put in enough hours at work due to taking care of their families. On the other hand, organizations see women's stereotypical attributes in a positive way—women are more cooperative and care more about people, for example. Whether the stereotypes are positive or negative is not the issue. The real issue is that the research evidence does not support the gender differences that are so widely believed.[76] Many men are cooperative and caring, for example. In addition, many women are risk-takers. On the average, men and women are more similar in their dispositions and skills than they are different.

Let's look at negotiation. A large-scale review of 123 studies found that in 100 studies, gender differences in negotiation were small. Men may be at a slight advantage when they are out for themselves, or when the stakes are higher. Women seem to be more effective in negotiation when they are bargaining for another person. However, differences are due more to the lack of experience with negotiation than they are to gender. With practice, women develop equal levels of expertise in negotiation.

A study looked at managerial motivations toward stereotypically male or female priorities. Results found that there were no differences in typical-masculine and typical-feminine motivation. Men did not give more value to typical-masculine attributes of motivation, such as opportunity for advancement, high earnings, and responsibility. Also, women did not give more value to typical-feminine attributes of motivation, such as time for personal life, cooperation, stability, and job security.[77]

What about cooperation? A study of over 50 years of research[78] on cooperation found that there were no gender differences. In other words, men were just as cooperative as women were. In addition, based on research, the risk-taking belief is a myth. Women and men are equal risk-takers in real-life organizational situations but not situations such as games of pure chance.[79] In a study of mutual fund investors,[80] women did exhibit less risk-taking than men. But this was due to their lack of knowledge of financial markets and investments and not the personal trait of risk-taking. Providing such information and mentoring can clearly correct this difference.

Differences between men and women at work seem to be more due to their exclusion from powerful social networks and their lack of mentoring and training than trait-related gender differences. When women are given the same opportunities as men, their representation in higher levels of organizations will rise.

In addition to gender differences, there are also some pervasive stereotypes of different age groups. We turn to a discussion of the different generations at work next.

Generations in the Workplace

Learning Objective 9.5: Name the characteristics of four generations at work, and describe how Generation Z will affect organizations.

Age is a demographic or surface-level diversity variable, but there are values and attitudes that appear to be related to what generation an employee belongs to. Different generations interacting in the workplace is a challenge for managers, and there has been a lot written about generational differences. It's important to dispel some myths about the different generations. Table 9.4 shows the four generations now in the workplace today, and how they view work and life in general.

The **veterans** were born between 1922 and 1945 and are now retiring or have passed on. However, trends indicate that people are retiring later than 65, since retirement plans were compromised by the great recession of 2007 to 2009, so many people in subsequent generations will remain in the workforce for some time.

The **Boomers** were born between 1946 and 1964 and are called this due to the baby boom that occurred after World War II (also called the "me" generation or "yuppies," which stands for *young upwardly mobile professionals*). This generation had significant influence throughout their lives and brought about the social changes experienced in the 1960s, including the Civil Rights Act of 1964.

The **Generation Xers**, or **Gen Xers**, were born between 1965 and 1980. This generation is sometimes referred to as the "Baby Busters" or "latchkey kids" because many of them had to let themselves into their homes after school because their Boomer parents were both at work.

Generation Y (the **Millennials**) entered the workforce and is having a clear impact on organizations (they are the largest group in the workforce today and in the general population). They were born between 1981 and 2000 and look for flexibility and choice.

Four Generations and Work Values

WORKPLACE CHARACTERISTICS			
	Veterans (1992–1945)	Baby Boomers (1946–1964)	Generation X (1965–1980)	Generation Y (1981–2000)
Work Ethic and Values	Hard work Respect authority Sacrifice Duty before fun Adhere to rules	Workaholics Work efficiently Crusading causes Personal fulfillment Desire quality Question authoiry	Eliminate the task Self-reliance Want structure and direction Skeptical	What's next Multitasking Tenacity Entrepreneurial Tolerant Goal oriented
Work is . . .	An obligation	An exciting adventure	A difficult challenge A contract	A means to an end Fulfillment
Leadership Style	Directive Command-and-control	Consensual Collegial	Everyone is the same Challenge others Ask why	*TBD
Interactive Style	Individual	Team player Loves to have meetings	Entrepreneur	Participative
Communications	Formal Memo	In person	Direct Immediate	E-mail Voice mail
Feedback and Rewards	No news is good news Satisfaction in a job well done	Don't appreciate it Money Title recognition	Sorry to interrupt, but how am I doing? Freedom is the best reward	Whenever I want it, at the push of a button Meaningful work
Messages That Motivate	Your experience is respected	You are valued You are needed	Do it your way Forget the rules	You will work with other bright, creative people
Work and Family Life	Ne'er the twain shall meet	No balance Work to live	Balance	Balance

*As this group has not spent much time in the workforce, this characteristic has yet to be determined.

Source: Critical Metrics (2014). Generational differences at work: Do they exist or not? https://www.critical-metrics.com/generational-differences-at-work-do-they-exist-or-not/.

As shown in Table 9.4, the average person within each of the four generations may have different attitudes about work and the balance between work and home life. Gen X employees want portable skills they can take with them to their next job and view work as a series of short-term contracts. The Boomers view work as an exciting adventure and strive for monetary gain and mobility. The Millennial generation does not view work as the be-all and end-all of their existence and see work as a means to an end. They are children of the Boomers, and most grew up more affluently than other generations. This generation is more interested in meaningful work than in employment with one organization long-term.

Figure 9.4 shows the results of a survey of 1,200 employees across four generations that measured their strengths and weaknesses. The Baby Boomers are now executives and can serve as mentors and role models. Gen X employees generate revenue and solve problems. In addition, the Millennials are high in tech savviness, having grown up on the internet. All generations have valuable attributes, and this survey reveals that the different generations can learn a lot from one another.

The Millennial generation has been written about in the popular media more than any other group. This is because they are now the largest cohort in the U.S. workforce, and there have been some rather unfair stereotypes of them. Let's look at what the research shows.

The Millennials

A study[81] found that Millennials are the only generational group that does not conceptually link organizational commitment with workplace culture. Millennials think about work

Generations in the Workplace

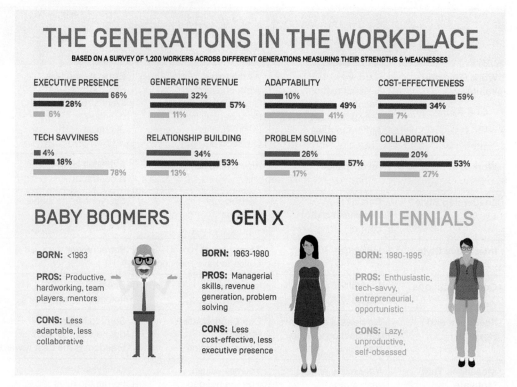

Source: Purvis, D. (2016). Workplace generations infographic: Which one are you? Retrieved from https://www.commsaxis.com/workplace-generations-infographic/.

differently than members of the other generations, and managers need to understand their attitudes toward duty, drive, and reward. For example, most Millennials received trophies for participation in high school sports, even if they did not win.[82] An in-depth study of the personalities of Millennials administered personality inventories online to more than 1,000 Millennials (up to 29 years old) and more than 3,000 persons from other generations (above 29 years old). The results indicated that Millennials are motivated by recognition, public acknowledgment, instant and frequent positive feedback, and instant gratification. A survey of undergraduates found that Millennials want praise when they do a good job and rewards for hard work. They show a clear communication preference for one-on-one, honest feedback from their bosses. They also enjoy communicating with coworkers and feel that they can learn from them.[83]

Millennials also state that they need to balance their personal and professional lives and have a comfortable work environment. They want flexible work schedules; however, they resent having to stay at work after hours. In particular, they desire a nonconformist environment without strict rules and traditional work approaches. They tend to challenge the status quo, and they will not be patient enough to keep the same job many years.[84] Millennials are the first wave of the digital generation born into the high levels of technology. They are far more qualified in digital knowledge than the generations that preceded them, and they quickly acquire new information technology. They have wide networks of friends and nurture these relationships using social media platforms such as Instagram.[85]

The next generation will be even more technologically savvy.

And . . . Here Comes Generation Z!

Some members of **Generation Z**, or **Gen Z**, are social media "influencers" that post information on brands for their generation, which is, loosely, people born from 1995 to 2010. They

have relied on the internet, social networks, and mobile phones their entire lives. Growing up this way has resulted in a generation very comfortable with collecting and cross-referencing many sources of information. They are adept at integrating real-life situations with virtual ones. They notice trends quickly and communicate their thoughts on social media.

Generation Z members spend time on mobile phones.

© Rawpixel.com/Shutterstock

The consulting firm McKinsey[86] recently conducted a survey investigating the behaviors of this new generation and its influence. The study found something interesting: There are four core Gen Z behaviors, all anchored in one element: this generation's search for truth. Gen Zs value individual expression and hate labels. They mobilize themselves for a variety of causes. They believe profoundly in the efficacy of dialogue to solve conflicts and improve the world. Finally, they make decisions and relate to organizations in a highly analytical and practical way. In contrast to the previous generation—the Millennials, sometimes called the "me" generation—Gen Z members are perhaps the "we" generation. They are idealistic, more confrontational, and less open to different opinions.

For Generation Z, the search for truth happens at the individual and community levels. This generation feels comfortable with diversity in all its forms. Their search for authentic experience results in greater freedom of expression and greater openness to understanding different kinds of people.

CRITICAL THINKING QUESTIONS

Do you agree or disagree with the characterization of Generation Z based on this research? Explain which characteristics you think are representative and which are not, based on your own values.

Limitations of Generational Differences

Recent research[87] has challenged the descriptions of the different generations. Jennifer J. Deal, researcher at the Center for Creative Leadership, explains that there are misconceptions and negative stereotypes associated with generations from veterans to Millennials. You may have heard the generalizations yourself: Veterans are dinosaurs. Baby Boomers think the whole world revolves around them. Gen Xers are the quintessential slackers, while Gen Y (aka Millennials) are even more narcissistic and entitled than Boomers.

But Deal's research reveals that these characterizations do not reflect the reality of the contemporary workplace. Over the course of seven years, Deal surveyed more than 3,000 corporate leaders to write her book *Retiring the Generation Gap: How Employees Young & Old Can Find Common Ground.* Deal discovered that employees across generations share similar professional values. People, regardless of age, want consistency and want leaders with integrity whom they can trust. Her research also indicates that "no one really likes change, we all like feedback, and the number of hours you put in at work depends more on your level in the organization than on your age."[88]

Deal's long-term study uncovered something surprising. It's not age that causes the generation gap; it's the battle for "clout." In other words, miscommunication and misunderstandings among generations are caused by (a) the desire for power and influence and (b) the insecurities stemming from this desire.[89]

Deal discovered that reality runs counter to many dominant ideas about the workplace generation gap. Here are some of the misconceptions that her research disproves:

- *Misconception 1: Values are determined by age.* Across the age groups Deal studied, she found that family tops the list of most important values. This shows that age groups have more in common than not.
- *Misconception 2: Different generations want different things from leadership.* What Deal found is that, among all generations, employees want trustworthy leaders.
- *Misconception 3: Some age groups are more resistant to change than others.* The results of Deal's study uncovered that *nobody likes change.* People across generations from Silents to Millennials find change to be challenging and uncomfortable.
- *Misconception 4: Younger generations aren't loyal to employers.* Research actually shows that it is one's level in the company and *not* their age that determines loyalty. For example, the number of hours an employee puts in is a function of their job title—not their generation.
- *Misconception 5: Some generations are more open to learning new skills than others.* What Deal's research actually shows is that all age groups value training and want to continue to develop professionally.
- *Misconception 6: The desire for feedback is a "Millennial thing."* Deal discovered that feedback is valued by employees regardless of their age.[90]

Managing Diverse Followers

Learning Objective 9.6: Explain the guidelines for managing diverse followers.

Diversity Mission Statements

A convincing example of the power of diversity is from a study of NFL draft picks for 12 players by well-known sports analysts from *NFL Countdown, Sporting News, Sports Illustrated,* CBSSports.com, About.com, and Fanball.com. Since their reputations depend on their being right, analysts care about whether or not they make the right predictions in the NFL draft. Researchers found that the average of all analysts' predictions was a better predictor than that of any individual analyst. Prediction diversity matters, and this example demonstrates that diverse points of view can enhance organizational functioning through better decisions: "*Diversity matters just as much as individual ability.* That is not a feel-good statement. It's a mathematical fact."[91]

The field of management recognizes that diversity is not something that must be "managed" but rather something that should be embraced because it makes business decision-making more effective. Many organizations today reflect diversity in their mission statements. For example, PepsiCo has won several awards for diversity, and their mission statement reflects the importance of valuing diversity as a core part of their company vision:

"People are PepsiCo's greatest asset. We believe in building a workforce that reflects the diverse consumers and communities we serve. Diversity and engagement is core to our company's values and how we operate as a global corporate citizen. A key driver of our company vision, Performance with Purpose, diversity and engagement helps create sustainable advantage for us.

PepsiCo has a strong legacy of leading in diversity practices starting in the 1940s by breaking the color barrier and hiring African American salespeople, in the 50s as the first major company to have a woman on its Board, to the 80s where we pioneered multicultural marketing. Together, with their different perspectives, experiences, and backgrounds, our people are building on this legacy and creating our future across the countries, markets and territories in which we operate."[92]

CAREERS IN MANAGEMENT

Chief Diversity Officer

Chief Diversity Officers (CDO) create an inclusive environment for employees through recruitment efforts, training, and activity planning. CDOs lead an organization's efforts to ensure that employees have a comfortable place to work and learn, regardless of their race, gender, age, ethnicity, socioeconomic status, sexual orientation, or disability.

CDOs cultivate workplaces that support diversity. This often includes developing and incorporating inclusion initiatives, such as diversity training and multicultural events. A CDO may also create strategic plans to recruit a diverse workforce. In some cases, this includes ensuring that an organization complies with affirmative action or equal employment opportunity regulations. CDOs proactively identify areas where more diversity is needed. For example, a tire company learned that there were no female managers. The CDO developed a plan for increasing the pool of applicants for managerial positions.

In cases of discrimination or harassment, the CDO makes investigations and attempts to resolve the issue. CDOs also coordinate programs such as support groups, commissions, veterans' affairs departments, and disability services.

The Daily Role

When Michelle Angier was a CDO at Intuit, she practiced the fine art of listening. From the moment she was hired, she began setting meetings with employee networks (e.g., the Women's Network, Pride Network) and a diverse group of stakeholders to hear what was working and what needed improvement. Angier also looked to Inuit's executive sponsors and external partners to help her get a pulse on the company. She credits listening to all of these voices with enabling her to discover opportunities for positive change and growth.

The experience of working as a diversity and inclusion leader can vary considerably from company to company and from industry to industry. Angier has taken on a wide variety of projects—from strategic planning to negotiation. She says she has done everything from developing strategy and presenting it to execs for buy-in to counseling people, helping them to "navigate deeply personal and emotional situations."

Building a Framework for Diversity and Inclusion

At Kaiser Permanente, diversity and inclusion are an integral part of the organizational business strategy. The company is currently number one on DiversityInc's Top 50 Companies for Diversity ranking.

Under the direction of Dr. Ronald Copeland, Kaiser Permanente's senior vice president and chief diversity and inclusion officer (DI), the company strategically plans for and implements inclusive practices. When it comes to providing care, Kaiser accommodates consumers' cultural and linguistic characteristics. In terms of talent acquisition and recruitment, diversity is also a top priority.

Copeland classifies the role of the diversity and inclusion officer as "mission-critical" when it comes to staying competitive in the marketplace. A DI officer can give the company an advantage in recruiting talent, meeting customers' demand for innovation and invention, building a culture of corporate citizenship, and even complying with laws and regulations. Copeland says stakeholders should know that their chief DI officer is a strategic partner with whom they can consult on all aspects of diversity.

Qualifications

Applicants for these positions typically need an advanced degree and years of experience. Projections indicate that the need for this C-suite job will grow in the coming years (by 6% between 2018 and 2024). Job growth is expected to come from corporate expansion and start-up companies, although job growth can vary according to industry.

Discussion Questions

1. Explain why organizations have created a C-suite position (i.e., like the chief executive officer and chief operating officer) for diversity.

2. Discuss how a chief diversity officer can be a change agent within an organization for implementing diversity policies.

3. How can a chief diversity officer help develop diverse leadership talent in an organization? Provide specific examples.

Sources: Adapted from Rayome, A. D. (2016). Does your company need a chief diversity officer? Retrieved from https://www .techrepublic.com/article/does-your-company-need-a-chief-diversity-officer/; Study.com. (n.d.). Chief diversity officer: Career outlook and salary. Retrieved from https://study.com/articles/Chief_Diversity_Officer_Job_Duties_Career_Outlook_and_Salary.html.

PepsiCo seems like they have a great mission statement regarding diversity. However, what specific actions can organizations take to promote diversity? One key thing decision-makers can do is ask themselves questions about diversity on a regular basis.

Promoting Open Discussions About Diversity

Managing a diverse workforce has challenges because it shifts the power in the organization, and some employees may not want to participate in diversity initiatives. They may even resist the organization's attempts to recruit, hire, and promote women and minorities. A study of human resource managers revealed several questions every manager should be asking themselves and others in their organization to promote open discussions about diversity[93]:

1. Are there challenging or pressing issues in managing a diverse workforce? If so, which do you find to be most challenging?
2. What are specific things you have done personally to ease those challenges?
3. In regard to diversity, are there things you wish had been done differently? If so, what? And how would you have handled those things differently?
4. What are specific things your company has done to ease those challenges?
5. What are your (or your company's) future plans for diversity? Do you have specific plans that will be implemented in the near future? If so, what?

Asking such questions (and thinking critically about the answers) should help a manager identify what challenges the organization faces and what might be done to address them.

CRITICAL THINKING QUESTIONS

In addition to asking questions, how can organizations promote an open discussion about diversity? Provide an example of how you would start a conversation about diversity. What would you say specifically?

Northern Trust is America's top employer for diversity. The Northern Trust Building in Miami, Florida.

© incamerastock/Alamy Stock Photo

A case study of a multicultural organization found that the organization implemented several key managerial actions:

- CEO support of diversity initiatives
- Managerial accountability
- Fundamental change in human resource practices
- Employee involvement and buy-in
- Overarching corporate philosophy regarding diversity
- Ongoing monitoring and improvement of diversity climate
- Multiple measures of success[94]

For example, managerial accountability is measured in this organization, by having 25% of the managers' salary increases linked to interaction with diverse individuals. It is important to have a plan for diversity and inclusion initiatives and to link them to hard organizational outcomes such as revenue.

America's Top 10 Best Employers for Diversity

Rank	Employer	Industry	Location
1	Northern Trust	Banking and Financial Services	Chicago, IL
2	Smithsonian Institution	Travel and Leisure	Washington, D.C.
3	Levy Restaurants	Restaurants	Chicago, IL
4	Intuit	IT, Internet, Software and Services	Mountain View, CA
5	Harvard University	Education	Cambridge, MA
6	Principal Financial	Banking and Financial Services	Des Moines, IA
7	Emory University	Education	Atlanta, GA
8	Wegmans Food Markets	Retail, Wholesale	Rochester, NY
9	Keller Williams Realty	Business Services and Supplies	Austin, TX
10	AbbVie	Drugs and Biotechnology	North Chicago, IL

Source: Kauflin, J. (2018). America's best employers for diversity. *Forbes.* Retrieved from https://www.forbes.com/sites/jeffkauflin/2018/01/23/americas-best-employers-for-diversity/.

In 2018, *Forbes*, working with their data partners at Statista, released the first-ever annual ranking of the best employers for diversity in America. They surveyed 30,000 employees at companies across the nation and researched those companies' workforces and practices, and then created a definitive listing honoring the top performers. The goal of the ranking is to create discussion of the importance of diversity and inclusion and reinforce employers' determination to improve their efforts. Their list of the top 10 employers for diversity is shown in Table 9.5.

To understand your attitudes toward diversity, complete Self-Assessment 9.3. Diversity also includes cultural diversity, and this is growing in importance due to globalization. You will learn more about cultural value differences in Chapter 13.

Managerial Implications

Understanding individual differences is an important part of every manager's job. Individual deep-level diversity differences set one person apart from another, and differences such as personality are relatively stable traits. Because they are stable, organizations are interested in understanding personality differences that are linked by research to unethical behavior. You may even be asked to take a personality test that assesses honesty and integrity when you apply for a job. Other individual differences such as PsyCap and EI are statelike and may be malleable through awareness and training.

This chapter also covered a wide variety of individual differences related to surface-level diversity. Specific chapter takeaways are:

- Personality was defined, and the contributions of heredity versus the environment on personality were discussed. The MBTI was discussed, since it is the personality test most often administered. However, managers should be aware of its limitations, and it should not be used for selecting individuals for employment or positions. On the other hand, the MBTI is useful in training on conflict resolution and team-building.
- The Big-Five personality theory has had more research support than the MBTI, and it can be remembered with the acronym OCEAN: openness to experience, conscientiousness, extraversion, agreeableness, and neuroticism. Conscientiousness has been related to job performance.

- Psychological capital (PsyCap) dimensions are traitlike, but they can be changed through training. These dimensions are hope, efficacy, resilience, and optimism (HERO). Research on PsyCap is showing relationships to both job performance and employee well-being.
- Another traitlike individual difference is emotional intelligence (EI). EI comprises self-awareness, other awareness, and emotion regulation. Research has shown that EI may be as important as intelligence (IQ) for job performance and career success. Most high-performing managers have high EI, and they make more money than those with low EI.
- Our contemporary understanding of diversity is defined in terms of surface-level and deep-level diversity. Surface-level diversity is what we can see in terms of demographic differences, and deep-level diversity is the underlying attitudes and values a person holds.
- Age as an important diversity characteristic was highlighted with descriptions of the four generations now in the workplace. Millennials will have a powerful impact on organizations, and their characteristics were explained.
- Guidelines for managing diverse followers were provided, with specific actions that organizations can take to embrace diversity.

People are unique. This chapter discussed individual differences that influence how people perceive and interact with others in organizations. These differences include both personality and diversity. Some of these differences are stable and don't change much over the course of a person's life, so managers must understand these differences and motivate diverse employees.

KEY TERMS

affinity groups 277

affirmative action 275

agreeableness 269

Boomers 280

conscientiousness 269

deep-level diversity 275

delay of gratification 265

emotion regulation 273

emotional intelligence (EI) 273

extraversion (E) 268

feeling (F) 268

fixed mindset 271

Generation Xers or Gen Xers 280

Generation Y or Millennials 280

Generation Z or Gen Z 282

growth mindset 271

introversion (I) 268

intuition (N) 268

judging (J) 268

locus of control 265

Machiavellianism 265

mentoring 277

Minnesota twin studies 267

neuroticism 269

openness 269

other awareness 273

perceiving (P) 268

personality 267

psychological capital (PsyCap) 272

self-awareness 273

sensing (S) 268

statelike 272

surface-level diversity 275

thinking (T) 268

traitlike 272

Type A 270

Type B 270

veterans 280

TOOLKIT

Activity 9.1

Emotional Intelligence Exercise

Asking what causes negative emotions can provide much information about someone's needs, beliefs, and values. When we ask questions, we increase our understanding of others. Understanding leads to an increased sense of compassion, empathy, and connection with others.

In this exercise, ask a classmate to be your partner. Have them tell you about a setback in their life that they felt strongly about. Listen for feelings, values, and beliefs. Make notes using the form below.

Focus on the feelings and the causes of them, not the details of the story. Try to get to the underlying thoughts, beliefs, and attitudes below the emotions. While listening, remember not to give advice or try to solve the person's problems.

Next, switch roles and tell the person about a setback in your life. After you have both told your stories, answer the discussion questions.

Discussion Questions

1. How did this person feel? (Try to name at least five feelings.)
2. What does this person value?
3. What needs were not met?
4. What are some of the person's beliefs?

Activity 9.2

Experiences of Diverse Managers

Use your networks to identify a manager in government, business, or the nonprofit sector who is a member of a group protected by antidiscrimination laws: race, color, religion, sex, or national origin. This person may remain anonymous (i.e., do not identify them or their organization in your responses). Interview this person to learn about their career experiences. You may start with the following questions, but feel free to add more based on your interests.

1. Tell me about the different jobs you have held in your career. Why did you make job changes?
2. Have you ever experienced discrimination at work? Describe your experience. What did you do about it?
3. Have you ever experienced sexual harassment at work? Describe your experience. What did you do about it?
4. (if female) Have you ever felt that having children would affect your career? Was this ever discussed with you by your boss? Describe what happened.
5. Have you ever felt that you were treated differently by your boss due to your race, color, religion, sex, and/or national origin? Explain what happened. How did you resolve it?
6. Have you ever felt that your race, color, religion, sex, and/ or national origin played a role in whether or not you were hired for a job? Explain.
7. Have you ever felt that your race, color, religion, sex, and/ or national origin played a role in how much you were paid or other benefits? Explain.
8. Have you ever felt that your race, color, religion, sex, and/or national origin played a role in your promotions? Explain.

Discussion Questions

1. Based on your interview, did diversity affect the career experiences of the person you interviewed? Explain.
2. Do you agree with how the person resolved the situations they experienced? What would you have done differently?

3. Explain whether you think being a member of more than one group (e.g., Black and female) would make a difference.

Case Study 9.1

Covering Up Diversity

The idea of "covering" up our identities is not a new one. It dates back to the early 1960s, when sociologist Erving Goffman defined "covering" as when a person belonging to a known stigmatized group makes great efforts to hide the stigma. For example, a Muslim employee hides in an empty office to pray instead of using a conference room—so that his coworkers will not see him. Covering is a form of identity management, and research shows that many employees cover up some aspect of their identity from bosses and coworkers. Kenji Yoshino further developed the concept of "covering." There are four ways employees cover at work.

- *Appearance covering* concerns how individuals alter their self-presentation—including grooming, attire, and mannerisms—to blend into the mainstream. For example, a Christian employee might hide the cross pendant she wears under her blouse.
- *Affiliation-based covering* concerns how individuals avoid behaviors widely associated with their identity, often to negate stereotypes about that identity. For example, a man might avoid talking about being a new parent because he does not want colleagues to think he is less committed to work.
- *Advocacy-based covering* concerns how much individuals "stick up for" their group. For example, a gay employee might not challenge a homophobic joke made about gays by a coworker because they do not want to be seen as overreacting to it.
- *Association-based covering* concerns how individuals avoid contact with other group members. For example, a White man married to a Black woman might not bring her to a work-related function because he does not want coworkers to know he is in a mixed-race marriage.

Yoshino did a survey spanning seven different industries to better understand covering at work. The 220 respondents included a mix of ages, genders, races/ethnicities, and orientations. Seventy-five percent of respondents reported covering along at least one axis at work. Ninety-four percent of Blacks, 91% of women of color, 91% of LGBT individuals, and 80% of women reported that they covered their identities at work. Covering occurred with greater frequency within groups that have been historically underrepresented in the workplace. But minorities are not the only people who cover. The study found that 50% of straight White men reported covering identities related to religion, disability, veteran status, or social rank. Covering is prevalent and affects everyone at work.

An Asian person covers when they act like they do not like math—proficiency in math being a stereotypically Asian trait. A person who needs a cane to walk refrains from using it so that others do not see them as disabled, causing themselves physical pain at work. A Jewish man calls in sick on a holy day rather than telling his boss he cannot work that day. An employee diagnosed with breast cancer hides it from her coworkers so they do not view her as not able to complete her job duties during chemotherapy. These examples show that covering is harmful to employees and their productivity. According to Elizabeth Segran at *Fast Company*, "employees who feel the need to hide parts of their private lives at work also struggle to build close bonds with their colleagues, which makes it hard for them to establish strong networks of support."

Organizations should promote inclusion in the workplace by reducing covering. After all, diversity cannot be embraced if it is hidden from view. Leaders need be positive role models and uncover their identities. This takes courage, but it will increase followers' sense of safety. In Yoshino's study, 21% of respondents in the study stated that they had "uncovered in a way that [had] led to success," both for them and for their organization. They felt that covering had been taking up energy that they could be devoting to work, and they felt less stress and more relaxed at work after they uncovered their diverse identities.

Discussion Questions

1. Have you (or has someone you know) ever engaged in covering? What type of covering was it? How did it make you feel (or how do you think it made the other person feel)?
2. Provide examples of each of the four types of covering: appearance, affiliation, advocacy, and association.
3. Explain how not being yourself at work can negatively affect workplace relationships. How might covering affect a person's satisfaction at work? Their productivity?

4. Do you agree that organizations can make a difference by having leaders uncover themselves? Explain. What other steps can organizations take?

Source: Adapted from Goffman, E. (1963). *Stigma: Notes on the management of spoiled identity.* New York, NY: Simon & Schuster; Segran, E. (2015). How hiding your true self at work can hurt your career. *Fast Company.* Retrieved from https://www.fastcompany.com/3051111/how-hiding-your-true-self-at-work-can-hurt-your-career; Tanenbaum Center for Religious Understanding. (2015, January). Identity covering at work: A majority phenomenon. *Tanenbaum Corporate Membership Report, 4*(1). Retrieved from https://tanenbaum.org/wp-content/uploads/2015/01/2015-January-Corporate-Member-Newsletter-Vol.-4-No.-1.pdf; Yoshino, K. (2006). *Covering: The hidden assault on our civil rights.* New York, NY: Random House; and Yoshino, K., & Smith, C. (2013). Uncovering diversity: A new model of inclusion. *Deloitte University, Leadership Center for Inclusion.* Retrieved from https://www.lcidnet.org/media/uploads/resource/Uncovering_Talent_Deloitte.pdf.

Self-Assessment 9.1

Big-Five Personality Test

This is a personality test; it will help you understand why you act the way you do and how your personality may be structured. Please follow the instructions below. The scoring and interpretation follow the questions. There are no right or wrong answers. You do not have to share your results with others if you do not wish to do so.

Instructions

In the following table, for each statement 1 through 25, rate each with the following scale of 1 through 5: 1 = disagree, 2 = slightly disagree, 3 = neutral, 4 = slightly agree, and 5 = agree.

Personality Statement	Disagree	Slightly Disagree	Neutral	Slightly Agree	Agree
1. I feel comfortable around people.	1	2	3	4	5
2. I have a good word for everyone.	1	2	3	4	5
3. I am always prepared.	1	2	3	4	5
4. I often feel blue.	1	2	3	4	5
5. I believe in the importance of art.	1	2	3	4	5
6. I make friends easily.	1	2	3	4	5
7. I believe others have good intentions.	1	2	3	4	5
8. I pay attention to details.	1	2	3	4	5
9. I dislike myself.	1	2	3	4	5
10. I have a vivid imagination.	1	2	3	4	5
11. I am skilled in handling social situations.	1	2	3	4	5
12. I respect others.	1	2	3	4	5

13. I get chores done right away.	1	2	3	4	5
14. I am often down in the dumps.	1	2	3	4	5
15. I enjoy hearing new ideas.	1	2	3	4	5
16. I am the life of the party.	1	2	3	4	5
17. I accept people as they are.	1	2	3	4	5
18. I carry out my plans.	1	2	3	4	5
19. I have frequent mood swings.	1	2	3	4	5
20. I am interested in abstract ideas.	1	2	3	4	5
21. I know how to captivate people.	1	2	3	4	5
22. I make people feel at ease.	1	2	3	4	5
23. I make plans and stick to them.	1	2	3	4	5
24. I panic easily.	1	2	3	4	5
25. I have excellent ideas.	1	2	3	4	5

Scoring and Interpretation

The question numbers are shown in parentheses below. Write your score (1 to 5) on the blank following the question. For example, if you answered question (1) with a score of 2, write 2 on the blank.

O = (5) ___ + (10) ___ + (15) ___ + (20) ___ + (25) ___ = ___ (Openness to Experience)
C = (3) ___ + (8) ___ + (13) ___ + (18) ___ + (23) ___ = ___ (Conscientiousness)
E = (1) ___ + (6) ___ + (11) ___ + (16) ___ + (21) ___ = ___ (Extraversion)
A = (2) ___ + (7) ___ + (12) ___ + (17) ___ + (22) ___ = ___ (Agreeableness)
N = (4) ___ + (9) ___ + (14) ___ + (19) ___ + (24) ___ = ___ (Neuroticism)

The scores you calculate for each personality characteristic should be between 5 and 25. Scores from 5 to 10 can be considered lower and scores above 10 can be considered higher.

Following is a description of each trait.

Openness to experience (O) is the personality trait of seeking new experience and intellectual pursuits. High scorers may daydream a lot. Low scorers may be very down-to-earth.

Conscientiousness (C) is the personality trait of being honest and hardworking. High scorers tend to follow rules and prefer clean homes. Low scorers may be messy and cheat others.

Extraversion (E) is the personality trait of seeking fulfillment from sources outside the self or in community. High scorers tend to be very social, while low scorers prefer to work on their projects alone.

Agreeableness (A) reflects that many individuals adjust their behavior to suit others. High scorers are typically polite and like people. Low scorers tend to "tell it like it is."

Neuroticism (N) is the personality trait of being emotional.

Discussion Questions

1. Discuss your personality profile based on the results of the Big-Five personality assessment.
2. Are there any traits you would like to improve on (e.g., low openness to experience)? How will you go about improving on them?
3. How will you use the results of the assessment to become a more effective manager?

Source: Adapted from Finholt, T. A., & Olson, G. M. (1997). From laboratories to collaboratories: A new organizational form for scientific collaboration. *Psychological Science*, *8*(1), 28–36; and International Personality Item Pool. (2019). The NEO Big 5 Scales. Retrieved from http://ipip.ori.org.

Self-Assessment 9.2

Type A or Type B Behavior Pattern

This assessment measures the extent to which you are a Type A or Type B personality. There are no right or wrong answers, and this is not a test. You don't have to share your results with others unless you wish to do so.

Instructions

Answer the following questions about yourself on a scale of 1, strongly disagree, to 7, strongly agree:

Statements	Strongly Disagree	Disagree	Somewhat Disagree	Neutral	Somewhat Agree	Agree	Strongly Agree
1. Having work to complete "stirs me into action" more than other people.	1	2	3	4	5	6	7
2. When a person is talking and takes too long to come to the point, I frequently feel like hurrying the person along.	1	2	3	4	5	6	7
3. Nowadays, I consider myself to be relaxed and easygoing (reversed).	1	2	3	4	5	6	7
4. Typically, I get irritated extremely easily.	1	2	3	4	5	6	7
5. My best friends would rate my general activity level as very high.	1	2	3	4	5	6	7
6. I definitely tend to do most things in a hurry.	1	2	3	4	5	6	7
7. I take my work much more seriously than most.	1	2	3	4	5	6	7
8. I seldom get angry (reversed).	1	2	3	4	5	6	7
9. I often set deadlines for myself workwise.	1	2	3	4	5	6	7
10. I feel very impatient when I have to wait in line.	1	2	3	4	5	6	7
11. I put much more effort into my work than other people do.	1	2	3	4	5	6	7
12. Compared with others, I approach life much less seriously (reversed).	1	2	3	4	5	6	7

Scoring and Interpretation

Subtract your answers to questions 3, 8, and 12 (marked reversed) from 8, with the difference being your new score for those questions. For example, if your original answer for question 12 was 3, your new answer is 5 (8 − 3). Then add up your answers for the 12 questions. Compare your answer to the following scale:

53 or above   Type A   You may perceive higher stress in your life and be susceptible to health problems due to stress.

52 or below   Type B   You experience less stress in your life, and you are less sensitive to stress you do experience.

Source: Jenkins, C. D., Zyzanski, S. J., & Rosenman, R. H. (1971). Progress toward validation of a computer-scored test for the Type A coronary-prone behavior pattern. *Psychosomatic Medicine, 22*, 193–202. Reprinted with permission of Lippincott, Williams and Wilkins.

Self-Assessment 9.3

Attitudes Toward Diversity Scale

This self-assessment exercise identifies your attitudes toward diversity with respect to your peers. There are no right or wrong answers, and this is not a test. You do not have to share your results with others unless you wish to do so.

Instructions

You will be presented with some questions representing different situations involving your peers (consider the classmates you are working with on your team). Answer each question using the scale below.

Statements	Strongly Agree	Agree	Neutral	Disagree	Strongly Disagree
1. All in all, I would say that minority peers are just as productive as other peers. (R)	1	2	3	4	5
2. I often pick up the slack for some of my female peers who are less productive.	1	2	3	4	5
3. Sometimes I have to compensate for the lack of productivity of minority peers.	1	2	3	4	5
4. The most qualified peers on my team seem to be male.	1	2	3	4	5
5. I find that minority peers seem to be less productive on average.	1	2	3	4	5
6. The minorities on my team have a greater degree of difficulty getting along with others.	1	2	3	4	5
7. If a member of my team were prejudiced, he or she would be less likely to fit in. (R)	1	2	3	4	5
8. If one of my peers were racist, I would confront that person and let him or her know of my disapproval. (R)	1	2	3	4	5
9. People who are prejudiced have no place in this school. (R)	1	2	3	4	5
10. I do not feel comfortable with peers who are racist. (R)	1	2	3	4	5

Scoring and Interpretation

First, recode your responses to the reverse-worded questions (marked R): 1, 7, 8, 9, and 10.

$1 = 5, 2 = 4, 3 = 3, 4 = 2, 5 = 1$

Then sum your responses. Your responses can range from 10 to 100. Scores ranging from 10 to 40 indicate a somewhat negative attitude toward diversity. Scores from 41 to 70 indicate a moderate attitude toward diversity. Scores from 71 to 100 indicate a positive attitude toward diversity.

Discussion Questions

1. Were you surprised by your results? Why or why not, based on your experiences with women and minorities in teams you have worked with?
2. How could this assessment be used to help a team that is experiencing conflict due to having diverse

members? What specific things could be done to reduce conflict based on the questions in this scale (for example, confronting racist remarks made by a team member)?

3. Based on your experiences, does having a diverse team increase or decrease team performance? Explain your answer and provide an example.

Source: Adapted from Montei, M. S., Adams, G. A., & Eggers, L. M. (1996). Validity of scores on the attitudes toward diversity scale (ATDS). *Educational and Psychological Measurement*, 56(2), 293–303.

⑤SAGE edge™

Get the tools you need to sharpen your study skills. SAGE edge offers a robust online environment featuring an impressive array of free tools and resources. Access practice quizzes, eFlashcards, video, and multimedia at **edge.sagepub.com/scanduragower**.

CHAPTER 10

MOTIVATION

CHAPTER **LEARNING OBJECTIVES**

After studying this chapter, you should be able to:

10.1 Describe the motivation process of energizing, directing, and sustaining behavior.

10.2 List and define the needs described in Maslow's hierarchy.

10.3 Discuss how expectations of the future relate to high job performance.

10.4 Provide examples for each motivating property of SMART goals.

10.5 Demonstrate understanding of positive reinforcement by providing an example.

10.6 Explain why fairness matters to employees.

Get the edge on your studies at **edge.sagepub.com/ scanduragower**.

- Take the chapter quiz
- Review key terms with eFlashcards
- Explore multimedia resources, SAGE readings, and more!

Can You Solve the Candle Problem?

Best-selling author Dan Pink describes the "Candle Problem" in his TED Talk. How do you attach a candle to a wall with a box of thumbtacks and matches so that it doesn't drip? The **candle problem** (also known as **Duncker's candle problem**) is a thought experiment that illustrates the influence of functional fixedness on a participant's problem-solving ability. Gestalt psychologist Karl Duncker created the test, which was published posthumously in 1945.[1] Later researchers examined the impact of incentives on solving the candle problem and this linked it to motivation. For example, a researcher had two groups of people try to solve the problem. He offered money to the people in one group who solved it with the fastest times. The other group had no monetary incentives. When the tacks were in the box as shown in Figure 10.1, virtually all of the people *not offered a cash reward* solved the problem

▼ FIGURE 10.1

The Candle Problem

Sources: Hoffeld, D. (2016). *The science of selling: Proven strategies to make your pitch, influence decisions, and close the deal.* New York, NY: Tarcher Perigee. Based on Duncker, K. (1945). On problem-solving (L. S. Lees, Trans.). *Psychological Monographs, 58*(5), i–113. doi:10.1037/h0093599.

faster. The reward seemed to block people's ability to think creatively to come up with solutions. Can you solve it? How long did it take?

This test consistently showed that the group being given money was three minutes *slower* than the other group. What is the solution? One idea is to light the candle and drip wax on one side of the box, then attach the box to the wall and drip wax into the bottom so that the candle can be securely attached. The candle is then able to drip into the box. This solution is not only elegant, but it also saves resources because you don't need to use the thumbtacks to solve the problem.

If you are surprised to learn that the group receiving money took longer to arrive at a creative solution, you might be further surprised to learn that 40 years of management research has consistently shown that, for most tasks, you can't incentivize people to perform better with only money.[2] This is one of the most surprising, yet consistent research findings, but also probably one of the most ignored. There is sometimes a mismatch between what science knows and what managers do.

Motivating with money does work well for manual work and simple solutions. This is extrinsic motivation defined as monetary rewards. Such rewards get people to focus toward the answer and push them to solve the task quicker. However, in today's workforce, most employees don't do simple, repetitive work like this. Certainly not managers. They do much more complicated tasks that have no easy answer and often require creativity. For simple tasks, a reward improves performance, but if creativity is needed, then the higher reward decreases performance. Today, management is leaning more toward intrinsic motivation—the desire to do work harder for personal reasons. Intrinsic motivation is the result of three forces:

- *autonomy*—the desire to direct our own lives,
- *mastery*—the urge to get better, or develop skills, and
- *purpose*—the need to do what we do for reasons bigger than ourselves.[3]

The ideas of autonomy, mastery, and purpose were first explained by Edward Deci and Richard Ryan in their cognitive evaluation theory (CET), which described intrinsic motivation as the drive to do things for their own sake. CET research demonstrated the critical roles played by feelings of the ability to work free from surveillance (autonomy), the feelings of competence experienced (mastery), and the need to experience relatedness to other people (purpose).[4]

To understand intrinsic motivation, think about the time you spend on hobbies such as cycling or cooking. Watch children while they are playing. At work, intrinsic motivation involves liking a certain type of work or specific tasks such as analyzing, inventing, or problem-solving. It means "liking the doing."[5]

People expect to be paid money for the work that they do. It results in compliance with organizational directions. But when managers give rewards, it decreases autonomy for most employees. They feel that they are being controlled. In modern management, an extra project chosen by the employees increases autonomy. It may also give them a sense of mastery over a new challenge as well as a higher purpose, since the project they choose may have a lot of personal meaning to them. For example, an employee may choose to work on improving the recycling program in their organization because they believe in sustainability.

Companies today are implementing intrinsic motivation through autonomy, mastery, and purpose. For example, the software company, Atlassian, gives engineers a day off from their normal work to develop whatever they want, as long as it is unrelated to their normal work and they deliver a progress report by the end of the day. Another example is known as ROWE, a Results Only Work Environment. Employees do whatever they want, wherever they want as long as they deliver the results. ROWE started at the Best Buy corporate headquarters. The goal was to improve recruitment of the best and brightest professionals and managers to run the company. The company gave employees a choice from a set of flexible schedules. The employees who selected flexibility in their work were happier and more productive. These employees were also less likely to quit.[6]

Wikipedia is another example of the power of intrinsic motivation. Microsoft is one of the most powerful software companies in the world. In the early 1990s, they developed a digital encyclopedia called Encarta, which was built by well-paid professionals and managers who were incentivized with standard extrinsic motivators such as salary and bonuses.[7] And then Wikipedia hit the scene in 2001.[8] Wikipedia was built by unpaid (autonomous) volunteers. The volunteers did it because they found that doing the research was interesting and fun, and this reinforced mastery feelings. They were motivated by their need to share knowledge with other people and believed in the crowd-sourced encyclopedia idea. This increased both mastery and a sense of purpose. It was cool. In 1999, no economist would have predicted that Encarta's model would be overtaken by Wikipedia's—yet it has, with all of the work being done by people receiving no financial incentives for their efforts.

If we get past the simplistic view of rewards and punishments and allow people to be more motivated by autonomy, mastery, and purpose, we can make our organizations stronger by encouraging creativity and problem-solving.

Sources: Adapted from Dan Pink. (2014). The puzzle of motivation. *TED Summaries.* https://tedsummaries.com/2014/06/06/dan-pink-the-puzzle-of-motivation/comment-page-1/#comments; Locke, E. A., & Schattke, K. (2018). Intrinsic and extrinsic motivation: Time for expansion and clarification. *Motivation Science.* doi:10.1037/mot0000116; Nyugen, S. (2017, January 4). Results only work environment: ROWE. *WorkplacePsychology.net.* Retrieved from https://workplacepsychology.net/2017/01/04/results-only-work-environment-rowe/; Ryan, R. M., & Deci, E. L. (2000). Intrinsic and extrinsic motivations: Classic definitions and new directions. *Contemporary Educational Psychology, 25*(1), 54–67; Weinberger, M. (2015, November 17). Microsoft had a secret, genius reason for making an encyclopedia in the nineties. *Business Insider.* Retrieved from https://www.businessinsider.com/history-of-microsoft-encarta-2015-11; Wikipedia. (2019). History of Wikipedia. Retrieved from https://en.wikipedia.org/wiki/History_of_Wikipedia.

Textbook Organization

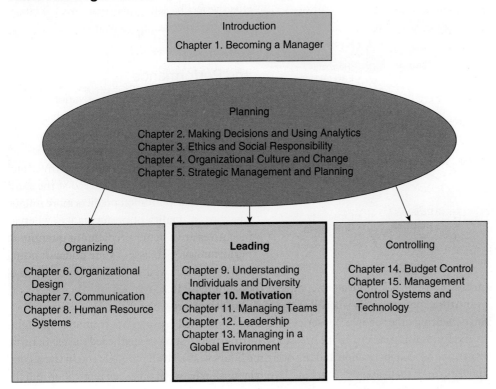

an Pink's TED Talk underscores the importance of the type of motivation for the best results. Some have argued that motivation is the number one problem facing organizations.[9] Every manager must understand how to motivate their followers toward goals that matter to the organization. This chapter explores motivation at work with practical applications of how to energize, direct, and sustain employee motivation. This is the motivation process and it is described in the following section.

What Is Motivation?

Learning Objective 10.1: Describe the motivation process of energizing, directing, and sustaining behavior.

Motivation has been defined as "what a person does (direction), how hard a person works (intensity), and how long a person works (persistence)."[10] The motivation process starts with energizing behavior by activating people's needs and drives. Once people are energized, it is important to direct their behavior toward goals that are important to the organization.[11] In this chapter, we will explore models of motivation that direct and sustain behavior. An overview of motivation theories is shown in Figure 10.2. Understanding this figure will help you keep track of the various theories of motivation. Some theories focus on energizing behavior and these are the need theories (Maslow's hierarchy of needs, McClelland's manifest needs, Alderfer's ERG theory, and Herzberg's motivator-hygiene theory). Other theories focus on processes (expectancy theory and goal setting). Research shows that goal-setting systems are necessary to direct efforts. To sustain behavior over the long term, rewards must be administered correctly using reinforcement theory and the process must be fair (organizational justice). Finally, for motivation to be effective, feedback is needed so that the processes of energizing and directing

Overview of Motivation Theories

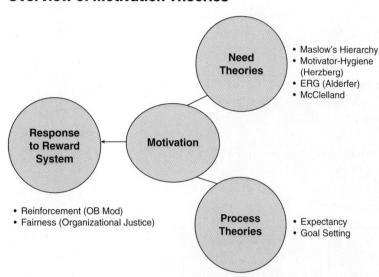

behavior stay on track. This chapter will pay particular attention to the process of providing effective feedback to employees, since it is essential in most theories of motivation.

Relationship Between Motivation and Performance

Managers are interested in motivation because it predicts job performance. Studies that review decades of research on motivation conclude that intrinsic motivation is a moderate to strong predictor of performance. When intrinsic and extrinsic motivation is considered at the same time, intrinsic motivation predicts more unique variance in quality of performance, whereas incentives are a better predictor of quantity of performance.[12] To assess your understanding of what workers want from their jobs in terms of intrinsic and extrinsic motivators, complete Toolkit Activity 10.1.

Intrinsic motivation also increases **prosocial motivation**, which is the desire to put efforts into benefiting other people.[13] A series of studies[14] examined prosocial motivation of firefighters and fundraising callers. In the first study, intrinsic motivation strengthened the relationship between prosocial motivation and the overtime hours worked by 58 firefighters. In the second study, intrinsic motivation strengthened the relationship between prosocial motivation and the performance of 140 fundraising callers. The callers were introduced to the students who would be receiving the scholarships from their efforts, so this increased the callers' feelings of purpose. Callers who reported high levels of both prosocial and intrinsic motivation raised more money one month later. They made more calls to potential donors. The effect lasted over time. Clearly, intrinsic motivation predicts job performance, and this is why it is an important part of a manager's job. Although people work for money, intrinsic motivation appears to be more important for the type of work that is becoming more common, which requires complex problem-solving and creativity. The contrast between intrinsic and extrinsic rewards is discussed next.

Intrinsic and Extrinsic Rewards

As pointed out in the discussion of the candle problem at the beginning of this chapter, rewards are an essential part of understanding motivation. There are generally two types: intrinsic rewards and extrinsic rewards. **Intrinsic rewards** come from performing the work itself. When employees find their work challenging and enjoyable, they feel a sense of achievement. For example, a nurse feels an internal sense of satisfaction when she helps patients in the postoperative recovery room. Another example would be a person who finds volunteer work to be satisfying although they receive no pay. **Extrinsic rewards**, on the other hand, are tangible benefits that an employee receives for their work. These rewards include salary, benefits, and bonuses. For example, a nurse might receive a pay raise due to excellent patient satisfaction ratings.[15] A salesperson might earn a bonus for having above-average sales performance at their company.

Does paying someone to do a job reduce their intrinsic motivation? Surprisingly, it can. Research has found that extrinsic rewards can

Firefighters have prosocial motivation to help others.

© Prath/Shutterstock

sometimes lead to reductions in intrinsic motivation. As odd as that might sound, remember that intrinsic motivation refers to people's internal desire to do something, generally because they enjoy the task and find it interesting. Paying them to do these tasks risks changing the focus away from these intrinsic rewards and shifting it to the far more tangible, but less motivating, extrinsic reward. How much less motivating? A research study[16] of three different work settings found that employees who were intrinsically motivated to do their jobs reported higher job performance and commitment than employees who were primarily motivated by financial rewards in all three groups. In other words, it is true that "you can't pay someone to like their job" but human psychology is just strange enough that it *is* possible to pay someone to stop liking their job.

We know that the previous paragraph might have left you a bit skeptical so let's consider some examples from your own life. Think about what you are doing this very second—reading this book. Are you reading this book because you want to get a good grade in your management class (extrinsic) or are you interested in learning more about motivation (intrinsic)? For example, money was found to undermine college students' intrinsic motivation to perform a fun task.[17] These experiments were replicated in work organizations.[18]

A review of 128 studies concluded that contingent rewards significantly reduced intrinsic motivation.[19] These findings may be surprising, since most people think that money matters more than other rewards. In fact, paying people money for doing something they enjoy may actually *reduce* their motivation. Clearly both extrinsic and intrinsic rewards matter, but extrinsic rewards may relate to the satisfaction of lower levels of needs and intrinsic rewards may relate to higher levels of needs such as the need to grow and learn from working. To further understand intrinsic motivation, we begin with an examination of the forces that energize behavior, which is the first step in the motivation process. This is perhaps best explained by need theories of motivation, which focus on the factors that underlie human drives.

To learn about your own intrinsic and extrinsic motivation, complete Toolkit Activity 10.2.

Need Theories

Learning Objective 10.2: List and define the needs described in Maslow's hierarchy.

Maslow's Hierarchy of Needs

Abraham Maslow summarized research related to the psychology of human motivation in his 1954 book *Motivation and Personality*.[20] At that time, researchers generally focused on such factors as biology, achievement, or power to explain what energizes, directs, and sustains human behavior. Maslow posited a **hierarchy of needs** based on two general types of needs: deficiency needs and growth needs. At the level of the deficiency needs, a lower-level need must be met before moving to the next level. However, once deficiency needs are met, a person will be motivated to fill them if they are threatened. The five levels in Maslow's hierarchy of needs are as follows:

1. **Physiological needs**—hunger, thirst, bodily comforts
2. **Safety/security needs**—to be safe and out of danger
3. **Social needs**—to affiliate with others, be accepted by them
4. **Esteem needs**—to achieve, gain approval and recognition, including self-esteem
5. **Self-actualization needs**—to appreciate life, be concerned about personal growth, have peak experiences

The presentation of Maslow's hierarchy is typically a triangle or pyramid. However, Maslow never considered that the needs at the bottom were more important than higher-level

Maslow's Ladder of Needs

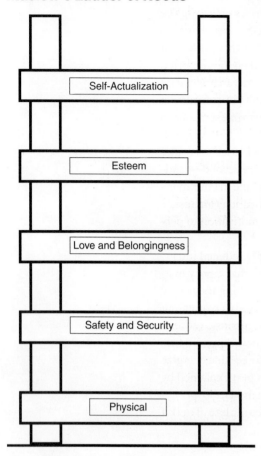

Self-Actualization

Esteem

Love and Belongingness

Safety and Security

Physical

Source: Based on Maslow, A. (1954). *Motivation and personality.* New York, NY: Harper; Leech, J. (2014). Maslow's hierarchy of need. Retrieved from https://mrjoe.uk/maslows-hierarchy-needs-psychology-myth-busting-1/.

Some people have a higher need for achievement than others.

© fizkes /Shutterstock

needs. Maslow himself never presented any figure summarizing his theory. This happened later, as the theory became popular in management.[21] A perhaps more accurate depiction of the theory is a ladder, as shown in Figure 10.3. According to Maslow, an individual is ready to act upon the higher-level growth needs only when lower-level needs are met. Maslow published his first conceptualization of his theory in 1943[22] and it has since become one of the most popular theories of human motivation.

Maslow's theory enjoys wide acceptance and appears in many courses, including psychology, marketing, and management.[23] This is because the theory is intuitive, and students find it easy to understand. It makes sense that managers can apply the theory to create work and reward systems that allow employees to satisfy their needs. This will lead to both satisfaction and higher performance. Managers are taught to understand where each of their employees is located on ladder and adapt their assignments and rewards to motivate employees at the next level. To learn about your needs, complete Self-Assessment 10.1.

Despite its popularity, Maslow's theory has received only limited research support.[24] As noted above, some researchers called into question whether Maslow's needs are arranged in a hierarchy.[25] However, one study found that satisfaction of the lower-level need immediately below any need in the hierarchy predicted satisfaction of the next-higher-level need, yielding some evidence for the hierarchical nature of Maslow's theory of need satisfaction. Another interesting finding was that satisfaction of the physiological needs was a significant predictor of the satisfaction of every one of the four higher-level needs, suggesting that if physiological needs are not met, this will limit a person's ability to satisfy any of the higher-level needs.[26]

McClelland's Need Theory

David McClelland says that, regardless of our gender, culture, or age, we all have three motivating drivers, and one of these will be our dominant motivating driver.[27] This dominant motivator is largely dependent on our culture and life experiences, which shape our needs over time. McClelland's research uncovered three needs, which are shown in Figure 10.4 (along with typical behaviors that can be expected of people with each need): the need for achievement, the need for affiliation, and the need for power. These needs are described below.

Most of McClelland's research was on the **need for achievement (nACH)**. There is some research support for the idea that people who have a higher need to achieve do perform at higher levels and people with higher nACH may be more successful entrepreneurs.[28] However, a high need to achieve is not necessarily related to being an effective leader, since those with a higher nACH may be more interested in their own attainment rather than coaching others to succeed. People motivated by nACH need challenging things to work on. They gain satisfaction from overcoming difficulties, so a manager should assign them to tasks that stretch their abilities. People motivated by achievement work very effectively alone or with other high achievers, but they may become frustrated if they are in a team that has nonachievers. They need a lot of feedback on their work—they want to know how they are doing so they can improve.

McClelland also specified the **need for affiliation (nAFF)**, which is a need for relationships, similar to Maslow's social needs. People with nAFF work best in teams, as opposed to having to work alone. Feedback should be provided to people with nAFF in a personal way. They want to know that the relationship with their manager is important. They may prefer to receive positive feedback in private rather than publicly.

The **need for power (nPOW)** is the need to have influence over others and to have status. Those with high nPOW want to take charge. They like to compete with other people and they want to win, so they thrive when they are assigned to projects with challenging goals (similar to people with nACH). They are natural persuaders, so they may do well in sales positions or negotiations. They like direct feedback and want the feedback to be linked to how they can move up in the organization (so they can gain even more influence over others).

McClelland's theory has received more research support than other need theories; however, the application of the theory to motivate followers is limited because these needs are believed to be learned at a young age and remain relatively stable over the life course. For example, it may not be possible to increase an adult's need for achievement. The three needs in McClelland's theory can be summarized as follows:

- *Need for achievement motivation (nACH)*—Those with a high need for achievement tend to engage in situations that offer personal accountability. This person sets difficult but achievable goals for themselves, and desires performance feedback.
- *Need for affiliation motivation (nAFF)*—Those with a need for affiliation have a preference for building strong relationships, value belonging to a group or organization, and have a heightened sense of empathy. This type of person works great in a group and wants to be respected and accepted.
- *Need for power motivation (nPOW)*—Individuals with a need for power desire to influence others, but they do not demonstrate a need to simply have control. They need to feel a sense of authority over others. These individuals possess the need to increase personal status and prestige.[29]

CRITICAL THINKING QUESTIONS

Compare Maslow's hierarchy of needs and McClelland's need for achievement (nACH). Is the nACH more related to esteem needs or self-actualization?

Alderfer's ERG Theory

Clayton P. Alderfer's existence, relatedness, and growth (ERG) theory[30] condenses Maslow's five human needs into three categories:

- **Existence needs** include material and physiological desires (examples are food, water, air, clothing, safety, physical love, and affection). (Maslow's first two levels)
- **Relatedness needs** include social and external esteem from others, and relationships with significant others like family, friends, and coworkers. This also means to be recognized and feel secure as part of a group or family. (Maslow's third and fourth levels)
- **Growth needs** include internal self-esteem and self-actualization. These motivate a person to make productive effects to progress toward one's ideal self. This includes the need to have meaningful work. (Maslow's fourth and fifth levels)

Existence needs are the most concrete and obvious. Relatedness needs are less concrete than existence needs, which depend on relationships. Finally, growth needs are concrete in that their goals are particular to a person and unique.

McClelland's Needs and Typical Behaviors

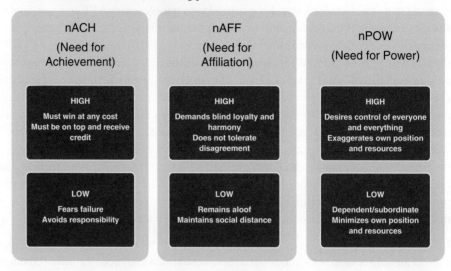

While Alderfer's ERG theory is similar to Maslow's hierarchy, it differs in some important ways. A lower-level need does not have to be gratified for a person to move on to the next need. The order of needs can differ for different people. For example, a student may eat Ramen noodles to save money and place growth needs above existence ones (protein).

Herzberg's Two-Factor Theory

Frederick Herzberg proposed a **two-factor theory** of motivation (sometimes referred to as the **motivator-hygiene theory**).[31] According to Herzberg, there some aspects of a person's job that result in satisfaction (which he called **motivators**), while there are others that *prevent dissatisfaction* (which he called hygiene factors). **Hygienes** is admittedly an odd word choice, but Herzberg used the term to describe conditions and practices that prevent people from being satisfied with their work. In other words, the opposite of "satisfaction" is not dissatisfaction but rather "no satisfaction," and the opposite of "dissatisfaction" is "no dissatisfaction." This relationship is explained by Figure 10.5. Satisfaction and dissatisfaction at work operate on two different continuums, rather than on the same one.

Based on Herzberg's research, examples of motivators and hygiene factors follow. According to Herzberg, the motivators (sometimes called satisfiers) produce job satisfaction.[32] These factors may be considered as intrinsic motivation because they relate to the work itself, and the rewards are intrinsic rather than extrinsic. They motivate the employees to higher levels of performance. Motivators are related to psychological growth needs. The following are some examples:

- *Recognition*—The employees should be applauded and receive credit for their accomplishments by the managers.
- *Sense of achievement*—The employees must feel they have achieved something when they complete their work.

▼ FIGURE10.5

Relationship of Motivators and Hygiene Factors to Satisfaction and Dissatisfaction

MOTIVATORS	
Satisfaction	No Satisfaction

HYGIENE FACTORS	
No Dissatisfaction	Dissatisfaction

- *Growth and promotional opportunities*—The employees should feel there are growth and advancement opportunities in an organization to motivate them to perform well. This includes learning new skills while working.
- *Responsibility*—The employees should feel responsibility for their work. Managers should increase the employees' ownership of the work by reducing control over them.
- *Meaningfulness of the work*—In order for the employees to have high motivation, the work should be purposeful, interesting, and challenging.

Growth opportunities are a motivator at work.

© Monkey Business Images/Shutterstock

Hygiene factors are factors that are essential for existence (they are sometimes called dissatisfiers or maintenance factors). These factors do not lead to job satisfaction, as noted above, but if they are absent, then they lead to dissatisfaction. In other words, hygiene factors must be adequate so that they keep employees content and don't give them a reason to complain. These factors are generally related to extrinsic rewards and are outside of the work itself. These factors relate to the context of the work environment the employees are in. They relate most to the lower-level physiological needs that the individuals must have fulfilled (recall Maslow's hierarchy of needs). The following are some examples:

- *Pay*—The pay or salary structure should be appropriate and reasonable. It must be competitive with other jobs in the same industry.
- *Company and administrative policies*—The company policies should not be too rigid. They should be fair and clear. Examples include flexible working hours, dress code, breaks, vacation time, and codes of ethics.
- *Benefits*—Employees are offered health care plans, benefits for family members, and employee assistance programs, as examples.
- *Physical working conditions*—The working conditions should be safe and clean. The work equipment and computers should be updated and well maintained.
- *Interpersonal relations*—The relationship of the employees with their peers, superiors, and subordinates should be appropriate, without conflict or humiliation.
- *Job security*—The organization provides job security to employees.

Herzberg found that hygiene factors can only make people dissatisfied if they are not present, and motivators produce job satisfaction. His research is summarized in Figure 10.6. To motivate employees, managers had to focus on the motivating factors such as achievement, recognition, the work itself, responsibility, advancement, and growth. As shown in the figure, safety was the only hygiene factor that somewhat related to job satisfaction (but it was mostly related to job dissatisfaction).

▼ FIGURE 10.6

Herzberg's Motivator-Hygiene Factors

Hygiene: Job Dissatisfaction	Motivation: Job Satisfaction
	Achievement
	Recognition
	Work Itself
	Responsibility
	Advancement
	Growth
Company Policy and Administration	
Supervision	
Interpersonal Relations	
Working Conditions	
Safety	
Status	
Security	

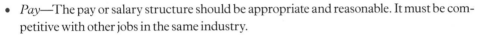

Source: Herzberg, F. M., Mausner, B., & Snyderman, B. B. (1959). *The motivation to work*. New York, NY: John Wiley. Reprinted with permission.

The need theories covered so far relate to what energizes behavior. Despite their popularity, these theories have not been well supported by research. Process theories have received more research support. Next, we turn to process theories that direct behavior. One of the most important of these is expectancy theory, which focuses on our expectations of what may happen in the future and the value we place on various rewards.

Expectancy Theory

Learning Objective 10.3: Discuss how expectations of the future relate to high job performance.

The choice to put in effort can be thought of as a decision process in which people weigh the value of the rewards they are likely to receive if they can attain a certain level of performance. There is a theory of motivation that examines the decisions that people make in terms of whether or not they will work hard. This is known as the **expectancy theory** of motivation. The key ideas in expectancy theory[33] are as follows:

- **Valence** is the value or strength one places on a particular outcome or reward.
- **Expectancy** relates efforts to performance. In other words, if a person tries, they believe they will achieve a given level of performance.
- **Instrumentality** refers to the belief that performance is related to rewards. In other words, a person believes that if they achieve a level of performance, they will receive a reward.
- Thus, the level of motivation is expressed in the form of an equation:

$$\text{Motivation} = \text{Expectancy} \times \text{Instrumentality} \times \text{Valence}$$

Remember that the expectancy theory model is multiplicative in nature: all three components of motivation must have high positive values to generate high motivation. If any one of the variables approaches zero, the possibility of the motivated performance also approaches zero. The expectancy theory of motivation does not concentrate on underlying drives (like the need theories of Maslow and McClelland). Instead, the focus is on outcomes (having valences), the strength of a person's belief that they can achieve them (expectancy), and how much they believe they will receive the outcomes in the future (instrumentality).

Expectancy theory explains why cash bonuses increase motivation.

© bunyarit klinsukhon /Shutterstock

▼ FIGURE 10.7

The Expectancy Theory of Motivation

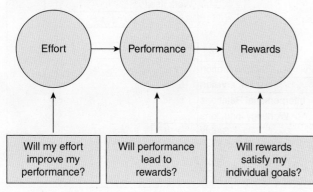

Source: Vroom's expectancy theory. Retrieved from https://ebrary.net/2842/management/argyriss_theory.

For example, let's say that you want an A on the midterm exam in your management class. You value an A on the exam highly because you need an A in the class to maintain your 3.8 GPA. So, the midterm A has a high valence. The expectancy is your confidence in your study habits that if you try (i.e., put in a lot of effort), then you will receive an A on the midterm exam. The instrumentality is your belief that getting an A on the midterm will help you get an A in the class. So it's the belief that your instructor will fairly assign the grades if you perform well on the exam. A summary of expectancy theory and how it predicts effort is shown in Figure 10.7.

Research on the ability of expectancy theory to predict performance is mixed.[34] This is likely because there are many factors that could be an input to performance such as the quality of supervision and the fairness of rewards

CAREERS IN MANAGEMENT

Understanding Entrepreneurial Motivation Using Expectancy Theory

Expectancy theory provides an excellent framework for understanding why some people choose to start their own business.[35] It makes sense that people who believe that they can be entrepreneurs will be more interested in becoming one. And the valence matters too—the choice to become an entrepreneur is a function of the belief that it will be rewarding in terms of both satisfaction and money. A study of 117 Spanish entrepreneurs[36] found that expectancy, instrumentality, and valence increased their motivation to become an entrepreneur. First, entrepreneurs believed in themselves—that they could be successful entrepreneurs. Second, they thought that starting their own business would be a rewarding and valuable career. Thus, they said they were interested in starting businesses. In the United States, an experimental study[37] investigated the entrepreneurial expectancy (i.e., the effort to performance linkage) for 179 undergraduate business students. The researchers found that feedback (positive versus negative) that the students received regarding their entrepreneurial ability (regardless of actual ability) changed expectancies regarding future business start-ups, but it did not alter task effort or quality of performance. In other words, students receiving positive feedback about their entrepreneurial abilities had higher entrepreneurial expectancies than individuals receiving negative feedback. For example, if your entrepreneurship professor tells you that you can start a business successfully, you are more likely to pursue your start-up idea.

Another study of 433 undergraduate business students[38] found that expectancy theory predicted undergraduate students' interest in becoming entrepreneurs. Expectancy was assessed by having the students complete a measure of entrepreneurial self-efficacy—how much they believed in their own abilities to succeed as an entrepreneur. The valences (values) associated with being an entrepreneur were making money, having financial security, being independent, and satisfying a need for achievement. Instrumentalities were assessed by having students rate the probability that being an entrepreneur would result in these four outcomes. Expectancy, instrumentality, and valence predicted individual motivations to pursue an entrepreneurial career. The study also found that entrepreneurship education had a positive impact on students' perceived expectancy and desirability of being an entrepreneur (valences). After students took a semester-long entrepreneurship course, they perceived higher expectancy and desirability, which in turn translated into stronger entrepreneurial motivation and intentions to become an entrepreneur.

These studies show that entrepreneurial skills might be taught and, once acquired, strengthen individual perceptions of competence and expectations for success. In such courses, it is important to learn the skills necessary to engage in entrepreneurial activities and be able to successfully apply those skills. Expectancies are strengthened by believing that you can successfully complete entrepreneurial tasks. Instrumentality is strengthened by understanding of the importance of certain activities for their success as entrepreneurs. Entrepreneurship is becoming a popular career choice and many students may have a high valence for entrepreneurship. Valence is determined mostly by students' individual perceptions of their fit to such a career.

Discussion Questions

1. In addition to taking a course in entrepreneurship, how can students' expectancies (belief that they can succeed in starting a business) be strengthened?

2. Besides making money, having financial security, being independent, and satisfying achievement needs, are there other factors that have valence for being an entrepreneur? What are the risks (i.e., are there any negative valences)?

3. What other careers/occupational choices do you think could be explained by expectancy theory? Provide an example.

Sources: Barba-Sánchez, V., & Atienza-Sahuquillo, C. (2017). Entrepreneurial motivation and self-employment: Evidence from expectancy theory. *International Entrepreneurship and Management Journal, 13*(4), 1097–1115; Gatewood, E. J., Shaver, K. G., Powers, J. B., & Gartner, W. B. (2002). Entrepreneurial expectancy, task effort, and performance. *Entrepreneurship Theory and Practice, 27*(2), 187–206; Hsu, D. K., Shinnar, R. S., & Powell, B. C. (2014). Expectancy theory and entrepreneurial motivation: A longitudinal examination of the role of entrepreneurship education. *Journal of Business and Entrepreneurship, 26*(1), 121–140; Locke, E. A., & Baum, J. R. (2007). Entrepreneurial motivation. In J. R. Baum, M. Frese, & R. A. Baron (Eds.), *SIOP Organizational Frontiers Series: The psychology of entrepreneurship* (pp. 93–112). Mahwah, NJ: Erlbaum.

(fairness will be discussed later in this chapter in the section on organizational justice). Yet expectancy theory has shown that effort may be a more important predictor of performance than ability.[39] A review of research on expectancy theory noted the following: "Expectancy theory has become a standard in motivation, as reflected by its incorporation as a general framework for a wide variety of research."[40]

Goal Setting

Management research has investigated the properties of motivating goals in numerous laboratory and field experiments.[41] For goals to motivate people, they must have certain properties. These goal-setting principles can be remembered with the acronym **SMART goals**, for Specific, Measurable, Actionable, Relevant, and Time-bound. Figure 10.8 provides a guide to setting goals that motivate by following these principles.

Definitions of the five motivating properties of goals along with examples from a retailer of a sports store that sells university logo apparel follow.[42]

- **S**pecific goals refer to something unique and detailed. Specific is the opposite of broad or vague. *A specific goal should detail where you want to go.* It goes without saying that your goal in business is to make a profit or to sell more products. These are general goals, not examples of SMART business goals. What do you want to sell? Where do you want to sell it? Who do you want to sell it to? An example of a SMART business goal that respects the specific characteristic could be:

  I want to increase sales of university logo apparel in my four mall stores. I'll do this by setting up a booth at a local football game to sell hats and T-shirts.

- **M**easurable refers to something as being measurable, such as year-over-year sales. It's more than just a measure of something or a number to be achieved. Measurement is about being able to develop a number objectively and compare it to a baseline. For example, if we just say that we want to sell sports apparel, we couldn't measure that. This statement is too subjective and impossible to measure. A measurable example looks something like this:

  I want to sell 20% more university logo apparel, compared to last year's retail sales, in my four mall stores. I want to take advantage of the university team's winning streak.

▼ FIGURE 10.8

SMART Goals Guide	
Specific	• What exactly needs to be accomplished? • Who else will be involved? • Where will this take place? • Why do I want to accomplish the goal?
Measurable	• How will I know I've succeeded? • How much change needs to occur? • How many accomplishments or actions will it take?
Attainable	• Do I have, or can I get, the resources needed to achieve the goal? • Is the goal a reasonable stretch for me (neither out of reach nor too easy)? • Are the actions I plan to take likely to bring success?
Relevant	• Is this a worthwhile goal for me right now? • Is it meaningful to me—or just something others think I should do? • Would it delay or prevent me from achieving a more important goal? • Am I willing to commit to achieving this goal?
Time-bound	• What is the deadline for reaching the goal? • When do I need to take action? • What can I do today?

Source: Seivert, J. (2014, December 12). Getting ready for the new year. Retrieved from https://sellinginteriordesign.com/2014/12/12/getting-ready-for-the-new-year/.

- **A**ttainable means that people need to feel able to attain SMART business goals. For example, if we were to suggest a 200% increase in something, this would be unattainable (most likely, depending on the circumstances). This goal could discourage anyone whose job it is to achieve it, therefore making it something useless and purposeless. And ultimately the goal is rejected. An attainable goal would be:

  I want to increase sales by 20% because the university team is on a winning streak.

- **R**elevant refers to a goal that has a practical meaning and benefits a company. SMART goals *must be important to the business.* For example, setting a goal to change the wall color in all of your restaurants could certainly be necessary and an important goal for maintenance personnel. Yet, for your business, this is an operational detail, not relevant to the bottom line. A goal should always be linked to something that will define the company's destination. Here's an example:

Goals are motivating if they have certain properties.

© Keepsmiling4u /Shutterstock

  Increasing retail sales is important to my bottom line. I want to be able to open another mall store in two years.

- **T**ime-bound means that there is a timeframe within which to meet the goal. This is the last element in our examples of SMART business goals: *It refers to a date, a time to reach the goal.* In our case, we could state the following:

  I want to achieve the 20% increase in retail sales by the end of the year.

Here are some other examples of SMART business goals:

- *Car-rental company:* Increase our lead base of priority rental members by increasing marketing efforts by 25% by the end of the year.
- *Gym:* Sell 30% more memberships during the month of January, when New Year's resolutions occur in our region.
- *Restaurant franchise:* Open 15 new stores by the end of the year: 10 in our state and 5 in our neighboring state, Oregon.

Limitations of Goal Setting

Despite a strong evidence base that supports the effectiveness of SMART goals in motivating performance, researchers have uncovered some limitations. Individual performance goals may harm team performance because they reduce the incentives to cooperate.[43] Goals may need to be set for the team and not for individuals if the team members depend on one another to complete a task. Another limitation is that people may set moderate or easy goals so that they can attain them.[44] Experimental research has also found that people may engage in unethical behavior just to meet goals. This happens even when there are no financial incentives present, and it becomes more prevalent when individuals just miss their goals.[45] In fact, the overuse of goal setting in an organization may actually reduce intrinsic motivation.[46]

Despite recent criticisms, goal setting has been defended as one of the best-researched areas of motivation. Its proponents responded to the criticisms and concluded: "Organizations cannot thrive without being focused on their desired end results any more than an individual can thrive without goals to provide a sense of purpose. Purposeful activity is the essence of living action. If the purpose is neither clear nor challenging, very little gets accomplished."[47] Those who defend goal setting cite the effective use of goals in organizational settings such as the "stretch goals" implemented at General Electric. By definition, **stretch goals** are goals that employees don't know how to reach because they are difficult.[48] An example of how goal setting is implemented in practice follows.

We can look to Microsoft for an example of successful implementation of goal setting.[49] Goal commitment is so important that Microsoft changed the name of the process from "goal setting" to "goal commitment." Managers are actively involved in the process of developing commitments with their followers. Each manager is expected to:

1. Discuss and document the commitments of all employees;
2. Revisit and refresh commitments over time;
3. Agree to success metrics for each commitment, including the "How?" behind execution (e.g., the plans to be used to attain the commitments), not just the "What?";
4. Align commitments across the company by cascading commitments, beginning with Microsoft's commitments and connecting to organizational, team, and ultimately individual commitments; and
5. Drive management team calibration discussions so interdependencies and metrics are vetted across individuals.[50]

It is clear from Microsoft's example that managers play an important role in setting and monitoring progress toward goal commitments with each of their direct reports. This process assures alignment with the organization's goals, employee commitment, and accountability for results. This is accomplished through regular one-on-one meetings between managers and their employees in which the goal commitment form shown in Figure 10.9 is discussed. First, employees identify five to seven areas that align with the commitments of their manager and the overall Microsoft organization. Next, employees discuss how they will achieve their commitments and set up key milestones, noting who they depend on to accomplish the commitment. Finally, success measures are defined to evaluate the progress and realization of the goal commitments.

CRITICAL THINKING QUESTIONS

> Given the criticisms of goal setting, explain your position on whether or not organizations should continue to implement stretch goals. What are some possible limitations to stretch goals?

▼ FIGURE 10.9

Goal Commitment Form Used at Microsoft

Reviewer and employee, edit this section to create a prioritized list of commitments.

Commitments	Execution Plan	Accountabilities
Identify 5-7 areas of focus which are aligned with commitments of your manager, organization, and *Microsoft Commitments*.	Identify how you will achieve your commitments (key milestones and dependencies).	Define success measures and metrics to evaluate the realization of your commitments.

Source: Shaw, K. N. (2004). Changing the goal-setting process at Microsoft. *Academy of Management Executive, 18*(4), 139–142. p. 142.

Research on goal setting has also clearly demonstrated that employees who receive **feedback** on their progress achieve higher levels of performance than those who don't.[51] Feedback guides performance and allows the person to correct behaviors that may not be working. Further, research has indicated that if employees are allowed to generate their own feedback, it may be more motiving than feedback from an outside source such as their supervisor.[52] Feedback is essential to the process of goal setting and motivation in general. The next section provides specific guidelines for a manager to follow in providing feedback to their followers.

Effective feedback is essential for goal setting and motivation.

© fizkes /Shutterstock

How to Give Effective Feedback

Susan M. Heathfield, a management and organization development consultant who specializes in human resources issues, offers the following guidelines for giving effective feedback:

1. Effective employee feedback is specific, not general. For example, say, "The report that you turned in yesterday had all of the necessary data we needed to make the decision to invest in the new venture." Don't say, "That was a good report."
2. Useful feedback always focuses on a specific behavior, not on a person or their intentions. For example, say, "When you send text messages during meetings, it is distracting to the team."
3. The best feedback is sincerely and honestly provided to help. For example, say, "I really want to help you improve by giving you these pointers on your presentation skills."
4. Successful feedback describes actions or behavior that the individual can do something about. For example, a person may not be able to change their personality trait such as being introverted. Focus on how they can contribute in other ways to team discussions.
5. Whenever possible, feedback that is requested is more powerful. Ask permission to provide feedback. Say, "Would you like some feedback on your sales performance this week? Is that okay with you?" This gives the person a feeling that they are in control of the feedback.
6. When you share information and specific observations, give feedback they can use. For example, say, "Here's what you might do differently when you speak to your employees."
7. Provide the feedback as soon as possible after the event happened. For example, say, "Do you have 10 minutes to talk about the presentation you just gave?"
8. Effective feedback involves what or how something was done, not why. For example, say, "Tell me what happened with the client you lost." or ask, "How could I have helped you avoid this situation?"
9. Check to make sure the other person understood what you communicated. For example, ask, "Can you tell me what I just told you?" Set a time to discuss the matter again.
10. Good feedback is consistent. For example, say, "This is not the first time we have encountered your rudeness to the secretary. Let's go over what we talked about regarding this matter last week."[53]

Reinforcement Theory

Learning Objective 10.5: Demonstrate understanding of positive reinforcement by providing an example.

Reinforcement theory is based on Thorndike's **law of effect**, which states that past actions that led to positive outcomes tend to be repeated, whereas past actions that led to negative outcomes will diminish.[54] The law of effect led to research that created a system known as **operant conditioning** (sometimes referred to as **reinforcement theory**).[55] In this approach to motivation, individual personality, thoughts, and attitudes are not considered as motivators of behavior. Instead, the emphasis in operant conditioning is on the environment.

The goal of reinforcement theory is to explain learned behavior. B. F. Skinner is the psychologist most associated with this approach. He conducted experiments with animals like rats and pigeons to understand how behavior could be shaped by setting up systems of rewards and punishments. This is known as **shaping**, in which closer and closer approximations of a desired behavior are rewarded. These rewards (or punishments) were contingent on the response of the animals he studied (probably the most well-recognized studies are those of rats who were taught to run mazes through the shaping of their behavior with pellets of food as rewards).

Reinforcers

Reinforcement is any event that strengthens or increases the behavior it follows. Skinner's research found there are **reinforcers** that increase behavior and those that decrease behavior.[56] The two kinds of reinforcement that *increase* behavior are as follows:

1. **Positive reinforcement** is a favorable event or outcome presented after the behavior (e.g., praise or a bonus).
2. **Negative reinforcement** is the removal of an unpleasant event or outcome after the display of a behavior (e.g., ending the daily criticism when an employee shows up for work on time).

Punishment

Punishment, in contrast, is the presentation of an adverse event or outcome that causes a *decrease* in the behavior it follows. There are two kinds of punishment:

1. **Punishment by application** is the presentation of an unpleasant event or outcome to weaken the response it follows (e.g., writing a letter to an employee's file for failing to meet a deadline).
2. **Punishment by removal** (also called extinction) is when a pleasant event or outcome is removed after a behavior occurs (e.g., withholding praise when an employee does not perform well).

CRITICAL THINKING QUESTIONS

Explain why punishment may not be the most effective way to motivate your employees. What would you do instead?

▼ FIGURE 10.10

Contingencies of Reinforcement

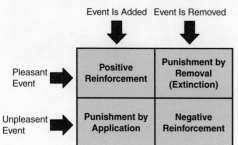

Source: Scandura, T.A. (2019). *Essentials of Organizational Behavior: An Evidence-Based Approach* p. 212. Thousand Oaks, CA: Sage.

A summary of these contingencies of reinforcement is shown in Figure 10.10. As the figure shows, it is important to consider whether the reward is applied or withheld and whether the event is pleasant or unpleasant. The previously given definitions and examples refer to the type of reward or punishment that is applied or removed. For example, a pleasant event that is applied would be a manager praising an employee when the employee completes an excellent project report (a positive reinforcement).

Schedules of Reinforcement

Skinner's research also found that how often a reward (or punishment) is applied also predicts learning and motivation. He referred to this as the schedules of reinforcement.[57] The first schedule is **continuous reinforcement** in which a specified behavior is rewarded or punished every time it occurs. This is not seen often in organizations; however, it is useful during the learning process (e.g., when an employee is learning to use a new computer program). In this example, the employee would be allowed to leave work 30 minutes early (a positive event) each time they complete a module of a computer training program successfully. Once the employee has attained an acceptable level of mastery, they are moved to a partial reinforcement schedule. For example, the employee is no longer rewarded or punished every time, but they are rewarded (punished) on a more random basis as described next.

As illustrated in Figure 10.11, the schedules of partial reinforcement are based on time (interval) or the number of times the response is given by the employee (ratio). Also, the schedule can be fixed or variable (random). These two dimensions result in four possible schedules of partial reinforcement as shown in the figure and described here.

Fixed-interval schedules are those where the first response is rewarded only after a specified amount of time has elapsed. This schedule causes high amounts of responding near the end of the interval. An example of this in a work setting is the way pay is typically disbursed—every two weeks or every month, for example. After a fixed amount of time, the employee receives a paycheck.

Variable-interval schedules occur when a response is rewarded after an unpredictable amount of time has passed. This schedule produces a slow, steady rate of response. An example of this would be bringing in donuts for breakfast once a week for employees but varying which day they are brought in (e.g., sometimes on Monday and sometimes Wednesday). The employees never know when they will be treated to donuts, so the element of surprise is motivating and they may come to work on time regularly so they don't miss out.

Gambling payouts follow a variable-ratio reinforcement schedule.

© antoniodiaz /Shutterstock

▼ FIGURE 10.11

Schedules of Partial Reinforcement

	Interval	Ratio
Fixed	Reinforced after a certain amount of time has passed	Reinforced after a certain number of responses have occurred
Variable (Random)	Reinforced after an average amount of time has passed	Reinforced after an average number of responses have occurred

Source: Scandura, T.A. (2019). *Essentials of Organizational Behavior: An Evidence-Based Approach* p. 213. Thousand Oaks, CA: Sage.

FACT OR FICTION?

Are There Benefits to Playing Video Games?

A study using a national sample[58] found that about 8% of video-game players aged 8 to 18 exhibited pathological patterns of play in video games: They spent twice as much time playing games compared with nonpathological gamers and received poorer grades in school. They also exhibited problems paying attention. Such studies have prompted the World Health Organization to propose a new mental disorder labeled "gaming disorder."[59]

Without question, video games are addicting. And principles of motivation explain why. Video games have reward systems that engage both intrinsic and extrinsic motivation. They are intrinsically enjoyable to play. In addition, gamers receive extrinsic rewards on a variable-ratio schedule for achieving goals or overcoming obstacles. For example, game players receive badges for attaining a level of competence in a game. The reward is not necessarily related to the game, but it serves as a signal to the player (and others) that the player has had success. Progress tracking is often enabled and guided by reward systems; progress toward an overall objective is mapped out by a sequence of intermediate goals. There has been much discussion of the potentially harmful effects of too much gaming on young people. But could there be a positive benefit from playing video games?

Researchers are using video games to help students learn. Gamification is "...using game-based mechanics, aesthetics and game thinking to engage people, motivate action, promote learning, and solve problems."[60] A research study of 100 undergraduate students[61] found that gamified learning interventions have a positive impact on student learning. The students participated in a competitive online game in which they offered contracts that had to be completed to receive virtual cash. The game created a market trading environment among the students in the game. To be successful, students had to search online for government and consulting reports about the national tax system that affected the success of

contracts. Successful contracts were rewarded with virtual cash that increased the students' portfolio. Unsuccessful trades resulted in the students losing their investments. Thus, the students received continuous feedback on the success of their decisions. After the game, students were tested on their knowledge of the national tax system. Overall, playing the game had an impact on learning about the tax system. However, the gains in learning due to the game varied depending on whether the student was motivated intrinsically or extrinsically—intrinsic motivation was more strongly related to learning than extrinsic. In other words, the fun of playing the game with others was more motivating than the "cash" they received.

Discussion Questions

1. What schedules of reinforcement are used in video games? How does this explain why they are so "addictive"?

2. Explain why intrinsic motivation was more related to participation in the game described and learning than extrinsic motivation (the amount of money earned in the game).

3. Do you think that gamification may be the future of learning? Explain your position.

Sources: Buckley, P., & Doyle, E. (2016). Gamification and student motivation, *Interactive Learning Environments, 24*(6), 1162–1175; Gentile, D. (2009). Pathological video-game use among youth ages 8 to 18: A national study. *Psychological Science, 20*(5), 594–602; Kapp, K. M. (2012). *The gamification of learning and instruction: Game-based methods and strategies for training and education.* San Francisco, CA: John Wiley; Lee, B. Y. (2017, December 24). Do you have gaming disorder? A newly recognized mental health condition. *Forbes.* Retrieved from https://www.forbes.com/sites/brucelee/2017/12/24/do-you-have-video-gaming-disorder-a-newly-recognized-mental-health-condition/#25fd2492316d.

Fixed-ratio schedules are those where a response is reinforced only after a specific number of responses. This schedule produces a high, steady rate of responding. An example of a fixed-ratio schedule would be payment to employees based on the number of items they produce (a piece-rate pay system). In piece-rate systems, the employee is paid for each article produced; for example, a worker sewing zippers into jeans is paid for each zipper correctly sewn in.

Variable-ratio schedules occur when a response is reinforced after an unpredictable number of responses. This schedule creates a high, steady rate of responding. Gambling and lottery games are good examples of a reward based on a variable-ratio schedule. This is why gambling results in such long-term and persistent behavior (it's the element of chance that motivates the behavior). In a work setting, this might be offering praise to an employee for good performance after one time and then again after four times and then another time after two times.

Partial schedules are more motivating than continuous reinforcement (e.g., the employee may become accustomed to praise from the leader, so praise loses its motivating power on behavior). Of the partial reinforcement schedules, research has demonstrated that the variable-ratio schedule of partial reinforcement produces the most persistent, long-term effects on behavior.[62] Receiving rewards in a random fashion tends to increase effort until the reward is received. This explains why playing video games is so addicting. See the Fact or Fiction? feature for a discussion of how video games are being used to enhance student learning.

As the previous examples indicate, reinforcement is used in organizations in a variety of ways to increase employee motivation and performance. It is also used to extinguish undesirable behaviors. Given the strong research base supporting the principles of reinforcement theory, it represents a powerful tool most leaders use to motivate performance.[63] The application of reinforcement theory in organizational behavior (OB) is known as **organizational behavior modification (OB Mod)**.

Organizational Behavior Modification

OB Mod has been employed to increase performance and reduce absenteeism. The first step is to pinpoint the specific behavior that needs to be changed. For example, coming to work on time every day is an example of a behavior that needs intervention if an employee is not doing it. Second, measure the baseline: How many days per month is the employee on time? Third, perform an **A-B-C analysis**, which answers the key questions shown in Figure 10.12. A-B-C stands for *antecedents*, *behavior*, and *consequences*:

- *Antecedents*—What is causing the behavior? Consider both internal and external factors.
- *Behavior*—What is the current behavior? What is the desired behavior?
- *Consequences*—What is currently reinforcing the behavior? What needs to be changed?

Fourth, develop an action plan based on reinforcement theory strategies to apply (using the contingencies of reinforcement and the schedules). Implement the plan and then evaluate the plan comparing the behavior to the baseline (after compared to before). This will provide feedback, and the plan may need to be changed or another behavior targeted for the future. A comprehensive review of OB Mod interventions[64] stressed the importance of following up after interventions to ensure the long-term durability of the intervention. The authors also concluded that follow-up is needed to provide the feedback necessary to adjust the intervention if warranted. Leaders use the principles of OB Mod to change employee behaviors by meeting with followers to discuss their performance. In some cases, this discussion takes place during performance management reviews.

▼ FIGURE 10.12

A-B-C Analysis

Time	Antecedent	Behavior	Consequence
	What comes before the behavior?	The specific behavior	What happened after the behavior?
		Paint a very clear picture of what happened	
			What did I use as a consequence?
	Where was it?		
	Who was there?		
	What was happening?		What did I say?

Source: Functional behavioral assessment and functional analysis. Retrieved from https://www.slideshare.net/jmcullenbsu/fba-and-fa-powerpoint.

FIGURE 10.13

Applied Behavior Modification Example

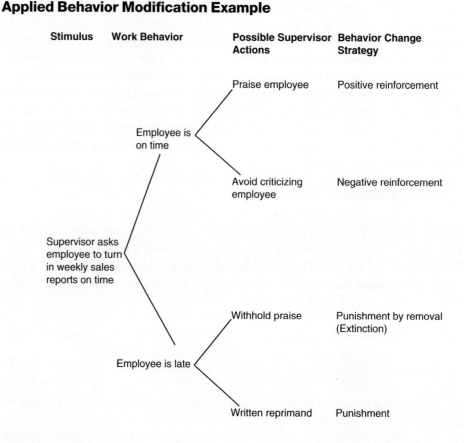

An example of applied OB Mod for an employee who turns in weekly sales reports late is shown in Figure 10.13. As this example shows, the specific behavior targeted is that the employee completes and turns in the weekly sales report each Friday (say, by 5:00 p.m. each Friday). If the employee is on time, the supervisor can praise them (positive reinforcement) or withhold criticism (this only works if the supervisor has consistently criticized the employee's late reports often, of course). If the employee is late, the objective is to decrease the behavior, so the supervisor can withhold praise to produce extinction of the behavior (punishment by removal), or write a reprimand and put it in the employee's file, which is unpleasant (punishment). Of course, the supervisor can use more than one behavior change strategy and should eventually move the employee to a variable-interval or variable-ratio schedule (i.e., apply or remove the reinforcement more randomly) once the employee is consistently submitting the weekly sales reports on time.

Ethical Concerns in OB Mod

Some critics have argued that the use of behavior modification in humans in the work setting is dehumanizing.[65] In essence, the ability to manipulate a person's behavior through rewards and punishments undermines individual autonomy, which is an important component of the treatment of human beings at work.[66] Others argued that the provision of contingent rewards is basically bribery, which is unethical.[67] Another major criticism of behavior modification is that it ignores an employee's thoughts and feelings during the process.[68] Like goal setting, the pursuit of rewards may lead to unethical behavior by employees. For example, an employee with the attitude of "doing what it takes to get the job done" in order to receive a bonus may engage in behavior that violates ethical norms.[69] There is no question that behavior modification is a powerful tool, and it is here to stay as part of organizational reward systems. Care should be taken in the implementation of behavior modification so that ethical issues are taken into consideration.

In addition to ethics concerns, the use of OB Mod may also threaten employee's sense of being treated fairly by managers if rewards and punishments are administered arbitrarily. Employees want to be treated fairly by their managers,[70] and motivation will break down if they are not. The next section reviews research on organizational justice, with a focus on both what people receive (outcomes) as well as how they are treated (processes).[71]

Organizational Justice

Learning Objective 10.6: Explain why fairness matters to employees.

Equity Theory

Can you recall a time when you didn't get the grade you thought you deserved on a course paper? People become unmotivated when they feel they are not rewarded fairly. Equity theory suggests that people lose motivation when they feel that what they give and what they get is not equal. According to the theory, a person (the focal person, or FP) compares themselves to a comparison other (CO) such as a peer. They compare their inputs (skills, abilities, effort) to the peer's inputs and outcomes (e.g., a merit raise). Three situations are possible when employees do this comparison:

- **Equity**—The inputs and outcomes for the FP equal the inputs and outcomes for the other (CO). This means that the FP puts in effort and receives a certain pay raise. This is compared with a CO who puts in more effort and receives a higher pay raise. There is balance because the FP recognizes that their peer CO works harder and gets a higher raise.
- **Underpayment inequity**—The input and outcomes for the FP are *lower* than the inputs and outcomes for the CO. For example, the FP views the ratio of their inputs and outcomes as less than the CO. The FP realizes that they are "underpaid," and this causes stress for the FP. This stress causes the FP to do something about the situation. The FP may become demotivated (reduce inputs) to bring the ratio back to equity. If the situation persists, they may even find another job that pays better.
- **Overpayment inequity**—The inputs and outcomes for the FP are *higher* than the inputs and outcomes for the peer CO. The FP compares their inputs to outcomes and views their ratio of inputs to outcomes as *higher* than their peer. The FP realizes that they are being "overpaid" for their contributions compared to their CO. This situation is interesting because while we might expect the FP to work harder, this typically does not happen. People are more likely to distort the perceptions of inputs and/or outcomes to justify or rationalize their relative overpayment inequity. For example, they may justify their higher pay by changing their views of inputs (higher skills) or downgrading the contributions of their peer.

Employees want these ratios to be equal or in balance as depicted in Figure 10.14. Inequitable comparisons affect employee attitudes, such as job satisfaction.[72] For example, in one study, employees in an underpayment condition engaged in theft to compensate for the inequity.[73] Also, employees who experience unfair situations don't help their coworkers out (organizational citizenship).[74] There is strong research support that indicates that perceptions of fairness affect motivation. When people experience something unfair in terms of what they receive at work, it creates tension that they need to resolve.[75] Research on equity (or distributive justice) was later expanded to include other forms of justice that help explain how employees come to view the workplace as fair.

FIGURE 10.14

Equity Theory of Motivation

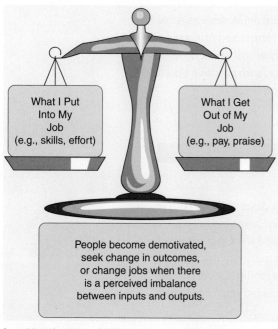

Source: Adapted from Adams, J. S. (1965). Inequity in social exchange. In L. Berkowitz, *Advances in experimental social psychology* (Vol. 2, pp. 267–299). New York, NY: Academic Press.

Organizational Justice

The need for fairness is a universal motive.[76] This need translates into the workplace. For example, an employee may feel that they did not receive a fair pay raise, given their efforts. Employee concerns for fairness permeate the workplace, and managers need to understand how followers evaluate whether or not what they are receiving is fair. There are three areas in which people seek fairness in organizations. The first area is the outcomes they receive (distributive justice), which is grounded in equity theory. **Distributive justice** can apply to any work-related outcome, from how much employees are paid to how work schedules are determined. The second area is **procedural justice**, which refers to the fairness of procedures used to determine how outcomes are allocated. At the heart of procedural justice are concepts of providing voice or representation in decision making, consistency of decision standards, and accurate, unbiased decision criteria. The third part of organizational justice is **interactional justice**, which refers to how decisions are communicated to employees. For example, employees want to be treated with respect during their performance evaluations.[77] As summarized in Figure 10.15, these three domains of organizational justice are all related and combine to produce an employee's overall perception of whether or not they are being treated fairly.[78]

CRITICAL THINKING QUESTIONS

Which component of organizational justice do you feel is most important to employees? Are they more concerned with what they receive or how they are treated? Explain your position.

FIGURE 10.15

Dimensions of Organizational Justice

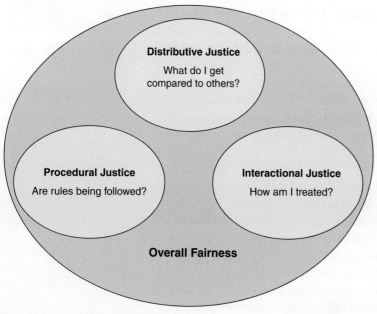

Source: Based on Ambrose, M. L., & Schminke, M. (2009). The role of overall justice judgments in organizational justice research: A test of mediation. *Journal of Applied Psychology, 94,* 491–500.

Managerial Implications

Motivating employees is a key aspect of a manager's job. This chapter covered the essentials that managers need to know. The key takeaway points are:

- The motivation process involves energizing, directing, and sustaining behavior. All motivation theories can be placed into this general framework. Need theories explain what energizes behavior. Process theories examine how behavior is directed through expectations and goals. For example, the direction of behavior can be accomplished through setting SMART goals. Finally, sustaining behavior can be achieved by setting up reward contingencies using reinforcement theory.
- Theories of motivation involve feedback. Employees need to know how they are

doing in terms of meeting their goals. Feedback on performance is needed for employees to correct their behaviors, and this chapter provided specific guidelines for giving effective feedback.

- Predominant need theories are Maslow's hierarchy and Alderfer's ERG theory. These needs are similar in that they address higher-level needs that are social and growth related.

- Expectancy theory predicts how much effort employees will put into their work. The values they want (e.g., pay or time off from work) have valences. The expectancy is the degree to which an employee believes that if they try, they will attain high performance. The instrumentality is how much the employee believes that performance will lead to rewards. Managers can motivate employees by determining what they value and providing it (valences). Next, managers can increase the employees' belief in themselves—that they can achieve high performance. Finally, managers must fairly and consistently reward employees to strengthen the instrumentalities.

- Goal-setting theory is one of the best-researched theories in management. To be motivating, needs must be specific, measurable, actionable, relevant, and time-bound. These motivating properties can be remembered with the acronym, SMART.

- Behavior modification principles are used pervasively in organizational reward systems known as OB Mod, and they are based on B. F. Skinner's research on reinforcement theory. By knowing behavioral contingencies and schedules of rewards, managers can design reward systems that motivate employees to high, consistent performance. Caveats are noted for OB Mod, which must be implemented with consideration of ethics.

- When situations are unfair in organizations, employees can become demotivated. Equity theory explains how employees compare their inputs and outcomes to others to decide if they are being treated fairly (also known as distributive justice). Other forms of organizational justice are important as well. Procedural justice has to do with whether the organization's procedures and policies are fair and followed by managers. Interactional justice is how employees are treated with respect and dignity by their managers. All three forms of justice combine to determine whether employees feel they are being treated fairly.

KEY TERMS

A-B-C analysis 315

candle problem 297

continuous reinforcement 313

distributive justice 318

Duncker's candle problem 297

equity 317

esteem needs 301

existence needs 303

expectancy 306

expectancy theory 306

extrinsic rewards 300

feedback 311

fixed-interval schedules 313

fixed-ratio schedules 314

growth needs 303

hierarchy of needs 301

hygienes 304

instrumentality 306

interactional justice 318

intrinsic rewards 300

law of effect 311

motivation 299

motivator-hygiene theory 304

motivators 304

need for achievement (nACH) 302

need for affiliation (nAFF) 303

need for power (nPOW) 303

negative reinforcement 312

operant conditioning 312

organizational behavior modification (OB Mod) 315

overpayment inequity 317

physiological needs 301

positive reinforcement 312

procedural justice 318

prosocial motivation 300

punishment by application 312

punishment by removal 312

reinforcement theory 312

reinforcers 312

TOOLKIT

Activity 10.1

What Do Workers Want From Their Jobs?

This activity aims to help identify what motivates people at work. Study the following table. Rank each item under the column titled "Individual Factors" from 1 to 10, with 1 being the most important and 10 being the least important. Then join a group of three or four other students and put the average rankings of the group in the column, "Group Factors." To compute the average ranking, add together the scores of each member and divide by the number of people in the group.

Individual Factors	Group Factors	What Do People Want From Their Jobs?
_____	_____	Promotion in the Company
_____	_____	Tactful Discipline
_____	_____	Job Security
_____	_____	Help With Personal Problems
_____	_____	Personal Loyalty of Supervisor
_____	_____	High Wages
_____	_____	Full Appreciation of Work Done
_____	_____	Good Working Conditions
_____	_____	Feeling of Being In on Things
_____	_____	Interesting Work

This same scale has been given to thousands of workers across the country. Their ranking is as follows:

Supervisors ranked the items in this order:

1. High Wages
2. Job Security
3. Promotion in the Company
4. Good Working Conditions
5. Interesting Work
6. Personal Loyalty of Supervisor
7. Tactful Discipline
8. Full Appreciation of Work Done
9. Help With Personal Problems
10. Feeling of Being In on Things

However, when employees were given the same exercise, their rankings tended to follow this pattern:

1. Full Appreciation of Work Done
2. Feeling of Being In on Things
3. Help With Personal Problems
4. Job Security
5. High Wages
6. Interesting Work
7. Promotion in the Company
8. Personal Loyalty of Supervisor
9. Good Working Conditions
10. Tactful Discipline

Discussion Questions

1. In comparing the different ratings, what might account for the different opinions?
2. What might be the cause of the supervisors' rankings being so different from the employees' rankings?
3. If this survey was given to your department, what would the results be?

Sources: "What do People Want from Their Jobs?" The Performance Juxtaposition Site, http://www.nwlink.com/~donclark/leader/want_job.html#sthash.86o3taW7.dpuf. Reprinted by permission of Don Clark.

Activity 10.2

Work Values Checklist

Whether we realize it or not, often our career choice is based on values rather than the work. Values are the beliefs, attitudes, and judgments we prize. Are you aware of your values? Do you act on them? Use this checklist to get a better idea of what's important to you. It's divided into three categories related to intrinsic, extrinsic, and lifestyle values.

Intrinsic Values

These are the intangible rewards—those related to motivation and satisfaction at work on a daily basis. They provide the inner satisfaction and motivation that make people say, "I love getting up and going to work."

How important (on a scale of 1 to 5, with 5 being most important) are these intrinsic values to you?

1. _____ Have variety and change at work
2. _____ Be an expert
3. _____ Work on the frontiers of knowledge
4. _____ Help others
5. _____ Help society
6. _____ Experience adventure and excitement
7. _____ Take risks or have physical challenges
8. _____ Feel respected for your work
9. _____ Compete with others
10. _____ Have lots of public contact
11. _____ Influence others
12. _____ Engage in precision work
13. _____ Gain a sense of achievement
14. _____ Have opportunities to express your creativity
15. _____ Work for a good cause

Extrinsic Values

These are the tangible rewards or conditions you find at work, including the physical setting, job titles, benefits, and earnings or earning potential. Extrinsic values often trap people into staying at jobs they don't like, saying, "I just can't give up my paycheck." These values are commonly called "golden handcuffs."

How important (on a scale of 1 to 5, with 5 being most important) are these golden handcuffs to you?

1. _____ Have control, power, or authority
2. _____ Travel often
3. _____ Be rewarded monetarily
4. _____ Be an entrepreneur
5. _____ Work as a team
6. _____ Work in a fast-paced environment
7. _____ Have regular work hours
8. _____ Set your own hours/have flexibility
9. _____ Be wealthy
10. _____ Have prestige or social status
11. _____ Have intellectual status
12. _____ Have recognition through awards, honors, or bonuses
13. _____ Wear a uniform
14. _____ Work in an aesthetically pleasing environment
15. _____ Work on the edge, in a high-risk environment

Lifestyle Values

These are the personal values associated with how and where you want to live, how you choose to spend your leisure time, and how you feel about money.

How important (on a scale of 1 to 5, with 5 being most important) are these lifestyle values to you?

1. _____ Save money
2. _____ Vacation at expensive resorts
3. _____ Have access to educational/cultural opportunities
4. _____ Live close to sports or recreational facilities
5. _____ Be active in your community
6. _____ Entertain at home
7. _____ Be involved in politics
8. _____ Live simply
9. _____ Spend time with family
10. _____ Live in a big city
11. _____ Live abroad
12. _____ Have time for spirituality or personal growth
13. _____ Be a homeowner
14. _____ Live in a rural setting
15. _____ Have fun in your life and at work

Discussion Questions

1. Prioritize your list. Write down all of the values you rated as 5s. If you have less than five, add the values you rated as 4s to the list. Which values are most important to you?
2. Which of the three categories is most important to you? Consider how each is reflected in the work you would like to do in the future. What seems to fit? For example, does "Be wealthy" conflict with "Spend time with family"?
3. If there is no overlap or compatibility between categories, or if everything is important to you, then reprioritize your list by selecting your top 10 values. Then narrow that list down to the five values you absolutely need both on and off the job.
4. Write two or three sentences describing or summarizing how your values will translate into your ideal job. Knowing what's important will help you prepare for your next interview or help you find increased satisfaction with the job you have.

As you follow the process, if you notice that what motivates you is actually a reward or already part of your lifestyle, it means you're living your values.

Source: Adapted from Bortz, D. (n.d.). Work values checklist. Retrieved from http://career-advice.monster.com/job-search/career-assessment/work-values-checklist/article.aspx.

Case Study 10.1

KPMG: Motivating Employees With a Deeper Sense of Purpose

KPMG, the audit, tax, and advisory firm, has long had high levels of employee job satisfaction. In 2019, the company again made *Fortune*'s "Best Companies to Work For" list and 89% of their employees said it is a great place to work. Why do employees feel this way?

The firm studied the question of why their employee morale is so high because they want to maintain their high motivation. Surveys indicated that employees felt best about the firm when the experienced a higher sense of purpose. As you may recall, the opening vignette of this chapter discussed the importance of purpose for intrinsic motivation. KPMG started their Higher Purpose initiative, an organization-wide effort to strengthen their employees' pride in what they do. The firm wanted to learn more about their employees' higher purpose and meaning in their work in relation to both clients and communities. Although KPMG had always been a purpose-driven organization, they had not previously focused on directly celebrating this strong sense of purpose among employees. The initiative brought answers to the question, "What do you do at KPMG?"

Analysis of employee surveys revealed that one survey item was strongly related to employee engagement, retention, and pride: "I feel like my job has special meaning and is not just a job." KPMG then asked its employees what made their job meaningful. One woman said, "I keep jobs in the U.S.A." A man answered, "I power innovation." And a team said, "We restore neighborhoods." The firm had a goal of gathering 10,000 stories and ended up with more than 40,000. Employee stories about the purpose in their work were built into an advertising campaign that included print, digital, and live communications about the great work KPMG employees were doing.

This company shows that purpose-driven work motivates employees to give their best. Research shows that employees who have a social impact are more satisfied at work.

This is known as prosocial motivation, which is the desire to expend effort to benefit other people. It is related to intrinsic motivation and is a stable individual difference, which means some people are more prosocially motivated than others. In other words, they have empathy and want to help. Their focus is on promoting the welfare of others.

KPMG delved deep into understanding the relationship between purpose and motivation. A 2015 *Harvard Business Review* article describes how the firm interviewed hundreds of employees, asking questions like, "How does KPMG operate when we are at our best?" and "What is unique about our firm's culture?" A few themes emerged, which resulted in a new purpose statement: "Inspire Confidence. Empower Change." More importantly, KPMG's research found that leaders played an important role in communicating purpose. Having leaders talk about purposeful work had a significant impact on their employees' sense of company pride and work satisfaction. The graph in Figure 10.16 shows the differences between people whose boss talked about purpose (the blue line) and people whose boss did not (the gray line). As you can see, the boss reinforcing the message of purpose in work was related to KPMG employees' feeling that it is a great place to work and their sense of pride. Also, purpose was related to lower thoughts of quitting.

▼ FIGURE 10.16

Higher Purpose Research Findings at KPMG

Communicating Higher Purpose Raises Engagement and Morale

Employees whose leaders talk about purpose are approximately 30–50 points higher on key items than those whose leaders do not discuss it. Here are some key areas:

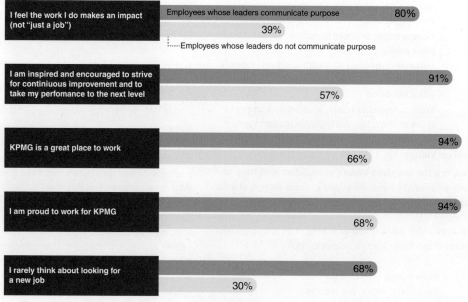

Source: re:Work. (n.d.). KPMG: Motivating employees through a deeper sense of purpose. Retrieved from https://rework.withgoogle.com/case-studies/KPMG-purpose/.

In a group of employees who claimed that their leaders discussed purpose, 94% said KPMG is a great place to work and also said they were proud to work for KPMG. In comparison, only 66% of employees who felt their leaders didn't discuss purpose agreed KPMG is a great place to work and just 68% were proud to work there. Those whose felt their leaders did not talk about purpose were three times more likely to report that they were thinking about looking for another job. The turnover rate in these two groups was dramatically different: there was a 5.6% attrition rate for those individuals whose leaders talked about purpose versus 9.1% among those whose leaders did not. It was also found that employees whose leaders communicated about purpose were significantly more motivated to strive for continuous improvement and high performance than colleagues whose leaders failed to discuss this important topic. And these differences hold steady across generations.

Discussion Questions

1. Why do you think that having a leader who communicates a sense of purpose in the work increases employee motivation?
2. The strongest relationships of a leader communicating purpose were for employees feeling that KPMG is a great place to work and feeling a sense of pride in working there. Why do you think these were the most related to purpose?
3. The research found that the motivation effect of having a sense of purpose in work holds steady across generations. Did this surprise you? Would you expect that millennials would be more or less motivated by a sense of purpose? Explain your reasoning.

Sources: *Fortune*. (2019). Best companies to work for. Retrieved from https://www.greatplacetowork.com/certified-company/1000377; Grant, A. M. (2008). Does intrinsic motivation fuel the prosocial fire? Motivational synergy in predicting persistence, performance, and productivity. *Journal of Applied Psychology*, *93*(1), 48–58; KPMG. (n.d.). KPMG purpose. Retrieved from https://advisory.kpmg.us/insights/future-hr/future-hr-purpose-culture/kpmg-purpose.html; Pfau, B. N. (2015, October 6). How an accounting firm convinced its employees they could change the world. *Harvard Business Review*. Retrieved from https://hbr.org/2015/10/how-an-accounting-firm-convinced-its-employees-they-could-change-the-world; re:Work. (n.d.). Motivating employees with a deeper sense of purpose. Retrieved from https://rework.withgoogle.com/case-studies/KPMG-purpose/.

Self-Assessment 10.1

Maslow's Hierarchy of Needs

This self-assessment exercise identifies your scores for each need in Maslow's hierarchy of needs. The goal of this assessment is for you to learn about your general assumptions about yourself and to understand how this may affect your style as a manager. There are no right or wrong answers, and this is not a test. You don't have to share your results with others unless you wish to do so.

Part I. Self-Assessment

Instructions: Circle the response that best describes how satisfied you are with this aspect of your life.

I am completely satisfied with . . .

Statements	Strongly Disagree	Disagree	Neutral	Agree	Strongly Agree
1. The quality of food that I eat every day.	1	2	3	4	5
2. The quality of the house/apartment I am living in.	1	2	3	4	5
3. The amount of rapport I share with the people I know.	1	2	3	4	5
4. The admiration given to me by others.	1	2	3	4	5
5. Being totally comfortable with all facets of my personality.	1	2	3	4	5
6. The quality of the water I drink every day.	1	2	3	4	5
7. The safety of my neighborhood.	1	2	3	4	5
8. The intimacy I share with my immediate family.	1	2	3	4	5
9. How much other people respect me as a person.	1	2	3	4	5

(Continued)

(Continued)

Statements	Strongly Disagree	Disagree	Neutral	Agree	Strongly Agree
10. Being the person I always wanted to be.	1	2	3	4	5
11. The amount of cooling I have when the weather is hot.	1	2	3	4	5
12. How secure I am from disasters.	1	2	3	4	5
13. The emotional support I receive from my friends.	1	2	3	4	5
14. The high esteem that other people have for me.	1	2	3	4	5
15. Completely accepting all aspects of myself.	1	2	3	4	5
16. The quality of sleep I get to feel fully refreshed.	1	2	3	4	5
17. My financial security.	1	2	3	4	5
18. The enjoyment I share with associates.	1	2	3	4	5
19. How much respect I have for myself.	1	2	3	4	5
20. Actually living up to all my capabilities.	1	2	3	4	5
21. The amount of exercise I get to keep me healthy.	1	2	3	4	5
22. My ability to get money whenever I need it.	1	2	3	4	5
23. The affection shown to me by my friends.	1	2	3	4	5
24. My sense of self-worth.	1	2	3	4	5
25. Living my life to the fullest.	1	2	3	4	5

Part II. Scoring and Interpretation

In Part I, you rated yourself on 25 questions. Add the numbers you circled in each of the columns to derive your score for each of Maslow's hierarchy of needs.

Physiological	Safety	Social	Esteem	Self-Actualization
1. _____	2. _____	3. _____	4. _____	5. _____
6. _____	7. _____	8. _____	9. _____	10. _____
11. _____	12. _____	13. _____	14. _____	15. _____
16. _____	17. _____	18. _____	19. _____	20. _____
21. _____	22. _____	23. _____	24. _____	25. _____
Total_____	Total_____	Total_____	Total_____	Total_____

The following are examples of needs in Maslow's hierarchy.

- *Physiological needs*—air, food, drink, shelter, warmth, sex, sleep.
- *Safety needs*—protection from elements, security, order, law, stability, freedom from fear.
- *Social needs*—friendship, intimacy, trust, acceptance, receiving and giving affection and love, affiliating, being part of a group (family, friends, work).
- *Esteem needs*—two categories: (i) esteem for oneself (dignity, achievement, mastery, independence) and (ii) the desire for reputation or respect from others (status, prestige).

- *Self-actualization needs*—realizing personal potential, self-fulfillment, seeking personal growth and peak experiences, a desire to become everything one is capable of becoming.

Discussion Questions

1. Which of Maslow's needs are the strongest for you? Were you surprised by your scores?
2. Do you feel that having a strong need at one level reduces the needs at the next-higher level? Explain.

3. Do you think that it is important for a manager to be self-actualized? Why or why not?

Sources: Maslow, A. H. (1987). *Motivation and personality* (3rd ed.). Delhi, India: Pearson Education; assessment adapted from Taormina, R. J., & Gao, J. H. (2013). Maslow and the motivation hierarchy: Measuring satisfaction of the needs. *American Journal of Psychology, 126*(2), 155–177.

Get the tools you need to sharpen your study skills. SAGE edge offers a robust online environment featuring an impressive array of free tools and resources. Access practice quizzes, eFlashcards, video, and multimedia at **edge.sagepub.com/scanduragower**.

CHAPTER 11

MANAGING TEAMS

CHAPTER LEARNING OBJECTIVES

After studying this chapter, you should be able to:

11.1 Explain the difference between a working group and a team.

11.2 Develop an example of how a team charter helps a team meet its goals.

11.3 Describe the five stages of team development.

11.4 Provide examples of team effectiveness.

11.5 Describe the symptoms of groupthink.

11.6 Understand the advantages and disadvantages of team decision-making.

Get the edge on your studies at **edge.sagepub.com/scanduragower.**

- Take the chapter quiz
- Review key terms with eFlashcards
- Explore multimedia resources, SAGE readings, and more!

When Teamwork Isn't Fair

Have you ever been on a team in which some members slacked off and did not pull their weight? In other words, did you do all of the work on a class team project, and the slacking members got an A? This is known as social loafing. Social loafing is the number one reason why students don't want to work on team projects—it's just not fair. A study was conducted[1] to investigate the causes of social loafing in student teams. Researchers found that the incidence of social loafing increases with the scope of the project and the size of the student team. Social loafing affected students' satisfaction with team members' contributions and the perceived fairness of the project grade. This study also found that there are ways to reduce social loafing, and these will be discussed later in this chapter. Social loafers are "invisible students." But they are not the only students you will meet in team projects. Teamwork isn't always pleasant. However, your team projects are providing you with a realistic view of the types of people you may meet in the workplace.

Students You Meet in Team Projects

In a *FastWeb* article,[2] Elizabeth Hoyt writes, "The truth is these group exercises are also exercises in life because, in the workplace, you're going to experience the same exact types of people." She refers to these problematic team members as the invisible student, the silent student, the procrastinator, the control freak, and our personal favorite, the person who likes to overpromise and underdeliver. Read her descriptions below and think about whether you have you ever worked with one of these group members or, perhaps more importantly, whether you have ever been one of them. Also think about how you have or how you could try to improve your working relationships with each type of team member.

The Invisible Student

These are the social loafers. You have asked your professor three times if they are actually still on your team because you never see them. Your professor swears that they are actually in your class, but she admits she hasn't seen them in class either. To make sure their name is still on your final project paper, they will answer an email now and then. They are vague and don't commit to showing up at team meetings. You and the other team members don't count on them and assign their work to others.

The Silent Student

This person probably attends all of your team meetings but says nothing. They really have no opinion on how the project is going and don't volunteer to help. What's interesting is that this silence doesn't seem to be attributed to shyness or an introverted personality but rather to disinterest or laziness. Be on the lookout for the person texting during the first team meeting—that's your clue.

The Procrastinator

They offer to take on tasks but they don't answer emails when you follow up. They wait until hours before the assignment is due to start the task and, of course, don't get it done very well. They give the appearance of doing the work, but you have a sense that you can't trust them. Everyone ends of scrambling an hour before the assignment is due to clean up their mess. The good thing about this person, unlike the invisible student and the silent one, is that they seem to care about the assignment and accept some of the workload—they just don't get it done on time. This causes the team to stress out at the last minute.

Procrastinators wait until the last minute to get the work done.

©iStockphoto.com/CJMGrafx

The Control Freak

You'll definitely recognize this person because they'll be the one in constant contact via all communication channels: email, Facebook, Twitter, and cell phone. They take charge at the beginning of the project, create an outline, and collect everyone's contact information. They assign who is going to do what on the project. The good news is that they care about the quality of the final project. The bad news is that they don't trust anyone to do the work as well as they think they can. They often end up doing most of the work. However, other team members resent not being allowed to participate and being micromanaged through the process.

The Teammate Who Overpromises and Underdelivers

This team member talks big and promises to deliver the best writing, graphics, analytics, and other key aspects of the project. They have a friend of a friend of a friend who can get you into a video studio to record your own vignettes for the presentation. No, you can't all meet this friend, just trust that she will make it happen. This team member is a classic overpromiser, underdeliverer (OPUD). In most cases, the promises are well intended but they are too much to deliver in the time allowed, and they will fall short. However, the real problem is that your group structured the project around these promises and you are left with big holes when they don't happen. On presentation day, OPUD shows up with no video ("My friend got the flu and I couldn't sit in the studio, but I tried so hard to make this happen. I am sorry, guys."). She does bring a flip chart with some marker drawings on it ("Looks great—it has color after all, right guys?"), and her proudest achievement is a PowerPoint slide with some clip art in it ("The clip art really adds interest, doesn't it?").

Sources: Aggarwal, P., & O'Brien, C. L. (2008). Social loafing on group projects: Structural antecedents and effect on student satisfaction. *Journal of Marketing Education, 30*(3), 255–264; and Hoyt, E. (2016). The 5 students you meet in group projects. *FastWeb*. Retrieved from https://www.fastweb.com/student-life/articles/the-5-students-you-meet-in-group-projects.

▼ FIGURE 11.0

Textbook Organization

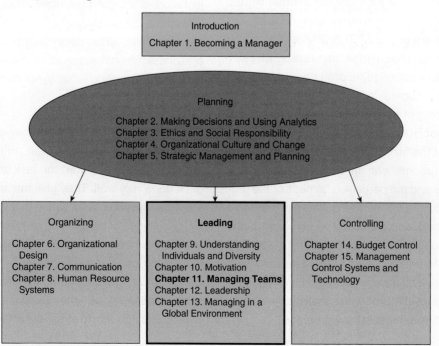

A lot of courses require students to complete team projects. Professors assign team projects because organizations want to hire graduates with teamwork experience. Let's start learning about teams and how to work with the types of students we will meet in them.

What Is a Team?

A common definition of a team is "a group of individuals who work together to produce products or deliver services for which they are mutually accountable."[3] Basically, a team has two or more people who share a specific goal, and they work together to attain it. The team having a common goal is important, since not all groups of people share a common goal. Managers must understand the difference between a group and team, and this will be discussed next.

Group Versus Team

Group and **team** don't mean the same thing. A group is a number of people located near one another or part of the same classification. A useful way to think about the difference is that groups and teams lie along a continuum based on how much team members depend on each other.[4] For example, a person can be part of a group but not depend on others to produce a product or service. A working group interacts primarily to share information with other members (e.g., members of a work group attend a monthly staff meeting and share what they are working on). They are not responsible for shared work (i.e., they are not interdependent). In other words, their individual contributions can just be added together. Members of a team, on the other hand, depend on one another to do their work. They must interact to create something that no one person on the team could create.

Teams produce something more than just adding up the contributions of individual team members and this is known as **synergy**. Synergy is defined as group performance that exceeds the performance of the best group member when working alone.[5] The gains from synergy come from social support from other team members, the perceived importance of the team goal, the inclusion of experts for both task and team processes, the use of multiple perspectives and information, team learning, and members identifying with the team.[6] One review concludes: "Just by putting a few people together to accomplish task(s) does not result in teamwork. Whether a team would lead to synergy or negative outcomes largely depends on the way it is managed."[7] Creating such synergy triggers performance to levels that exceed what can be expected based on the individual team members' capabilities alone. Some of the differences between groups and teams are summarized in Table 11.1.

CRITICAL THINKING QUESTIONS

> What different task and team process skill sets do you think are needed for a team to experience synergy? Provide an example of a team that has synergy.

▼ TABLE 11.1

Differences Between Groups and Teams

Groups	Teams
• Work on individual goals	• Work on team goals
• Monthly staff meetings	• Frequent team meetings
• Members are independent	• Members are interdependent
• Members accountable to the manager	• Members accountable to team
• Performance measured by individual output (sum of individual contributions)	• Performance greater than sum of individual contributions (synergy)
• Effectiveness defined by the manager	• Effectiveness defined by the team

There are different types of teams in people's lives. Many of these teams relate to the workplace and these will be reviewed next.

Types of Teams

In organizations, **formal teams** are created by the organization (e.g., a sales team), and other **informal teams** are created by workers (e.g., a friendship group of employees who go to happy hour after work each Friday).[8] Workers are more satisfied at work when they have friendships with coworkers. Research conducted by Gallup found that close work friendships boost employee satisfaction by 50% and people with a best friend at work are seven times more likely to engage fully in their work.[9] These informal groups may focus on issues that run counter to the organizational objectives or they may improve morale. Examples of informal work groups are groups organized to do charity work or run in 5K corporate races.[10] Sometimes friendship groups form in which members provide social support to one another and engage in social activities after work. One review of team types identified 42 different types of teams that have been studied in the organizational sciences. These types included student teams, project teams, decision-making teams, ad hoc teams, cross-functional teams, self-managing teams, and top management teams, to name a few.[11]

Teams in organizations are defined by their goals. An in-depth study of teams[12] found that formal groups used in organizations have different goals:

- **Problem-resolution teams:** the goal of problem-resolution teams is to resolve problems on an ongoing basis, by enabling trust and focusing on issues.
- **Creative teams:** the goal of creative teams is to create something, and such teams emphasize autonomy and exploration.
- **Tactical teams:** the goal of tactical teams is to execute well-defined plans by having high-level tasks and ensuring that team members understand their roles.

Different types of organizational teams and examples are shown in Table 11.2. Some teams provide advice, such as committees and advisory councils, and are known as **advice/involvement teams**. These teams may also be **committees** that recommend solutions to a specific problem. When these teams include members from different functional areas of the organization, they are called **cross-functional teams**. Other teams focus on the core mission

▼ TABLE 11.2

Types of Formal Teams, Team Processes, and Typical Outputs

Type/Examples	Skill Differentiation	External Integration	Work Cycles	Typical Outputs
Advice/involvement Committees Advisory councils	Low	Low	Brief or long, single cycle	Decisions Suggestions Proposals
Production/service Assembly teams Flight attendant crews Data processing teams	Low	High	Repeated, continuous, brief	Retail sales Customer service Repairs
Project/development Research teams Engineering teams Task forces	High	Low	Differs by project, single cycle	Plans Designs Reports
Action/integration Negotiating teams Sports teams Surgery teams	High	High	Brief performance events, often repeated	Lawsuits Concerts Surgery

Source: Adapted from Sundstrom, E., De Meuse, K. P., & Futrell, D. (1990). Work teams: Applications and effectiveness. *American Psychologist, 45*(2), 120–133. p. 125.

of the organization in producing products or delivering services. Such teams are known as **production/service teams** and include assembly teams and flight attendant crews, as examples. This type of team is also known as a **command group** or **traditional work group**. In some cases, production/service teams have managerial responsibilities and these are known as **management teams**, which provide direction for their organizational department, and they have hierarchical rank over the unit.

Another team type that is formally created by the organization are **project/development teams**, where the goal is to invent new products or services and include research and development (R&D) teams and **task forces**. Task forces are temporary teams that focus on solving problems. Finally, teams are sometimes created to put on events or resolve disputes and such teams are called **action/negotiation teams**. Examples of these teams are sports teams and negotiating teams. Teams that interact through electronic means more than face-to-face are called **virtual teams**. Virtual teams present challenges to managers, and these will be covered in more detail later in this chapter in the section on team challenges.

Some organizations have experimented with allowing production/service teams to have managerial responsibilities and these are known as **self-managed work teams (SMWTs)**. In a self-managed team, the members make their own decisions about the control and execution of their daily work. They are fully responsible for the output of the team. Organizations have experienced positive results from self-managed teams, including higher productivity, quality of work, and improved safety.[13]

As indicated in Table 11.2, this framework also shows the team processes that can be expected in different types of teams. **Differentiation** refers to the different types of skill sets that are needed on the team. **External integration** refers to the degree to which the team must interact with other teams or those outside of the organization, including suppliers, managers, peers, staff, and customers.

Work cycles or time spent in team activities also vary in different types of teams (brief, repeated events or longer-term development). The outputs expected from the teams also vary depending on the type of team. Advice/involvement teams produce decisions or suggestions. Production/service teams produce the actual products or deliver the services. Project/development teams develop research reports and designs for new products and services. Action/negotiation teams may produce events such as concerts or resolve lawsuits.

The types of teams described above are created by the managers in organizations to meet organizational goals. Their members have a shared interest in common. Goals are central to the effectiveness of teams and they are discussed in the next section.

Team Goals

Learning Objective 11.2: Develop an example of how a team charter helps a team meet its goals.

Goal setting increases both motivation and performance, as we learned in Chapter 10 on motivation. Setting goals for teams is just as important as it is for individuals. It's important to keep in mind that team goals should also be SMART (specific, measurable, actionable, relevant, and time bound). Recalling the definition of a team, they have a sense of shared purpose for which members are mutually accountable. Specific team goals predict specific team performance (e.g., setting challenging goals for quantity results in higher team output).[14] Also, feedback on performance affects the allocation of resources when individuals strive to accomplish both individual and team goals. Finally, goals provide feedback on team performance, which is essential for managers. Team members who receive no team performance feedback can't effectively set team goals and, as a result, they set unrealistic goals.[15]

A review[16] of the effects of team goal setting on team performance concluded that specific difficult goals resulted in significantly higher team performance compared with nonspecific goals. Also, individual goals aimed at maximizing individual performance had a negative effect on team performance unless the individual goals were for the good of the group. Thus, team goals have a clear effect on team performance, but individual goals should be used with caution. Team goals need to include both **results measures** (e.g., sales revenue) and **process measures** (e.g., orders fulfilled). Results measures tell the managers where they stand in terms of organizational goals, whereas process measures monitor the tasks and activities employed to get the results obtained.[17] One of the best ways for team members to set results and process goals is to create a team charter in the first team meeting.

The Team Charter

A manager can make performance expectations clear and communicate them to team members by engaging the team to develop a **team charter**. A team charter is a document that describes the team goals and work processes (the ground rules for acceptable team behaviors). In creating a team charter, not only is the team purpose clarified but the expectations for behavior are set forth (e.g., required level of participation in meetings). The team charter sets forth the team norms that provide important regulation of team behavior. These rules and guidelines that a team establishes shape the way that team members interact with one another and with others outside of the team.[18] Once expectations are developed through a charter and agreed upon, misunderstandings should be fewer and a team member violating the ground rules in the charter (e.g., lack of follow-through) can be reminded of the team's commitment.

A business strategy simulation was used to study the influence of having a team charter and performance strategies of 32 teams of MBA students.[19] Taking the time to develop a high-quality team charter and performance strategies paid off in terms of more effective team performance over time. Teams that had quality charters and strategies outperformed teams with poor-quality charters and strategies. Charters are an important tool the leader can use to get their team off to a good start by developing a sense of purpose and setting forth the ground rules for team interaction. An abbreviated example of a team charter for a team given the goal of improving the times that patients must spend in hospital waiting rooms is shown in Figure 11.1. The team was charged with the goal of minimizing wait times to within 15 minutes of arrival and given resources to try different interventions with doctors, nurses, and reception staff. Representatives for each of these groups were part of the team.

You can develop a team charter for your team in this class by completing Toolkit Activity 11.1.

CRITICAL THINKING QUESTIONS

> Create a results measure and a process measure for the team charter example shown in Figure 11.1. Explain how the process measure helps the team reach the team goal of improving wait times.

Setting specific and challenging goals will set a working group on the path to becoming a real team. Next, models of how teams develop over time will be discussed.

▼ FIGURE 11.1

Team Charter Example

Team Purpose
This team will improve the wait times in outpatient office waiting rooms so that a doctor will see patients within 15 minutes of arrival.

Time Commitment
The project will last 6 months. Team members will devote 4 hours per week to the project.

Supporting Resources
Data from patient surveys, access to receptionists for interviews, use of East Wing conference room for meetings, and a project budget of $5,000,000.

Reporting Plan
The team will submit a weekly report describing progress and intervention results. A monthly review with hospital leadership will be conducted.

Deliverables
The team will deliver a final report summarizing the interventions and quantify the percentage improvements in hospital waiting time for each unit of the hospital.

Team Members
Maria Gonzalez, MD, Team Leader David Beckham, Reception Manager Belinda James, DNP Debra Markowitz, RN Melinda Smith, MBA Mark Spencer, MD, CEO, Project Sponsor

Team Development

Five-Stage Model

The five-stage model of team development is probably the most well known and recognized in team management.[20] The five stages are as follows:

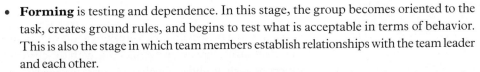

During storming, a team experiences conflict.

©iStockphoto.com/CreativalImages

- **Forming** is testing and dependence. In this stage, the group becomes oriented to the task, creates ground rules, and begins to test what is acceptable in terms of behavior. This is also the stage in which team members establish relationships with the team leader and each other.
- **Storming** is characterized as a time of intergroup conflict. There is a lack of team unity and there are difficulties around interpersonal issues. Group members resist the leadership of the team and may even become hostile toward one another to assert their individualism.
- **Norming** occurs when the team becomes cohesive and establishes roles and norms for interaction. In this stage, the team develops a "we" feeling and wants to stay together. Conflict may be avoided to maintain harmony during the norming phase.
- **Performing** is the next stage and the team begins to solve problems and coordinate tasks. The team develops a structure that supports task performance.
- **Adjourning** is the final stage in which the team disbands after completing its tasks.[21]

Some of the specific behaviors that you can expect to see during each of these stages of team development are shown in Figure 11.2. It's important to recognize that storming is a natural team occurrence and to be prepared to address it by enforcing team norms and emphasizing performance goals.

Punctuated Equilibrium Model

By observing teams in action, researcher Connie Gersick learned that teams don't always develop in an orderly sequence of stages. Her research, which is based on the concept of punctuated equilibrium from biology, found that teams have an initial period of inactivity (inertia) until about the midpoint of the time allowed for their task.[22] Punctuated equilibrium in teams is illustrated in Figure 11.3. The research is based on a study of over 12 task forces assigned to complete a specific project. Each team began with a unique approach to accomplishing its project in its first meeting (Phase 1). Phase 1 continues until one-half of the allotted time for project completion expires. At this midpoint, a major transition occurs where the team's old norms are dropped, and they increase progress toward completing the project. This happens due to the pressure of having a deadline.[23] Toward the end of the time allowed to complete the project, there is significant activity toward completion of the task (Phase 2).

▼ FIGURE 11.2

Stages of Team Development

Finish ↑

Development of Team →

Stage 5 Adjourning: Having completed their task the team dissolves. Members will share either a sense of loss or relief, depending on the outcome of the task.

Stage 4 Performing: Confidence grows both individually and with other members of the team as they work towards a common goal.

Stage 3 Norming: The team finds ways of resolving conflict and begins to emerge as a cohesive unit. Criticisms and feedback are given constructively and members start co-operating with one another.

Stage 2 Storming: Conflict occurs as personal agendas come to light. Members assert themselves and start questioning decisions and challenging authority.

Stage 1 Forming: Members start interacting and try to work out what is expected of them. Excitement and enthusiasm is mixed with fear and uncertainty.

Start

Source: Tuckman, B. W., & Jensen, M. C. (1977). Stages of small-group development revisited. *Group & Organizational Studies,* 2, 419–427.

Punctuated Equilibrium Model

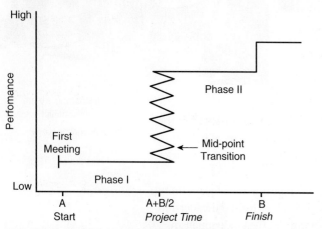

Source: Adapted from Gersick, C. J. G. (1991). Revolutionary change theories: A multilevel exploration of the punctuated equilibrium paradigm. *Academy of Management Review, 16*(1), 10–36.

Each team experienced its transition at the same point, which was halfway between the first meeting and the completion deadline. The teams procrastinated at the beginning, then experienced a crisis at the midpoint, and then ramped up their activity to complete the project. The midpoint effect was the emergence of an awareness that time was limited and the teams needed to start doing real work. Given these findings, managers should try to anticipate the midpoint effect by establishing a series of benchmarks so that teams do not delay their work. An example of how to do this is taking a 12-month construction project and then breaking it down into six significant milestones every two months, with the challenge of meeting each deadline. This would create the needed tension for moving the team toward performance.[24]

Research has discovered some of the underlying reasons for the midpoint effect.[25] When a large number of people on the team are procrastinators, teams are then more likely to procrastinate. Also, the teams' motivation matters—teams that have the goal of learning are less likely to procrastinate. This research also found that team procrastination has negative effects in terms of higher stress and lower performance.

CRITICAL THINKING QUESTIONS

> Have you ever been on a team that procrastinated on starting work? What did you do? Do you think that you could have moved the team forward more rapidly by setting midpoint goals? Explain.

Team Performance Curve

The team performance curve[26] is shown in Figure 11.4. These stages of development recognize that performance may decline during the storming phase.

- **Working groups** have no significant performance standards. They primarily exist to share information and best practices and to make decisions to help individuals perform their work in the best way possible. They do not produce a joint work product or have team goals. Many work groups are large and they may break down into smaller groups with some real team characteristics. Such groups are very common in organizations and do contribute to organizational goals, but they don't have team performance goals. They usually have one person who is the supervisor or manager and they direct the working group's activities.
- **Pseudo-teams** are groups that could have performance objectives and a common purpose but they emerge during the team storming stage. Due to conflicts, they are dysfunctional and produce almost nothing.
- **Potential teams** recognize the need for team goals and try to improve their team efforts. They accomplish some team goals and produce about as much as the working group. However, they need more clarity in their purpose and objectives. They may also need to develop norms and a working approach to solving team problems.
- **Real teams** by definition are small groups of people with complementary skills who are equally committed to a common purpose, goals, and working approach for which they hold themselves mutually accountable.

- **High-performance teams** are real teams who perform beyond the level of real teams and team members are personally committed to one another's individual learning and success. These teams outperform all expectations of both the organization and the individual members.

High-performance teams are rare. Most organizations strive to create real teams with the hope that some of them will evolve into high-performance teams. There are six characteristics that define a real team. They are:

- *Small number.* This is practical and based on real teams in organizations. Under some circumstances, large teams can perform but organizing work with a large group of people can be difficult. Team members must be able to communicate often and meet regularly. Large groups tend to break down into cliques or rely on policies and procedures to accomplish their goals. Most real teams have fewer than 10 members.
- *Complementary skills.* There are three types: functional/technical, problem-solving/decision-making, and interpersonal skills. All three are needed within the team. While it is possible for team members to develop these skills, having a good mix of skill types at the beginning gets the team off to a good start.
- *A common meaningful purpose.* A purpose that is meaningful to all members of the team is the most important aspect of a real team. A team purpose articulates the goals of the team and gives it direction. This is best accomplished when the team develops its own common purpose by creating a team charter. When asked, team members should be able to state the common purpose of the team.
- *Specific performance objectives.* Performance objectives are part of the common purpose and they are also an important part of defining a real team. The team needs to own their performance objectives even if they are set by the organization. They should be clear, simple, and measurable so that the team can receive feedback on their progress. They should be aspirational but must also be realistic and set forth specific work products to be created.
- *A common working approach.* The team process must be understood by all members. Real teams must have ground rules. For example, there should be an expectation that all members participate in team meetings. Team members must understand these rules and contribute to the work of the team.
- *A sense of mutual accountability.* Team members should feel responsible for the work of team. They need to feel individually responsible for the team's purpose, working approach, and results. Team success is more important to the members of a real team than individual success.

▼ FIGURE 11.4

Team Performance Curve

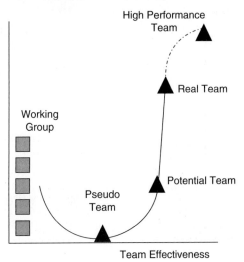

Source: Katzenbach, J. R., & Smith, D. K. (1993). *The wisdom of teams: Creating the high-performance organization.* Boston, MA: Harvard Business School Press. p. 84.

In high-performance teams, members celebrate when the team succeeds.

©iStockphoto.com/Delmaine Donson

In high-performance teams, individual team members celebrate when the team succeeds. It is important to realize that success can be determined in various ways in teams. Next, the dimensions of team effectiveness are discussed.

Team Effectiveness

Learning Objective 11.4: Provide examples of team effectiveness.

So far in this chapter, you have probably noticed a recurring focus on high-performance, successful, and otherwise effective teams. Naturally these are desirable goals, but how do we define and measure team effectiveness?

Broadly speaking, there are three contributors to overall team effectiveness: attitudes, behaviors, and performance, as shown in Figure 11.5.[27] These are not independent, of course. Just as with individual people, the attitudes of team members influence their behaviors, which, in turn, impact their performance. In this section, we will explore these components in more detail to get a sense of how managers can measure team performance and shape the attitudes and behaviors of members to increase the overall effectiveness of a team.

Team Attitudes: Affect and Viability

It is no great secret that positive attitudes toward a person, place, or thing generally translate into favorable behaviors toward that person, place, or thing. Think back to your favorite subjects in school, for example, even as a child. If you loved science, you probably kept up with your homework, paid attention in class, and maybe even read some parts of your textbook that were not required. In subjects you disliked, however, you might have missed a few due dates, daydreamed in class, and generally did only what was necessary to get through it. The workplace is no different.[28] As such, it can be helpful to examine the **affective reactions**, which are emotional responses of teams and their individual members to their work and to each other as an indicator of team effectiveness.[29] This is especially true when a team's performance is difficult to observe or quantify, as is often the case in fields such as consulting and research.[30]

Team members' collective attitudes toward the team and its work can help give managers a sense of whether or not a team has the motivation and viability necessary to succeed. **Team viability** refers to members' collective sense of belonging and desire to continue working together.[31] In short, teams that enjoy working together tend to experience less turnover and higher productivity levels. From a manager's perspective, these are both outcomes that can make managing a team much easier.

Team Behaviors: Creativity and Learning

One way of assessing a team's effectiveness is to examine the creativity of its behaviors and outputs. Defined as "members working together in such a manner that they link ideas from multiple sources, delve into unknown areas to find better or unique approaches to a problem, or seek out novel ways of performing a task,"[32] **team creativity** is a sign of a well-designed and well-managed team. Because they consist of members with different knowledge, skills, and abilities, teams have the potential to draw on a wider set of resources than individual employees typically can access by themselves.

In addition to sharing knowledge amongst themselves, teams can collectively acquire, combine, and apply new knowledge through an ongoing process called **team learning**.[33] By engaging in behaviors like asking questions, analyzing past mistakes and errors, seeking

▼ FIGURE 11.5

Contributors to Team Effectiveness

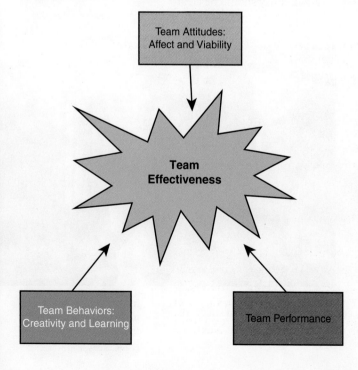

feedback, and solving problems together, teams can learn in two unique ways. One is relational job learning, in which members develop an understanding of how their individual job functions are interconnected and interdependent upon those of other employees in the organization. The other is personal skill development, in which team members increase their own knowledge and skills, enabling them to work more effectively with each other and employees outside the team.[34]

Team Performance

Many of the same performance measures used to evaluate individual employees are used to evaluate teams. These include supervisor and customer ratings of the quality, accuracy, efficiency, profitability, and error rates of the work performed by the team.[35] There are times, however, when a blend of team-based and individual employee performance measures is useful. Measures of **role-based performance**, the ability of each member to perform their assigned task, are commonly used in situations where one or more team members has a specialized task that must be done competently.

Six beneficial team roles have been identified by research:[36]

- *Organizer*—someone who acts to structure what the team is doing. An organizer also keeps track of accomplishments and how the team is progressing relative to goals and timelines.
- *Doer*—someone who willingly takes on work and gets things done. A doer can be counted on to complete work, meet deadlines, and take on tasks to ensure the team's success.
- *Challenger*—someone who will push the team to explore all aspects of a situation and to consider alternative assumptions, explanations, and solutions. A challenger often asks "why" and is comfortable debating and critiquing.
- *Innovator*—someone who regularly generates new and creative ideas, strategies, and approaches for how the team can handle various situations and challenges. An innovator often offers original and imaginative suggestions.
- *Team builder*—someone who helps establish norms, supports decisions, and maintains a positive work atmosphere within the team. A team builder calms members when they are stressed and motivates them when they are down.
- *Connector*—someone who helps bridge and connect the team with people, groups, or other stakeholders outside of the team. Connectors ensure good working relationships between the team and "outsiders," whereas team builders work to ensure good relationship within the team.

To learn more about your effective behavior in these roles, complete Self-Assessment 11.1.

A team's overall performance often depends on these individual member roles. For example, a struggling goal keeper will hurt a sports team's performance no matter how talented the other athletes are; a talented goalie can compensate for the weaknesses of other team members. Because the performance of individual members is not always as obvious as this example might suggest, role-based performance measures can be used in addition to team-based measures to provide managers with important diagnostic information about what is causing a team to fail or succeed. Another tool that a manager can use to measure various aspects of team performance is a team dashboard. Dashboards help teams receive frequent feedback, which leads to excellent performance.[37] An example of a dashboard for a fishing operation with measures of team satisfaction, conflict, and performance is shown in Figure 11.6. Each week the dashboard is updated so that team members can track their progress.

Example of a Team Dashboard

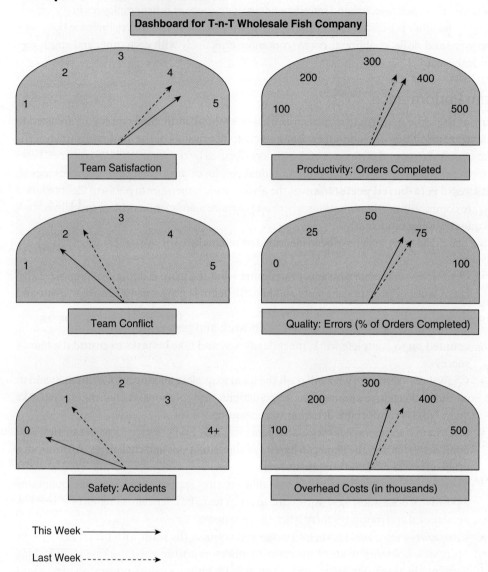

Dashboard for T-n-T Wholesale Fish Company

Team Satisfaction

Productivity: Orders Completed

Team Conflict

Quality: Errors (% of Orders Completed)

Safety: Accidents

Overhead Costs (in thousands)

This Week ────────→

Last Week ------------→

How to Build Effective Teams

To build an effective team, a manager must pay attention to both **task functions** and **maintenance functions**. Task functions relate to what the team is working on. Maintenance functions relate to the support that the manager provides to the team. These functions are both essential to team effectiveness and are summarized in Figure 11.7.

According to team consultant Rosalind Cardinal, there are five steps to building effective teams.[38] A manager should implement these steps to ensure that the team experiences positive affect and viability.

Step 1: Establish and demonstrate your leadership skills. Trust between employees and managers is essential. When employees trust a leader's decision-making skills and integrity, they will want to do a good

▼ FIGURE 11.7

Task and Maintenance Team Functions

Task Functions	Maintenance Functions
• Goal achievement • Specific tasks • Production • Problem-solving • Sharing ideas • Innovation	• Support • Assistance • Relationship building • Encouragement • Reinforcement of team purpose • Monitoring of alignment with team charter

FACT OR FICTION?

Forget What You Learned in Grade School: Five Teamwork Myths

Since we were all kids, we've been told that we need to work well as part of a team, that the team trumps the individual, and that every leader is only as good as their team.[39] Can we really believe that this idea of team is the key to productivity and success? Anyone whose days are spent trying to squeeze in work between all of their meetings can tell you that teamwork can be a waste of time. Can teams be too much of a good thing? Let's look at some of the facts and fiction about teamwork.

Top Five Myths of Teamwork

1. **Teams are always needed.** Managers should analyze every task to make sure that they really need a team to do it. Teamwork may not always be efficient. Sometimes it's better to delegate a task to one or two people, especially if the task is simple or routine. In his book *The Myths and Realities of Teamwork*, David Wright states: "If a task or a process is simple, an organizational can cope without teamwork."[40] For example, a manager should not have a team meeting to discuss a trivial issue such as what color to paint the walls in the conference room.

2. **Teams should come to a consensus.** Time spent trying to reach consensus on decisions could be better spent acting on the decisions. There are other decision-making methods that are less time-consuming and the job gets done. For example, rather than reach consensus, a manager can speak to each team member individually. If all are in agreement, there is no need for a meeting to reach consensus.

3. **There's no "I" in team.** This is an old idea that has been refuted by recent research. It is important for a manager to attend to the needs of the individuals within the team. By understanding the I's in team, the benefits of individual motivation are not lost. People still need individual coaching and development, even if they are on a team. Wright states: "There is no I in team, but there is a ME and ignore the me at your own peril."[41] For example, a team member may feel that they are not being personally recognized for their contributions to the team on the performance evaluation. They are a top performer but quit the team.

4. **You must get along with your teammates.** We don't have to like everyone on our team—personality clashes are real. But team members have to respect one another and their opinions. There should be clear guidelines for appropriate behavior (remember the team charter). You don't have to spend happy hour with your team for it to be productive. Conflict actually enhances team performance. Wright states, "Conflict is an energy source, so harness it."[42] For example, a team that has a healthy debate on an issue may avoid making a poor decision.

5. **The more the merrier.** Large teams don't outperform smaller ones. It might seem like adding more people will increase performance, but teams lose some of their effectiveness when they get larger than seven members. The larger a team gets, the harder it is to coordinate efforts. Just finding a time when eight people can all meet may be impossible. For example, in a large team of 15 people, half of the people break out and form their own clique with the people they like the best.

Discussion Questions

1. Discuss whether you agree or disagree with each of the five team myths and why.

2. Provide an example of a task that would be better assigned to an individual than a team. (Myths 1 and 2)

3. Explain how you would keep team members happy, invested in the task, and excited about their team work. Do you agree that this is the only way for a team to be effective? If you disagree, what are some other ways to ensure team effectiveness? (Myth 3)

4. Do you agree that "conflict actually helps a team stay innovative"? Describe how a manager can keep conflict in a team healthy so that it does not tear the team apart. (Myth 4)

Sources: Adapted from Palfini, J. (2007). Forget what you learned in grade school: Five teamwork myths. *CBS News*. Retrieved from https://www.cbsnews.com/news/forget-what-you-learned-in-grade-school-five-teamwork-myths/; and Wright, D. (2013). The myths and realities of teamwork. Retrieved from https://pdfs.semanticscholar.org/074d/138a0f218fb7e38582dd170a4b974fc09621.pdf.

---

job—even when their manager isn't around. In order to build a strong team, you, as a manager, need to develop strong leadership skills. Leadership isn't about asserting authority; it's about creating a culture of trust by being honest, clear, and forthcoming.

Step 2: Build a strong working relationship with each of your employees. Get to know all of your team members. What are their unique skills? What motivates them? What stifles their creativity or makes them feel unappreciated? What do they like about their jobs? What do they simply tolerate or even dislike about their jobs? A strong leader will discover each employee's expertise and abilities in order to pair them with specific tasks, duties, and problems to be solved. When a manager can match employees' individual skills and talents with their work, employees will be more satisfied and productive. As a manager, you should also look for opportunities to include the team in decision-making and to allow the team to work on open-ended projects rather than simply assigning tasks. To establish a strong, productive working relationship with employees, you should encourage their interests, engage them in making decisions, and empower them to solve problems.

Step 3: Foster relationships between your employees. Take a look at how employees work together. Seek out opportunities to make communication stronger, encourage collaboration, and build trust among team members. If and when there are conflicts, as a manager, you should step in to help employees find a workable solution. Encourage respect and cooperation. In order to do so, remain objective and act as a mediator rather than taking sides. Empower team members by encouraging them to brainstorm solutions, which may lead to innovative problem-solving.

Step 4: Value and encourage teamwork. Once team members have strong, conflict-free relationships and/or the skills to effectively resolve conflicts, it's time for teamwork. As a manager, you should foster the open flow of communication and encourage collaboration. Support the team by encouraging them to share information amongst themselves, and also throughout the company. When it comes to creating a culture of open communication, think beyond simply holding meetings. Good leaders are always open to feedback, questions, and concerns. Check in often with employees, and offer your assistance when they need it. Most importantly, model transparency for your team by communicating constantly, clearly, and honestly.

Step 5: Create and stick to ground rules for the team. When you have strong individual and team relationships, as well as open communication, you can establish group values and goals. You can also evaluate performance on an individual and team level. You can engage your team in developing ground rules, guidelines, and best practices. Be sure that each team member is part of the process, understands the expectations, and agrees they can meet them.

Despite a manager's best efforts to build the team's effectiveness, teams face challenges that the manager should be prepared to address. These challenges are discussed next.

Team Challenges

Learning Objective 11.5: Describe the symptoms of groupthink.

Managers should understand that leading a team has a number of challenges. These will be described in the following sections, along with remedies that may be applied to avoid them.

Groupthink

Groupthink is a team decision-making challenge that arises due to a high degree of cohesiveness and group norms that result in conformity.[43] Groupthink is defined as the conformity-seeking tendency of the group, which results in compromised decision-making. Due to group pressure, the team does not survey all alternatives and expressions of views that go against the majority of team members are suppressed. Team members apply direct pressure on dissenters and urge them to go along with the majority. The following are symptoms of groupthink:

1. *Group rationalization.* The team members generate explanations that support their preferred course of action.
2. *Direct pressure.* Those who speak out against the group decision are pressured into conformity.
3. *Suppression.* Members with differing views don't share them with the group for fear of ostracism and/or ridicule.
4. *Illusion of unanimity.* The team members believe that they are in agreement but, in fact, they are not. Dissenting views have been suppressed. Not speaking is interpreted as support for the team decision.

Groupthink occurs most often in highly cohesive groups and when the group is confident about their course of action early in the process.[44] Experimental research has supported the existence of groupthink.[45] For example, an experiment tested groupthink and found partial support for the theory in that direct pressure from managers increased the symptoms of groupthink.[46] Teams with directive managers proposed and discussed fewer alternatives than groups with leaders who encouraged member participation. These teams were also willing to comply with their managers' proposed solutions when the leaders stated their preferences early in the group discussion. The *Challenger* space shuttle disaster was one of the worst disasters in the history of the U.S. space program. The case has been interpreted using groupthink.[47] In this scenario, the decision by NASA to launch the space shuttle when temperatures were too low for O-rings to function properly resulted in the death of six astronauts and a civilian teacher. The analysis concludes that directive leadership and time pressure contributed to the impaired decision-making process of NASA engineers.

The *Challenger* space shuttle disaster has been explained by groupthink.

© Everett Historical/Shutterstock

To minimize groupthink, the leader can:

- avoid being too directive and encourage everyone to participate fully in team discussions;
- assign a member of the team to play the devil's advocate, which is a role that challenges team assumptions and decisions throughout the process; and
- employ decision-making techniques other than consensus decision-making to provide more structure and avoid conformity.

CRITICAL THINKING QUESTIONS

Why are directive leadership and time pressure the strongest antecedent to groupthink? What else can leaders do to prevent putting undue pressure on a team in the decision-making process?

Most students recognize groupthink symptoms because they have probably occurred in student project teams. Think about a time when you felt like disagreeing with your team but stayed silent because the team was cohesive or you didn't want to create conflict. You may have been a victim of groupthink. A second group challenge that is common in student project teams is social loafing. You will recognize this one if you have ever been in a team where you (or a subgroup of team members) did all the work but others that didn't contribute got the credit.

Social loafing is defined as a "decrease in individual effort when performing in groups as compared to when they perform alone."[48] The social loafing effect is not new. It has plagued teamwork since people started working in groups. Max Ringelmann, a French agricultural engineer, conducted the earliest research that found that increasing numbers of workers does not increase productivity as expected.[49] In fact, social loafing is sometimes called the **Ringelmann effect**, and he collected his data on the performance of agricultural workers between 1882 and 1887, but did not publish his research until 1913. He studied the maximum performance of human beings as a function of the method that the worker used to push or pull a load horizontally.

How did Ringelmann study this? He measured the performance of one person pulling a load, and then added workers to the pulling of the load one at a time, up to eight workers. Ringelmann asked workers to pull as hard as they could on a rope, alone or with one, two, or seven other people, and then used a gauge to measure how hard they pulled in kilograms of

Group Size and Performance Demonstrating the Social Loafing Effect

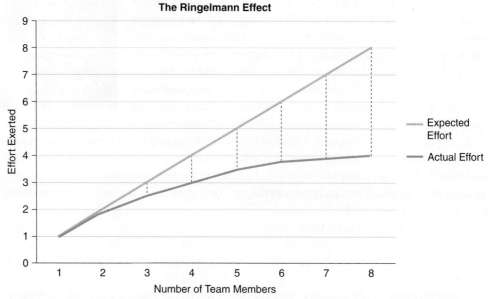

Note: As the group gets larger, the amount of work per person decreases from its maximum of 1.

Source: Adapted from Ringelmann, M. (1913). Recherches sur les moteurs animes: Travail de rhomme [Research on animate sources of power: The work of man]. Annales de l'Institut National Agronomique, 2e serie-tome XII, 1–40.

pressure.[50] He found that performance did not increase as one might expect: adding a second worker did not double the performance of pulling weight. In fact, when the eighth worker was added, there was no increase in performance at all.[51] He explained this by stating that "coordination losses" occur as more workers are added to groups.[52] The effect is shown in Figure 11.8.

Ringelmann's research has been replicated in modern settings. A study examined rope-pulling by students to see if participation in team sports reduced the effect of social loafing.[53] Male participants had to pull a rope individually and then with others. Groups of two, three, four, and six persons were formed and grouped into those with no previous team sports experience, those with individual sports experience, and those with team sports experience. For each team, the sum of individual contributions of the participants constituting a team was computed using a device designed to measure back strength (a dynamometer). The researchers stated, "This sum served as the anticipated result (expected value). The expected values were later compared to the actual achievements (i.e., the value achieved by the whole team). The results of the study suggested that previous experience in collective (team) sports eliminated the effect of social loafing."[54] It is interesting that students who had participated in individual sports had the most dramatic performance decrement when the size of the group got larger.

Research on the Ringelmann effect has been ongoing for over 100 years. Another interesting study examined the causes of social loafing. In other words, is social loafing due to just coordination losses or do people really put in less effort in groups? In the study, groups of six undergraduate males were recruited from introductory psychology classes at a Midwestern public university. They were seated in a semicircle, one meter apart, in a large soundproofed laboratory and told that researchers were interested in studying the noise people make in social settings (like football games) by cheering and applause. They were asked to cheer, clap their hands, and be as loud as possible, and researchers measured the noise level with a sound meter for five seconds. After some practice, there were 36 trials of yelling and 36 trials of clapping. Within each type of noise, each person performed twice alone, four times in pairs, four times in groups of four, and six times in groups of six. The experiment produced results consistent with the Ringelmann effect. Of course, the more people making noise resulted in more noise overall; however, it did not grow in proportion to the number of people: the average sound pressure generated *per person* significantly decreased with increasing group size. In other words, two-person groups performed at only 71% of the sum of their individual capacity, four-person groups at 51%, and six-person groups at 40%. The researchers concluded, "As in pulling ropes, it appears that when it comes to clapping and shouting out loud, many hands do, in fact, make light the work."[55] A second experiment was conducted, in which the students wore noise-canceling headphones so that they could not hear one another and this limited their ability to coordinate efforts. This experiment demonstrated that the effect was due to lower effort, and not coordination losses.

Can social loafing be prevented in teams? Research has examined this question, and there are steps that a manager can take to reduce social loafing. A research study[56] of 420 college students was conducted to see what reduces social loafing during group projects. This research identified three factors that reduce social loafing:

- *Limiting the scope of the project.* Instructors can reduce social loafing by either dividing a big project into two or more smaller components or replacing semester-long projects with a smaller project and some other graded work. Also, breaking up a big project into smaller components can be beneficial. For example, allocating responsibility so that each individual is spearheading certain aspects of a larger project ensures accountability and helps prevent social loafing.[57]
- *Smaller group size.* Limiting the group size can make it harder for social loafers to hide behind the shield of anonymity provided by a large group. In smaller groups, each member will feel that their contribution will add greater value.[58]
- *Peer evaluations.* Peer evaluations send a signal to group members that there will be consequences for nonparticipation. It has been found that as the number of peer evaluations during a project goes up, the incidence of social loafing goes down.[59]

Virtual Teams

In today's world of work, more is being done through the internet in virtual teams. Virtual teams are "functioning teams that rely on technology-mediated communication while crossing several different boundaries."[60] Such teams rely on technology to communicate, and this has significantly changed how teamwork is conducted. A real advantage of virtual teams is that members can be located in different countries.

Virtual teams have more challenges.[61] A comparison of computer-based teams to face-to-face teams found that performance depended on experience with the technology.[62] The results also suggested that the newness of the computer program to team members and not the newness of the group led to poorer task performance for computer groups. A review of studies on computer-mediated groups reported that computer-based groups generated more ideas but had more limited interactions and took longer to complete their work compared with teams that met face-to-face.[63] Virtual teams may have less social support and direct interaction among team members, which is needed to build trust.[64] Virtual teams share less information.[65] Also, virtual work and the use of email in combination may change how information is shared.[66]

Virtual teams rely on technology to communicate.

© Syda Productions/Shutterstock

Virtual teams face a number of obstacles. Members are less familiar with one another; they may have never met face-to-face. This makes it difficult to develop strong working relationships. In many cases, virtual team members are geographically dispersed and may even be working in different countries and time zones. The differences in time zones create a challenge when the organization wants to use audio or video conferencing for team meetings.[67] In some situations, team members must stay awake all night to participate in a team meeting. Organizations are now rotating meeting times to be fair to all team members to avoid resentment from the members who must always be on call at all hours of the day and night. Virtual teams often do not actually work together and lack interdependence. Virtual team members are tempted to just break down a project into components and everyone works independently.[68]

A study of virtual teams found that the following team member behaviors improved trust and performance in virtual teams:[69]

- Carefully select members for participation in virtual teams. Not all employees have the desire and skills to participate effectively in this type of team.
- Provide clear guidelines for responsibilities, and make sure that team members understand goals.
- Give the team guidelines on how to communicate, and develop regular patterns of communication.
- Engage in open and thoughtful messages early in the team's life cycle.
- Effectively handle conflict; don't delay addressing it, since virtual team members communicate less frequently than face-to-face teams.
- Ensure that team members provide other team members with timely accounts of the work they are doing individually.
- Provide feedback to the team often on their progress.
- Emphasize the quality and predictability of communication rather than the quantity.

It's also important to use the right technology in virtual teams. In addition to email, the following tools are available[70] and are the most frequently used to communicate:

- *Videoconferencing.* In addition to email, managers of virtual teams should use conference calling with systems that don't require access codes (sometimes team members are driving) but do record meetings for those who can't attend. Videoconferencing provides visual cues that help establish empathy and trust.
- *Direct calls and text messages.* By supporting real-time conversation between team members, direct calls are one of the simplest and most powerful tools. Texting is a surprisingly effective way to maintain personal relationships.
- *Discussion forums or virtual team rooms.* Software is now available that allows team members to present issues to the entire group, and records the meeting for team members to comment on when they have time. This is critical for completing complex projects. All interaction is documented and therefore becomes a searchable database.

In today's global environment, virtual teams often have members who are located in different countries. So, the challenges of a virtual team have the added challenge of being multicultural as well. Next, the challenge of multicultural teams is discussed.

Multicultural Teams

Cross-cultural issues affect teams for a number of reasons. Team members may be assigned to work in another country. Another reason is that teams are made up of people from different cultures. As noted above, virtual teams may be spread out all over the world. Culture represents a challenge because it may be more difficult to get all the team members "on the same page" with respect to the team purpose and common working approach. Culturally diverse teams struggle with the following:

- performing complex tasks,
- face-to-face interactions that can feel awkward,
- conflict when members are required to work together closely, and
- team size; if the team is too large members from some cultures may withdraw from participation.[71]

In addition to the above challenges, managers must realize that not all team processes translate cross-culturally. For example, in the United States, teams are often empowered to make their own decisions in Self Managed Work Teams (SMWTs). Such teams have no leader. This works in the United States, but a study found that leaderless teams were resisted in the Philippines.[72] Resistance to SMWTs was affected by culture because Filipino team members viewed the manager as incompetent when they delegated authority to the team. Also, the degree of determinism (i.e., the belief that "people should not try to change the paths their lives are destined to take") affected reactions to the implementation of SMWTs. Similar reactions to the offer of team participation were reported in studies done in Russia and Mexico.[73] Caution should be exercised when implementing team participation in some cultures. Managers should check cultural assumptions before offering participation to multicultural teams. You will learn more about cultural value differences in Chapter 13.

Team Conflict

Conflict in teams creates stress and arguments that distract the team from working and harms performance.[74] Conflict is detrimental to member satisfaction.[75] However, moderate levels of task conflict actually improve team performance because this stimulates information exchange among team members. Task conflict and differences of opinion may improve decision quality by forcing members to see other viewpoints and think creatively.[76] In other words, conflict can result in higher performance in teams. What matters is how the conflict is managed. Teams can improve or maintain top performance by using three conflict resolution strategies:

1. Focus on the content of interactions rather than delivery style.
2. Explicitly discuss reasons behind any decisions in distributing work assignments.
3. Assign work to members who have the relevant task expertise rather than assigning by other common means such as volunteering, default, or convenience.[77]

High-performing teams are more proactive in resolving their conflicts and search for strategies that apply to everyone.[78] Task conflict may improve performance if relationship conflict can be kept to a minimum. When performance goals are more specific, there is a stronger effect of team conflict on performance. This provides support for the idea that team conflict is productive to a point, and then starts to harm team performance. Two separate studies of work teams in Taiwan and Indonesia[79] found team effectiveness depends on relationship conflict in the team. Team members who bicker so intensely cannot have even the slightest task conflict without harming performance.[80] Both task and relationship conflict matter in terms of understanding how conflict may harm team performance. Self-Assessment 11.2 will help you learn how much team conflict you are experiencing due to the task, the relationships, and your team process.

CRITICAL THINKING QUESTIONS

How would you address one essential team member who continually interrupts others, creating conflict within the team, which harms the team's productivity? Outline the talking points you would use to discuss their behavior.

Ethical Concerns From Peer Pressure

Being in a team exerts a powerful force on individuals to go along with the team. This is due to the combined forces of cohesion and norms. **Cohesion** is defined as "the resultant of all the forces acting on the members to remain part of the group."[81] These forces depend on the attractiveness or unattractiveness of the prestige of the group, the group members, and/or the group's activities. The mutual attraction of the member to the group is the most important determinant of cohesion.[82] When cohesion is strong, the group is motivated to perform and better coordinate activities for success. In cohesive teams, there is a sense of "we-ness" and team members tend to use *we* rather than *I* to describe the team and its activities.[83] Reviews of these studies have found that team cohesion and team performance are positively related.[84] For example, one review reports that the average cohesive team performed 18% higher than the average noncohesive team.[85]

In addition to cohesion, **team norms** also have a powerful effect on team member attitudes and behaviors. **Norms** are defined as informal and interpersonal rules that team members are expected to follow.[86] These standards may be explicit and formally stated by the leader or members of the team. But norms may also be implicit. They are not written down, and communication of the norms to team members depends on the ability of the leader (or team members) to effectively convey the expected behaviors. Norms have a powerful influence on team behavior, and they are often difficult to change. For example, at football games, everyone is expected to wear hats and shirts with the team's logo on them. While this isn't written down anywhere and football games do not post dress codes, you will notice that most people wear team apparel at the game. This is an example of an implicit norm. If you show up at game in the opposing team's apparel and sit in the student section, your peers may give you the "side eye" for not understanding the norms of supporting your team by wearing the team colors. Implicit norms are tricky in that they are difficult to detect, and it is easy to misinterpret them.

With the combined effects of cohesion and strong team norms, sometimes team members experience peer pressure that results in unethical behavior.[87] Unethical behavior by managers has been linked to pressure from bosses and/or peers.[88] Another example is cheating behavior in school. Cheating is unethical, and a study of over 5,000 students found that business students cheat more than their nonbusiness-student peers. Student perceptions that peers were cheating had the strongest relationship to cheating behaviors.[89]

Five Dysfunctions of a Team

Patrick Lencioni developed a good summary of team challenges in his best-selling book, *The Five Dysfunctions of a Team*.[90] This approach is shown in Figure 11.9, and the five dysfunctions are described as follows:

▼ FIGURE 11.9

Five Dysfunctions of a Team

Source: Lencioni, P. (2005). *The five dysfunctions of a team*. New York, NY: John Wiley.

CAREERS IN MANAGEMENT

Team Coach

A team coach is an internal consultant to the team. Despite millions being spent on team training, trainers cannot anticipate every situation that will arise for the team. Having a team coach is a great way to reinforce training and provide ongoing assistance as the team moves through its stages of development. The coach helps team members put their training into action. The team coach also helps teams work through conflict and overcome obstacles.[91] The team coach is an advisor and challenges the team. Teach coaches are change agents who work at the team level to make sure the team is aligned with organizational change. Having team coaches sends the right message that the top management is committed to change. An example of team coaching in practice is Google's Guru Program.

Google is investing in managers to create internal team coaches with their Guru Program. A recent report, *The Conference Board's Global Executive Coaching Survey 2016*,[92] describes the program as a cutting-edge strategy of developing employees into team coaches. Google launched Career Guru in 2010 and expanded it into Guru-plus with 350 internal coaches in 60 offices around the world. The team coaching is accomplished virtually using Google Hangouts. Depending on the topic, the one-on-one sessions can range from one to eight sessions.

The program covers 12 different topics that employees can receive coaching on. Topics include career, team development, leadership, manager, parenting, innovation, new employees, well-being, presentations (reports and TED Talks, for example), and respect. For example, a sales employee working in Australia who is preparing to make a big sales pitch may get coaching from a "sales guru" working in the same industry in another country.

It's a revolutionary program but it makes a lot of sense for Google. The process to become a guru is rigorous. To become a team coach, applicants must have been at Google for at least two years, serve at the organization's senior level or be subject matter experts, have their manager's support for serving as a guru, and be considered an employee in good standing by their manager and human resources. Gurus undergo training and are evaluated by those they coach.

The Conference Board expects to see more personalized coaching with measurable outcomes. Rebecca L. Ray, executive vice president of knowledge organization at the Conference Board, noted in a news release that there is much anecdotal evidence on the power of coaching: "But turning this tool of individual development into an organizational catalyst will depend on rich analytics, scalable deployments and objective, repeatable results. The next frontier [in coaching] will bring in the latest in technology, neuroscience, mindfulness and more."

Discussion Questions

1. How do you feel about the "virtual" coaching used by Google versus traditional face-to-face coaching? What are some pros and cons of each?

2. If "Coaching is not telling people what to do and barking orders," what do you think an effective team coach *does* need to be able to do?

3. Who are some effective coaches or "gurus" you have met in your life? How did they help you?

Sources: Adapted from Gurchieck, K. (2016). Does your organization use internal coaches? *Society for Human Resource Management*. Retrieved from https://www.shrm.org/resourcesandtools/hr-topics/organizational-and-employee-development/pages/does-your-organization-use-internal-coaches.aspx; and Kelly, A. (2009). The role of the agile coach. *Agile Connection*. Retrieved from https://www.agileconnection.com/article/role-agile-coach.

---

1. The first dysfunction is an **absence of trust** among team members. Essentially, this stems from their unwillingness to be vulnerable within the group. Team members who are not genuinely open with another about their mistakes and weaknesses make it impossible to build a foundation for trust.

2. This failure to build trust is damaging because it sets the tone for the second dysfunction: **fear of conflict**. Teams that lack trust are incapable of engaging in unfiltered and passionate debate of ideas. Instead, they resort to veiled discussions and guarded comments.

3. A lack of healthy conflict is a problem because it ensures the third dysfunction of a team: **lack of commitment**. Without having aired their opinions in the course of passionate

and open debate, team members rarely, if ever, buy in and commit to decisions, although they may feign agreement during meetings.

4. Because of this lack of real commitment and buy-in, team members develop an **avoidance of accountability**, the fourth dysfunction. Without committing to a clear plan of action, even the most focused and driven people often hesitate to call their peers on actions and behaviors that seem counterproductive to the team.

5. Failure to hold one another accountable creates an environment where the fifth dysfunction can thrive. **Inattention to results** occurs when team members put their individual needs (e.g., ego, career development, or recognition) or even the needs of their divisions above the collective goals of the team.[93]

Some managers consider these dysfunctions separately, but this is not how Lencioni explains them. They cannot be addressed separately because they form an interrelated set of team challenges in which having one dysfunction makes the team vulnerable to the others. When teams face challenges, they may bring in a consultant known as a team coach to help them address problems and become functional. The Careers in Management feature explains what a team coach does.

Team Decision-Making

Learning Objective 11.6: Understand the advantages and disadvantages of team decision-making.

As you have probably noticed in your own experiences, decision-making in groups or teams is a bit more complicated than it is when you are working alone. More people means more ideas, opinions, and more conflict. A manager should carefully consider the advantages and disadvantages of using a team to make a decision. Table 11.3 shows the advantages and disadvantages of team decision-making. The key advantage to using a team to make a decision is gaining insights from a number of people who can brainstorm more alternatives to consider. Also, research has shown that participation in decisions increases team innovation due to minority opinions being considered.[94] The next sections discuss procedures that a manager can use to reduce the disadvantages of team decision-making—the devil's advocate and dialectical inquiry approaches.

Devil's Advocacy

As noted earlier, **devil's advocate**[95] is an antidote for groupthink. A devil's advocate is a person (or persons) assigned by the manager to critique the team's ideas. Devil's advocacy can reduce groupthink and other pressures to conform. How does devil's advocacy work? After a team has developed a solution to a problem, it is then sent to one (or more) people who were not on the original team, with instructions to point out its flaws. If the proposal can withstand the scrutiny of the devil's advocates, it can then be implemented. Although devil's advocacy can be used as a critiquing technique after alternative solutions to a problem have been developed, it can also be used during the early stages of the decision-making process. For example, during a decision-making session, one member could be assigned the role of devil's advocate, expressing as many objections to each alternative solution to a problem as possible.[96]

Dialectical Inquiry

Dialectical inquiry is another way to ensure that the team reaps the benefits of team decision-making and avoids the problems.[97] This approach generates two diametrically opposed viewpoints and then attempts to reconcile them in the final solution. The process is as follows:[98]

Advantages and Disadvantages of Team Decision-Making

Advantages	Disadvantages
• More knowledge and expertise available • A greater number of alternatives considered • Final decision better understood and accepted • More commitment to make final decision work • Improved decision quality	• Social pressure to conform • Domination of one member or a dominant clique • Decisions take longer • Team conflict results in stress

Source: Lunenburg, F. C. (2011). Decision making in organizations. *International Journal of Management, Business, and Administration, 15*(1), 1–9. Reprinted with permission.

1. Two or more groups with divergent views are formed to express the full range of possible alternatives to a problem. The groups are intentionally different from one another but similar within the group. Collectively they cover all positions that might have an impact on the ultimate solution to a problem.

2. Each group meets separately, identifies the assumptions behind its position, and rates them on their importance and feasibility. Each group then presents a "for" and an "against" position to the other groups.

3. Each group debates the other group's position and defends its own. The goal is not to convince others but to confirm that what each group expresses as its position.

4. The information that is generated by both groups is then analyzed. This process results in the identification of information gaps and identifies areas where further research on the problem is needed.

5. An attempt to achieve consensus among the two positions takes place. Solutions are sought that best meet the requirements of both positions. Further refinement of information needed to solve the problem is then generated. Although agreement on a plan is a goal of this approach, a complete consensus does not always result from the process. However, this procedure can produce useful ideas regarding the pitfalls of an approach.

We now turn to the various options that a manager can use to implement team decisions. One of the most famous of these procedures is Robert's Rules of Order.

Robert's Rules of Order

The first edition of the book *Robert's Rules of Order*[99] was published in 1876 by U.S. Army Major Henry Martyn Robert. Its procedures are based on parliamentary procedures and are modeled after those used in the U.S. House of Representatives. It's amazing that these procedures are still used in many organizations today.

Here are the basic elements of Robert's Rules:[100]

1. *Motion.* To introduce a new action, a motion must be made by a group member ("I move that..."). A second motion must then be made (raise your hand and say, "I second it."). After discussion, the group votes on the motion. A majority vote is required for the motion to pass.

In a dialectical inquiry, divergent views are formed to express the range of alternatives to a problem.

©iStockphoto.com/fizkes

2. *Postpone indefinitely.* This basically kills a motion during the meeting. When passed, the motion cannot be reintroduced at that meeting. It may be brought up again at a later date. This is made as a motion ("I move to postpone indefinitely..."). A second is required for this postponement to move to vote. A majority vote is required to postpone a motion indefinitely. It may not ever be brought up again.

3. *Amend.* To change a motion, a person suggests an amendment. Let's say you support an idea in principle but not exactly as presented. Raise your hand and make the motion: "I move to amend the motion on the floor." This also requires a second. After the motion to amend is seconded, a majority vote is needed to decide whether the amended proposal is accepted. Then a vote is taken. Sometimes, a "friendly amendment" is made. If the person who made the original motion agrees with the changes, it can be voted on without a second.

4. *Commit.* This is used to place a motion in committee. It requires a second motion. There must be a majority vote for it to be carried forward to the next meeting. A committee is required to prepare a report on the motion committed before the next meeting. If an appropriate committee exists, the motion goes to that committee. If not, a new committee is established.

5. *Question.* To end a debate, the question is called (say "I call the question") and needs a second. A vote is held without additional discussion. A two-thirds vote is required for passage.

6. *Table.* To table a discussion is to lay aside the matter so that it is considered later ("I make a motion to table this discussion until the next meeting. In the meantime, we will get more information so we can better discuss the issue."). A second is needed and a majority vote is required to table the item.

7. *Adjourn.* A motion is made to end the meeting. A second motion is required. A majority vote is then required for the meeting to be adjourned (ended).

Although these rules date back to the 1800s, many organizations follow Robert's Rules of Order, particularly universities and government organizations. The rules involve decision-making by majority voting, but voting creates winners and losers, and so an alternative to simple majority voting is discussed next.

Multivoting

In practice, it is often required that votes be taken. Given that voting has a number of disadvantages including dissatisfaction with decisions and lack of commitment, a manager should know that **multivoting** is another option. The steps for multivoting follow.[101] As with other team decision-making techniques, you need a flip chart or whiteboard, marking pens, 5 to 10 slips of paper for each individual, and a pen or pencil for each individual.

1. *Display the list of options.* Combine duplicate items. Organize large numbers of ideas, and eliminate duplication and overlap. List reduction may also be useful.
2. *Number (or letter) all items.*
3. *Decide how many items must be on the final reduced list.* Decide also how many choices each member will vote for. Usually, five choices are allowed. The longer the original list, the more votes will be allowed—up to 10.
4. *Working individually, each member selects the five items (or whatever number of choices is allowed) they think are most important.* Then each member ranks the choices in order of priority, with the first choice ranking highest. For example, if each member has five votes, the top choice would be ranked 5, the next choice 4, and so on. Each choice is written on a separate paper, with the ranking underlined in the lower right corner.

5. *Tally votes.* Collect the papers, shuffle them, and then record the votes on a flip chart or whiteboard. The easiest way to record votes is for the scribe to write all the individual rankings next to each choice. For each item, the rankings are totaled next to the individual rankings.

6. *If a decision is clear, stop here. Otherwise, continue with a brief discussion of the vote.* The purpose of the discussion is to look at dramatic voting differences, such as an item that received both 5 and 1 ratings and avoid errors from incorrect information or understandings about the item. The discussion should not pressure anyone to change their vote. Also, if a team member or members feel strongly that an option should be considered, the team can put it back in the voting process.

7. *Repeat the voting process in Steps 4 and 5.* If greater decision-making accuracy is required, this voting may be done by weighting the relative importance of each choice on a scale of 1 to 10, with 10 being most important. As can be seen from this process, multivoting allows for multiple rounds of discussion as the list gets reduced. It allows team members to have more of a voice in the final decision through a series of votes rather than just one.

CRITICAL THINKING QUESTIONS

What are the advantages and disadvantages of multivoting? Would you consider using this technique? Why or why not?

Brainstorming

Brainstorming is one of the most common forms of an enhancement to team decision-making.[102] Brainstorming should be used when the team needs to produce a creative solution. It enhances the creative process because idea generation is separated from idea evaluation. Members are trained not to critique ideas but just to write them down as the group generates solutions to a problem. Ideas are typically written on flip-chart paper or a whiteboard so that everyone can see them. The team meets in a separate session to evaluate the ideas generated and decide on a course of action.

Consensus

Consensus decision-making is another technique that is commonly used in organizations. In many cases, consensus is preferable to voting (although voting is more common). In a consensus decision-making process, everyone can say they have been heard and will support the final decision. The consensus model involves collaboratively generating a proposal, identifying unsatisfied concerns, and then modifying the proposal to create as much agreement as possible. The following steps are suggested for reaching consensus:[103]

- Step 1: Have a discussion.
- Step 2: Identify emerging proposals.
- Step 3: Identify any unsatisfied concerns.
- Step 4: Collaboratively modify the proposal.

Brainstorming enhances team decision-making.

©iStockphoto.com/PeopleImages

- Step 5: Assess the degree of support.
- Step 6: Finalize the decision.

or

- Circle back to Step 1 or 3.
- Finalize a decision.

To finalize a decision, a variety of decision rules can be applied. The following are some possible options:[104]

- Unanimous agreement
- Unanimity minus one vote
- Unanimity minus two votes
- Super majority thresholds (90%, 80%, 75%, two-thirds, and 60% are common)
- Simple majority
- Executive committee decides
- Person-in-charge decides

After the discussion, if someone still disagrees, they can abstain from supporting the decision. However, when using consensus decision-making, it's best to discuss the issue until everyone can support the implementation of a decision.

Consensus is one of the most commonly used and effective decision-making processes in organizations. The consensus guidelines should be followed in situations in which the support of all members of a team is needed for effective implementation of the decision. You will have the opportunity to practice consensus decision-making in a team in Toolkit Activity 11.2.

CRITICAL THINKING QUESTIONS

> Explain why following the consensus guidelines will result in more support for the implementation of a decision rather than simply voting on it. Which other team decision-making techniques would be effective for implementation?

Nominal Group Technique

The **nominal group technique (NGT)** is a more structured process that may be effective if there are status differences in the team or if the team has one or more dominating participants. The group meets face-to-face, but the discussion is more restricted than in brainstorming or consensus decision-making. This process reduces status differentials because participates write their ideas on index cards and a facilitator collects the cards. This process is particularly effective when the team has a dominating participant who shuts down the team discussion with criticism. Research has indicated that NGT works better than brainstorming.[105] NGT is often used by senior management teams as a preparation tool for productive strategy meetings. The steps for the NGT follow:[106]

1. Each team member independently writes their ideas on the problem on 3 × 5 cards or slips of paper.
2. Each member presents one idea to the team. The cards are collected by the facilitator who can either read them or redistribute them randomly to the team members

who then read the ideas on the card. This way, no one is identified with a particular idea.

3. The discussion continues until all ideas are heard and recorded.

4. The team discusses the ideas and asks questions to clarify them.

5. Each team member then silently ranks the ideas independently. The idea with the highest total ranking is the final decision.

Stepladder

The **stepladder technique** that may also be an effective way to combat the challenge of dominating participants in the team. The process is shown in Figure 11.10.

Stepladder decision-making has five steps:[107]

▼ FIGURE 11.10

Stepladder Decision-Making Technique

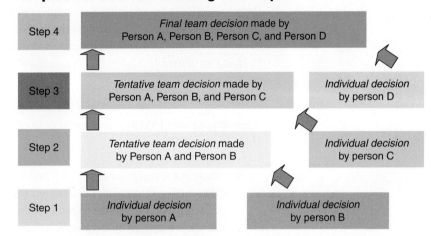

Source: Adapted from Rogelberg, S. G., & O'Connor, M. S. (1998). Extending the stepladder technique: An examination of self-paced stepladder groups. *Group Dynamics, 2*, 82–91.

1. *Present the task.* Before getting together as a group, present the task or problem to all members. Give everyone sufficient time to think about what needs to be done and to form their own opinions on how to best accomplish the task or solve the problem.

2. *Have a two-member discussion.* Form a core group of two members. Have them discuss the problem.

3. *Add one member.* Add a third group member to the core group. The third member presents ideas to the first two members *before* hearing the ideas that have already been discussed. After all three members have laid out their solutions and ideas, they discuss their options together.

4. *Repeat, adding one member at a time.* Repeat the same process by adding a fourth member and so on to the group. Allow time for discussion after each additional member has presented his or her ideas.

5. *Reach a final decision.* Reach a final decision only after all members have been brought in and presented their ideas.

An experiment was conducted to see if the stepladder technique resulted in higher-quality decisions compared to consensus decision-making.[108] Stepladder groups produced significantly higher-quality decisions than did conventional groups in which all members worked on the problem at the same time. Stepladder group decisions surpassed the quality of their best individual members' decisions 56% of the time. In contrast, conventional group decisions surpassed the quality of their best members' decisions only 13% of the time.

Delphi Method

The **Delphi method**[109] is a decision-making technique that employs a panel of independent experts. It was developed by the RAND Corporation in the 1950s for the Department of Defense as a decision-making tool. Experts are given a proposal and complete an assessment of it over several rounds. These experts can be colocated or they can be dispersed geographically and submit their ideas from anywhere in the world. After each round, a facilitator provides an anonymous summary of the experts' predictions or problem solutions from the previous round as well as the rationale each provided. Participants are encouraged to revise their earlier answers in light of the replies of other members of the group. Over time, the expert panel converges on the best prediction. This technique allows a manager to gather information from a wide range of expert sources to make better decisions, thereby utilizing the wisdom of many.

Managerial Implications

This chapter provided an overview of managing teams. The key takeaway points from this chapter are as follows:

- There is a difference between a working group and a team. One of the most important differences is that a team has a shared goal, and members of a working group work independently without having to produce a shared product. Teams create synergy, in which the whole is greater than the sum of the parts.
- One of the most important tools a manager has is to have their team create a team charter. A team charter states the team's mission or goal and clearly lays out the expectations for team behavior. Examples of the ground rules are participation, rules for attendance, and how the team will resolve conflict. Toolkit Activity 11.1 takes you through the steps to create an effective team charter.
- Teams have life cycles and move through predictable stages. One approach is the team development model, which has stages of forming, storming, norming, performing, and adjourning. Another approach is the punctuated equilibrium model, in which the team suddenly becomes more active in working on the task at the midpoint from the start and finish of a team project. The team performance curve explains how teams may suffer performance losses during storming as they move from a working group to a pseudo-team. Some teams become potential teams and the real teams that have higher performance. Finally, high-performance teams are rare, but they outperform all other types of teams.
- Team effectiveness is measured by the output or performance of the team. Other indicators of team effectiveness are team affect, viability, creativity, and learning. A useful tool to monitor team effectiveness is the creation of a team dashboard.
- Teams face a number of challenges that may inhibit performance such as groupthink and social loafing. Managers need to anticipate these challenges and employ evidence-based strategies to avoid or minimize them. Other challenges are due to diversity in multicultural teams and/or working online in virtual teams. Teams also experience conflict, which must be effectively managed. Self-Assessment 11.2 allows you to measure your team conflict, which could be included on your team dashboard. Managers should also be aware that peer pressure due to team cohesion and strong team norms may lead to unethical behavior by individuals.
- Teams are often used to make decisions. They brainstorm new ideas and then have a number of techniques available to make decisions, including Robert's Rules of Order, multivoting, consensus, the nominal group technique, and the stepladder technique. Practice consensus decision-making by getting together with your team and conducting Toolkit Activity 11.2.

Teams are now common in organizations and employers expect managers to be able to work in and effectively lead teams. Chapter 12 will go into more detail on how to become an effective managerial leader.

KEY TERMS

TOOLKIT

Activity 11.1

The Team Charter

Getting Started: Developing Ground Rules

Anyone who plays sports has to learn the rules. Anyone who learns to play an instrument has to learn the techniques. The rules of "how we do things here" (the etiquette of the situation and the appropriate behaviors) are the ground rules.

Teams often begin by making assumptions about ground rules. Members believe that everyone knows how it should be and how everyone should behave. When someone else's behavior fails to conform to one's own expectations, people tend to be surprised. Even more importantly, because the rules are not clear and because there has been no discussion as to how problems will be managed, unnecessary conflict follows. This assignment serves the following objectives:

- It gives you the opportunity to get to know your team members.
- It provides a short but *important* task so that the team can learn to function quickly without a large portion of your grade resting on the initial outcome.

- It enables the team to develop and understand the rules of conduct expected of each team member.

Your team will be required to submit a team charter. The following points that must be included in your charter are listed next, with some examples of the kinds of questions that might be addressed. However, use these as starting points; be sure to address any other important issues that come up in your discussions.

Attendance

How often should we meet?
How long should our meetings be?
When is it okay to miss a meeting?

Lateness

Since team meetings should start on time, how do we deal with lateness?
What does "on time" mean?

Interruptions

How do we deal with interruptions?
What is allowed? Phone calls? Messages?

Food, Coffee, and Breaks

Do we have food or coffee?

Who cleans up?

How many breaks should we have?

How much socializing is permissible?

Participation

What do we mean by participation?

How do we encourage participation?

Are there group norms that we can establish to encourage participation?

Goals

What are the team's goals and objectives?

What is the team's mission?

How will the team keep members motivated?

How will the team reward itself (and individual members) for a job well done?

Norms

What behaviors are permissible?

How do we deal with inappropriate humor?

How do we deal with people who dominate, resist, are too quiet, are too noisy, and so on?

How will we monitor our progress?

What important roles need to be assumed by team members during the semester? How will these roles be assigned?

Decision-Making

How do we make decisions?

What decisions must be agreed to by all?

What does consensus mean?

Conflict

How will the team encourage positive (creative) conflict and discourage negative (dysfunctional) conflict? How can the team encourage and manage differences of opinion and different perspectives?

Sanction Issues (What Will the Team Do With Deviates?)

How will the team deal with members who violate the agreed-upon norms of the team? For example, how will social loafing or inadequate participation be dealt with?

Firing Team Members

What are the specific rules or criteria for firing a team member? (You must give two written notices to the person and a copy to the professor prior to dismissal.)

Team Member Strengths and Weaknesses

Each team member should be identified (name, phone number, email) along with an assessment of their strengths and areas for improvement.

Other

Are there other issues that have a positive or negative impact on the team?

The Next Step: A Name and a Logo

After your team has prepared its team charter, create a name for your team and design a logo. The name and logo should be meaningful to the team, reflecting an attribute that the team members believe is important (humor is allowed and encouraged, but both the team logo and name should be meaningful). The name is limited to one or two words. Write a brief explanation of your name and logo choice. Give a copy to your instructor (along with your team charter). Your team charter should also include the following:

- A cover page with the following printed on it: the team name, team logo, team member names, and course name, number, and section
- A page with team member names, phone numbers, and email addresses
- Team charter rules and expectations
- A brief explanation of your team name and logo choice

Source: Adapted from Cox, P. L., & Bobrowski, P. E. (2000). The team charter assignment: Improving the effectiveness of classroom teams. *Journal of Behavioral and Applied Management, 1*(1), 92–103.

Activity 11.2

Team Decision-Making by Consensus: Hurricane Survival

The Situation

You have been monitoring local news broadcasts for a week and Hurricane Tracy is certain to strike your area. You have covered the windows of your home with plywood and put sandbags around your doors. You live in an evacuation area and your governor has ordered evacuation for your area. You have discussed the situation with your neighbors and most of them have decided to stay and "ride it out." You decide to assemble a hurricane survival kit so that you will be ready for the hurricane. *Do not read ahead to see the expert rankings!*

First rank the following list of items individually, without discussing it with your team. Give the item that you think is most important to your survival a 1, the item that you think is second most important to your survival a 2, and so on until you have ranked all 12 items. You must rank all items and there can be no ties. Enter your rankings in the first column, "Individual." After you have done this ranking, meet with a team of at least five people and rank the items using the consensus decision-making method described in this chapter. You can assume that your team members are the people that live in your home, and you have all decided to stay together. Even if you are persuaded by your team members during the discussion, don't change your individual rankings. Enter your team rankings in the column labeled "Team."

	Individual	Difference 1	Expert	Difference 2	Team
Ax					
Radio with NOAA band					
Bug spray					
Maps of state and region					
Cash					
Gas in gas cans					
Power bank charger					
Car with full tank of gas					
One backpack per person					
Water (2 gallons per person)					
Flashlight with batteries					
Cans of tuna fish and beans					
Add the Columns (Absolute Values; Ignore + and -)		Individual Score:_____			Team Score:_____

Interpretation

You will now compare your results to a survival expert's rankings using a difference score method. Enter the survival expert's rankings in the column labeled "Expert." The expert ranking is provided below. These rankings are generally based on a YouTube video that provides more explanation of the rankings (https://www.youtube.com/watch? v=litakVUrWg8). Here are the expert's rankings:

1. Maps of state and region
2. Backpacks
3. Car (inspected and in good condition)
4. Water
5. Canned tuna and beans (nonperishable food)
6. Flashlight with batteries
7. Gas (in car and in cans)
8. Cash
9. Ax
10. Radio with NOAA band
11. Power bank charger (for cell phones)
12. Bug spray

Write the above rankings in the center column, labeled "Expert." To compute the degree to which you agreed with the survival expert, do the following calculations:

- Subtract your individual ranking from the expert ranking and enter it in the second column, "Difference 1." Take the absolute value (i.e., ignore pluses and minuses).
- Then do the same for your team ranking (subtract the team ranking from the expert ranking) and enter it in the column labeled "Difference 2."

- Add down both columns to obtain an individual score and a team score. Note: Lower scores are better because this means that the score is lower than the expert ranking.
- Subtract the individual score from the team score to determine whether you did better alone or as a member of the team. Positive scores indicate that your survival chances were enhanced by discussing the situation with your team members. Negative scores mean that you could have survived alone. The person with the lowest score knew the most about hurricane survival prior to this exercise.

Discussion Questions

1. Did your team do better than your individual score? How did team decision-making help or hinder the decision?
2. How many members in your team had a score that was better (i.e., lower) than the team score? Who had the lowest (best) score? Did the team listen to this person? Why or why not?
3. If all of the individual scores were higher than the team score, you achieved "synergy" (the team did better than anyone could have done alone). Did you? Explain why you did or did not improve your overall chances for survival in this situation.
4. What did you learn about team decision-making that will enable you to effectively use teams to make organizational decisions?

Source: Adapted from Thorn, C. (2017). *Top 10 best hurricane survival tip items*. Retrieved from https://www.youtube.com/watch? v=litakVUrWg8.

Case Study 11.1

For Companies, Virtual Teams Shrink the Map

When corporations want to bring together the brightest and best talent for a particular project, it no longer matters where the workers are located, thanks to the growing use of virtual teams. "Virtual teams aren't an extra for a global company; they're the real core of how we work and the value proposition we offer our customers," says Patricia Rossman, chief diversity officer with the German chemical manufacturer BASF. "Virtual teams give you the reach to pull together a variety of different perspectives on how we meet market needs. Because we don't all think alike, we're able to anticipate needs in different parts of the world, and we're able to look through different lenses."

Nearly half of all organizations surveyed by the Society for Human Resource Management (SHRM) in 2012 used virtual teams, but they were much more common for multinational corporations, used by two-thirds of such organizations. More than half of the multinationals turned to virtual teams because their work is becoming more globalized, requiring more collaboration across business units.

But effectively managing a virtual team is not so easy. More than 60% of respondents in the SHRM study found that developing trust among team members was extremely challenging. Other major issues included resolving personality conflicts, settling disputes over tasks and information, and monitoring the performance of team members. On the flipside, the teams were most successful in brainstorming to address issues, setting goals, and developing plans for projects.

Teleconferences and video conferences facilitate the creation of "virtual teams" of employees in diverse locations for multinational corporations.

"The big challenge without the benefit of face-to-face regular interaction is that it's hard to build trust and rapport," says Madeline Boyer, teamwork consultant at the Wharton School's executive education program and coauthor of *Committed Teams: Three Steps to Inspiring Passion and Performance*. One way to improve teamwork is by establishing a virtual water cooler that relies on off-topic email chains, chat platforms, and other social tools.

Committed Teams cites the example of GitHub, a software company based in San Francisco with workers around the globe: "Employees are encouraged to shamelessly boast about their accomplishments on the company's internal messaging platforms. In response, their global teammates post selfies in which they raise a glass to acknowledge the success." At BASF, much of a team's success relies on its leadership, says Luciana Amaro, the company's vice president of talent development and strategy. Some of the key skills required by a team leader include being able to successfully tap into the diversity of team members, create trust, listen effectively, empower team members, set up processes to monitor members' work, and manage conflict.

It's also important for the team leader to pull together employees of different generations. "We do have some situations where we have new people joining our research and development team, for example, and they're working with people who wrote the textbook that they studied under," Rossman says. And she's found that employees are often interested in taking part in virtual teams "as a way to get exposure and network and participate at earlier experience levels."

Virtual team membership also can be used as a development opportunity for employees in remote parts of the world, says William Castellano, associate dean of executive and professional education at Rutgers University. One thing corporations need to keep in mind when setting up virtual teams is the cultural differences of team members. "Processes that might be very successful here may not work in different parts of the world," Castellano says. For example, it might be natural for members from some cultures to speak up during a meeting, but "often for people from cultures that are a little bit less assertive, they won't offer an opinion if they're not asked."

At BASF, English is the working language, but employees may be hesitant to speak if it isn't their mother tongue. To address that, a team leader may hold a round-robin session so everyone takes a turn speaking or may call on different people for their input at different parts of the meeting, Amaro says.

The real driver of virtual teams has been the advancement of technology, Castellano says. Corporations no longer have to rely just on conference calls and email. Instead, videoconferencing, document sharing, and other technological developments improve organizations' ability to share knowledge across borders.

It also allows the incorporation of contract workers into virtual teams. "With knowledge workers, there's often no choice but to engage outside people," Castellano says. At BASF, virtual teams seldom meet in person, if at all. Members may come together for a kickoff meeting or for certain milestones in a project. By relying on virtual teams, the company reduces travel costs and makes international collaboration easier for employees—particularly those who have families and may not want to travel, Amaro says. "If we had to really be mobile to be able to deliver what we deliver in a virtual way, I believe it wouldn't be sustainable from a cost perspective and also from a willingness of employees' perspective," she says.

Discussion Questions

1. Why do you think it is more difficult to develop trust in a virtual team compared to a team that meets

face-to-face? Explain how you would develop trust in a virtual team.

2. Discuss the advantages and disadvantages of working in virtual teams.

3. Do you prefer to work on a virtual team or meet face-to-face? Explain why.

Sources: Ladika, S. (2016, June 6). For companies, virtual teams shrink the map. *SAGE Business Researcher.* Retrieved from http://businessresearcher.sagepub.com/sbr-1775-99951-2733738/20160606/short-article-for-companies-virtual-teams-shrink-the-map; Moussa, M., Boyer, M., & Newberry, D. (2016). *Committed teams: Three steps to inspiring passion and performance* (p. 95). Hoboken, NY: John Wiley; and Society for Human Resource Management. (2012, July 13). Virtual teams. Retrieved from https://www.shrm.org/hr-today/trends-and-forecasting/research-and-surveys/Pages/virtualteams.aspx.

Self-Assessment 11.1

Effective Team Role Behaviors

This self-assessment exercise assesses how well you execute different role behaviors in your team. The goal of this assessment is for you to learn about your general orientation to team roles and to understand how this may affect how your behavior in a team. There are no right or wrong answers, and this is not a test. You don't have to share your results with others unless you wish to do so.

Part I. Taking the Assessment

Circle the response to the following prompt that best describes your role orientation.

Based on my prior experiences, as a member of different teams . . .

Statements	None	Almost None	A Small Amount	Neutral	Some	A Fair Amount	A Lot
1. I'm comfortable being critical of my teammates.	1	2	3	4	5	6	7
2. I like it when we keep busy and get things done.	1	2	3	4	5	6	7
3. I like to challenge peoples' assumptions.	1	2	3	4	5	6	7
4. I like to be the one that sorts out the details of a team project.	1	2	3	4	5	6	7
5. I like to be the one who decides who will do which tasks on a team.	1	2	3	4	5	6	7
6. I'm always ready to support a good suggestion in the common interest of the team.	1	2	3	4	5	6	7
7. I like to try out new ideas and approaches.	1	2	3	4	5	6	7
8. I can be counted on when a task needs to be done.	1	2	3	4	5	6	7
9. I'm comfortable dealing with interpersonal conflicts and helping people work through them.	1	2	3	4	5	6	7
10. I enjoy coordinating team efforts with people or groups outside of the team.	1	2	3	4	5	6	7
11. I can be counted on to spread ideas between my team and people outside of my team.	1	2	3	4	5	6	7
12. I'm comfortable being the spokesperson for a team.	1	2	3	4	5	6	7
13. I'm often the first to volunteer for a difficult or unpopular assignment if that is what the team needs.	1	2	3	4	5	6	7

14. I like to be the one who keeps track of how well my team is doing.	1	2	3	4	5	6	7
15. I bring a sense of organization to any job a team undertakes.	1	2	3	4	5	6	7
16. I get bored when we do the same task the same way every time.	1	2	3	4	5	6	7
17. I'm not afraid to question my teammates' authority.	1	2	3	4	5	6	7
18. I typically find out what is going on outside my team and share that with my teammates.	1	2	3	4	5	6	7
19. I like coming up with new ways that our team can accomplish our tasks.	1	2	3	4	5	6	7
20. I like helping different kinds of people work effectively together.	1	2	3	4	5	6	7
21. I'm comfortable producing and sharing new ideas with my team.	1	2	3	4	5	6	7
22. It bothers me when I see teammates getting frustrated or depressed.	1	2	3	4	5	6	7
23. I'm always committed to my team tasks.	1	2	3	4	5	6	7
24. I can typically provide a strong rationale to refute ideas that I believe are unsound.	1	2	3	4	5	6	7

Part II. Scoring Instructions

In Part I, you rated yourself on 24 questions. Add the numbers you circled in each of the columns to derive your scores for the six team behaviors. During class, we will discuss each role and how this may affect your team.

Organizer	Doer	Challenger	Innovator	Team Builder	Connector
4. _____	2. _____	1. _____	7. _____	6. _____	10. _____
5. _____	8. _____	3. _____	16. _____	9. _____	11. _____
14. _____	13. _____	17. _____	19. _____	20. _____	12. _____
15. _____	23. _____	24. _____	21. _____	22. _____	18. _____
Total O_____	Total D_____	Total CH _____	Total I_____	Total T_____	Total CO_____

Interpretation

- *Organizer*—You act to structure what the team is doing. An organizer also keeps track of accomplishments and how the team is progressing relative to goals and timelines.
- *Doer*—You willingly take on work and get things done. A doer can be counted on to complete work, meet deadlines, and take on tasks to ensure the team's success.

- *Challenger*—You will push the team to explore all aspects of a situation and to consider alternative assumptions, explanations, and solutions. A challenger often asks "why" and is comfortable debating and critiquing.
- *Innovator*—You regularly generate new and creative ideas, strategies, and approaches for how the team can handle various situations and challenges. An innovator often offers original and imaginative suggestions.

- *Team Builder*—You help establish norms, support decisions, and maintain a positive work atmosphere within the team. A team builder calms members when they are stressed and motivates them when they are down.
- *Connector*—You help bridge and connect the team with people, groups, or other stakeholders outside of the team. Connectors ensure good working relationships between the team and "outsiders," whereas team builders work to ensure good relationship within the team.

Scores can range from 7 to 28 for each dimension. In general, if your score is above 18, you demonstrate a high level of this behavior in your team. If your score is below 10, you demonstrate a below-average level of this behavior on your team.

Discussion Questions

1. Which two role behaviors do you demonstrate most in your team? Describe a situation of when your team or you demonstrated this behavior.
2. Which two role behaviors do you demonstrate the least? Discuss whether you would like to improve this behavior.

3. Discuss your role behaviors with members of your team. Are there any team members exhibiting the same behaviors? Are there any roles that are not being played by any member of the team? What can you do to ensure that all roles are being represented on the team?

Source: Adapted from Mathieu, J. E., Tannenbaum, S. I., Kukenberger, M. R., Donsbach, J. S., & Alliger, G. M. (2015). Team role experience and orientation: A measure and tests of construct validity. *Group & Organization Management, 40*(1), 6–34.

Self-Assessment 11.2

Team Conflict

This self-assessment exercise assesses how much conflict exists in your team. Think of a team that you are a part of. This can be a team at work, in class, or in an outside group. The goal of this assessment is for you to learn about your general assumptions about people and work and to understand how this may affect how you lead them. There are no right or wrong answers, and this is not a test. You don't have to share your results with others unless you wish to do so.

Part I. Taking the Assessment

Circle the response that best describes your team situation.

Statements	None	Almost None	A Small Amount	Neutral	Some	A Fair Amount	A Lot
1. How frequently are there conflicts about ideas in your team?	1	2	3	4	5	6	7
2. How much friction is there among members of your team?	1	2	3	4	5	6	7
3. How often do members disagree about who should do what?	1	2	3	4	5	6	7
4. How often do people in your team disagree about opinions regarding the work to be done?	1	2	3	4	5	6	7
5. How much are personality conflicts evident in your team?	1	2	3	4	5	6	7
6. How frequently do members disagree about the way to complete a team task?	1	2	3	4	5	6	7
7. How much conflict is there about the work you do?	1	2	3	4	5	6	7
8. How much tension is there among members of your team?	1	2	3	4	5	6	7
9. How much conflict about delegation of tasks exists in your team?	1	2	3	4	5	6	7
10. To what extent are there differences of opinions regarding tasks?	1	2	3	4	5	6	7
11. How much emotional conflict is there among members of your team?	1	2	3	4	5	6	7

Part II. Scoring Instructions

In Part I, you rated yourself on 11 questions. Add the numbers you circled in each of the columns to derive your scores for three types of team conflict. During class, we will discuss each approach, its strengths and weaknesses, and how this may affect your team.

Task Conflict	Relationship Conflict	Process Conflict
1. _____	2. _____	3. _____
4. _____	5. _____	6. _____
7. _____	8. _____	9. _____
10. _____	11. _____	
Total TC _____	Total RC_____	Total PC _____
÷ 4 _____	÷ 4 _____	÷ 3 _____

Total Team Conflict: Add TC_____ + RC _____ + PC _____ = _____ (can range from 3 to 17)

Source: Adapted from Wakefield, R. L., Leidner, D. E., & Garrison, G. (2008). Research note—a model of conflict, leadership, and performance in virtual teams. *Information Systems Research,* *19*(4), 434–455.

Interpretation

- *Task conflict* (TC) arises when task knowledge—an understanding of the necessary activities to reach team goals—is not fully understood or shared by team members. The result may be disagreements among members about work content, appropriate tasks, or assignment of team activities.
- *Relationship conflict* (RC) arises when relational knowledge—personal understanding of team members including individual cultures and norms—is insufficient. Relational conflict may evoke negative emotions and interpersonal disagreements between members not directly related to tasks.
- *Process conflict* (PC) stems from a lack of agreement concerning how work should be done. This type of conflict surfaces when members disagree on the methods and processes required to complete tasks.

Discussion Questions

1. Which type of conflict does your team experience the most: task, relationship, or process? Describe a situation of when your team had this type of conflict.
2. Which type of conflict does your team experience the least: task, relationship, or process? What team behaviors do you believe have led to the avoidance of this type of conflict?
3. If your total team conflict score is over 10, it can be considered a high amount of conflict. Does your team experience a lot of conflict? What can you do to reduce the amount of team conflict?

Source: Adapted from Wakefield, R. L., Leidner, D. E., & Garrison, G. (2008). Research note—a model of conflict, leadership, and performance in virtual teams. *Information Systems Research, 19*(4), 434–455.

Get the tools you need to sharpen your study skills. SAGE edge offers a robust online environment featuring an impressive array of free tools and resources. Access practice quizzes, eFlashcards, video, and multimedia at **edge.sagepub.com/scanduragower.**

Introducing…

⑤SAGE vantage™

Course tools done right.

Built to support teaching. Designed to ignite learning.

SAGE vantage is an intuitive digital platform that blends trusted SAGE content with auto-graded assignments, all carefully designed to ignite student engagement and drive critical thinking. Built with you and your students in mind, it offers easy course set-up and enables students to better prepare for class.

SAGE vantage enables students to engage with the material you choose, learn by applying knowledge, and soar with confidence by performing better in your course.

PEDAGOGICAL SCAFFOLDING	CONFIDENCE BUILDER	TIME-SAVING FLEXIBILITY	QUALITY CONTENT	HONEST VALUE
Builds on core concepts, moving students from basic understanding to mastery.	Offers frequent knowledge checks, applied-learning multimedia tools, and chapter tests with focused feedback.	Feeds auto-graded assignments to your gradebook, with real-time insight into student and class performance.	Written by expert authors and teachers, content is not sacrificed for technical features.	Affordable access to easy-to-use, quality learning tools students will appreciate.

To learn more about **SAGE vantage**, hover over this QR code with your smartphone camera or visit **sagepub.com/vantage**

CHAPTER 12

LEADERSHIP

CHAPTER LEARNING OBJECTIVES

After studying this chapter, you should be able to:

12.1 Discuss why leadership tends to be a difficult concept to define, and explain the difference between being a manager and being a leader.

12.2 Describe how the trait approach differs from other theories of leadership and how Dark Triad traits play a role in leadership.

12.3 Explain the difference between structure-initiating and consideration leadership behaviors.

12.4 Use path–goal theory to identify situational factors that help determine the appropriate leadership style.

12.5 Explain why and how leaders form high- and low-quality exchange relationships with different employees.

12.6 Discuss why trust is important, and how to repair it.

12.7 Illustrate the elements and progression of transactional and transformational leadership.

12.8 Compare and contrast the role of morality in ethical, servant, and authentic leadership.

Get the edge on your studies at **edge.sagepub .com/scanduragower**.

- Take the chapter quiz
- Review key terms with eFlashcards
- Explore multimedia resources, SAGE readings, and more!

What Makes an Effective Leader?

In this chapter, you will see that there are many theories about how leadership works. Each of these attempts to explain how different leadership styles, characteristics, and behaviors can help or hurt a leader's effectiveness. One thing that might surprise you, though, is finding that leadership is very hard to study empirically because it includes many tangible and intangible personal traits and factors, organizational performance, follower opinions, and the context in which the leader is operating.

Intangible factors such as trustworthiness, supportiveness, sensitivity, and ethicality are all critical to effective leadership but are very difficult to measure and analyze accurately. Objective performance indicators measure effectiveness, such as an organization's profitability and employee retention. However, the availability and relevance of these metrics varies considerably from one organization to another. In addition, all leaders have "followers" (for example, employees under their supervision) who can provide opinions (sometimes very different) regarding the leader's effectiveness.

For this reason, much of the research used to test the theories presented in this chapter has measured the effectiveness of leaders from the perspective of employees. There are advantages to this approach. Perhaps most importantly, employees are directly impacted by the decisions, behaviors, and characteristics of their supervisors, giving them insight that no observer can get on their own. The potential problem, however, is that people's evaluations of leaders are not always reliable.

As you might expect, asking employees to rate their managers' ethicality, trustworthiness, supportiveness, or effectiveness often produces conflicting data—even between employees who work together and share the same supervisor.[1] If you and a peer have ever shared divergent opinions about a manager or coach, you have seen how easily it can happen. A recent investigation[2] showed that research on leadership styles, behaviors, characteristics, and performance is impacted by this subjectivity. The authors replicated studies of several leadership behaviors, characteristics, and styles discussed in this chapter with and without a simple measure of "leader affect," a measure of how much employees like their manager as a person. Their findings suggested that employees' evaluations of how authentic, abusive, and ethical their managers were heavily impacted by how much they liked them as people. The influence was so strong that in some cases the measures could be swapped (for example, replacing the measure of ethical leadership with the measure of whether employees liked or disliked their managers) and produce the same results.[3]

Finally, all leaders share different situations in which they must lead, and this is known as context, or the circumstances that form the setting for an event, statement, or idea, and in terms of which it can be fully understood.[4] For example, the settings that military leaders might be making immediate personnel decisions under could include the pressures of life and death, whereas leaders of organizations might be making personnel decisions based on a more long-term, and peaceful, outcome.

▼ FIGURE 12.0

Textbook Organization

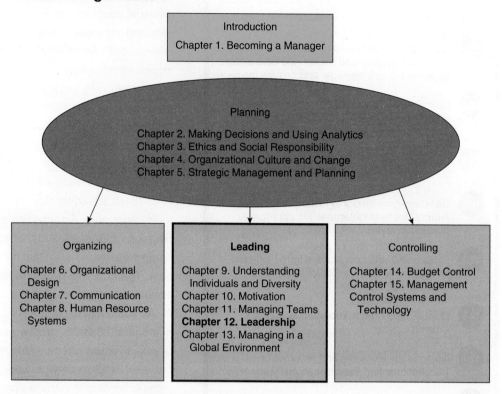

Introduction

Chapter 1. Becoming a Manager

Planning

Chapter 2. Making Decisions and Using Analytics
Chapter 3. Ethics and Social Responsibility
Chapter 4. Organizational Culture and Change
Chapter 5. Strategic Management and Planning

Organizing

Chapter 6. Organizational
Design
Chapter 7. Communication
Chapter 8. Human Resource
Systems

Leading

Chapter 9. Understanding
Individuals and Diversity
Chapter 10. Motivation
Chapter 11. Managing Teams
Chapter 12. Leadership
Chapter 13. Managing in a
Global Environment

Controlling

Chapter 14. Budget Control
Chapter 15. Management
Control Systems and
Technology

All of this serves as a reminder of how complex leadership truly is, and that there is no magic formula. What works in one situation is likely to fail in another and it is not always clear why. That is why we study all of the different facets of what makes an effective leader, and you will find an interesting section in this chapter that shows that effective leaders are not always "good" leaders.

What Is Leadership?

Learning Objective 12.1: Discuss why leadership tends to be a difficult concept to define, and explain the difference between being a manager and being a leader.

Leadership can mean different things to different people. No one can attest to this as well as Gary Yukl,[5] who examined half a century's worth of leadership books and studies to see how different authors define this concept. After identifying the common elements of hundreds of definitions, he developed the following description of leadership:

> Leadership is the process of influencing others to understand and agree about what needs to be done and how to do it, and the process of facilitating individual and collective efforts to accomplish shared objectives.[6]

Although this definition does not roll off the tongue, it does captures two key elements of leadership. First, it clarifies that it is an influence process, involving power and influence tactics that are covered in this chapter. Second, it recognizes that leadership involves directing individuals and groups toward organizational goals. Nevertheless, why is it important to define leadership if the term means different things to different people? One reason is that it helps us clarify the distinction between managers and leaders, as we discuss in the next

A pastor and leadership blogger named Ron Edmondson was inspired—by an internet post of all things—to summarize his observations about commonly held leadership myths in his book, *The Mythical Leader: The Seven Myths of Leadership.*[7] Here are the beliefs he hopes to dispel:

- **Leadership and management are the same thing.**[8] One may assume that all managers are leaders but that is not correct, since some managers do not exercise leadership and some people lead without having any management positions. Therefore, there is a continuing controversy about the difference between leaders and managers.[9]

- **A leadership position will make me a leader.** It will make you a manager, yes, but it takes more than a title to motivate and inspire.

- **If no one is complaining, no one is unhappy.** How many times have you walked up to your boss and criticized them to their face? Probably not too many. Leaders or not, people in positions of power can make life difficult for employees below them in the organizational hierarchy. For this reason, employees are not always forthcoming with constructive criticism. Leaders who have demonstrated a desire to learn from (and about) their mistakes, however, can benefit from the honest candor of their employees.

- **Being the leader makes me popular.**[10] Ingratiation is defined as illicit attempts by subordinates to increase their interpersonal attractiveness in the eyes of their superiors. In other words, the subordinate is trying to obtain the superior's approval. The end goal is to obtain valued career outcomes such as promotions, raises, and desirable assignments. This is not being popular; this is the popular term "kissing up." Never mistake ingratiation for respect, and leaders should always want to be respected, not necessarily liked.[11]

- **I can lead everyone the same way.** By the end of this chapter, you will have learned just how false this assumption is for most leaders. For example, the section on path–goal theory describes how employees with different skill levels often respond better to different leadership styles than more experienced employees.

- **Leaders must be charismatic extraverts.** While charisma and extraversion might help you as a leader, research shows that charisma is not always a positive characteristic and that introverts can also be effective leaders.

- **Leaders accomplish things by controlling others.** Edmondson explains that while this may be true for dictators, dictators are not true leaders. Only those who inspire followers to share their vision and goals fit the definition of a leader.[12]

Discussion Questions

1. What characteristics do you think an effective leader should have? Who do you know that exhibits these characteristics?

2. Myths often exist because they have the appearance of being true. Where do you think these myths come from? What do you think causes so many people to believe them?

3. Who are some examples of recent public figures that seemed to be leaders, but then their behaviors proved they were not?

Sources: Algahtani, A. (2014). Are leadership and management different? A review. *Journal of Management Policies and Practices*, *2*(3), 71–82; Deluga, R. J. (2003). Kissing up to the boss: What it is and what to do about it. *Business Forum*, *26*(3), 14–18; and Edmondson, R. (2017). *The mythical leader: The seven myths of leadership.* Nashville, TN: HarperCollins.

---

section. Another is that, absent a shared definition, misconceptions about leadership have a way of spreading. If you or anyone you know has ever experienced a "bad boss" (check out https://www.thoughtco.com/bad-bosses-in-movies-2432060 for a fun review of the top 10 bad boss movies), chances are that boss had a fundamental misunderstanding about what it means to be a leader. See the Fact or Fiction? feature for some common examples of these misunderstandings.

Managers Versus Leaders

Leading and motivating employees toward the attainment of organizational goals is a fundamental aspect of management. So, what is the difference between a manager and a leader? Are all managers leaders? Are all leaders managers? In his examination of leadership research, Yukl observed that even people who write about these topics for a living sometimes blur the lines between leadership and management. To help clarify the distinction, Warren Bennis's classic book, *On Becoming a Leader*, provides the following summary of the differences between being a manager and being a leader:[13]

Leadership and Management

- The manager administers; the leader innovates.
- The manager is a copy; the leader is an original.
- The manager maintains; the leader develops.
- The manager focuses on systems and structure; the leader focuses on people.
- The manager relies on control; the leader inspires trust.
- The manager has a short-range view; the leader has a long-range perspective.
- The manager asks how and when; the leader asks what and why.
- The manager has their eye always on the bottom line; the leader's eye is on the horizon.
- The manager imitates; the leader originates.
- The manager accepts the status quo; the leader challenges it.
- The manager is the classic good soldier; the leader is their own person.
- The manager does things right; the leader does the right thing.

Managers embody characteristics of both leadership and management.

©iStockphoto.com/filadendron

A second researcher, Abraham Zaleznik, posed a similar question in a *Harvard Business Review* article, "Managers and Leaders: Are They Different?"[14] He concedes that there is some overlap between the definition of managers and leaders (see Figure 12.1), but he makes the important point that an organization typically needs both to function optimally.

On the surface, this argument may seem a bit counterintuitive. Looking at the list above, it is easy to conclude that managers' duties tend to be more task oriented, or as we have said, planning, organizing, and controlling (POC) oriented, compared to the innovative and exciting roles played by leaders. This view, however, ignores the vital and challenging role of managers who are often tasked with translating leaders' visions into reality. Zaleznik explains that managers are day-to-day problem solvers, while leaders focus on developing new approaches and options for the future. As shown in Figure 12.1, leadership involves inspiring others to follow their vision for the organization. This is certainly a valuable ability to possess, but managers are the ones charged with POC of the operations of the organization, ensuring that employees and processes function effectively in pursuit of the leader's vision and the organization's shared goals. Both of these roles are critical, as is depicted in Figure 12.1.

You should have a pretty good idea that "leaderment," while sounding funny, is very much a place where some managers and some leaders find themselves. By learning what the leader's vision is and, in return, understanding the POC roles of the manager, organizations are much more likely to succeed.

The next section talks about leadership traits, a popular group of theories of how leaders come to be.

Leadership Traits

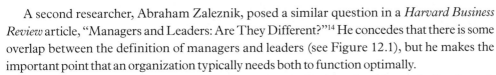

Learning Objective 12.2: Describe how the trait approach differs from other theories of leadership and how Dark Triad traits plays a role in leadership.

Judging by cave paintings depicting power differences among tribes of Neanderthals, it would appear that leadership has been of interest to human beings since the dawn of civilization.[15] It is only in the past few decades, however, that we have begun to study it from a scientific perspective. Prior to this, leadership was often viewed as something "great men" achieved, by virtue of their noble characteristics and heroic deeds. This line of thinking gave rise to the

Traits of U.S. Presidents (1953–2000)

	IQ	Extraversion	Agreeableness	Conscientiousness	Neuroticism	Openness
Average U.S. citizen	98	50	50	50	50	50
Average U.S. president (1953–2000)	134.73	78	26	57	46	39
Average U.S. president (1776–2000)	134.54	69	24	72	56	28
Eisenhower	131.90	71	33	98	30	29
Kennedy	150.56	99	11	5	27	82
Johnson	127.83	99	1	72	95	7
Nixon	131.00	7	.02	98	97	14
Ford	127.08	91	53	69	15	8
Carter	145.10	58	56	99	76	77
Reagan	130.00	98	28	9	4	10
H. W. Bush*	130.13	N/A	N/A	N/A	N/A	N/A
Clinton	148.80	99	24	5	24	82

*The authors did not estimate personality scores for George H. W. Bush, citing a lack of reliable data.

Sources: Lynn, R., & Meisenberg, G. (2010). National IQs calculated and validated for 108 nations. *Intelligence, 38*(4), 353–360; Rubenzer, S. J., & Faschingbauer, T. R. (2004). *Personality, character, and leadership in the White House: Psychologists assess the presidents.* Washington, DC: Potomac Books; and Simonton, D. K. (2006). Presidential IQ, openness, intellectual brilliance, and leadership: Estimates and correlations for 42 US chief executives. *Political Psychology, 27*(4), 511–526.

"great man" theory of leadership, so named by a 19th century author who wrote that, "The history of the world is but the biography of great men."[16] Although the simplicity of this approach, not to mention the sexist title, seems bizarre by today's standards, it was not entirely inaccurate. Throughout history, there is evidence of common traits shared by effective leaders.[17]

A more refined perspective, known as the **trait approach**, attempts to identify these characteristics. Early research identified traits such as drive (achievement, ambition, energy, tenacity, initiative), vigor, originality, and cognitive ability (IQ) in people who held leadership positions.[18] Its focus on stable traits, which are generally characteristics that people are born with or develop at a young age, as predictors of leadership effectiveness remains somewhat controversial, however. Although the question of whether great leaders are "born or made" has been debated for centuries, the view that effective leadership can be taught dominates modern thinking, and outcomes, on the subject. For example, reading the *Steve Jobs* book by Walter Isaacson[19] leads many to believe that Jobs was born a leader—charismatic, ambitious, and smart—but a review of his successor, Tim Cook, reveals an introverted and quiet man who still successfully leads the Apple organization.

The trait approach, however, suggests that factors such as personality and intelligence largely predetermine our capacity for leadership. This, in turn, implies that organizations should focus their energy on selecting the right people for leadership positions rather than attempting to train them. Although the proliferation of leadership training programs in modern companies such as IBM, Unilever, and John Deere[20] shows us that this view has its detractors, it is difficult to fully refute the importance of traits. Consider the profiles of U.S. presidents during the second half of the 20th century shown in Table 12.1, which shows how they scored on the Big Five personality test introduced in Chapter 9 as compared to the average U.S. citizen.

Table 12.1 summarizes estimates of two types of traits: IQ and the Big Five personality traits. With the exception of IQ scores, these numbers represent percentiles. This means that for the five personality traits (see Chapter 9 for a review of these), a score of 50 is the population average, scores in the range from 51 to 100 are above average, and scores between 0 and 49 are below average.

What does this information tell us about the traits of elected presidents versus the average U.S. citizen?

- Although it is important to remember that these data are based on imperfect estimates,[21] it would appear that above-average intelligence is a requirement of the job.
- What about personality traits? Unsurprisingly, late 20th-century U.S. presidents tend to be extraverts, although recent research points to introverts (like Tim Cook) as being successful organization leaders.[22]
- We can also assume, however, that not all of this extraverted engagement is friendly banter. Looking at the next trait, agreeableness, we see that U.S. presidents are consistently below average when it comes to being cooperative, modest, or trusting of others.[23]

So far, it appears that traits play a major role in determining a candidate's odds of being elected president. If a candidate is an agreeable introvert with average intelligence, history is not on their side to be president. If we continue to the right side of the table, however, we see that not all traits are shared so consistently.

- The conscientiousness trait provides a particularly striking example of this, with most of these presidents scoring at the very high or very low ends of the scale. Conscientious people are goal oriented, organized, and dependable, and research has consistently linked this to effective leadership.[24] It is therefore interesting to see that three of the eight presidents' conscientiousness scores rank in the bottom 10% of the population. Stranger still, these same three (Kennedy, Reagan, and Clinton) were, by most measures, among the most popular presidents of the 20th century.[25]
- The neuroticism (or its inverse, emotional stability) scores show a bit more consistency, with most presidents possessing relatively stable emotional tendencies. It is notable that the three presidents with relatively high neuroticism scores (Nixon, Johnson, and Carter) left office with some of the lowest approval ratings of the 20th century.[26] Only one, Nixon, was elected to a second term, and that term ended prematurely with the Watergate scandal (you might have learned about this in history class, but the full story is pretty interesting and you can find it here: https://www.history.com/topics/1970s/watergate).
- Finally, take a look at the scores for the openness to experience trait. What trends or patterns do you see? None? Given the range of openness levels and the lack of any obvious impact on a president's success, we might conclude that this particular trait is less important for the job of U.S. president. It may also be that the value of openness fluctuates at different points in history. For example, Kennedy's strong openness to experience was apparent in his successful challenge to land a person on the moon, whereas Ford's stoic, stay-the-course personality has been viewed as the perfect antidote to the scandals that plagued his predecessor, Nixon.[27]

CRITICAL THINKING QUESTIONS

Think of some leaders currently in the news. What traits have you noticed to be common or uncommon compared to other leaders? What makes these traits important or unimportant?

What can we learn from this section? That traits *do* have important implications for leadership, but that it is not always easy to understand which traits are important in a given context, or even what that impact might be. It is clear, for example, that extraverts are more likely than introverts to seek out and/or be chosen for leadership positions.[28] Extraverts may also be more effective leaders but the evidence is less clear, suggesting that the relationship between this trait and leadership performance may depend on the type of leadership position in question.[29] The importance of other traits like openness to experience also appear to be situation specific. You will have the opportunity to reflect on the traits that you think make the best leaders in Toolkit Activity 12.1.

One thing trait research has consistently shown us is that there are no absolutes when it comes to leadership. A review of decades of research on traits suggests that it may be the combination of traits rather than a single one that best explains how traits may influence leadership.[30] What combination is best? The answer to that question, like so much in the realm of leadership, often depends on the challenges, demands, and general context of the specific situation. For example, the combination of traits that make an effective leader today is different than it was 20 years ago and varies considerably between countries and cultures.[31]

To make a long story short, leader traits are important but do not tell us everything we need to know about what make a leader effective. In addition, we have only discussed the customary range of personality traits that are measured for individuals. In the next section, we discuss the potentially dangerous combination of personality traits found in some leaders, and they are known as the Dark Triad.

The Dark Triad

There are three traits that make up the Dark Triad: Machiavellianism (sometimes shortened to "Mach"), which refers to a person who believes that the "ends justify the means"; narcissism, which is the expression of grandiosity, entitlement, dominance, and superiority[32]; and psychopathy, which is impulsivity and thrill-seeking combined with low empathy and anxiety.[33]

A Mach person will do whatever it takes to win. As you learned in the Chapter 9 opening, the trait is named for Niccolo Machiavelli who wrote a book called *The Prince*,[34] which detailed his strategies for gaining and holding onto power in the 16th century. Individuals classified as being high in Machiavellianism (high Mach) believe that other people can be manipulated, and that it is permissible to do so to realize their goals. Recent research has conceptualized Mach as being composed of a complex set of characteristics: a tendency to distrust others, a willingness to engage in amoral manipulation, a desire to accumulate status for oneself, and a desire to maintain interpersonal control (see Figure 12.2).

Thus, Mach appears to involve behaviors as well as internal beliefs and motivations.[35] This research also found that high-Mach employees

Narcissists do not make the best managers in the long run due to their inability to maintain relationships or trust others.

©iStockphoto.com/Orbon Alija

engage in counterproductive work behaviors (for example, purposely wasting office supplies). However, they reported lower job satisfaction and experienced more stress on the job. The relationship of Mach and task performance was interesting: high-Mach employees' performance improved over time, suggesting that they need time to learn the organization's political system and work themselves into power networks. Despite the positive long-term relationship with task performance, Mach has been related to negative outcomes for other people. High-Mach behavior has been linked to workplace bullying[36] and abusive supervision.[37] Therefore, individuals with the high-Mach personality may engage in unethical behavior to achieve their goal. Remember that they believe that the ends justify the means, even if it involves lying to manipulate others.

However, because it is important in research to examine both sides, not all modern scholars believe Mach is a bad thing. Close examination of Machiavelli's work indicates that he aimed to implement an ethical system for leadership that involved eradicating corruption and initiating rule of law. He utilizes what he has learned from history and current affairs to obtain a realistic understanding of human behavior that forms a basis for a consequentialist ethics (a contextual view), and although he claims a good leader might do bad things, this is in situations where necessity constrains a leader to choose the "least bad" course of action. Machiavelli also advocates winning the goodwill of followers through leadership as a source of power. In fact, based on today's Mach IV scale, Machiavelli would probably not score as especially "Machiavellian." Additionally, many of his ideas contain seeds for theories that are now considered important for leadership today.[38]

While narcissists can appear charming or pleasant in small doses, they have difficulty trusting others and are unable to develop effective working relationships in the long term.[39] Researchers have described psychopathy as impulsive, thrill-seeking behaviors combined with low empathy and anxiety.[40] Such individuals do not feel guilt, make impulsive decisions, and seek immediate gratification.[41] A study of Dark Triad personalities found that psychopathy and Machiavellianism were associated with the use of hard tactics such as threats and manipulation. However, Machiavellianism and narcissism were also related to the use of soft tactics such as charm, ingratiation, and giving compliments. The study also found that men tend to use hard tactics (being more forceful) more often than women do.[42]

You might be wondering if such toxic employees or "bad guys" win at work. A study of 793 employees in their early careers found that narcissism was positively related to salary, Machiavellianism was positively related to leadership position and career satisfaction, however, psychopathy was negatively related to all career outcomes. Thus, the Dark Triad as a combination did not predict positive outcomes such as career satisfaction and success, but individual traits may have a relationship with higher salary and career satisfaction. Psychopathy, however, has no relationship with positive individual outcomes in research… so far.[43]

In the next section, we turn our focus to an alternative set of approaches that are focused on understanding the behavior of leaders rather than their traits and talents. In contrast to trait theories, the behavioral approach assumes that leaders are made and not born. In other words, they suggest that anyone can learn the behaviors needed to be an effective leader, and research on leader behaviors seeks to understand what effective leaders do and not who they are.

▼ FIGURE 12.2

The Structure of Machiavellianism

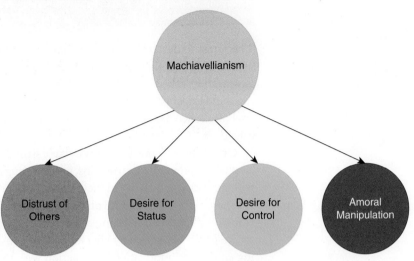

Source: Dahling, J. J., Whitaker, B. G., & Levy, P. E. (2009). The development and validation of a new Machiavellianism scale. *Journal of Management, 35*(2), 219–257.

Leadership Behaviors

Learning Objective 12.3: Explain the difference between structure-initiating and consideration leadership behaviors.

The quest to determine which behaviors were consistently linked to effective leadership began, as you might expect, by observing the behaviors of people in leadership positions.[44] Researchers asked employees to describe what their bosses did and created a list of over a thousand leader behaviors. These behaviors were numerically coded and, using a form of data analytics called factor analysis, researchers found that the majority of them fell into one of two categories.[45]

One category consists of **structure-initiating behaviors**, such as defining tasks for employees, providing instructions, and focusing on goals. These behaviors provide employees with guidance and clarity in their work. They provide structure, in other words. The second category consists of **consideration behaviors**, such as providing encouragement, listening to employees' concerns, and expressing trust, respect, and sensitivity toward employees.

Research has generally concluded that consideration behaviors are helpful for increasing employees' motivation, satisfaction with their jobs, and satisfaction with their leaders. Although each of these can indirectly lead to high levels of employee performance, the same research suggests that structure-initiating behaviors have a more direct impact on employees' performance.[46] Thus, consideration behaviors may boost employee performance by helping them to enjoy their jobs, whereas structure-initiating behaviors help employees perform their tasks more effectively.

Based on this evidence, it might seem logical to conclude that people in leadership positions should engage in both structure-initiating and consideration behaviors. There are two problems with this line of thinking, however. One is that, like the leadership traits discussed above,

▼ FIGURE 12.3

The Managerial Grid

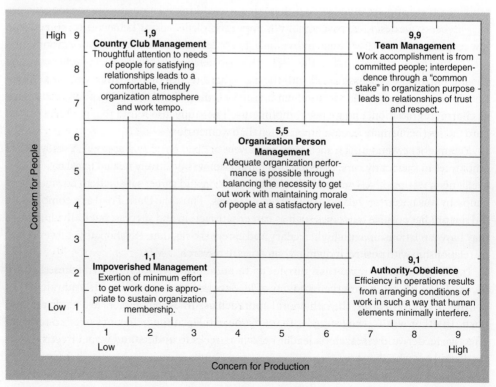

Source: Blake, R. R., & Mouton, J. S. (1975). An overview of the grid. *Training and Development Journal, 29*(5), 29–37.

we cannot say for sure how effective a given leadership behavior will be without knowing important details about the **context** the leader is working in. For example, we are far more likely to see structure-initiating leadership behaviors than consideration behaviors among military officers because the former is better suited to the specific demands of the job.[47]

Once again, it is important to remember that there is no one leadership style that is superior to the rest, a topic we discuss in more detail later in the chapter. The other issue is that most of us have a leadership style that comes naturally and fits our personalities.[48] You might find that you are good at initiating structure and focusing on the task at hand but do not enjoy listening to employees' concerns, for example. Or the opposite might be true. Even if both approaches suit you equally, there are logistical challenges to consider. Structure-initiating and consideration behaviors both require time and energy on the part of leaders. The managerial grid, shown in Figure 12.3, provides an illustration of these challenges.

The Managerial Grid

Although the managerial grid was first developed in 1964, it remains a popular tool for self-assessment and leadership training in modern organizations. It is useful for our purposes because it helps us think about the tradeoffs faced by leaders who favor structure-initiating approaches (referred to as "concern for production" in the managerial grid), consideration approaches (referred to as "concern for people"), and those who attempt to pursue both (or neither) strategies. Using the terminology of the managerial grid, let's consider some of these tradeoffs:[49]

- **Country club management** (high people, low production): This style of leader is most concerned about the needs and feelings of members of their team. These people operate under the assumption that as long as team members are happy and secure, then they will work hard. What tends to result is a work environment that is very relaxed and fun but where production suffers due to lack of direction and control.[50]
- **Authority-obedience management** (high concern for production, low concern for people): The opposite of the country club leader, with a near-total focus on getting the job done, these leaders frequently achieve short-term gains in efficiency. They may struggle to maintain them, however. If employees feel they are being treated like machines instead of humans, they are likely to become unhappy and unmotivated, neither of which is good for productivity.[51]
- **Team style management** (high concern for production, high concern for people): According to the Blake-Mouton model, this is the pinnacle of managerial style. These leaders stress production needs and the needs of the people equally highly. The premise here is that employees are involved in understanding organizational purpose and determining production needs. When employees are committed to and have a stake in the organization's success, their needs and production needs coincide. This creates a team environment based on trust and respect, which leads to high satisfaction and motivation and, as a result, high production.[52]
- **Middle-of-the-road management** ("organization person management," with equal concern for production and concern for productivity): This might look like the "sweet spot" of the managerial grid. Aiming to balance concern for employees with concern for production without overextending oneself does have some intuitive appeal. As is often the case, however, pursuing two different goals without fully committing to either one runs the risk of falling short of both. You have probably experienced this in some of your classes. You might find yourself trying to help the team put together a huge project (no procrastination involved, certainly) so you do not study as hard for a test as you should, confident that you will be fine. In the end, either or both of these things might fail because you tried to balance, rather than thinking about prioritizing which was more important—production of the team project or your own well-being.[53]

- **Impoverished management** (low concern for production, low concern for people): This leader is mostly ineffective. They do not have a high regard for creating systems for getting the job done or for creating a work environment that is satisfying and motivating. The result is a place of disorganization, dissatisfaction, and disharmony.[54]

As the research on leadership evolved, it became clear that the behavior approach to leadership was limited because it did not take into account the context of leadership. In other words, different situations may require different leadership behaviors. For example, a focus on production is needed when a manager gives feedback to a poor-performing employee. However, other situations need a focus on the people, such as a team-building training for the members of a work group. Leadership theories that consider the situation, or context, are discussed next.

It All Depends—Contingency Leadership

Learning Objective 12.4: Use path–goal theory to identify situational factors that help determine the appropriate leadership style.

In this section, we present a leadership approach called **path–goal theory (PGT)**. This was one of the first attempts at moving beyond the simplistic view that effective or ineffective leadership can be understood solely by observing the characteristics or behaviors of effective or ineffective leaders.[55] Instead, it recognized that the success or failure of a given leadership trait or behavior is often contingent on the fit between that trait or behavior and the situational context in which the leader is working.[56] As such, PGT represents a school of thought known as the **contingency approach** to leadership.[57] Although there are several examples of this approach, they all share PGT's goal of finding the right match between leader and context.

Path–Goal Theory

Path–goal theory is based on the simple premise that leaders motivate followers to accomplish goals by establishing the *paths* to the *goals*.[58] By doing so, leaders are thought to increase motivation by rewarding the achievement of goals and productivity by removing obstacles to goal attainment.[59] PGT identifies four different approaches leaders can use to do this (refer to Figure 12.4):

1. **Directive leadership**—giving followers specific instructions about their tasks, providing deadlines, setting standards for performance, and explaining rules.
2. **Supportive leadership**—showing consideration, being friendly and approachable, and paying attention to the well-being of followers.
3. **Participative leadership**—allowing followers to have a voice in decisions that affect them, sharing information, and inviting followers' ideas and opinions.
4. **Achievement-oriented leadership**—challenging followers to perform at high levels, setting standards for excellence, and showing confidence in followers' ability to reach goals.[60]

Importantly, PGT and other contingency perspectives do not stop there. Rather than simply listing these four options, PGT includes guidelines for choosing the approach that best fits

CRITICAL THINKING QUESTIONS

Think of some companies that you have studied, or perhaps even worked at. What path–goal approach do these leaders use to motivate their employees? Try to think of an example for each situation.

Path–Goal Theory

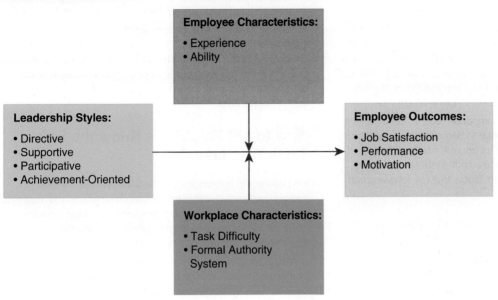

Employee Characteristics:

• Experience
• Ability

Leadership Styles:

• Directive
• Supportive
• Participative
• Achievement-Oriented

Employee Outcomes:

• Job Satisfaction
• Performance
• Motivation

Workplace Characteristics:

• Task Difficulty
• Formal Authority
  System

Sources: House, R. J. (1971). A path–goal theory of leadership effectiveness. *Administrative Science Quarterly, 16,* 321–328; House, R. J., & Mitchell, T. R. (1974). Path–goal theory of leadership. *Journal of Contemporary Business, 3,* 81–97.

a situation, based on the ability level of followers the leader is working with, and House, the originator of the theory, understood the need to modernize these guidelines to fit the changing leadership environment.[61]

Because highly trained and/or experienced employees often require or prefer different leadership styles, PGT recognizes that leaders must often change their behaviors to fit these evolving needs and preferences. For example, a new employee might be unable to provide much information, making participative leadership a poor choice in these contexts. Until they have gained sufficient training and experience, achievement-oriented leadership is likely to be ineffective as well. Conversely, highly experienced employees who are experts at their jobs might benefit from these approaches while viewing directive leadership as overbearing and annoying.[62]

The PGT framework also considers the actual task employees are working on at any given time. If an employee's task is not clear, a directive or supportive style explains what needs to be done. In highly repetitive tasks, leaders can show concern for followers' well-being (supportive leadership). The formal authority system is another situation characteristic to consider. In other words, if the formal authority system is strong, the leader can enforce rules through a directive approach.[63]

Research on PGT has shown it to be reliable and effective in most workplace settings.[64] One of its key strengths lies in the application of motivation theory (expectancy theory in Chapter 10, in particular) to leadership. Think back to this section and the extent to which motivational psychology is built into the PGT approach. PGT is also practical in that it emphasizes the removal of barriers to effective performance, a common source of stress and performance degradation among employees.[65]

CRITICAL THINKING QUESTIONS

How can a leader intervene using PGT if followers are having difficulty getting help from the purchasing department to get the supplies they need to do their job?

CAREERS IN MANAGEMENT

Top "Soft Skills" Employers Look For

Leadership requires a diverse skill set. Successful leaders have not only mastered technical skills, they have also mastered "soft skills." Soft skills are sometimes referred to as people skills. These interpersonal skills include negotiating, motivating, engaging, and building positive relationships with others at work. They are key to being an effective manager.

Here are the top seven most important soft skills employers are looking for today. It's important to demonstrate these when you interview for a position. And, of course, it is important to demonstrate them once you are on the job. Mike Steinerd, Indeed's director of recruiting, states that the following soft skills matter most:[66]

1. *Be a team player.* This means not only being cooperative but also displaying strong team leadership ability when it is needed by the team.

2. *Be flexible.* This is an extremely valuable asset to employers. Managers who can adapt to change are the most dependable in all circumstances.

3. *Communication.* This is critical to the job of manager. Communication involves speaking well, writing well, being a good listener, and using the right body language.

4. *Problem-solving.* Regardless of the industry you work in, the ability to solve problems that arise is essential.

5. *Accept feedback.* It is important to be able to hear both positive and constructive feedback. The best managers apply feedback to grow professionally.

6. *Confidence.* The best managers have a clear sense of their strengths. They understand their skills and abilities. By showing confidence, your supervisors, employees, and clients will believe in your vision.

7. *Creative thinking.* Managers need to "think outside of the box" sometimes to come up with unique solutions or alternatives. This soft skill is valuable since it drives innovation.[67]

Employment Skills Matter for All Jobs

When you are seeking a leadership position, you will want to highlight your soft skills. Being an effective leader will include things like being able to delegate and offer constructive criticism.

All jobs require soft skills, even technical ones. For example, information technology positions require soft skills such as creativity and the ability to present ideas and solutions to individuals as well as groups. Strong communication skills, both written and oral, are an important asset in virtually any field, at every level.[68]

How to Let Employers Know the Soft Skills You Have

It is essential to reference the skills the employer is seeking in your job application materials such as cover letters and résumés. The same is true when you are interviewing. Review the job posting and be prepared to give specific examples of your skills that match the job posting—and do not forget the soft skills!

Give examples of your soft skills during job interviews. Demonstrate your positive attitude and enthusiasm throughout the interview. Do not just say that you have the skills the company needs—prove it to them. Prepare some examples of instances when you used your soft skills effectively. Learn about the position and the company and get a sense of the organizational culture so that you communicate comfortably with the interviewer. Actions speak louder than words.[69]

Discussion Questions

1. Of the list of soft skills, which three do you think are most important? Explain your choices.

2. Explain why employers are looking for managers who have both hard (technical) and soft skills. Find a posting for a job you are interested in applying for someday. Which soft skills are listed in the job posting?

3. Develop two or three examples of how you can highlight your soft skills on your résumé. What activities or experiences can you start now that will enhance your ability to show that you have soft leadership skills when you graduate?

Sources: Doyle, A. (2019, August 24). The most important soft skills employers seek. *The Balance Careers*. Retrieved from https://www.thebalancecareers.com/top-soft-skills-2063721; and Noel, K. (2015). Soft skills leaders need for success. *Business Insider*. Retrieved from https://www.businessinsider.com/soft-skills-leaders-need-for-success-2016-4.

The Role of Relationships

Learning Objective 12.5: Explain why and how leaders form high- and low-quality exchange relationships with different employees.

It is commonly said that leadership does not happen in a vacuum, meaning that no one can call themselves a "leader" if nobody is willing or able to be led. Because the working relationship between leaders and followers is so central to the effectiveness of the overall organization, managers and researchers have a vested interest in learning how to cultivate the best relationships a given situation will allow.[70]

It is an interesting quirk of management research that, in the context of relationships between leaders and those they lead, the terminology almost always changes from follower to "member." As the study of leadership evolved and developed an appreciation for the importance of relationships, researchers and practitioners began to realize that people who are classified as "followers" generally do not seek to form strong relationships with those who are labeled "leaders," and vice versa. Thus, in the spirit of dispensing with potentially counterproductive terminology (remember the "great man" approach described earlier in this chapter?), it gradually became the norm to refer to employees as "followers" or "members" of that leader's workgroup.

Trust is an important component of leader-follower relationships.

©iStockphoto.com/nortonrsx

Leader-Member Exchange

Much of what we know about how leaders form relationships with followers has come from research on **leader-member exchange (LMX)**.[71] LMX theory is based on the premise that leaders do not treat every follower the same way, but instead form exchange relationships of varying quality with each of them.[72] An **exchange relationship** between two people is, as the name suggests, based on the transfer of valued resources (performance, money, information, supplies, etc.) between two people.[73] High-quality exchange relationships exist when two individuals, such as a leader and follower, have developed sufficient trust that each is willing to help the other without requiring immediate reciprocation. Even if you have never held a leadership position, you have almost certainly formed both high- and low-quality exchange relationships with people in your life.

Many of us, for example, have sold possessions such as old computers, cars, or textbooks to other people. If you sell one of these items to a friend, you might not insist on being paid right away assuming you trust your friend to pay you at a later date. This is because you have a high-quality exchange relationship with your friend. Very few people would grant such flexibility to a stranger purchasing your item, however. You do not know that person and therefore have no way to determine how trustworthy they might be or if they will ever pay you, which means you have a low-quality exchange relationship with them. If you fulfill your part of the exchange and hand over your item, you might never receive your payment.

The nature of an exchange relationship between leaders and followers can be far more complex than this simple illustration, but the fundamental principles are the same. High-quality LMX relationships are those in which leaders and followers each trust the other to "do right" by them. If you have such a relationship with your manager and they ask you to help train a new employee, you probably would not demand extra compensation on the spot as a condition of doing so. Instead, you would trust that your manager will reciprocate at some future time.

In a low-quality relationship, it might still be difficult to say "no" to this request (this is your boss, after all) but you would do so with little expectation of receiving any recognition, compensation, or other benefits in return. For this reason, low-quality LMX relationships are generally harmful to employees' job satisfaction, motivation, and productivity.[74]

Knowing this, why would anyone in a leadership position form anything other than high-quality exchange relationships with employees? Largely for the same reason that most people have only one "best friend." Your best friend is someone who can count on you to listen to all of their problems, lend them money, and rescue them from their broken-down car in a bad part of town at 3:00 a.m. Imagine having that kind of exchange relationship with 10, 20, or 100 people, or employees. Remember that we are talking about the exchange of resources and, as basic economics tells us, resources are scare. A leader has only so much time, energy, knowledge, and financial resources to share.

Leader-Member Exchange Relationships

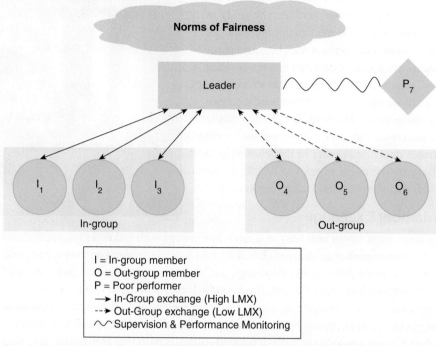

Source: Scandura, T. A. (2019). *Essentials of organizational behavior: An evidence-based approach* p. 135. Thousand Oaks, CA: Sage.

The logic of LMX theory is that, rather than spread these resources around equally, leaders tend to give more to some employees and less to others. As the preceding example suggests, the higher-quality exchange relationships tend to be formed with employees a leader has reason to trust, collectively referred to as that leader's **in-group**.[75] **Out-group** employees, with whom low-quality relationships are formed, are not necessarily "bad" employees or people who are disliked by their leader. They may be newer employees who have yet to prove themselves or simply employees who do not have much to contribute to an exchange relationship.[76] This may sound harsh, but it is the reason why very few employees in a large company can say they have a strong relationship—or have even met—their CEO. We all have to choose which people in our lives to prioritize, and LMX simply recognizes that the same is true for those of us in leadership positions (Figure 12.5).

A natural question for both leaders and followers at this point might be, "How do I form high-quality leader-member exchange relationships in my workplace?" As the preceding discussion has made clear, developing trust is perhaps the most important step in the process.

Trust

Learning Objective 12.6: Discuss why trust is important, and how to repair it.

Trust is considered "the willingness to be vulnerable."[77] This might seem like a strange definition since we often talk about people "earning our trust," but the truth is we must make ourselves vulnerable in order to create a trusting relationship. How much do you trust others? Find out by completing the Toolkit Activity 12.2, the Trust Fall.

Trust within organizations is related to important outcomes, including risk-taking and job performance.[78] A review of the various definitions of trust offers the following summary: **trust** is a psychological state comprising the intention to accept vulnerability based on positive expectations of the intentions or behavior of another.[79] A meta-analytic study found that trust is related to LMX as well as job satisfaction and performance.[80] Several other theories of leadership mention trust (e.g., servant leadership, which is discussed later in this chapter). Trust is therefore fundamental to the development of effective working relationships with teams, bosses, and others.

There are some helpful frameworks to organize your thinking about how trust operates in organizations. A three-part view of trust is a useful way to think about trust development with another person: calculus-based, knowledge-based, and identification-based trust.[81]

- **Calculus-based trust (CBT)** is "trust in one-time transactions that typically derives from the calculus of gains and losses, weighed by perceived risks. Market-based exchanges may emphasize calculus more, whereas communal relationships might emphasize identification (below)."[82]
- **Knowledge-based trust (KBT)** is the second level of trust. This level of trust is grounded in how predictable the other person is. Over time, through interactions where benefits are exchanged between two parties, people come to expect the other person to come through for them. KBT is based on information gathered about the other person in a variety of circumstances. An example of KBT in an organization would be a follower becoming the go-to person for the boss in terms of creating the boss's Power-Point decks for important presentations. The boss can jot down a list of bullet points in a document and send them to the follower. Within a day, the boss receives a professional-looking presentation deck to review and edit.
- **Identification-based trust (IBT)** is the highest degree of trust in this model. This form of trust is characterized by the leader and follower sharing the same goals and objectives,[83] or a full internalization of the other's desires and intentions,[84] meaning both are working toward the same things with each other's best interests in the forefront.

Trust develops over time.[85] As shown in Figure 12.6, trust may transform over time and develop different "faces" as it matures. In other words, the types of trust build upon one another over time based on the nature of the working relationship. Calculus-based trust develops to a point, and the trust level becomes KBT as the behavior of the parties becomes predictable. Most relationships in organizations fall into the KBT range of trust. Once stable, a

▼ FIGURE 12.6

Types of Trust

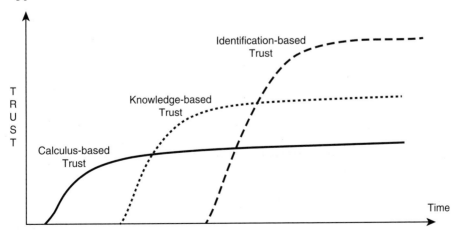

Sources: Hernandez, J. M. D. C., & Santos, C. C. D. (2010). Development-based trust: Proposing and validating a new trust measurement model for buyer-seller relationships. *BAR-Brazilian Administration Review*, 7(2), 172–197; and Lewicki, R. J., & Bunker, B. B. (1996). Developing and maintaining trust in work relationships. In: R. M. Kramer & T. R. Tyler (Eds.), *Trust in organizations: Frontiers of theory and research* (pp. 114–139). Thousand Oaks, CA: Sage.

Building trust with new employees within the first few hours of them starting helps establish a strong relationship from the beginning.

©iStockphoto.com/fizkes

few relationships will reach the next point and will become IBT relationships (in other words, high LMX in-group relationships). At this point, both parties fully understand what the other party cares about, and there is a level of empathy that emerges (i.e., the ability to put oneself in the boss's place and see the organization the way they do), and there is a sense of harmony in thoughts, emotions, and behavior. This level of IBT is strengthened by the creation of joint projects, shared goals, and shared work values.[86]

A longitudinal study of new hires found that the cues that are perceived early in employment predict the emergence of trust. In fact, information attended to in the first hours on a job is crucial.[87] Trust becomes stable, but it is important to remember that trust is vulnerable. Even in high-quality leader-follower relationships, IBT can revert to the CBT stage, so followers and bosses must be careful about maintaining relationships.[88] According to this model, movements between the stages of trust can be smooth and incremental or they can be dramatic and transformational. Remember that the development of trust takes time and that trust does require testing to see how durable it is.

As we have discussed, trust plays an important role in the development of working relationships with bosses (and others, including peers) in the organization, and relationships in general. It requires making yourself vulnerable, deciding what level of trust you want to have with somebody, and working to maintain it or build it to the next level. It is hard to imagine any

▼ TABLE 12.2

Steps to Repair Broken Trust

Statements
1. **Acknowledge** that trust has been broken. Acknowledging that there is a problem is the first step to healing. Don't use the "ostrich" technique of burying your head in the sand and hoping the situation will resolve itself because it won't. The longer you wait to address the situation, the more people will perceive your weakness as wickedness.
2. **Admit** your role in causing the breach of trust. For some leaders this may be a challenging step. It's one thing to acknowledge that there is a problem, it's a whole other thing to admit you caused it. Our ego and false pride are usually what prevent us from admitting our mistakes. Muster up the courage, humble yourself, and own up to your actions. This will pay huge dividends down the road as you work to rebuild trust.[89] An important substep as you proceed is to understand *exactly* why and how the trust was broken. Before you can continue to apologize, assess, and amend, be sure you know what you are trying to fix. There is a model available called the TrustWorks! ABCD Trust Model. It is a helpful way to think about how you might have broken the trust by not being Able, Believable, Connected, or Dependable.[90]
3. **Apologize** for what happened. A sincere apology involves admitting your mistake, accepting responsibility, asking for forgiveness, and taking steps to make amends to the offended party. Explaining the reasons why something happened is fine, but don't make excuses by trying to shift the blame to something or someone other than yourself.
4. **Assess**. People form perceptions of our trustworthiness when we use, or don't use, behaviors that align with these four elements of trust. Knowing the specific element of trust you violated will help you take specific actions to fix the problem.
5. **Amend** the situation by taking corrective action to repair any damage that has been done, and create an action plan for how you'll improve in the future. Your attempts at rebuilding trust will be stalled unless you take this critical step to demonstrate noticeable changes in behavior.[91]

Sources: Blanchard, K., Blanchard, K., & Olmstead, C. (2013). *TrustWorks!* London, England: HarperCollins; and Conley, R. (2011). Five steps to repairing broken trust. Retrieved from https://leadingwithtrust .com/2011/07/24/five-steps-to-repair-trust/.

relationship functioning without trust, so it is important to understand what you need to do should you damage trust. Research on trust repair has examined what strategies work to get the relationship back on track. Table 12.2 provides a step-by-step approach to repairing broken trust.

CRITICAL THINKING QUESTIONS

> Think of a time when you tried to restore trust after it was broken. Based on this section, what would you do differently?

Trust is a basis for good and effective leadership and relationships, and by now you should understand that there is a full range of behaviors that go along with being viewed as a leader. The next section discusses both management (i.e., transactional behaviors) and leadership (i.e., transformational behaviors) behaviors, and then is followed by a section on the more contemporary theories of leadership, one or more of which might describe the type of leader you are or aspire to be.

Transformational Leadership

Learning Objective 12.7: Illustrate the elements and progression of transactional and transformational leadership.

The **full-range model of leadership** is based on over 25 years of research on **transformational leadership**.[92] People are more engaged when their leaders behave in certain ways at the highest end of the full-range model. The full-range model starts at the lower end of leadership, which is termed **transactional leadership**. Leadership is a continuum, with transactional leadership being the foundation upon which transformational leadership is built. These behaviors range from passive to active and ineffective to effective, as depicted in Figure 12.7. For example, laissez-faire leadership is very passive and inspirational leadership is more active. Management by exception is less effective, compared with idealized influence. The specific components of transactional and transformational leadership are described in the following sections.[93]

Transactional Leadership

Transactional leadership is defined as behaviors that motivate followers through rewards and corrective actions. The transactional leader behaviors (from ineffective to more effective) are as follows:

- *Nonleadership/laissez-faire leadership.* This is the "near-avoidance of leadership,"[94] the least active and least effective of all of the leadership styles in the full-range model.
- *Management by exception.* This has two forms: active and passive. In management by exception, active (MBE-A), the leader looks for the follower to make errors and then corrects them. In management by exception, passive (MBE-P), the leader does not actively look for errors or deviations from work standards but takes corrective action when noticed.
- *Contingent reward.* This is promising or delivering rewards to followers contingent on their performance.[95]

There are times when a manager must use the transactional approach. For example, if they have a low-performing employee, a leader may need to employ the management-by-exception approaches. Also, it is important that managers deliver rewards to employees that are contingent

Full-Range Model of Leadership

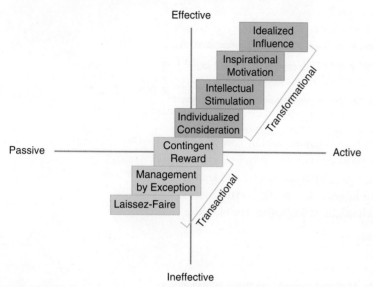

Full Range of Leadership Model

Source: Adapted from Bass, B.M. & Avolio, B.J. *Improving Organizational Effectiveness through Transformational Leadership.* Copyright © 1994, Sage Publications.

on their performance. As leadership becomes more active, managers employ the transformational leadership behaviors that are described next.

The Four "I's"

Transformational leadership is defined as behaviors that mobilize extra effort from followers through emphasis on change through articulating a new vision for the organization. As noted earlier, these behaviors are most related to positive attitudes, commitment, and performance of followers. Leadership is active, and this leads to greater effectiveness. These behaviors include the following (known as the four I's):

- *Individualized consideration.* Transformational leaders treat each follower as a unique person. They get to know employees on a one-on-one basis and mentor them.
- *Intellectual stimulation.* Transformational leaders encourage innovation and new ideas. They listen to followers openly and don't criticize creative solutions to problems.
- *Inspirational motivation.* Leaders inspire others to work hard toward organizational goals by providing challenge. They are positive and upbeat and get others to feel optimistic.
- *Idealized influence.* Being admired and respected by followers is the core of this leadership component. These leaders are change agents in the organization.[96]

Transformational leaders increase intrinsic motivation by aligning followers' tasks with the things employees value most. Meta-analyses have confirmed that transformational leadership behaviors are positively and significantly related to both productivity and performance ratings by supervisors.[97] Transformational leadership also predicts employee creativity, especially when leaders communicate high expectations for creative behaviors.[98] Are you a transformational leader? Find out by completing Self-Assessment 12.1.

A recent trend in leadership research and practice has been a focus on moral approaches to understanding the effectiveness of managers. As you learned in Chapter 3 of this textbook, ethics has become a central concern in the area of management, and a number of leadership theories have emerged that consider the moral implications of leadership. Following the scandals of Enron, Wells Fargo, and others, management researchers responded by working on new theories that incorporate a moral component and placing followers first. The study of ethics and morality in leadership will continue to be of interest in management since research is showing that ethical leadership is related to employee well-being and performance.[99] These approaches are discussed next.

Contemporary Approaches to Leadership

Learning Objective 12.8: Compare and contrast the role of morality in ethical, servant, and authentic leadership.

Modern approaches to leadership address the importance of leaders having a moral compass when they make decisions. These approaches also address the role of leaders in treating followers with dignity in the workplace.

Ethical Leadership

Since the early 2000s, a series of large organizations have failed or were on the brink of failure due to the unethical and/or immoral behaviors of their leaders. This led leadership researchers to dig deeper into these two phenomena in order to discover the roles that ethics and morality play in effective leadership. Despite what researchers have found, and what many other good leaders will tell you, some leaders still persist in operating with little or no consideration of trust, ethics, or morality. This link will take you to an interesting article from *Fortune* magazine,[100] in which you will find some organizations you are familiar with whose leadership is floundering (http://fortune.com/2016/03/30/most-disappointing-leaders/).

Leadership and ethics are intertwined—ethical decision-making is important to the practice of leadership, and contemporary theories of leadership address morality. Research on ethical leadership has found four components:

- Moral sensitivity involves recognizing that our behavior *impacts* others.
- Moral judgment involves determining the right decision.
- Moral motivation is having the need to do the right thing.
- Moral action is doing the right thing.[101]

Ethical leadership is positively related to ethical behavior of work groups and negatively related to relationship conflict among coworkers.[102] A review of the research on ethical leadership concludes that if employees indicate that their leaders are ethical and fair role models who communicate and reward ethical behavior, there is less deviance and more cooperative behavior, and employees perform better and are more willing to both expend effort and report problems to management.[103]

If leaders at the top of the organization are viewed as ethical by their followers, then ethics have a cascading effect throughout the organization and lower-level employees also view their manager as ethical.[104] The moral component is also emerging as a key aspect of contemporary leadership theories. Next, we discuss two other recent approaches to leadership that directly incorporate aspects of morality: servant and authentic leadership.

Servant Leadership

As indicated previously, modern leadership research emphasizes morality. In addition to ethical leadership, two other theories have emerged: servant leadership[105] and authentic leadership.[106] While research on these theories is relatively new, findings indicate that followers respond positively to these leader behaviors. **Servant leadership** dates back to the 1970s when Robert Greenleaf was inspired about leadership while reading Hermann Hesse's *Journey to the East*. In this novel, a group of travelers begin a long journey. A servant named Leo sings to them and inspires them while doing his tasks. Leo disappears along the way, and the group falls into chaos and cannot complete their journey. The basic idea is that followers are just as important as, if not more important than, leaders. Greenleaf's definition of the servant leader is as follows:

> The servant-leader *is* servant first. . . . It begins with the natural feeling that one wants to serve, to serve *first*. Then conscious choice brings one to aspire to lead. That person is sharply different from one who is *leader* first, perhaps because of the need to assuage an unusual power drive or to acquire material possessions.[107]

The idea of putting followers first and empowering them in contrast with typical top-down leadership is shown in Figure 12.8. An example of a company that has servant leadership at the core of its management philosophy is the retail chain Wawa, who trains all managers in

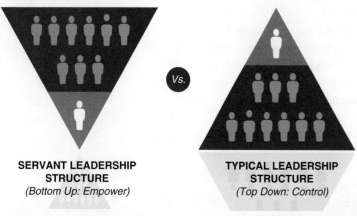

▼ FIGURE 12.8

Servant Leadership Versus Typical Leadership Structure

SERVANT LEADERSHIP STRUCTURE
(Bottom Up: Empower)

Vs.

TYPICAL LEADERSHIP STRUCTURE
(Top Down: Control)

Source: Gailey, T. (2015, Spring). The servant leader: Transforming executive style. *St. Joseph's University Haub School Review.* Retrieved from https://www.sju.edu/news-events/magazines/haub-school-review/haub-school-review-spring-2015.

servant leadership principles. Dorothy Swartz, the company's senior director of talent management and development, says Wawa pursued this training to ensure the entire company was aligned around one leadership philosophy.[108]

Researchers have recently developed measures of servant leadership, and they relate to positive attitudes and performance of followers.[109] There are seven servant leadership dimensions:

- Emotional healing
- Creating value for the community
- Conceptual skills
- Empowering
- Helping subordinates grow and succeed
- Putting subordinates first
- Behaving ethically[110]

Servant leaders facilitate team confidence, affirming the strengths and potential of the team and providing developmental support.[111] This developmental support is also characteristic of **humble leadership**, where a leader's humility allows them to show followers how to grow from working in an organization. This leads followers to believe that their own developmental journeys are legitimate in the workplace.[112] Leader humility might create shared leadership in teams by encouraging proactive team members to take responsibility, but this is often based on the skills of the individuals in the team. As an example, one study found that shared leadership was most strongly related to team performance when team members had high levels of task-related competence.[113] Are you a servant leader? Find out by completing Self-Assessment 12.2.

Authentic Leadership

Authentic leadership involves knowing oneself and behaving in a way that is consistent with what is intuitively right.[114] Authentic leaders are most effective when they develop an effective vision that relates to the shared interests of their team. Dan Vesella, CEO of the pharmaceutical company Novartis, is an example of such a leader because he is successful but also demonstrates compassion by assisting people suffering from life-threatening diseases.[115] Authentic leadership has four dimensions:

- **Self-awareness**—seeks feedback to improve interactions with others.
- **Relational transparency**—says exactly what he or she means.
- **Internalized moral perspective**—demonstrates beliefs that are consistent with actions.
- **Balanced processing**—solicits views that challenge their deeply held positions.[116]

These contemporary leadership theories seem to sound alike, but they also have some differences so it is important to compare and contrast them. Transformational leadership is probably the most unique but does share some aspects of servant leadership. Researchers conducted several meta-analyses to compare these approaches and found that authentic and ethical leadership may not offer unique contributions to understanding the relationship of leadership to employee performance, organizational citizenship behaviors, and attitudes. However, servant leadership did appear to be significantly different than transformational leadership.[117] A second study[118] using 100 independent samples and 25,452 individuals found that authentic and

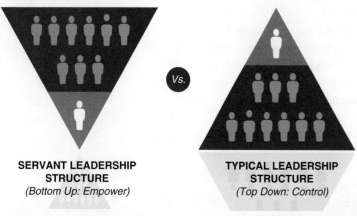

transformational leadership are highly related, but transformational leadership is a better predictor of follower satisfaction, follower satisfaction with the leader, task performance, and leader effectiveness. However, authentic leadership was better at predicting group or organization performance and organizational citizenship behaviors. Thus, both approaches appear to be useful in understanding the relationship of leadership to organizational outcomes.

CRITICAL THINKING QUESTIONS

> Compare and contrast ethical, servant, and authentic leadership. What do they have in common, and what are the key differences?

Managerial Implications

This chapter attempted to provide some clarity to the ambiguous but critical topic of leadership. Having completed the chapter, you should understand the following points:

- Leaders and managers are *not* the same thing. It is important to recognize the difference and also understand that when leadership and management overlap, it defines the objectives of the managerial leader, which are to organize resources and enable followers to understand the mission of the organization.
- Leaders' traits, such as their personality or intelligence levels, can impact their effectiveness, but determining which traits matter in which situations is a challenging and often-unproductive endeavor.
- Some categories of leader behavior, such as structure-initiating and consideration behaviors, can improve employee productivity and morale *if* they are used in the appropriate situations. Understanding the role of context (situations) in leadership is known as the contingency approach, and one of the best-known contingency theories is the path–goal theory (PGT) of leadership.
- Leaders form different types of relationships—some better than others—with different employees. Although it may seem unfair at first glance, it reflects the reality that leaders have limited resources to share with employees. This approach, known as the LMX model of leadership, discusses how leaders can learn to offer all employees an opportunity to be in the in-group to ensure fairness in their work unit.
- Knowing how to develop and repair trust is among the most important skills a leader (or a follower) can have. Trust develops in stages, over time, in the forms of calculus-based, knowledge-based, and identification-based trust. Most relationships in organizations are knowledge-based, but highly developed leader-member exchange relationships are characterized as having identification-based trust.
- A rash of corporate scandals at the turn of the century has caused business leaders and researchers to think more carefully about the role of ethics and morality in leadership. Contemporary approaches to leadership consider morality and include ethical, servant, and authentic leadership. These approaches are related to transformational leadership, but they are also distinct in the way that they predict different organizational outcomes such as job satisfaction and group performance.

The intersection of management and leadership is where the managerial leader accomplishes goals, explains their vision, mobilizes resources, and motivates the workforce. Today's organizations need managers who are leaders and especially those who embrace morality.

KEY TERMS

achievement-oriented
leadership   376

authentic leadership   386

authority-obedience
management   375

balanced
processing   386

calculus-based trust
(CBT)   381

consideration
behaviors   374

context   375

contingency approach   376

country club
management   375

directive leadership   376

ethical leadership   385

exchange relationship   379

full-range model of
leadership   383

"great man" theory of
leadership   370

humble leadership   386

identification-based trust
(IBT)   381

impoverished
management   376

in-group   380

internalized moral
perspective   386

knowledge-based trust
(KBT)   381

leader-member exchange
(LMX)   379

middle-of-the-road
management   375

out-group   380

participative leadership   376

path–goal theory
(PGT)   376

relational transparency   386

self-awareness   386

servant leadership   385

structure-initiating
behaviors   374

supportive leadership   376

team style management   375

trait approach   370

transactional leadership   383

transformational
leadership   383

trust   380

TOOLKIT

Activity 12.1

The Best Leaders

Get together with your team or a classmate and think of good leaders and managers you have worked for or observed in the past. Begin writing a combined list of the traits and behaviors these people had (or have) that made them both effective and respected by their employees. Come up with as long a list as possible (try to beat the other teams!).

Now look at the list. Circle the traits you feel you have, and put a star next to the ones you are not as comfortable with. Looking at the starred words, write down some notes on how you can build this trait or behavior to become a better leader. For example, if your group comes up with the trait that the leader was always the first person in the office every day and greeted everybody in a positive manner when they came in, but you are usually running late for things, what can you do about it?

Compare your lists with each other and work together to come up with solutions to all of the things you listed as a team that you need to improve on. Check back with your list and team periodically, or even work on giving each other feedback the rest of the semester, on how you are progressing on your leadership growth project.

Discussion Questions

1. Are your friends or colleagues in your campus groups or at work noticing a difference in your leadership styles?

2. Think back on situations you encounter where you are taking a leadership role, or would like to. Which positive traits from your list are you using? Have you noticed any others that your list did not include?

3. Write up an action plan to help you develop your leadership skills over the course of your college career. Post it somewhere you can see it every day and review it every Sunday. How are you doing?

Activity 12.2

The Trust Fall

Have you ever done the trust fall? It is an exercise that is often done during team-building or ice-breaking exercises between people who do not know each other well, or at all. There are several variations, but the simplest involves one person standing with their back toward the person behind them and then falling into their arms, trusting the person behind them to catch them. There is also a group variation, which you will do here.

One member of the team is selected and stands on a raised platform; they then fall backward, relying on the support of their team to catch them. This quick team-building activity is all about support and trust and is great when you are in the forming stage of team development. You will need the following:

- Equipment required: raised platform—step or table
- Space required: minimal—delivered either indoors or outdoors
- Group size: 5 members

Instructions

- One person is selected (or volunteers) to try the challenge first. They stand on the raised platform, waiting for their teammates. The rest of the group should form two vertical lines facing each other on the ground level.
- The volunteer (faller) should stand with their back to the rest of the team, with their arms crossed.
- A stable landing area should be provided by the rest of the team using their arms to protect the faller.
- Once everyone is ready and in position, the volunteer should freely fall in the direction of the catchers.
- The aim of the catchers is to catch the faller, so they may need to adjust themselves to ensure the volunteer lands safely in the landing area.
- Allow all members of the team to take turns as the faller.

Discussion Questions

1. Did you have any hesitation before falling? How did you feel having to rely on others to support you?
2. How did you manage the fallers' safety? What did you do to protect them?
3. Can you relate this challenge to a time when you have had to rely on others?
4. Is there anything that stops you from trusting others around you in the workplace or classroom?

If you think about it, this exercise puts the definition of trust as the willingness to be vulnerable into an actual behavior. You need to make yourself vulnerable and "trust" that the stranger behind you will catch you. If you have time in class, try the trust fall. You might find that you are nervous doing this exercise, even with people you know, because trust is a complex feeling. As a leader or member, though, trust is critical to effective teamwork.

Sources: Priestly, D. (2015). Trust fall. Retrieved from http://www.ventureteambuilding.co.uk/trust-fall/; Trust fall. (n.d.). *Urban Dictionary*. Retrieved from https://www.urbandictionary.com/define.php? term=trust fall.

Case Study 12.1

Bad Blood: The Dark Side of Charisma at Theranos

The blood-testing startup Theranos and its charismatic founder, Elizabeth Holmes, were on the fast track. Holmes idolized Steve Jobs and came up with a genius idea for Theranos. She was considered a transformational leader by the industry. Her story made headlines: Holmes was the world's youngest female self-made billionaire. She was a 19-year-old Stanford University dropout with incredible connections in the industry. She incorporated the company Theranos (combining "therapy" and "diagnosis"). She rented the basement of a group college house, hired the first employee, and rented lab space.

What was Theranos? Holmes claimed her company could do almost any diagnostic test on a few drops of blood from a finger prick. The value of her company surged to a valuation of $9 billion. However, skepticism about the blood-testing process grew because Theranos executives refused to disclose details on how the diagnostic tests were being done. Medical researchers were suspicious. And Theranos's own employees were also suspicious because the details of the testing were not shared with them either.

Then, Theranos crashed and burned. The valuation of Theranos was built on almost nothing, which came to light as details from the process were revealed. Theranos's own employees blew the whistle on the company's deception. A *Wall Street Journal* article exposed the truth about Theranos. The blood-testing machines they invented did not test blood as they had claimed. Even worse, the company faked test results by using other commercial machines to do the tests it claimed were being done on its machines. At first, Holmes fought the allegations, but the evidence was convincing and the company began to fall apart. Contracts from medical providers were terminated. Investors lost millions. Holmes and her cofounder were charged with massive criminal fraud lawsuits. Holmes stepped down as CEO and the company was forced to close.

On its surface, Theranos seemed representative of Silicon Valley startups: A young and charismatic CEO comes up with a new idea creating disruptive change and innovation that would improve the health of millions by providing easier access to diagnostic testing. The claims made by Holmes were miraculous, and investors and the media believed them. Of course, her claims were false. But how did Holmes and Theranos get so far in their deception?

Holmes was, without a doubt, a charismatic leader who caught the media's imagination. She was on the covers of *Fortune* in 2014 and *Forbes* in 2015. She cultivated her image as a young Steve Jobs by wearing a black turtleneck. The belief in her company and its promise became distant from the reality that such testing could not be done with current technology. In his book, *Bad Blood: Secrets and Lies in a Silicon Valley Startup*, John Carreyrou describes how Holmes used a bold idea and her personal charisma to maintain the support of investors, as well as powerful board members—even when the lack of supporting data should have caused them to question the ability of the company to deliver.

The book also portrays Holmes's unbridled ambition and what happens when "fake it 'til you make it" becomes extreme. Holmes's ambition prevented anything from stopping the company. Employees revealed that Holmes was ruthless in covering up the company's secrets. Theranos was a revolving door, as Holmes and her cofounder fired anyone who voiced doubts. They created a culture of fear in the company. Employees' emails were monitored, and legal threats against employees who spoke out against them or to the press were frequent and aggressive.

The deceptions around the company's blood testing, which was stated as being designed to help people, are troubling. One employee recalls how a laboratory was hidden from federal regulators to prevent them from seeing it was fake. For presentations to investors, lab technicians would perform standard blood tests in the lab, and Holmes would pretend that the Theranos machine generated the results. Employees even developed an app to make it look like the machine was just slowly processing, when really it had malfunctioned. Engineers became desperate to make it look like the machine was working and started using existing commercial blood-testing devices with smaller samples. The problem is that this made test results less accurate. Patients received erroneous blood test results, causing real harm.

The Theranos case reminds us that charisma has a dark side. When a charismatic leader does not allow criticism, we should be concerned.

Discussion Questions

1. What were the sources of Elizabeth Holmes's charisma? What behaviors did she engage in to build and maintain the confidence of the public and her investors?
2. Discuss the pros and cons of the advice, "Fake it 'til you make it." What is the balance of showing confidence and ethical reasoning? Give examples from the Theranos case.
3. Discuss Elizabeth Holmes's behavior in terms of the Dark Triad. Which of the Dark Triad behaviors did she exhibit?
4. Provide an example of another charismatic leader (either historical or current) who engaged in deception. What are/were the outcomes of their charisma?

Sources: Carreyrou, J. (2018). Theranos Inc.'s partners in blood. *Wall Street Journal.* Archived from the original on May 18, 2018; Carreyrou, J. (2018). *Bad blood: Secrets and lies in a Silicon Valley startup.* New York, NY: Pan Macmillan; Hartmans, A. (2019). The rise and fall of Elizabeth Holmes, who started Theranos when she was 19 and became the world's youngest female billionaire before it all came crashing down. *Business Insider.* Retrieved from https://www.businessinsider.com/theranos-founder-ceo-elizabeth-holmes-life-story-bio-2018-4; Juetten, M. (2018). Failed startups: Theranos. *Forbes.* Retrieved from https://www.forbes.com/sites/maryjuetten/2018/12/13/failed-startups-theranos/#14c3c3865ca6; and Waltz, E. (2017). After Theranos. *Nature Biotechnology, 35*(1), 11–16.

Self-Assessment 12.1

Are You a Transformational or a Transactional Leader?

In this chapter, you learned about transformational and transactional leadership styles. If you have held leadership positions in the past, you might have some idea which style you tend to use. Even if you have no leadership experience, these self-assessments have been designed to help you see whether you are more likely to adopt one or the other. Or you can also consider your leadership behavior with your teammates. There are no right or wrong answers, and this is not a test. You don't have to share your results with other classmates unless you wish to do so.

Instructions

Read each of the following statements and circle the response that best describes you.

Statements	Strongly Disagree	Disagree	Neutral	Agree	Strongly Agree
1. I have a clear understanding of where my group is going.	1	2	3	4	5
2. I always give others positive feedback when they perform well.	1	2	3	4	5
3. I paint an interesting picture of the future for our group.	1	2	3	4	5
4. I give special recognition to group members when their work is very good.	1	2	3	4	5
5. I am always seeking new opportunities for the group.	1	2	3	4	5
6. I commend others when they do a better-than-average job.	1	2	3	4	5
7. I inspire others with my plans for the future.	1	2	3	4	5
8. I frequently acknowledge others' good performance.	1	2	3	4	5

Transformational Leadership	Transactional Leadership
1. _____	2. _____
3. _____	4. _____
5. _____	6. _____
7. _____	8. _____
Total _____	Total_____

Scoring and Interpretation

Write the number you circled for each question on the blanks in the box below.

- *Transformational leadership (identifying and articulating a vision)*: identifying new opportunities for a leader's unit/division/company, and developing, articulating, and inspiring others with their vision of the future.
- *Transactional leadership (contingent reward)*: promising or delivering rewards to followers, contingent on their performance.

Your scores for each dimension (transformational or transactional) can range from 4 to 20. In general, scores from 4 to 12 represent lower levels of your preference for the leadership style, and scores above 13 indicate higher levels of your preference for the leadership style.

Discussion Questions

1. According to your results, which leadership style do you prefer: transformational or transactional?
2. What are some potential strengths and weakness of your transactional or transformational style preference?

3. Identify one or two career paths that interest you. Would this leadership style be a good fit for it? Why or why not?

Source: Adapted from Podsakoff, P. M., MacKenzie, S. B., Moorman, R. H., & Fetter, R. (1990). Transformational leader behaviors and their effects on followers' trust in leader, satisfaction, and organizational citizenship behaviors. *The Leadership Quarterly, 1*(2), 107–142.

Self-Assessment 12.2

Servant Leadership

In this chapter, you learned about servant leadership. If you have held leadership positions in the past, you might have some idea which style you tend to use. Even if you have no leadership experience, try to imagine how you would behave in a leadership position. Or you can also consider your leadership behavior with your teammates. There are no right or wrong answers, and this is not a test. You don't have to share your results with other classmates unless you wish to do so.

Instructions

Answer each of the following questions by circling the response that best describes you.

Statement	Strongly Disagree	Disagree	Somewhat Disagree	Neutral	Somewhat Agree	Agree	Strongly Agree
1. I can tell if something work-related is going wrong.	1	2	3	4	5	6	7
2. I make the career development of my team members a priority.	1	2	3	4	5	6	7
3. My team members would seek help from me if they had a personal problem.	1	2	3	4	5	6	7
4. I emphasize the importance of giving back to the community.	1	2	3	4	5	6	7
5. I put the interests of my team members ahead of my own.	1	2	3	4	5	6	7

(Continued)

(Continued)

Statement	Strongly Disagree	Disagree	Somewhat Disagree	Neutral	Somewhat Agree	Agree	Strongly Agree
6. I give team members the freedom to handle difficult situations in the way that they feel is best.	1	2	3	4	5	6	7
7. I would *not* compromise ethical principles in order to achieve success.	1	2	3	4	5	6	7

Scoring and Interpretation

Add your scores for each of the questions together. Then divide by 7. Your score will range from 1 (very low) to 7 (very high). An average score would be 4.

In the validation of this measure, researchers collected data from 598 employed undergraduates at a Midwestern university. Their mean score was 4.69 with a standard deviation of 1.17.

Servant leadership is related to employee engagement, creativity, and helping behaviors. It enhances team performance. Our society now demands higher ethical behavior by leaders. Servant leadership is thus a desirable set of behaviors for leaders to emulate. This style "promotes integrity, focuses on helping others, and prioritizes bringing out the full potential of followers."[119] Servant leadership may also reduce unethical behavior because it guards against the negative outcomes of leaders promoting their own self-interests.

Discussion Questions

1. Were you surprised by your results for servant leadership? Which of the seven questions were you highest on (i.e., 6 or 7)?
2. Ask your team members to complete mirroring questions about you on the same 1 to 7 rating scale (strongly disagree to strongly agree):

1. This person can tell if something work-related is going wrong.
2. This person makes the career development of my team members a priority.
3. I would seek help from this person if I had a personal problem.
4. This person emphasizes the importance of giving back to the community.
5. This person puts the interests of their team members ahead of their own.
6. This person gives team members the freedom to handle difficult situations in the way that they feel is best.
7. This person would *not* compromise ethical principles in order to achieve success.

Does your self-perception agree with how others see you with respect to your total score divided by 7? Explain any differences you see in the responses to each of the questions.

3. How did your results compare with the large sample of employed undergraduates at the Midwestern university? These students were employed. Explain why this might have resulted in similarities to or differences from your own results.

Source: Adapted from Liden, R. C., Wayne, S. J., Meuser, J. D., Hu, J., Wu, J., & Liao, C. (2015). Servant leadership: Validation of a short form of the SL-28. *The Leadership Quarterly, 26*(2), 254–269.

⑤SAGE edge™

Get the tools you need to sharpen your study skills. SAGE edge offers a robust online environment featuring an impressive array of free tools and resources. Access practice quizzes, eFlashcards, video, and multimedia at **edge.sagepub.com/scanduragower**.

Introducing…

$ \text{⑤} $ SAGE vantage™

Course tools done right.

Built to support teaching. Designed to ignite learning.

SAGE vantage is an intuitive digital platform that blends trusted SAGE content with auto-graded assignments, all carefully designed to ignite student engagement and drive critical thinking. Built with you and your students in mind, it offers easy course set-up and enables students to better prepare for class.

SAGE vantage enables students to *engage* with the material you choose, *learn* by applying knowledge, and *soar* with confidence by performing better in your course.

PEDAGOGICAL SCAFFOLDING

Builds on core concepts, moving students from basic understanding to mastery.

CONFIDENCE BUILDER

Offers frequent knowledge checks, applied-learning multimedia tools, and chapter tests with focused feedback.

TIME-SAVING FLEXIBILITY

Feeds auto-graded assignments to your gradebook, with real-time insight into student and class performance.

QUALITY CONTENT

Written by expert authors and teachers, content is not sacrificed for technical features.

HONEST VALUE

Affordable access to easy-to-use, quality learning tools students will appreciate.

To learn more about **SAGE vantage**, hover over this QR code with your smartphone camera or visit **sagepub.com/vantage**

CHAPTER 13

MANAGING IN A GLOBAL ENVIRONMENT

CHAPTER LEARNING OBJECTIVES

After studying this chapter, you should be able to:

13.1 Explain why understanding cultural differences is important for being an effective manager.

13.2 Provide examples of cultures that scored high and low on each of Hofstede's dimensions of national culture.

13.3 Discuss the key findings from the Global Leadership and Organizational Behavior Effectiveness (GLOBE) project international study.

13.4 Explain how globalization has affected the manager's job.

13.5 Provide examples of the three dimensions of the global mindset.

13.6 Describe the three dimensions of cultural intelligence.

Get the edge on your studies at **edge.sagepub .com/scanduragower**.

- Take the chapter quiz
- Review key terms with eFlashcards
- Explore multimedia resources, SAGE readings, and more!

Alexa Is Making New International Friends

Will Alexa be able to communicate well in other cultures around the world? Alexa can be asked to tell customers the weather, set a timer, play music, and operate smart-home devices. Amazon started to sell a handful of Echo devices in India in October 2017 by invitation only, but the company planned to expand there and sell the new Echo, Echo Plus, and Echo Dot. The devices started shipping in the country later that month. India is the world's second most populated country so figuring out how Alexa could communicate there is a strategic priority. However, in India, Amazon faces tough competition from e-commerce companies such as Flipkart and Snapdeal. The goal is to get Indian customers to buy Echo devices and then connect to Amazon's online store and other services such as

Prime memberships. Amazon had primed this by starting its Prime membership service in India in 2016.[1]

Echo devices had been available for sale in the United States, United Kingdom, and Germany. Amazon also sent Alexa to Japan, which has been a valuable international market for Amazon for years with Prime launching there over 10 years ago. Yes, Alexa now speaks Japanese.

In addition to Japanese, Alexa now speaks in English in three accents (American, British, and Indian), as well as German, depending on which market a customer lives in. With Alexa's increased ability to understand context and intent, she will be able to understand sentences that include proper nouns in Hindi, Tamil, Telugu, Kannada, Malayalam, or Punjabi, according to an Amazon spokesperson.[2] Amazon announced a bold plan for Alexa to travel to 80 additional countries.

Alexa going global has created exciting career opportunities at Amazon. In May 2018, Amazon's website listed open positions for "The Alexa International Expansion Team." The ad states that the team:

> …focuses on expanding Alexa's capabilities on a global scale, launching into new countries and languages. We take on the unique challenge of understanding the nuances of how Alexa can serve customers' needs in different cultures and locations. Our Technical Product Managers and Voice Designers lead the charge on international expansion. Our Content Editors work on making Alexa as local and authentic as possible, matching her voice and personality to the countries where she resides like the UK, Germany, India, Japan, and Canada. We are also hiring technical talent including Software Development Engineers and Managers located in Seattle, who focus on infrastructure for deploying Alexa internationally.[3]

These new job opportunities are perfect for culturally diverse applicants. The Amazon website also has a post about one of the international expansion team members, "Jenny L." Since she graduated from the Stanford Graduate School of Business, Jenny primarily led product development and engineering in Search, Advertising, and now Alexa. "With Amazon perpetually entering new industries, I am always challenged to learn something new and become an expert in new industries and functional skills," she says. "This is where the skills I acquired in my first career as a strategy consultant have become surprisingly applicable throughout my career at Amazon."[4]

Amazon's latest quest is to form and lead a new technology team for Alexa International Expansion. Although Alexa is already popular across the world, the plans to expand Alexa are vast, including increased linguistic innovations.[5] "I am tri-lingual and majored in International Studies in college, so it's super exciting that my language skills are applicable to my daily work," Jenny says, and the Amazon job site is still searching for Team Alexa Product Managers all around the world.[6]

Is the globalization of Alexa working? Yes, based on the sales estimates. Amazon CEO Jeff Bezos estimates that 20.54 Amazon Echo devices and 4.60 Google Home devices were sold globally through the third quarter of 2017.[7] Amazon estimates that the global installed base of smart speakers will could easily surpass 40 million. The key variable in total sales will be Asian markets, particularly China and Japan.[8]

Sources: Amazon. (2018). Alexa International Expansion. Retrieved from https://www.amazon.jobs/en/teams/alexa-international-expansion; Amazon. (2019). Alexa International Expansion. Retrieved from https://www.amazon.jobs/en/teams/alexa-international-expansion; Kinsella, B. (2017, October 27). Bezos says more than 20 million Amazon Alexa devices sold. Retrieved from https://voicebot.ai/2017/10/27/bezos-says-20-million-amazon-alexa-devices-sold/; Rubin, B. F. (2017, October 4). Amazon spreads Echo's global reach with expansion to Asia. *CNet.* Retrieved from https://www.cnet.com/news/amazon-echo-alexa-expansion-india-japan-asia/.

The Alexa and Amazon experiences internationally provide a solid base for the importance of understanding cultures. This book has covered organizational cultures and their strength in dictating many parts of the organization. Because culture is largely invisible, it is important for managers to be aware of national cultures, too, and their significant impact on employees and other stakeholders.

▼ FIGURE 13.0

Textbook Organization

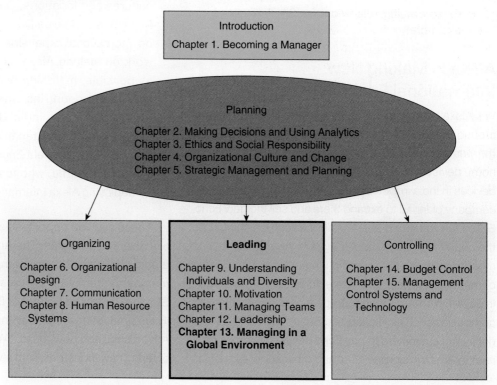

What Is Culture?

National culture is an elusive concept in terms of definition. Definitions typically employed in management have their roots in sociology or anthropology. Sociologists define **culture** as follows:

- It is shared by almost all members of a social group.
- Older members of the group pass it on to younger members.
- It shapes behavior or structures one's perception of the world (such as morals, laws, and customs).[9]

Culture can be considered to be the commonly shared understandings of the ways of doing things in an organization.[10] Culture is composed of the things that we can see (e.g., the clothes a person wears or what holidays they celebrate) and things we cannot see (e.g., how they define morality and what they value).

Using the analogy of an iceberg helps us understand culture (see Figure 13.1).[11] When we see an iceberg, the portion that is visible above water is only a minor part of something much larger. Similarly, people often think of culture as what they can see—the observable characteristics of people from that culture (e.g., food, music, arts, or the way that people greet one another). Actually, these are merely external representations of much more deeply held core values and assumptions. Below the "water line" are a culture's core values as shown in Figure 13.1. People learn these values at a young age regarding what is good, right, desirable, and acceptable. Sometimes different cultures share similar core values (such as "honesty" or "respect"), but these values may be expressed differently in everyday life. A given culture's interpretations of these core values become observable behaviors such as the way that people behave or communicate with one another. Core cultural values are not easy to change, and if they do,

▼ FIGURE 13.1

The Culture Iceberg

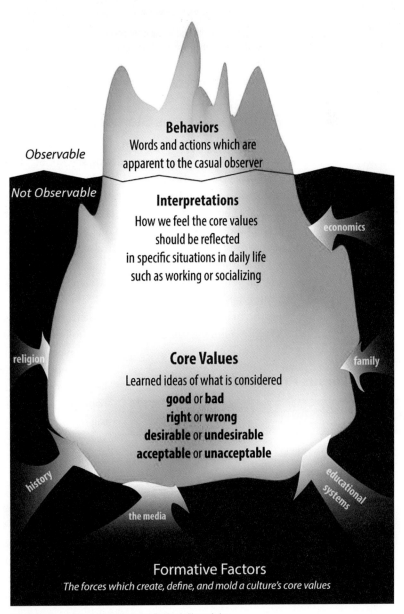

Observable

Behaviors
Words and actions which are apparent to the casual observer

Not Observable

Interpretations
How we feel the core values should be reflected in specific situations in daily life such as working or socializing

economics

religion

family

Core Values
Learned ideas of what is considered
good or **bad**
right or **wrong**
desirable or **undesirable**
acceptable or **unacceptable**

history

educational systems

the media

Formative Factors
The forces which create, define, and mold a culture's core values

Source: © 2015, Language & Culture Worldwide. Reprinted with permission.

it takes a long time. This is because they are passed down from generation to generation by parents, grandparents, and teachers. By the time we are adults, these values have become the formative factors that guide us in making decisions. The media and laws enacted by legislators reinforce these ideas. Therefore, like an iceberg, there are things that we can see and describe readily, but there are also many deeply rooted ideas that we can only understand by learning about the underlying cultural values.[12]

National cultures are complex. But it is clear that cultural values affect managers and how they make decisions. In addition, a manager cannot assume that what works in their own culture will work everywhere in the world. Fortunately, there is management research that helps us to understand the values that lie underneath the culture iceberg. The next sections will review this research and provide evidence-based guidelines that are essential to a manager being effective in today's global context.

CRITICAL THINKING QUESTIONS

Think of a person you know from another culture and explain how you could learn about their cultural values. Provide an example of a cultural value held by this person and discuss how it might affect your working relationship.

Prototypes Versus Stereotypes

Before we begin our discussion of cultural differences, it is important to point out that cultural averages may not reflect an individual's values. Research on culture is based on prototypes. A **prototype** describes something that is an example or model for identical things to be made in the near future. In terms of culture, someone could reflect a prototype when they exhibit desirable behaviors, talents, or characteristics. On the other hand, a **stereotype** describes things repeatedly attributed to one group of people. These things are usually negative or demeaning. They do not reflect an absolute pertaining to all people.[13]

It is important to recognize that cultural values are based on averages. A particular person you encounter may not conform to the average value for their culture. Cultural value prototypes are our "first best guess" for what a person may be like. For example, a Chinese person may have received their degree from a university in London, so they exhibit European as well as Chinese values. Consider the following situation:

Stereotype: Imagine that you are collaborating with an organization in the Middle East. Going into negotiations, you might operate on the stereotype that the managers in Arabic countries are Muslim. You might then assume that negotiating the partnership will be a long and complex task because, according to stereotype, bargaining and haggling are commonplace in Arabic culture.[14]

Figure 13.2 gives you a view of the difference between stereotypes, like what you have done above, and prototypes, like what will be revealed in the rest of the scenario below.

Prototype: This stereotype could be completely off-base for a variety of reasons. What if the new partner is Lebanese and Christian, or a European who happens to have established a business in the Middle East? It's also possible that the partner was educated in the United States or is simply an

▼ FIGURE 13.2

Stereotypes Versus Prototypes

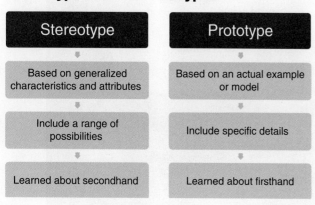

Stereotype	Prototype
Based on generalized characteristics and attributes	Based on an actual example or model
Include a range of possibilities	Include specific details
Learned about secondhand	Learned about firsthand

Examples of High- and Low-Context Cultures

High Context-Low Context Continuum

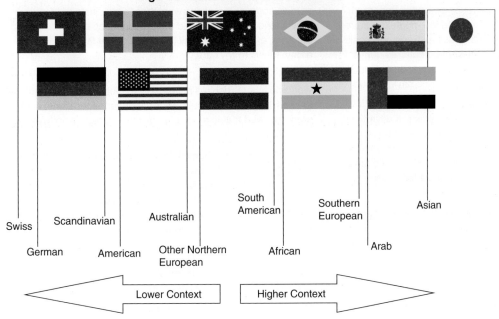

Sources: National Association of Realtors. (2018, December 13). Communication clashes. Retrieved from https://www.nar.realtor/global-perspectives/communication-clashes; Hall, E. T., & Hall, M. R. (1990). *Understanding cultural differences*. Boston: MA: Intercultural Press.

experienced international business person who has adopted a more efficient approach to negotiating. If you rely on a stereotype alone, you could be entering into a new relationship with faulty assumptions based on a narrow point of view.

By contrast, if you take a prototype approach to interactions with your new partner, you can widen your perspective.[15] You might begin by assuming that, in the Middle Eastern culture, a lot of back-and-forth discussions will take place because negotiating is a valuable part of the culture. However, your thought process does not *end* with this stereotype. You can approach the relationship-building process with this idea in mind, but you'll need to carefully consider other factors, too. Does the company operate in other places? Who is the CEO and what is their background? Who will you work with on a typical day? What does that person value as a manager? What is the office environment and culture of the team you'll work with most often? Using a prototype lens versus a stereotype lens helps you zoom out and consider the big picture rather than a single dominant detail.[16]

Please keep this "stereotype versus prototype" difference in mind as we begin our discussion of cultural differences and as you continue learning about the world. You will get a chance to practice your understanding of cultural differences in Activity 13.1.

High-Context and Low-Context Cultures

In **high-context cultures,** people rely on situational cues to ascribe meaning to situations when they are communicating with others. For example, in a high-context culture, a person may need to get to know their teammates well before they can work effectively together. In contrast, **low-context cultures** rely mainly on written and spoken words and they develop shared meanings from the literal words that are used. When teams meet in a low-context culture, you can expect that the team leader will develop formal action plans early in the process as a

FACT OR FICTION?

Do Advertisements Have the Same Meaning in Different Cultures?

There has been fascinating research on the impact of advertisements used in high- and low-context cultures. Ads in high-context cultures place a strong emphasis on relationships. Also, people in high-context cultures derive meaning from the social environment. Advertisements in high-context cultures typically show families having good times together.

In low-context cultures, however, the emphasis in advertising tends to be on the individual. People from low-context cultures tend to take things literally and are more socially distant from other people.[17] Advertisements in low-context cultures tend to show one person isolated from others with a focus on themselves.

Research shows that when evaluating direct ads, consumers in low-context communication cultures indicated a higher persuasion effect than those in high-context communication cultures. What this means is that low-context cultures are more likely to buy products based on seeing an advertisement. Furthermore, in low-context cultures, the persuasion effect for direct comparative ads is greater than indirect comparative ads. However, counter to common beliefs, the cultural context plays no role in differentiating consumers' attitudes toward comparative ads.

The expectation of how advertising affects different cultures in some cases is predictable, yet in other instances it is not.[18] A great example of the relationship aspect from above comes to us from a McDonald's ad with the same slogan, "I'm lovin' it." The ad from Sweden, a low-context culture, featured a young woman relaxing and listening to headphones, while an ad from high-context India showed a man with a shopping cart running in a supermarket with a small boy in the seat of the cart. Thus, "loving it" in a low-context culture means blocking out the outside world, whereas "loving it" in a high-context culture involves close family relationships taking place in public. Recall that a high-context culture reflects the degree to which people see themselves as embedded and connected, so the advertising in high-context cultures shows people in relationships and groups rather than separate and alone.[19]

Another study describes a milk advertisement in the United States, from a campaign created by the California Milk Processor Board. From the country mentioned and the explicit way the picture in the advertisement was presented, it belongs to low-context communication. In this advertisement for milk, famous singer Taylor Swift has a milk moustache and the slogan reads, "Got milk?" In the ad, there is a section of written words by Taylor Swift. In the ad, Taylor Swift says: "In this business, you've got to be decisive. So I choose milk. Some studies suggest that teens who choose milk instead of sugary drinks tend to be leaner and the protein helps build muscle. So eat right, exercise and drink 3 glasses of low fat or fat free milk a day. Music to my ears."[20]

Although some organizations feel that the globalization of the world no longer requires advertisers to distinguish between low- and high-context cultures for younger generations, a 2005 study showed that this blending of low and high is not ready for prime time.[21]

The milk producers showed their awareness of that even in the verbiage of the Taylor Swift ad. Notice that Swift uses the first-person noun "I" instead of "we" (i.e., "I choose milk"), which reflects the individualism of a low-context culture where emphasis is on the goals and accomplishments of the individual rather than the group. In individualistic cultures, individuals are expected to be independent of others and take care of themselves. Personal values are more important than collective values, and it makes the audience from the low-context U.S. culture more comfortable.

However, this same ad might have a different effect if placed in a magazine in a high-context culture. For example, if milk is advertised in China in this way, most Chinese parents may not be persuaded to purchase milk, according to the research. Due to the collectivist culture they share, they would feel more comfortable if milk is advertised as something that everyone drinks.[22]

Discussion Questions

1. Select an ad you are familiar with and provide another example of (a) a high-context communication and (b) a low-context communication.

2. Describe how the text of the Taylor Swift milk ad could be adapted so that it would appeal to a high-context culture such as China.

3. Provide an example of how a low-context culture would approach a business negotiation.

Sources: Bai, H. (2016). A cross-cultural analysis of advertisements from high-context cultures and low-context cultures. *English Language Teaching, 9*(8), 21–27; Choi, S. M., Wei-Na, L., & Hee-Jung, K. (2005). Lessons from the rich and famous: A cross-cultural comparison of celebrity endorsement in advertising. *Journal of Advertising, 34*(2), 85–98; and Würtz, E. (2005). A cross-cultural analysis of websites from high-context cultures and low-context cultures. *Journal of Computer-Mediated Communication, 11*(1), article 13.

reference for the team. These examples show that employees bring their national culture values with them to work every day. To succeed as a manager, it is important to understand cultural values. Examples showing the range from high- and low-context cultures (from low to high) are shown in Figure 13.3.[23]

Cultural Tightness–Looseness

Cultural tightness–looseness is defined as the strength of social norms and the level of sanctioning within societies.[24] **Cultural tightness** produces order and efficiency, conformity, and resistance to change. In contrast, **cultural looseness** is associated with social disorganization, deviance from social norms, innovation, and being open to change. Tightness–looseness is reflected in the clarity and pervasiveness of norms and the degree of tolerance for deviation from these norms. For example, one factor indicating tight and loose societies is the level of accountability in organizations and the extent to which individuals have a sense of accountability. A large-scale study assessed cultural tightness–looseness in 33 cultures with the following survey questions (respondents were asked to agree or disagree with the questions on a 6-point scale):

1. There are many social norms that people are supposed to abide by in this country.
2. In this country, there are very clear expectations for how people should act in most situations.
3. People agree upon what behaviors are appropriate versus inappropriate in most situations in this country.
4. People in this country have a great deal of freedom in deciding how they want to behave in most situations (reverse-scored; higher scores indicate more cultural tightness).
5. In this country, if someone acts in an inappropriate way, others will strongly disapprove.
6. People in this country almost always comply with social norms.[25]

This research found the 33 cultures studied varied with respect to tightness–looseness. Tight cultures had more social controls and were more likely to have autocratic leaders. They were also more likely to have more rules and laws, for example. Examples of tight cultures are India, Malaysia, and Pakistan. Examples of relatively loose cultures are Hungary, Israel, and Ukraine. The United States had a score of 5.1, which was a bit below the overall average score of 6.5 across all respondents from all cultures. So the United States can be seen as somewhat loose.

Cultural tightness is likely a response to ecological and historical threats such as population density, conflict, natural disasters, and disease (as examples). Governments, the media, education, laws, and religion also shape cultural tightness. These aspects relate to the structure of norms and tolerance for deviation from them, and this affects the degree of structure in everyday situations, including management. The researchers conclude that "understanding tight and loose cultures is critical for fostering cross-cultural coordination in a world of increasing global interdependence."[26] Research on cultural tightness–looseness is relatively new, but this approach shows a great deal of promise for enhancing our understanding of cross-cultural management.

Geert Hofstede stated one of the most often-quoted definitions of culture: "Culture is the collective programming of the mind that distinguishes the members of one group or category of people from others."[27] This definition has become famous among managers, and Hofstede is now one of the most-cited researchers in the social sciences.

In addition to offering a definition of culture, Hofstede articulated four cultural values that have received much research attention: power distance, collectivism–individualism, uncertainty avoidance, and relationship orientation. In 1988, a fifth cultural value, time orientation (called Confucian dynamism), was added.[28] These cultural values remain the best-known frameworks for understanding cross-cultural differences in a variety of disciplines, including management. Next, we will review them and the research on these cultural values, which has had a large impact on how we view the effects on national culture in organizations.

Hofstede's Cultural Values

Over the years, Hofstede and his colleagues have developed five cultural values, which are summarized below and in Table 13.1. Brief definitions and examples of countries with the United States as the referent culture for comparison purposes follow.

- *Power distance*—deference to authority (e.g., the United States is low, China is high)
- *Collectivism–individualism*—group orientation (e.g., the United States is low, Russia is high)
- *Uncertainty avoidance*—risk aversion (e.g., the United States is low, France is high)
- *Relationship orientation* (masculinity–femininity)—a focus on people over material things (e.g., the United States is low and the Netherlands is high on femininity/relationship orientation)
- *Confucian dynamism* (long-term orientation)—a focus on the future rather than the past and present (e.g., the United States is low, Japan is high)[29]

To define these cultural values, Hofstede collected surveys from employees all over the world—initially from 40 countries.[30] Later, his research expanded to 62 countries (116,000 managers and employees working for the large multinational company, IBM).[31] This research showed that cultural values remain fairly stable over time. The research team also created cultural clusters of countries in the survey based on the five cultural dimensions described above. For example, the United States, Great Britain, Canada, and Australia are lower on power distance and higher on individualism compared to other countries. Venezuela, Peru, Mexico, and Argentina are higher power distance and higher collectivist cultures.[32] Spain, France, Belgium, and Italy are higher on power distance but also relatively more individualistic compared with other cultures.

In management research, there has been a great deal of research interest in the dimensions of national culture and collectivism in particular.[33] For example, being a loyal team member is expected to be more important in collectivist cultures compared to individualist cultures.[34] Research has linked collectivism to positive team outcomes.[35] The high level of individualism in the United States may help explain why the move to team-based organizations has been more difficult compared with some Asian cultures such as China. Also, having a personal relationship with the boss is more important in individualistic cultures, since employees' see the boss as the link to advancement and monetary rewards.[36] In contrast, in a collectivist culture, rewards may be tied more closely to the performance of the team. A recent review of research on team performance showed that showed that cooperation was higher in collectivistic cultures.[37]

Power distance relates to leadership and team behavior. Individuals with high power distance may not expect to have high-quality relationships with their boss, and they do not attempt to manage their boss because they tend to have unquestioning deference to authority.[38] In contrast, for employees with low power distance, status in the organization is not important and they may see themselves as equal to their supervisors.[39]

Cooperation and performance are higher in collectivistic cultures, such as China.

©iStockphoto.com/imtmphoto

There is no doubt that Hofstede's research has had a significant influence on management practice. The cultural values framework has been important to the implementation of many business systems, including compensation, budget control, entrepreneurial behavior, training design, conflict resolution, work group dynamics, innovation, and leadership.[40]

Hofstede's Cultural Values

Low Score on Cultural Value	High Score on Cultural Value
Individualism: Social organization is loose, and people care for themselves and their immediate family.	**Collectivism:** Social organization is tight, and people are loyal to their in-group and/or organization.
Low power distance: People prefer that power be equally distributed in an egalitarian way.	**High power distance:** People accept power differences and respect authority.
Low uncertainty avoidance: People tolerate uncertainty and ambiguity. They are willing to take risks.	**High uncertainty avoidance:** People feel threatened by uncertainty and ambiguity. They are risk averse and create rules to create stability.
Masculinity: People value assertiveness and strive to acquire money and things.	**Femininity:** People value caring for one another and the quality of life.
Short-term oriented: People value the past and present, expecting short-term gain.	**Long-term oriented:** People plan for the future, persist, and value being thrifty.

Sources: Hofstede, G. (1980). *Culture's consequences: International differences in work-related values*. Beverly Hills, CA: Sage; Hofstede, G. (1991). *Culture's consequences: International differences in work-related values* (2nd ed.). Newbury Park, CA: Sage; and Hofstede, G., & Bond, M. H. (1988). The Confucius connection: From cultural roots to economic growth. *Organizational Dynamics, 16*(4), 5–21.

CRITICAL THINKING QUESTIONS

Do you think that cultures around the world are becoming more "westernized" (in other words, like the United States)? Why or why not?

There have been many applications of the Hofstede cultural values framework. Yet the model has been criticized for not being current, since the values were developed in 1980. Some people believe that researchers cannot describe all people in a single culture as having the same set of values. The focus on countries is another limitation of the research (i.e., the United States and Canada are similar). The original studies lacked context since they didn't discuss potential political influences on the data. The initial study used only one company (IBM) so this might tell us more about IBM's culture than national culture. Culture is complex and it may not be possible to measure it with only four or five dimensions.[41] In fact, an additional dimension, Indulgence, has been added more recently. Indulgence refers to the degree of restraint in a culture as compared to engaging in free gratification of basic drives to enjoy life and have fun. Hofstede's measures and statistical analyses have also been criticized for their lack of validity and rigor.[42] On the other hand, Hofstede's work was published when there was little work on national culture and spurred a great deal of research interest, his approach was systematic and rigorous for the 1980s time period, and other studies have generally confirmed the initial results.

A large review of research covering 30 years on the Hofstede cultural values analyzed 598 studies (and over 200,000 employees and managers). This review found that the original cultural value dimensions were all important to understand work outcomes. The five cultural values were significantly and positively related to organizational commitment, identification, citizenship behavior, team-related attitudes, and feedback seeking. However, personality and demographics were better predictors of performance, absenteeism, and turnover than cultural values.[43]

Despite these criticisms, Hofstede's research has had a large effect on the practice of management. His book, *Culture's Consequences*, is considered to be one of the 25 most-cited books in the realm of social science research, with over 42,000 citations.[44] This cultural values framework has been instrumental for worldwide implementation of a number of management practices including compensation, budget control, entrepreneurial behavior, training design, conflict resolution, work group dynamics, innovation, and leadership training.[45]

CRITICAL THINKING QUESTIONS

Explain why the study of national culture became so important during the 1980s. Give an example of how a manager's cultural background affects their management style.

Hall and Hofstede laid the foundations for research on cross-cultural management that followed. Building on this prior work, a large-scale study of cultural differences called the **Global Leadership and Organizational Behavior Effectiveness (GLOBE) project** was conducted to better understand how differences in culture may affect organizational outcomes in many parts of the world. We will review this study next.

Project Globe

Learning Objective 13.3: Discuss the key findings from the Global Leadership and Organizational Behavior Effectiveness (GLOBE) project international study.

GLOBE involved 170 social scientists and management scholars from 61 cultures throughout the world to collect, analyze, and interpret data collected from employees and managers. The goal of the GLOBE project was to provide an in-depth examination of the relationship

▼ TABLE 13.2

GLOBE Cultural Dimensions and Sample Questionnaire Items

Culture Construct Definitions	Sample Questionnaire Item
Power distance: The degree to which members of a collective expect power to be distributed equally.	Followers are expected to obey their leaders without question.
Uncertainty avoidance: The extent to which a society, organization, or group relies on societal norms, rules, and procedures to alleviate unpredictability of future events.	Most people lead highly structured lives with few unexpected events.
Humane orientation: The degree to which a collective encourages and rewards individuals for being fair, altruistic, generous, caring, and kind to others.	People are generally very tolerant of mistakes.
Institutional collectivism: The degree to which organizational and societal institutional practices encourage and reward collective distribution of resources and collective action.	Leaders encourage group loyalty even if individual goals suffer.
In-group collectivism: The degree to which individuals express pride, loyalty, and cohesiveness in their organizations or families.	Aging parents generally live at home with their children.
Assertiveness: The degree to which individuals are assertive, dominant, and demanding in their relationships with others.	People are generally dominant.
Gender egalitarianism: The degree to which a collective minimizes gender inequality.	Boys are encouraged more than girls to attain a higher education. (reverse-scored)
Future orientation: The extent to which a collective encourages future-oriented behaviors such as delaying gratification, planning, and investing in the future.	More people live for the present than for the future. (reverse-scored)
Performance orientation: The degree to which a collective encourages and rewards group members for performance improvement and excellence.	Students are encouraged to strive for continuously improved performance.

Source: Adapted from House, R., Javidan, M., Hanges, P., & Dorfman, P. (2002). Understanding cultures and implicit leadership theories across the globe: An introduction to project GLOBE. *Journal of World Business, 37*(1), 3–10.

GLOBE Culture Clusters

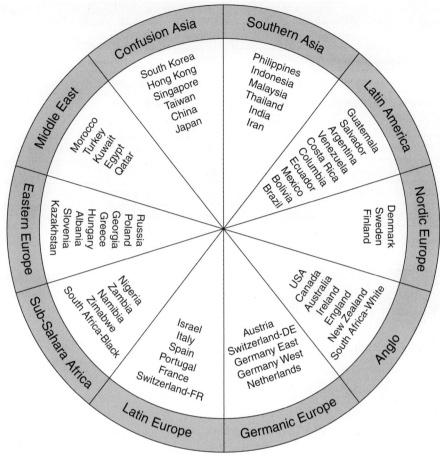

Source: Adapted from House, R. J., Hanges, P. J., Javidan, M., Dorfman, P. W., & Gupta, V. (Eds.). (2004). *Culture, leadership, and organizations: The GLOBE study of 62 societies.* Thousand Oaks, CA: Sage.

of cultural values to leadership and organizational effectiveness. The researchers refined and extended the Hofstede cultural value framework and identified nine cultural concepts. As with Hofstede, this research identified power distance and uncertainty avoidance as cultural values. Collectivism was split into two dimensions—loyalty to the group (the people you work with) and loyalty to institutions (such as the organization you work for). In addition, the GLOBE project identified humane orientation, assertiveness, gender egalitarianism, future orientation (similar to Hofstede's Confucian dynamism), and performance orientation. The nine GLOBE cultural dimension definitions and sample questionnaire items are shown in Table 13.2.[46]

Just as with Hofstede's research, however, pay careful attention to the GLOBE constructs and items, as the survey results have their own detractors (even Hofstede), based on some research that found negative correlations between "values" and "practices" in the GLOBE dimensions.[47]

Based on the GLOBE research and the 61 countries included in the study, cultures appear to vary on the nine dimensions. High- and low-scoring country examples are shown for each of the dimensions in Table 13.3. Some cultures were found to be similar to others, and the GLOBE research team created a set of "country clusters," as shown in Figure 13.4.

Examples of Countries Highest and Lowest on GLOBE Cultural Values

Cultural Dimension	Highest	Lowest
Power distance	Argentina, Spain, Russia	Denmark, Israel, Costa Rica
Uncertainty avoidance	Switzerland, Denmark, Austria	Russia, Hungary, Venezuela
Humane orientation	Philippines, Ireland, Egypt	Spain, France, Singapore
Institutional collectivism	Sweden, South Korea, Japan	Greece, Argentina, Italy
In-group collectivism	Iran, India, China	Finland, Netherlands, Sweden
Assertiveness	Germany (former East), Spain	New Zealand, Japan, Kuwait, United States
Gender egalitarianism	Hungary, Poland, Sweden	Morocco, India, China
Future orientation	Canada, Singapore, Denmark	Russia, Argentina, Italy
Performance orientation	Hong Kong, Taiwan, United States	Argentina, Greece, Venezuela

Source: Adapted from House, R. J., Hanges, P. J., Javidan, M., Dorfman, P. W., & Gupta, V. (Eds.). (2004). *Culture, leadership, and organizations: The GLOBE study of 62 societies.* Thousand Oaks, CA: Sage.

Companies have a shortage of global managers.

©iStockphoto.com/ipopba

For example, Latin American countries such as Argentina and Columbia are more similar to one another than countries in Sub-Saharan Africa, which includes Nigeria and Zimbabwe.[48]

You can learn how your cultural values compare with other cultures by taking Self-Assessment 13.1, the GLOBE Cultural Values Assessment. After completing the assessment, you can compare your results to selected country clusters. Visualizations of the data by country and for these country clusters can be viewed at https://globeproject.com/results.

CRITICAL THINKING QUESTIONS

What are the advantages of knowing cultural values that generalize across cultures? Is it more useful to learn about cultural values that are unique to a culture? Why or why not?

Now that we have a good foundation in understanding cultural differences, we next turn to the development of global managers. Today's managers often lack the global leadership skills needed to be effective in the multinational business context.[49] One study estimated that 85% of Fortune 500 companies have a shortage of global managers.[50] The critical skills needed for effective global managers and how you can learn them are discussed in the following sections.

The Impact of Globalization on Management

Learning Objective 13.4: Explain how globalization has affected the manager's job.

Globalization and the rise of the **multinational corporation (MNC)** has affected the work performed by most managers. An MNC has facilities and other assets in at least one country other than its home country. Such companies have offices and/or factories in different countries and usually have a centralized head office where they coordinate global management.[51]

Examples of the largest MNCs in the world include China National Petroleum, Coca-Cola, and Toyota. The rise of MNCs has resulted in increased globalization in management, which is described as follows:

In the 1990s, leaders of organizations found themselves crossing borders across all dimensions of business and government more rapidly, more constantly, and more frequently than they had in previous decades. Global supply chains became the norm. Global markets became the norm. Immediate, real-time global communication with all stakeholders became the norm. Global knowledge sharing became the norm.[52] In fact, global knowledge sharing, in just a few short years has changed the world view of sustainable development, health initiatives, and virtual teams, just to name a few.[53] Global finance systems became the norm. Global competitors became more ubiquitous and dangerous. Global careers became increasingly important. Social media, branding, marketing, selling, and communication became the norm. Something was changing—the world of business seemed less "international" in nature and more, somehow, "global" in nature. For many businesspeople and scholars the term, "global" replaced "international" as the adjective commonly used to describe organizational and leadership strategies, thinking, and behavior.[54]

The changes in business that have resulted in the need for a worldview for managers has been termed, not surprisingly, **globalization**.[55] Carlos Ghosn, the chairman and CEO of the Renault-Nissan alliance, was asked about the importance of cross-cultural management education for managers. Here was his reply:

More and more, managers are dealing with different cultures. Companies are going global, and teams are spread across the globe. If you're head of engineering, you have to deal with divisions in Vietnam, India, China or Russia, and you have to work across cultures. You have to know how to motivate people who speak different languages, who have different cultural contexts, who have different sensitivities and habits. You have to get prepared to deal with teams who are multicultural, to work with people who do not all think the same way as you do.[56]

Other top executives who view the ability to influence people from other cultures as the most important skill required for their own success share Ghosn's view.[57] A *Sloan Management Review* article has been widely cited as a call for managers and leaders with a more global mindset: Global business requires the management and leadership mindset of explorers, guiding their organizations through unfamiliar and turbulent environments. With markets, suppliers, competitors, technology, and customers around the world constantly changing, traditional leadership models no longer work.[58] Ghosn's perspective was written 10 years after this latter article, as organizations continue to struggle with keeping up with change, especially now that it is a global matter.

Therefore, it is now necessary for a manager to understand cultural differences and cultivate their global mindset.

The Global Mindset

Learning Objective 13.5: Provide examples of the three dimensions of the global mindset.

The **global mindset** is a set of individual attributes that enhance a manager's ability to influence others who are different from them.[59] To learn about how the global mindset develops, a team of researchers at the Thunderbird Graduate School of Management led by Mansour

Javidan conducted interviews with over 200 senior executives and 5,000 managers in Asia, Europe, and the United States. They inquired about the success and failure of these managers. In particular, they asked about what was limiting their progress in managing in other cultures. "When you think about globalization, the implication of the company's global strategy is that managers will be increasingly asked to work with people from other parts of the world," according to Javidan. "The problem is that children grow up mostly learning how to live and work with people who are like them. So when a company asks its managers to work effectively with people from other parts of the world, it's asking managers to do something that's different from what they're naturally developed for."[60]

A person with a lower global mindset typically considers interaction with people from other cultures as frustrating and intimidating; thus, many of the difficulties associated with cross-border business operations may be traced to differences in culture. International companies must therefore develop information processing capabilities that will enable them to acquire the knowledge they need to overcome their psychic distance as well as liabilities of foreignness to be able to operate effectively in foreign markets.[61]

In contrast, a person with a higher global mindset finds diversity interesting and not intimidating. They view interacting with people from other cultures as an exciting challenge. Researchers also learned that a person with a global mindset is passionate about diversity. Managers with a global mindset know a great deal about cultures and political and economic systems. Due to their openness and extensive knowledge, they are able to build trusting relationships with people in other cultures because they show respect for that culture.

As shown in Figure 13.5, there are three dimensions of the global mindset:

1. *Global psychological capital*—the feeling or affective aspect of the global mindset. A manager with strong psychological capital is willing to engage in a global environment and has a positive attitude toward diversity.[62] One study found that coaching support may enhance managers' psychological capital and global competencies.[63]
2. *Global social capital*—the behavioral aspect of the global mindset. A manager with strong global social capital acts in a way that helps build trusting relationships with people from other parts of the world.[64] Their success in building strong social capital was found to be characterized by a broad and diverse network of both internal and external ties.[65]
3. *Global intellectual capital*—the cognitive aspect of the global mindset. A manager with strong global intellectual capital knows a lot about the global business in their industry and its broader macro environment, making it easier for them to analyze, digest, and interpret this information.[66]

These characteristics relate to the global effectiveness of managers. For example, in global virtual sales teams (GVSTs), an increasing phenomenon, an integrated framework for increasing effectiveness found that collective intellectual capital and social capital influence the GVST environment (affective GVST climate, GVST efficacy, and GVST potency). These are important factors in virtual teams in general because they impact attitude, effectiveness, and the strength of the team.[67]

Global psychological capital helps a manager leverage their global intellectual capital. A manager may be knowledgeable about other cultures and world events, but without a strong global psychological capital, they may be disinterested in working with people from other countries and may find global roles stressful. To learn about your global mindset, complete Self-Assessment 13.2 and answer the discussion questions.

The Global Mindset

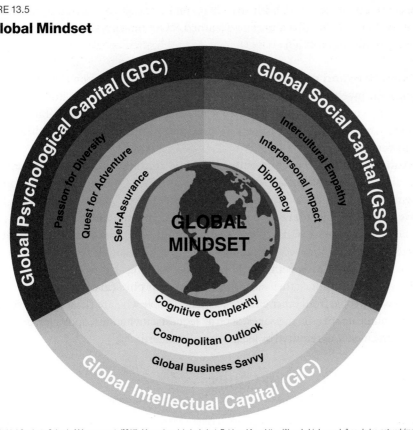

Source: Thunderbird Graduate School of Management. (2017). Measuring global mindset. Retrieved from https://thunderbird.asu.edu/knowledge-network/measuring-global-mindset-article.

Cultural Intelligence

Learning Objective 13.6: Describe the three dimensions of cultural intelligence.

Cultural intelligence (CQ) is defined as an individual's capabilities to function and manage effectively in culturally diverse settings.[68] CQ is developed by first assessing one's strengths and weaknesses in CQ, undergoing training in cross-cultural interactions, and then applying CQ learning to real-life cross-cultural situations to build confidence.[69] CQ is composed of four dimensions: metacognitive, cognitive, motivational, and behavioral, as shown in Figure 13.6. **Cognitive CQ** refers to self-awareness and the ability to detect cultural patterns. This dimension includes **metacognitive CQ**, which refers to the cognitive processing necessary to recognize and understand expectations appropriate for different cultural situations. **Motivational CQ** refers to persistence and goal setting for cross-cultural interactions. **Behavioral CQ** is the ability to adjust to others' cultural practices.[70]

The cognitive aspect of CQ predicts cultural judgment, whereas motivational CQ predicts cultural adaptation. Both cognitive and behavioral CQ predict task performance.[71] But can CQ be acquired through training? Two multinational studies compared students' CQ before taking cross-cultural management courses to their scores afterward. Student CQ was significantly higher after taking courses that included CQ, with stronger effects found for cognitive CQ than motivational or behavioral CQ. Another study found that individuals with certain characteristics are more likely to benefit from CQ training. Individuals with greater propensity to change stereotypes are more likely to develop higher levels CQ when they take training.[72] Thus, research has found that CQ can be learned.[73] CQ training should include assessment and training on all facets of CQ:

- **Cognitive (and metacognitive)**—acquiring information on the new culture and engaging in self-reflection.[74] Cognitive CQ consists of two parts: culture-general knowledge (i.e., understanding the different elements that make up a cultural environment) and context-specific knowledge (i.e., knowledge about how culture manifests in certain environments).[75]
- **Motivational**—developing culture-specific confidence (self-efficacy) and setting goals for cross-cultural adjustment.[76] Motivational CQ encourages people to interact with people who are culturally different from themselves.[77]
- **Behavioral**—includes role-plays to model and practice effective behaviors, verbally and nonverbally, with those from another culture.[78] Verbal behavior flexibility allows people to adjust the speed, inflection, warmth, enthusiasm, and formality of their speech when communicating with people from other cultures. Nonverbal behavior flexibility allows people to adjust their sitting proximity, their physical contact, and their eye contact with people from other cultures. Finally, people who are flexible in speech acts can communicate specific messages, such as requests, invitations, apologies, gratitude, and disagreements, as required by local cultural standards.[79]

CRITICAL THINKING QUESTIONS

> Explain why it is important for a manager to have cultural intelligence. Which dimension do you feel is most important and why?

CQ involves the ability to learn about other cultures and develop the confidence and skills to try new behaviors. Adaptation is a key aspect of success in working with others to achieve a third culture both one-on-one and in teams. To see if you have a high degree of CQ, complete Self-Assessment 13.3.

Culture Shock

Culture shock has become a common term, and most people are now familiar with the concept. The term was coined by an anthropologist who defined **culture shock** as the distress experienced by a traveler from the loss of familiar patterns of social interaction. Oberg described several "symptoms" of culture shock, including the following:

Cultural intelligence involves the ability to learn about other cultures and develop the confidence and skills to try new behaviors.

©iStockphoto.com/FatCamera

1. Stress due to the effort required to make necessary adjustments
2. Having a sense of loss from missing family and friends—"homesickness"
3. Wanting to avoid interactions with persons from the host culture
4. Feeling helpless and wanting to depend on those from one's home country
5. Having a fear of being robbed or injured, or becoming ill
6. Being angry at delays and inconveniences experienced
7. Feeling incompetent from not being able to cope with the new environment[80]

The process of culture shock from predeparture (before you leave) to reentry (getting home) is shown in Figure 13.7. As this figure illustrates, the impact of cultural transitions on well-being follows a series of ups and downs. During the predeparture phase, there is a sense of excitement and anticipation of experiencing a new adventure in another culture. On arrival, there is typically a sense of confusion due to jet lag and getting used to one's surroundings. Most expatriates experience a honeymoon phase followed by a plunge when they begin to encounter difficulties in understanding cultural practices and values. Over time, reconciliation occurs, and the expatriate begins to adjust and accommodate to the new environment.[81]

As shown in Figure 13.7, the expatriate can expect a series of "culture bumps" and research suggests the following steps to cope with them:

1. Pinpoint the specific time when you felt different or uncomfortable.
2. Define the situation.
3. List the behaviors of the other person(s).
4. List your own behavior.
5. List your feelings in the situation.
6. List the behaviors you expect from people in your own culture in that same situation.
7. Reflect on the underlying values in your culture that prompt that behavior expectation.[82]

Expatriation

Expatriation occurs when a person who has citizenship in at least one country is living in another country. Typically, an **expatriate** only stays in the foreign country for a certain period and plans to return to their home country eventually, although there are some who never return

▼ FIGURE 13.6
Cultural Intelligence

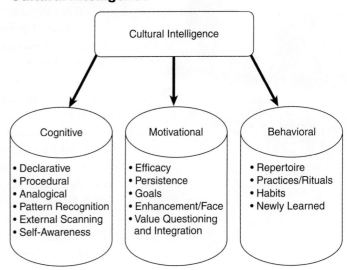

Source: Earley, P. C., & Ang, S. A. (2003). *Cultural intelligence: Individual interactions across cultures.* Stanford, CA: Stanford University Press.

▼ FIGURE 13.7
Stages of Culture Shock

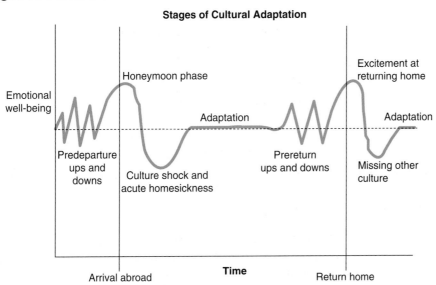

Source: Mitchell, L., & Myles, W. (2010). *Risk sense: Developing and managing international education activities with risk in mind.* Ontario, Canada: University of Guelph.

To cope with culture shock, reflect on the underlying values in your culture.

©iStockphoto.com/Tassii

to their country of citizenship.[83] Despite the prevalence and importance of expatriates on international assignments, culture shock often results in dissatisfaction and lower performance.[84] This can be costly for organizations that make a significant investment in training, relocating, and compensating expatriates. Some estimate the failure rate (leaving an assignment early) to be between 8% and 12%.[85] Recently, a study of global leadership trends, released by the consulting firm Right Management, found that managers often fail in overseas assignments. In this research, a survey of 202 CEOs and senior human resource management professionals was conducted and found that just 58% of overseas assignments were considered successful, and there was little difference based on the region.[86] For the United States, expatriate failure costs have been estimated to be about $1 million per failure,[87] and the total economic impact of failure ranges between $2 billion and $2.5 billion.[88] These costs led to the development of sophisticated measures of the return on investment for expatriate assignments, which include such costs as selection, moving expenses, housing, compensation, bonuses, and readjustment costs after the assignment.[89] In addition to these costs, the stress on expatriates results in decreased productivity not accounted for in these estimates.[90]

An expatriate assignment can be assigned by the organization or initiated by the manager. **Self-initiated expatriates (SIEs)** choose to go abroad and assigned expatriates (AEs) are offered the opportunity by their organization. A study of 193 expatriates (67 AEs and 126 SIEs)[91] indicates that self-initiated foreign work experience is significantly more likely to be chosen by women and those in lower ranks in organizations. In addition, SIEs have higher organizational mobility. Therefore, there may be a difference in career outcomes for those who have the flexibility to volunteer for an expatriate assignment.

What makes people want to volunteer for an expatriate assignment? Based on a study of 514 university students,[92] CQ influences the degree to which career adaptability relates to intentions to go abroad for their careers. In other words, being flexible and culturally intelligent seems to influence the intention to become an expatriate. CQ relates to the ability to adjust to the expatriate assignment in the host country.[93] Being an expatriate relates to compensation as well as career mobility. A study of 440 graduates of elite MBA programs from around the world[94] found that expatriates receive more total compensation but only if they have experienced more than one expatriate assignment and acquired knowledge and new skills utilized during post-repatriation. They also tend to be at higher organizational levels. In other words, expatriation relates to compensation attainment because it is an intense developmental experience, and not merely a signaling mechanism for who is on the fast track.

What can organizations do to help expatriates adjust to their international assignments? A study of the adjustment experiences of 213 expatriates from three U.S.-based Fortune 500 companies found that perceived support from the organization influenced their adjustment.[95] Expatriates' adjustment was, in turn, related to their performance as rated by their supervisors. Surface-level cultural differences (e.g., food, housing, and climate) were most strongly related to general adjustment. However, deep-level cultural differences (e.g., values and assumptions) affected work and interaction adjustment, and expatriates who reported self-transcendence had an easier time adjusting to their expatriate assignment. Self-transcendence includes universalism (understanding, appreciation, tolerance, and protection for the welfare of all people and for nature) and benevolence (preservation and enhancement of the welfare of people with whom one is in frequent personal contact).[96]

Expatriate managers do not have to go it alone. There is evidence to support that having a personal partner move with the expat alleviates many of the adjustments. Personal partners have help in five support areas:

CAREERS IN MANAGEMENT

Expatriate Manager

Have you ever considered boosting your career by moving abroad? Choosing to live in another country is becoming more common: a 2015 survey among more than 14,000 expatriates (expats) reveals a lot of positives for students looking for an international education, by following their dreams to live in another country.[97]

Expatriates are assigned to work in other countries on long- or short-term business projects, by either personal choice or employer request. They help their companies establish operations in other countries, enter overseas markets, or transfer skills and knowledge to their companies' business partners. Such international experience helps organizations develop managers who can succeed in a global workplace.[98]

A study conducted by InterNations, the largest global network and information site for people who live and work abroad, found that nearly one in four senior executives was an expatriate at some point in their career when needed by their employer. The study also found that one in five senior executives mentions the search for a personal challenge as one of their reasons for accepting the expatriate assignment.

However, not all expatriate assignments result in success. The statistics on the career advancement of expatriates show that only 18% of those interviewed by InterNations climbed the corporate career ladder to middle management. According to mobility studies from the global talent industry Worldwide ERC (2012), failure rates for international assignments are estimated to range from 25% to as much as 50%.[99] To help avoid this, Worldwide ERC offers several intercultural tools to assist employees before they take an international assignment.[100] It is important to have the right expectations for expatriation.

Expatriate managers work hard. Regardless of industry, managers living and working abroad spend 49.4 hours per week at work. However, they are satisfied with their jobs and work-life balance. Expatriate managers receive support from their employers in the forms of relocation expenses, cross-cultural and language training, and mentorship. Other benefits include overseas health care, tax equalization, living allowances, tax equalization, housing assistance, career planning, spouse and child relocation services, and even leave for rest and relaxation. Such benefits and higher compensation make expatriate manager assignments very appealing.[101]

What are the characteristics that lead to being a successful expatriate manager? A study of expatriates found that there are three skill sets that relate to the success of an expatriate manager:

1. Self-orientation—ability to reduce stress and deal with isolation, physical mobility, technical competence, and realistic expectations.

2. Other-orientation—strong relationship skills, strong verbal and nonverbal communication skills, and respect and empathy for others.

3. Perceptual orientation—flexible, high tolerance for ambiguity, nonjudgmental, open-minded, and independent.[102]

Another research study conducted by J. Stewart Black and Hal Gregerson[103] found that top firms look for these traits in expatriate leaders:

- *Motivation to communicate, despite challenges.* Certainly, expatriates make some effort to learn the language and communicate with their new colleagues and neighbors. But what separates the adequate communicator from the extremely effective? The most professionally successful expats are those who simply *refuse* to give up on communication even if they fail miserably or make embarrassing mistakes. According to the research, organizations sought out people who weren't afraid to take risks. They looked for the people who were willing to speak French, even if it was fractured and imperfect, or who did their best to understand a colleague whose English skills were limited. Companies want to work with expatriates who will commit to overcoming language and cultural communication barriers.

- *Willingness to expand social connections.* Often, when people move overseas, their relationships are quite isolated. They meet a clique of fellow expats and stick together, missing opportunities to widen their social circle. The most successful global employees, however, are eager to mingle with the locals. They aren't reluctant to socialize with everyone in their new home base, from neighbors to waiters and merchants to government officials. In getting to know their fellow local residents, employees glean insider knowledge of the local market and adjust to their city.[104]

- *Cultural flexibility.* When different people from different cultural backgrounds work together on international projects, the diversity of values and habits may cause conflict. In order to reduce culturally based conflicts and misunderstandings, project team members must be aware of their cultural differences and actively work to understand and accept those differences. Identifying differences such as values or behavioral norms can lead to acceptance and respect toward other cultures.[105]

- *Cosmopolitan mindset.* Expats with cosmopolitan perspectives accept and embrace cultural differences. The companies in the study found that people with this mindset can be successful in other countries because they respect and value diversity.

- *A collaborative style of negotiating.* When expats negotiate, they can find themselves in precarious situations. Dealing with different cultural values and social norms can spell conflict if communication isn't clear and open. It is

(Continued)

(Continued)

critical for expats to adopt a collaborative negotiation style so that all parties can contribute to the conversation and set expectations.[106]

Expatriate managers help transfer knowledge from the multinational parent company to the local subsidiaries. Their days are busy and filled with experiences of new customs, new foods, and learning about the culture in which they find themselves immersed. It is important to keep in mind that having the right technical skills may be the reason a person is chosen for an expatriate assignment. However, the self-awareness and cross-cultural skills are the ones that most often lead to both success and satisfaction with the expatriate experience.

Discussion Questions

1. Would you consider becoming an expatriate manager? Why or why not?

2. Do you have the characteristics that firms are looking for in an expatriate? Which ones do you think you would need to develop and why?

3. Are there specific countries in which you would want to be an expatriate manager? Why did you choose these countries? How similar are they to your own culture?

4. How can you improve your chances of being successful in an expatriate assignment? List at least three strategies you would use to learn about the other culture and how to be successful in an expatriate assignment.

Sources: Black, J. S. & Gregerson, H. (1999, March/April). The right way to manage expatriates. *Harvard Business Review*, 52–60; Böhm, C. (2013). Cultural flexibility in ICT projects: A new perspective on managing diversity in project teams. *Global Journal of Flexible Systems Management, 14*(2), 115–122; Grobbel, M. (2015). Managers on the move: An exclusive look at expat executives. *Experteer.com.* Retrieved from https://us.experteer.com/magazine/managers-on-the-move-an-exclusive-look-at-expat-executives/; Mendenhall, M., & Oddou, G. (1986). Acculturation profiles of expatriate managers: Implications for cross-cultural training programs. *Columbia Journal of World Business, 21*(4), 73–79; and Worldwide ERC. (n.d.). Intercultural tools. Retrieved from https://www.worldwideerc.org/intercultural-tools/.

- Bureaucratic assistance
- Language mentoring
- Cultural guidance
- Networking assistance
- Cross-cultural competence and mobility of the partner

Through these five forms of support, expatriates can save time and energy outside of work, allowing them to focus on performing at work. The strongest forms of support were given by the host country national partners, who are completely adjusted in the host country and can act as mentors in the first four support areas.[107]

These adjustments in personal interactions with mentors from a host culture were a significant predictor of expatriate retention in a study of 321 U.S. expatriates assigned to the Pacific Rim or Western Europe.[108] In addition, having a mentor who provides both career and social support is essential.[109] Mentors are key resources before, during, and after international assignments and are often indispensable for facilitating promotions after the assignment ends. Expatriates must think in terms of having a network of mentors who can provide support for adaptation in terms of host country culture, task assistance, and office culture (these may or may not be the same mentor and can be supervisors, peers, or someone outside of the organization).[110] Finally, training in cross-cultural interactions, culture, and language improves adjustment for expatriates.[111]

Nearing the time of the return home, there is a similar excitement as that of predeparture where the expatriate puts things in order in the host country and makes preparations to return to their home country (repatriation), which is described in the next section.

CRITICAL THINKING QUESTIONS

Would you take an expatriate assignment if offered by the organization you work for? Would you volunteer for an expatriate assignment? Explain your answers.

Repatriation

Even when an expatriate has adjusted and performed well on assignment, they must also be prepared for **repatriation**. Repatriation, or reentry to the organization after the expatriate assignment, refers to the transition when the expatriate has completed the international assignment and returns home.[112] Expatriates are at risk of leaving the organization after they return. It has been estimated that 10% of expatriates leave their firm shortly after completing an international assignment, and another 14% leave between two and three years of their return.[113] Expatriates may experience a similar sequence of culture shock feelings when they return to their home culture. Successful expatriates become accustomed to their host culture and are tolerant of unfamiliar situations and work habits. **Reverse culture shock** is the realization that time has moved on and things have not stood still while the expatriate was away from the home office.[114] Things have changed, and the returning expatriate experiences confusion and disappointment that may lead to a temporary state of depression and a sense of loss. Upon return to the home country, they may even look judgmentally upon their home culture as they realize some of the negative aspects of their own national culture. They may be disappointed in the reactions of coworkers and superiors upon their return. In addition, they feel that their work abroad is not understood or appreciated and expected rewards and promotions may not follow.[115] Other employees who stayed home may have been promoted, and the expatriate was "out of sight, out of mind" in the eyes of their supervisor. Finally, there is a readjustment phase (whether the expatriate leaves the job or not) in which there is resolution of the reentry culture shock and the expatriate puts the experience into perspective.

Communication and validation are important to successful repatriation.[116] Communication is how much information the expatriate has regarding what is happening at home while on assignment. With higher levels of communication, those who return are more proactive, effective, and satisfied with their jobs after they return.[117] Fortunately, today we have Skype and Google Hangouts (virtual face-to-face chat rooms), which allow expatriates to have face-to-face contact with their families and colleagues while on assignment. If the family is living abroad with the expatriate, the spouse has a significant influence on the expatriate adjustment process.[118] Culture shock may be more difficult for the spouse, who may feel isolated while the expatriate has peers at work to interact with.[119] Validation refers to the amount of recognition the expatriate gets for success on the international assignment. This may include a promotion— those who are promoted after an expatriate assignment adjust better than those who are not.[120]

It is important to keep this in mind and anticipate the "highs" and "lows" that will likely be experienced while on an expatriate assignment. Being able to work through culture shock is critical for expatriates, since many organizations now expect significant international experience as a prerequisite to promotion to the highest rank. It has been reported that "companies like GE, Citigroup, Shell, Siemens, and Nokia are using international assignments of high potential employees as the means to develop their managers' global leadership mindset and competencies."[121] International assignments are the most effective source for developing global leaders.[122] So if you have aspirations to be an executive-level leader, it is important for you to understand the process of expatriate cross-cultural adjustment and be ready for the adjustment process of culture shock. Fortunately, management researchers have been studying this process of expatriation for a number of years.

Jack Welch, former CEO of General Electric Co. (GE), stated that the CEOs of the future will be able to adjust to other cultures:

> The Jack Welch of the future cannot be like me. I spent my entire career in the U.S. The next head of General Electric will be somebody who spent time in Bombay, in Hong Kong, in Buenos Aires. We have to send our best and brightest overseas and make sure they have the training that will allow them to be the global leaders who will make GE flourish in the future.[123]

Former General Electric
CEO Jeffrey Immelt speaks
during a GE Ecomagination
forum in Paris, France.

©Bloomberg /Getty Images

Welch was right. His successor, Jeffrey Immelt, held a series of leadership positions with GE that included marketing and global product development and he served as vice president of worldwide marketing and product management for GE Appliances.

Managerial Implications

National culture affects many aspects of management. Today, due to globalization, an important part of every manager's job is the ability to understand and work effectively with people from different cultures. This chapter reviewed research that helps a manager understand the different cultural values that exist and how they affect cross-cultural interactions and adjustment.

- National culture was defined, underscoring the reasons for why understanding cultural differences is important for being an effective manager.
- The difference between high-context and low-context cultures was explained. The degree of reliance on context has important implications for the way in which employees communicate with one another. High-context cultures are more indirect, whereas low-context cultures are more direct.
- Models of culture were explained, including Hofstede's dimensions of national culture and the Global Leadership and Organizational Behavior Effectiveness (GLOBE) project international study.
- The key concepts of the global mindset and cultural intelligence (CQ) were explained and guidelines for how they can be developed were provided.
- The process of culture shock and its impact on expatriate managers, noting the high costs of expatriate failure, was highlighted. Guidelines for how organizations can prepare managers for expatriate assignments were provided.

In summary, the skills needed for successful interactions with another culture are a global mindset and cultural intelligence. It is also important to anticipate and develop a plan to cope with culture shock if you embark on an expatriate assignment. These guidelines are also helpful for the reentry process for those returning from an international assignment. This chapter has increased your awareness of the effects of national culture on management. The effective manager must be able to suspend judgment and use their CQ to effectively adjust to those from other cultures whether assigned in the United States or abroad. By now, you realize that in today's global environment, cross-cultural differences affect every aspect of management.

KEY TERMS

behavioral CQ   409

cognitive CQ   409

cultural intelligence (CQ)   409

cultural looseness   401

cultural tightness   401

cultural tightness–
looseness   401

culture   397

culture shock   410

expatriate   411

expatriation   411

Global Leadership and
Organizational Behavior
Effectiveness (GLOBE)
project   404

global mindset   407

globalization   407

high-context cultures   399

low-context cultures   399

metacognitive CQ   409

motivational CQ   409

multinational corporation
(MNC)   406

prototype   398

repatriation   415

reverse culture shock   415

self-initiated expatriates
(SIEs)   412

stereotype   398

Activity 13.1

Understanding Cultural Differences: Party Time!

Instructions

Divide the class into two groups, A and B. Send one group outside the room. Hand out instructions to Group B and review instructions with them, answering any questions they may have. Have them begin to interact with each other so they can practice these instructions with each other. Meanwhile, brief the other group and hand out instructions for Group A. Once Group A has been briefed and prepped, have Group A rejoin Group B for the "party." (*Note:* It is helpful to provide munchies and soft drinks to lend a "cocktail" party atmosphere.) The goal during the "party" is for participants to meet as many other persons as possible, not necessarily just ones from the other group. Depending on the size of the groups, let them mingle for approximately 10 minutes. Then, debrief the exercise, using the "Three R's" approach described below.

Party Instructions for Group A

1. Always speak softly and quietly.
2. Stand at least an arm's length away (or further) whenever you are in conversation with someone.
3. Don't look persons in the eye when talking with them.
4. Try not to touch anyone, especially when talking with them—keep your hands by your side at all times.
5. Smile only at persons you know.
6. Have fun and meet as many people as you can during the "party"!

Party Instructions for Group B

1. Speak loudly and excitedly.
2. Stand close to someone when talking with that person—and it's fine to touch them on the shoulder or arm when talking.
3. It's very important to look persons in the eye when talking with them.
4. It's fine to use gestures when talking and it's okay to literally bump into people at the party (no need to apologize).
5. Smiling and being friendly is wonderful!
6. Have fun and meet as many people as you can during the "party"!

After 15 minutes of interaction, use the "three R's" approach to understand the "culture" of the people from the other group.

The Three R's

Cross-cultural communication is essential, but it can present some challenges. For example, when Americans collaborate with their colleagues from Japan, they should consider nonverbal cues, whereas Japanese people communicating with American coworkers should expect more straightforward verbal communications. Each culture has different social norms and values, but these types of barriers to communication are not insurmountable. With mutual effort and care, clear and open cross-cultural communication can help international colleagues form effective working relationships. Here are some steps to consider when working with partners around the world.

- *Recognize your cultural differences.* Start by simply noticing the diversity in communication styles across cultures. Make an effort to grow your awareness and understanding of other cultures.
- *Respect your cultural differences.* When you are attuned to cultural differences, you can work on respecting and accepting these differences. Embrace the diversity in communication styles and celebrate it. This will enable you to actively listen to your colleague's perspectives.
- *Reconcile your cultural differences.* It's not enough to simply recognize and respect differences—you have to reconcile them, too. Work together with your international colleagues to resolve your differences with empathy and understanding so you can work toward your shared goals.

Discussion Questions

1. Did you find it easier to interact with people from your own group? Explain why or why not.
2. Describe the differences between your group and the other group. (Recognize)
3. When you noticed a difference in communication style, how did you react? Did you try to understand the other person's point of view? (Respect)
4. Did you empathize with the other culture? Did you adapt your communication style to match theirs? Provide an example. (Reconcile)

Sources: Deardorf, D. K. (2003). Cross-cultural communication activity: The "Uncocktail Party." Retrieved from http://www.ufic.ufl.edu/pd/downloads/ici-Activities/UncocktailParty.pdf; Fernando, A. (2018, October 18). Think global: How to overcome cultural communication challenges. Retrieved from https://opensource.com/article/18/10/think-global-communication-challenges.

Case Study 13.1

Why Did Walmart Fail in Germany?

Walmart Moves Into Germany

Walmart is the biggest food retailer in the world and has a presence in several nations. In some nations (e.g., the United States, Canada, China), Walmart is a great success. However, Walmart has failed in some countries (e.g., Germany, South Korea). First, we describe Walmart's failure in Europe's largest economy. Second, we use Walmart's experiences in Germany to illustrate some key principles related to product failure and product deletion (see Table 13.4). Walmart's experiences are also an example of the importance to adapt to culture when starting a business in a new country.

The German Grocery Industry

There is fierce competition in the German grocery industry, due to the increasing number of discount supermarket chains.[124] As a result, there is low profitability in the food retail sector; profit margins range from 0.5 to 1%, which is one of the lowest profit margins in Europe.[125] For reference, consider the United Kingdom. There, profit margins in the food retail sector are about 5%. While companies are certainly interested in other financial metrics, like shareholder wealth and market share, profitability and margins are a top priority in the retail industry.

Walmart's Strategy

Walmart, as an international retail giant, has upwards of 6,000 stores around the globe.[126] Their signature strategy and marketing approach is continuous cost cutting. Their business model relies on consistently offering lower prices than competitors. To achieve this goal, Walmart must maintain extremely efficient logistics processes. The corporation has put forth cutting-edge technology to optimize its systems, including radio-frequency identification (RFID). This RFID technology uses special tags and transponders to automatically access data. Other cost-cutting methods include pushing suppliers to charge less for goods and reducing labor costs by providing employees with minimal benefits. Some of these cost-reducing measures result in lower prices for Walmart shoppers.

Walmart's Entry Into the German Market

Rather than starting from scratch by building new stores, Walmart entered into the German market by acquiring stores from existing retail corporations. Between 1997 and 1998, Walmart acquired nearly a hundred stores from two supermarket chains—21 from Wertkauf and 74 from Interspar—to become the fourth largest supermarket corporation in Germany.[127] Walmart's original goal was to set up 500 stores, but they never surpassed their initial purchases. Over the years, this stalled progress led to a rapidly declining position in the market. By 2002, Walmart began layoffs, and by late 2006, Walmart's financial difficulties were too much to overcome and it was bought out by Metro, Walmart's main competition in Germany.

Missteps in the German Market

Walmart's exit from the German marketplace can be traced to five key missteps:

1. Failure to adapt to market structure.
2. Failure to adjust business model.
3. Communication breakdown due to lack of cultural awareness.
4. Lack of adequate legal and regulatory knowledge.
5. Product and service failures.

Failure to Adapt to Market Structure and Adjust Business Model

The first two missteps are closely related. In short, Walmart's business model was no match for the German retail grocery market structure. Rapid expansion is an integral component of Walmart's continuous cost-cutting objective. When the company entered the German market, it could not acquire enough locations to reach its expansion goals (large volumes purchased from suppliers equals lower prices to Walmart). Because the company didn't build its own stores, and instead acquired them from the German retail chains, they were locked into the structures, which were too small to provide a wide range of goods. Additionally, there was too much distance between them, once again depleting the savings from buying large quantities from suppliers to share amongst stores, driving up logistical costs.

Before expanding to a new market, it is essential to study and predict how competitors will respond. Metro was also working on expansion and, in turn, preventing Walmart from expanding.[128] Walmart often had to eliminate products because of Metro's competition.

Walmart's "everyday low prices" slogan is astronomically successful in the United States and around the world. In Germany, however, competition is fierce, as was evidenced in the very low profit margins, in the retail food market. That competition drives down prices for German consumers. Because shoppers have a wide variety of discount grocery options, Walmart's continuous cost-cutting method did not result in its typical competitive advantage (see Table 13.4).

Communication Breakdown Due to Lack of Cultural Awareness

Walmart failed to adequately consider how its corporate culture would operate in Germany and did not make adjustments to keep store managers happy. Walmart's executives decided to run the German stores from Great Britain, using English for corporate communications. The corporation neglected to adequately accommodate German store managers who did not speak English, resulting in communication barriers. Several critical business relationships (with key suppliers like Adidas, Nike, and Samsonite) took a nosedive as a result. This meant that the retailer lost not only suppliers, but crucial categories of product.[129] By failing to communicate effectively with the German managers, who had extensive knowledge of the local market and connections to important suppliers, Walmart lost integral relationships and essential products (see Table 13.4).

Lack of Adequate Legal and Regulatory Knowledge

Due to insufficient knowledge of German laws and regulations, Walmart faced a host of compliance issues.

Because Walmart achieves continuous cost cutting largely by drastically reducing labor costs, the company has a union-free policy. In Germany, however, labor unions are a large and dominant force. Collective bargaining equips unions with considerable influence in the political sphere.

German business regulations underscore the importance of financial transparency. German Commercial Code requires all corporations to put forth an annual public financial statement, including profits and losses. Walmart failed to comply and found itself in hot water with Verdi, a German union in the service sector, which 2.4 million members, making it one of the largest independent trade unions globally.[130] For 1999 and 2000, Walmart refused to provide financial statements and Verdi sued the corporate retailer, resulting in a fine. Walmart never recovered from the bad press.

In addition to its anti-union ways and bad press, Walmart faced a third culture clash. While price wars are a common feature of the American economy, German law works to keep them at bay. When their expansion plans failed, Walmart waged a price war to quash its smaller competitors. Walmart intended to undercut prices, drive the chains out of business, and then take over their stores. To this end, Walmart began selling "Smart Brand" (a private brand label) merchandise below manufacturing cost, prompting competitors to reduce their prices, too. The result was an industry-wide profit decrease so drastic that it led Germany's Federal Cartel Office to intervene.

Product and Service Failure

German supermarket chains are known for their lack of customer service. Walmart, looking for its niche, thought that providing good customer service combined with low prices would make for a competitive edge. Stores implemented the "10-foot rule," meaning that, every 10 feet throughout the store, employees offered service or assistance to shoppers. Walmart did not anticipate a widespread negative reaction to this program. German shoppers were used to self-service at discount stores and found the overly involved Walmart employees annoying, the opposite of Walmart's intentions. Another Walmart mainstay, the "greeter" program (which stations employees at store entrances to greet customers), also proved unpopular with German shoppers.

Summary: How Walmart Failed in Germany

Walmart attempted to import its American formula for success into the German market without considering cultural differences and regulatory practices. As a result, the corporation was ultimately unsuccessful at establishing its presence in Germany. Without adequate knowledge of German law, politics, and customs, Walmart could not provide appropriate service for the market. In addition, communication and cultural barriers negatively impacted relationships with suppliers, causing further revenue reduction due to lost product lines.[131]

Table 13.4 provides an outline of the many ways in which Walmart's investment in Germany failed, and it gives a good checklist to follow if your organization is planning an international expansion or if you will be working abroad in a country with a culture different than your own. The cumulative effect of poor management and total absence of analyses of the local market or culture had serious impacts on Walmart's profitability in Germany. Frustrations of both employees and the customers played a major role in the eventual downfall. Mismanagement of cultural diversity and adaptation of inappropriate leadership are considered the overall causes of this significant business failure.

As for financial performance, Walmart never officially published the losses it experienced during its stay in Germany. Walmart had been losing approximately $200 million every year of its operation in Germany, and the transaction to divest itself of its German chain cost the company approximately $1 billion (U.S.).[132] Walmart failed in Germany, and cultural factors played a major role.

▼ TABLE 13.4

Product Failure: Examples From Walmart's Investment in Germany

Product Failure	Examples
Insufficient demand	Walmart's low price strategy didn't create any competitive advantage since many German local retailers were already using that strategy.
Existing competitors are too strong	Walmart's biggest competitor, Metro, took specific counter-measures to prevent Walmart from executing their expansion plan.
Failure to develop and communicate unique selling propositions	The profit margins in the German retail industry were already low before Walmart entered. Walmart was not able to convince German consumers that their prices were really that much lower than the competition.

(Continued)

Change in culture (i.e. change in corporate culture, change in consumer taste or fashion)	Walmart did not adapt well to the German corporate culture.
Changing standard of government regulations	Managers were not familiar with German laws and regulations, so there were violations. In general, Walmart's anti-union policies conflicted with the strong German union. Walmart also tried to sell their products below manufacturing costs, which is illegal in Germany.
Poor promotion/communication	There was a language barrier between English-speaking managers and older German business people who don't speak English.
In retailing, failure to secure attractive sites	There were not enough appropriate locations for Walmart stores available in Germany.
Product failure	Stores were often located far apart. As a result, logistics costs were high. One of Walmart's main success factors is to minimize costs, but this goal was restricted by high logistical costs.
Poor service quality—during or after sales	Some of Walmart's methods for providing service were not accepted by German customers. For instance, the customers did not like the concept of the "greeter."
Failure to get corporation from key supply-chain members	Several key suppliers refused to supply goods, for fear of tarnishing their corporate image.

Source: ShareAlike 4.0 International. (2015). Case, example of product failure: Walmart in Germany, 1997 to 2006. CC BY-SA 4.0. Retrieved from http://www.opentextbooks.org.hk/ditatopic/7191.

Discussion Questions

1. Explain why you think Walmart tried to implement the same practices that worked in the United States in the German stores. Why do you think they did not ask for input from German employees?

2. Compare the cultures of the United States and Germany based on the dimensions of national culture studied by Hofstede. What differences in cultural values such as power distance and collectivism help explain what happened in Germany?

3. Describe three ways that Walmart could have modified their management practices to fit the German culture. Do you think this may have helped them succeed? Explain.

Source: ShareAlike 4.0 International. (2015). Case, example of product failure: Walmart in Germany, 1997 to 2006. CC BY-SA 4.0. Retrieved from http://www.opentextbooks.org.hk/ditatopic/7191.

Self-Assessment 13.1

GLOBE Cultural Values Assessment

Instructions

The following questions ask you to describe the cultural values of your society. Indicate the degree to which you agree or disagree with the statements by circling the response that best represents your views. There are no right or wrong answers, so provide your immediate impressions. (*Note:* These items are adapted from the GLOBE studies but the GLOBE studies used five items to analyze each cultural dimension.)

Uncertainty Avoidance

Statements	Strongly Disagree	Disagree	Somewhat Disagree	Neutral	Somewhat Agree	Agree	Strongly Agree
1. In this society, orderliness and consistency are stressed, even at the expense of experimentation and innovation.	1	2	3	4	5	6	7
2. In this society, most work is highly structured, leading to few unexpected events.	1	2	3	4	5	6	7

Power Distance

Statements	Strongly Disagree	Disagree	Somewhat Disagree	Neutral	Somewhat Agree	Agree	Strongly Agree
1. In this society, a person's influence is based primarily on the authority of one's position.	1	2	3	4	5	6	7
2. In this society, subordinates are expected to obey their boss without question.	1	2	3	4	5	6	7

Institutional Collectivism

Statements	Strongly Disagree	Disagree	Somewhat Disagree	Neutral	Somewhat Agree	Agree	Strongly Agree
1. In this society, managers encourage group loyalty even if individual goals suffer.	1	2	3	4	5	6	7
2. The pay and bonus system in this organization is designed to maximize collective interests.	1	2	3	4	5	6	7

In-Group Collectivism

Statements	Strongly Disagree	Disagree	Somewhat Disagree	Neutral	Somewhat Agree	Agree	Strongly Agree
1. In this society, group members take pride in the individual accomplishments of their group manager.	1	2	3	4	5	6	7
2. In this society, group cohesion is more valued than individualism.	1	2	3	4	5	6	7

Gender Egalitarianism

Statements	Strongly Disagree	Disagree	Somewhat Disagree	Neutral	Somewhat Agree	Agree	Strongly Agree
1. In this society, women are encouraged to participate in professional development activities to the same degree as men.	1	2	3	4	5	6	7
2. In this society, most people believe that work would be more effectively managed if there were many more women in positions of authority than there are now.	1	2	3	4	5	6	7

Assertiveness

Statements	Strongly Disagree	Disagree	Somewhat Disagree	Neutral	Somewhat Agree	Agree	Strongly Agree
1. In this society, people are generally assertive.	1	2	3	4	5	6	7
2. In this society, people are generally dominant.	1	2	3	4	5	6	7

Future Orientation

Statements	Strongly Disagree	Disagree	Somewhat Disagree	Neutral	Somewhat Agree	Agree	Strongly Agree
1. The way to be successful in this society is to plan ahead.	1	2	3	4	5	6	7
2. In this society, the accepted norm is to plan for the future.	1	2	3	4	5	6	7

Performance Orientation

Statements	Strongly Disagree	Disagree	Somewhat Disagree	Neutral	Somewhat Agree	Agree	Strongly Agree
1. In this society, employees are encouraged to strive for continuously improved performance.	1	2	3	4	5	6	7
2. In this society, major rewards are based on only on performance effectiveness.	1	2	3	4	5	6	7

Humane Orientation

Statements	Strongly Disagree	Disagree	Somewhat Disagree	Neutral	Somewhat Agree	Agree	Strongly Agree
1. In this society, people are usually very concerned about others.	1	2	3	4	5	6	7
2. In this organization, people are generally very friendly.	1	2	3	4	5	6	7

Scoring

This assessment is designed to measure your perceptions of different cultural values in your culture. Score the questionnaire by doing the following. First, sum the two responses you gave for the two items in each dimension. Second, divide the sum of the responses by two. The result is your mean score for the dimension.

For example, if your uncertainty avoidance ratings were 2 in response to question 1 and 3 in response to question 1, you would score the dimension as follows:

$$2 + 3 = 5$$

$$5 / 2 = 2.5$$

Interpretation

When you are finished, you should have nine average (mean) scores. Place your mean scores for each of the dimensions in the following table in the column, "Your Score." You can compare your mean scores to the mean scores for selected cultural clusters from the GLOBE data.

GLOBE Cultural Dimension	Anglo	Latin America	Middle East	Southern Asia	Latin Europe	GLOBE Overall	Your Score
Uncertainty avoidance	4.42	3.62	3.91	4.10	4.18	4.16	
Power distance*	4.97	5.33	5.23	5.39	5.21	5.13	
Institutional collectivism	4.46	3.86	4.28	4.35	4.01	4.25	
In-group collectivism	4.30	5.52	5.58	5.87	4.80	5.13	
Gender egalitarianism	3.40	3.41	2.95	3.28	3.36	3.37	
Assertiveness	4.14	4.15	4.14	3.86	3.99	4.14	
Future orientation	4.08	3.54	3.58	3.98	3.68	3.85	
Performance orientation	4.37	3.85	3.90	4.33	3.94	4.10	
Humane orientation	4.20	4.03	4.36	4.71	3.71	4.09	

*Note: Power distance means not available in data reported by House et al. (2004). These power distance values are taken from the GLOBE Project. (n.d.) Southern Asia cluster. Retrieved from https://globeproject.com/results/clusters/southern-asia? menu=list

Discussion Questions

1. How do your mean scores compare with your country cluster? Are you similar to or different than others who reported on these cultural dimensions in the GLOBE study?
2. How do you compare to the average across all cultural clusters (GLOBE overall); Do you think that these results have changed since the data was collected? Explain.
3. Explain how you can use this knowledge of your own culture in comparison with other cultural values to improve your ability to work effectively with people from different cultures.

Sources: Adapted from GLOBE Research Survey. (2006). Form Alpha. University of Victoria. Retrieved from https://www.uvic .ca/gustavson/globe/assets/docs/GLOBE-Phase-2-Alpha-Questionnaire-2006.pdf; House, R. J., Hanges, P. J., Javidan, M., Dorfman, P. W., & Gupta, V. (Eds.). (2004). *Culture, leadership, and organizations: The GLOBE study of 62 societies*. Thousand Oaks, CA: Sage.

Self-Assessment 13.2

Do You Have A Global Mindset?

This self-assessment exercise identifies your approach to interacting with people from different cultures. There are no "right or wrong" answers, and this is not a test. You don't have to share your results with others unless you wish to do so.

Part I. Taking the Assessment

Please answer the following questions about yourself.

To what extent do you (or are you):

Statements	Not at All	Small Extent	Moderate Extent	Large Extent	Very Large Extent
1. Know and understand local markets in several parts of the world.	1	2	3	4	5
2. Know how to assess risks of doing business internationally.	1	2	3	4	5
3. Know how to transact business in different parts of the world that have different economic, political, and institutional systems.	1	2	3	4	5
4. Know about the geography, history, and important persons of several countries.	1	2	3	4	5
5. Know about the major religions of the world and their influence on society.	1	2	3	4	5
6. Know the economic and political issues, concerns, hot topics, etc. of major regions of the world.	1	2	3	4	5
7. Stay up-to-date on world news and events.	1	2	3	4	5

(Continued)

(Continued)

8. Know how to work well with people from different parts of the world.	1	2	3	4	5
9. Understand the nonverbal expressions of people of several cultures.	1	2	3	4	5
10. Emotionally connect to colleagues and friends from other cultures.	1	2	3	4	5
11. Enjoy exploring different parts of the world.	1	2	3	4	5
12. Enjoy spending time getting to know people from other parts of the world.	1	2	3	4	5
13. Like to travel.	1	2	3	4	5
14. Have experience negotiating contracts/ agreements in cultures other than your own.	1	2	3	4	5
15. Work effectively with people who are very different from you.	1	2	3	4	5
16. Viewed by your coworkers as collaborative.	1	2	3	4	5
17. Challenge yourself in new and different ways.	1	2	3	4	5
18. Test the limits of your abilities.	1	2	3	4	5
19. Grasp complex concepts quickly.	1	2	3	4	5
20. Have strong analytical and problem-solving skills.	1	2	3	4	5
21. Feel comfortable in any setting.	1	2	3	4	5
22. Feel comfortable even though you are not in control of a situation.	1	2	3	4	5

Part II. Scoring and Interpretation

Write your ratings from the above questions for each question in the grid below. Then total your ratings for each dimension of the global mindset. Divide by the number of items in each column to obtain your score.

Global Intellectual Capital (GIC)	Global Social Capital (GSC)	Global Psychological Capital (GPC)
1. ____	8. ____	11. ____
2. ____	9. ____	12. ____
3. ____	10. ____	13. ____
4. ____	14. ____	17. ____
5. ____	15. ____	18. ____
6. ____	16. ____	21. ____
7. ____		22. ____
19. ____		
20. ____		
Total____ Divide by 9 GIC ____	Total____ Divide by 6 GIC ____	Total ____ Divide by 7 GPC ____

The Global Mindset

- *Global intellectual capital* (GIC)—the cognitive aspect of the global mindset. It refers to how much and what the manager knows about the global business in their industry and its broader macro environment, and how easy it is for them to analyze, digest, and interpret this information.
- *Global social capital* (GSC)—the behavioral aspect of the global mindset. It reflects the manager's ability to act in a way that helps build trusting relationships with people from other parts of the world.
- *Global psychological capital* (GPC)—the affective (feeling) aspect of the global mindset. It refers to the manager's emotional energy and their willingness to engage in a global environment. It reflects a positive and constructive attitude toward diversity of thought and action.[133]

Discussion Questions

1. Which of the three dimensions were you strongest on (global intellectual capital, global social capital, or global psychological capital)? Which were you lowest on? Did your scores surprise you? Why or why not?
2. What did you learn about yourself by rating your global mindset? Rate another person in your class using this assessment. What feedback do you want to provide them with so that they can improve their global mindset?
3. Which questions were rated 3 or lower (if any)? How could you improve those behaviors? Give two or three specific strategies. If all of your ratings were 3 or higher, describe how you would help another person to improve on their global mindset. Give two or three specific strategies.

Source: Javidan, M. (2018). Taking a snapshot of your global mindset. Used with permission.

Self-Assessment 13.3

What Is Your Cultural Intelligence?

This self-assessment exercise identifies your approach to interacting with people from different cultures. There are no "right or wrong" answers, and this is not a test. You don't have to share your results with others unless you wish to do so.

Part I. Taking the Assessment

You will be presented with some questions representing different situations involving cross-cultural interaction. Answer each question using the scale that corresponds with each question.

Statements	Not at All Like Me	Not Like Me	Somewhat Not Like Me	Neutral	Somewhat Like Me	Like Me	Most Like Me
1. I am conscious of the cultural knowledge I use when interacting with people with different cultural backgrounds.	1	2	3	4	5	6	7
2. I know the legal and economic systems of other cultures.	1	2	3	4	5	6	7
3. I enjoy interacting with people from different cultures.	1	2	3	4	5	6	7
4. I change my verbal behavior (e.g., accent, tone) when a cross-cultural interaction requires it.	1	2	3	4	5	6	7
5. I adjust my cultural knowledge as I interact with people from a culture that is unfamiliar to me.	1	2	3	4	5	6	7

(Continued)

(Continued)

	1	2	3	4	5	6	7
6. I know the rules (e.g., vocabulary, grammar) of other languages.	1	2	3	4	5	6	7
7. I am confident that I can socialize with locals in a culture that is unfamiliar to me.	1	2	3	4	5	6	7
8. I use pause and silence differently to suit different cross-cultural situations.	1	2	3	4	5	6	7
9. I am conscious of the cultural knowledge I apply to cross-cultural interactions.	1	2	3	4	5	6	7
10. I know the cultural values and religious beliefs of other cultures.	1	2	3	4	5	6	7
11. I am sure I can deal with the stresses of adjusting to a culture that is new to me.	1	2	3	4	5	6	7
12. I vary the rate of my speaking when a cross-cultural situation requires it.	1	2	3	4	5	6	7
13. I check the accuracy of my cultural knowledge as I interact with people from different cultures.	1	2	3	4	5	6	7
14. I know the marriage systems of other cultures.	1	2	3	4	5	6	7
15. I enjoy living in cultures that are unfamiliar to me.	1	2	3	4	5	6	7
16. I change my nonverbal behavior when a cross-cultural situation requires it.	1	2	3	4	5	6	7
17. I know the arts and crafts of other cultures.	1	2	3	4	5	6	7

18. I am confident that I can get accustomed to the shopping conditions in a different culture.	1	2	3	4	5	6	7
19. I alter my facial expressions when a cross-cultural interaction requires it.	1	2	3	4	5	6	7
20. I know the rules of expressing nonverbal behaviors in other cultures.	1	2	3	4	5	6	7

Part II. Scoring Instructions

In Part I, you rated yourself on 20 questions. Add the numbers you circled in each of the columns to derive your score for the four aspects of cultural intelligence (CQ).

These dimensions have been shown through research to be related to cross-cultural adjustment and leader effectiveness and are described in the section on CQ in this chapter.

Metacognitive	Cognitive	Motivational	Behavioral
1. _____	2. _____	3. _____	4. _____
5. _____	6. _____	7. _____	8. _____
9. _____	10. _____	11. _____	12. _____
13. _____	14. _____	15. _____	16. _____
17. _____	18. _____	19. _____	20. _____
Total _____	_____	_____	_____

Discussion Questions

1. Which of the dimensions did you score highest on? Lowest? What does this tell you about areas that you may need to improve?
2. Add the scores together for each dimension to compute an overall score for cultural intelligence. Scores can range from 20 to 100. In general, scores from 60 to 100 are very high and scores less than 40 are considered low. Do you have a high degree of cultural intelligence?

3. Discuss how you can increase your cultural intelligence. List two or three specific action steps you will take to improve your scores.

Source: Eisenberg, J., Lee, H. J., Brueck, F., Brenner, B., Claes, M. T., Mironski, J., & Bell, R. (2013). Can business schools make students culturally competent? Effects of cross-cultural management courses on cultural intelligence. *Academy of Management Learning and Education, 12*(4), 603–621.

⑤SAGE edge™

Get the tools you need to sharpen your study skills. SAGE edge offers a robust online environment featuring an impressive array of free tools and resources. Access practice quizzes, eFlashcards, video, and multimedia at **edge.sagepub.com/scanduragower**.

PART V

CONTROLLING

CHAPTER 14

BUDGET CONTROL

CHAPTER **LEARNING** OBJECTIVES

After studying this chapter, you should be able to:

14.1 Understand budgets and their role in successful organizational function.

14.2 Explain the different budgeting systems.

14.3 Comprehend the critical components of a budget.

14.4 Apply different budgeting systems depending on the circumstances.

14.5 Use budgets for management decision-making.

14.6 Understand the ethics of using budgets as control.

Get the edge on your studies at **edge.sagepub.com/ scanduragower.**

- Take the chapter quiz
- Review key terms with eFlashcards
- Explore multimedia resources, SAGE readings, and more

What Is Budget Control?

If you have made it this far in the book, you are going to be a rock star and here's why. The typical 15-week semester rarely allows you to get to the last two chapters of a textbook; since you have, Chapters 14 and 15 will give you a **competitive advantage** over the rest of the college graduates out there.

Budget control, or **budgetary control**, is the extent to which budgets are used to monitor costs and operations during an accounting period. Managers use the budgetary control process to set budgets for financial and performance goals, compare results, and adjust performance as needed.[1]

The term *budget* might make you flashback to accounting, but just think about your everyday life instead. Everything you do is based on a budget—of money, time, and energy—so talking about budgeting

as a manager is not that different. In fact, by the end of this chapter, you will have some new tools for your own budgeting purposes as well as for your role as an effective manager and leader.

You use budgets personally in order to live your healthiest and best life. When you get your paycheck, do you run out and spend it on as much Mexican food as you can afford (ideally, yes) or do you stop at the grocery store, pay the electric bill, and make sure you have some money left over to get you through to the next paycheck (more likely, yes)? Do you invite all your friends over to eat all of the groceries you bought in one night? Your answer is likely "I wish!" but instead, you plan some meals or at least make sure there is enough food to keep you fed until your next paycheck.

As important as budgets are to you personally and to organizations at the department and upper levels, they are oddly misunderstood and unfortunately seem to be undertaught in many business schools. To drive home the point of how important it is to understand and be able to effectively develop and apply budgets in your college afterlife, the following comment is from a recent *Wall Street Journal* blog in response to that day's prompt: "What Your College Isn't Teaching." Based on your reading of this chapter so far, you probably will not be surprised by the first answer:

> We force undergraduates to take plenty of entry-level classes, but where's one on practical financial responsibility? How about a test on setting a budget? My concern extends to my classmates on the less quantitative side of campus, but even as a finance major, I could benefit from this sort of education.[2]

Moreover, you might find it interesting that the *Wall Street Journal* article was emailed to one of this book's authors by a former graduate student, also advocating for more education on "the treatment and application of small business budgeting."

Sources: My Accounting Course. (n.d.). Budgetary control. Retrieved from https://www.myaccountingcourse.com/ accounting-dictionary/budgetary-control; WSJ Opinion. (2019, April 23). What your college isn't teaching you. *Wall Street Journal*. Retrieved from https://www.wsj.com/articles/ what-your-college-isnt-teaching-11556057975.

Textbook Organization

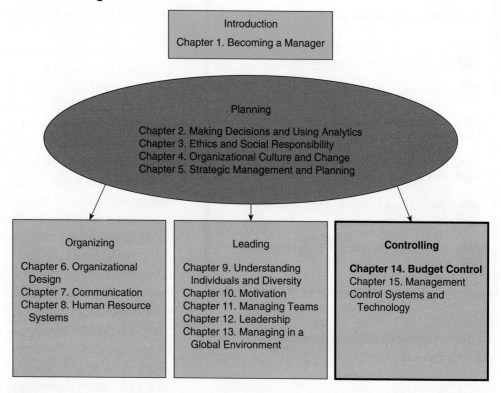

Introduction

Chapter 1. Becoming a Manager

Planning

Chapter 2. Making Decisions and Using Analytics
Chapter 3. Ethics and Social Responsibility
Chapter 4. Organizational Culture and Change
Chapter 5. Strategic Management and Planning

Organizing

Chapter 6. Organizational Design
Chapter 7. Communication
Chapter 8. Human Resource Systems

Leading

Chapter 9. Understanding Individuals and Diversity
Chapter 10. Motivation
Chapter 11. Managing Teams
Chapter 12. Leadership
Chapter 13. Managing in a Global Environment

Controlling

Chapter 14. Budget Control
Chapter 15. Management Control Systems and Technology

Now that you see the importance of budgeting from your personal perspective and have seen some feedback from your colleagues at other universities who have entered the professional world and been struck by how important a solid knowledge of smart budgeting is to them, let's create a better understanding of the many roles that budgets play. In this chapter, we will focus more on the financial aspects of budgeting. In Chapter 15, we will show how important budgets are as organizational control mechanisms.

What Are Budgets and What Can They Do?

Learning Objective 14.1: Understand budgets and their role in successful organizational function.

Good budgets are designed to account for both **planning** and **controlling**. Planning gets back to the objectives discussed in Chapter 5 and uses various budgets to achieve those objectives. Controlling refers to the steps taken by management to increase the likelihood that organizational objectives are met and that all parts of the organization are working together toward those objectives.[3]

Budgets are often used to filter and analyze information throughout the organization. The budgeting process uses information that is already available and often relies heavily on historical performance to forecast future needs. Budgeting plays an important tactical role in business operations. On a strategic level, budgeting helps to clarify competitive priorities, cost forecasts, and the feasibility of capital expansion projects.[4]

Advantages of Budgeting

Budgets determine where resources will be spent and work to help visualize and maximize the use of these resources. Among the many advantages of budgeting, Steven Bragg[5] highlights the following:

The budgeting process can be used to expand capacity or work around bottlenecks.

©3dkombinat/Shutterstock

- *Planning orientation.* Budgeting forces managers to think longer-term and better plan for the future.
- *Profitability review.* A good budget highlights the areas of the business the produce the most money and the areas that use the most money, giving managers a better sense of which departments are the most profitable.
- *Assumptions review.* Because the budgeting process forces managers to think about the company's primary objectives and why it's in business, re-evaluating these issues during budgeting sometimes results in changed assumptions. Challenging long-held assumptions is healthy and can lead to positive change as managers reevaluate the best way to operate their business.[6]
- *Performance evaluations.* Budgets establish standards and expectations that are used to evaluate results and performance.[7] Companies often tie performance with bonuses or other incentives. Managers often focus on financial goals, but operational goals (e.g. reduce warehouse waste) can also be part of the budget for performance appraisal purposes. This system of evaluation is called responsibility accounting.
- *Funding planning.* A good budget should derive the amount of cash that will be spun off or which will be needed to support operations.
- *Cash allocation.* Companies only have a limited amount of cash available to invest. The budgeting process forces managers to prioritize the assets most worth investing in.
- *Bottleneck analysis.* Bottlenecks, which can slow down productivity and efficiency, affect businesses of all types and sizes. Budgeting can be used to focus resources on improving the capacity of that bottleneck.[8]

As you can see, to help deal with the continuous changes in an organization, budgets are controlling mechanisms in and of themselves and they are incredibly important financial tools in the planning, organizing, and controlling roles of managers. Now that you understand how important the budget process is, let's take a look at some of the different ways that companies construct their budgets.

CRITICAL THINKING QUESTIONS

Do you feel you have a good grasp of the importance of budgets? Do you understand how budgets are not just about money but also time and resources? Give an example of how your personal time and resources did not match up with how you budgeted, or didn't budget, them.

The Many Different Types of Budgeting Systems

Learning Objective 14.2: Explain the different budgeting systems.

Responsibility accounting is just what the name suggests. It is a system that involves identifying the entities responsible for decision-making within an organization and learning about their objectives, developing performance measurement schemes, and preparing and analyzing performance reports for decision-makers.[9] Your responsibility center should only include items that you can be held directly responsible for and have at least some control over.

This principle also applies to the budget, or budgets, you are in charge of developing, implementing, and controlling.

Unfortunately, many organizations forget this premise when they talk about **cost centers** (spend money) and **revenue centers** (make money). Ideally, the manager is responsible for both sides of the budget as the ultimate control. Say, for example, the sales manager knows that developing prototypes of the items they sell will increase sales, but the marketing department is in charge of the design and expense of making the prototypes. In this case, the sales manager wants to make more revenue for the company, but the marketing manager has only a certain budget allowance (as a cost center) to spend. The sales manager is frustrated because they have no control over the decision or costs, while the marketing manager knows their year-end bonus is tied, in part, to staying under their annual budget.

These types of frustrations are very common at small and large companies, and you can imagine why. When you consider our comment regarding managers who have bonuses tied to their budgets (revenue increases, cost decreases) and our earlier discussion of how budgets are often used as performance appraisal tools, you can see why budgets can create an atmosphere where different departments are working toward different goals. This is further complicated because the organization only cares about making more profit and not individual gains.

Although budgeting can cause stress and tension in an organization (try contacting a manager during the month their annual budget is due), budgets are valuable tools to assess the following at the organizational level:

- Coordination of departments
- Formulation of a profitable revenue versus expense
- Coordination of specific departments that might have seemingly opposite goals
- Proper control of expenditures
- Formulation of investment and financing programs
- Coordination of all operations within the business[10]

Of course, not all organizations have the same mission, goals, and objectives or even the same **bottom line** objectives (defined as the "line at the bottom of a financial report that shows the net profit or loss"[11]). However, all organizations do share the need for budgets as part of both their planning and organizing as well as their controlling. According to Shim, Siegel, and Shim, this is why effective budgeting requires the following:

1. Predictive ability
2. Clear channels of communication, authority, and responsibility
3. Accounting-generated accurate, reliable, and timely information
4. Compatibility and understandability of information
5. Support at all levels of the organization: upper, middle, and lower[12]

This list, and the proper application of the right budgeting technique for the right situation, should help eliminate the problems outlined above by adding transparency to the budgeting process and ensuring that all levels of the organization understand what each budget represents to the department and organization as a whole. As Shim et al. note, "In the end, a sound budget process communicates organizational goals, allocates resources, provides feedback, and motivates employees."[13]

After reading about the differing budget needs of organizations based on their mission, it is probably no surprise that many different budget models are used depending on the organization in question. The next section includes a comprehensive list of the types of budgets that are used and the situations they fit best.

Types of Budgets and Purpose

To understand an organization as a whole and how different budgeting methods have different purposes, it is important to be familiar with the various types of budgets. Table 14.1 outlines the types of budget models and the purpose of each. Although the range might seem extreme, it once again highlights the importance of budgeting as a financial control. Once you read the explanations, you will likely be able to see how each model adds unique value to the budgeting process.

Next, we will discuss each budget type, including benefits, disadvantages, and use cases.

Master budget: The master budget serves as a summary of sub-budgets. It provides an overview of the spending plans for the calendar or fiscal year.

Operating budget and **financial budget:** An operating budget lays out the spending plan for all costs related to the production of goods and services. A financial budget documents the projected assets, liabilities, and stockholders' equity as well as balance sheet items. Each of these budgets is an essential document for assessing the financial well-being of a business.[14]

Cash budget: Your cash budget is probably a critical part of your life, and the same goes for organizations. Cash budgets, more commonly known as "cash flow," track estimated money flowing in and flowing out over a given period of time. The purpose of the cash budget is to determine whether the business has sufficient cash to cover operating expenses (day-to-day expenses).

▼ TABLE 14.1

Types of Budgets and Purposes

Type of Budget	Purpose
Master budget	Serves as a summary of all sub-budgets
Operating budget	Projects revenue and costs associated with operations
Financial budget	Shows assets, liability, equity, and balance sheet
Cash budget	Projects anticipated cash in and cash out
Static (fixed) budget	Projects revenue and expenses before a budget period begins and does not reflect changes to the budget as they happen
Flexible (expense) budget	Projects revenue and expenses and adjusts projections based on activity or volume
Capital expenditure budget	Projects capital expenditures such as the purchase of land, buildings, or equipment
Program budget	Projects revenue and expenses for a specific program
Incremental budget	Projects budget in terms of dollars or percentages assigned to project increments
Add-on budget	Uses the previous year's budget and "adds on" increments, expenses, or revenue to adjust for inflation, volume, or other concerns
Supplemental budget	Allocates funds for budget areas not captured in the regular budget
Bracket budget	Projects higher and lower levels than the base budget
Stretch budget	Is typically an informal budget that challenges employees to achieve a target or objective that is higher than predicted forecasts for sales or production
Strategic budget	Reflects the company's strategic plan
Activity-based budget	Begins with a specific objective or target, lists all of the activities needed to achieve it, and assigns a cost to each
Target budget	Aligns significant expenditures with the organization's objectives
Rolling (continuous) budget	Extends the existing budget model in increments

Source: Adapted from Shim, J. K., Siegel, J. G., & Shim, A. I. (2012). The what and why of budgeting: An introduction. In *Budgeting basics and beyond* (pp. 1–27). Hoboken, NJ: John Wiley.

To build a cash budget, organizations look at revenue projections (sales, donations, grants, services rendered, etc.) as well as data about accounts receivable and upcoming expenses. If the cash flow budget indicates that a company does not have enough cash, it must either borrow money or sell stock (for organizations with stock).[15] Cash budgets help management anticipate potential cash shortages and surpluses.

Cash flow is easiest to forecast when a business is stable, when operations are routine, and when the attitude toward risk is conservative.[16] Cash flow can be much harder to predict in fast-moving industries and organizations but it is what keeps the doors open.

Static (fixed) budget: Companies that are relatively stable utilize static budgets. Static budgets don't change due to increases or decreases in products or services sold or produced. The downside to using a static budget is inflexibility. When a business experiences unpredictable sales, a static budget doesn't work well.[17]

Fixed budgets are problematic because they don't account for a dynamic marketplace. They work best for departments that are not closely intertwined with variable volume (sales, manufacturing, etc.). For this reason, administration, marketing, and management departments can typically utilize fixed budgets. Fixed costs allocated to specific programming or projects (e.g., think repairs, advertising for a specific program, or purchase of land, buildings, or equipment) can also become fixed budgets.

Flexible (expense) budget: Companies typically use a flexible budget, also called an expense budget.[18] A flexible budget is revisited and revised regularly throughout the year to capture changes in revenue and expenditures. This flexibility enables managers to adapt the budget as their business needs change.[19]

This type of budget works best when volumes (e.g., the number of sales or the production of goods and/or services) change but do so within a fairly typical range. It is easy to develop a flexible budget with readily available computer programs or even a simple spreadsheet.

When managers use a flexible budget, they need to be vigilant about continuously updating their estimates with actual expenditures. The biggest benefit of flexible budgets is that they account for the unexpected. Industries, markets, and circumstances can change quickly, and flexible budgets allow managers the ability to respond to conditions they did not foresee as well as take advantage of surprising opportunities.[20]

Capital expenditure budget: Capital expenditures include funds spent to acquire or maintain fixed assets such as land, buildings, or equipment. These expenditures are captured in a capital expenditure budget, documenting the amount and timing of each purchase. Businesses typically complete this type of budget as part of the annual master budget so they can plot their spending for the coming year.[21]

The capital expenditure budget shows the estimated cost of the purchase as well as how the expenditure will be paid (e.g., cash, credit, or loan). Firms typically budget 3 to 10 years in advance and budgets are laid out by a special committee (capital projects committee) rather than the budget committee. Often, the budget categorizes capital projects by business objective (e.g., expand product offerings, reduce costs, develop innovative products, improve employee safety). At most firms, special authorization is required for large capital projects and the budget is accompanied by a detailed proposal that requires final approval from management and executives, depending on the scale.[22]

Capital expenditure budgets involve planning for the construction of new facilities.

©3dkombinat/Shutterstock

Program budget: Program budgets are simple and straightforward, listing only the revenue and expenses for a given program. Program activities such as research, development, marketing, and training are tracked on a program budget. Typically, these budgets are designed with cost-effectiveness in mind and all amounts must be weighed carefully against program goals. In general, a program budget won't be used for control purposes because it charts program-level spending and revenue activity, not individual-level spending and activity.[23]

Incremental budget: Incremental budgeting examines the increase in budget in terms of dollars or percentages assigned to project increments. Incremental budgets spell out the resources (e.g., labor, equipment, capital) allocated to each increment and the benefits the increment will produce (e.g., sales, revenue). Projects can be broken up into multiple increments.[24]

Add-on budget: An add-on budget modifies the previous year's budget, adjusting for factors like inflation, employee cost-of-living increases, or other concerns.[25] An add-on budget doesn't really incentivize efficiency, but it can instill a sense of competition that requires managers to innovate.

Supplemental budget: A supplemental budget allocates funds for budget areas not captured in the regular budget.

Bracket budget: Bracket budgets show projections at a higher level and a lower level than the base budget. This type of budget helps managers conceptualize a contingency plan in case forecast sales or production projections do not come to fruition. A bracket budget can be used when there are foreseeable risks or threats that require consideration and planning.[26]

Stretch budget: Stretch budgets are used to motivate employees. The budgeter "stretches" the conception of what is possible by projecting sales or production figures that are higher than forecasts predict. Meanwhile, expenses are estimated at the budget target. Looking at a stretch budget should challenge employees to increase effort and production. Ideally, a stretch budget shows objectives that are formidable yet achievable.[27]

Strategic budget: Strategic budgeting combines strategic planning with budgeting. When a company is in flux and dealing with financial insecurity or uncertainty, building a strategic budget can be an effective tool for keeping an organization on track or helping it course-correct in cases of uncertainty.

Activity-based budget: Sometimes it is necessary to think about the budget in terms of the spending required to achieve a specific business objective such as a sales target or production value. Whereas traditional budgets connect expenses to functions (e.g., administration, manufacturing, logistics, etc.), activity-based budgeting (ABB) focuses on the cost of all of the activities that are undertaken to achieve an outcome. For example, imagine that a jewelry company needs to fulfill a large order. The budgeters begin with the total number of pieces they must produce for their client and then work backward to establish all of the activities they will need to do in order to achieve their objective. They then budget a cost for each activity.[28]

Budgets help you understand an organization as a whole.

©iStockphoto.com/serdjophoto

Target budget: A target budget aligns significant expenditures with the company's business objectives.[29] Devising methods to fund projects in order to maintain positive momentum for the company is the budgeter's primary goal. To that end, the budgeter must be diligent about justifying large expenditures and carefully assess all requests for special projects to make sure they align with the company's financial vision.

Rolling (continuous) budget: A rolling budget involves incrementally extending the existing budget model. Also referred to as a continuous or perpetual budget, a rolling budget is revised on a periodic basis (e.g., monthly or quarterly). Usually, an organization adds a new budget period as soon as the most recent one is completed. For instance, if the rolling budget is quarterly, the updated budget for the new quarter will be available when the current quarter ends (e.g., the Q1 budget ends in March and the Q2 budget update begins the first of April).

Why do managers use a rolling budget? It keeps them focused on the big picture and helps them look ahead so they do not become so focused on short-term objectives that they lose sight of the company's long-term plans.[30]

A rolling budget moves beyond the static projection of revenue and expenditures to provide a continuous snapshot of the future.[31] Fixed budgets are outmoded in today's dynamic, fast-paced world. Many events, ranging from natural disasters to new inventions to stock market crashes, can change a budget on a dime. Rolling budgets can account for the everchanging nature of the marketplace to help managers ensure that their planning is continuous and forward-thinking.[32]

In the 1950s, formal budgets made their way to corporate America. Since then, budgeting has evolved extensively. Managers have adopted a wide variety of budgets to suit the specific needs of their businesses. A budget can be as simple as a cash flow sketched on a notepad or as complex as a vast array of bracket budgets drawn up for each program in a giant corporation or the behemoth that is the federal government yearly budget.[33]

Budgets can be tailored to specific industries. Some industries use them for tightly controlling expenses. Other industries budget to plan and communicate their strategic goals or even to motivate employees to improve performance.[34]

Now that you have reviewed the many types of budgets and their best uses, let's take a closer look at the components of a budget so you will be equipped to analyze or build a budget yourself.

CRITICAL THINKING QUESTIONS

> Which of these types of budgets do you think your university uses and why? How would any of these budgets pose a potential problem if used incorrectly?

Components for Managing a Budget

Learning Objective 14.3: Comprehend the critical components of a budget.

To add some levity to the idea of budgets and their roles, Colville likened a budget to a play, in that each part of the budget had its role, and therefore many voices and parts come together to create a dialogue, or discourse, that tells a story.[35] While this might seem a little existential, it is in fact very true. As we go through the primary parts of a budget, you will see how each one tells an important story, how one role is dependent on another, and how all of the parts come together to produce the bottom line, or conclusion of the play. In this section, we will start at the end of the play and work our way backward.

Budget Reports

After budgets are developed, managers use regular reports, called financial statements, to see how their division is operating based on their budget. **Financial statements** are summary accounting reports that are prepared periodically to inform executives, managers, creditors, and other interested parties on a business's financial condition and operating results.[36]

The most popular type of financial statement is an **income statement**, also known as a **profit and loss statement (P&L)** or **operating statement**,[37] which summarizes management's performance based on profitability over a certain period of time, typically a month, quarter, or year. The income statement itemizes historical revenues and expenses that led to the current profit or loss. An income statement can be used to identify how management can improve their income. Income statements are based on this fundamental accounting equation: Income = Revenue – Expenses.[38]

There are other financial reports, but the income statement is the one managers reference most often because the items in it typically mirror what is in their budget and what they will be questioned on regularly. The income statement allows managers to see fairly quickly what line items need intervention for controlling purposes.

Figure 14.1 shows the parts of an income statement. You will note that it says "typical" income statement because, just like anything else, different organizations might need additional categories, or fewer categories, to suit their purpose, as explained below.

Although there are several parts to an income statement, the three main parts you almost always see in an organization's report are revenue, expenses, and profit/loss.

▼ FIGURE 14.1
Parts of a Typical Income Statement

Sample Income Statement	
Revenue *The money a business earns from selling products or services.*	$100,000
Cost of Goods Sold *The cost of producing the goods or services.*	($25,000)
Gross Profit *Net sales (revenue) minus the cost of goods sold.*	$75,000
Operating Expenses *The costs associated with running the business.*	($22,000)
Pre-Tax Profit *The gross profit minus the operating expenses.*	$53,000
Taxes *The contribution to the goverment's revenue service.*	$14,000
Net Profit (Loss) *The gross profit minus the operating expenses minus the taxes.*	$39,000

Revenue

Determining revenue might seem as easy as just looking at what you make, but in fact it has many parts. Depending on what type of organization you work for, revenue can come from product sales, service sales, grants, donations, and so on. In short, revenue includes all money received.[39]

Expenses, Operating Expenses, and Cost

Expenses fall heavily on the control side of the budgeting process, and the income statement is an excellent way to keep track. Business **expenses** can be defined as the costs of doing business, or what we used and then paid for or charged so we could run our business; some examples are office supplies, salaries and wages, advertising, building rent, and utilities.[40] However, most income statements have many, many other categories, including the following:

- Office supplies
- Telephone
- Building/Office rent
- Utilities
- Depreciation expense
- Maintenance and repairs
- Interest expense
- Memberships
- Donations
- Bank fees and charges
- Salaries and wages

- Employment taxes
- Equipment rental
- Contract labor
- Professional fees
- Travel
- Entertainment
- Other expenses (i.e., any other type of expense that a business incurs)

Cost of Goods Sold

Businesses that sell products, including retailers, wholesalers, or manufacturers, have a special section included in their income statement called **cost of goods sold** (COGS).[41] According to Murray, "COGS is sometimes referred to as cost of sales and refers to the production costs for products manufactured and sold or purchased and re-sold by the company. These costs are an expense of the business, and they reduce the revenue the company makes from selling its products."[42]

The COGS section of the income statement calculates the cost of goods, whether purchased or produced, sold. Companies that sell goods, like retailers or wholesalers, calculate the cost of goods sold by comparing their inventory at the beginning and end of an accounting period. Manufacturers need to look at their finished-goods inventories as well as their raw materials inventories and goods-in-process inventories.[43]

Figure 14.2 shows how the calculations come together to arrive at COGS and provides the calculations for wholesale and retail pricing.

Depending on your role, you may or may not need to perform these calculations. If you do, you have a good example to follow. If you do not, be thankful for your great accounting department.

Pretax Profit and the Bottom Line

Although the bottom line is important to the organization as a whole, the biggest importance it carries for a manager is probably how it impacts their bonus structure and their ability to keep their job. When managers are responsible for both sides of their department's income statement, they probably watch their expenses very closely. While this might seem like smart management, you must also spend money to make money; savvy managers pay attention to both sides of the budget to maximize revenue and minimize expenses.

Net Profit

Many income statements have a couple of net profit categories. That is because net profit is calculated on just your revenue minus your expenses; however, the corporate income statement takes into account other expenses to the organization like taxes. Again, for our purposes and managers' purposes, the net profit shown from revenue minus expenses is enough for the department controls.

Understanding an Income Statement

Figure 14.3 shows many of the same categories you would see on any organization's income statement. These are important to you as a manager and will probably explain things you hear in the news, so it is important to understand the role these categories play in running an organization.

As you can see, the first four entries under "fixed expenses" (wages, payroll, sales and marketing, and rent) comprise a much higher percentage of the expense category than the rest of the items. One reason why organizations cut jobs when they are not doing well financially is that labor is almost always the largest expense item the company carries. However, as a smart

Calculating the Cost of Goods Sold

ZIPPERED GUSSET TOTE COST SHEET

DATE: 2/26/15				STYLE #: 02
DESCRIPTION: ZIPPERED GUSSET TOTE				SEASON: S/S 2016
				SELLING PRICE: 925.00

SIZE RANGE: NIA

MARKERS: N/A AT THIS TIME

MATERIAL	SQ FT	PRICE	AMOUNT
PRINTED COATED/CORRECTED VINYL	4	6.00	24.00
LINING	2	5.00	10.00
STIFFENER	2	5.00	10.00

TOTAL MATERIAL COST

FRONT

TRIMMINGS	QANT	PRICE	AMOUNT
SIX INCH SILVER ZIPPER	2	.50	2.00
SEVEN INCH SILVER ZIPPER	2	.50	2.00
1/4 INCH CHICAGO SCREW	4	.10	.40
LINEN WAXED THREAD(SO YDS)	5	7.00	3.50
1/2 INCH SILVER FEET	4	.50	2.00

TOTAL TRIMMING COST

BACK

LABOR			
CUTTING			4.00
SEWING			26.00
GRADING		N/A	N/A
MARKING		N/A	N/A

TOTAL LABOR AND MATERIAL COST

TOTAL COST	83.90
MARKUP	TOTAL COST + 120%
WHOLESALE PRICE	184.58
SUGGESTED RETAIL	WHOLESALE x 5, 925.00

manager, you understand that cutting jobs means cutting production and/or sales, which means, most likely, cutting revenue.

Intuit notes that the true cost of each of your employees is much higher than their paycheck. Even a company that doesn't provide benefits or paid vacation days for their employees has unavoidable expenses like Social Security and Medicare taxes.[44] These expenses are called payroll expenses. Shelton estimates that employers should expect to pay 10% or more to cover

Income Statement Basics

Income Statement	2016		2017		2018		Average
Number of Months	12		12		12		
Net Sales	500,000	100.00%	550,000	100.00%	620,000	100.00%	556,666.7
(– Cost of Goods Sold)	(110,000)	(22.00%)	(104,500)	(19.00%)	(124,000)	(20.00%)	(112,833.3)
Gross Margin	390,000	78.00%	445,500	81.00%	496,000	80.00%	443,833.3
Fixed Expenses							
Wages	165,000	33.00%	187,000	34.00%	207,080	33.40%	186,360.0
Payroll	28,500	5.70%	33,550	6.10%	39,246	6.33%	33,765.3
Sales and Marketing	45,000	9.00%	55,000	10.00%	60,388	9.74%	53,462.7
Rent	50,000	10.00%	60,500	11.00%	72,540	11.70%	61,013.3
Utilities	60,000	12.00%	8,250	1.50%	9,300	1.50%	25,850.0
Insurance	6,000	1.20%	7,150	1.30%	8,804	1.42%	7318.0
Interest on Loans	9,000	1.80%	10,450	1.90%	11,780	1.90%	10,410.0
Depreciation and Amortization	5,000	1.00%	5,500	1.00%	6,200	1.00%	5,566.7
Total Fixed Expenses	368,500	73.70%	367,400	66.80%	415,338	66.99%	383,746.0
Gross Margin	390,000	78.00%	445,500	81.00%	496,000	80.00%	443,833.3
(– Fixed Expenses)	(368,500)	(73.70%)	(367,400)	(66.80%)	(415,338)	(66.99%)	(383,746.0)
Net Income	21,500	4.30%	78,100	14.20%	80,662	13.01%	60,087.3

payroll taxes, federal and state unemployment taxes, and workers' compensation insurance.[45] "Because unemployment taxes and Social Security taxes phase out after a certain compensation level, you will pay a higher relative percentage for low-paid employees than you will for well-paid ones," according to Intuit.[46]

These are just some of the tough control decisions you will need to make as a manager. By looking at labor and additional employment expenses, you can see how a quick budget cut in those categories gives you the most budget reduction "bang for your buck." However, fewer people mean lower production, which means lower revenue, which means soon you will be asked again to lower your budget because the revenue has decreased.

Also take a look at the "rent" category. You may think that this category does not pertain to you as a manager, but most businesses take a portion of their **fixed organizational expenses** and apportion them off between their departments. Fixed organizational expenses are typically the same amount each month, can't be easily changed, and are paid on a regular basis.[47] For example, if you work for an organization with five departments, this means that each of those five departments will have a portion of the rent, utilities, and other fixed costs charged to their budget. Companies choose to divide up those expenses in a variety of different ways. In the next section, we will look at why most of the different budgets we discussed earlier are necessary, depending on the purpose of the department and/or organization.

Why is it important to understand the different parts of an income statement? If you were asked to reduce your budget by 20% for the upcoming fiscal year, what categories would you consider reducing and in what order?

Applying Appropriate Budget Systems

Learning Objective 14.4: Apply different budgeting systems depending on the circumstances.

Earlier we discussed the tension that can exist between the revenue and expense sides of a budget, depending on who controls which side. Ideally, of course, the organization is aware of this tension and managers are encouraged to work together to do what is best for the organization. We also discussed a wide range of budgets and their use. In this section, we will look at four of the most popular budgeting models and provide you with information and examples on how best to use them. You will experience many different budget models in your career, so having knowledge of the most prominent ones is part of the financial competitive advantage you will have in your professional (and perhaps even personal) life.

Even with the most careful planning, smart managers know that while there are things they can control, there are many they cannot. Hurricane Katrina, Hurricane Sandy, and California wildfires are just a few of the natural disasters in recent years that caused untold losses to organizations and the people that work for them.

The Four Most Common Types of Budgets

The Corporate Finance Institute recognizes four common types of budgets that companies primarily use: (1) incremental, (2) activity-based, (3) value proposition, and (4) zero-based. These four budgeting methods (featured in Figure 14.4) each have their own advantages and challenges, but each has a built-in, short-term amount of flexibility to keep the budget as updated and feasible as possible.[48] As you read through the descriptions, compare them to the budgets we have already discussed to see which are the most similar and which you think is the best to use.

Incremental budgeting: Incremental budgeting uses the previous year's budget as a starting point. A percentage is added to or subtracted from the previous figure to determine the current budget. Incremental budgeting is widely used because it is a straightforward and simple process. This type of budget works when primary cost drivers stay the same from year to year. Although this type of budget is the most common, there are a few disadvantages:

- It creates perpetual inefficiency by reducing employees' motivation to economize. When managers are given an incremental increase every year (e.g., 10%), they get in the habit of simply taking the increase whether they actually need it or not.
- It can contribute to budgetary slack[49] (we will return to this later in the chapter). A manager might, for instance, inflate the budget, overstating actual costs and expenditures so that their team appears to be on or under budget.
- It is unlikely to account for external factors that affect cost and production. For

▼ FIGURE 14.4

The Four Most Commonly Used Budgeting Methods

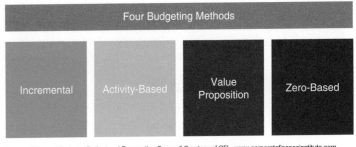

Source: "Types of Budgets. Budget and Forecasting Course." Courtesy of CFI - www.corporatefinanceinstitute.com.

THE BEST-LAID PLANS

Many small and large retail and service organizations used the flexible expense and revenue model when budgeting and planning for fiscal year 2000 and 2001. After completing an optimistic, pessimistic, and highly conservative estimate based on historical figures, they planned and hired staff, purchased inventory, and bought a series of marketing materials and advertising spots.

On September 11, 2001, the entire United States ground to a halt. Terrorists crashed four commercial airliners, loaded with fuel for cross-country flights from the East Coast to the West Coast, into the World Trade Center towers, the Pentagon, and a desolate field in rural Pennsylvania.[50] Journalist Marc Davis describes the impact of 9/11 on the stock market:

> Anticipating market chaos, *panic selling,* and a disastrous loss of value in the wake of the attacks, the NYSE and the Nasdaq remained closed until September 17, the longest shutdown since 1933. Moreover, many trading, brokerage, and other financial firms had offices in the World Trade Center and were unable to function in the wake of the tragic loss of life and collapse of both towers.

> On the first day of NYSE trading after 9/11, the market fell 684 points, a 7.1% decline, setting a record for the biggest loss in exchange history for one trading day. At the close of trading that Friday, ending a week that saw the biggest losses in NYSE history, the Dow Jones was down almost 1,370 points, representing a loss of over 14%. The Standard and Poor's (S&P) index lost 11.6%. An estimated $1.4 trillion in value was lost in those five days of trading.[51]

Small businesses were equally devastated. Even the most conservative and pessimistic revenue forecasts came in at half their estimates. According to Davis, small businesses, especially those closest to the World Trade Center, suffered the most. Nearly 18,000 small businesses were closed or destroyed."[52]

Sources: Davis, M. (2017, September 11). How September 11 affected the U.S. stock market. *Investopedia.* Retrieved from https://www .investopedia.com/financial-edge/0911/how-september-11-affected- the-u.s.-stock-market.aspx; Davis, M. (2019, June 25). The impact of 9/11 on business. *Investopedia.* Retrieved from https://www .investopedia.com/financial-edge/0911/the-impact-of-september-11- on-business.aspx; Webb Pressler, M. (2011, September 8). What was 9/11? *Washington Post.* Retrieved from https://www.washingtonpost .com/lifestyle/style/what-was-911/2011/08/31/gIQAQL5RDK_story .html?noredirect=on&utm_term=.0110a35c6b22.

---

example, an incremental budget doesn't account for inflation. It simply assumes that costs will rise an incremental amount. This could leave a company vulnerable to external factors like inflation.[53]

Activity-based budgeting: This top-down framework for budgets starts with considering how much the company will have to spend on activities required to achieve its objectives (e.g., production volume, sales targets, etc.). An activity-based budget begins with a detailed catalog of all of the activities needed to meet a particular metric and a cost assigned to each.[54] This approach requires the budgeter to do a values and ethics assessment and use it as a framework for examining each activity in the budget and prioritizing the importance of each activity. It allows managers to think carefully about ethics and values when establishing the activities needed to accomplish their objectives and incorporate them into the budget accordingly.[55]

Value proposition budgeting: Value proposition budgeting is about ensuring that each expenditure provides some kind of return on investment, adding value in some tangible way. To develop a **value proposition budget**, the budgeting team weighs the following issues:

- Why is this expenditure included in the budget?
- What value does this expenditure add? Does it add value for customers, staff, leadership, and other stakeholders inside or outside the company?
- What does a cost-benefit analysis reveal? Does the value added by the expense justify the expense? If not, is there some other reason that the expense is necessary?

Although value proposition budgeting does help to prevent unnecessary spending, its primary focus is adding value rather than eliminating expenses (for an approach that focuses on eliminating unnecessary expenses, see zero-based budgeting).[56]

Zero-based budgeting: Zero-based budgeting is a hard reset for each business unit. A **zero-based budget** requires the justification of each and every dollar amount, not by looking back at what the company has done in the past but by looking critically at present need. Rather than making incremental adjustments to the previous year's budget, each unit starts over from scratch (at "zero," so to speak). This type of budgeting requires a ruthless, cutthroat approach, so it can result in tension and defensiveness from team members.[57] Because no expenses are accepted without justification, zero-based budgeting may trigger a scarcity mindset in managers rather than encouraging cooperation and careful reflection. The goal of zero-based budgeting is to "strip down" the budget by eliminating each and every superfluous expense. With this approach, everything that is nonessential to profitable operation must go.

When should you use a "bottom-up" approach? Whenever there is a pressing need to cut costs—if a company is restructuring, facing economic downturn, or dealing with market instability.

Zero-based budgeting should focus on discretionary costs instead of essential expenditures. It is a tedious, lengthy process and most companies reserve it for situations when a dramatic shake up is necessary.[58]

Zero-Based Versus Incremental Budgeting Comparison

In the following excerpt, Patrick Williams provides a detailed comparison of zero-based versus incremental budgeting.

Given the pressure to budget effectively, firms scrutinize the process. Ultimately, there are two common approaches for establishing an annual budget: zero-based and incremental.

Zero-based budgeting assumes that the budget is built from "zero." That is, nothing is carried over or assumed from previous periods. Often, there is a temptation within organizations to justify activity with "that's what we've always done" or "last year, we did this." Those justifications imply that past activity, and the associated spend, will be repeated. However, within a zero-based budget approach, past activity and spend should *NOT* be assumed. The budget is not based on previous budgets or past performance. Instead, each expense needs to be justified before it will be added to the official budget.

The benefit of a zero-based budget is that it forces decision-makers to scrutinize their assumptions about what has and will make their plan effective, prioritizing specific activities. For instance, consider a retailer that runs an annual back-to-school promotion, including granola bars, toaster pastries, and fruit snacks. Let's assume that they invest $45,000 to advertise the sale, not including product discounts:

- Granola Bars
  - Sales revenue: $258,691.23
  - Gross margin: $ 63,638.04
  - Gross margin percent: 6%

- Toaster Pastries
  - Sales revenue: $103,724.51
  - Gross margin: $ 20,774.90
  - Gross margin percent: 0%

- Fruit Snacks
  - Sales revenue: $97,319.61
  - Gross margin: $32,115.47
  - Gross margin percent: 0%

Let's assume this was a successful promotion—it did generate $116,528.41 in gross margin ($63,638.04 + $20,774.90 + $32,115.47), not including other items that shoppers may have added to their carts during the trip.

But how might the investment change the next year, using a zero-based budget assumption? Think about the $45,000 advertising expense. Shouldn't that be applied across each segment (granola bars, toaster pastries, and fruit snacks)? Do you start to feel differently about any of the product segments, knowing that $15,000 in advertising costs will need to be subtracted from their gross margin?

Said another way, would you still argue to invest $15,000 to advertise toaster pastries if you'll only generate $20,774.90? As it stands, you have $5,774.90 ($20,774.90 – $15,000.00) to pay against other operating expenses, after allocating $15,000 in advertising costs. Would you be eager to defend that to your boss? With a zero-based budgeting approach, you'd need to defend the activity and spend, if you wanted to include it in the budget. That might be a tough task, indeed.

Incremental budgeting uses previous budgets and actual performance as a baseline from which to build forward-looking budgets. Each line item, meaning each planned expense, is adjusted to reflect expected competitive activity, economic factors, consumer trends, and other applicable issues that potentially affect performance. Thus, incremental budgeting takes into consideration the changing competitive landscape and the organization's needs.

In this approach, decision-makers make adjustments to year over year (YOY) budgets, meaning compared to the last year, to reflect anticipated changes to the business environment. In the example used above, the manager might reflect the cost of advertising as $50,000, believing that media rates will increase in the coming year. Or they may increase the expected sales revenue for each of the product segments, having seen positive trends for each throughout the year. These small changes are built into an overall budget that provides a comprehensive view of all activity and associated costs.

The benefit of incremental budgeting is that it challenges decision-makers to go in-depth to analyze planned activity and associated expenses. Further, it encourages those same managers to consider what trade-offs they'd make within their budget to prioritize certain activities over others. If leaders have determined that the total budget will not increase by more than 4% YOY, then a manager with an estimated budget of +7% will be expected to update their plan, prioritizing the plans that best assures they meet their annual goals, while reducing exposure on others to meet the +4% target. This is particularly effective when multiple decision-makers are competing for a limited supply of dollars to invest. Simply, leadership will challenge the managers to identify the best opportunities for growth, ultimately allocating funding for them while managing the budget to its target.[59]

The Ongoing Budgeting Process

To facilitate budgeting, the manager needs to engage in an ongoing budget process, as described by Patrick Williams in the following excerpt:

That means that the manager must closely monitor actual sales, cost of goods sold, and expenditures to see how closely actual performance aligns with the budget or plan that was originally created. Differences and their causes are noted so that decision-makers can make adjustments to operations. For instance, if an item is under-performing budget assumptions, the manager might promote the item, reduce its price, or seek to cancel future orders.

The company may use this same information about performance relative to budget to make adjustments at a more macro-level. Changes to the budget can be made across categories, division, or business units, allocating funds to certain areas while reducing funds for other areas. For example, if the cereal category is under-performing while the produce category is exceeding expectations, a retailer may reallocate funds from cereal to spur even greater growth in produce. Similarly, if a chain of stores operates several banners, funds may be shifted between those business units.

As you can see, budgeting is an ongoing process for a firm. The job is not over when the budget is finalized. Instead, performance is continually monitored, relative to the budget. To ensure financial goals are attained, adjustments are made when necessary. Further, differences between the budget plan and actual results, and their causes, are taken into consideration for future budget preparation.[60]

Because this section is designed to help you become familiar with budgets and their appropriate application, the above scenario shows how important it is to understand the use, many times, of multiple budgets in an organization not just as accounting tools but also as complete organizational control tools. Following the money is the most important thing managers and leaders in an organization do, since revenue and expenses track the performance of the organization and signal when it is time to make changes and revisit the strategic plan. Continuous budget reviews help leaders carefully control the financial aspects of their organization, down to the department level. The next section furthers the idea of how budgets are crucial in the decision-making and control process for all members of the organization.

CRITICAL THINKING QUESTIONS

What is the benefit of zero-based budgeting? Why would you choose incremental budgeting instead?

Using Budgets to Make Organizational Decisions

Learning Objective 14.5: Use budgets for management decision-making.

Strategic decisions play a key role in a firm's success. Members of the top management team are responsible for making strategic decisions that are unique, are complex, and provide direction.[61] Accounting professor Mark Bettner notes that "unfortunately, many business professionals lack the fluency in the unique language of accounting and finance required to perform basic financial analysis, prepare budgetary forecasts, or compare competing capital investment alternatives."[62]

Although we have briefly outlined some of the decisions managers will need to make, planning and controlling via the budget process is an ongoing and imperative part of an organization's daily function and sustainable future. Some decisions that managers will need to make, sometimes on a daily basis, include the following areas:

- Adding or dropping product lines
- Opportunity costs

- Relevant versus irrelevant costs
- Special orders
- Utilization of constrained resources

The importance of each of these areas of decision-making is discussed below.

Adding or Dropping Product Lines

Managers should consider relevant benefits and costs when deciding whether to add a new product line or drop an existing one. Product lines or business segments should be evaluated based on direct revenue and direct cost. Allocated fixed costs (remember our earlier discussion of fixed costs such as rent) should not be included in the analysis of income, because the organization will pay that amount with or without the product line.[63]

Opportunity Costs

An important economic concept is **opportunity cost**. An opportunity cost is the loss of a possible gain from another alternative. For example, if you decide to go to the movies instead of staying at home reading a book, the opportunity cost of going to the movies is the money spent on a ticket plus the time you no longer have to read the book. Opportunity cost, in other words, is what you have to give up when choosing how to spend limited resources like time and money.[64]

Opportunity costs are a big deal in organizations and in your personal life. They drive many of your decisions. Do you buy that new car you wanted, or do you take out a line of credit on your home to put on a new roof? Will the old car hold up for a few more years? How are you going to spend that money to get the best investment for your dollars? At the risk of wildly disappointing you, there is probably a new roof versus a new car in your future.

Relevant Versus Irrelevant Costs

Relevant versus irrelevant costs is also known as opportunity costs versus **sunk costs**, and this is another decision-making challenge you will find in your personal and professional life also on a regular basis. Relevant costs are things like opportunity costs. They are relevant to your decision because they mean giving up one thing for another.

Sunk costs, however, are irrelevant costs. Even if you have spent money on a project, organizations (and you) are not supposed to consider the spent money (sunk costs) when making their next decision.

Dr. Emma Hutchinson poses the following questions in a discussion of two options you may have when you wake up:

> Do you work out or sleep in? Have you ever convinced yourself to get out of bed by reminding yourself that you paid $60 for your monthly gym membership? Well, you fell victim to a common logical fallacy.
>
> A sunk cost is a cost that no matter what is unrecoverable. As such, it should have *no impact* on future decision making. This may sound strange but consider the [sic] your two options using the analysis learned above for making decisions.[65]

This seems like a really hard thing to do, and it is. Keep in mind, though, that many, many executives have lost their jobs going against this solid rule of decision-making. To sharpen your opportunity cost versus sunk cost decision-making skills, take the test in Table 14.2.

Opportunity Cost Versus Sunk Cost Decision-Making

1. Which of the following statements about opportunity cost is TRUE?
   I. Opportunity cost is equal to implicit costs plus explicit costs.
   II. Opportunity cost only measures direct monetary costs.
   III. Opportunity cost accounts for alternative uses of resources such as time and money.
   a) I, II, and III.
   b) I
   c) III only.
   d) I and III only.

2. Which of the following statements about opportunity costs is TRUE?
   I. The opportunity cost of a given action is equal to the value foregone of all feasible alternative actions.
   II. Opportunity costs only measure direct out-of-pocket expenditures.
   III. To calculate accurately the opportunity cost of an action we need to first identify the next-best alternative to that action.
   a) III only.
   b) I and III only.
   c) II only.
   d) None of the statements is true.

3. Suppose that you deciding between seeing a movie and going to a concert on a particular Saturday evening. You are willing to pay $20 to see the movie and the movie ticket costs $5. You are willing to pay $80 for the concert and the concert ticket costs $50. The opportunity cost of going to the movie is:
   a) $5.
   b) $30.
   c) $35.
   d) $65.

4. Suppose that you are willing to pay $20 to see a movie on Saturday night. A ticket costs $10, and the next-best alternative use of your time would be to go to dinner with a friend. The cost of the dinner is $20 and you value the experience of having dinner with your friend at $60. The opportunity cost of seeing the movie is equal to:
   a) $50.
   b) $30.
   c) $20.
   d) $10.

5. Suppose that you are willing to pay $50 to see a movie on Saturday night. A ticket costs $15, and the next-best alternative use of your time would be to go to a concert which costs $80 and you value at $100. The opportunity cost of seeing the movie is equal to:
   a) $15.
   b) $20.
   c) $35.
   d) $70.

6. Suppose you play a round of golf costing $75. The golf takes four hours to play. If you were not playing golf you could be working and earning $40 per hour. The opportunity cost of your golf game is:
   a) $75.
   b) $235.
   c) $155.
   d) $160.

7. Suppose you have bought and paid for a ticket to see Lady Gaga in concert. You were willing to pay up to $200 for this ticket, but it only cost you $110. On the day of the concert, a friend offers you a free ticket to the opera instead. Assuming that it is impossible to resell the Lady Gaga ticket, what is the minimum value you would have to place on a night at the opera, in order for you to choose the opera over Lady Gaga?
   a) $200.
   b) $110.
   c) $90.
   d) $0.

(Continued)

8. Suppose that you are willing to pay $350 to see Leonard Cohen play at the Save-On-Foods Arena. Tickets cost $100, and the next-best alternative use of your time would be to work in paid employment earning $50 over the evening. The opportunity cost of seeing Leonard Cohen is equal to: a) $50. b) $100. c) $150. d) $200.
9. I am considering loaning my brother $10,000 for one year. He has agreed to pay 10% interest on the loan. If I don't loan my brother the $10,000, it will stay in my bank account for the year, where it will earn 2% interest. What is the opportunity cost to me of the loan to my brother? a) $200. b) $800. c) $1,000. d) $1,200.
10. In January, in an attempt to commit to getting fit, I signed a year-long, binding contract at a local gym, agreeing to pay $40 per month in membership fees. I also spent $300 on extremely stylish gym clothes. This morning, I was trying to decide whether or not to actually go to the gym. Which of the following was relevant to this decision? a) The $40 that I paid the gym this month. b) The $300 I spent on gym clothes. c) The fact that I also had to take a *Management Today* midterm exam today. d) All of the above were relevant.
11. Suppose you have bought and paid for a ticket to see Kanye in concert. You were willing to pay up to $350 for this ticket, but it only cost you $100. On the day of the concert, a friend offers you a free ticket to Lady Gaga instead. You can resell your Kanye ticket for $80. What do your sunk costs equal? a) $0. b) $20. c) $80. d) $100.
12. Which of the following statements about sunk costs is FALSE? I. Sunk costs are those that cannot be recovered, no matter what future action is taken. II. Because sunk costs cannot be recovered, they are irrelevant for future decision-making. III. The presence of sunk costs can affect future decision-making, if they are large enough. a) II and III only. b) II only. c) III only. d) I and III only.
13. As a member of the local Sports Club, I pay $30 per month in membership fees. In a typical month I spend about $50 on beer at the Club. Every month I also have the option of attending a meeting of the whiskey club (open only to Club members), at a cost per meeting of $15, payable at the beginning of each meeting. Given this, what do my monthly SUNK COSTS equal? a) $15. b) $30. c) $45. d) $95.

Source: Hutchinson, E. (2016). Exercise 1.2 in Module 1.2: Opportunity costs and sunk costs. In *Principles of Microeconomics*. OpenStax Economics, Principles of Economics. OpenStax CNX. Licensed under Creative Commons license CC BY 4.0. Retrieved from https://pressbooks.bccampus.ca/uvicecon103/chapter/1-2-opportunity-costs-sunk-costs/.
Answers: 1. d; 2. a; 3. c; 4. a; 5. c; 6. b; 7. a; 8. c; 9. a; 10. c; 11. b; 12. c; and 13. b.

How did you do? Hopefully you really understand the huge difference between the two when it comes to decision-making, even if you are not comfortable with spending a lot of money on something and then not being allowed to consider that in your decision!

Special Orders

A **special order** is a one-time customer order. Special orders usually involve buying a large quantity of goods at a low price. Because special orders can be chances for organizations to make money or lose money, they can be hard decisions to make.[66] Managers need to carefully evaluate all relevant information like costs and revenue. The following example is adapted from a Freedom Learning

Group case study and outlines the decision-making process a manager might follow when deciding whether or not to place a special order.[67]

A call just came in to CoolShoes.com for a special-order shoe. A basketball team would like CoolShoes.com to make 50 pair of their shoes, with the awesome soles, but a high-top version in fuchsia. CoolShoes.com has never made high tops before, nor do they have the material in fuchsia. The team is willing to pay $150 a pair for these custom shoes. What information does CoolShoes.com need to decide if taking this special order is a good idea or not?

When you first look at this interesting order, it looks good, right? CoolShoes.com can make a quick $7,500 for 50 pair of shoes. That is $50 per pair *more* than they currently charge, and it shouldn't take long to make 50 pairs.

Ben, the purchasing manager, starts to make some calls about the fuchsia material for the shoes. He finds out that this particular color is hard to come by. The raw material is going to cost $3 per unit, and it will take seven units per pair, since they are high tops.

Cost for a regular pair of shoes $2 per unit × 5 units = $10 per pair

Cost for the fuchsia high tops $3.50 per unit × 7 units = $24.50 per pair

Ben also finds out that to cut the new pattern for the high tops will require a die for their material cutter. The cost of this special die is $1,200. Oh, and Mary let us know that the production workers would need to work overtime to make the special order, so the direct labor cost would be $30 an hour, since they would be paid time and a half for the hours, and they are going to take an hour per pair to make, as opposed to the half hour for the regular shoes.

Let's take a look at Table 14.3 to see where we are with our special-order fuchsia high tops.

So even with all of the extra costs, the special-order fuchsia high tops will add $3,725 to the net income. It's a *go* for the high tops.

What else might happen because of this special order? This is really great advertising for CoolShoes.com, because their shoes will be on the basketball court for all the world to see.

Special orders are not just limited to production organizations. Service organizations frequently get last-minute calls for help with consulting or installations, and the same process for calculating costs is necessary. Clients will often pay a premium for time-sensitive service items, so the revenue incurred for the extra work might be well worth the overtime.

Utilization of Constrained Resources

The following example from Freedom Learning Group illustrates how **constrained resources** are used.

A constrained resource is something that you have a limited amount of. In a manufacturing business it may be machine time, labor hours, or raw materials. Whenever there is a constrained resource, as a manager, you need to determine the best way to use the limited (constrained) resource to bring the most money to your net profit (bottom line).

So you are the manager of a small retail clothing store. You have 1,000 square feet of space to use for inventory (excluding walkways, register area, and fitting rooms), and you need to use it in the most effective manner to create the best net income for your store.

▼ TABLE 14.3

Making a Special-Order Decision

Revenue (50 pair @ $150 each)	$7,500
Expenses	
Material: fuchsia (50 × 7 units × $3.5 per unit)	$1,225
Direct labor (50 × .8 × $30)	$1,200
Variable overhead (30 hours × $3 per hour)	$150
Total variable expenses	$2,575
Fixed expenses	
Die for material cutter	$1,200
Total variable and fixed expenses for special order	($3,775)
Incremental net operating income	**$3,725**

Source: Adapted from Freedom Learning Group. (n.d.) Special order decisions. *Lumen Learning.* ShareAlike 4.0 International under Creative Commons license CC BY SA 4.0. Retrieved from https://courses.lumenlearning.com/wm-accountingformanagers/chapter/special-order-decisions/.

Fuchsia high-top sneakers.

©iStockphoto.com/Yury Gubin

You have the following inventory:

- **Jeans:** Each pair contributes $40 to net income and you can get two in one square foot of space.
- **Shirts:** Each shirt contributes $10 to the net income, but you can get five in one square foot of space.

If your entire store was jeans you would have 2,000 pair of jeans contributing $40 per pair or $80,000 to your net income.

If your entire store was shirts, you would have 5,000 shirts each contributing $10 or $50,000 to your net income.

How would you stock your store? Well, if you were simply looking at using your space to maximize net income, and you thought jeans would work by themselves, you would stock it with jeans right?

What else may you want to look at in your retail space? Perhaps for every pair of jeans you sell, you also sell two shirts. Is one more difficult to prepare for sale? Maybe shirts need to be pressed and hung, while jeans are simply folded on a shelf.

There are many things to think about when you stock a small retail store, with space constraints you will need to experiment with the best product mix![68]

You can probably picture yourself pouring over the budget numbers and making decisions that impact your company. What if you are in a different industry, one where your decisions about adding and dropping lines, opportunity costs, and utilization of constrained resources actually directly impact peoples' lives? When and where does the budget take a back seat to the well-being of your stakeholders?

As the *Kaiser Health News* article in the Fact or Fiction box illustrates, high prescription drug prices in general are an issue for nearly all Americans, regardless of whether or not they have insurance. Managers in industries like health care make life-changing decisions based on budget information. A recent collaborative study between the Association of State and Territorial Health Officials, the Department of Health Policy and Management, and Johns Hopkins Bloomberg School of Public Health on politics, budget development, and health care concluded that a better understanding of how and why politics interacts with the budget- and priority-setting processes is critical to a sustainable public health system. In addition, the authors stated that in the context of harsh economic realities, budget and priority setting is both difficult and constant.[69]

To emphasize the ways budgets drive decisions from both revenue and cost perspectives, a question that is often asked is: "How much is a human life worth?" While this might seem a little morbid, this calculation is used to make many decisions that regulate our lives, from what we eat to how fast we drive.

The Cost of a Human Life, Statistically Speaking

Lawmakers and government regulators are supposed to operate on the cost-benefit principle. For each new regulation they consider—from childproof locks on lighters to what should go on a nutrition label to how many life jackets a plane should carry—officials are supposed to weigh how much it will cost against how much it will benefit. To do that, they have to ask difficult questions about how they measure costs and benefits, and how they make the intangible, tangible. The most difficult among these questions is: How do you put a dollar value on human life, and how much will we spend to save it?[70]

Legislators and regulators grapple with these ethical, philosophical questions every time they make a choice related to human health and safety. How do they do it? They use a method quite familiar to budget professionals: they come up with a number and they make it official.

FACT OR FICTION?

The Cost of Insulin

There is a lot of attention being paid to the cost of prescription drugs in America, and the cost of insulin is one of the hottest debates. Since its price doubled between 2012 and 2016, insulin has commanded attention from Capitol Hill to Hollywood, becoming a mainstay in health care conversations and even garnering a mention in a Netflix comedy show.

Voters consider rising prices for life-sustaining medications like insulin to be a pressing issue at the ballot box. Democratic presidential candidates are paying attention and addressing the issue with regularity.[71] At a televised town hall event in 2019, Senator Kamala Harris (D-Calif.) cited the skyrocketing price of insulin when answering an audience question about health care. She argued that a shocking number of diabetes patients "cannot afford their insulin." Harris put the number at one in four.[72]

Given the high rate of diabetes in America, researchers point out that one-quarter of patients with diabetes not being able to afford their insulin is an astronomical number. But it might not be as high as it seems on face value, since the number of patients with diabetes who need insulin to survive is smaller than the total number of people who are diabetic. According to the American Diabetes Association (ADA), about 1.25 million Americans have type 1 diabetes, meaning they cannot live without insulin.[73]

Because Harris's statement is so alarming, it has the potential to become a mainstay in the Democrats' campaign season. In an article for *Kaiser Health News*, Shefali Luthra examined the data to see if Harris's statement holds up to scrutiny.

Three Distinct Data Sets Prove Harris's Claim

When Harris's claim was questioned, her staff responded with the results of a December 2018 peer-reviewed study by the Yale Diabetes Center.[74] The study surveyed 199 participants and found that 51 had discontinued or lowered their dosage of insulin because they could not afford to pay for it. That's a bit more than the one-in-four figure that Harris cited in her statement (25.62%).

Although the study was conducted with a small sample in one city, three academics who study health care agree that it is fairly accurate and that the findings hold true nationally. Stacey Dusetzina, a Vanderbilt University professor whose specialty is health policy, contends that the sample included a representation of people that matches the demographics that researchers would look for in a national sample, such as age, insurance status and type, race, and ethnicity. In other words, the study corroborates and aligns with others of its kind.

The ADA did an online survey of a sample that represented the demographics of diabetes patients nationally.[75] The organization polled 530 people. Around 27% of those participants cited cost as a factor in their choice to take or buy insulin. Diabetes patient advocacy group T1 International also conducted similar research.[76] Although the opt-in T1 study is still being peer reviewed, James Elliott, a T1 trustee, believes that it will likely corroborate the one-in-four figure revealed in the studies conducted by the Yale Diabetes Center and the ADA.

Harris's Talking Point Relies on Extrapolation, But It's "More True Than Not"

Harris's comment requires extrapolation simply because it is based on limited data. Only one of the three studies she's cited has been peer reviewed and the sample size is very small.

Although the cost of insulin has soared since 2012, there is a lack of peer-reviewed data tracking the affordability of insulin. Dr. Jing Luo, an affiliate of the Yale study who teaches at Harvard Medical School, has done general research on insulin prices and calls Harris's talking point "more true than not."

What about Harris's phrase "cannot afford their insulin"? The supplied research doesn't address this question exactly. It simply accounts for people who have cited cost as a reason why they stopped purchasing insulin or begun using less insulin.

Experts like Dr. Kasia Lipska, an endocrinologist who led the Yale study, say that this question is a good method for judging whether or not people can afford insulin.[77] The question focuses on insulin, rather than asking participants about other financial choices related to the purchase of insulin. For example, it doesn't ask whether patients reduce grocery or gas purchases in order to buy their insulin.

The Verdict

It is difficult to rate Harris's statement as completely true or give it too much weight. In the absence of a national peer-reviewed study, one has to extrapolate to accept that the findings of the peer-reviewed Yale study apply throughout the country.[78] Another important caveat is that Harris's claim only applies to people with type 1 diabetes (since they are the ones who use insulin) rather than all patients with diabetes.

According to experts, the three studies cited provide constitute ample proof of Harris's claim. The widely accepted usage of the phrase "cannot afford" may actually mean that rising insulin prices are an even bigger public health crisis and financial crisis than we think. The data sets provided only measure people who stopped taking insulin altogether or reduced their dosage. The findings do not track the other financial problems that high insulin prices create (e.g., a person who chooses to forgo another necessary medication in order to be able to purchase insulin or a family that skimps on the parents' health care in order to buy insulin for a child).

(Continued)

Because the available peer-reviewed data back up Harris's statement but the amount of data available is limited, this claim was rated as *mostly true*.[79]

Sources: Adapted from American Diabetes Association. (2018a). Statistics about diabetes. Retrieved from https://www.diabetes.org/resources/statistics/statistics-about-diabetes; American Diabetes Association. (2018b). Insulin affordability survey. Retrieved from http://main.diabetes.org/dorg/PDFs/2018-insulin-affordability-survey.pdf; CNN. (2019). Transcript from "CNN Hosts a Town Hall with Sen. Kamala Harris (D-CA) Presidential Candidate (Aired April 22, 2019, 10-11p ET)." *CNN*. Retrieved from http://www.cnn.com/TRANSCRIPTS/1904/22/se.04.html; Herkert, D., Vijayakumar, P., Luo, J., Schwartz, J. I., Rabin, T. L., DeFilippo, E., & Lipska, K. J. (2019). Cost-related insulin underuse among patients with diabetes. *JAMA Internal Medicine*, *179*(1), 112–114; Luthra, S. (2019, April 29). Is insulin's high cost keeping diabetes patients from taking their medicine? *Kaiser Health News*. Retrieved from https://khn.org/news/is-insulins-high-cost-keeping-diabetes-patients-from-taking-their-medicine/; T1 International. (2019). The USA insulin price crisis. Retrieved from https://www.t1international.com.

In America, your life is worth $7 million to $9 million, according to the figure set by the U.S. Office of Management and Budget.

Why not $300,000? Why not $42 million? How do economists derive these seemingly arbitrary figures? To answer this difficult question, economists make their calculations based on the choices we make about behavior that poses risks to our health and safety. Think smoking, driving, eating undercooked meat or egg products, or working in a high-risk job.

Adam Smith, known as the father of modern economics, argued centuries ago that workers' wages reflected "the ease or hardship, the cleanliness or dirtiness, the honorableness or dishonorableness of the employment."[80] Is he right? Economists have conducted more than 100 studies linking the value of human life to decisions that humans make about risk, including job risks and personal risks.

For example, how much more does one earn for coal mining or oil drilling than working at a safer desk job? Let's calculate that a dangerous mining job pays $10,000 more annually than a relatively safe office job. Assume that miners have a 1% greater chance of dying on the job than office workers. If $10,000 accounts for 1% of the value of a human life, then the value of a human's life is $1 million ($10,000 = .01 × X).

We can also consider what we are willing to pay for safety features and how we adjust our behavior in response to risk. What will we pay for a life-saving bike helmet? How about antilock brakes? How do we adjust our choices with risk assessment in mind? If we're allowed to drive faster, even though we know it makes us more likely to die in an accident, how much do we choose to speed up?[81]

After seeing how budgets are used to make small decisions all the way through to life and death decisions, you should be wondering where and how ethics play a role in the budget as control system. The next section will cover some examples and allow you to put yourself in these ethical dilemmas as a manager, a stakeholder, perhaps a shareholder, and a person.

CRITICAL THINKING QUESTIONS

> What are some significant decisions you have had to make lately? What information did you consider before making the final decision? Were there health risks involved? How would that alter your choices?

Budgets as Decision-Making Tools: An Ethical Perspective

Learning Objective 14.6: Understand the ethics of using budgets as control.

Throughout the chapter, there have been a few mentions of how budgeting and control can have effects that are not intended as managers "pad" their expenses and perhaps understate their potential revenue in an effort to look better at how they managed their budget at the end of the fiscal year. Although this might not seem like much, by now you should understand that managers are often in charge of millions of dollars of expenses and revenues. Just a small ethical violation could create huge financial problems for the organization.

However, at the end of the previous section, you saw how making decisions based on budgets has life-altering and life-threatening consequences, too. It is not just a matter of a manager padding expenses for personal gain, but rather organizations making decisions for their gain versus human lives. This brings a sobering element to the ethics involved with organizational decision-making.

Despite public demand for stronger business ethics and the widespread adoption of a code of ethics by many organizations, the integration of ethical values into the corporate planning process has received little attention in real life or in the research literature. This has significant effects since ethical values govern managers' behaviors and decisions. Ethical decisions made by organizations have economic, social, and legal effects on not only the organization, but society as a whole.[82]

Although the main objective of managers and leaders in an organization is to maximize stakeholder value, now that you have reviewed the role that budgets play and their potential to drive questionable ethical decision-making choices when it comes to human lives, you should be able to see the many ethical issues that arise when employees and organizations use budgets for their own personal gain (i.e., shareholder value versus stakeholder value).

Stakeholder Considerations

If applied *too* broadly, the term stakeholder can literally apply to everyone with any kind of relationship to a company, making the distinction useless. How can managers narrow the scope and effectively manage stakeholders? The first step is to prioritize stakeholders and accurately assess their claims.

Balancing stakeholders' claims fairly and ethically is essential to stakeholder management. Ideally, managers should do their best to make sure that no one gets special treatment at the expense of others. They should strive to address the needs of as many stakeholders as they can. That said, despite their best intentions and their commitments to equity, companies have limited time and money. It is impossible to meet every stakeholder's needs all of the time, so instead companies must strive for balance.

Prioritizing Stakeholders' Claims

To begin the complex process of prioritizing stakeholder claims, it is important to consider stakeholders' expectations of the company. What do they think about their prospects? What assumptions or predictions have they made about what the company can provide for them or how they will be treated? While stakeholders' expectations can vary widely, it is reasonable to assume that all stakeholders expect some form of satisfaction or gratification for the company. For example, when stakeholders are also shareholders (i.e., own stock in the company), they are typically hoping for a high return on their investment. Employees, on the other hand, may be less invested in profitability (other than as it relates to their job security, of course). Instead, they tend to base their satisfaction on their benefits and wages, the tasks and projects they are assigned, working conditions, and stability. If the stakeholders are members of the community in which the business operates, they are likely to base their satisfaction on the company's effects on the community—both positive and negative. Does the business work to reduce negative impacts on the environment? Does it do anything to improve quality of life within the community?

Managers have to consider a wide array of stakeholder expectations. They must make ethical, fair decisions and often they must do so in the face of conflicting expectations (e.g., pitting shareholders' demands for profitability against workers' desire for higher salaries and benefits packages that cost more). Knowing that it is virtually impossible to address all of the stakeholders' claims all of the time, managers must do the delicate work of deciding which stakeholders to consider and in what order. This process is known as **stakeholder prioritization**.

CAREERS IN MANAGEMENT

Budget Control

There are many jobs available in the budget control field, such as a budget analyst or comptroller, but they are also tied to many other titles that include budget control. Best of all, these jobs are available in all types of organizations, including for profit, not for profit, and local, state, and national government.

Budget analyst: If you want to do a minimum amount of travel for your job, local government entities are always looking for budget analysts. A recent and simple Google search showed this posting within 10 miles of the search zone:

> The City is seeking qualified professionals for an exciting and challenging management opportunity. Under the limited supervision of the Assistant City Manager, this position will prepare annual operating budgets, capital budgets, and capital improvement plans for review and adoption by City Council. Other management tasks will also be assigned for the City as required. The successful applicant for the position will hold a Bachelor's Degree in public administration, finance, business, or a related field. Three or more years of experience in local government at a management level, including experience in local government budgeting, is preferred. Experience with the Tyler Munis financial software system is a plus.[83]

As you can see, a budget analyst needs a degree in a business field, not necessarily accounting or finance, and this ad stresses that the lucky candidate will have minimum supervision. This means they are looking for someone who does not like to be micromanaged and has the motivation and problem-solving skills to work on their own. The best part is the average salary for this position, listed under the job posting, which ranges between $74,000 and $144,000!

Comptroller: What about being a comptroller? If you check O*NET OnLine (http://onetonline.org) and search for "comptroller," you will find that comptroller is related to other job titles such as chief financial officer (CFO), controller, director of finance, finance director, finance manager, finance vice president, and treasurer.[84]

These are pretty lofty titles, which show you how valuable employees with budget control experience are to organizations.

The following are just a few of the duties described in these job descriptions:

- Supervise employees performing financial reporting, accounting, billing, collections, payroll, and budgeting duties.

- Coordinate and direct the financial planning, budgeting, procurement, or investment activities of all or part of an organization.

- Develop internal control policies, guidelines, and procedures for activities such as budget administration, cash and credit management, and accounting.

- Maintain current knowledge of organizational policies and procedures, federal and state policies and directives, and current accounting standards.

- Prepare or direct preparation of financial statements, business activity reports, financial position forecasts, annual budgets, or reports required by regulatory agencies.[85]

Perhaps you noticed that these bullets include planning and control functions. Additionally, they are looking for employees who can develop internal control procedures as well as external control procedures like keeping up with current account standards and federal and state policies and directives, and preparing appropriate financial reports for regulatory agencies.

The projected job growth in these budget control positions is much higher than average, at least until 2026, and the median wage? How about nearly $130,000?

If you have an interest in working in budget control, you can see that the available jobs and job titles are plenty and this is a high-growth field with great income potential. It looks like budget control is a pretty interesting field to pursue after all.

Sources: Google. (n.d.). Careers in budget control search terms. Retrieved from https://www.google.com/search?q=careers+in+budget +control&oq=careers+in+budget+control&aqs=chrome..69i57j33l2.50 99j0j7&sourceid=chrome&ie=UTF-8&ibp=htl;jobs&sa=X&ved=2ahUK EwiFq-bc9IzIAhVNq1kKHYxvBTMQiYsCKAF6BAgGEBA#fpstate=tldet ail&htidocid=cwuJFHsIAcBhtxMsAAAAAA%3D%3D&htivrt=jobs; and O*NET OnLine. (2019). Summary report for: 11-3031.01 - Treasurers and Controllers. Retrieved from https://www.onetonline.org/link/ summary/11-3031.01.

First, managers have to decide if a particular individual is actually part of a specific stakeholder group. For instance, a clothing brand might get hundreds of mentions on Twitter. How should managers decide which Tweets are relevant? How do they know that the feedback in a particular message is representative of key stakeholders (e.g., people who are influencers or part of their target market, etc.)? Managers need to consider context to answer these questions. To do so, they might analyze a Twitter user's communication patterns to determine if they are actually part of a customer base that the company values.

Once a manager has discerned that an individual is, in fact, a stakeholder, it is time to consider the company's relationship with the stakeholder. What does the company need from this individual? Are the needs urgent or long term? If the company needs something immediately, that is a good sign that it should prioritize this particular stakeholder's claims. If not, that does not mean that the stakeholder is not important. It simply means that perhaps this stakeholder's claims should not be labeled as urgent or immediate.

Assessing and prioritizing stakeholders is not a static project; it is a recurring process and it often happens in real-time. Managers must practice stakeholder prioritization in dynamic conditions, and this process does not have to be formalized. Sometimes, it is a simple matter of determining which customer has a large order to fill or whether a particular supplier might need incentive to complete a rush job. In short, managers are constantly determining the answers to these questions on an ad hoc basis: Who is a stakeholder? Is their interest important to address immediately? Is this relationship essential to the growth of the business?

When a stakeholder relationship is essential to the business—if, for example, an individual is indispensable, irreplaceable, or influential—this stakeholder should be prioritized. Examples of such stakeholders include but are not limited to integral suppliers, loyal customers, and officials who regulate compliance. That is not to say that managers should kowtow or pander to these individuals; managers should simply recognize that it is in the best interest of the business to attend to their concerns. Imagine, for instance, that a state legislator in the company's district is launching a bill to raise business taxes to generate revenue for the state. This type of legislation could have a big impact on the company's finances. Therefore, this legislator is a stakeholder that the company should prioritize. Even though, on their own, the legislator might not be able to move the bill, it is still important for the company to form a strong working relationship. Over time, the legislator could build political clout and develop a coalition, so the business will want to have a connection and rapport with the legislator if they are ever in the position to pass the bill. Prioritizing this particular stakeholder will ensure that the company has a voice in the political process.

It is impossible to give each and every stakeholder undivided attention because no company has limitless time and capital. That is exactly why prioritization is essential. Companies must consider two factors in the stakeholder management process: the priority level of the stakeholder relationship and the urgency of the stakeholder's claim. In other words, managers must decide: how important is the relationship and how urgent is the stakeholder's concern? Once a manager has these answers, they can decide how to allocate labor and resources.

Two other variables to consider in the stakeholder prioritization process are circumstance and time. Context is everything. For instance, a grocery retailer faced with the emergence of aggressive competitors must prioritize customer service and value, making customers their priority stakeholder and perhaps temporarily putting other concerns on the backburner. Consider Whole Foods, a multinational grocery chain famous for selling products free from hydrogenated fats and artificial colors, flavors, and preservatives. Amazon recently acquired the chain, drastically slashing prices. These lower, attractive prices combined with the store's existing reputation for high quality could potentially draw in a new base of customers. In essence, potential customers who had focused on value over quality in the past may no longer need to economize by shopping at other stores. By contrast, Whole Foods' competitors like Walmart and ALDI will have to prioritize their customer service because they can no longer compete with low prices alone. Changes to the market, like this Whole Foods acquisition, can necessitate changes in stakeholder management.

Figure 14.5 demonstrates another method for prioritizing stakeholder relationships: the power and interest matrix. This figure shows how to map stakeholders based on their influence and interest in the company. As you can see, a stakeholder group's influence (a.k.a. power) can be given more weight than its interest. When the matrix shows that a stakeholder has both power

▼ FIGURE 14.5

Determining a Stakeholder Prioritization by Assessing the Relationship Between the Stakeholder Group's Power (a.k.a. Influence) and the Stakeholder Relationship Interest

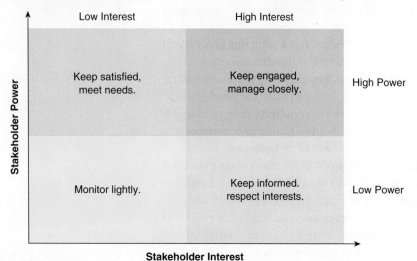

Source: Adapted from Rice University. (2018). Ethical decision-making and prioritizing stakeholders. In *Business ethics* (module 3.3). Licensed under Creative Commons license CC BY SA 4.0. Retrieved from https://openstax.org/details/books/business-ethics.

and interest, that stakeholder becomes a key stakeholder. When key stakeholders experience a problem, meeting their concerns becomes a higher priority. In other words, the more power and interest a stakeholder group has, the more essential it is to address their claims above others.

In order to be successful, businesses must ethically consider stakeholders' claims. Doing so is not only fair and just, but it also leads to stakeholder satisfaction. From stock owners to employees to residents of the community where the firm is located, content and fulfilled stakeholders are integral to financial success.[86]

An Example of Unethical Budget Practices

The business press is full of stories about how managers and leaders manipulate budgets and earnings in dysfunctional, questionably ethical, and sometimes even illegal ways to make themselves look better on performance evaluations and obtain bonuses.[87] Yet despite what we have studied so far and the many stories about budget improprieties, most organizational and behavioral views of budgeting fail to fully acknowledge the ethical components of the problem.[88]

Budgetary slack (sometimes called **budget gaming**) is defined as the deliberate underestimation of budgeted revenue or overestimation of budgeted expenses. Managers will use budgetary slack as a tactic to ensure they have a better chance of "making their numbers," which is particularly important for managers whose performance appraisals and bonuses are contingent on whether or not they achieve their budgeted numbers.[89]

Budget slack costs organizations money because assets are misallocated when managers intentionally include more organizational resources in the budget than they really need. Along with wasting the significant time and effort that goes into a company's budgeting process, the budget is often the primary tool for determining how to best distribute organizational resources like time, money, and materials.[90]

Other organizational losses come when the managers do "make their numbers" and are rewarded for it, as the following section illustrates.

The Potential Problems With Bonuses for Managers

Rewarding managers with bonuses can certainly inspire increased productivity, but are bonuses truly in the company's best interest? Doling out manager bonuses can lead to problems that impact the company's bottom line and threaten its potential for success. Before choosing to give bonuses, it is essential for executives to explore the potential pitfalls. Doing so will help ensure that an incentive program both benefits managers and protects the company.

The Potential for Decreased Performance

It may sound counterintuitive to say that incentive bonuses can actually lead to a decline in performance, but here's how it works. When a bonus is attached to productivity in one specific area, it can lead to a quality decline in other areas. For instance, if managers receive a share of the profits when firms stay below budget, they may choose to slash costs by skimping on quality. They might deliberately spend less on advertising even though it's bad for the company. They could order less expensive but inferior materials, demand that their direct reports work overtime (leading to disgruntled employees), or even put off critical repairs.

The Potential for Declining Morale

If you aren't clear and specific about your incentive program, you might unintentionally defeat one of your primary purposes for developing it in the first place: boosting morale. For example, consider a sales bonus program. If you aren't clear exactly how bonuses will be rewarded, you might wind up with a sales manager who thinks the bonus is for gross sales, not just new sales. Discovering this miscommunication after the incentive period ends could make for one disgruntled manager.

Another thing to consider is how will direct reports' labor play a role in manager bonuses? If subordinate employees are pushed to take on more work or complete work faster and only the manager gets a bonus, that could spell trouble for morale. Employees might feel used or cheated.

Ongoing bonus programs can also have a detrimental effect on morale. If you have to end an ongoing bonus program at any point, employees who have come to think of the bonus as part of their salary could face negative consequences. They might wind up in a precarious financial situation, leading them to feel resentful, decide to leave, or have any of a number of other consequences.

Before you institute any kind of bonus program, carefully consider how it could affect morale in the long run.

The Impact on Cash Flow

When you don't attach a fixed dollar amount and firm pay date to a bonus, you may find yourself scrambling for cash. If managers dramatically exceed your projections or achieve their metrics sooner than you had anticipated, you'll be left struggling to cover the bonus promised. Make sure that your finance department plays an active role in designing your incentive program to avoid surprises.

The Potential for Fraud

While it's unpleasant to think about lack of integrity, the fact of the matter is that an employee might rely on fraud to earn a bonus. There are a host of ways for employees to manipulate metrics in their favor. For example, if they are rewarded for staying under budget, employees might underreport expenses or ask a vendor to hold off on billing until their incentive period is over (this happens all the time, by the way).

If they are rewarded for sales in a given period, employees could offer unauthorized discounts to boost sales or ask customers to wait on a big purchase until they can receive credit for the sale. Some employees might set goals that are intentionally low in order to blow past them. While everyone hopes their employees are ethical, take care to make sure that your incentive system can withstand those who are not.[91]

The other problem this creates is that of positive reinforcement for bad behavior. Once a manager receives a bonus by taking advantage of the budget, they have more incentive to continue the behavior to continue receiving those rewards.

Employees could commit fraud to earn a bonus.

©ARENA Creative/Shutterstock

Considerations and Solutions to Budgetary Slack

There is a good deal of research into the ethical perceptions of a manager versus their participation in budgetary slacking despite, once again, the lack of organizations recognizing the strong role that ethics play.

Reputations and Ethics

One study examined a manager's perception of their reputation and ethics versus their propensity for budgetary slack. The research showed that reputation concerns are positively associated with the subordinate's perception that budgetary slack is unethical, meaning that a person concerned with their reputation is more likely to perceive budgetary slack as unethical. According to Stevens,[92] these reputation concerns are negatively associated with the amount of slack the subordinate builds into the budget, meaning the more concerned a person is with their reputation, the less slack they will build into the budget. Finally, a manager's ethical concerns were found to be negatively associated with budgetary slack, so the higher the ethical concerns, the less the budgetary slack.[93]

Organizational Environments

Since there is seemingly enough evidence to support the importance of ethics in budgeting, solutions to help organizations be more confident in their employees and their budgets, and save untold time and resources, are critical and fairly straightforward.

Research shows that one way to reduce budgetary gaming is to have a strong ethical cultural. Strong ethical cultures have formal ethics codes, ethics training, good management role models, and reward socially responsible behavior.[94] Organizations can strengthen their ethical cultures by being aware of the pressure their employees feel to make their numbers. Studies also show that empowering employees to have more ownership over the budgeting process can reduce unethical practices.[95]

Integrating Values in Decision-Making

Finally, in an article dedicated to incorporating ethics into the budgeting process using a values-based approach, Santosuosso calls for the practice to consider at least five stages:

1. The first stage concerns the identification of ethical values. The choice of what constitutes a "value" should not be left to the whim of managers and employees, but should be the result of a moral judgment in the true sense. In brief, moral duty helps people who have a developed moral reasoning and enjoy freedom of choice to correctly identify values and persuade the will to act for their achievement.
2. The identification of ethical values leads to the creation of an ethical framework. An ethical framework, in contrast with the contents of a code of ethics, shows in detail the values and circumstances concerning people, causes, effects, mode and places that are relevant for describing them. The ethical framework, as a dynamic, not static document, represents the first document for effective corporate planning with an ethical dimension.
3. The decision process needs a prior examination of the whole structure of an action, in all its distinctive parts, for the achievement of the values that are going to be implemented in budgeting. No action taken to introduce a value should prevent the affirmation of other values, whether in the system of values shown in the ethical framework or the values specifically involved in the preparation of the budget.
4. Due to several constraints on the quantity and/or quality of the factors of production available to the firm, it is likely that managers have to choose a preference order for values. The budget can be prepared by starting with the implementation of the values

that have priority over others. Choices about priorities are made on the basis of a moral judgment in the sense indicated earlier.

5. The key factor in this model is on the introduction of values into activity-based budgeting. More specifically, the budgeting process is carried out by incorporating the values into each single element of every activity.[96]

CRITICAL THINKING QUESTIONS

What areas of management in this book have involved the discussion of values? What types of organizational values do you feel will work well with your values? How can value differences hinder an organization and its employees?

Managerial Implications

Many of the mysteries of the seemingly simple budget have been disclosed and analyzed in this chapter. Budgets have been shown to be extremely important mechanisms of financial control, they have been shown to be excellent vehicles for managers to use for decision-making, they have proven to have an unethical side, and they have been examined to find some consistencies in how to have the right people using the right tools to create budgets that maximize stakeholder value.

Some takeaways from this chapter include remembering that effective budgeting requires the existence of the following:

1. Predictive ability
2. Clear channels of communication, authority, and responsibility
3. Accounting-generated accurate, reliable, and timely information
4. Compatibility and understandability of information
5. Support at all levels of the organization: upper, middle, and lower[97]

We have also determined that the most ethical budgets are created by the most ethical people, so organizations should work to:

- Enhance ethical environments (for example, formal ethics codes, ethics training, and socially responsible behavior)
- Provide good management role models
- Reveal truthful information
- Fully cultivate an ethical atmosphere that is sensitive to the pressures employees may feel to game the budget
- Empower employees with greater budgetary responsibility because this also tends to reduce unethical slack creating behaviors

After reviewing the many ways to budget, the importance of understanding financial data like what an income statement provides, and how organizational decision-making is often driven by the "numbers," the final important takeaway is how to ensure those numbers are used for good and not evil. We are a long way off from having a mutually agreed-upon code of ethics for organizations to follow that guarantee stakeholder well-being. However, as the upcoming managers and leaders of the world, *you* will know how to use your values and instill values in your employees and organization so that your budgeting process guarantees that all stakeholders win.

KEY TERMS

TOOLKIT

Activity 14.1

Malaysia Airlines

Malaysia Airlines is owned by individual investors and the Malaysian government, which took over the company in 2014 after two mysterious jet crashes. The airline has lost money and struggled since that time, going through three CEOs. The current CEO, Peter Bellew, is experienced in tourism and travel and has been asked to cut costs and increase revenues. His strategy is to maximize the number of Malaysian Muslims (who make up more than 60% of the population) flying to Mecca for hajj, the annual holy pilgrimage and an obligation for all Muslims who are well enough to travel and can afford the trip. Bellew plans to provide charter flights to make the pilgrimage easier on travelers.

Discussion Questions

1. What are the passenger stakeholder claims on Malaysia Airlines?
2. What are the government stakeholder claims on Malaysia Airlines?
3. What would you advise Bellew to identify as a priority— the demand from pilgrims for easy travel at a reduced price or the demand from the government for profitable operations?

Source: Reprinted from Rice University. (2018). Ethical decision-making and prioritizing stakeholders. In *Business-ethics* (module 3.3). Licensed under Creative Commons license CC BY SA 4.0. Retrieved from https://openstax.org/details/books/business-ethics.

Case Study 14.1

Rising Prescription Costs in America

In a 2016 *JAMA* article, Kesselheim, Avorn, and Sarpatwari reported that Americans spend more money on prescription medications per capita than any other nation on Earth.[98] These costs, according to the authors, are out of sync with the consumer price index (CPI), which charts the average prices of goods in a particular market. Brand-name drug prices are rising far beyond the CPI. Prices have climbed so high that medicines, rather than insurance premiums or even hospital bills, are the largest out-of-pocket health care cost for many Americans.[99]

What Is Causing the Dramatic Price Increases?

It's simple: there is no cost ceiling for medicines in America. Manufacturers of pharmaceuticals can charge whatever they want, and it is likely that the market will bear it because medicines are a necessity. In other words: drug companies raise prices simply because they can, and there is nobody to stop them.

Pharmaceutical companies will, of course, argue that increased costs to the consumer fund research and development. They will cite the high costs of developing innovative, life-saving medicines, arguing that passing this cost onto the consumer keeps them profitable and ensures that they can continue to innovate. But do costs really need to be so high? According to a 2017 AARP cover story, drug companies are incredibly profitable, even considering their extensive research costs. When AARP compared the profits of drug companies to the margins of corporate giants like Coca-Cola, GE, Exxon, and GM, they discovered that drug companies hold five of the top six highest profit margins. The report also demonstrates that most pharmaceutical companies spend more on marketing their existing medicine than developing new drugs.[100]

Of course, researching, developing, and bringing cutting-edge drugs to the marketplace saves and improves the quality of lives. This work absolutely must be encouraged and continue, and it's arguably easier than ever. The number of drug approvals has steadily increased in the last 5 to 10 years. Pharmaceutical companies can often circumvent costly and lengthy regulatory processes, especially in the trial phase, and get drugs to market sooner.[101]

While pharma tends to argue that rising costs are necessary to develop new drugs, we also see astronomical price hikes for drugs that have been on the market for years. For example, recent price increases for the EpiPen (a product containing epinephrine, a decades-old synthetic substitute for adrenaline used to treat life-threatening allergies) made news headlines. Out-of-pocket costs for the medicine rose a whopping 535% between 2007, when generic drug maker Mylan acquired the rights to sell it, and 2014, when Mylan raised the consumer costs from less than $100 to more than $600, according to *JAMA Internal Medicine*.[102] Jacob Sherkow, a law professor at New York Law School, studies the relationship between patent law, scientific developments, and litigation. He summarizes the problem with the EpiPen succinctly, pointing out that people are outraged that a 40-year-old mechanism for using a 100-year-old medicine now costs over $600.

And it's not just prescriptions. Health care costs are rising rapidly across the board. Consumers, physicians, health insurance providers, drug makers, and lawmakers are all grappling with this complex topic. Emergency room physicians, in particular, have a unique vantage point to see the devastating consequences of these soaring costs. They often see families forced to choose between comfortable lifestyles and the cost of care. Families shouldn't have to worry about losing or downgrading their homes in order to afford treatment and prescription copays.[103]

Skyrocketing prices are a huge problem, but even if prices stay stagnant, they have already risen to an unaffordable level. According to a 2017 report from Johns Hopkins University, prescription drugs accounted for 10% of total health care spending, costing Americans $425 billion. The report also cited the unpredictable future of the Affordable Care Act, pointing out that things may get even worse when it comes to drug costs and the expense of health care in general.[104]

Cost fluctuations make it challenging for Americans to create and stick to a health care budget. Unpredictable prescription prices are one of the most difficult aspects of this task. Due to the high costs of care and prescriptions, people are forced to choose between their financial health and their physical health. In the case of a life-sustaining medicine, the choice isn't much of a

choice at all: go broke or die. When a medication needed to treat potentially deadly allergies jumps from $94 to $609, how can one stick to a budget?[105]

The EpiPen is just one of many examples. In 2015, pharma company Valeant raised the price of an essential heart drug, isoproterenol, from about $450 to more than $2,700 per dose—a 600% increase.[106] Erin Fox, who directs the Drug Information Department at University of Utah, helps the hospital develop and reevaluate its drug budget and policies and tracks drug shortages. In an article for the *Harvard Business Review*, she explores the fallout from the uncontained cost of drug prices. In Fox's hospital system alone, the annual inpatient pharmacy cost of one drug the hospital uses for treatment increased 600%, from $300,000 to more than $1,900,000.[107]

Discussion Questions

1. You are the marketing director for Valeant. Part of your compensation plan is profit sharing and is based on the overall profitability of the company from the master budget bottom line. When you hear the announcement about the increase in revenue due to a price hike for your popular drug, isoproterenol, how do you feel?

2. As marketing director, you find out that your budget will be increased by 50% due to the increase in revenue from the sales of isoproterenol. An increase in a department manager's budget is often a sign of a pending promotion. What are your thoughts about the company's increase of the cost of isoproterenol from $444 per dose to $2,700 per dose now that you realize you will probably receive a hefty increase in your profit sharing and a promotion?

3. While you are sitting at your desk at Valeant, you receive a call. Your favorite relative has just been rushed to the local hospital because of chest pains. You drive to the hospital as quickly as possible and are told that your loved one's heart has stopped and they need a dose of an expensive heart medication as soon as possible to revive them. As their medical proxy, you know they are living on a fixed income and have limited prescription coverage, which is how they have ended up in this precarious position. The medicine that will help them the most is $2,700 per dose and is not covered by their insurance. What are your thoughts about the increase in the cost of isoproterenol, and the skyrocketing cost of prescription drugs?

Sources: Adapted from Bose, S. (2017, August 29). The high cost of prescription drugs in the United States. *Huff-Post*. Retrieved from https://www.huffpost.com/entry/the-high-cost-of-prescription-drugs-in-the-united-states_b_59a606aae4b0d81379a81c1f; Chua, K. P., & Conti, R. M. (2017). Out-of-pocket spending among commercially insured patients for epinephrine autoinjectors between 2007 and 2014. *JAMA Internal Medicine, 177*(5), 736–739; Editors of AARP. (2017, April). Why drugs cost so much. *AARP Bulletin*. Retrieved from https://www.aarp

.org/content/dam/aarp/health/healthy-living/2017/04/drug-prices-download-final.pdf; Fox, E. (2017, April 6). How pharma companies game the system to keep drugs expensive. *Harvard Business Review*. Retrieved from https://hbr.org/2017/04/how-pharma-companies-game-the-system-to-keep-drugs-expensive; Gosk, S. (2013). The high cost of prescription drugs. *YouTube*. Retrieved from https://www.youtube.com/watch?v=DheVxefnbD4; Hub Staff Report. (2017, April 3). Examining the rising costs of prescription drugs in the U.S. and possible alternatives. *Johns Hopkins Magazine*. Retrieved from https://hub.jhu.edu/2017/04/03/drug-pricing-health-policy-expert-gerard-anderson/; Kesselheim, A. S., Avorn, J., & Sarpatwari, A. (2016). The high cost of prescription drugs in the United States: Origins and prospects for reform. *JAMA*, *316*(8), 858–871; Rapaport, L. (2017). Another look at the surge in EpiPen costs. *Reuters Health News*. Retrieved from https://www.reuters.com/article/us-health-epipen-costs-idUSKBN16Y24O; WebMD. (n.d.). What conditions does isoproterenol Hcl solution treat? Retrieved from https://www.webmd.com/drugs/2/drug-13986/isoproterenol-injection/details/list-conditions.

Case Study 14.2

Going King Sized in the United States and Crashing on the Couch in China

IKEA is a multinational corporation with a proven track record of listening to stakeholders in ways that improve relationships and the bottom line. The Swedish company has had success in the United States and, more recently, in China by adapting to local cultural norms. For example, in the United States, IKEA solicited the concerns of many of its approximately 50,000 in-store customers and even visited some at home. The company learned, among other things, that U.S. customers assumed IKEA featured only European-size beds. In fact, IKEA has offered king-size beds for years; they simply were not on display. IKEA then began to focus on displaying furniture U.S. consumers were more familiar with and so grew its bedroom furniture sales in 2012 and 2013.

As IKEA expands into China, it has welcomed a different trend—people taking naps on the furniture on display.

"While snoozing is prohibited at IKEA stores elsewhere, the Swedish retailer has long permitted Chinese customers to doze off, rather than alienate shoppers accustomed to sleeping in public."

Adapting to local culture, as these examples demonstrate, is one way a company can respond to stakeholder wishes. The firm abandons some of its usual protocols in exchange for increasing consumer identification with its products.

IKEA appears to have learned what many companies with a global presence have concluded: Stakeholders, and particularly consumer-stakeholders, have different expectations in different geographic settings. Because a firm's ethical obligations include listening and responding to the needs of stakeholders, it behooves all international companies to appreciate the varying perspectives that geography and culture may produce among them.

Discussion Questions

1. Does IKEA have a system to influence stakeholder behavior? If so, describe the system and explain who changes more under the system, IKEA or its consumers.
2. Does IKEA's strategy reflect a normative approach to managing stakeholder claims? If so, how?

Source: Reprinted from Rice University. (2018). Ethical decision-making and prioritizing stakeholders. In *Business ethics* (module 3.3). Licensed under Creative Commons license CC BY SA 4.0. Retrieved from https://openstax.org/details/books/business-ethics.

Self-Assessment 14.1

Managing Budgets

Are you ready to be a manager? A large part of your job will be developing, implementing, reviewing, and reporting to others about various budgets. Rate yourself on the skills and abilities below, as listed by O*NET OnLine,[108] with 5 being the highest ("I am awesome") and 1 being the lowest ("I need some serious help here").

Statements	Strongly Disagree (Help)	Disagree	Neutral	Agree	Strongly Agree (Awesome)
1. I feel I am able to summarize budgets and submit recommendations for the approval or disapproval of funds requests.	1	2	3	4	5
2. I feel I am able to analyze monthly department budgeting and accounting reports to maintain expenditure controls.	1	2	3	4	5
3. I feel I am able to examine budget estimates for completeness, accuracy, and conformance with procedures and regulations.	1	2	3	4	5

4. I feel I am able to direct the preparation of regular and special budget reports.	1	2	3	4	5
5. I feel I am able to provide advice and technical assistance with cost analysis, fiscal allocation, and budget preparation.	1	2	3	4	5
6. I feel I am good at active listening—giving full attention to what other people are saying, taking time to understand the points being made, asking questions as appropriate, and not interrupting at inappropriate times.	1	2	3	4	5
7. I feel I am good at reading comprehension—understanding written sentences and paragraphs in work-related documents.	1	2	3	4	5
8. I feel I am good at critical thinking—using logic and reasoning to identify the strengths and weaknesses of alternative solutions, conclusions, or approaches to problems.	1	2	3	4	5
9. I feel I am good at mathematics—using mathematics to solve problems.	1	2	3	4	5
10. I feel I am good at communicating—talking to others to convey information effectively.	1	2	3	4	5

Source: Adapted from O*NET OnLine. (2019). Budget analysts. Retrieved from https://www.onetonline.org/link/summary/13-2031.00.

Now list your scores below and add them up. The first five items and number 9 were the technical and analytical side of budgeting, and 6, 7, 8, and 10 were the softer skills. This is because when you are gathering, using, or communicating your budget numbers, you need to be able to do this in the most effective way possible.

Technical Skills

1. _____
2. _____
3. _____
4. _____
5. _____
9. _____

Total: _____ (30 is the highest; you would like 25 or higher)

Soft Skills

6. _____
7. _____

8. _____
10. _____

Total: _____ (20 is the highest; you would like 16 or higher)

Discussion Questions

1. What skills do you need to work on most to become a manager with budgeting responsibilities?
2. How can you improve your scores on those items where your scores were lower?
3. Which items did you score well on?
4. Why do you think that is?
5. Summarize your budgeting knowledge, from the chapter and the assessment. Keep your results in mind and add them to your SWOT analysis.

$SAGE edge™

Get the tools you need to sharpen your study skills. SAGE edge offers a robust online environment featuring an impressive array of free tools and resources. Access practice quizzes, eFlashcards, video, and multimedia at **edge.sagepub.com/scanduragower**.

CHAPTER 15

MANAGEMENT CONTROL SYSTEMS AND TECHNOLOGY

CHAPTER LEARNING OBJECTIVES

After studying this chapter, you should be able to:

15.1 Understand the critical role of "control" in planning, organizing, and leading.

15.2 Describe the different types of control systems.

15.3 Recognize the correct types of control systems for an organization depending on its context.

15.4 Understand how to establish control systems for performance success.

15.5 Recognize the critical role technology plays in effective quality management.

15.6 Apply data analytics to control for maximum firm performance.

Get the edge on your studies at **edge.sagepub.com/ scanduragower.**

- Take the chapter quiz
- Review key terms with eFlashcards
- Explore multimedia resources, SAGE readings, and more!

What Is Management Control?

Remember our opening discussion in Chapter 14 about how budgets and management control would give you the competitive advantage over your colleagues? You can probably already tell that knowing about budgets is crucial, and this final chapter takes everything we have discussed throughout the whole book and teaches you to create a variety of control systems to help you apply the knowledge and skills you have learned and use them to manage and adjust the resources, stakeholders, plans, and financials of your organization.

Think about your own life again. You now have a good grasp of how much budgeting knowledge goes into everything, but then we also know how much life changes. If the car breaks down, do you repair it or get another one? If you have one class that takes up 80% of your time, do you continue to balance your studying like that or reallocate your resources? After you graduate, do you still get to run home and nap between projects or get regular vacations, or do you need to build up your stamina for 50 weeks of work a year and look forward to paid holidays and two weeks of vacation? (Sorry for that reality blast!)

Organizations, as you know by now, have even more moving parts, and these parts need oversight and control to keep them running smoothly. Even organizations that sound like they would be great to work for because of the **laissez-faire** (easygoing) attitude they seemingly take toward controls end up having to implement controls. An employee of a super-hip new technology company recently related this story:

> In 2016, we were a small dotcom that offered unlimited time off and vacation. We could work from anywhere, and every year our annual meeting was held in Cancun. Our employees were all over the country, so the organization flew us there for a half day of meetings and then gave us a couple of paid days in a nice resort hotel and then flew us home.

> By 2019, the annual meeting was a virtual conference call, and despite the growth of the business internationally there were layoffs. Now employees put in for time off—even for short-term things like doctor's appointments.

This is a fairly common story. Companies who want to stay laid back soon realize that any of a variety of changes in how, where, and why they exist forces them to step back and begin putting guidelines and rules in place (controls) to keep track of what they are doing and make sure they continue to maximize stakeholder wealth.

Controlling is the umbrella over planning, organizing, and leading.
©iStockphoto.com/Sabin_Acharya

Think of controlling as the umbrella over planning, organizing, and leading. Each of these areas needs controls each step of the way. That's why management textbooks show controlling as a separate function of the management process.

In this chapter, controlling will be shown as an integral part of each of the management roles. In the next section, we will talk more about why control is critical and why your understanding of the control process and its overall importance and application will give you the competitive advantage over your college graduate peers.

Management Control as the Umbrella of Management

Learning Objective 15.1: Understand the critical role of "control" in planning, organizing, and leading.

Organizational control comprises the "development of rules, guidelines, procedures, limits, or other protocols for directing the work and processes of employees and departments. These controls can include setting rules or procedures for financial transactions, employee behavior, and specific practices for all or individual departments. A control can depend on an individual employee following the guideline, or require multiple parties to agree on an action."[1]

Although control is often lumped in as one of the managerial functions, it is the critical function because it helps to check errors and take corrective action. According to modern concepts, control is a "foreseeing" action, whereas earlier concepts of control were simply systems put into place once errors were detected. Control means "to check, verify, and regulate." In management terms, this means setting standards, measuring actual performance, and taking corrective action.[2]

Although the first definition sounds pretty intense, the second one breaks it down into management language. The challenging part now is to understand that controls are needed at every step of the management process. If you break down the definitions above, just a single control can be aimed at an employee, a group of employees, a department, all departments, behaviors, and finances.

The group of controls working together is known as a **management control system** (MCS). The goal of the MCS is to allow an organization to live its best life by raising the performance of the company, with an objective to define and align the entire organization toward a common strategy that is sustainable for all.[3] In other words, all of the stakeholders benefit from the control system. The system also ties back into the organization's strategic plan, as we discussed in Chapter 5, because the plan drives the controls and the controls provide the feedback loop needed to act as a checks-and-balances system for the strategic plan.

Another phrase often used in place of MCS (and noted in the definition above) is **performance measurement** (PM).[4] Interestingly, despite being a part of the accounting literature for decades, there has been little explicit theoretical and empirical research on the concept of MCS[5] or PM as holistic approaches to organizational control. Even now, strategic management researchers say that firms still need appropriate controls for capabilities to materialize into performance,[6] as effective control systems lag behind the strategic developments and growth of a globalized society.

Let's take another look at our management model in Figure 15.0, which features a list of all of the chapters in this book.

Based on what we have discussed in this book and even in this chapter so far, you can probably imagine that the controlling aspect of management is now a piece of the management function that needs to be moved to the top of the management model because it pertains to every aspect of what a manager and leader must monitor constantly to achieve maximum stakeholder satisfaction and performance. Table 15.1 outlines each chapter and a potential area in that chapter that can be impacted by lack of controls and feedback.

▼ FIGURE 15.0
Management Functions

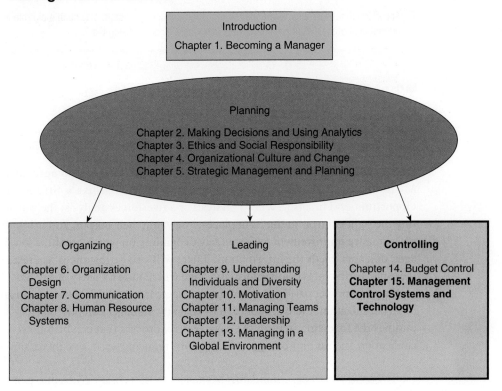

▼ TABLE 15.1

Control Examples in the Management Model

Chapter	Topic	Area Impacted by Lack of Controls and Feedback
1	Becoming a Manager	Task performance, team performance, and operational efficiency
2	Making Decisions and Using Analytics	Using budgets and data
3	Ethics and Social Responsibility	Establishing values for the manager, employees, and organization
4	Organizational Culture and Change	Managing communication, values, and resources
5	Strategic Management and Planning	Accounting for all stakeholders and resources in the mission and vision
6	Organization Design	Having the right skills and abilities in the right format for the mission and vision
7	Communication	Keeping in mind the audience, purpose, and feedback for all messaging
8	Human Resource Systems	Hiring, performance, retention, and off-boarding
9	Understanding Individuals and Diversity	Instilling knowledge and values so each stakeholder is recognized as a valued member
10	Motivation	Using fair and equitable rewards, systems, and oversight to keep employees satisfied and motivated
11	Managing Teams	Creating effective team dashboards
12	Leadership	Taking responsibility and accountability for what you are leading
13	Managing in a Global Environment	Understanding the large world and the impact it can have on your organization, resources, and stakeholders
14	Budget Control	Using the financials to manage all the departments and organization to reach objectives, goals, and the mission
15	Management Control Systems and Technology	Taking Chapters 1–14 and putting them all together to create a system of controls that offer oversight, planning, and feedback to the stakeholders who need it

> According to researchers, why does the management control system play such a big role in accounting but not in strategy? What are some ways you would go about fixing that?

What Types of Control Systems Are Used by Organizations?

Learning Objective 15.2: Describe the different types of control systems.

Here is where the really interesting part comes in. There is no agreement on the ideal MCS, and no tried-and-true MCS currently exists. Unlike a Strengths-Weaknesses-Opportunities-Threats (SWOT) analysis or a five-forces analysis, the way to go about putting the right controls in the right places, analyzing their output, and using the feedback for performance improvement varies widely depending on which organization, industry, manager, or leader needs the information. There will also be instances where a combination of these need different types of information and will require a variety of MCSs.

Since the proper performance of the management control function is critical to the success of an organization, there are some steps that any manager can put in place. Talia Lambarki outlines the following steps in the basic control process that can be followed for almost any application, such as improving product quality, reducing waste, and increasing sales:

1. *Setting performance standards.* Managers must translate plans into performance standards. These performance standards can be in the form of goals, such as revenue from sales over a period of time. The standards should be attainable, measurable, and clear.
2. *Measuring actual performance.* If performance is not measured, it cannot be ascertained whether standards have been met.
3. *Comparing actual performance with standards or goals.* Accept or reject the product or outcome.
4. *Analyzing deviations.* Managers must determine why standards were not met. This step also involves determining whether more control is necessary or if the standard should be changed.

5. *Taking corrective action.* After the reasons for deviations have been determined, managers can then develop solutions for issues with meeting the standards and make changes to processes or behaviors.[7]

Timing of Controls

When you think about control processes or activities, think about timing. Controls can be instituted for a past action or process, a future problem or scenario, or an ongoing concern in the present. **Feedback control** relates to something that has already happened. **Proactive control** concerns the future. **Concurrent control** is focused on the present.[8]

As mentioned earlier, thinking about things and being able to plan for them *before* they happen are a huge benefit to an organization. For example, suppose you know there is a new, competitive product entering the industry in about a year. Instead of waiting for feedback control (after the product has launched) that the new product is eating into your sales, you want to proactively control for that

Control systems measure performance and compare it to standards.

©iStockphoto.com/baranozdemir

and add new features or even come up with a new product before that happens. Below is additional information about the importance of feedback timing.

Feedback

Feedback is a reactive control. It happens when a process or activity has already been completed. For example, a manager might assess a sales team's performance by comparing their target sales to their actual sales figures. Did they hit the target or do they need to continue working on the goal? If they were successful, the techniques they used can continue. If not, tweaks can be made to adjust the process going forward.

Here's another example of feedback control. Imagine a production team that has to fulfill a large order quarterly. The production manager decides to break the quarterly goal into three monthly targets. The team works for one month on the first target. At the end of the month, the manager reviews the production progress to determine whether or not the team hit the target. If the team was successful, they move on to the next target. If not, the manager may tweak the process, provide additional resources, bring on more workers, or make other adjustments. Once the changes are implemented, the manager will set another timeframe to come back and re-evaluate.

One pitfall of feedback control is that it is reactive rather than proactive. Adjustments and improvements can only be made after the process is finished or the action is complete. A project may be finished before the manager spots a problem with the work, for example. Feedback control works best for projects that are cyclical (e.g., repeated quarterly) rather than one-off activities or tasks.

Proactive Control

Proactive control is about stopping a problem before it starts. You may also hear proactive control referred to as preliminary, prevention, or feed-forward control. It involves getting out in front of potential troubles, rather than waiting for a bad result. Proactive control is about preventing a problem or intervening rather than trying to repair it after the fact. For example, an automotive engineer performs crash tests on the brake system of a new vehicle prototype *before* the vehicle is mass produced.

It is often said that "prevention is the best medicine," and this is the spirit of proactive control. While not every bad outcome is foreseeable, thinking one step ahead is an important aspect of managing and planning.

Concurrent Control

Concurrent control happens in real time. It may include monitoring, standards, rules, codes, and policies put in place to control processes while they are happening. Fleet tracking is just one example of current control. GPS technology enables managers in the transportation industry to monitor destinations, routes, and more. Managers can exercise concurrent control by detouring drivers to avoid traffic or road hazards and keep tabs on drivers' compliance with company policies (e.g., not running their own errands during work time).

Monitoring employee internet activity is another example of concurrent control. At Keen Media, for instance, employees keep a digital record of their work day with the goal of increasing efficiency and eliminating distractions. IT can issue reports showing how much time employees spent online away from work-related activities.

Figure 15.1 illustrates the control process. The process is at the center and the controls happen around it.[9]

So far, the explanations of how controls work, and a rundown of their importance in every area of management, might seem like a daunting endeavor. The graphic in Figure 15.2 might make it look a little easier, or perhaps will at least help you understand why managers make the big bucks.

▼ FIGURE 15.1

The Control Process Loop

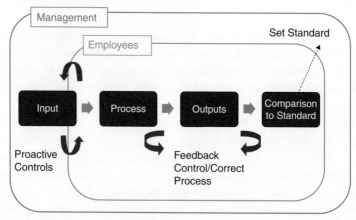

Source: Adapted from Carroll, R. (n.d.). The control process. *Lumen Learning*. Licensed under Creative Commons license CC BY 4.0. Retrieved from https://courses.lumenlearning.com/wm-principlesofmanagement/chapter/the-control-process/.

In the next section, we will discuss the varying levels of control in an organization. Understanding these different levels will help you decide what level of control you need to implement for your department or project.

Types of Controls Based on Organizational Need

Learning Objective 15.3: Recognize the correct types of control systems for an organization depending on its context.

Managers can implement varying levels of control ranging from high-level strategic control to midlevel operational control and low-level tactical control. Consider this sample scenario. A company president sets out to build new headquarters. She calls on the company's board to help her make big-picture decisions, such as the location of the new building, the size, and architectural elements (strategic control). The project manager helps the president develop a detailed project schedule to stay on task and on budget (operational control). Finally, a general contractor supervises workers, shops for materials and equipment, and implements rules to keep workers safe (tactical control). Learn more about each level of control below.

Strategic Control

Strategic control helps managers stay aligned with high-level goals, making sure that the company is headed in the right direction.[10] This level of control involves observing and assessing strategy as it is being implemented. Managers must also carefully consider any deviations from the plan and make adjustments as needed.

Sometimes unforeseen events or circumstances call for immediate reassessment of strategy. Instances like this might include drastic changes in the market (e.g., a stock market crash, the emergence of a new competitor, or a product failure).

Implementation of a strategy is sometimes a cumulative process with a series of activities happening over a set increment of time. Managers can set milestones, evaluating the strategy at regular intervals to gauge effectiveness and make determinations about whether or not the strategy is progressing as planned.

Strategic control entails tracking internal and external events. Information from inside and outside the organization is required. Possible sources of this valuable data include communications with customers, trade and industry publications, trade shows, conferences, observation of competitors, and even feedback *from* competitors. For instance, Toyota provides tours of its plants, sharing details about its business strategy, called "The Toyota Way," to the public and even its competitors.

Errors made with regard to strategic control are typically serious (think: failing to adequately assess a competitor's product and losing customers). One example of such a failure is BlackBerry. The electronics company once held a formidable position in the corporate cell phone market but didn't notice that consumers were switching to iPhone, a competitor. BlackBerry never recovered from this strategic control error.[11]

Operational Control

While strategic control provides the overall direction for the organization, **operational control** involves assessing immediate operations and processes.[12] Operational control systems make sure that business activities and projects are consistent with strategic plans. Middle management implements operational controls to evaluate decisions in the short term (over one to two years), so they can take action to correct any performance problems. Actions may include training, disciplinary tactics, improvement plans, incentives, or even termination.

Operational control focuses on internal sources of information rather than looking outside the company at the marketplace or the competition. Rather than the company as a whole, it affects smaller business units or departments (sales, marketing, etc.) or other aspects of the organization such as production goals or materials and equipment options.[13] Errors or mismanagement of operational controls can result in missed deadlines or failure to produce deliverables. For example, if employees responsible for production are not trained properly and in a timely fashion, production targets may go unmet.

While strategic control requires internal and external information, operational control focuses on what's going on within an organization.

©iStockphoto.com/AndreyPopov

Tactical Control

A tactic is the approach for meeting a particular objective. **Tactical control** deals with the current day-to-day operations implemented to work toward specific strategic objectives. Managers determine who must do what in order for the organization to be successful in the near future (within the next year or sooner). For instance, consider a wholesale bakery. The CEO sets a marketing strategy to develop an eCommerce platform to sell products to restaurants and hotels. Tactical control in this situation would entail regularly meeting with the marketing team to develop a plan for meeting this objective—including steps, roles, and processes—and routinely assessing progress. Tactics for the eCommerce marketing strategy might include the following:

- Building a targeted list of local restaurants and hotels
- Outlining a process for how the website would be used to process orders making in-person visits to chefs at targeted venues
- Monitoring sales via the eCommerce platform to determine whether or not sales are on target[14]

Strategic control is always the first level of control. Next comes operational control. Finally, there's tactical control. Consider the following example:

1. *Strategic.* A company decides to pursue a strategy of becoming more energy efficient.
2. *Operational.* The company makes an operational decision to get a Leadership in Energy and Environmental Design (LEED) certification. To obtain the certification, the

company must earn a certain number of points. Points are awarded for energy initiatives such as time thermostats, sensors that shut off lights when a room is unoccupied, and replacing chemicals with green cleaning solutions.

3. *Tactical.* The company's tactical decision is to decide which energy efficient equipment should be purchased.

Control can be objective or normative. Objective control involves objectives that can be quantified or measured (e.g., a particular sales volume, a specific profit margin, a given level of inventory efficiency). Normative control involves the company's social norms—employees learn the values and beliefs of a company and learn what is expected of them by observing other employees.[15]

Objective and Normative Control

Objective control is based on measurements that can be quantified and tested. Objective control isn't about subjective rules or ambiguous policies. Rather, it focuses on measurable progress, behavior, or output. For example, assume that a clothing store wants its employees to be friendly to shoppers. What does friendly mean? How does one measure "friendly"? To make the control objective, management could create a clear, measurable method for friendliness. For example, they could implement the following policies:

1. Employees must smile at all customers and greet them no more than 15 seconds after they have entered the store.
2. Employees must ask each customer they encounter "How may I help you today?"

Output control is a form of objective control. Some organizations, such as tech company Yahoo, have ditched set rigid rules about work hours and instead set output goals for employees. Programmers' output can be measured whether they work from 9 a.m. to 5 p.m. or prefer to come into the office from noon to 8 p.m.

Normative controls regulate actual behavior and behavioral expectations rather than objective written policies and procedures. This type of control uses values and beliefs called norms, which are established standards of behavior. Informal rules demonstrate how workers are expected to behave and complete their duties. Team interactions and relationships are built over time organically, rather than dictated by a formal handbook or manual. Team members come to a natural, informal consensus about how work will be completed and divided, often according to team members' strengths, weaknesses, and interests. These unwritten "rules" are strong influences on behavior and interaction.

Normative control reflects the organization's culture, the shared values among the members of the organization. Every organization has its own culture and its own behavioral norms. It can take time for employees to get a feel for how their organization works. One company may expect employees to be self-starters who jump in and solve problems on their own without talking things through with a supervisor to solve problems. Another may require a manager's buy-in for solutions or insist on approval from leadership before workers discuss changes outside the department. Some topics might be considered off-limits, while others are talked about openly.[16] Companies differ in the approaches to control. Most have a mix of objective and normative controls, but some are more traditional, relying strictly on a top-down approach.

Top-Down Controls

Top-down control relies on rules, regulations, and formal policies to establish authority and govern employee performance. This is also known as bureaucratic control. Budgets, statistical reports, and performance appraisals are all results-oriented examples of top-down controls.

Top-down control is seen in organizations where senior leadership makes important decisions, develops policies, and maintains authority over implementing these decisions and policies. Lower-level managers may make suggestions for their departments, but leadership rests primarily in the hands of senior management.

Top-down control has some advantages. For example, employees don't make big-picture strategic decisions or help develop process and policy. Therefore, they can focus exclusively on their job duties rather than concerning themselves with the direction of the company. Executives don't have to provide context for the ideas they have implemented. Businesses that operate in heavily regulated industries typically find this approach more useful than other kinds of companies.

Yet there are also disadvantages to top-down control. Because lower-level employees often work more closely with customers and are frequently better positioned to spot new trends or notice new competition, senior management can miss opportunities or threats. A heavy-handed top-down approach can also hamper communication, discouraging employees from sharing information, input, and suggestions with upper management.[17]

So far, we have talked about the need for controls and the types of controls that can be used throughout the organization. At this point, though, you might be asking yourself how organizations keep track of all those controls and make sure the organizational system as a whole is balancing all of its critical needs. Next, we will talk about a tool for this—a balanced scorecard.

Using Controls to Forecast, Track, and Balance Organizational Systems

Learning Objective 15.4: Understand how to establish control systems for performance success.

The human body is made up of separate, complex systems that work together to keep it functioning. The same is true of business organizations. Just as you must have regular checkups to make sure that your body is healthy, organizations should monitor all of the systems that keep them up and running. Although we may not always head to the doctor until we have a cough or aches and pains, regular health maintenance exams are essential.

In the case of an organization, a balanced scorecard is its regular physical. A **balanced scorecard** is a tool for keeping a continuous record and measurement of the company's condition.[18]

The Balanced Scorecard

The balanced scorecard (BSC) is a strategic planning and management system that organizations use to:

- Clearly establish and communicate their goals and objectives
- Consider strategy as the organizing principle for everyone's day-to-day work
- Map out projects, products, and services
- Track and evaluate progress toward the achievement of strategic targets[19]

The Gartner Group estimates that over half of large business organizations in America implement the BSC method of assessment. In fact, many large businesses around the world also make use of the balanced scorecard to monitor and assess operations. Focusing on financial results alone,[20] rather than considering a broader view of overall company health and stakeholder values, can result in mistakes. The scorecard system was developed to help prevent this kind of shortsightedness. The balanced scorecard enables organizations to set goals that relate to customers, financial health, strategy, and learning and growth opportunities (see Figure 15.2).

The Balanced Scorecard

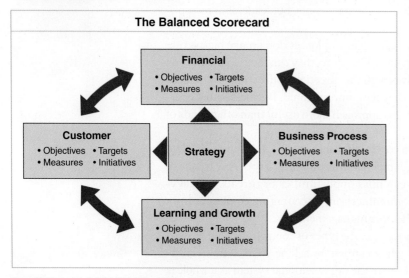

Source: Mackinnon, L. A. K. (2007). Think Differently! Personal Balanced Scorecard. Licensed under Creative Commons Attribution Share-Alike 3.0 Australia. Retrieved from https://www.think-differently.org/2007/09/7-steps-to-developing-and-using-your/.

As we discussed in Chapter 5 regarding how strategy drives an organization, and in the same way it provides a checkpoint for the organization to be sure it is maintaining its balance.

Balanced Scorecard Components

The balanced scorecard is still a popular management method. In 2014, it was rated sixth on global consultant organization Bain & Company's top 10 list of management tools.[21] A balanced scorecard generally entails the following components.

Learning and Growth Culture Assessment

Taking stock of learning and growth opportunities helps managers evaluate company culture. Is the company fostering an environment where learning and growth are valued? Are employees developing professionally? Is the company expanding its capacities? Is the organization taking advantage of the latest, most innovative technology? Can and do employees access continuing education? Is the company aggressive about recruiting the most qualified talent? Managers must be intentional and diligent about evaluating organizational culture in the areas of learning and growth.

Learning and growth are the lifeblood of a healthy, functioning company. To be competitive and endure, a company must value and continually seek opportunities in this arena.

Internal Business Processes Assessment

What does the day-to-day running of the company look like? Managers must critically analyze quality, efficiency, and the company's ability to adapt to changes (both internal and external).

Customer Satisfaction Assessment

Customer satisfaction is often measured via surveys to existing customers, but another valuable and often-overlooked tool is checking in with customers who have switched to another brand or disengaged altogether. According to "The Value of Keeping the Right Customers," a report from the *Harvard Business Review*, securing new customers is much more expensive than maintaining relationships with existing customers. It can cost between five and a whopping 25 times more to find a new customer than to keep a current customer happy.[22] That's why it is essential for companies to assess customer satisfaction, determine whether they are meeting customers' needs and wants efficiently, and take steps to correct any problems. Without customers, the business will go under.

Financial Assessments

Financial success is, of course, the backbone of for-profit organizations. If companies aren't succeeding financially, they aren't succeeding. Focusing on great customer service or innovative products means nothing if a company is not financially healthy. Managers can use metrics such as revenue, profit, and return on investment to assess financial health. They may also evaluate asset turnover, liquidity, and gross profit margin.

Why Do Companies Need a Balanced Scorecard?

Before 1992, Fannie Mae, a financial services company, tied employee compensation directly to a wide variety of performance metrics. In 1992, they implemented a new compensation structure, tying all incentive pay for executives to just two measurements. This quadrupled bonuses and incentives for Fannie Mae execs. In 1993, executives received a total of $8.5 million in incentives. By 2000, the number had climbed to $35.2 million. Just three years later, in 2003, the regulator monitoring Fannie Mae discovered accounting fraud.[23]

In the absence of a balanced scorecard, executives can develop tunnel vision, focusing on only a few aspects of the organization and missing important information about others. Just because a company is performing well financially doesn't mean there aren't performance problems in other areas. Ultimately, if left unchecked, areas of weakness could threaten strengths and potentially destroy the company. A company could, for instance, excel at meeting customer expectations or being a good corporate citizen but have a low profit margin, preventing it from being competitive or overcoming challenges.

A BSC necessitates a comprehensive examination of the company's performance and overall state. It enables management to assess effectiveness and implement improvement programs as needed. You can see that the scorecard takes into account nearly all the aspects of the organization. However, the scorecard is also based on feedback, for the most part, on things that have already happened. So, although the balanced scorecard gives you a good picture of your current health, it does not give you a prognosis of what might happen as a result of the scores or a forecast of what might lie ahead.[24]

In 2010, the same Bain survey ranked the balanced scorecard first in the world of management tools; by 2017, it had fallen out of the top 10.[25] Many organizations still use it as a control mechanism, so be prepared for your after-college-career to include balanced scorecard systems, but companies with the finances and technology have moved on to more sophisticated tools of control that can provide prognoses and forecasts, known as big data and data analytics.

Technology and Data Analytics as Management Control

Learning Objective 15.5: Recognize the critical role technology plays in effective quality management.

If you are already a little taken aback by the amount of information a balanced scorecard approach to management control needs, welcome to big data, data analytics, and 2020. It is not surprising that evolving technology would bring management control along for the ride, but what a ride it is. In Chapter 2, you had a brief overview of big data and business analytics as decision-making tools.

This chapter, however, will introduce you to the comprehensiveness of big data, the many tools available to analyze the types of big data, and how it is used as a control mechanism not just for marketing and sales-type decisions but also for the many moving parts of an organization. We will also discuss how data analytics helps an organization with seeing the future, planning for the future, and making rapid changes to any parts of the organization that are not working according to those plans or that will foster the success of new plans.

Imagine for a second that you could have every single part of your life—school (books, classes, teachers, costs), friends (ages, locations, heights, favorite foods), and transportation (car, insurance, gas, tolls, parking), for example—feed into one software system for organizational purposes. That is big data.

Big data is used as a control mechanism in organizations.

©iStockphoto.com/Artem Peretiatko

Now imagine that all of that big data is being analyzed so that you know where all your friends are at any given time, you can decide who to invite out for Mexican food that night (based on their food preferences), you know how you are going to get to the restaurant (where to get gas, where to park, etc.), and you know how much time you could spend socializing because you also need to study for your management exam the next day. This information prints out on your computer screen or pops up on your smartwatch to help you make the best decision you need to make, or might need to make, for everything in your life. That is **data analytics**.

For more about how all of this works, let's look at what big data is and examine the ways it is transformed for analytical purposes.

What Is Big Data?

A huge repository of terabytes of data is generated *each day* from modern information systems and digital technologies such as the Internet of Things (IoT), which is a system of computers and digital machines that are connected to an internet service provider (yes, it's a thing), and cloud computing. Analysis of these massive data requires a lot of effort at multiple levels to extract knowledge for decision-making.[26]

There is no quantitative measurement for exactly how large a database must be in order to be considered "big." Rather, big data is defined by the need for the development of innovative tools and methods to process it. To use big data, you need programs and machinery that can communicate quickly and efficiently to sort, categorize, and summarize data.

It takes a lot of work to turn a mass of raw data into useful information. Special programming techniques are required to get multiple machines and programs to "collaborate" when it comes to data processing and analyzing. It is usually faster for programs to process data stored locally instead of on a network. One major aspect of thinking about big data is how to distribute it across a cluster of machines and how to make those machines network together efficiently.[27]

What Does "Big Data" Mean?

What kinds of datasets are considered "big data"? The possibilities for using big data are almost as large in scale as the data itself. You've likely heard of the ways that large tech corporations like Facebook and Google use big data. Social media networks sort through and analyze users' data to show them relevant ads and targeted content. Search engines analyze the relationship between queries and results to present users with more relevant answers to their questions. Have you ever wondered why you searched for shoes on one website and then all of the sudden advertisements for those shoes show up on your social media feeds? Boom! Data analytics is crunching big data and selling that data to the social media site.

Yet this is only the tip of the big data iceberg. Possibilities for the use of big data are much deeper. Two of the largest datasets in today's world are transactional data and sensor data. Transactional data include a range of information, from stock prices and bank data to an individual store's record of purchases. Sensor data comes from the IoT. Sensor data could include anything and everything from location data on a cellular network, to passenger boarding information taken on a public transit system, to information taken from internet-connected robots in a factory, to the electrical usage data from your own home.[28]

The Four "V's" About Big Data

Data scientists describe "big data" as data containing four main characteristics, known as the "four V's": volume, velocity, veracity, and variety.

Volume refers to the scale of the data and is the main characteristic that makes data "big." Big data domains are those able to store data in the order of size, ranging from a petabyte to an exabyte. One exabyte equals 1 billion gigabytes, which is quite large considering our smartphones work with memories of 16 gigabytes, on average. Storage volumes, such as those in smartphones, are much smaller than volumes produced by the acquiring of data, which globally sum up to the order of zettabytes (one zettabyte equals 1,000 exabytes), due to the fact that storage data are often heavily cut back due to quality control and data reduction processes.[29]

The Big Data Framework describes volume this way:

> The volume of data refers to the size of the data sets that need to be analyzed and processed, which are now frequently larger than terabytes and petabytes. The sheer volume of the data requires distinct and different processing technologies than traditional storage and processing capabilities. In other words, this means that the data sets in Big Data are too large to process with a regular laptop or desktop processor. An example of a high-volume data set would be all credit card transactions on a day within Europe.[30]

The uses of big data are varied.

Image by Mary Pahlke from Pixabay

Velocity, the second "V," refers to the frequency of incoming data that needs to be processed. If you think about how many Instagram stories, text messages, and credit card purchases are being sent every day, you can have a good appreciation of velocity. Extremely large data volumes require extreme remedies. Uploading 100 petabytes of data over the internet today would still take about 30 years even with high-speed internet.[31]

The other two "V's" are more critical: veracity and variety. **Veracity** refers to the trustworthiness of the data[32] or the quality of the data being analyzed. High-veracity data is viewed as trustworthy and meaningful, whereas low-veracity data is untrustworthy and meaningless. The low-veracity data is referred to as noise. One example of a high-veracity data set would be data from a scientific experiment.[33]

Variety is the many sources, as noted above, and the many different forms[34] that data can take.

> Variety makes Big Data really big. Big Data comes from a great variety of sources and generally is one out of three types: structured, semi structured, and unstructured data. The variety in data types frequently requires distinct processing capabilities and specialist algorithms. An example of high variety data sets would be the CCTV audio and video files that are generated at various locations in a city.[35]

Perhaps you have noticed during your latest television and movie viewing that nearly every modern investigative show has somebody saying "check the CCTV (closed-circuit television) camera feeds in the area."

Lucy Roberts offers a brief history of CCTV that helps you understand why:

> Nothing changed the concept of or the public's awareness of video surveillance as much as the tragic events of September 11, 2001 when the World Trade Center was attacked by terrorists. Where once people saw video surveillance as an issue that might never affect them, it was now an issue of immediate and lasting importance. Software developers began refining programs that would enhance video surveillance, including facial recognition programs that could compare various key facial feature points in order to match

recorded faces to known mug shots or photographs of terrorists or criminals. While the earlier versions weren't always reliable, the later versions became more refined and were phased into use by law enforcement in some areas.[36]

Now imagine all the CCTV cameras lining streets, attached to businesses, and outside peoples' homes, and you can imagine the incredible amount of just video data that is recorded each day.

Data About Data: Structured, Semi-Structured, and Unstructured Data

The previous discussion of data variety mentioned structured data, semi-structured data, and unstructured data. Figure 15.3 shows how these types of data all flow into what is known as metadata.

A data structure is defined as "a particular way of organizing and storing data in a computer such that it can be accessed and modified efficiently. More precisely, a data structure is a collection of data values, the relationships among them, and the functions or operations that can be applied to the data."[37] For the analysis of data, it is important to understand that there are three common types of data structures: structured, semi-structured, and unstructured. Finally, it is most important to understand that these three are all used to flow into what organizations need to use to control their systems—metadata.

Structured Data

Structured data is data that adheres to a predefined data model and is therefore straightforward to analyze. Structured data conforms to a tabular format with a relationship between the different rows and columns. Common examples of structured data are Excel files or Structured Query Language (SQL) databases. Each of these have structured rows and columns that can be sorted.

Structured data depends on the existence of a data model—a model of how data can be stored, processed and accessed. Because of a data model, each field is discrete and can be accesses separately or jointly along with data from other fields. This makes structured data extremely powerful because it is possible to quickly aggregate data from various locations in the database. Structured data is considered the most "traditional" form of data storage, since the earliest versions of database management systems were able to store, process and access structured data.

Unstructured Data

Unstructured data is information that either does not have a predefined data model or is not organized in a predefined manner. Unstructured information is typically text heavy but may also contain data such as dates, numbers, and facts. This results in irregularities and ambiguities that make it difficult to understand using traditional programs compared to

▼ FIGURE 15.3

How Structured Data Becomes Metadata

| Structured Data | Textual Data | Image File | Video | Audio | XML Data | JSON Data | Sensor Data | Metadata |

Source: Big Data Framework. (2019). Data types: Structured vs. unstructured data. Licensed under a Creative Commons Attribution-ShareAlike 4.0 International License. Retrieved from https://www.bigdataframework.org/data-types-structured-vs-unstructured-data/.

data stored in structured databases. Common examples of unstructured data include audio files, video files, or Non-SQL databases.

The ability to store and process unstructured data has grown greatly in recent years, with many new technologies and tools coming to the market that are able to store specialized types of unstructured data. MongoDB, for example, is optimized to store documents. Apache Giraph, as an opposite example, is optimized for storing relationships between nodes.

The ability to analyze unstructured data is especially relevant in the context of big data, since a large part of data in organizations is unstructured. Some examples include pictures, videos, or PDF documents. The ability to extract value from unstructured data is one of main drivers behind the quick growth of big data (Figure 15.4).

Semi-Structured Data

Semi-structured data is a form of structured data that does not conform with the formal structure of data models associated with relational databases or other forms of data tables, but nonetheless contain tags or other markers to separate semantic elements and enforce hierarchies of records and fields within the data. Therefore, it is also known as self-describing structure. Examples of semi-structured data include Java-Script Object Notation (JSON) and eXtensible Markup Language (XML).

The reason that this third category exists (between structured and unstructured data) is because semi-structured data is considerably easier to analyze than unstructured data. Many big data solutions and tools have the ability to "read" and process either JSON or XML, which reduces the complexity to analyze structured data compared to unstructured data.

Metadata: The Real Data About Data

The final data type is **metadata**. From a technical point of view, this is not a separate data structure but it is one of the most important elements for big data analysis and big data solutions. Metadata is data about data. It provides additional information about a specific set of data.

In a set of photographs, for example, metadata could describe when and where the photos were taken. The metadata then provides fields for dates and locations, which by themselves can be considered structured data. For this reason, metadata is frequently used by big data solutions for initial analysis.[38]

In summary, "Data that is high volume, high velocity and high variety must be processed with advanced tools (analytics and algorithms) to reveal meaningful information. Because of these characteristics of the data, the knowledge domain that deals with the storage, processing, and analysis of these data sets has been labeled Big Data."[39]

▼ FIGURE 15.4
Analytics at Work

With 80 percent of new data growth existing as unstructured content—from text files to 3D images, to medical records, to email keystrokes—the challenge is trying to pull it al together and make sense of it.

Source: Courtesy of Igneous, Inc. Reproduced with permission.

Metadata from internet service providers and social media platforms is fed into big data analytics.

©iStockphoto.com/bymuratdeniz

Before you read the article from Henry Steele below,[40] you might want to sit down. Young business professionals who are good with communicating, understanding big ideas, planning, and working with data and/or software are making *a lot* of money and will continue to do so as organizations continue to implement data analytics as their entire management control system.

Data science professionals are being relied upon by businesses to make critical decisions about creating products, expanding into other markets, and even acquiring other companies. Data science workers are essential, so they are well compensated. It is estimated that the median salary for data science professionals overall in the United States is $118,000.

Which careers and jobs offer the highest compensation? Below are 10 of them.

1. A **big data engineer** is responsible for analyzing large amounts of data and changing it so that it can be used for valuable insights that are relied upon by top executives to enhance their business operations. A big data engineer also analyzes, procures, reports, and digests on the data that is flowing to and from the company. They also provide oversight of hardware, software, and data infrastructure to make sure that the information is being adequately streamlined and used. The salary range for this job is $135,000 to $196,000, with a 5.8% salary increase between 2016 and 2017.

2. A **data architect** has one of the most desirable data science jobs out there. These data experts assist in designing and maintaining data and its ever-changing structure while developing and strategizing efficiency models and constant design improvements with a strong focus on visualization. This position is usually an executive-level job, and professionals in this field will report to board members and C-level employees. The annual salary range for this career is $131,000 to $184,000, with a 4.1% salary increase between 2016 and 2017.

3. **Data warehouse manager.** For data science professionals who eat, breathe, and sleep big data, this is a great career option. A data warehouse manager is responsible for housing huge amounts of data safely in a secure facility. The core tasks of the data warehouse manager include the safe and efficient managing of data while providing as much efficiency as possible. The data warehouse manager must also work closely with the maintenance IT and security teams to assure as much uptime and accessibility as possible. This career has a salary range of $129,000 to $179,000, with a 4.1% salary increase between 2016 and 2017.

4. A **database manager** is in charge of maintaining the organization's databases and also diagnosing and fixing issues as they come up. Database managers also are in charge of managing the database and its hardware, while also making sure the databases are modern and compatible with newer systems and software. The salary range for database managers is estimated at $122,000 to $155,000, with a 3.7% increase between 2016 and 2017.

5. The job of **business intelligence analyst** comes with a good salary and core requirements. You are responsible for analyzing data from the business and molding it into information that is useful. It will be relied upon by top company executives to enhance business operations. You also will need to produce data reports that are independent that help to show trends, patterns, and modernization methods that can boost business operational protocols. The salary range for this data science job is $118,000 to $145,000, with a 4.3% salary increase between 2016 and 2017.

6. **Data scientist.** One of the most sought-after jobs in this field is that of data scientist. These data professionals nearly always command a top salary as they develop groundbreaking algorithms that pair with predictive modeling systems. This results in the creation of new data proficient prototypes and new data analytical methods.

   Data scientists use analytical, statistical, and programming skills to collect, analyze, and interpret large amounts of data. They use this information to develop solutions to the most demanding business challenges. Data scientists have a high level of technical skill in statistics, machine learning, coding languages, databases, and reporting technologies. Data scientists should have skills in the programming languages R and Python, as well as SQL. The salary range for a data scientist is between $116,000 and $163,000. The average increase in salary between 2016 and 2017 was a healthy 6.4%.

7. A career in **data modeling** requires you to have mastery of data science because you will be handling large amounts of business data and then converting it into usable insights that help to identify and predict trends in the business and overall market. These types of reports are used by executives to enhance processes and boost efficiency. The typical salary range for a data modeler is $111,000 to $155,000, with a 3.9% increase in salary on average between 2016 and 2017.

8. **Database developer.** In this data position, you will be improving current database processes and also modernizing the business infrastructure and to boost the efficiency of coding. Also, you will be troubleshooting databases and problems, as well as debugging systems and engaging in logical reasoning to fix any issues that arise along the way.

   This data science job is different from a database administrator. The latter is focused on routine database maintenance and support for a current database. Database developers concentrate on improving a database, expanding

(Continued)

(Continued)

the range and functionality, and developing submissions for the IT architecture of the company. The typical salary range for database developers is $108,000 to $145,000, with a 1% increase in salary between 2016 and 2017.

9. **Database administrators** are tasked with optimizing the database for a company and getting to peak performance. It also is necessary to streamline and repair various issues, and also to safeguard the system and serves from everyday wear and tear, as well as high volumes of traffic and corruption of data. You also will be working with an IT team and a security team to make sure that the company's data is never stolen or compromised. Databases also have to be available to employees at all times. The typical salary range for this position is $98,500 to $140,000, with a 3.6% increase in salary between 2016 and 2017.

10. **Data analysts.** Companies bring in data analysts to convert large quantities of business data and to deliver valuable insights into their business operations. The good thing about being a data analyst is that it is not just limited to technology companies. Large companies in all industries around the world, from IT to healthcare, to automotive to retail to finance and insurance all need data analysts to run their daily business operations.

Data analysts must create useful insights from the vast reams of data they collect. These reports are used to enhance company efficiency and processes, and also help to decrease the cost to profit ratio. Business executives will use this information to ensure the company is profitable and will also use it to integrate better business systems and protocols. The annual salary range for data analysts is $77,500 to $118,000. The increase in salary between 2016 and 2017 was 3.8%.

If you choose one of the above data science careers and jobs, it is likely that you will enjoy a long career with good pay and your job will be in demand.

Source: Adapted from Steele, H. (2018, September 21). 10 highest paying data science careers. *BusinessStudent.com*. Licensed under Creative Commons Attribution 4.0 International License CC BY 4.0. Retrieved from https://www.businessstudent.com/careers/highest-paying-data-science-careers/.

Data Analytics

Learning Objective 15.6: Apply data analytics to control for maximum firm performance.

Big data analytics is transformative. "By analyzing this data, organizations can learn trends about the data they are measuring, as well as the people generating this data. The hope for this big data analysis is to provide more customized service and increased efficiencies in whatever industry the data is collected from."[41]

There are companies (such as Amazon, Facebook, or Uber) that thoroughly based their success on big data and their analysis; others, particularly in the telecommunication or financial sectors, have drastically changed their competitive strategies using big data analysis. Industries and institutions of any sort can expect at least one of the following outcomes from the collection, creation, and analysis of big data: improving effectiveness and performances, thus increasing revenue; significantly reducing costs of processes; or reducing costly risks such as lack of compliance, and production or service delivery risks.[42]

MapReduce: How Big Data Gets Analyzed

MapReduce is both a specific program and a general model for *how* to program. It is a method for taking large raw datasets and performing computations on multiple computers simultaneously to turn that data into useful information. MapReduce consists of two steps that give the method its name. First, the "Map" function filters raw data into categories so it can be analyzed. Next, there's the "Reduce" function, which combines the data into a summary. Although MapReduce started as proprietary research at Google, it's now a generic name for a popular model used throughout the tech industry.[43]

Big Data Analysis Tools

The widely used and influential Apache Hadoop is a premier data analysis tool. It is a collection of open source software that stores and analyzes data on a large scale.[44] Hadoop is capable of running on commodity software (i.e., software that is widely available from many suppliers and relatively interchangeable), making it easy to integrate into an existing data center. It can even be used to conduct data analysis in the cloud. Apache Hadoop consists of these four parts:

1. *Hadoop Distributed File System (HDFS)*. Hadoop's file distribution system was developed for high aggregate bandwidth (i.e., it is designed to transfer data at a very fast rate).
2. *YARN (short for "Yet Another Resource Network") Platform*. YARN is Hadoop's resource management and job scheduling technology.
3. *MapReduce*. Hadoop relies on the MapReduce method described above, filtering data into categories for analysis and compiling the data into a summary.
4. *Libraries*. These are common libraries that other Hadoop subsystems need to function.[45]

However, Apache Hadoop is not the only game in town. Another attention-getting framework is Apache Spark. Its primary benefit is that it stores data in its memory rather than on a disk. This method of storage can make specific kinds of data analysis go much more quickly—in some cases, up to 100 times faster. Spark can work with Hadoop's component for storage (HDFS), but it's also compatible with other data sources such as Apache Cassandra or OpenStack Swift. Another benefit is that Spark can be run on one local computer, which makes testing and development a much simpler process.[46]

Hadoop and Spark are just two popular big data tool options. There is a vast array of open source data frameworks for storing and analyzing big data. Many of these tools meet niche needs for specific hardware configurations or provide other specialized features. The Apache Software Foundation supports many of these tools.

Below is a list of other popular open source big data platforms and tools:

- Elasticsearch, another enterprise search engine modeled on Lucene, develops insights through data analysis (using both structured and unstructured data). It is part of the Elastic stack (once referred to as the ELK stack, so named for Elasticsearch, Kibana, and Logstash).
- Cruise Control is a LinkedIn creation that enables users to run clusters from its other source stream-processing software platform, Apache Kafka.
- TensorFlow, open sourced by Google in 2015, is a repository of machine learning software. It has garnered praise for making machine learning more accessible because it is so user-friendly.[47]

You probably are not surprised at the big list of tools used to analyze big data because, after all, it is big data. Why are we showing you so many? Because when your feet hit the front door of your next employer, chances are you will need to be familiar with these systems and how to analyze the output. Yet again, this is another competitive advantage for you in the workplace.

Open Source

Another important thing to note about the systems mentioned above is that they are **open source**. "As big data continues to grow in size and importance, the list of open source tools for working with it will certainly continue to grow as well."[48] More importantly, the information available to you via the IoT will become more open source, meaning you can use and modify information you find, sometimes in its entirety, as long as you use the proper attribution.[49]

There is a reference at the end of the last sentence to the website for one such open source website, Creative Commons (CC). Much of the research in this chapter has come from organizations, universities, government agencies, researchers, and consulting sites that want their information to be readily available to students and scholars, so they use CC so that you have access to the material, in its entirety, as long you use the appropriate CC license (Figure 15.5).

When photos, articles, and quotes are not open source, you must be careful to properly use them and cite them according to fair use guidelines, which is "(in US copyright law) the doctrine that brief excerpts of copyright material may, under certain circumstances, be quoted verbatim for purposes such as criticism, news reporting, teaching, and research, without the need for permission from or payment to the copyright holder."[50]

The proper citation for the definition above includes all the CC licenses that are available, built into the following web link: https://www.google.com/search?as_rights=(cc_publicdomain|cc_attribute|cc_sharealike).-(cc_noncommercial|cc_nonderived)&q=fair%20use&hl=. This means we can use the definition for any purpose and change or modify the definition if we choose (those are the CC options that were chosen, as seen in Figure 15.6).

Knowing how you can and can't use information from the internet is an important control as well, since any materials your company uses for its literature, training, internet site, and so on may not use photos or language that came from the IoT unless it is done from an open source site or follows the fair use guidelines.

Software source coding was an early entrant to the idea of open source data sharing, as further described by the Open Source Initiative:

> Development based on the sharing and collaborative improvement of software source code has a history essentially as long as software development itself. The "open source" label was created at a strategy session held on February 3rd, 1998 in Palo Alto, California, shortly after the announcement of the release of the Netscape source code. The strategy session grew from a realization that the attention around the Netscape announcement had created an opportunity to educate and advocate for the superiority of an open development process.[51]

▼ FIGURE 15.5

Creative Commons License Sample Page

Source: Creative Commons. Retrieved from https://creativecommons.org/choose/results-one? license_code=by-sa&jurisdiction=&version=4.0&lang=en.

▼ FIGURE 15.6

Creative Commons Search Page

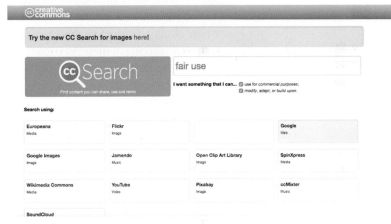

Source: Creative Commons. Retrieved from https://oldsearch.creativecommons.org/.

How Data Analytics Has Changed Performance Forever

Throughout this book, we have mentioned the one imperative a leader faces: maximize shareholder/stakeholder wealth. One of the most important ways to do that is to maximize firm performance, as further described by Kilimci and colleagues:

> Since competition is increasing day by day among retailers at the market, companies are focusing more predictive analytics techniques in order to decrease their costs and increase their productivity and profit. Excessive stocks (overstock) and out-of-stock (stockouts) are very serious problems for retailers. Excessive stock levels can cause revenue loss because of company capital bound to stock surplus. Excess inventory can also lead to increased storage, labor, and insurance costs, and quality reduction and

degradation depending on the type of the product. Out-of-stock products can result in lost for sales and reduced customer satisfaction and store loyalty. If customers cannot find products at the shelves that they are looking for, they might shift to another competitor or buy substitute items.[52]

One way to avoid these problems is through demand forecasting, one of the main issues of supply chains.

It aimed to optimize stocks, reduce costs, and increase sales, profit, and customer loyalty. There has been extensive set of methods and research performed in the area of demand forecasting, but traditional forecasting methods are based on time-series forecasting approaches. These forecasting approaches predict future demand based on historical time series data which is a sequence of data points measured at successive intervals in time.[53]

When you take into consideration that it seems that the retail industry will face more competition in the future, you can quickly see that forecasting based on historical data points will not provide proper quality management controls over most of the management functions.[54]

Moreover, using data analytics will change the entire way your organization functions. We can again look back on the chapters in this book, and not even have to work too hard, to see where quality data and analysis will provide information to help good managers and leaders control *all* aspects of their organization to help improve performance and stakeholder satisfaction. In the following subsections, we will provide examples of and even research results showing how data analytics impacts the management control process as we have discussed throughout the book.

Decision-Making

Principles of Digital Development describes the importance of data and decision-making as follows:

> No amount of data will lead to accelerated impact if it is not used to inform decision making. When an initiative is data driven, quality information is available to the right people when they need it, and they are using those data to take action. The data produced by a digital initiative should be used for more than just outputs, such as published work or donor reporting. Examples of the types of data that can be collected to inform decision making include surveillance, research, operations, project management and data from secondary sources collected outside of the program.[55]

While decisions can be made using historical data, in today's world those types of decisions will leave you far behind the competition. This is one of the reasons we reviewed the different types of data (structured, unstructured, etc.) and the different ways that data is analyzed. Historical data is certainly important, but when you can get up-to-the-second data on *who* (demographics) is buying your *what* (product or service) and *how* (online, big box store, etc.), your decisions are up-to-the-second as well.

The benefits of data-driven decision making (DDD) have been demonstrated pretty conclusively. Economist Erik Brynjolfsson and his colleagues from MIT and Penn's Wharton School recently conducted a study of how DDD affects firm performance.[56] They developed a measure of DDD that rates firms as to how strongly they use data to make decisions across the company. They show statistically that the more data driven a firm is, the more productive it is—even controlling for a wide range of possible confounding factors. And the differences are not small: one standard deviation higher on the DDD scale is associated with a 4–6% increase in productivity. DDD is also correlated with higher return on assets, return on equity, asset utilization, and market value, and the relationship seems to be causal, meaning one causes the other.[57]

In a sense, knowing that DDD is so effective for firm performance, you can extrapolate that DDD plays a role in every aspect of the management purview. However, we can do better than make you extrapolate since there is additional data on the power that DDD has on direct management issues.

Organizational Culture and Change

It might take you a minute to think of how data analytics can impact organizational culture and change, but it does. We have discussed how many people do not look forward to change, but research studies have shown that a firm's favorable experience (i.e., benefit perceptions) in utilizing external source data could encourage future acquisition of big data analytics. In other words, if employees are provided with data from an outside source that helps them do a better job and make better decisions, then bringing a data analytics department, system, or team into the organization is met with more of a positive attitude.[58]

It has also been proposed that to lead the data-driven culture, corporations need to establish a stream of clean, accurate, reliable, and active data feeds reflecting all major business activities (the umbrella of control). If all of these qualities are present, employees are more likely to trust the data, the technology, and the tools. This trust will help support the data-driven vision of the organization's leaders.[59]

Strategic Management and Planning

This is sort of a given, since we already ruined the surprise by discussing vision in the last section, but once again the data is in, and the empirical survey results show that better-performing companies are characterized by a more sophisticated analytical planning process. Lower-performing firms acknowledge big analytics as a competitive advantage for the higher-performing firms.[60]

Speaking of competitive advantage and strategy, top-performing organizations use analytics five times more than lower performers. Senior executives now want businesses run on data-driven decisions, they want to understand optimal solutions based on complex business parameters or new information, and they want to take action quickly.

However, for analytics-driven insights to trigger new actions across the organization, they must be closely linked to business strategy, easy for end-users to understand, and embedded into organizational processes so that action can be taken at the right time.[61]

With these results we can also see *organizational design, human resource systems, motivation,* and *leadership* intertwined with the data analytics performance boost. Data shows that end-users are happier when the information is easy to use (motivation) and that the information needs to be embedded in all of the organizational processes (organizational design). These are both products of close work with the human resource systems and good leadership.

Finally, from a performance and strategy standpoint, organizations that strongly agreed that the use of business information and analytics differentiates them within their industry (competitive advantage) were twice as likely to be top performers as lower performers. They were also twice as likely to use analytics to guide future strategies and twice as likely to use insights to guide day-to-day operations. Finally, to support the power and speed of DDD, these organizations make decisions based on rigorous analysis at more than double the rate of lower performers.[62]

Communication

Just like in life, communication plays a myriad of roles in data analytics. First, of course, is the communication it takes throughout the organization to onboard the effective use of data analytics, as was discussed above. Perhaps even more important is the communication of the data results to those who need them.

> Despite the respect it commands in concept, analytics can be difficult to explain and understand. As a result, analytical capabilities may not get used effectively as decision makers fall back on their intuition or experience. Yet there are approaches that can help quantitative analysts tell a story with data and tactics that can help decision makers develop beneficial relationships with analysts.[63]

Storytelling, or a narrative, still remains a powerful way to communicate in organizations, even in the age of analytics. People remember stories, and that makes it easier to share information with others. In fact, we can add *understanding individuals and diversity* and *managing in a global environment* to this section as well, because both numbers and storytelling are universal languages used and appreciated across every country around the world. As Davenport explains, among the more effective analysts are those who can tell a story with and about data:

> Regardless of the details of the analysis method and the means of getting it across, the elements of good analytical stories are similar. They have a strong narrative, typically driven by the business problem or objective. A presentation of an analytical story on customer loyalty might begin, "As you all know, we have wanted for a long time to identify our most loyal customers and ways to make them even more loyal to us—and now we can do it."[64]

Great Managers Use Great Data

To create a culture in your department or organization where the use of big data and data analytics is seen as a welcome addition to employees doing their jobs and the future of the company, here are a few tips from Principles for Digital Development on how to make the big data transition and implementation as smooth as possible:

- Design programs so that impact can be measured continuously and incrementally, focusing on outcomes, not just outputs.
- Make use of existing data, including open data sets and data from interoperable systems.
- Use rigorous data collection methods. Consider and address potential biases and gaps in the data collected, perform data quality checks, and maintain strong documentation behind collected data.
- Close knowledge gaps by contributing data to the development community and using data and interoperability standards.
- Use quality real-time or timely data to support rapid decision-making, [and] improve programming for users and inform strategy.
- Present data in formats that are easy to interpret and act on, such as data visualizations and stories.
- Create a data use culture by prioritizing capacity building and data use efforts across all stakeholder groups, including the groups whose data are being collected.
- Be holistic about data collection and analysis. Collect data from multiple sources, and use a mix of data collection and analysis methods. Analyze your data collaboratively with stakeholders.

- Identify and use open data and interoperability standards.
- Collect and use data responsibly according to international norms and standards.[65]

Managerial Implications

Congratulations! At this point, you can go out and say you have the knowledge and tools you need to be an effective manager (well, if you actually read the book). This chapter took all of the preceding management components of planning, organizing, and leading and showed how controlling these critical functions is what helps make the organization, and you, as effective and successful as possible. Great takeaways from this chapter include the following:

- Understanding the different types of management control and performance management systems and their basic uses.
- Recognizing the correct types of control systems for an organization depending on the needs: strategic, operational, and tactical.
- Deciding on objective or normative data needs for the different areas of control.
- Understanding the use of a balanced scorecard approach to management control.
- Learning how to establish control systems and feedback systems across the organization for performance success.
- Recognizing the critical role technology plays in modern management control.
- Implementing data analytics to control for maximum firm performance.
- Communicating the importance of data analytics as an organizational change tool and organizational performance-enhancing tool.
- Using data analytics to allow for rapid decision-making across the organization.

Once again, way to go on making it through this awesome book, learning so much that you can walk into an interview with confidence, and becoming a management superstar!

KEY TERMS

balanced scorecard   475

concurrent control   470

data analytics   478

feedback control   470

laissez-faire   467

management control
system   468

metadata   481

normative control   474

objective control   474

open source   484

operational control   473

organizational control   468

performance
measurement   468

proactive control   470

semi-structured data   481

strategic control   472

structured data   480

tactical control   473

top-down control   474

unstructured data   480

variety   479

velocity   479

veracity   479

volume   478

TOOLKIT

Activity 15.1

What Big Data Might Work Where?

Below are 13 management concepts we have reviewed in the book (not including Chapters 1 and 15) before discussing the management control process. After each one, list at least two pieces of big data that you think would provide you with important analytical output you need to make better decisions and have better control over the process. They can be structured or unstructured.

Chapter	Topic	Big Data Sources
2	Making Decisions and Using Analytics	
3	Ethics and Social Responsibility	
4	Organizational Culture and Change	
5	Strategic Management and Planning	
6	Organization Design	
7	Communication	
8	Human Resource Systems	
9	Understanding Individuals and Diversity	
10	Motivation	
11	Managing Teams	
12	Leadership	
13	Managing in a Global Environment	
14	Budget Control	

Case Study 15.1

Pajama Email Hackers

Have you ever wanted a job where you could sit around in your pajamas and bunny slippers and make good money? A group of hackers figured out how, and it triggered a huge investigation by the Securities and Exchange Commission, not to mention a loss of over $100 million by companies who should have known much better, but did not have the proper controls in place to stop the pajama hackers.

So Here Is What Happened...

The United States Securities and Exchange Commission's ("Commission") Division of Enforcement ("Division"), in consultation with the Division of Corporation Finance and the Office of the Chief Accountant, investigated whether certain public issuers that were victims of cyber-related frauds may have violated the federal securities laws by failing to have a sufficient system of internal accounting controls. As discussed more fully below, the issuers—a group that spans numerous industries—each lost millions of dollars as a result of cyber-related frauds.

In those frauds, company personnel received spoofed or otherwise compromised electronic communications[66] (Business E-mail Compromise or BEC[67]) purporting to be from a company executive or vendor, causing the personnel to wire large sums or pay invoices to accounts controlled by the perpetrators of the scheme. Spoofed or manipulated electronic communications are an increasingly familiar and pervasive problem, exposing individuals and companies, including public companies, particularly those that engage in transactions with foreign customers or suppliers, to significant risks and financial losses.[68]

The Federal Bureau of Investigation (FBI) recently estimated that these so-called "business email compromises" had caused over $5 billion in losses since 2013, with an additional $675 million in adjusted losses in 2017—the highest estimated out-of-pocket losses from any class of cyberfacilitated crime during this period.[69] In connection with the investigation, the Commission considered whether the issuers complied with the requirements of Sections 13(b)(2)(B)(i) and (iii) of the Securities Exchange Act of 1934 ("Exchange Act").[70] Those provisions require certain issuers to devise and maintain a system of internal accounting controls sufficient to provide reasonable assurances that transactions are executed with, or that access to company assets is permitted only with, management's general or specific authorization.[71]

As the Senate emphasized over four decades ago when passing these provisions, "[a] fundamental aspect of management's stewardship responsibility is to provide shareholders with reasonable assurances that the business is adequately controlled."[72]

While the cyber-related threats posed to issuers' assets are relatively new, the expectation that issuers will have sufficient internal accounting controls and that those controls will be reviewed and updated as circumstances warrant is not. The Commission has determined not to pursue an enforcement action in these matters based on the conduct and activities of these public issuers that are known to the Commission at this time. The Commission, however, deems it appropriate and in the public interest to issue this Report of Investigation ("Report") pursuant to Section 21(a) of the Exchange Act to make issuers and other market participants aware that these cyber-related threats of spoofed or manipulated electronic communications exist and should be considered when devising and maintaining a system of internal accounting controls as required by the federal securities laws. Having sufficient internal accounting controls plays an important role in an issuer's risk management approach to external cyber-related threats, and, ultimately, in the protection of investors.[73]

Investigating the Perps

The Division's investigation focused on the internal accounting controls of nine issuers that were victims of one of two variants of schemes involving spoofed or compromised electronic communications from persons purporting to be company executives or vendors. The issuers covered a range of sectors including technology, machinery, real estate, energy, financial, and consumer goods, reflecting the reality that every type of business is a potential target of cyber-related fraud.[74]

At the time of the cyberscams, each issuer had substantial annual revenues and had securities listed on a national securities exchange. Each of the nine issuers lost at least $1 million; two lost more than $30 million. In total, the nine issuers lost nearly $100 million to the perpetrators, almost all of which was never recovered.[75]

While this might seem like a huge amount of money, in just a six-month period in 2016, the FBI Internet Crime Complaint Center (IC3) received victim complaints totaling:

Total U.S. financial complaints:	3,044
Total U.S. financial recipient exposed dollar loss:	$346,160,957
Total non-U.S. financial complaints:	774
Total non-U.S. financial recipient exposed dollar loss:	$448,464,415[76]

Some of the investigated issuers were victims of protracted schemes that were only uncovered as a result of third-party actions, such as through detection by a foreign bank or law enforcement agency. For example, one company made 14 wire payments requested by the fake executive over the course of several weeks—resulting in over $45 million in losses—before the fraud was uncovered by an alert from a foreign bank. Another of the issuers paid eight invoices totaling $1.5 million over several months in response to a vendor's manipulated electronic documentation for a banking change; the fraud was only discovered when the real vendor complained about past due invoices.[77]

Emails From Fake Executives

The first type of business email compromise the Division reviewed involved emails from persons not affiliated with the company purporting to be company executives. In these situations, the perpetrators of the scheme emailed company finance personnel, using spoofed email domains and addresses of an executive (typically the CEO) so that it appeared, at least superficially, as if the email were legitimate.[78]

In all of the frauds, the spoofed email directed the companies' finance personnel to work with a purported outside attorney identified in the email, who then directed the companies' finance personnel to cause large wire transfers to foreign bank accounts controlled by the perpetrators. The perpetrators used real law firm and attorney names, and legal services-sounding email domains like "consultant.com," but the contact details connected company personnel with an impersonator and co-conspirator. These were not sophisticated frauds in general design or the use of technology. In fact, from a technological perspective they only required creating an email address to mimic the executive's address. Each of the schemes had some common elements:[79]

- The spoofed emails described time-sensitive transactions or "deals" that needed to be completed within days, and emphasized the need for secrecy from other company employees. They sometimes implied some level of government oversight, such as one fraudulent email claiming the purported transaction was "in coordination with and under the supervision of the SEC."
- The spoofed emails stated that the funds requested were necessary for foreign transactions or acquisitions, and directed the wire transfers to foreign banks and beneficiaries. Although all of the issuers had some foreign operations, these purported foreign transactions would have been unusual for most of them. The emails also provided minimal details about the transactions.[80]
- The spoofed emails typically were sent to midlevel personnel, who were not generally responsible or involved in the purported transactions (and who rarely communicated with the executives being spoofed). The emails also often included spelling and grammatical errors.[81]

Emails From Fake Vendors

The second type of cyber-related fraud involved electronic communications impersonating the issuers' vendors. This form of scam was more technologically sophisticated than the spoofed executive emails because, in the instances the Division reviewed, the schemes involved intrusions into the email accounts of issuers' foreign vendors.

After hacking the existing vendors' email accounts, the perpetrators inserted illegitimate requests for payments (and payment processing details) into electronic communications for otherwise legitimate transaction requests. The perpetrators of these scams also corresponded with unwitting issuer personnel responsible for procuring goods from the vendors so that they could gain access to information about actual purchase orders and invoices. The perpetrators then requested that the issuer personnel initiate changes to the vendors' banking information, and attached doctored invoices reflecting the new, fraudulent account information. The issuer personnel responsible for procurement relayed that information to accounting personnel responsible for maintaining vendor data.

As a result, the issuers made payments on outstanding invoices to foreign accounts controlled by the impersonator rather than the accounts of the real vendors. Unlike the fake executive scams, the spoofed vendor emails had fewer indicia of illegitimacy or red flags. In fact, several victims only learned of the scam when the real vendor raised concerns about nonpayment on outstanding invoices. Because vendors often afford issuers months before considering a payment delinquent, the scams, in certain circumstances, were able to continue for an extended period of time.

Let's Get This Under Control

The Commission recently emphasized that "cybersecurity presents ongoing risks and threats to our capital markets and to companies operating in all industries, including public companies regulated by the Commission."[82] Accordingly, the Commission Statement and Guidance on Public Company Cybersecurity Disclosures advised such public companies that "[c]ybersecurity risk management policies and procedures are key elements of enterprise-wide risk management, including as it relates to compliance with the federal securities laws.[83]

In light of the risks associated with today's ever-expanding digital interconnectedness, public companies should pay particular attention to the obligations imposed by Section 13(b)(2)(B) to devise and maintain internal accounting controls that reasonably safeguard company and, ultimately, investor assets from cyber-related frauds. More specifically, Section 13(b)(2)(B)(i) and (iii) require certain issuers to "devise and maintain a system of internal accounting controls sufficient to provide reasonable assurances that (i) transactions are executed in accordance with management's general or specific authorization," and that "(iii) access to assets is permitted only in accordance with management's general or specific authorization."[84] As the Senate underscored when these provisions were passed, "[t]he expected benefits from the conscientious discharge of these responsibilities are of basic importance to investors and the maintenance of the integrity of our capital market system."[85]

Virtually all economic activities now take place through digital technology and electronic communication, leaving business transactions and assets susceptible to a variety of cyber-related threats.[86] This is a growing global problem, and cyberscams like the ones described above that target an issuer's assets are an ever-increasing part of the cybersecurity threats faced by a wide variety of businesses, including issuers with Section 13(b)(2)(B) obligations.[87]

The financial and other impacts of these frauds can be significant, as the instances described above attest. As noted above, these frauds were not sophisticated in design or the use of technology; instead, they relied on technology to search for both weaknesses in policies and procedures and human vulnerabilities that rendered the control environment ineffective. Having internal accounting control systems that factor in such cyber-related threats, and related human vulnerabilities, may be vital to maintaining a sufficient accounting control environment and safeguarding assets. These examples underscore the importance of devising and maintaining a system of internal accounting controls attuned to this kind of cyber-related fraud, as well as the critical role training plays in implementing controls that serve their purpose and protect assets in compliance with the federal securities laws. The issuers here, for instance, had procedures that required certain levels of authorization for payment requests, management approval for outgoing wires, and verification of any changes to vendor data. Yet they still became victims of these attacks.

The existing controls could be (and were) interpreted by the company's personnel to mean that the (ultimately compromised) electronic communications were, standing alone, sufficient to process significant wire transfers or changes to vendor banking data. To that end, after falling victim to these frauds, each of the issuers sought to enhance their payment authorization procedures, and verification requirements for vendor information changes. Moreover, as noted above, many of these issuers only learned of the fraud as a result of third-party notices, such as from law enforcement or foreign banks. Thereafter, these issuers took steps to bolster their account reconciliation procedures and outgoing payment notification processes to aid detection of payments resulting from fraud.[88]

Systems of internal accounting controls, by their nature, depend also on the personnel that implement, maintain, and follow them. In the context of the business email compromises the Division reviewed, the frauds succeeded, at least in part, because the responsible personnel did not sufficiently understand the company's existing controls or did not recognize indications in the emailed instructions that those communications lacked reliability.

For example, in one matter, the accounting employee who received the spoofed email did not follow the company's dual-authorization requirement for wire payments, directing unqualified subordinates to sign-off on the wires. In another, the accounting employee misinterpreted the company's authorization matrix as giving him approval authority at a level reserved for the CFO. And there were numerous examples where the recipients of the fraudulent communications asked no questions about the nature of the supposed transactions, even where such transactions were clearly outside of the recipient employee's domain and even where the employee was asked to make multiple payments over days and even weeks.

In two instances the targeted recipients were themselves executive-level employees—chief accounting officers—who initiated payments in response to fake executive emails. To this end, while most of the issuers had some form of training regarding controls and information technology in place prior to the scams, all of them enhanced their training of responsible personnel about relevant threats, as well as about pertinent policies and procedures following the frauds.

And One Final Note About Control

By this report, the Commission is not suggesting that every issuer that is the victim of a cyber-related scam is, by extension, in violation of the internal accounting controls requirements of the federal securities laws. What is clear, however, is that internal accounting controls may need to be reassessed in light of emerging risks, including risks arising from cyber-related frauds. Public issuers subject to the requirements of Section 13(b)(2)(B) must calibrate their internal accounting controls to the current risk environment and assess and adjust policies and procedures accordingly.

Ultimately, issuers themselves are in the best position to develop internal accounting controls that account for their particular operational needs and risks in complying with Section 13(b)(2)(B).[89] In performing this analysis, issuers should evaluate to what extent they should consider cyber-related threats when devising and maintaining their internal accounting control systems. Given the prevalence and continued expansion of these attacks, issuers should be mindful of the risks that cyber-related frauds pose and consider, as appropriate, whether their internal accounting control systems are sufficient to provide reasonable assurances in safeguarding their assets from these risks.

Discussion Questions

1. How surprised are you to know that large, well-funded organizations can be that easily hacked for so much money?
2. What specific management control systems do these organizations need to implement immediately to avoid these easy scams (think about your own email and cyber accounts)?
3. What management control systems do you think these organizations should implement to create a stronger control system?

4. What role does or could communication play in these BEC attacks?
5. Were you aware that the federal government requires controls at large companies to protect against these scams?
6. Why do you think this story did not get more press?

Source: Reprinted from Securities and Exchange Commission. (2018). *Report of investigation pursuant to Section 21(a) of the Securities Exchange Act of 1934 Regarding certain cyber-related frauds perpetrated against public companies and related internal accounting controls requirements.* Retrieved from https://www.sec.gov/litigation/investreport/34-84429.pdf.

Case Study 15.2

Social Media Data and Its Predictive Capability

And the New American Idol Is...

The 11th season of the hit television show *American Idol* began on January 18, 2012. Forty-two contestants embarked on a journey to become the next musical sensation. The show's judges made the first round of cuts, winnowing the field to a final set of 13 singers. Subsequent eliminations were in the hands of the viewers, who chose their favorite vocalists using a straightforward voting system.

This final phase of the competition consisted of two episodes each week. Every Wednesday, the contestants took to the stage to perform. Viewers were invited to judge the performances, voting for the best contestant using one of these methods: voting via toll-free phone calls, voting via text message, or voting online. According to the competition's regulations, only voters living in the United States, Puerto Rico, or the U.S. Virgin Islands were eligible to participate.

Each voter was allowed to make unlimited texts or calls; however, online votes were limited to 50 per unique IP address.

Each week, hundreds of millions of votes rolled in. After the tally, the contestant who gathered the fewest votes was asked to leave the show. Since the show aired at 8 p.m. local time on each coast and votes could be submitted for up to two hours after the show aired, the voting window extended from 10 p.m. EST to 3 a.m. EST. Customarily, after the last performance aired, the voting window was expanded to four hours after the show aired, so the voting window was 9 p.m. EST to 4 a.m. EST.[90]

Can Twitter Predict the Winner?

This experiment began with a simple question: Does a contestant's popularity on Twitter predict that they're a favorite of the voters? In the quest to answer this question, 677,000 tweets with numbers corresponding to each of the perspective idols were collected.

The experiment involved extracting tweets from the Twitter feed used for the entirety of Season 11. There were a total of 224,189 tweets in this dataset. The tweets in the feed constituted about 10% of total tweets, providing a statistically relevant sample of the Twitter "ecosystem." This dataset was used to conduct a postevent analysis of the show's previous nine eliminations. They [the researchers] supplemented their data by running a script to query Twitter search API every ten minutes. For this process, keywords related to *American Idol* were used. The search ran between May 16 when the top four finalists performed and the penultimate episode, resulting in 453,616 tweets.

Location, Location, Location

The tweets collected in the dataset revealed location information (e.g., auto geotagging by smart phones or self-reported location data). All location data. When geolocation data wasn't available for a particular tweet, location data revealed in previous tweets from that user was assigned to it.

Analysis of geolocalized tweets revealed geographical polarization among voters. In the weeks before the "Top 3" show, contestant Phillip Phillips garnered the most buzz in the midwestern and southern regions of the country, whereas Jessica Sanchez was popular on the west coast and in large metropolitan areas throughout the nation. Joshua Ledet received strong support in Louisiana.

The "Top 3" week analysis revealed a departure from the previous geographical distribution, which could potentially be explained by contestants' performance. As expected, viewers reacted to each week's episode. According to the geolocalized data, each participant's city was a hotbed of Twitter attention (Phillips was born and raised in Georgia, Sanchez is from Chula Vista, California, and Ledet is from the Lake Charles metropolitan area in Louisiana).

Taking a Worldwide View of the Data

Analysis of location data revealed not only American interest in the show, but interest throughout the globe. While one might expect only Americans to be interested in *American Idol*, the show enjoyed popularity in several foreign countries, namely the Philippines. One of the final contestants has Filipino heritage, which may explain the interest. Jessica Sanchez's mother was born in the Bataan province of the Philippines. In fact, Sanchez was so popular in the country that she even received congratulations from President Benigno Aquino III who praised her performance and wished the singer luck in her bid for the top spot. Tweets in support of Sanchez revealed her popularity, making up about 45% of the total of tweets from America and 64% worldwide.

According to the aforementioned official rules, only residents of the United States, the Virgin Islands, and Puerto Rico are allowed to vote for the next idol. Therefore, officially, Sanchez's popularity abroad should not have affected the official vote tallies. However, when tweets

from the Philippines were isolated, they corresponded to a peak in the two voting sessions for east and west time zones. Websites that speculated about votes from other countries and even provided instructions on how to subvert the rules were cropping up online. Therefore, it is possible that these tweets points to a potential anomaly that could indicate fraudulent votes; however, there is no hard evidence of such a thing.

Never, Ever, Make Assumptions!

The research began with an underlying premise: the number of votes each contestant receives is proportionate to the number of tweets that mention them—in essence, the larger the Twitter "volume," the more popular the contestant and the more votes they will receive. The study of this dataset was limited to a simple measure: number of tweets. By design, it did not control for the array of factors that might affect tweet volume—including negative, positive, or neutral tweet content or attempts to affect voting outcome by spamming the Twittersphere with exposure for a specific contestant with autogenerated tweets. Rather, one of the goals of the analysis was actually to test whether simple, minimal measurements applied to Twitter data could be predictors of actual voting outcome. The intent of this experiment was to develop another simple prediction system to again test the premise that sheer volume of Twitter mentions can be predictive of popularity in official tallies.

While the dataset did span the entire duration of the current season, analysis focused on the "Top 10" phase of *American Idol*, specifically, to test the predictive power Twitter in the last nine eliminations. For seven of those eliminations, the three contestants with the fewest votes were revealed during the customary "elimination day" episode of the show. This experiment considered the viability of Twitter as a proxy for the voting results not only for the single eliminated contestant, but for the bottom three contestants.

The dataset was limited to a specific time window (8 p.m. to 3 a.m. EST each Wednesday) in order to minimize the number of tweets generated after the elimination. This timeframe was selected intentionally because votes could be submitted until midnight on the west coast (3 a.m. on the east coast). Interestingly, the number of tweets associated to the eliminated contestant (Joshua) was practically always the smallest. The inset provided a detailed view of the live show time period. At this resolution, the sequence of peaks of each contestant correlated with time and sequence of their performances that night.

For each of the last nine weeks, the researchers integrated the number of tweets related to each user in the *show+voting* time window. They then ranked the contestants in decreasing order. The last three counted as the bottom three and the last contestant was the most likely to be eliminated. They confronted our prediction with the real outcomes. In order to account for errors induced by sampling of the real number of tweets, they evaluated the 99% confidence intervals assuming a homogeneous and fair sampling and report the results. Twitter data served as a correct indicator for the last three eliminations and identified correctly most of the bottom three/two contestants.

And the Next American Idol Is… Not Correct According to the Data

On May 23, 2012, the season finale aired. At 10 p.m. EST, Phillip Phillips was declared the newest American Idol.

Just three days before (May 20), the first draft of a paper outlining this experiment was submitted before the final two episodes of the show. It broke down the methodology and the postevent analysis of the previous nine eliminations on the show.

Predictions for the winning contestant were made using data gathered on May 22 when the show began at 8 p.m. EST until the voting period came to a close at 4 a.m. EST. They were discussed in an updated version of the paper submitted to *arXiv* hours before the official announcement.[91]

Although Phillips won the title, the entire dataset showed that Jessica Sanchez was clearly the most popular contestant on Twitter during the measurement window.[92] This indicates that the original premise of the experiment did not hold up.

However, the analysis did not take into account a critical factor. As previously indicated, Jessica was the only contestant with a strong Twitter signal coming from outside the United States, specifically the Philippines. Since voting was restricted to the United States and its territories, data that was not geolocated in the United States could not be used to test the premise. With the tweets outside the United States and the tweets without geolocation discarded, the data showed that Phillips was indeed the most popular contestant on Twitter, which aligned with the show's result, proving the initial premise.[93]

Discussion Questions

1. What different types of data sources can you find in this case, based on what you read in the chapter?
2. How did the results of this study support the importance of thorough data collection and analysis?
3. If you decide to set up a similar social media data analysis for a live show with a winner, what structured data would you be sure to include? What unstructured data would you include?
4. How well do you think your model will work compared to the one in the case? Why?

Source: Adapted from Ciullo, F., Mocanu, D., Baronchelli, A., Gonçalves, B., Perra, N., & Vespignani, A. (2012a). Beating the news using social media: The case study of *American Idol*. *EPJ Data Science*, *1*, 8. Licensed under a Creative Commons Attribution 2.0 Generic (CC BY 2.0) license. Retrieved from https://doi.org/10.1140/epjds8v; Ciulla, F., Mocanu, D., Baronchelli, A., Gonçalves, B., Perra, N., & Vespignani, A. (2012b). Beating the news using Social Media: The case study of *American Idol*. *arXiv*, 1205.4467. Retrieved from https://arxiv.org/abs/1205.4467; and Reuben. (2016). Idol analytics: *American Idol* predictions, statistics, and analysis. Retrieved from http://idolanalytics.com/.

Self-Assessment 15.1

What a Quality Control Manager Needs

Instructions

Are you ready to take on management control? Rate yourself on the following skills, listed by O*NET OnLine as being the most important things a quality control systems manager needs. Use 5 as the highest ("I am awesome") and 1 being the lowest ("I need some serious help here").

Statements	Strongly Disagree (Help)	Disagree	Neutral	Agree	Strongly Agree (Awesome)
1. Reading Comprehension—Understanding written sentences and paragraphs in work-related documents.	1	2	3	4	5
2. Judgment and Decision-Making—Considering the relative costs and benefits of potential actions to choose the most appropriate one.	1	2	3	4	5
3. Quality Control Analysis—Conducting tests and inspections of products, services, or processes to evaluate quality or performance.	1	2	3	4	5

(Continued)

(Continued)

4. Active Listening—Giving full attention to what other people are saying, taking time to understand the points being made, asking questions as appropriate, and not interrupting at inappropriate times.	1	2	3	4	5
5. Monitoring— Monitoring/assessing performance of yourself, other individuals, or organizations to make improvements or take corrective action.	1	2	3	4	5
6. Complex Problem-Solving—Identifying complex problems and reviewing related information to develop and evaluate options and implement solutions.	1	2	3	4	5
7. Critical Thinking—Using logic and reasoning to identify the strengths and weaknesses of alternative solutions, conclusions, or approaches to problems.	1	2	3	4	5
8. Speaking—Talking to others to convey information effectively.	1	2	3	4	5
9. Time Management—Managing one's own time and the time of others.	1	2	3	4	5
10. Writing—Communicating effectively in writing as appropriate for the needs of the audience.	1	2	3	4	5
11. Systems Evaluation—Identifying measures or indicators of system performance and the actions needed to improve or correct performance, relative to the goals of the system.	1	2	3	4	5
12. Active Learning—Understanding the implications of new information for both current and future problem-solving and decision-making.	1	2	3	4	5
13. Social Perceptiveness—Being aware of others' reactions and understanding why they react as they do.	1	2	3	4	5
14. Systems Analysis—Determining how a system should work and how changes in conditions, operations, and the environment will affect outcomes.	1	2	3	4	5
15. Coordination—Adjusting actions in relation to others' actions.	1	2	3	4	5
16. Instructing—Teaching others how to do something.	1	2	3	4	5

17. Learning Strategies—Selecting and using training/instructional methods and procedures appropriate for the situation when learning or teaching new things.	1	2	3	4	5
18. Persuasion—Persuading others to change their minds or behavior.	1	2	3	4	5
19. Management of Personnel Resources—Motivating, developing, and directing people as they work, identifying the best people for the job.	1	2	3	4	5
20. Mathematics—Using mathematics to solve problems.	1	2	3	4	5
21. Negotiation—Bringing others together and trying to reconcile differences.	1	2	3	4	5
22. Operation Monitoring—Watching gauges, dials, or other indicators to make sure a machine is working properly.	1	2	3	4	5

Scoring

Total score (add up the circled numbers) _____

Out of the 22 questions, your score will be between 22 and 110. This assessment is more about your individual skills than your total score, though. Take a look back through and see what skills you scored lower on, and revisit your SWOT analysis and add them, and your goal and objective to fix each one, to your weaknesses. You may also go back and add the high scores to your strengths and be sure to continue taking opportunities to maintain those strengths.

One thing you hopefully noticed in this assessment is that many of these are skills you will need for *every job*. They are not just part of the management control job market, but rather every professional position you will likely apply for. It is important to keep in mind how many of your skills are transferrable. Perhaps you are not thinking about management process control, but you are thinking about a position that involves at least 20 of the skills listed. Look back over the assessment and circle which ones. Hopefully those were your high scores!

Source: O*NET OnLine and U.S. Department of Labor, Employment and Training Administration. Licensed under a Creative Commons Attribution 4.0 International License CC BY 4.0. Retrieved from https://www.onetonline.org/link/summary/11-3051.01.

Get the tools you need to sharpen your study skills. SAGE edge offers a robust online environment featuring an impressive array of free tools and resources. Access practice quizzes, eFlashcards, video, and multimedia at **edge.sagepub.com/scanduragower**.

THE SCIENTIFIC METHOD

APPENDIX LEARNING OBJECTIVES

After studying this appendix, you should be able to:

 A.1 Understand how the scientific method is used in businesses to aid in critical thinking and problem-solving.

 A.2 Define the types of data used in business analytics.

Get the edge on your studies at **edge.sagepub.com/scanduragower**

- Take the chapter quiz
- Review key terms with eFlashcards
- Explore multimedia resources, SAGE readings, and more!

The Scientific Method

Learning Objective A.1: Understand how the scientific method is used in businesses to aid in critical thinking and problem-solving.

The use of business analytics dates back to the late 1800s but is an emerging trend in management today.[1] Historically, when the rate of productivity gains from assembly line production started to slow after the Industrial Revolution (roughly 1760–1840), managers looked for ways to increase profitability and began to focus on the humans who operated the machinery.

At the start this was not entirely positive for the people who worked in the factories. Recall from Chapter 1 that scientific management is a field of study founded by engineer Frederick Winslow Taylor. Scientific management was adopted by CEOs like Henry Ford, who tended to view employees as machines rather than human beings.[2] The earliest examples of business analytics involved the measurement and analysis of data such as the average number of seconds employees took to shovel coal with their right hand versus their left hand. Another example is how small adjustments to the angle of seamstresses' posture were scrutinized to squeeze small production gains out of each employee per hour of labor.[3]

The scientific method has been with us for many years, but years passed before managers acknowledged employees as human beings with thoughts and feelings. It was not entirely intentional, since little was known about human psychology at the time. The tools were not available to measure employee attitudes. Humans are infinitely more complex than machines. They bring emotions, perceptions, needs, and other complexities into the workplace that, until relatively recently, were thought to be impossible to measure and understand.[4]

The mid- to late 1900s brought breakthroughs on both the psychological and technological aspects of work and it has become possible to simultaneously treat management as a science while engaging employees as human beings.[5] We have reached a point where researchers and managers can study employees, with all of their human attributes, using tools readily available to anyone with a basic computer and an understanding of the scientific method, which we review next. To produce the research discussed in this textbook, the scientific method is applied to rigorously study the experiences of employees at the workplace.

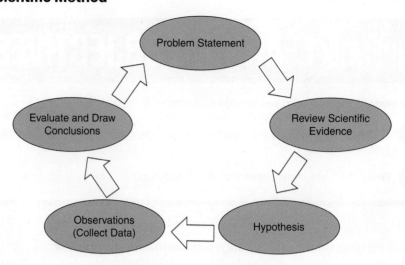

The Scientific Method

If you have taken courses in science, Figure A.1 probably looks familiar. The scientific method is simple to understand, and yet powerful enough to solve seemingly insurmountable challenges, from eradicating smallpox to landing human beings on the moon.[6]

Familiarity with the scientific method is also important for understanding the role of data analytics in solving business and workplace challenges.[7] A brief overview of its key elements—observation, prediction, testing, analysis, and conclusion—is provided in Table A.1.

The Role of Variables

In the testing phase, data are collected. Being able to generate the data to be analytic requires that a question or problem is decomposed into measurable parts that can be analyzed. These "parts" are **variables**—quantifiable factors whose values fluctuate, often in relation to other variables. Scientists and managers might examine the relationship between an **independent variable** and a **dependent variable** to understand something that is occurring at the workplace. Changes in the independent variable (also called a predictor variable) are hypothesized to impact the dependent variable (also called an outcome variable). Let's begin with a simple example. Managers may be interested in improving employee performance and hypothesize that increasing employees' salaries by 10% (the independent variable) will increase their job performance (the dependent variable). This hypothesis implies that the reverse is likely true as well—if managers institute a pay cut, it will reduce performance levels. In this situation, the independent variable is thought to predict a dependent variable (i.e., salary increases predict performance).

In the workplace, however, there are not many problems that can be investigated with only two variables. The relationship between salary and performance generally depends on many other factors.[8] Employees with more training and job experience, for example, might have higher performance increases compared to inexperienced employees who are still learning how to do their jobs. Factors such as these are called **moderating variables** because their presence alters (or "moderates") the relationship between an independent variable and a dependent variable, as shown in Figure A.2.

We encounter moderators in every aspect of our lives. The best drivers should not get behind the wheel if they drink too much alcohol—the normally simple relationship between driving skill (independent variable) and the likelihood of getting into an accident (dependent variable) changes dramatically once alcohol (moderating variable) enters the equation. This is what makes moderators so important from a management perspective: the solution to

Steps of the Scientific Process

Step	Description	Example
1. Observation/question	What is the problem or phenomenon we want to learn more about?	Employee performance is below average.
2. Prediction	After engaging in research and critical thinking, formulate a testable prediction (or predictions) to explain the observation in Step 1.	Based on a comparison of salary levels at competing companies, management suspects that the employees are unmotivated because they feel underpaid.
3. Testing	Data are collected to test the prediction(s) developed in the previous step.	Managers increase wages by 10%. They measure performance levels for six months after the increase.
4. Analysis	The data from Step 3 are analyzed.	Mean performance levels during the six-month periods before and after the increase are compared.
5. Conclusion	Based on the results of the data analysis, hypotheses are either supported or rejected. If rejected, the decision-maker returns to Step 2 and develops new predictions to test. Ideally, the process continues until a solution is reached.	Results indicate that performance increased by 5% but that the effect was not uniform. Employees with at least one year of experience showed an average improvement of 9%, but newer employees improved by only 1%. Management concludes that salary impacted performance as expected, but only among more experienced employees. This conclusion leads to the new hypothesis that recent hires need better training.

▼ FIGURE A.2

A Moderated Relationship

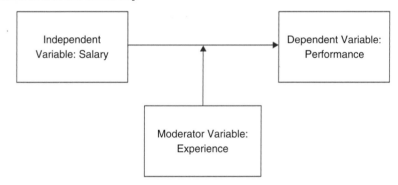

workplace problems often seems obvious (Unproductive employees? Pay them more, problem solved!)—that is, until we start considering moderating factors.

The preceding examples are simplified and leave out many of the steps in applying the scientific method in the workplace. To use the scientific method, managers should pay careful attention to important considerations at each step in the process. The testing phase is critical and rigor is necessary to guard against producing flawed results. For example, if poor measures are used, then the results of the study are compromised ("garbage in, garbage out"). The analysis phase is also a step where proper selection and execution of statistical techniques is needed to ensure the data tell us what we want to know.[9] The remainder of this appendix therefore focuses primarily on these two steps of the scientific method—testing and analysis.

As you read through the chapters in this book, however, you should note that the other stages of the scientific method are also important. Throughout each chapter, you will find examples of real workplace challenges that managers and researchers have solved by implementing the scientific method.

Data Used by Managers

Before data can be analyzed, it must be carefully collected in the testing phase of the scientific method. In organizations, several types of data are gathered to solve problems faced by managers. Each type of data has advantages and disadvantages. It is important for managers to understand the limitations of certain types of data. This section provides an overview of some of the most common forms of data used by managers.

Cross-Sectional Versus Longitudinal Data

Cross-sectional data is collected by a decision-maker on all of the independent and dependent variables they plan to study at the same point in time. **Longitudinal data** is collected over a period of time. For example, a manager announces that free snacks will be made available all day long in the employee cafeteria. They ask employees to complete a one-time survey to see how happy this has made them. This is an example of collecting cross-sectional data. If, after implementing free snacks in the cafeteria, the manager surveys the same employees every two weeks for a year to see if their job satisfaction is changing over time, longitudinal data is being collected. By collecting longitudinal data, the manager can determine whether the snacks have a long-term impact on satisfaction or whether it is short-lived.

Cross-sectional data has the advantage of being easy to collect. Surveys are collected at one time and this minimizes disruption to the employees and their work. This efficiency involves a significant tradeoff however. The biggest disadvantage of cross-sectional data is its inability to establish *causality*.[10] When two pieces of data are collected at the same time, it is almost impossible to determine whether a change in one (the independent variable) actually causes a change in the other (the dependent variable). Returning to the cafeteria snacks example, the manager might observe that job satisfaction was extremely high after the big announcement and conclude that it was an unqualified success. But how do we know for sure that the snacks created satisfaction? Here are three possibilities that each demonstrate a key limitation of cross-sectional data for establishing causality:

- *Alternative explanations:* Maybe the offering of snacks convinced employees that the organization, not the manager, cared about them and *this* caused their happiness.
- *Lack of baseline data:* Maybe the employees were actually happier *before* the announcement of the snacks.
- *Reverse causality:* Maybe employees' preexisting happiness made the manager think they would enjoy having snacks, meaning that the assumed dependent variable (job satisfaction) actually caused the independent variable (snacks).

Longitudinal data gives the manager a shot at figuring out what is causing what. This is because it allows for fluctuations in independent and dependent variables to be tracked over time. Longitudinal data can provide a better idea of whether changes in one variable are truly causing changes in the other variable. If, for example, job satisfaction was measured on a monthly basis before snacks in the cafeteria was announced, during the munch fest, and then again after the snacks are discontinued, we would have a much better idea of how (or if) its implementation impacted employees' satisfaction levels. The tradeoff, however, is the expense and logistical difficulty of collecting longitudinal data. Taking measurements at multiple times means that employees are interrupted and the time that employees spend providing data is time that they are not working. Most management research is, therefore, cross-sectional.[11]

Self-Reported Versus Other-Reported Data

Self-reported data and **other-reported data** refer to information that is measured by employees about themselves or about other employees, respectively. Cross-sectional and longitudinal data have clear advantages and disadvantages as discussed above. However, the relative advantages of self- and other-reported data depend largely on what is being measured.[12] Job satisfaction, for example, is a highly personal experience that other people cannot easily assess.[13] An employee likely knows how much they like or dislike their job. The boss may think they are happy at work when they are not. Performance, on the other hand, can often be measured accurately—perhaps more accurately—by observers than by employees themselves. This is because employees have biased views of their own performance and inflate ratings.

Whether a manager uses self- or other-reported data is often guided by which source is likely to produce the most accurate responses. Self-reported data is best for employee attitudes and reports on their experience at work. Performance, on the other hand, may be better assessed by the boss. No offense, but this is also why your performance in this class is most likely to be evaluated by someone other than yourself. In other words, would you give yourself a "C" if your performance was average? The challenge with other-reported data is that it may be difficult or impossible to collect. Another problem is confidentiality. Many leadership studies, for example, ask employees to rate the leadership style of their bosses. Protections must be put in place to ensure that there will not be retaliation from bosses who are rated by their followers.

Physiological Data

Physiology is the science of living creatures and the biological processes that keep them alive. **Physiological data**, therefore, refers to information from and about these biological processes. Common examples in management studies include heart-rate, blood-oxygen saturation, and cortisol (a stress-related hormone) levels.[14] Most employees find the process of having their pulse measured, being hooked up to an EKG monitor, giving blood, or spitting into a cup to be strange. Due to the intrusiveness of collecting physiological data, it is rarely used in ordinary business analytics although it is more common in academic studies of management.[15] We mention it primarily to explain why business analytics must often settle for the limitations of the other data types described above (self- and other-reported). That said, a cortisol spit test is probably more accurate than self- or other reports of job-induced stress could ever be, for example. The cost and logistical challenges—not to mention the unpleasant reaction employees are likely to have—associated with such data mean that compromises must often be made. For example, to understand the effects of stress on employee performance, we have to settle for self-reports in surveys.

Contextual Data

To understand employee reactions, it is important to consider the context in which they work. The collection, analysis, and interpretation of **contextual data** have changed dramatically in recent years.[16] In fact, the very meaning of the term has evolved as technological advances such as smartphones and watches give access to the "context" of our lives in ways that were not imaginable until recently. For example, a Fitbit watch records how many hours of sleep people get each night. Basically, contextual data today serves the same purpose it always has—the data literally allow other data to be put into their proper context. An often-cited, and sometimes controversial, example of contextual data analysis is the university admissions process.[17] Without contextual data, variables like standardized test scores would likely make admissions an easy job—every applicant above a certain score is accepted, everyone below is out. You probably recall sending *far* more data than just test scores when you went through the college admissions process. Much of this data was contextual, even if you did not realize it. Maybe there was an essay about challenges you have overcome. The committee may have received recommendation letters from your teachers, coaches, or supervisors. Your postal code may have even been considered. Each of these is designed to provide a more "complete" picture of you as an applicant, with the goal of avoiding over-reliance on easily quantifiable but incomplete data.[18]

Technological advances, however, have greatly expanded the range of data that can be classified as "easily quantifiable." Even decidedly qualitative information, such as the afore-mentioned college essay or the essay portion of standardized tests, are frequently codified and analyzed by computers with less and less human intervention as the technology matures.[19] Sim-ilar developments have occurred in related areas such as the selection (e.g., hiring/promotion) of employees using artificial intelligence. Some of the most amazing advances in contextual data analysis, however, have occurred in the marketing field. Although these applications gen-erally fall outside the scope of this book, there are signs that the primary focus of contextual analysis has become targeted marketing.[20] Smartphone GPS technology has enabled the ability to factor a consumer's location, buying habits, and movements into advertising and promotions and is testing the limits of both technology and consumer ethics (e.g., you stop and look at a window display in a local clothing store, and then an ad for that clothing appears in the feed in one of your social media apps on your phone). Contextual data is being constantly collected and analyzed to enable target marketing.

SUMMARY

This appendix described the scientific method used in management research. It is important for a manager to understand how the recommendations for effective management are derived from research. A recurring theme throughout this textbook is the importance of analytics for successful managers—not in the future but right now. Having completed this appendix, you should understand the following points:

- The scientific method is used to generate research evidence on management.

- Managers also use the scientific method to improve decision-making.
- The scientific method consists of the following elements: observation, prediction, testing, analysis, and conclusion.
- Testing and analysis are the most critical steps in the process.
- It is important to understand the different types of data that managers can collect to apply the scientific method to solve problems.

KEY TERMS

contextual data   503

cross-sectional data   502

dependent variable   500

independent variable   500

longitudinal data   502

moderating variables   500

other-reported data   503

physiological data   503

self-reported data   503

variables   500

Get the tools you need to sharpen your study skills. SAGE edge offers a robust online environment featuring an impressive array of free tools and resources. Access practice quizzes, eFlashcards, video, and multimedia at **edge.sagepub.com/scanduragower**.

GLOSSARY

Chapter 1: Becoming a Manager

analytics: the analysis of data or statistics to facilitate or improve decision-making processes.

benchmarking: examining the success of other organizations to identify best practices.

building shared vision: the sharing of a long-term view of the future that is uplifting and encourages experimentation and innovation.

change behavior: monitoring the external environment of the organization and developing innovative strategies.

controlling: the steps taken by management to increase the likelihood that the objectives are attained and that all parts of the organization are working together toward the goal.

critical thinking: the process of learning by questioning everything.

decisional roles: managerial roles that require the use of information.

disruptive change: change that disrupts the markets for an organization's products.

disseminator: a manager who communicates key information to their colleagues.

disturbance handler: a managerial role in which managers help mediate disputes.

effectiveness: "doing the right things"; achieving results, making the right decisions, and successfully carrying them out so they achieve the organization's goals.

efficiency: "doing things right"; maximum utilization of the organization's resources to attain its mission.

entrepreneur: a managerial role in which managers create and lead change within the organization by solving problems, generating new ideas, and implementing them.

evidence-based management (EBM): the translation of management research to management practice.

field theory: a framework for the implementation of organizational change; examines the forces driving and restraining change.

figurehead: a managerial role in which managers have social, ceremonial, and legal responsibilities.

Hawthorne effect: positive responses in attitudes and performance by employees when observers pay attention to their group; based on the findings of two studies conducted in the early 20th century.

informational roles: managerial roles that involve processing information.

interpersonal roles: managerial roles that involve providing information to others.

leader: a managerial role in which managers provide leadership for their team, their department, or perhaps their entire organization.

leading: when managers command their team through daily tasks and during periods of significant change.

learning organization: a group that fosters continual learning for employees while encouraging new and expansive patterns of thinking.

liaison: a managerial role involving communication with internal and external contacts.

management: (1) the efficient and effective pursuit of organizational goals by (2) integrating the work of people through (3) planning, organizing, leading, and controlling the organization's resources.

mental models: deeply ingrained assumptions, generalizations, or even images that influence how we act and how we understand the world.

mission: overall goal.

monitor *or* nerve center: a managerial role in which managers regularly seek out information related to the organization and industry.

negotiator: a managerial role in which managers engage in important negotiations within their team, department, and organization.

organizational behavior (OB): the study of individuals and their behaviors at work.

organizational culture: the norms, behaviors, and values that create the unique environment of an organization.

organizational development (OD): the application of psychological theories to workplace issues.

organizing: ensuring the organization runs smoothly by managing the internal processes and structures.

personal mastery: competence plus the discipline of continually clarifying and deepening personal vision, focusing energies, developing patience, and seeing reality objectively.

planning: determines which responsibilities are given to employees, sets priority levels for tasks, and creates timelines for task completion.

relations behavior: managerial behaviors that provide support and encouragement.

resource allocator: a managerial role in which managers determine where organizational resources are best applied.

scientific management: an approach based on efficiency studies of how employees move during their work, as described by Frederick Taylor in his 1914 book *The Principles of Scientific Management*.

spokesperson: a managerial role in which managers must communicate key information to their colleagues and their team.

sustainability: meeting "the needs of the present without compromising the ability of future generations to meet their own needs" (Brundtland, 1987).

systems thinking: learning from experience by utilizing and understanding cause and effect.

task behavior: managerial behaviors that guide employees in doing their jobs.

team learning: developing teams to generate desired results; people on the team act, learn, and grow rapidly from interactions.

Theory X: refers to leaders who have a pessimistic view of human nature, as described in Douglas McGregor's book *The Human Side of Enterprise*; Theory X managers tend to be directive and engage in surveillance and coercion.

Theory Y: refers to leaders who have an optimistic view of human nature, as described in Douglas McGregor's book *The Human Side of Enterprise*; Theory Y managers tend to allow discretion, participation, and creativity.

Chapter 2: Making Decisions and Using Analytics

behavioral analytics: the collection and analysis of data about human behavior, particularly its predictors and outcomes.

big data: collections of large amounts of data; it has been defined in terms of high volume, high velocity, and high variety.

bounded rationality: the context decision-makers use to simplify complex problems by limiting the amount of information-processing needed.

business analytics: the use of data to help managers gain improved insight about business operations.

creative-thinking skills: refers to how adaptable and imaginative individuals are.

creativity: generally thought of as a different but useful solution to a problem, or novel and effective ideas.

equality heuristic: resources should be allocated equally.

escalation of commitment: when individuals continue a failing course of action after receiving feedback that shows it is not working.

expertise: refers to knowledge (technical, processes, or academic).

fluency: when the quickest decision is selected, as when there is a pressing need to bring a new product to market before competition enters.

framing: the choice to present questions as gains or losses.

heuristics: decision rules.

hindsight bias *or* **I-knew-it-all-along effect:** "the tendency for individuals with outcome knowledge to claim they would have estimated a probability of occurrence for the reported outcome that is higher than they would have estimated" before knowing the outcome (Hawkins & Hastie, 1990).

imitating the majority: heuristic entailing doing what most people do.

imitating the successful: heuristic entailing following best practices.

intrinsic motivation: the urgent need to solve the problem faced, regardless of the monetary rewards expected.

intuition: responses that are reached with little apparent effort, and typically without conscious awareness; they involve little or no conscious deliberation.

management analytics: encompasses behavioral and operational analytics.

operational analytics: the application of advanced analytical methods to make better decisions about business operations.

overconfidence bias *or* **hubris:** an inflated level of confidence.

people analytics *or* **workforce analytics** *or* **talent management:** the application of analytics to better understand employees and potential employees.

prospect theory: a way of understanding the perceptions people have of risks when making decisions.

recognition heuristic: if one of two alternatives is recognized, infer that it has the higher value on the criterion in question.

risk analysis: evaluation of the likelihood that a damaging event might negatively affect an organization.

satisficing: making a decision that is satisfactory but not optimal.

sunk-costs fallacy: when people continue to invest in failing courses of action to recoup their losses, hoping to show they have made the right decision all along.

Chapter 3: Ethics and Social Responsibility

bounded ethicality: an unconscious psychological process that hinders the quality of decision-making by limiting the information being considered; ethical errors are often made as a result, due to the limited capacity to process information.

caring ethical climate: the organization creates a climate where people look out for each other.

consequentialist ethics: an ethical school of thought that revolves around the belief that doing what is best for the greatest number of people constitutes the right thing to do, regardless of whether it breaks rules.

conventional reasoning: the stage when conformity to social rules is motivated by a person's desire to maintain relationships with other people and social systems.

corporate social responsibility: the duty of corporations to act in an economically, legally, ethically, and philanthropically responsible manner.

deontological ethics *or* **duty-based ethics:** an ethical school of thought that revolves around the belief that doing right is based solely on what a series of rules state, rather than based on the consequences of an action.

ethical climate: the moral environment of a workplace, which creates clear boundaries for actions that are right and wrong.

ethical leadership: leadership practices that emphasize moral sensitivity, judgment, motivation, and action.

ethics: the rules or principles that define right and wrong.

ethics of care: ethics that focuses on the need to maintain relationships with others to guide decisions.

independence ethical climate: the organization expects people to exercise their own personal and moral beliefs.

instrumental ethical climate: the organization expects people to do anything to further the company's interests.

law and code: an ethical framework that considers only whether a decision violates a law.

moral courage: the personal fortitude to face ethical issues, challenges, or dilemmas and to pursue virtuous action in response.

moral development: the thinking process that occurs when people are deciding what is right or wrong; it develops in stages.

moral intensity: the extent to which action is a moral imperative.

moral outrage: a severe reaction to perceived injustice.

PLUS decision-making model: takes into account the way that many organizations do business today, such as empowering employees to make their own decisions, keeping open lines of communication, and always keeping in mind the values of the organization.

post-conventional reasoning: the stage when an individual moves beyond the perspective of their own society and morality is defined by abstract principles that apply to all situations and societies.

pre-conventional reasoning: the stage when an individual's morality is externally controlled by authority figures who mete out punishment and distribute rewards.

rights view: the belief that humans are entitled to a certain number of rights based solely on their humanity.

rules ethical climate: company rules and regulations guide decision-making.

shareholders: individuals who own shares in a company.

stakeholders: individuals with an interest in a company.

theory of justice: the idea that fairness is equivalent to justice.

triple bottom line (TBL) *or* **3Ps:** people, planet, and profit, which Professor Joseph Potchen identifies as key components of corporate responsibility.

utilitarian view: consideration of decisions that do the most good for the most people.

virtue ethics: emphasizes the role of personal values (such as integrity) in decision-making.

Chapter 4: Organizational Culture and Change

anticipatory socialization: the process an individual goes through as they attempt to find an organization to join.

artifacts and creations: a component of organizational culture consisting of its physical manifestations, such as artwork, building architecture, and the way employees dress.

assimilate: to completely absorb the ideas, values, and other elements of culture.

assumptions: underlying values, which are often unconscious because people do not question them.

change curve: the four stages that precipitate change—status quo, disruption, exploration, and rebuilding; based on the stages of death and dying identified by Elizabeth Kübler-Ross.

changing: the second step of Lewin's three-step model, where individuals move toward a desired state.

commitment to change: supporting change and helping the organization implement it.

competing values framework: a four-quadrant framework that demonstrates how an individual's values compete with other peoples' values and/or the values of the company; the quadrants include open systems, internal processes, rational goal-setting, and human relations.

compliance with change: going along with a change but secretly hoping it will end soon.

enacted values: the unconscious values that people act out.

entry: occurs when a new member starts work and begins to assimilate into the organizational culture.

espoused beliefs and values: the reasons people give for their behavior.

force-field analysis: an examination of the forces for and against the implementation of an organizational change.

human relations: the competing values framework quadrant that focuses on internal, flexible processes such as team-building communication.

impression management: the process (either conscious or unconscious) where an individual deliberately attempts to influence the perceptions and opinions of others.

internal processes: the competing values framework quadrant that focuses on performance management and coordination to maximize control.

language: terms and usage that may be unique to the organization and represent the organizational culture and how it is transmitted to newcomers.

metamorphosis: the stage in which a person transforms from a new employee to an established contributor who is valued and trusted by other members of the organization.

norms: informal and interpersonal rules that team members are expected to follow.

onboarding: the process of welcoming and orienting new organizational members to facilitate their adjustment to the organization, its culture, and its practices.

open systems: the competing values framework quadrant that deals with external forces and keeping the organization nimble during change.

organizational culture: the norms, behaviors, and values that create the unique environment of an organization.

organizational socialization: the process an organization utilizes to ensure that new members acquire necessary attitudes, behaviors, knowledge, and skills to become productive organizational members.

preentry: occurs from the time someone is offered the job to when they actually start working.

proactive: actively attempting to make alterations to the workplace and its practices.

psychological contract: an unwritten set of expectations in the employment relationship as distinct from the formal, codified employment contract.

rational goal-setting: the competing values framework quadrant that fosters a productive work environment through planning and goal-setting.

reactive: when an organization makes changes in its practices after some threat or opportunity as already occurred.

refreezing: the third stage of Lewin's three-step model, where individuals wishing to make a change reinforce and restructure based on the changes they have introduced.

resistance to change: opposition to new ways of doing things.

rituals: when a group's values and identities are publicly demonstrated or enacted within the context of a specific occasion or event.

socialization: the process that follows the steps of anticipatory socialization, entry and assimilation, and metamorphosis.

stories: knowledge and experiences shared through narrative and anecdotes to communicate lessons, complex ideas, concepts, and causal connections.

strong cultures: work cultures based on high levels of agreement among employees about what they value and high intensity toward those values.

subcultures: smaller cultures that exist within a larger culture.

symbols: images, diagrams, or objects that represent a cultural value or idea, ultimately speaking to shared knowledge between individuals.

unfreezing: the first stage of Lewin's three-step model, where individuals wishing to make a change challenge the status quo by shaking up assumptions.

values: a person's or group's morals or standards.

Chapter 5: Strategic Management and Planning

blue-ocean strategy: a strategy whereby leaders aim to create products or services that enjoy little competition, precisely because they meet a need that is not being met.

competitive advantage: a condition that allows a company to maintain a more profitable position in the market than other companies.

cost leadership: achieving the lowest cost of goods or services sold in the firm's competitive industry or industry segment.

descriptive analytics: includes a summary of historical data, providing information about what has happened.

differentiation: ensuring that a company is different from its competitors.

emergent strategy: a strategy whereby leaders aim to identify unexpected outcomes, analyze them, and apply what they have learned to future strategies.

environmental scans: constant measurement and assessment of the work environment.

fact-based management: management decisions based on research.

feedback loop: analyzing what one puts into the system and what comes out as a result.

five-forces analysis: analysis of the five forces that define an industry by enabling users to break down its weaknesses and strengths.

goals: broad accomplishments an individual hopes to achieve.

intelligence gap: the difference between the information needed and what is available.

knowledge management: a process, cycle, and discipline of knowledge acquisition, knowledge creation, knowledge-sharing, and knowledge application.

long-term financial objectives: company-wide financial goals that are meant to be accomplished over the course of several years.

long-term growth-related objectives: company-wide goals that are meant to be accomplished over the course of several years.

mantra: three or four words that sums up an organization's vision, mission, culture, or product.

mission statement: defines what line of business a company is in, why it exists, and what purpose it serves.

not-for-profit organizations (NPOs): organizations that exist to accomplish a goal unrelated to making a profit.

objectives: what an individual specifically wants to get done.

organizational citizenship behavior (OCB): a complex phenomenon characterized by altruism, conscientiousness, sportsmanship, and courtesy.

organizational values: morals or standards that guide the decisions of leadership.

performance management: creating, monitoring, and refining a workplace environment to ensure that employees perform their best.

Porter's five forces: spells out five forces that define an industry by enabling users to break down its weaknesses and strengths.

predictive analytics: analytics that identify what is probably to occur.

predictive modeling: modeling used to anticipate future trends.

prescriptive: referring to rules or a plan.

prescriptive analytics: analytics that identify what should be done about what is likely to occur.

profit: the surplus left after a company pays for wages.

shareholders: individuals who own shares in a company.

stakeholders: individuals with an interest in a company.

strategic knowledge gaps: the difference between the strategic knowledge needed and what is available.

strategic management: management that includes long-term planning,

continuous reflection, and assessment of an organization's progress toward meeting its goals.

strategic plan: a process or document that communicates an organization's goals and maps out the actions needed to reach those goals.

sustainable development: growth that ensures positive outcomes for both the current moment and into the future.

SWOT analysis: an examination of strengths, weaknesses, opportunities, and threats.

values: enduring, passionate, and distinctive core beliefs.

vision statement: describes what a company hopes to achieve in the long run.

wicked problems: large, multifaceted problems.

Chapter 6: Organizational Design

approach job-crafting: when an employee's job-crafting involves role and social expansion.

autonomy: the extent to which the employee has the freedom to plan and perform their own work.

avoidance job-crafting: when an employee's job-crafting involves role reduction or work withdrawal.

boundary spanners: individuals who are especially sensitive to and skilled in bridging interests, professions, and organizations.

centralization: when most or all key decisions are made by an organization's top leadership rather than by the managers or employees of individual work units.

complexity: the range of activities conducted within an organization.

context satisfaction: the degree to which employees are satisfied with various aspects of their job.

corporation: a company or group authorized to act as a single entity.

C-suite: the CEO and other top management team members, such as the chief executive officer (CEO), who report to the organization's board of directors, which is led by the chairman of the board.

direct reports: employees who report to an individual higher in the organization's hierarchy.

divisional structure: organized according to specific products, product groups, services, markets, customers, or major programs, with decentralization of day-to-day decisions.

dotted-line relationships: communication channels that exist without a direct power relationship.

economies of scale: more units of a good or a service are produced on a larger scale, yet with (on average) fewer input costs.

entrepreneurial organization: another term for a "simple structure"; consists of one large unit with one or two top managers; these organizations are relatively unstructured and informal.

feedback from the job: information provided by the job on how effective the employee's work is.

formalization: the amount of rules, regulations, and procedures an organization requires its employees to follow.

functional organization: organizes work into different units (e.g., departments) based on business functions or expertise.

geographic organization: an organization that stays close to their customers because the delivery of fresh products is important.

growth-need strength: a person's need to learn new things, grow, and develop from working.

hierarchy of authority: the power structure of an organization where the amount of authority increases with each level.

horizontal loading *or* **combining tasks:** the addition of tasks to an existing job that require the same level of skill.

innovative organization: another term for an "adhocracy"; companies that work in emerging industries, which require leadership to adjust practices "ad hoc," or as needed.

integration: the combination of one functional area's work into the greater whole of the organization.

job: "a set of task elements grouped together under one job title and designed to be performed by a single individual" (Ilgen & Hollenbeck, 1991).

job-crafting: the extent to which individuals can demonstrate initiative in designing their own work.

job enrichment: includes the addition of tasks outside an employee's scope of work that are of interest to the employee or are generally reserved for employees in position of authority.

job redesign: the practice of loading jobs with core job characteristics that have been shown to motivate employees.

job rotation: cross-training or allowing workers to do different jobs.

limited-liability corporation (LLC): a hybrid of a partnership and a corporation.

machine organization: an organization that features standardization, formalization, and routine procedures while utilizing centralized decision-making.

M-form: multidivisional organizations; a wide array of brands, products, or divisions in different geographical locations.

middle line: middle managers.

operating core: the people who produce a company's products.

organization chart: a diagram that depicts an organization's hierarchy.

organizational design: the process of constructing and adjusting an organization's structure to achieve its goals.

organizational structure: the rules, relationships, communication channels, and duties that allow members to work toward their shared goals.

partnership: a relationship between two or more investors who have a stake in a company.

product organization: also called a service or brand organization; organizes the work into units that are responsible for producing specific products and services.

professional organization: an organization that features highly trained professionals, high specialization, decentralized decision-making, and complex rules and procedures.

silo mentality: the sense that knowledge-sharing and goal development are relevant only within a division, rather than at the company level.

skill variety: the extent to which people use different skills and abilities at work; the employee is not doing the same repetitive tasks over and over.

sociotechnical systems design: type of organizational design based on the premise that an organization comprises both the structure and social interactions among employees.

sole proprietorship: when a company has one owner; it is easy to form and offers complete managerial control to the owner.

span of control: the number of direct reports each person has.

specialization: when jobs are narrowly defined and depend on unique expertise.

standardization: when work is performed in a routine manner, following the same steps each time.

strategic apex: the top management team.

support staff: staff involved in the operations and maintenance of a workplace, including the administration and human resources.

task identity: when an employee has ownership over a task and begins to identify with an entire work product.

task significance: the degree to which the job is seen as having an impact on others; when the work does something good for society.

technostructure: analysts whose job is to standardize the work of others in the organization.

uncertainty: the gap between the amount of information possessed and that required to perform a task.

vertical loading: adding decision-making responsibility to the job.

virtual organization: a temporary cooperation of enterprises that share resources, knowledge, and competencies to better respond to business opportunities.

Chapter 7: Communication

absorptive capacity: the capacity of an organizational unit to learn.

active listening: a way of listening that is empathetic, nonjudgmental, and engaged.

centralized networks: networks in which the information has to pass through a person in the center of the communication channel before going to any other member.

channel: the medium that transmits the message.

communication: the sharing or exchanging of information.

communication apprehension (CA): an individual's anxiety toward anticipated communication with others.

communication network: a pattern of interaction that determines who communicates with whom.

cross-cultural communication: an exchange of information between individuals or organizations belonging to different cultural groups.

cyberslacking: use of the internet for personal reasons during working hours.

decentralized networks: networks in which members of the organization can communicate with anyone.

decoding: according to the Shannon-Weaver model of communication, decoding occurs after encoding, allowing the receiver to translate and understand a message.

downward communication: communication that follows the chain of command from the C-suite executives down to employees at the operating level.

encoding: according to the Shannon-Weaver model of communication, the encoder transforms the message into a signal, which is transmitted to the receiver.

external communication: communication that flows between employees inside the organization and with a variety of people outside the organization.

horizontal communication: occurs laterally across an organization's hierarchy.

jargon: the language, especially the vocabulary, peculiar to a particular trade, profession, or group.

knowledge management: a systematic process of organization-wide coordination in pursuit of major organizational goals.

knowledge transfer: how organizational units gain knowledge from other units to enhance innovation and performance.

netiquette: a system of online etiquette, particularly over email.

noise: any communication barrier that may affect how a person interprets a message.

nonverbal communication: includes the use of visual cues such as body language, posture, distance, eye contact, facial expressions, and touch.

one-way communication: in the workplace context, one-way communication is when a manager sends a message and it is received by employees; employees do not question or share feedback with the manager.

organizational communication: the process through which people transmit meaning to other individuals through messages in the context of a formal organization.

public relations: "a strategic communication process that builds mutually beneficial relationships between organizations and their publics" (Public Relations Society of America, n.d.).

receiver: the receiver of a transmitted message in the Shannon-Weaver model of communication.

sender: the source of message transmission in the Shannon-Weaver model of communication.

Shannon-Weaver model of communication: describes the two-way communication process by defining the steps of sender, encoding, channel, decoding, and receiver.

social networking: websites and applications that enable interaction and increase socialization.

trigger words: phrases and words that result in communication breakdowns.

two-way communication: in the workplace context, two-way communication is when a manager sends a message to employees and allows for questions to be asked and feedback to be shared.

upward communication: communication that begins at the lowest levels of an organizational hierarchy (such as the entry level) and travels up the hierarchy.

Chapter 8: Human Resource Systems

360-degree feedback: includes ratings from higher management, peers (coworkers), the employee's followers, and customers, rather than solely from supervisors.

assessment center: a selection method in which applicants are presented with a variety of exercises designed to measure different management competencies.

behaviorally anchored rating scale (BARS): an assessment tool that provides specific examples of performance to supervisors, allowing them to rate employee performance in relation to these examples.

central tendency error: when the manager rates all dimensions of performance as average.

compensation: pay and other rewards provided to employees for their efforts on the job.

cross-cultural training (CCT): education that promotes intercultural learning through behavioral, cognitive, and affective skill-building.

development: "activities leading to the acquisition of new knowledge or skills for purpose of personal growth" (Aguinis & Kraiger, 2009).

flexible working hours: formal or informal working arrangements that differ from the standard employee schedule.

forced ranking: an assessment method in which all employees in a work group are ranked relative to one another.

gain-sharing plan: compensation is tied to unit-level performance rather than individual performance.

graphic rating scale: when an employee's performance is rated against multiple points along a continuum.

halo error: the overall tendency to give an employee a high rating on all aspects of job performance.

human capital: the economic value of employees' experience, knowledge, skills, and abilities.

human capital management (HCM): the alignment of employees' experience, knowledge, skills, and abilities with the current needs and strategic goals of an organization.

human resource management (HRM): the use of employees to achieve organizational goals.

job sharing: splitting one full-time job into two jobs.

knowledge, skills, and abilities (KSAs): by developing the knowledge, skills, and abilities of employees, leaders can reduce resistance to organizational change.

new finish line: when the knowledge and skills an employee must master continue to unfold; instead of reaching a point of mastery (or finish line), employees today must constantly be learning to meet a moving target.

performance management: the creation of a system that enables employees to perform to the best of their abilities; this can include an employee review process.

person–job fit (P–J fit): the mutual fulfillment of needs by employee and employer.

person–organization fit (P–O fit): the alignment of employees' personalities with the workplace culture of an organization.

profit-sharing plan: when employee bonuses are based on reaching a company financial target, such as return on assets or net income.

recruitment: to attract, with the goal of hiring, a candidate for a position.

remote working _or_ telecommuting: the ability to work from home, or anywhere.

sabbatical: a long-term break from work, which may be paid or unpaid.

salary range: the span between the minimum and maximum base salary an organization will pay for a specific job or group of jobs.

salary range structures: a hierarchal group of jobs and salary ranges within an organization.

selection: in the context of employment, the decision to hire a candidate based on a pool of applicants.

situational judgment test (SJT): a selection method in which applicants are given realistic work-related situations and then asked to choose the most effective among several behavioral choices for addressing the situation.

staffing: broadly defined as attracting, selecting, and retaining competent individuals to achieve organizational goals.

strategic HRM: "the pattern of planned human resource deployments and activities intended to help the firm to achieve its goals" (Wright & McMahan, 1992, p. 298).

stock options: a variation of profit-sharing where employees are given stock options as part of their compensation package.

training: education focused on specific tasks.

transfer of training: "the application of knowledge, skills, and attitudes learned from training on the job and subsequent maintenance of them over a certain period of time" (Cheng & Ho, 2001, p. 103).

work sample test: when applicants must demonstrate specific knowledge and skills by performing a limited number of job-related tasks during the application process.

Chapter 9: Understanding Individuals and Diversity

affinity groups: groups that are organized around employees' similar circumstances and common goals, most often among employees who share an ethnicity, gender, or other identity.

affirmative action: an active effort to improve the employment or educational opportunities of members of minority groups and women.

agreeableness: one of the personality traits highlighted in the Big-Five personality test; entails being affable, tolerant, sensitive, trusting, kind, and warm.

Boomers: people born in the United States between 1946 and 1964 during the so-called "baby boom" that occurred after World War II.

conscientiousness: one of the personality traits highlighted in the Big-Five personality test; entails being organized, systematic, punctual, achievement oriented, and dependable.

deep-level diversity: differences in the underlying attitudes and values a person holds.

delay of gratification: an individual's willingness to postpone immediate satisfaction of their needs in order to receive greater rewards later.

emotion regulation: being able to recover rapidly from experienced emotions.

emotional intelligence (EI): the ability to control emotions.

extraversion (E): one of the personality preferences highlighted in the Myers-Briggs Type Indicator test and the Big-Five personality test; extraverts are outgoing, talkative, and sociable and enjoy social situations.

feeling (F): one of the personality preferences highlighted in the Myers-Briggs Type Indicator test; feeling types tend to use emotion.

fixed mindset: the belief that one's abilities are carved in stone and predetermined at birth.

Generation Xers *or* **Gen Xers:** people in the United States who were born between 1965 and 1980.

Generation Y *or* **Millennials:** people in the United States who were born between 1981 and 2000.

Generation Z *or* **Gen Z:** people in the United States who were born between 1995 and 2010.

growth mindset: the belief that one's abilities can be developed by making a great deal of effort.

introversion (I): one of the personality preferences highlighted in the Myers-Briggs Type Indicator test; introverts tend to be shy.

intuition (N): one of the personality preferences highlighted in the Myers-Briggs Type Indicator test; intuitive people tend to be "idea people."

judging (J): one of the personality preferences highlighted in the Myers-Briggs Type Indicator test; judging people tend to make quick decisions.

locus of control: an individual's belief about the relationship between their behavior and its consequences.

Machiavellianism: the degree to which someone uses manipulation, dishonesty, and cynicism to advance; people high in Machiavellianism tend not to trust other people and want to win at all costs.

mentoring: when an influential individual in an employee's work environment shares their advanced work experience and knowledge and commits to providing upward mobility and support to the employee's career.

Minnesota twin studies: long-term studies of twins in Minnesota born between 1936 and 1955 that have enabled researchers to examine the heritability of personality traits.

neuroticism: one of the personality traits highlighted in the Big-Five personality test; entails being anxious, irritable, temperamental, and moody.

openness: one of the personality traits highlighted in the Big-Five personality test; entails being curious, original, intellectual, creative, and open to new ideas.

other awareness: being aware of emotions experienced by others.

perceiving (P): one of the personality preferences highlighted in the Myers-Briggs Type Indicator test; perceiving individuals tend to be flexible.

personality: "regularities in feeling, thought, and action that are characteristic of an individual" (Snyder & Cantor, 1998).

psychological capital (PsyCap): the psychologically beneficial characteristics of hope, efficacy, resiliency, and optimism.

self-awareness: in the context of emotional intelligence, recognizing your emotions when you experience them.

sensing (S): one of the personality preferences highlighted in the Myers-Briggs Type Indicator test; sensing people tend to be practical.

statelike: characteristics that are relatively changeable; a person can develop them through either awareness and/or training.

surface-level diversity: overt differences between people, usually related to their physical features.

thinking (T): one of the personality preferences highlighted in the Myers-Briggs Type Indicator test; thinking people tend to use logic.

traitlike: characteristics that are relatively permanent and will likely not be changed through awareness or training.

Type A: People who are competitive and aggressive.

Type B: People who are relaxed and easygoing.

veterans: individuals born between 1922 and 1945.

Chapter 10: Motivation

A-B-C analysis: when seeking to modify undesirable employee behavior, managers should explore the antecedents, behavior, and consequences of the behavior to determine what may be causing it.

candle problem: also called Duncker's candle problem; in a study in which participants were required to affix a candle to a wall using thumbtacks while preventing drip, results showed that money does not motivate people to better perform a task.

continuous reinforcement: when a specified behavior is rewarded or punished every time it occurs.

distributive justice: related to the fairness or equity of outcomes someone receives.

Duncker's candle problem: see *candle problem.*

equity: related to fairness and impartiality; what an employee gives is equivalent to what an employee gets.

esteem needs: the need to have esteem for oneself and the need to be respected by others.

existence needs: all material and physiological desires (e.g., food, water, air, clothing, safety, physical love, and affection).

expectancy: relates efforts to performance; in other words, if a person tries, they believe they will achieve a given level of performance.

expectancy theory: a theory used to predict the likelihood that an employee will work hard using the formula: Motivation = Expectancy × Instrumentality × Valence.

extrinsic rewards: rewards coming from outside, including things like paychecks, benefits, or job titles.

feedback: information about reactions to a person's performance of a task which is used as a basis for improvement.

fixed-interval schedules: where the first response is rewarded only after a specified amount of time has elapsed.

fixed-ratio schedules: where a response is reinforced only after a specific number of responses.

growth needs: the need for self-esteem or self-actualization.

hierarchy of needs: derived from the work of Abraham Maslow, the hierarchy of needs refers to five needs that are ordered by their necessity: physiological needs, safety/security needs, social needs, esteem needs, and self-actualization needs.

hygienes: conditions and practices that prevent people from being satisfied with their work.

instrumentality: the belief that performance is related to rewards.

interactional justice: refers to how decisions are communicated to employees.

intrinsic rewards: rewards coming from within, such as the feeling of satisfaction or engagement in one's work.

law of effect: past actions that led to positive outcomes tend to be repeated.

motivation: defined as "what a person does (direction), how hard a person works (intensity), and how long a person works (persistence)."

motivator-hygiene theory: a motivation theory that considers aspects of a person's job that result in satisfaction (motivators), and others that prevent dissatisfaction (hygienes); also known as two-factor theory.

motivators: aspects of a person's job that result in satisfaction.

need for achievement (nACH): people who are motivated by being seen as a high achiever.

need for affiliation (nAFF): people who are motivated by strong relationships, admire belonging to groups or organizations, and are sensitive to the needs of others.

need for power (nPOW): people who need to have influence over others and to have status.

negative reinforcement: the removal of an unpleasant event or outcome after the display of a behavior.

operant conditioning: also known as reinforcement theory; the environment is considered to be the leading motivator of behavior.

organizational behavior modification (OB Mod): when reinforcement theory is used in the organizational context to modify behavior.

overpayment inequity: when one receives a higher reward than should be expected based on the work completed.

physiological needs: factors that are related to a body's basic functioning (e.g., air, food, drink, shelter, warmth, sex, and sleep).

positive reinforcement: a favorable event or outcome presented after a behavior.

procedural justice: the fairness of procedures used to determine how outcomes are allocated.

prosocial motivation: the desire to expend effort to benefit other people.

punishment by application: the presentation of an unpleasant event or outcome to weaken the response it follows.

punishment by removal: when a pleasant event or outcome is removed after a behavior occurs.

reinforcement theory: also known as operant conditioning; the environment is considered to be the leading motivator of behavior.

reinforcers: events or outcomes that strengthen or increase the behavior they follow.

relatedness needs: includes social esteem from others and relationships with significant others such as family, friends, coworkers, and managers.

safety/security needs: to be safe and out of danger.

schedules of reinforcement: how often a reward (or punishment) is applied; this has been found to predict learning and motivation.

self actualization needs: realizing personal potential, self-fulfillment, and seeking personal growth and peak experiences; a desire to become everything one is capable of becoming.

shaping: in behavior modification, when closer and closer approximations of a desired behavior are rewarded.

SMART goals: guidelines for setting achievable goals; goals should be Specific, Measurable, Actionable, Relevant, and Time-bound.

social needs: the need to affiliate with others and be accepted by them.

stretch goals: goals that employees do not know how to reach because they are difficult.

two-factor theory: see *motivator-hygiene theory*.

underpayment inequity: when one receives a lower reward than should be expected based on the work completed.

valence: the value or strength one places on a particular outcome or reward.

variable-interval schedules: when a response is rewarded after an unpredictable amount of time has passed.

variable-ratio schedules: when a response is reinforced after an unpredictable number of responses.

Chapter 11: Managing Teams

absence of trust: one of the five dysfunctions of teams, identified by Lencioni; when individuals on a team do not trust each other.

action/negotiation teams: these teams are created to put on events or resolve disputes.

adjourning: the final stage in the five-stage model of team development; when the team disbands after completing its tasks.

advice/involvement teams: these teams provide advice; examples include committees and advisory councils.

affective reactions: emotional responses of teams and their individual members to their work and to each other as an indicator of team effectiveness.

avoidance of accountability: one of the five dysfunctions of teams, identified by Lencioni; when teams avoid commitment and accountability.

brainstorming: a group discussion to generate ideas.

cohesion: "the resultant of all the forces acting on the members to remain part of the group" (Festinger, 1950, p. 274).

command group: another term for production/service teams; these teams focus on the core mission of the organization in producing products or delivering services.

committees: another term for advice/ involvement teams; these groups recommend solutions to a specific problem.

consensus: decision-making where all participants come to agreement.

creative teams: the goal of creative teams is to create something, and such teams emphasize autonomy and exploration.

cross-functional teams: teams that include members from different functional areas of an organization.

Delphi method a decision: making technique that employs a panel of independent experts.

devil's advocate: a person (or persons) assigned by the manager to critique the team's ideas.

dialectical inquiry: a decision-making approach that generates two diametrically opposed viewpoints and then attempts to reconcile them in the final solution.

differentiation: the different types of skill sets that are needed on the team.

external integration: the degree to which the team must interact with other teams or those outside of the organization, including suppliers, managers, peers, staff, and customers.

fear of conflict: teams that lack trust are incapable of engaging in unfiltered and passionate debate of ideas; instead, they resort to veiled discussions and guarded comments.

formal teams: teams created by an organization.

forming: the first stage in the five-stage model of team development; when the group becomes oriented to the task, creates ground rules, and begins to test what is acceptable in terms of behavior.

group: a number of people located near one another or part of the same classification.

groupthink: the conformity-seeking tendency of the group; due to group pressure, the team does not survey all alternatives and expressions of views that go against the majority of team members are suppressed.

high-performance team: a team that performs at a particularly high level, producing excellent work.

inattention to results: one of the five dysfunctions of teams, identified by Lencioni; when team members pay more attention to their individual needs than to the needs of the group.

informal teams: teams created by workers.

lack of commitment: without having aired their opinions in the course of passionate and open debate, team members rarely, if ever, buy in and commit to decisions, although they may feign agreement during meetings.

maintenance function: relate to the support that the manager provides to the team.

management teams: teams involved in the production or delivery of services, while also performing managerial duties.

multivoting: group decision-making that allows for discussion and multiple rounds of voting.

nominal group technique: a structured process for decision-making that involves employees writing their ideas down prior to discussing as a group.

norming: a stage in the five-stage model of team development, when the team becomes cohesive and establishes roles and norms for interaction.

norms: informal and interpersonal rules that team members are expected to follow.

performing: a category in the five-stage model of team development, when the team begins to solve problems and coordinate tasks; the team develops a structure that supports task performance.

potential team: part of the team performance curve; potential teams need more clarity of purpose but are able to complete some work.

problem-resolution teams: resolve problems on an ongoing basis, by enabling trust and focusing on issues.

process measures: monitor the tasks and activities employed to get the results obtained.

production/service teams: another term for command groups; these teams focus on the core mission of the organization in producing products or delivering services.

project/development teams: teams where the goal is to invent new products or services.

pseudo-team: part of the team performance curve; small groups of people with complementary skills who are equally committed to a common purpose, goals, and working approach for which they hold themselves mutually accountable.

real team: part of the team performance curve; small groups of people with complementary skills who are equally committed to a common purpose, goals, and working approach for which they hold themselves mutually accountable.

results measures: measure results; tell managers where they stand in terms of organizational goals.

Ringelmann effect: also known as social loafing; slacking or underperforming in a group context with the assumption that others will complete the work.

role-based performance: the ability of each member to perform their assigned task within the team.

self-managed work teams (SMWTs): leaderless teams that make collective decisions.

social loafing: also known as the Ringelmann effect; slacking or underperforming in a group context with the assumption that others will complete the work.

stepladder technique: a decision-making technique that combats the challenge of managing dominating personalities within teams.

storming: a stage in the five-stage model of team development, when there is a lack of team unity and there are difficulties around interpersonal issues.

synergy: in the context of teams, synergy refers to group performance that exceeds the performance of the best group member when working alone.

tactical teams: teams that execute well-defined plans by ensuring that team members understand their roles.

task forces: temporary teams that focus on solving problems.

task function: relate to what the team is working on.

team: a group of people who come together to achieve a common purpose.

team charter: states the team's mission or goal, and clearly lays out the expectations for team behavior.

team creativity: a trait of good teams; includes innovative approaches to problem-solving.

team learning: developing teams to generate desired results; people on the team act, learn, and grow rapidly from interactions with each other.

team norms: provide important regulation of team behavior. These rules and guidelines that a team establishes shape the way that team members interact with one another and with others outside of the team.

team viability: the collective sense of belonging among team members and the desire to continue working together.

traditional work group: teams that focus on the core mission of the organization in producing products or delivering services. Such teams are known as production/service teams or command groups.

virtual teams: teams that rely on technology in order to meet and complete their work.

work cycles: time spent in team activities.

working group: members of working groups work independently without having to produce a shared product.

Chapter 12: Leadership

achievement-oriented leadership: challenging followers to perform at high levels, setting standards for excellence, and showing confidence in followers' ability to reach goals

authentic leadership: involves knowing oneself and behaving in a way that is consistent with what is intuitively right.

authority-obedience management: management that is highly concerned with production and not very concerned with people.

balanced processing: leaders who solicit views that challenge their own deeply held beliefs.

calculus-based trust (CBT): trust in one-time transactions, which typically derives from the calculus of gains and losses and is weighed by perceived risks.

consideration behaviors: providing encouragement, listening to employees' concerns, and expressing trust, respect, and sensitivity toward employees.

context: the circumstances that form the setting for an event, statement, or idea, and in terms of which it can be fully understood.

contingency approach: when the success or failure of a given leadership trait or behavior is contingent on the fit between that trait or behavior and the situational context in which the leader is working; the path–goal theory is an example of such an approach.

country club management: management that is highly concerned with people and not very concerned with production.

directive leadership: involves giving followers specific instructions about their tasks, providing deadlines, setting standards for performance, and explaining rules.

ethical leadership: leadership practices that emphasize moral sensitivity, judgment, motivation, and action.

exchange relationship: a relationship based on the transfer of valued resources such as performance, money, information, or supplies between two people.

full-range model of leadership: a model for understanding various components and traits of leadership; people are more engaged when their leaders behave in certain ways at the highest end of the full-range model.

"great man" theory of leadership: based on the idea that leadership was something "great men" achieved, by virtue of their noble characteristics and heroic deeds.

humble leadership: where a leader's humility allows them to show followers how to grow from working in an organization.

identification-based trust (IBT): characterized by the leader and follower sharing the same goals and objectives, or a full internalization of the other's desires and intentions, meaning both are working toward the same things with each other's best interests in the forefront.

impoverished management: management that has little concern for either people or production.

in-group: in the management context, employees a leader has reason to trust.

internalized moral perspective: leaders who demonstrate beliefs that are consistent with actions.

knowledge-based trust (KBT): a level of trust that is grounded in how predictable another person is.

leader-member exchange (LMX): the premise that leaders do not treat every follower the same way, but instead form exchange relationships of varying quality with each of them.

middle-of-the-road management: balancing concern for employees with concern for production.

out-group: employees who are perceived to have little to contribute to an exchange relationship.

participative leadership: leadership that allows followers to have a voice in decisions that affect them, by sharing information and inviting followers' ideas and opinions.

path–goal theory (PGT): a model in which the success or failure of a given leadership trait or behavior is contingent on the fit between that trait or behavior and the situational context in which the leader is working; it is considered a part of the contingency approach.

relational transparency: leaders who say exactly what they mean.

self-awareness: a leader who seeks feedback to improve interactions with others.

servant leadership: a desirable set of behaviors for leaders to emulate.

structure-initiating behaviors: defining tasks for employees, providing instructions, and focusing on goals; these behaviors provide employees with guidance and clarity in their work.

supportive leadership: leaders who make a practice of showing consideration, being friendly and approachable, and paying attention to the well-being of followers.

team style management: management that is highly concerned with both people and production.

trait approach: the attempt to identify the common traits of good leaders and then emulate these traits.

transactional leadership: behaviors that motivate followers through rewards and corrective actions.

transformational leadership: behaviors that mobilize extra effort from followers through emphasis on change while articulating a new vision for the organization.

trust: a psychological state comprising the intention to accept vulnerability based on positive expectations of the intentions or behavior of another (Rousseau et al., 1979).

Chapter 13: Managing in a Global Environment

behavioral CQ: the ability to adjust to the cultural practices of others.

cognitive CQ: self: awareness and the ability to detect cultural patterns.

cultural intelligence (CQ): the ability to function and manage effectively in culturally diverse settings.

cultural looseness: associated with social disorganization, deviance, innovation, and openness to change.

cultural tightness: associated with order and efficiency, conformity, and low rates of change.

cultural tightness–looseness: the strength of social norms and the level of sanctioning within societies.

culture: the unstated ways of doing things

culture shock: the disorientation people may feel when experiencing a new cultural environment.

expatriate: a person who lives outside the country in which they were born.

expatriation: when a person who has citizenship in at least one country is living in another country.

Global Leadership and Organizational Behavior Effectiveness (GLOBE) project: a large-scale study of cultural differences, which explored differences in culture and organizational outcomes worldwide.

global mindset: a set of individual attributes that enhance a manager's ability to influence others who are different from them.

globalization: the development of a global scale of communication, business, or relationships.

high-context cultures: cultures that rely heavily on situational cues for meaning when perceiving and communicating with others.

low-context cultures: cultures in which written and spoken words are the primary vehicles for communication.

metacognitive CQ: refers to the cognitive processing necessary to recognize and understand expectations appropriate for different cultural situations.

motivational CQ: persistence and goal-setting for cross-cultural interactions.

multinational corporation (MNC): a corporation that has facilities and other assets in at least one country other than its home country.

prototype: a preliminary model of something.

repatriation: reentry to the organization after the expatriate assignment

reverse culture shock: the realization that time has moved on and things have not stood still while an expatriate was away from home.

self-initiated expatriates (SIEs): people who choose to go abroad.

stereotype: describes things repeatedly attributed to one group of people, often unfairly or incorrectly.

Chapter 14: Budget Control

activity-based budget: a budget that estimates costs for individual activities.

add-on budget: a budget based on a previous year's budget, adjusted for current information.

bottom line: line at the bottom of a financial report that shows the net profit or loss.

bracket budget: a contingency plan with costs projected at higher and lower levels than the base amount, providing a clear picture of what will occur should forecasts not be achieved.

budget control: also known as budgetary control; the extent to which budgets are used to monitor and control costs and operations in a given accounting period.

budget gaming: the deliberate underestimation of budgeted revenue or overestimation of budgeted expenses.

budgetary control: see *budget control*.

budgetary slack: the deliberate underestimation of budgeted revenue or overestimation of budgeted expenses.

capital expenditure budget: a formal plan that states the amounts and timing of fixed asset purchases by an organization.

cash budget: an estimation of the cash inflows and outflows for a business over a specific period of time.

competitive advantage: a condition that allows a company to maintain a more profitable position in the market than other companies.

constrained resources: a resource available in limited quantities.

controlling: the process of management increasing the likelihood that objectives are attained and that all parts of an organization are working together toward that goal.

cost centers: a unit that spends money.

cost of goods sold: the production costs for products manufactured and sold or purchased and resold by the company.

expenses: money spent on something.

financial budget: a budget that examines the expected assets, liabilities, and stockholders' equity of the business.

financial statements: summary accounting reports, prepared periodically to inform the executives, managers, creditors, and other interested parties as to the financial condition of a business.

fixed organizational expenses: unchanged, repetitive expenses.

flexible (expense) budget: a series of budgets prepared for various levels of activities, revenues, and expenses.

income statement: also known as an operating statement or profit and loss (P&L); a summary of management's performance as reflected in the profitability (or lack thereof) over a certain period.

incremental budget: a budget that uses a previous year's actual figures and adds or subtracts a percentage to obtain the current year's budget.

master budget: an overall financial and operating plan for a forthcoming calendar or fiscal year.

operating budget: the costs for merchandise or services produced.

operating statement: see *income statement.*

opportunity costs: the value of the next-highest-valued alternative use of that resource.

planning: anticipating future needs and conditions.

profit and loss statement (P&L): see *income statement.*

program budget: a budget designed for a specific activity or program.

responsibility accounting: a system that involves identifying entities responsible for decision-making within an organization and learning about their objectives, developing performance measurement schemes, and preparing and analyzing performance reports of decision-makers.

revenue centers: a unit that makes money.

rolling (continuous) budget: involves incrementally extending the existing budget model at set periods of time.

special order: one-time customer order, often involving a large quantity and a low price.

stakeholder prioritization: management's ethical decision about which stakeholders to focus on and in which order.

static (fixed) budget: a budget that does not change or flex for increases or decreases in volume.

strategic budget: a budget that integrates strategic planning and budgeting control.

stretch budget: a budget based on sales and marketing forecasts that are higher than estimates.

sunk costs: costs that should not influence future financial decisions.

supplemental budget: a budget that allocates funds for budget areas not captured in the regular budget.

target budget: a budgeting process that matches major expenditures to a company's goals.

value proposition budget: a budgeting process that is centered around ensuring that everything included in the budget delivers value for the business, cutting unnecessary expenditures in the process.

zero-based budget: a budget that is built from zero, rather than through incremental adjustments.

Chapter 15: Management Control Systems and Technology

balanced scorecard: a business health checklist, monitoring and measuring the health of the company.

concurrent control: when monitoring takes place during the process or activity; may be based on standards, rules, codes, and policies.

data analytics: information that can provide prognoses and forecasts.

feedback control: control of something in the past; may include evaluating or adjusting.

laissez-faire: easygoing or relaxed.

management control system: a group of controls, which include developing rules, guidelines, procedures, limits, or other protocols for directing the work and processes of employees and departments working together.

metadata: data about data; provides additional information about a specific set of data.

normative control: when employees must learn the values and beliefs of a company and know what is right from observing other employees.

objective control: involves elements of the company that can be objectively measured, such as call volume, profitability, and inventory efficiency.

open source: software or applications for which the code is publicly available.

operational control: the development of the project schedule and budget.

organizational control: the development of rules, guidelines, procedures, limits, or other protocols for directing the work and processes of employees and departments.

performance measurement: a technique used to raise the performance of an organization with an objective to align toward a common strategy that is sustainable for all; all stakeholders benefit from the control system.

proactive control: prevention or intervention; anticipating trouble, rather than waiting for a poor outcome and reacting afterward.

semi-structured data: neither structured nor unstructured data, but somewhere in between.

strategic control: the monitoring of a strategy as it is being implemented, while evaluating deviations and making necessary adjustments.

structured data: adheres to a predefined data model.

tactical control: the direction of workers, ordering of materials and equipping for delivery; also, the establishment of rules to ensure site safety.

top-down control: also known as bureaucratic controls; the use of rules, regulations, and formal authority to guide performance.

unstructured data: information that either does not have a predefined data model or is not organized in a predefined manner.

variety: in this context, refers to the many sources and many different forms that data can take.

velocity: the infrastructure speed when efficiently transferring big files.

veracity: data uncertainty or the quality of the data that is being analyzed.

volume: data at scale, obtained from many sources with high number of data points.

Appendix: The Scientific Method

contextual data: data that allow other data to be put into their proper context.

cross-sectional data: data collected by a decision-maker on all of the independent and dependent variables they plan to study at the same point in time.

dependent variable: the outcome variable.

independent variable: the predictor variable.

longitudinal data: data collected over a period of time.

moderating variables: a variable whose presence alters (or "moderates") the relationship between an independent variable and a dependent variable.

other-reported data: information that is measured by employees about other employees.

physiological data: information from and about human biological processes.

self-reported data: information that is measured by employees about themselves.

variables: quantifiable factors whose values fluctuate, often in relation to other variables.

REFERENCES

Chapter 1

1. Fayol, H. (1948). *Industrial and general administration*. London, England: Pitman. (Original work published 1916)
2. American Intercontinental University. (2018, August 8). The four functions of management: What managers need to know. Retrieved June 1, 2019 from https://www.aiuniv.edu/degrees/business/articles/functions-of-management
3. Taylor, F. W. (1914). *The principles of scientific management*. New York, NY: Harper.
4. Bedian, A. G., & Wren, D. A. (2001). Most influential books of the 20th century. *Organizational Dynamics, 29*(3), 221–225.
5. Bedian & Wren (2001) and Taylor (1914).
6. Follett, M. P. (1918). *The new state, group organization the solution of popular government*. New York, NY: Longmans, Green.
7. Weber, M., Henderson, A., & Parsons, T. (1947). *The theory of social and economic organization* (1st American ed.). New York, NY: Oxford University Press.
8. Follett, M. P. (1940). *Dynamic administration: The collected papers of Mary Parker Follett*. E. M. Fox & L. Urwick, Eds. London, England: Pitman.
9. Dipboye, R. L. (2016). Exploring industrial & organizational psychology: Work & organizational behavior. Retrieved from https://ssrn.com/abstract=2767463
10. Mayo, E. (1949). *Hawthorne and the Western Electric Company: The social problems of an industrial civilization*. New York, NY: Routledge.
11. Maslow, A. (1954). *Motivation and personality*. New York, NY: Harper & Row.
12. McGregor, D. (1960). *The human side of enterprise*. New York, NY: McGraw-Hill.
13. Russ, T. L. (2011). Theory X/Y assumptions as predictors of managers' propensity for participative decision making. *Management Decision, 49*(5), 823–836.
14. Gürbüz, S., Şahin, F., & Köksal, O. (2014). Revisiting of Theory X and Y: A multilevel analysis of the effects of leaders' managerial assumptions on followers' attitudes. *Management Decision, 52*(10), 1888–1906.
15. Bobic, M. P., & Davis, W. W. (2003). A kind word for Theory X; or, Why so many newfangled management techniques quickly fail. *Journal of Public Administration Research and Theory, 13*(3), 239–264; and Thomas, J. M., & Bennis, W. G. (1972). *The management of change and conflict: Selected readings*. Harmondsworth, England: Penguin Books.
16. Kopelman, R. E., Prottas, D. J., & Falk, D. W. (2012). Further development of a measure of Theory X and Y managerial assumptions. *Journal of Managerial Issues, 24*(4), 450–470.
17. Bedeian, A. G., & Wren, D. A. (2001). Most influential management books of the 20th century. *Organizational Dynamics, 29*(3), 221–225.
18. Peters, T., & Waterman, R. H. (1982). *In search of excellence: Lessons from America's best run companies*. New York, NY: Warner Books.
19. Miller, D. (2001). Successful change leaders: What makes them? What do they do that is different? *Journal of Change Management, 2*(4), 359–368; and Vera, D., & Crossan, M. (2004). Strategic leadership and organizational learning. *Academy of Management Review, 29*(2), 222–240.
20. Senge, P. M. (1990). *The fifth discipline*. New York, NY: Doubleday, p. 3.
21. Garvin, D. A. (1993). Building a learning organization. *Harvard Business Review*. Retrieved from https://hbr.org/1993/07/building-a-learning-organization
22. Arlow, P. (1991). Personal characteristics in college students' evaluations of business ethics and corporate social responsibility. *Journal of Business Ethics, 10*(1), 63–69.
23. Treviño, L. K. (1992). Moral reasoning and business ethics: Implications for research, education, and management. *Journal of Business Ethics, 11*(5–6), 445–459.
24. Treviño, L. K., & Nelson, K. A. (2016). *Managing business ethics: Straight talk about how to do it right*. New York, NY: John Wiley.
25. Brown, M. E., & Treviño, L. K. (2006). Ethical leadership: A review and future directions. *Leadership Quarterly, 17*(6), 595–616.
26. McCabe, D. L., Treviño, L. K., & Butterfield, K. D. (2001). Cheating in academic institutions: A decade of research. *Ethics and Behavior, 11*(3), 219–232.
27. Bartlett, C. A., & Glinskam, M. (2001). *Enron's transformation: From gas pipeline to new economy powerhouse*. Boston, MA: Harvard Business School Press.
28. Sims, R. R., & Brinkmann, J. (2003). Enron ethics; or, Culture matters more than codes. *Journal of Business Ethics, 45*(3), 243–256, p. 244.
29. Christensen, C. M. (1997). *The innovator's dilemma: When new technologies cause great firms to fail*. Boston, MA: Harvard Business School Press.
30. Christensen & Overdorf (2000), as cited in Christensen (1997).
31. Christensen & Overdorf (2000), as cited in Christensen (1997).
32. Cramer, J., & Krueger, A. B. (2016). Disruptive change in the taxi business: The case of Uber. *American Economic Review, 106*(5), 177–182.
33. Bass, B. M. (1997). Does the transactional–transformational leadership paradigm transcend organizational and national boundaries? *American Psychologist, 52*(2), 130.
34. Burns, J. M. (1978). *Leadership*. New York, NY: Harper & Row.
35. Bass, B. M. (1990). From transactional to transformational leadership: Learning to share the vision. *Organizational Dynamics, 18*(3), 19–31.

36. As quoted in UCLA Sustainability. (n.d.). What is sustainability? Retrieved from https://www.sustain.ucla.edu/about-us/what-is-sustainability/

37. Kuhlman, T., & Farrington, J. (2010). What is sustainability? *Sustainability, 2*(11), 3436–3448, p. 3436.

38. Brundtland, G. H. (1987). *Our common future: Report of the World Commission on Environment and Development.* Oxford, England: Oxford University Press.

39. Kirby, J. (2010). The decade in management ideas. *Harvard Business Review.* Retrieved from https://hbr.org/2010/01/the-decade-in-management-ideas

40. Gerdeman, D. (2014, October 8). What do chief sustainability officers do? *Forbes.* Retrieved from https://www.forbes.com/sites/hbsworkingknowledge/2014/10/08/what-do-chief-sustainabilty-officers-do/#32c1e20433ab

41. Mintzberg, H. (1973). *The nature of managerial work.* New York, NY: Harper & Row.

42. MindTools. (n.d.). Mintzberg's management roles: Identifying the roles managers play. Retrieved from https://www.mindtools.com/pages/article/management-roles.htm

43. Alexander, L. D. (1979, August). The effect level in the hierarchy and functional area have on the extent Mintzberg's roles are required by managerial jobs. *Academy of Management Proceedings, 1979*(1), 186–189.

44. Tengblad, S. (2006). Is there a "new managerial work"? A comparison with Henry Mintzberg's classic study 30 years later. *Journal of Management Studies, 43*(7), 1437–1461.

45. Dunphy, S. M., & Meyer, D. (2002). Entrepreneur or manager? A discriminant analysis based on Mintzberg's managerial roles. *Journal of Business and Entrepreneurship, 14*(2), 17–37.

46. Mintzberg, H. (1994). Rounding out the manager's job. *Sloan Management Review, 36*(1), 11–26.

47. Yukl, G., Gordon, A., & Taber, T. (2002). A hierarchical taxonomy of leadership behavior: Integrating a half century of behavior research. *Journal of Leadership and Organizational Studies, 9*(1), 15–32.

48. Judge, T. A., Piccolo, R. F., & Ilies, R. (2004). The forgotten ones? The validity of consideration and initiating structure in leadership research. *Journal of Applied Psychology, 89*(1), 36.

49. Kraut, A. I., Pedigo, P. R., McKenna, D. D., & Dunnette, M. D. (1989). The role of the manager: What's really important in different management jobs. *Academy of Management Executive, 3*(4), 286–293.

50. Briner, R. B., Denyer, D., & Rousseau, D. M. (2009). Evidence-based management: Construct cleanup time? *Academy of Management Perspectives, 4,* 19–32.

51. Barends, E., Rousseau, D. M., & Briner, R. B. (2014). Evidence-based management: The basic principles. Retrieved from https://www.cebma.org/wp-content/uploads/Evidence-Based-Practice-The-Basic-Principles-vs-Dec-2015.pdf

52. Barends et al. (2014).

53. Rousseau, D. M., & Gunia, B. C. (2016). Evidence-based practice: The psychology of EBP implementation. *Annual Review of Psychology, 67,* 667–692.

54. Wright, A. L., Zammuto, R. F., Liesch, P. W., Middleton, S., Hibbert, P., Burke, J., & Brazil, V. (2016). Evidence-based management in practice: Opening up the decision process, decision-maker and context. *British Journal of Management, 27*(1), 161–178.

55. Aasekjær, K., Waehle, H. V., Ciliska, D., Nordtvedt, M. W., & Hjälmhult, E. (2016). Management involvement—a decisive condition when implementing evidence-based practice. *Worldviews on Evidence Based Nursing, 13*(1), 32–41.

56. HakemZadeh, F., HakemZadeh, F., Baba, V. V., & Baba, V. V. (2016). Toward a theory of collaboration for evidence-based management. *Management Decision, 54*(10), 2587–2616.

57. Pfeffer, J., & Sutton, R. (2006, January). Evidence-based management. *Harvard Business Review,* 1–16.

58. Sutton, R. (2006). Breakthrough business ideas? Retrieved from http://bobsutton.typepad.com/my_weblog/2006/07/breakthrough_bu.html

59. Glaser, E. M. (1941). *An experiment in the development of critical thinking.* New York, NY: Columbia University, Teachers College.

60. Paul, R., & Elder, L. (2006). *The miniature guide to critical thinking concepts and tools.* Dillon Beach, CA: Foundation for Critical Thinking Press.

61. Kurland, D. (2000). What is critical thinking? Retrieved from http://www.criticalreading.com/critical_thinking.htm

62. Paul & Elder (2006).

63. Stupple, E. J., Maratos, F. A., Elander, J., Hunt, T. E., Cheung, K. Y., & Aubeeluck, A. V. (2017). Development of the Critical Thinking Toolkit (CriTT): A measure of student attitudes and beliefs about critical thinking. *Thinking Skills and Creativity, 23,* 91–100.

64. Mitroff, I. (1998). *Smart thinking for crazy times: The art of solving the right problems.* San Francisco, CA: Berrett-Koehler.

65. Carter, M. Z., Armenakis, A. A., Feild, H. S. & Mossholder, K. W. (2013). Transformational leadership, relationship quality, and employee performance during continuous incremental organizational change. *Journal of Organizational Behavior, 34*(7), 942–958.

66. Aslam, U., Ilyas, M., Imran, M. K., & Rahman, U. U. (2016). Detrimental effects of cynicism on organizational change: An interactive model of organizational cynicism (a study of employees in public sector organizations). *Journal of Organizational Change Management, 29*(4), 580–598.

Chapter 2

1. Maxwell, J. C. (2007). *Failing forward.* New York, NY: HarperCollins, p. 75.

2. Blenko, M. W., Mankins, M. C., & Rogers, P. (2010). The decision-driven organization. *Harvard Business Review, 88*(6), 54–62.

3. Mintzberg, H. (1975, July–August). The manager's job: Folklore and fact. *Harvard Business Review,* pp. 49–61.

4. Shafir, E., & LeBoeuf, R. A. (2002). Rationality. *Annual Review of Psychology, 53*(1), 491–495; and Simon, H. A. (1986). Rationality in psychology and economics. *Journal of Business, 59*(4), S209–S224.

5. Bass, B. (1983). *Organizational decision making.* Homewood, IL: Richard D. Irwin.

6. Russo, J. E., Carlson, K. A., & Meloy, M. G. (2006). Choosing an inferior alternative. *Psychological Science, 17*(10), 899–904; and Thompson, L., &

Hrebec, D. (1986). Lose-lose agreements in interdependent decision making. *Psychological Bulletin, 120*(3), 396–409.

7. Ordonez, L., & Benson, L. (1997). Decisions under time pressure: How time constraint affects risky decision making. *Organizational Behavior and Human Decision Processes, 71*(2), 121–140.

8. Phillips, W. J., Fletcher, J. M., Marks, A. D., & Hine, D. W. (2016). Thinking styles and decision making: A meta-analysis. *Psychological Bulletin, 142*(3), 260–290.

9. Simon, H. A. (1977). *The new science of management decisions* (2nd ed.). Englewood Cliffs, NJ: Prentice Hall.

10. Augier, M. (2001). Simon says: Bounded rationality matters. *Journal of Management Inquiry, 10*(3), 268–275.

11. Plous, S. (1993). *The psychology of judgment and decision making.* New York, NY: McGraw-Hill.

12. March, J. G. (1978). Bounded rationality and the psychology of choice. *Bell Journal of Economics, 9*(2), 587–608.

13. Lu, J., Liang, Y., & Duan, H. (2017). Justifying decisions: Making choices for others enhances preferences for impoverished options. *Social Psychology, 48*(2), 92–103.

14. Kahneman, D., & Tversky, A. (1979). Prospect theory: An analysis of decision under risk. *Econometrica, 47*(2), 263–291.

15. Kahneman, D. (2011). *Thinking, fast and slow.* New York: NY: Macmillan.

16. Stanovich, K. E., & West, R. F. (2000). Individual differences in reasoning: Implications for the rationality debate? *Behavioral and Brain Sciences, 23,* 645–665.

17. Hogarth, R. M. (2010). Intuition: A challenge for psychological research on decision making. *Psychological Inquiry, 21,* 338–353, p. 339.

18. Dane, E., & Pratt, M. (2007). Exploring intuition and its role in managerial decision making. *Academy of Management Review, 32*(1), 33–54, p. 36.

19. Gladwell, M. (2007). *Blink: The power of thinking without thinking.* New York, NY: Little, Brown.

20. Simon, H. A. (1987). Making management decisions: The role of intuition and emotion. *Academy of Management Executive, 1*(1), 57–64, p. 63.

21. Zhao, S. (2009). The nature and value of common sense to decision making. *Management Decision, 47*(3), 441–453.

22. Hayashi, A. (2001, February). When to trust your gut. *Harvard Business Review,* pp. 59–65.

23. Burke, L. A., & Miller, M. K. (1999). Taking the mystery out of intuitive decision making. *Academy of Management Executive, 13*(4), 91–99, p. 95.

24. Shah, A. J., & Oppenheimer, D. (2008). Heuristics made easy: An effort reduction framework. *Psychological Bulletin, 134*(2), 207–222.

25. Kruglanski, A. W., & Gigerenzer, G. (2011). Intuitive and deliberate judgments are based on common principles. *Psychological Review, 118*(1), 97–109.

26. Bonesteel, M. (2017, December 27). Miami is bringing back the turnover chain in 2018. *Washington Post.* Retrieved from https://www.washingtonpost.com/news/early-lead/wp/2017/12/27/miami-is-blinging-back-the-turnover-chain-in-2018/?noredirect=on&utm_term=.16d6542e256e

27. Wood, G. (1978). The knew-it-all-along effect. *Journal of Experimental Psychology, Human Perception and Performance, 4,* 345–353.

28. Hawkins, S. A., & Hastie, R. (1990). Hindsight: Biased judgments of past events after the outcomes are known. *Psychological Bulletin, 107,* 311–327, p. 311.

29. Guilbault, R. L., Bryant, F. B., Brockway, J. H., & Posavac, E. J. (2004). A meta-analysis of research on hindsight bias. *Basic and Applied Social Psychology, 2/3,* 103–117.

30. Russo, J. E., & Schoemaker, P. J. H. (1992). Managing overconfidence. *Sloan Management Review, 33,* 7–17.

31. Spacey, J. (2018). 13 examples of hubris. Retrieved from https://simplicable.com/new/hubris

32. Laseter, T. (2017). The line between confidence and hubris. Retrieved from https://www.strategy-business.com/article/The-Line-between-Confidence-and-Hubris?gko=86a0e

33. Gilpin, K. (1992, October 9). Company news: Schwinn files under chapter 11. *New York Times.* Retrieved from https://www.nytimes.com/1992/10/09/business/company-news-schwinn-files-under-chapter-11.html

34. Shipman, A. S., Byrne, C. L., & Mumford, M. D. (2010). Leader vision formation and forecasting: The effects of forecasting extent, resources, and timeframe. *Leadership Quarterly, 21,* 439–456.

35. Fast, N. J., Sivanathan, N., Mayer, N. D., & Galinsky, A. D. (2012). Power and overconfident decision making. *Organizational Behavior and Human Decision Processes, 117,* 249–260.

36. Staw, B. M. (1981). The escalation of commitment to a course of action. *Academy of Management Review, 6,* 577–587.

37. Staw, B. M. (1976). Knee-deep in the big muddy: A study of escalating commitment to a chosen course of action. *Organizational Behavior and Human Performance, 16,* 27–44.

38. Brockner, J. (1992). The escalation of commitment to a failing course of action: Toward theoretical progress. *Academy of Management Review, 17,* 39–61.

39. Arkes, H. R., & Blumer, C. (1985). The psychology of sunk costs. *Organizational Behavior and Human Decision Processes, 35,* 124–140.

40. Moon, H. (2001). Looking forward and looking back: Integrating complete and sunk-cost effects within an escalation-of-commitment progress decision. *Journal of Applied Psychology, 86,* 104–113.

41. Khanin, D., & Mahto, R. V. (2013). Do venture capitalists have a continuation bias? *Journal of Entrepreneurship, 22*(2), 203–222.

42. Staw, B. M., Barsade, S. G., & Koput, D. W. (1997). Escalation at the credit window: A longitudinal study of bank executives' recognition and write-off of problem loans. *Journal of Applied Psychology, 82*(1), 130–142.

43. Wong, K. F. E., & Kwong, J. Y. Y. (2007). The role of anticipated regret in escalation of commitment. *Journal of Applied Psychology, 92*(2), 545–554.

44. Grant, A. (2013, July). How to escape from bad decisions [Blog post]. *Psychology Today.* Retrieved from www.psychologytoday.com/blog/give-and-take/201307/how-to-escape-bad-decisions

45. Gino, F. (2013). Sidetracked: Why our decisions get derailed, and how we can stick to the plan. Boston, MA: Harvard University Press, pp. 227–228.

46. Amabile, T. M. (1996). *Creativity in context.* Boulder, CO: Westview Press.

47. Cropley, A. J. (2003). *Creativity in education & learning.* Cornwall, England: Routledge Falmer.

48. Amabile, T. M. (1998, September/October). How to kill creativity. *Harvard Business Review,* pp. 77–87.

49. Basadur, M. (2004). Leading others to think innovatively together: Creative leadership. *Leadership Quarterly, 15*, 103–121.

50. Amabile (1998).

51. Burkus, D. (2013). *The myths of creativity: The truth about how innovative companies and people generate great ideas.* San Francisco, CA: Jossey Bass.

52. Evans, J. R. (2012). Business analytics: The next frontier for decision sciences. *Decision Line, 43*(2), 4–6, p. 5.

53. Acito, F., & Khatri, V. (2014). Business analytics: Why now and what next? *Business Horizons, 5*(57), 565–570, p. 566.

54. Acito & Khatri (2014) and Evans (2012).

55. Lustig, I., Dietrich, B., Johnson, & Dziekan, C. (2010, November/December). The analytics journey. *Analytics Magazine,* pp. 11–13.

56. Kohavi, R., Rothleder, N. J., & Simoudis, E. (2002). Emerging trends in business analytics. *Communications of the ACM, 45*(8), 45–48.

57. Hill, K. (2012, February 16). How Target figured out a teen girl was pregnant before her father did. *Forbes.* Retrieved from https://www.forbes .com/sites/kashmirhill/2012/02/16/ how-target-figured-out-a-teen-girl-was-pregnant-before-her-father-did/#3622196a6668

58. Lewis, R. E., & Heckman, R. J. (2006). Talent management: A critical review. *Human Resource Management Review, 16*(2), 139–154.

59. Schweyer, A. (2004). Are you managing your company's talent? An interview with HR-IT consultant and author Allan Schweyer. Retrieved from http://www.optimizemag .com/ article/ showArticle. jhtml?articleId=18100229

60. Institute for Operations Research and the Management Sciences. (2013). What is operations research? Retrieved from https://www.informs.org/About-INFORMS/What-is-Operations-Research

61. White, C. (2007). Operational analytics: Yesterday, today, and tomorrow. Retrieved from http:// www.b-eye-network.com/view/6536

62. Hanna, D., Shevlin, M., & Dempster, M. (2008). The structure of the statistics anxiety rating scale: A confirmatory factor analysis using UK psychology students. *Personality and Individual Differences, 45*, 68–74.

63. PricewaterHouseCoopers. (2014). Gut & gigabytes. *SAGE Business Researcher.* Retrieved from http:// businessresearcher.sagepub.com /sbr-1645-94783-2641913/20150209/ big-data, p. 33.

64. Bi, Z., & Cochran, D. (2014). Big data analytics with applications. *Journal of Management Analytics, 1*(4), 249–265.

65. Russom, P. (2011, September 14). *Big data analytics: TDWI best practices report.* Retrieved from http://tdwi.org/ research/2011/09/best-practices-report-q4-big-data-analytics.aspx

66. Stephens-Davidowitz, S. (2018). *Everybody lies: Big data, new data, and what the Internet can tell us about who we really are.* New York, NY: HarperCollins.

67. Watson, H. J. (2014) Tutorial: Big data analytics: Concepts, technologies, and applications. *Communications of the Association for Information Systems, 34*, Article 65.

68. Watson (2014).

69. Watson, H. J., & T. Leonard. (2011). U.S. Xpress: Where trucks and BI hit the road. *Business Intelligence Journal, 16*(1), 4–7.

Chapter 3

1. Ethics quotes. (n.d.). Edward Hennessy quote. Retrieved from https://www .decision-making-solutions.com/ethics_ quotes.html

2. Ethics quotes (n.d.).

3. Mill, J. S. (2016). Utilitarianism. In *Seven masterpieces of philosophy* (pp. 337–383). New York, NY: Routledge.

4. Edmundson, W. (2004). *An introduction to rights* (Cambridge introductions to philosophy and law). Cambridge, England: Cambridge University Press, pp. 105–107.

5. Rawls, J. (2009). *A theory of justice.* Cambridge, MA: Harvard University Press.

6. Dobrin, A. (2012). 3 approaches to ethics: Principles, outcomes and integrity. *Psychology Today.* Retrieved from https:// www.psychologytoday.com/us/blog/ am-i-right/201205/3-approaches-ethics-principles-outcomes-and-integrity

7. Gilligan, C. (1977). In a different voice. *Harvard Educational Review, 47*(3), 365–378.

8. Fritzsche, D. J., & Becker, H. (1984). Linking management behavior to ethical philosophy: An empirical investigation. *Academy of Management Journal, 27*(1), 166–175.

9. Stead, W. E., Worrell, D. L., & Stead, J. G. (1990). An integrative model for understanding and managing ethical behavior in business organizations. *Journal of Business Ethics, 9*(3), 233–242.

10. Noval, L. J. (2016). On the misguided pursuit of happiness and ethical decision making: The roles of focalism and the impact bias in unethical and selfish behavior. *Organizational Behavior and Human Decision Processes, 133*, 1–16.

11. Chugh, D., Bazerman, M. H., & Banaji, M. R. (2005). Bounded ethicality as a psychological barrier to recognizing conflicts of interest. In D. A. Moore, D. M. Cain, G. Loewenstein, & M. H. Bazerman (Eds.), *Conflicts of interest: Challenges and solutions in business, law, medicine, and public policy* (pp. 74–95). Cambridge, England: Cambridge University Press.

12. Shalvi, S., Dana, J., Handgraaf, M. J., & De Dreu, C. K. (2011). Justified ethicality: Observing desired counterfactuals modifies ethical perceptions and behavior. *Organizational Behavior and Human Decision Processes, 115*(2), 181–190.

13. Bazerman, M. H., & Sezer, O. (2016). Bounded awareness: Implications for ethical decision making. *Organizational Behavior and Human Decision Processes, 136*, 95–105.

14. Levine, M. (2016, September 9). Wells Fargo opened a couple million fake accounts. *Bloomberg.* Retrieved from https://www.bloomberg.com/ view/articles/2016-09-09/wells-fargo-opened-a-couple-million-fake-accounts

15. Sanders, C. E. (n.d.). Lawrence Kohlberg's stages of moral development. Encyclopedia Britannica. Retrieved from https://www.britannica.com/ science/Lawrence-Kohlbergs-stages-of-moral-development

16. Sanders (n.d.).

17. Weber, J. (1990). Managers' moral reasoning: Assessing their responses to three moral dilemmas. *Human Relations, 43*(7), 687–702.

18. Treviño, L. K., & Youngblood, S. A. (1990). Bad apples in bad barrels: A causal analysis of ethical decision-making behavior. *Journal of Applied Psychology, 75*, 378–385.

19. Kish-Gephart, J. J., Harrison, D. A., & Treviño, L. K. (2010). Bad apples, bad cases, and bad barrels: Meta-analytic

evidence about sources of unethical decisions at work. *Journal of Applied Psychology, 95*(1), 1–31.

20. Kirchner, B. (2010). *The Bernard Madoff investment scam.* Upper Saddle River, NJ: FT Press.

21. Psychology Notes HQ. (2019, July 25). Kohlberg's stages of moral development. Retrieved from https://www.psychologynoteshq.com/kohlbergstheory/

22. Treviño & Youngblood (1990).

23. Brass, D. J., Butterfield, K. K., & Skaggs, B. C. (1998). Relationships and unethical behavior: A social network perspective. *Academy of Management Review, 23*, 14–31.

24. Victor, B., & Cullen, J. B. (1988). The organizational bases of ethical work climate. *Administrative Science Quarterly, 33*, 101–125.

25. Wimbush, J. C., & Shepard, J. M. (1994). Toward an understanding of ethical climate: Its relationship to ethical behavior and supervisory influence. *Journal of Business Ethics, 13*(8), 637–647.

26. Cullen, J. B., Parboteeah, K. P., & B. Victor, B. (2003). The effects of ethical climates on organizational commitment: A two-study analysis. *Journal of Business Ethics, 46*(2), 127–141; and Koh, H. C., & Boo, E. H. Y. (2001). The link between organizational ethics and job satisfaction: A study of managers in Singapore. *Journal of Business Ethics, 29*(4), 309–324.

27. Schminke, M., Ambrose, M. L., & Neubaum, D. O. (2005). The effect of leader moral development on ethical climate and employee attitudes. *Organizational Behavior and Human Decision Processes, 97*(2), 135–151.

28. Peterson, D. K. (2002). The relationship between unethical behavior and the dimensions of the Ethical Climate Questionnaire. *Journal of Business Ethics, 41*(4), 313–326.

29. Martin, K. D., & Cullen, J. B. (2006). Continuities and extensions of ethical climate theory: A meta-analytic review. *Journal of Business Ethics, 69*(2), 175–194.

30. Brown, M. E., & Treviño, L. K. (2006). Ethical leadership: A review and future directions. *Leadership Quarterly, 17*(6), 595–616.

31. Mayer, D. M., Aquino, K., Greenbaum, R., & Kuenzi, M. (2012). Who displays ethical leadership, and why does it matter? An examination of antecedents and consequences

of ethical leadership. *Academy of Management Journal, 55*(1), 151–171.

32. Den Hartog, D. N. (2015). Ethical leadership. *Annual Review of Organizational Psychology and Organizational Behavior, 2*(1), 409–434, p. 428.

33. Mayer, D. M., Kuenzi, M., Greenbaum, R., Bardes, M., & Salvador, R. (2009). How low does ethical leadership flow? Test of a trickle-down model. *Organizational Behavior and Human Decision Processes, 108*(1), 1–13.

34. Lattall, D. (2013). Ethical decision making in the workplace. *PM eZine.* Retrieved from http://aubreydaniels.com/pmezine/ethical-decision-making-workplace

35. NPR Ethics Handbook. (2019). *NPR.* Retrieved from https://www.npr.org/ethics

36. GM layoff announcement sparks outrage—and stock increase. (2018, November 27). *CBS News.* Retrieved from https://www.cbsnews.com/news/gm-layoff-announcement-sparks-controversy/

37. Bies, R. J. (1987). The predicament of injustice: The management of moral outrage. *Research in Organizational Behavior, 9*, 289–319.

38. Ambrose, M. L., Seabright, M. A., & Schminke, M. (2002). Sabotage in the workplace: The role of organizational justice. *Organizational Behavior and Human Decision Processes, 89*(1), 947–965.

39. Hernandez, H. (2018, December 7). GM CEO Mary Barra was forced to shut US plants: Bob Nardelli. *Fox Business.* Retrieved from https://www.foxbusiness.com/business-leaders/gm-ceo-mary-barra-was-forced-to-shut-us-plants-bob-nardelli

40. Sekerka, L. E. (2016). Professional moral courage. In *Ethics is a daily deal* (pp. 171–197). New York, NY: Springer.

41. Essex, R. (2018, November 30). Folks are angry at GM, Mary Barra, but GM can't afford to be bothered. *Detroit Free Press.* https://www.freep.com/story/money/cars/general-motors/2018/11/30/gm-mary-barra-donald-trump/2150045002/

42. Treviño, L. K., & Nelson, K. A. (2004). *Managing business ethics: Straight talk about how to do it right.* Hoboken, NJ: John Wiley.

43. Ethics Resource Center. (n.d.). The PLUS decision making model. Retrieved from http://www.burtbertram.com/teaching/ethics/Article_02-PLUS_DecisionMakingModel.pdf

44. Ethics and Compliance Initiative. (n.d.). The PLUS ethical decision making model: Ethics and compliance toolkit. Retrieved June 1, 2019 from https://www.ethics.org/resources/free-toolkit/decision-making-model/

45. Ethics Resource Center (n.d.).

46. Jones, T. M. (1991). Ethical decision-making by individuals in organizations: An issue-contingent model. *Academy of Management Review, 16*(2), 366–395, p. 372.

47. McMahon, J. M., & Harvey, R. J. (2007). The effect of moral intensity on ethical judgment. *Journal of Business Ethics, 72*(4), 335–357.

48. Rhodes, C. (2016). Democratic business ethics: Volkswagen's emissions scandal and the disruption of corporate sovereignty. *Organization Studies, 37*(10), 1501–1518.

49. Boston, W. (2015, September 23). Volkswagen CEO resigns as car maker races to stem emissions scandal. *Wall Street Journal.* Retrieved from http://www.wsj.com/articles/volkswagen-ceo-winterkorn-resigns-1443007423

50. Carroll, A. B. (1991, July/August). The pyramid of corporate social responsibility: Toward the moral management of organizational stakeholders. *Business Horizons, 34*, 39–48, p. 40.

51. Caroll (1991), p. 43.

52. Michigan State University. (2019, July 12). 6-step guide to ethical decision-making. Retrieved from https://www.michiganstateuniversityonline.com/resources/leadership/guide-to-ethical-decision-making/

53. Michigan State University (2019).

54. Michigan State University (2019).

55. Business Dictionary. (n.d.). Stakeholder. Retrieved from http://www.businessdictionary.com/definition/stakeholder.html

56. Slaper, T. F., & Hall, T. J. (2011). The triple bottom line: What is it and how does it work? *Indiana Business Review.* Retrieved from http://www.ibrc.indiana.edu/ibr/2011/spring/article2.html

57. Kidder, R. M. (2003). *How good people make tough choices: Resolving the dilemmas of ethical living.* New York, NY: HarperCollins.

58. Treviño, L. K., Weaver, G. R., & Reynolds, S. J. (2006). Behavioral ethics in organizations: A review. *Journal of Management, 32*(6), 951–990.

59. Reynolds, S. J., Dang, C. T., Yam, K. C., & Leavitt, K. (2014). The role of moral knowledge in everyday immorality: What does it matter if I know what is right? *Organizational Behavior and Human Decision Processes, 123*(2), 124–137.

60. The ethics issue: The 10 biggest moral dilemmas in science. (n.d.) *New Scientist.* Retrieved from https://www.newscientist.com/round-up/ethics-issue/

61. The ethics issue: The 10 biggest moral dilemmas in science (n.d.).

62. Baron, J. (2018, December 27). Tech ethics issues we should all be thinking about in 2019. *Forbes.* Retrieved from https://www.forbes.com/sites/jessicabaron/2018/12/27/tech-ethics-issues-we-should-all-be-thinking-about-in-2019/#2f4d880d4b21

63. Michigan State University (2019).

Chapter 4

1. Ryan, L. (2016, October 19). Ten unmistakable signs of a toxic culture. *Forbes.* Retrieved from https://www.forbes.com/sites/lizryan/2016/10/19/ten-unmistakable-signs-of-a-toxic-culture/#3c76bb92115f

2. CultureIQ. (n.d.). What is employee engagement? Retrieved from https://cultureiq.com/employee-engagement-company-culture/

3. Schein, E. H. (1984). Coming to a new awareness of organizational culture. *Sloan Management Review, 25*(2), 3–16, p. 3.

4. Hogg, M. A., & Reid, S. A. (2006). Social identity, self-categorization, and the communication of group norms. *Communication Theory, 16*(1), 7–30.

5. Chatman, J. A., & O'Reilly, C. A. (2016). Paradigm lost: Reinvigorating the study of organizational culture. *Research in Organizational Behavior, 36,* 199–224.

6. Schein (1984).

7. Chatman, J. A., & Jehn, K. A. (1994). Assessing the relationship between industry characteristics and organizational culture: How different can you be? *Academy of Management Journal, 37*(3), 522–553.

8. Denison, D. R., Hooijberg, R., & Quinn, R. E. (1995). Paradox and performance: Toward a theory of behavioral complexity in managerial leadership. *Organization Science, 6*(5), 524–540.

9. Cameron, K., & Quinn, R. (2011). *Diagnosing and changing organizational culture: Based on the competing values framework* (3rd ed.). San Francisco, CA: Jossey-Bass.

10. Helfrich, C. D., Li, Y.-F., Mohr, D. C., Meterko, M., & Sales, A. E. (2007). Assessing an organizational culture instrument based on the competing values framework: Exploratory and confirmatory factor analyses. *Implementation Science, 2,* 13–14.

11. Cameron & Quinn (2011).

12. Helfrich et al. (2007).

13. Denison et al. (1995).

14. Helfrich et al. (2007).

15. ten Have, S., ten Have, W., & Stevens, F. (2003). *Key management models.* Edinburgh Gate, England: Financial Times Prentice Hall.

16. O'Reilly, C. (1989). Corporations, culture, and commitment: Motivation and social control in organizations. *California Management Review, 31*(4), 9–25.

17. Barney, J. B. (1986). Organizational culture: Can it be a source of sustained competitive advantage? *Academy of Management Review, 11*(3), 656–665; Gordon, G. G., & DiTomaso, N. (1992). Predicting corporate performance from organizational culture. *Journal of Management Studies, 29*(6), 783–798; and Sørensen, J. B. (2002). The strength of corporate culture and the reliability of firm performance. *Administrative Science Quarterly, 47*(1), 70–91.

18. O'Reilly, C. A., Chatman, J. A., & Caldwell, D. F. (1991). People and organizational culture: A profile comparison approach to assessing person–organization fit. *Academy of Management Journal, 34*(3), 487–516; and Vandenberghe, C. (1999). Organizational culture, person–culture fit, and turnover: A replication in the health care industry. *Journal of Organizational Behavior, 20*(2), 175–184.

19. Sørensen (2002).

20. Warrick, D. D., Milliman, J. F., & Ferguson, J. M. (2016). Building high performance cultures. *Organizational Dynamics, 45*(1), 64–70.

21. Zappos. (2019, June 7). What we live by: About us. Retrieved July 1, 2019 from https://www.zappos.com/about/what-we-live-by

22. Rosenbaum, S. (2010). The happiness culture: Zappos isn't a company, it's a mission. *Fast Company.* Retrieved from http://www.fastcompany.com/1657030/happiness-culture-zappos-isnt-company-its-mission

23. See https://www.holacracy.org/.

24. Hofstede, G. (1998). Identifying organizational subcultures: An empirical approach. *Journal of Management Studies, 35*(1), 1–12.

25. Boisnier, A., & Chatman, J. (2003). Cultures and subcultures in dynamic organizations. In E. Mannix & R. Petersen (Eds.), *The dynamic organization* (pp. 87–114). Mahwah, NJ: Lawrence Erlbaum.

26. Lafley, A. G. (2008, August 26). P&G's innovation culture: How we built a world-class organic growth engine by investing in people. *Strategy + Business.* Retrieved from https://www.strategy-business.com/article/08304?gko=a6111

27. Wanberg, C. R. (2012). Facilitating organizational socialization: An introduction. In C. R. Wanberg (Ed.), *The Oxford handbook of organizational socialization* (pp. 17–21). New York, NY: Oxford University Press.

28. Schein, E. H. (2003). Organizational socialization and the profession of management. In L. W. Porter, H. L. Angle, & R. W. Allen (Eds.), *Organizational influence processes* (pp. 283–294). New York, NY: M. E. Sharpe.

29. Jablin, F. M. (1987). Organizational entry, assimilation, and exit. In L. L. Putnam, K. H. Roberts, & L. W. Porter (Eds.), *Handbook of organizational communication: An interdisciplinary perspective* (pp. 679–740). Newbury Park, CA: Sage.

30. Kramer, M. W. (2010). *Organizational socialization: Joining and leaving organizations.* Malden, MA: Polity.

31. Ellis, A. M., Nifadkar, S. S., Bauer, T. N., & Erdogan, B. (2017). Newcomer adjustment: Examining the role of managers' perception of newcomer proactive behavior during organizational socialization. *Journal of Applied Psychology.* Retrieved from http://dx.doi.org/10.1037/apl0000201

32. Bauer, T. N., & Erdogan, B. (2011). Organizational socialization: The effective onboarding of new employees. In S. Zedeck (Ed.), *APA Handbooks in Psychology: Handbook of industrial and organizational psychology: Vol. 3. Maintaining, expanding, and contracting the organization* (pp. 51–64). Washington, DC: American Psychological Association.

33. HRZone. (n.d.). What is a psychological contract? Retrieved from https://www.hrzone.com/hr-glossary/what-is-a-psychological-contract

34. Delobbe, N., Cooper-Thomas, H. D., & De Hoe, R. (2016). A new look at the psychological contract during organizational socialization: The role of newcomers' obligations at entry. *Journal of Organizational Behavior, 37*(6), 845–867.

35. Bauer, T. N., Bodner, T., Erdogan, B., Truxillo, D. M., & Tucker, J. S. (2007). Newcomer adjustment during organizational socialization: A meta-analytic review of antecedents, outcomes, and methods. *Journal of Applied Psychology, 92*(3), 707–721.

36. Boje, D. M. (1995). Stories of the storytelling organization: A postmodern analysis of Disney as "Tamara-Land." *Academy of Management Journal, 38*(4), 997–1035.

37. Sole, D., & Wilson, D. G. (2002). Storytelling in organizations: The power and traps of using stories to share knowledge in organizations. Retrieved from http://www.providersedge.com/docs/km_articles/Storytelling_in_Organizations.pdf

38. Barker, R. T., & Gower, K. (2010). Strategic application of storytelling in organizations: Towards effective communication in a diverse world. *Journal of Business Communication, 47*(3), 295–312.

39. Weick, K. (1995). *Sensemaking in organizations*. Thousand Oaks, CA: Sage.

40. Merchant, A., Ford, J. B., & Sargeant, A. (2010). Charitable organizations' storytelling influence on donors' emotions and intentions. *Journal of Business Research, 63*(7), 754–762.

41. Schleckser, J. (2015). Using stories and symbols to build a powerful culture. *Inc.* Retrieved from https://www.inc.com/jim-schleckser/use-stories-and-symbols-to-build-a-powerful-culture.html

42. Barker & Gower (2010).

43. Barker & Gower (2010).

44. Lämsä, A. M., & Sintonen, T. (2006). A narrative approach for organizational learning in a diverse organisation. *Journal of Workplace Learning, 18*(2), 106–120.

45. Islam, G., & Zyphur, M. J. (2009). Rituals in organizations: A review and expansion of current theory. *Group and Organization Management, 34*(1), 114–139, p. 116.

46. Erhardt, N., Martin-Rios, C., & Heckscher, C. (2016). Am I doing the right thing? Unpacking workplace rituals as mechanisms for strong organizational culture. *International Journal of Hospitality Management, 59*, 31–41.

47. Alvesson, M., & Sveningsson, S. (2015). *Changing organizational culture: Cultural change work in progress*. New York, NY: Routledge.

48. Anand, N., & Watson, M. R. (2004). Tournament rituals in the evolution of fields: The case of the Grammy Awards. *Academy of Management Journal, 47*(1), 59–80.

49. Sole & Wilson (2002).

50. Rafaeli, A., & Worline, M. (2000). Symbols in organizational culture. In N. M. Ashkanasy, C. P. M. Wilderom, & M. F. Peterson (eds.), *Handbook of organizational culture and climate*. Thousand Oaks, CA: Sage.

51. Rafaeli, A., & Pratt, M. G. (Eds.). (2013). *Artifacts and organizations: Beyond mere symbolism*. New York, NY: Psychology Press.

52. Rafaeli, A., & Pratt, M. G. (1993). Tailored meanings: On the meaning and impact of organizational dress. *Academy of Management Review, 18*(1), 32–55.

53. Schleckser (2015).

54. Van Maanen, J. (1996). The smile factory: Work at Disneyland. In P. J. Frost, L. F. Moore, M. R. Louis, & C. C. Lundberg (Eds.), *Reframing organizational culture* (pp. 58–76). Newbury Park, CA: Sage.

55. Alvesson, M. (1995). Cultural perspectives on organizations. CUP Archive.

56. Ratliff, H. (n.d.). The slow decline of America Online. Retrieved from https://fusion360.atavist.com/the-slow-decline-of-america-online-

57. Beer, M., Eisenstat, R. A., & Spector, B. (1993). Why change programs don't produce change. In C. Mabey & B. Mayon-White (Eds.), *Managing change*. London, England: P.C.P.

58. Argyris, C. (1990). *Overcoming organizational defenses*. Boston, MA: Allyn & Bacon.

59. Oswick, C., Grant, D., Michelson, G., & Wailes, N. (2005). Looking forwards: Discursive directions in organizational change. *Journal of Organizational Change Management, 18*(4), 383–390; and Weick, K. E., & Quinn, R. E. (1999). Organizational change and development. *Annual Review of Psychology, 50*(1), 361–386.

60. Malhotra, N., & Hinings, C. B. (2015). Unpacking continuity and change as a process of organizational transformation. *Long Range Planning, 48*(1), 1–22.

61. Robertson, P. J., Roberts, D. R., & Porras, J. I. (1993). Dynamics of planned organizational change: Assessing empirical support for a theoretical model. *Academy of Management Journal, 36*(3), 619–634.

62. Lines, R. (2004). Influence of participation in strategic change: Resistance, organizational commitment and change goal achievement. *Journal of Change Management, 4*(3), 193–215.

63. Herscovitch, L., & Meyer, J. P. (2002). Commitment to organizational change: Extension of a three-component model. *Journal of Applied Psychology, 87*(3), 474–487.

64. Coch, L., & French, J. R. (1948). Overcoming resistance to change. *Human Relations, 1*(4), 512–532.

65. Burnes, B. (2015). Understanding resistance to change—Building on Coch and French. *Journal of Change Management, 15*(2), 92–116.

66. Burke, W. W. (2010). *Organization change: Theory and practice*. Thousand Oaks, CA: Sage; Katz, D., & Kahn, R. L. (1978). *The social psychology of organizations* (2nd ed.). New York, NY: John Wiley; and Nadler, D. A. (1987). The effective management of organizational change. *Handbook of organizational behavior* (pp. 358–369). Englewood Cliffs, NJ: Prentice Hall.

67. Rafferty, A. E., & Jimmieson, N. L. (2016). Subjective perceptions of organizational change and employee resistance to change: Direct and mediated relationships with employee well-being. *British Journal of Management, 28*, 248–264.

68. Turgut, S., Michel, A., Rothenhöfer, L. M., & Sonntag, K. (2016). Dispositional resistance to change and emotional exhaustion: Moderating effects at the work-unit level. *European Journal of Work and Organizational Psychology, 25*(5), 735–750.

69. Wride, M. (2018, February 15). What's the difference between human resources and organizational development? Retrieved from https://www.decision-wise.com/difference-between-human-resources-and-organization-development/

70. Organization Development Network. (n.d.). What is organization development? Retrieved from https://www.odnetwork.org/page/WhatIsOD

71. Organization Development Network (n.d.).

72. JobHero. (n.d.). Organizational development specialist job description. Retrieved from https://www.jobhero.com/organizational-development-specialist-job-description/

73. SHRM. (n.d.). Job descriptions. Retrieved from https://www.shrm.org/resourcesandtools/tools-and-samples/job-descriptions/

74. Jones, S. L., & Van de Ven, A. H. (2016). The changing nature of change resistance: An examination of the moderating impact of time. *Journal of Applied Behavioral Science, 52*(4), 482–506.

75. Bakari, H., Hunjra, A. I., & Niazi, G. S. K. (2017). How does authentic leadership influence planned organizational change? The role of employees' perceptions: Integration of theory of planned behavior and Lewin's three step model. *Journal of Change Management, 17*(2), 155–187.

76. Espedal, B. (2017). Understanding how balancing autonomy and power might occur in leading organizational change. *European Management Journal, 35*(2), 155–163, p. 159.

77. Kim, T. (2015). Diffusion of changes in organizations. *Journal of Organizational Change Management, 28*(1), 134–152.

78. Mindtools. (n.d.a). Lewin's change management model: Understanding the three stages of change. Retrieved from https://www.mindtools.com/pages/article/newPPM_94.htm

79. Seyfried, M., & Ansmann, M. (2018). Unfreezing higher education institutions? Understanding the introduction of quality management in teaching and learning in Germany. *Higher Education, 75*(6), 1061–1076.

80. Shirey, M. R. (2013). Lewin's theory of planned change as a strategic resource. *Journal of Nursing Administration, 43*(2), 69–72.

81. Burnes, B. (2004). Kurt Lewin and the planned approach to change: A re-appraisal. *Journal of Management Studies, 41*(6), 977–1002, p. 977.

82. Marshak, R. J. (2012). The Tao of change redux. *OD Practitioner, 44*(1), 44–51.

83. Lewin, K. (1951). *Field theory in social science*. New York, NY: Harper & Row.

84. Fisher, J. M. (2005). A time for change. *Human Resource Development International, 8*, 257–264.

85. Kübler-Ross, E. & Kessler, D. (2014). *On grief & grieving: Finding the meaning of grief through the five stages* of loss. New York, NY: Scribner.

86. Elrod, P. D., & Tippett, D. D. (2002). The "death valley" of change. *Journal of Organizational Change Management, 15*(3), 273–291.

87. Mindtools. (n.d. b). The change curve: Accelerating change, and increasing its likelihood of success. Retrieved from https://www.mindtools.com/pages/article/newPPM_96.htm

88. Harris, L. C., & Ogbonna, E. (1998). Employee responses to culture change efforts. *Human Resource Management Journal, 8*(2), 78–92.

89. Mindtools (n.d. b).

90. Harris & Ogbonna (1998).

91. Mindtools (n.d. b).

92. Armenakis, A. A., & Harris, S. G. (2002). Crafting a change message to create transformational readiness. *Journal of Organizational Change Management, 15*(2), 169–183.

93. Jaruzelski, B., Loehr, J., & Holman, R. (2011). The global innovation 1000: Why culture is key. Retrieved from https://www.strategy-business.com/article/11404?gko=62080

94. Armenakis & Harris (2002).

95. Elrod & Tippett (2002).

96. Conversations Staff. (2012, November 14). The real story of new Coke. Retrieved from https://www.coca-colacompany.com/stories/coke-lore-new-coke

97. Schanz (2017).

98. Schanz (2017).

99. Meyersohn (2018).

Chapter 5

1. Braun, M., & Latham, S. (2012). Pulling off the comeback: Shrink, expand, neither, both? *Journal of Business Strategy, 33*(3), 13–21.

2. Business Dictionary. (n.d.). Strategic planning. Retrieved from http://www.businessdictionary.com/definition/strategic-planning.html

3. Peel, M. J., & Bridge, J. (1998). How planning and capital budgeting improve SME performance. *Long Range Planning, 31*(6), 848–856.

4. Kunisch, S., Bartunek, J. M., Mueller, J., & Huy, Q. N. (2017). Time in strategic change research. *Academy of Management Annals, 11*(2), 1005–1064.

5. Chen, J., & Nadkarni, S. (2017). It's about time! CEOs' temporal dispositions, temporal leadership, and corporate entrepreneurship. *Administrative Science Quarterly, 62*(1), 31–66.

6. Mosakowski, E., & Earley, P. C. (2000). A selective review of time assumptions in strategy research. *Academy of Management Review, 25*(4), 796–812.

7. Kukalis, S. (1991). Determinants of strategic planning systems in large organizations: A contingency approach. *Journal of Management Studies, 28*(2), 143–160.

8. Corporate Finance Institute. (n.d.). What is a vision statement? Retrieved from https://corporatefinanceinstitute.com/resources/knowledge/strategy/vision-statement/

9. Corporate Finance Institute. (n.d.). What is a mission statement? Retrieved from https://corporatefinanceinstitute.com/resources/knowledge/strategy/mission-statement/

10. Thompson, A. (2019, February 13). Google's mission statement and vision statement (an analysis). Retrieved from http://panmore.com/google-vision-statement-mission-statement

11. Google Search. (n.d.). Mission statement. Retrieved from https://wwwhttps://www.google.com/search/howsearchworks/mission/.google.com/search/howsearchworks/mission/

12. Google Search (n.d.).

13. Comparably. (n.d.). Google mission, vision & values. Retrieved from https://www.comparably.com/companies/google/mission

14. Stanford University. (2019, May). Our vision. Retrieved from https://ourvision.stanford.edu/vision-initiatives/mission-values

15. immoreau. (2011, May 13). Guy Kawasaki Company mission statement [YouTube video]. Retrieved from https://www.youtube.com/watch?v=-JBYC6WpIaY4

16. Germain, R. & Cooper, M.B. (1990). How a customer mission statement affects company performance. *Industrial Marketing Management, 19*(1), 47–54.

17. Bart, C. K., Bontis, N., & Taggar, S. (2001). A model of the impact of mission statements on firm performance. *Management Decision, 39*(1), 19–35.

18. Porter, M. E. (1980). *Competitive strategy: How to analyze industries and competitors*. New York, NY: Free Press.

19. Porter (1980).

20. Hammonds, K. H. (2001, February 28). Michael Porter's big ideas. *Fast Company*. Retrieved from https://www.fastcompany.com/42485/michael-porters-big-ideas

21. Porter, M. E. (1985). *Competitive advantage: Creating and sustaining superior performance*. New York, NY: Free Press.

22. Mintzberg, H., Quinn, J. B., & Ghoshal, S. (1995). *The strategy process: Concepts, contexts and cases* (European ed.). Englewood Cliffs, NJ: Prentice Hall.

23. Prahalad, C. K., & Hamel, G. (1990, May–June). The core competence of the corporation. *Harvard Business Review, 68*(3), 79–91.

24. Meier, J. D. (n.d.). Organizational values: Actions are louder than words. Retrieved from http://sourcesofinsight.com/organizational-values/

25. Olsen, E. (n.d.). Core values. Retrieved from https://onstrategyhq.com/resources/core-values/

26. Heathfield, S. M. (2019, May 9). How to understand your current company culture. *The Balance Careers*. Retrieved from https://www.thebalancecareers.com/how-to-understand-your-current-culture-1918811

27. Loehr, A. (2016, March 7). 6 steps to defining your organizational values. Retrieved from https://www.cornerstoneondemand.com/rework/6-steps-defining-your-organizational-values

28. Kronos. (2015, November 3). CEO lessons: Culture, values, and profits are intertwined. Retrieved from https://www.hrbartender.com/2015/employee-engagement/ceo-lessons-culture-values-and-profits-are-intertwined/.

29. Loehr (2016).

30. Loehr (2016).

31. Williams, S. L. (2002). Strategic planning and organizational values: Links to alignment. *Human Resource Development International, 5*(2), 217–233.

32. Sharma, D. (2018). When fairness is not enough: Impact of corporate ethical values on organizational citizenship behaviors and worker alienation. *Journal of Business Ethics, 150*(1), 57–68.

33. Organ, D. W. (1988). *Organizational citizenship behavior: The good soldier syndrome*. Lexington, MA: Lexington Books.

34. Chappelow, J. (2019, April 11). Porter's 5 forces. *Investopedia*. Retrieved from https://www.investopedia.com/terms/p/porter.asp

35. iWise2. (n.d.). Porter's 5 forces. Retrieved from https://www.iwise2.com/library/business-strategy-planning-and-goal-deployment/strategy/porters-5-forces

36. Chappelow (2019).

37. Wilkinson, J. (2013, July 24). Threat of new entrants definition. Retrieved from https://strategiccfo.com/threat-of-new-entrants-one-of-porters-five-forces/

38. Chappelow (2019).

39. Porter (1985).

40. Creately. (2019, June 17). SWOT analysis templates to download, print or modify online. Retrieved from https://creately.com/blog/examples/swot-analysis-templates-creately/

41. Redman, B. (n.d.). Keys to a good SWOT analysis. *Chron*. Retrieved from https://smallbusiness.chron.com/keys-good-swot-analysis-25139.html

42. Parsons, N. (2018, April 5). What is a SWOT analysis, and how to do it right (with examples). Retrieved from https://www.liveplan.com/blog/what-is-a-swot-analysis-and-how-to-do-it-right-with-examples/

43. Jurevicius, O. (2013, February 13). SWOT analysis: Do it properly! Retrieved from https://www.strategicmanagementinsight.com/tools/swot-analysis-how-to-do-it.html

44. Jurevicius (2013).

45. Parsons (2018).

46. Jurevicius (2013).

47. Parsons (2018).

48. Jurevicius (2013).

49. Hall, M. (2019, April 11). Porter's 5 forces vs. SWOT analysis: What's the difference? *Investopedia*. Retrieved from https://www.investopedia.com/ask/answers/041015/whats-difference-between-porters-5-forces-and-swot-analysis.asp; and Kokemuller, N. (2019). What is the differences between SWOT and fives forces analysis? *Chron*. Retrieved from https://smallbusiness.chron.com/difference-between-swot-fiveforces-analysis-78277.html

50. Tips for writing goals and objectives. (n.d.). Retrieved from https://www.google.com/search?q=Tips-for-writing-goals-and-objectives.pdf.&oq=Tips-for-writing-goals-and-objectives.pdf.&aqs=chrome..69i57j69i60.9813j0j4&sourceid=chrome&ie=UTF-8

51. Mindtools. (n.d.). Smart goals. Retrieved from https://www.mindtools.com/pages/article/smart-goals.htm

52. Mulder, P. (n.d.). Management by objectives (MBO). Retrieved from https://www.toolshero.com/management/management-by-objectives-drucker/

53. Mulder (n.d.).

54. West, G. E. (1977). Bureau pathology and the failure of MBO. *Human Resource Management, 16*(2), 33.

55. Weldon, D. J. (1982). MBO: Success or failure? *Leadership and Organization Development Journal, 3*(4), 2–8.

56. Leonard, J. W. (1986). Why MBO fails so often. *Training and Development Journal, 40*(6), 38–39.

57. David, F. R. (2007). *Strategic management: Concepts and cases*. New York, NY: Pearson Prentice Hall.

58. Ingram, D., & Seidel, M. (2019). Financial business objectives. *Chron*. Retrieved from https://smallbusiness.chron.com/financial-business-objectives-4072.html

59. Business Dictionary. (n.d.). Long term objectives. Retrieved from http://www.businessdictionary.com/definition/long-term-objectives.html

60. Shujahat, M., Hussain, S., Javed, S., Malik, M. I. Thurasamy, R., & Ali, J. (2017). Strategic management model with lens of knowledge management and competitive intelligence. *VINE Journal of Information and Knowledge Management Systems, 47*(1), 55–93.

61. Al-Hakim, L. A. Y., & Hassan, S. (2014). Who are the crew members on implementation of knowledge management strategies to enhance innovation and improve organizational performance? *Journal of Resources Development and Management, 3*, 54–63; Malhotra, Y. (2004). Why knowledge management systems fail: Enablers and constraints of knowledge management in human enterprises. In C. Holsapple (Ed.), *Handbook on knowledge management* (Vol. 1, pp. 577–599). Heidelberg, Germany: Springer Berlin; and Momeni, A., Fathian, M., & Akhavan, P. (2012). Competitive intelligence and knowledge management's affinities and relations: Developing a model. *Invertis Journal of Science and Technology, 5*(1), 1–7.

62. Hildebrand, C. (2003, January 23). How to hire a knowledge management professional. Retrieved from https://searchcio.techtarget.com/tip/How-to-hire-a-knowledge-management-professional

63. Leidos. (2019, May). Knowledge management engineer—US citizen required [Job posting]. Retrieved from https://www.ziprecruiter

.com/c/Leidos/Job/Knowledge-Management-Engineer-US-CITIZEN-REQUIRED/-in-Chantilly,VA?ojob=1b925b088c68eda3ee68ce6e0490ee84

64. Booz, Allen, Hamilton. (2019). Knowledge management engineer [Job posting]. Retrieved April, 19, 2019 from knowledge+management+engineer+job&oq=knowledge+management+engineer+job&aqs=chrome..69i57j0.7777j1j4&sourceid=chrome&ie=UTF-8&ibp=htl;jobs&sa=X&ved=2ahUKEwiIkr-TgqXiAhVqmeAKHdP_B68Qp4wCMAJ6BAgJEB8#fpstate=tldetail&htidocid=554TRb_mGAsXTBkQAAAAAA%3D%3D&htivrt=jobs

65. Leidos (2019).

66. Booz, Allen, Hamilton (2019).

67. Leidos (2019).

68. Hildebrand (2003).

69. Momeni et al. (2012).

70. Grèzes, V. (2015). The definition of competitive intelligence needs through a synthesis model. *Journal of Intelligence Studies in Business*, 5(1), 40–46.

71. Liebl, F. (2004). *Knowledge management for strategic marketing*. Paper presented at the 32nd Academy of Marketing Science (AMS) Annual Conference, Vancouver, Canada.

72. Halawi, L. A., McCarthy, R. V. & Aronson, J. E. (2006). Knowledge management and the competitive strategy of the firm. *The Learning Organization*, 13(4), 384–397; and Liebl (2004).

73. Goodson, L. (2017). Feedback. *Strategy and Leadership*, 45(2), 51–55.

74. Kanter, Z. (2017, May 14.). Why Amazon is eating the world. *TechCrunch*. Retrieved from https://techcrunch.com/2017/05/14/why-amazon-is-eating-the-world/

75. Kenton, W. (2019, March 27). Not-for-profit. Retrieved from https://www.investopedia.com/terms/n/not-for-profit.asp

76. Bogdan, M., & Lungescu, D. C. (2018). Is strategic management ready for big data? A review of the big data analytics literature in management research. *Managerial Challenges of the Contemporary Society*, 11(2), 65–73.

77. McMillan, C., & Overall, L. J. (2016). Wicked problems: Turning strategic management upside down. *Journal of Business Strategy*, 37(1), 34–43.

78. McMillan & Overall (2016).

79. Bogdan & Lungescu (2018).

80. Davenport, T. H., & Harris, J. G. (2007). *Competing on analytics: The new science of winning*. Cambridge, MA: Harvard Business School Press.

81. Davenport, T. H., & Kim, J. (2013). *Keeping up with the quants: Your guide to understanding and using analytics*. Cambridge, MA: Harvard Business School Press.

82. Bogdan & Lungescu (2018).

83. Wheatley, M. (1992). *Leadership and the new science: Learning about organization from an orderly universe*. San Francisco, CA: Berrett-Kohler.

84. Brown, A. M. (2017). *Emergent strategy: Shaping change, changing worlds*. Chico, CA: AK Press.

85. Kim, W. C., & Mauborgne, R. (2015). *Blue ocean strategy: How to create uncontested market space and make the competition irrelevant (Expanded ed.)*. Cambridge, MA: Harvard Business School Press.

86. Schwieters, N. (2017, January 3). The end of conventional industry sectors [Blog post]. Retrieved from https://www.strategy-business.com/blog/The-End-of-Conventional-Industry-Sectors/

87. Baker, W. H., Addams, H. L., & Davis, B. (1993). Business planning in successful small firms. *Long Range Planning*, 26(6), 82–88.

88. Dockery, E., Herbert, W., & Taylor, K. (2000). Corporate governance, managerial strategies and shareholder wealth maximisation: A study of large European companies. *Managerial Finance*, 26(9), 21–35.

89. Kenton, W. (2019, April 12). Profit definition. *Investopedia*. Retrieved from https://www.investopedia.com/terms/p/profit.asp

90. Waas, T., Huge, J., Verbruggen, A., & Wright, T. (2011). Sustainable development: A bird's eye view. *Sustainability*, 3(10), 1637–1661.

91. Konkolewsky, H.-H. (2004). Protecting people, planet and profit. *The Safety and Health Practitioner*, 22(5), 36–38.

92. Elkington, J. (1994). Towards the sustainable corporation: Win-win-win business strategies for sustainable development. *California Management Review*, 36(2), 90–100.

93. Elkington (1994).

94. National Bureau of Economic Research. (n.d.). Changing business volatility. Retrieved from https://www.nber.org/digest/apr07/w12354.html

95. Porter, M. E. (1990). *The competitive advantage of nations*. New York, NY: Free Press.

96. Porter (1990).

97. Adhikari, D. R., Gautam, D. K., & Chaudhari, M. K. (2016). Corporate social responsibility domains and related activities in Nepalese companies. *International Journal of Law and Management*, 58(6), 673–684.

98. For more information on the statistics and progress since the 2015 earthquake, check out World Vision. (n.d.). 2015 Nepal earthquake: Facts, FAQs, and how to help. Retrieved from https://www.worldvision.org/disaster-relief-news-stories/2015-nepal-earthquake-facts

99. Martínez-Ferrero, J., Banerjee, S., & Garcia-Sanchez, I. (2016). Corporate social responsibility as a strategic shield against costs of earnings management practices. *Journal of Business Ethics*, 133(2), 305–324.

100. Sun, L., & Yu, T. R. (2015). The impact of corporate social responsibility on employee performance and cost. *Review of Accounting and Finance*, 14(3), 262–284.

101. Stonehouse, G., & Snowdon, B. (2007). Competitive advantage revisited: Michael Porter on strategy and competitiveness. *Journal of Management Inquiry*, 16(3), 256–273.

102. Wellesley High School. (2012). Commencement speech: You are not that special [YouTube video]. Retrieved from https://www.youtube.com/watch?v=_lfxYhtf8o4

103. immoreau (2011).

104. Jiang, D. Y., Lin, Y. C., & Lin, L. C. (2011). Business moral values of supervisors and subordinates and their effect on employee effectiveness. *Journal of Business Ethics*, 100(2), 239–252.

105. Maxham, J. G., & Netemeyer, R. G. (2003). Firms reap what they sow: The effects of shared values and perceived organizational justice on customers' evaluations of complaint handling. *Journal of Marketing*, 67(1), 46–62.

106. Sharma (2018).

107. Organ (1988).

108. Williams, S. L. (2002). Strategic planning and organizational values: Links to alignment. *Human Resource Development International*, 5(2), 217–233.

109. Oliver, J. (2017). Is "transgenerational response" a hidden cause of failed corporate turnarounds and chronic underperformance? *Strategy and Leadership*, 45(3), 23–29.

110. Vågerö, D., & Rajaleid, K. (2017). Transgenerational response and

life history theory: A response to Peeter Hõrak. *International Journal of Epidemiology, 46*(1), 233–234.

111. Yehuda, R., Engel, S. M., Brand, S. R., Seckl, J., Marcus, S. M., & Berkowitz, G. S. (2005). Transgenerational effects of posttraumatic stress disorder in babies of mothers exposed to the World Trade Center attacks during pregnancy. *Journal of Clinical Endocrinology and Metabolism, 90*(7), 4115–4118.

112. Oliver (2017).

113. Oliver (2017).

114. Brunning, H., & Perini, M. (2010). *Psychoanalytic perspectives on a turbulent world.* London, England: Karnac.

115. Oliver (2017).

116. Tonello, M. (2015). New statistics and cases of CEO succession in the S&P 500. Harvard Law School Forum on Corporate Governance and Financial Regulation. Retrieved from https://corpgov.law.harvard.edu

117. Oliver (2017).

118. Delaney, K., Guth, R. A., & Karnitschnig, M. (2008, February 2). Microsoft makes grab for Yahoo; software giant's bid is aimed at Google; tapping ads, customers. *Wall Street Journal,* p. A.1.

119. Oliver (2017).

120. Schloetzer, J. D., Tonello, M., & Aguilar, M. (2013). *CEO succession practices: 2012 edition* (Conference Board Research Report R-1492-12-RR). Retrieved from https://ssrn.com/abstract=2250357

121. Oliver (2017).

Chapter 6

1. Hartman, J. L., & McCambridge, J. (2011). Optimizing millennials' communication styles. *Business Communication Quarterly, 74*(1), 22–44.

2. Bencsik, A., Horváth-Csikós, G., & Juhász, T. (2016). Y and Z generations at workplaces. *Journal of Competitiveness, 8*(3), 90–106.

3. Twenge, J. M. (2010). A review of the empirical evidence on generational differences in work attitudes. *Journal of Business and Psychology, 25*(2), 201–210, p. 201.

4. Hershatter, A., & Epstein, M. (2010). Millennials and the world of work: An organization and management perspective. *Journal of Business and Psychology, 25*(2), 211–223.

5. Hershatter & Epstein (2010).

6. Bolman, L. G., & Deal, T. E. (2017). *Reframing organizations: Artistry, choice, and leadership.* New York, NY: John Wiley.

7. Schwenk, C. R. (1988). The cognitive perspective on strategic decision making. *Journal of Management Studies, 25*(1), 41–55.

8. DeCanio, S. J., Dibble, C., & Amir-Atefi, K. (2000). The importance of organizational structure for the adoption of innovations. *Management Science, 46*(10), 1285–1299; and O'Neill, J. W., Beauvais, L. L., & Scholl, R. W. (2016). The use of organizational culture and structure to guide strategic behavior: An information processing perspective. *Journal of Behavioral and Applied Management, 2*(2), 132–152.

9. Blau, P. M., & Scott, W. R. (1962). *Formal organizations: A comparative approach.* Stanford, CA: Stanford University Press.

10. Fredrickson, J. W. (1986). The strategic decision process and organizational structure. *Academy of Management Review, 11*(2), 280–297.

11. Galbraith, J. (1977). *Organizational design.* Reading, MA: Addison-Wesley.

12. Mintzberg, H. (1979). *The structuring of organizations: A synthesis of the research.* Englewood Cliffs, NJ: Prentice Hall.

13. Dudovskiy, J. (2019, April 4). Apple organizational structure: A brief overview. Retrieved from https://research-methodology.net/apple-organizational-structure-a-hierarchical-structure-that-may-change-in-near-future/

14. Bolman & Deal (2017).

15. Hrebiniak, L. G., & Joyce, W. F. (1985). Organizational adaptation: Strategic choice and environmental determinism. *Administrative Science Quarterly, 30*, 336–349.

16. Pugh, D. S., Hickson, D. J., Hinings, C. R., & Turner, C. (1968). Dimensions of organization structure. *Administrative Science Quarterly, 30*, 65–105.

17. Pugh et al. (1968).

18. Mintzberg, H. (1979). *The structuring of organizations: A synthesis of the research.* Englewood Cliffs, NJ: Prentice Hall.

19. Mintzberg (1979).

20. Mindtools. (n.d.). Mintzberg's organizational configurations. Retrieved from https://www.mindtools.com/pages/article/newSTR_54.htm; and Mintzberg (1979).

21. Weber, M. (1946). Essay on bureaucracy. In *Max Weber: Essays in Sociology,* 196–244.

22. Matheson, C. (2007). In praise of bureaucracy? A dissent from Australia. *Administration and Society, 39*(2), 233–261.

23. Stone, F. (2004). Deconstructing silos and supporting collaboration. *Employment Relations Today, 31*(1), 11–18.

24. Adler, P. S. (2012). Perspective—the sociological ambivalence of bureaucracy: From Weber via Gouldner to Marx. *Organization Science, 23*(1), 244–266.

25. Flood, A. B., Scott, W. R., Ewy, W., & Forrest, W. H., Jr. (1982). Effectiveness in professional organizations: The impact of surgeons and surgical staff organizations on the quality of care in hospitals. *Health Services Research, 17*(4), 341–366.

26. Scott, W. R. (1965). Reactions to supervision in a heteronomous professional organization. *Administrative Science Quarterly, 10*, 65–81.

27. Ouchi, W. G. (1984). The M-form society: Lessons from business management. *Human Resource Management, 23*(2), 191–213.

28. Andrews, P. H., & Herschel, R. T. (1996). *Organizational communication: Empowerment in a technological society.* Boston, MA: Houghton Mifflin.

29. Choose your business structure. (n.d.). *Entrepreneur.* Retrieved from https://www.entrepreneur.com/article/38822

30. Anand, N., & DAFT, R. L. (2007). What is the right organization design? *Organizational Dynamics, 4*(36), 329–344, p. 342.

31. Anheuser-Busch InBev. (n.d.). *Forbes.* Retrieved from https://www.forbes.com/companies/anheuser-busch-inbev/#3ee66caf3325; and Anheuser-Busch InBev. (n.d.). *Wikipedia.* Retrieved from https://en.wikipedia.org/wiki/Anheuser-Busch_InBev

32. Grinter, R. E., Herbsleb, J. D., & Perry, D. E. (1999). The geography of coordination: Dealing with distance in R&D work. In *Proceedings of the International ACM SIGGROUP Conference on Supporting Group Work* (pp. 306–315). Retrieved from http://www-cgi.cs.cmu.edu/afs/cs.cmu.edu/Web/People/jdh/collaboratory/research_papers/Group_99(final).pdf

33. Galbraith, J. R. (1971). Matrix organization designs: How to combine functional and project forms. *Business Horizons, 14*(1), 29–40.

34. Knight, K. (1976). Matrix organization: A review. *Journal of Management Studies, 13*(2), 111–130.

35. Burton, R. M., Obel, B., & Håkonsson, D. D. (2015). How to get the matrix organization to work. *Journal of Organization Design, 4*(3), 37–45.

36. Galbraith, J. R. (2008). *Designing matrix organizations that actually work: How IBM, Proctor & Gamble and others design for success.* San Francisco, CA: Jossey-Bass.

37. Barker, J., Tjosvold, D., & Andrews, I. R. (1988). Conflict approaches of effective and ineffective project managers: A field study in a matrix organization. *Journal of Management Studies, 25*(2), 167–178.

38. Burton et al. (2015).

39. Katz, R., & Allen, T. J. (1985). Project performance and the locus of influence in the R&D matrix. *Academy of Management Journal, 28*(1), 67–87.

40. Nami, M. R. (2008). Virtual organizations: An overview. *International Federation for Information Processing, 288*, 211–219, p. 211.

41. Orlowski, A. (2008, June 24). Farewell, then, Symbian. *The Register.* Retrieved from https://www.theregister .co.uk/2008/06/24/andrew_on_ symbian/.

42. Shim, T. (2018, August 23). How does Wikipedia work? Retrieved from https:// www.webhostingsecretrevealed.net/ blog/web-business-ideas/how-does-wikipedia-work/

43. Likert, R. (1961). *New patterns of management.* New York, NY: McGraw-Hill.

44. Chun, J. U., Yammarino, F. J., Dionne, S. D., Sosik, J. J., & Moon, H. K. (2009). Leadership across hierarchical levels: Multiple levels of management and multiple levels of analysis. *Leadership Quarterly, 20*(5), 689–707.

45. Webb, A. (1991). Coordination: A problem in public sector management. *Policy and Politics, 19*(4), 229–241, p. 231.

46. Lysonski, S. J., & Johnson, E. M. (1983). The sales manager as a boundary spanner: A role theory analysis. *Journal of Personal Selling and Sales Management, 3*(2), 8–21.

47. Trist, E., Higgin, B., Murray, J., & Pollack, A. (1963). *Organizational choice.* London, England: Tavistock.

48. Appelbaum, S. H. (1997). Socio-technical systems theory: An intervention strategy for organizational development. *Management Decision, 35*(6), 452–463.

49. Ilgen, D. R., & Hollenbeck, J. R. (1991). Job design and roles. *Handbook of Industrial and Organizational Psychology, 2*, 165–207, p. 173.

50. Hackman, J. R., & Oldham, G. R. (1976). Motivation through the design of work: Test of a theory. *Organizational Behavior and Human Performance, 16*(2), 250–279.

51. Hackman & Oldham (1976).

52. Renn, R. W., & Vandenberg, R. J. (1995). The critical psychological states: An underrepresented component in job characteristics model research. *Journal of Management, 21*(2), 279–303.

53. Bond, F. W., Flaxman, P. E., & Bunce, D. (2008). The influence of psychological flexibility on work redesign: Mediated moderation of a work reorganization intervention. *Journal of Applied Psychology, 93*(3), 645.

54. Hackman, J. R., & Oldham, G. R. (1980). *Work redesign.* Reading, MA: Addison-Wesley.

55. Grant, A. M. (2008). Does intrinsic motivation fuel the prosocial fire? Motivational synergy in predicting persistence, performance, and productivity. *Journal of Applied Psychology, 93*(1), 48–58.

56. Hackman, J. R., & Suttle, J. L. (Eds.). (1977). *Improving life at work.* Glenview, IL: Scott Foresman.

57. Campion, M. A., & McClelland, C. L. (1993). Follow-up and extension of the interdisciplinary costs and benefits of enlarged jobs. *Journal of Applied Psychology, 78*(3), 339–351; Fried, Y., & Ferris, G. R. (1987). The validity of the job characteristics model: A review and meta-analysis. *Personnel Psychology, 40*(2), 287–322; Griffin, R. W. (1983). Objective and social sources of information in task redesign: A field experiment. *Administrative Science Quarterly, 28*(2), 184–200; Orpen, C. (1979). The effects of job enrichment on employee satisfaction, motivation, involvement, and performance: A field experiment. *Human Relations, 32*(3), 189–217; Pritchard, R. D., Harrell, M. M., Diaz-Grandos, D., & Guzman, M. J. (2008). The productivity measurement and enhancement system: A meta-analysis. *Journal of Applied Psychology, 93*(3), 540–567; and Subramony, M. (2009). A meta-analytic investigation of the relationship between HRM bundles and firm performance. *Human Resource Management, 48*(5), 745–768.

58. Wrzesniewski, A., & Dutton, J. E. (2001). Crafting a job: Revisioning employees as active crafters of their work. *Academy of Management Review, 26*, 179–201, p. 180.

59. Wrzesniewski & Dutton (2001).

60. Oldham, G. R., & Hackman, J. R. (2010). Not what it was and not what it will be: The future of job design research. *Journal of Organizational Behavior, 31*(2–3), 463–479, p. 470.

61. Dierdorff, E. C., & Jensen, J. M. (2018). Crafting in context: Exploring when job crafting is dysfunctional for performance effectiveness. *Journal of Applied Psychology, 103*(5), 463–477.

62. Bruning, P. F., & Campion, M. A. (2018). A role–resource approach–avoidance model of job crafting: A multimethod integration and extension of job crafting theory. *Academy of Management Journal, 61*(2), 499–522.

Chapter 7

1. Merriam-Webster online dictionary. (n.d.). Communication. Retrieved from https://www.merriam-webster.com/ dictionary/communication

2. Barnard, C. I. (1938). *The functions of the executive.* Cambridge, MA: Harvard University Press, p. 236.

3. Richmond, V. P., McCroskey, J. C., & McCroskey, L. L. (2005). *Organizational communication for survival: Making work, work.* New York, NY: Allyn & Bacon, p. 20.

4. O'Reilly, C. A. (1980). Individuals and information overload in organizations: Is more necessarily better? *Academy of Management Journal, 23*(4), 684–696; Pincus, J. D. (1986). Communication satisfaction, job satisfaction, and job performance. *Human Communication Research, 12*(3), 395–419; and Pincus, J. D., Knipp, J. E., & Rayfield, R. E. (1990). Internal communication and job satisfaction revisited: The impact of organizational trust and influence on commercial bank supervisors. *Journal of Public Relations Research, 2*(1–4), 173–191.

5. Redding, W. C. (1985). Stumbling toward identity: The emergence of organizational communication as a field of study. In R. D. McPhee & P. K. Tompkins (Eds.), *Organizational communication: Traditional themes and new directions* (pp. 15–54). Beverly Hills, CA: Sage.

6. Blair, R., Roberts, K. H., & McKechnie, P. (1985). Vertical and network communication in

organizations: The present and the future. In R. D. McPhee & P. K. Tompkins, *Organizational communication: Traditional themes and new directions* (pp. 55–77). Beverly Hills, CA: Sage, p. 55.

7. Lawler, E. E., Porter, L. W., & Tennenbaum, A. (1968). Managers' attitudes toward interaction episodes. *Journal of Applied Psychology, 52*(6), 432–439.

8. Rader, M. H., & Wunsch, A. P. (1980). A survey of communication practices of business school graduates by job category and undergraduate major. *Journal of Business Communication, 17*(4), 33–41.

9. McCroskey, J. C. (1977). Oral communication apprehension: A summary of recent theory and research. *Human Communication Research, 4*(1), 78–96, p. 78.

10. Allen, M. T., & Bourhis, J. (1996). The relationship of communication apprehension to communication behavior: A meta-analysis. *Communication Quarterly, 44*, 214–225.

11. Pate, L. E., & Merker, G. E. (1978). Communication apprehension: Implications for management and organizational behavior. *Journal of Management, 4*(2), 107–119.

12. Blume, B. D., Baldwin, T. T., & Ryan, K. C. (2013). Communication apprehension: A barrier to students' leadership, adaptability, and multicultural appreciation. *Academy of Management Learning and Education, 12*(2), 158–172.

13. Haney, W. V. (1964). A comparative study of unilateral and bilateral communication. *Academy of Management Journal, 7*(2), 128–136.

14. Weaver, W. (1949). Recent contributions to the mathematical theory of communication. *Mathematical Theory of Communication, 1*, 1–12.

15. Watson-Manheim, M. B., & Bélanger, F. (2007). Communication media repertoires: Dealing with the multiplicity of media choices. *MIS Quarterly, 31*(2), 267–293.

16. Treviño, L. K., Webster, J., & Stein, E. W. (2000). Making connections: Complementary influences on communication media choices, attitudes, and use. *Organization Science, 11*(2), 163–182.

17. DeFleur, M. (1970). *Theories of mass communication.* New York, NY: McKay; and McQuail, D., & Windahl, S. (1981). *Commutations models.* New York, NY: Longman.

18. Leavitt, H. J., & Mueller, R. A. (1951). Some effects of feedback on communication. *Human Relations, 4*(4), 401–410.

19. Shannon and Weaver model of communication. (2018, January 6). *Businesstopia.* Retrieved from https://www.businesstopia.net/communication/shannon-and-weaver-model-communication

20. Dictionary.com. (n.d.). Jargon. Retrieved from http://www.dictionary.com/browse/jargon

21. dp916. (2010, November 22). Drill down. *Urban Dictionary.* Retrieved from https://www.urbandictionary.com/define.php?term=drill%20down

22. Webopedia. (n.d.). Drilldown. Retrieved from https://www.webopedia.com/TERM/D/drill_down.html

23. Brannen, M. Y., & Doz, Y. L. (2012). Corporate languages and strategic agility: Trapped in your jargon or lost in translation? *California Management Review, 54*(3), 77–97.

24. Sim, N. (2014). 8 ingenious ways Disney theme parks shield you from the real world. Retrieved from https://www.themeparktourist.com/features/20140418/17604/8-ingenious-ways-disney-theme-parks-shield-you-real-world

25. Tannen, D. (1990). *You just don't understand: Women and men in conversation.* New York, NY: Ballantine Books.

26. Tramel, M. E., & Reynolds, H. (1981). Communication freezers. In R. J. Lewicki, D. Sanders, & J. Minton (Eds.), *Executive leadership* (pp. 208–209). Englewood Cliffs, NJ: Prentice Hall.

27. Schroth, H. A., Bain-Chekal, J., & Caldwell, D. F. (2005). Sticks and stones may break bones and words can hurt me: Words and phrases that trigger emotions in negotiations and their effects. *International Journal of Conflict Management, 16*(2), 102–127.

28. Wentworth, D. (2016). Top spending trends in training 2016–2017. Retrieved from https://trainingmag.com/top-spending-trends-training-2016-2017

29. Vdovin, A. (2017). Why companies invest millions in employee communication. Retrieved from https://www.alert-software.com/blog/employee-communication-training-why-companies-invest-millions-in-employee-communication

30. Vdovin (2017).

31. Rogers, C. R. (1980). *A way of being.* Boston, MA: Houghton Mifflin.

32. Brooks, B. (2003). The power of active listening. *American Salesman, 48*(6), 12–14.

33. Weger, H., Jr., Castle Bell, G., Minei, E. M., & Robinson, M. C. (2014). The relative effectiveness of active listening in initial interactions. *International Journal of Listening, 28*(1), 13–31.

34. Knippen, J. T., & Green, T. B. (1994). How the manager can use active listening. *Public Personnel Management, 23*(2), 357–359.

35. Fleming, T. (2012). Why I'm a listener: Amgen CEO Kevin Sharer. Retrieved from http://www.mckinsey.com/insights/leading_in_the_21st_century/why_im_a_listener_amgen_ceo_kevin_sharer

36. Cascio, W. F., & Montealegre, R. (2016). How technology is changing work and organizations. *Annual Review of Organizational Psychology and Organizational Behavior, 3*, 349–375.

37. Hauben, M., & Hauben, R. (1995). *The Netizens and the world of the Net: An anthology on the history and impact of the Net.* New York, NY: Columbia University Press. Retrieved from http://www.columbia.edu/~rh120/

38. Silverman, R. E. (2012). Why you won't finish this article. *Wall Street Journal.* Retrieved from https://www.wsj.com/articles/SB10001424127887324339204578173252223022388

39. Silverman (2012).

40. Sproull, L., & Kiesler, S. (1986). Reducing social context cues: Electronic mail in organizational communication. *Management Science, 32*(11), 1492–1512.

41. Goldman, L. (2007, October 16). Netiquette rules—10 best rules for email etiquette. Retrieved from http://ezinearticles.com/?Netiquette-Rules—10-Best-Rules-for-Email-Etiquette&id=785177

42. Mano, R. S., & Mesch, G. S. (2010). E-mail characteristics, work performance and distress. *Computers in Human Behavior, 26*(1), 61–69.

43. Jackson, J., Dawson, R., & Wilson, D. (2003a). Reducing the effect of e-mail interruptions on employees. *International Journal of Information Management, 23*(1), 55–65.

44. 3/M. (2003b). Understanding e-mail interaction increases organizational productivity. *Communications of the ACM, 48*(6), 80–84; and Szóstek, A. M. (2011). "Dealing with my emails": Latent user needs in email management.

Computers in Human Behavior, 27(2), 723–729.

45. Phillips, J. G., & Reddie, L. (2007). Decisional style and self-reported email use in the workplace. *Computers in Human Behavior, 23*(5), 2414–2428.

46. Wajcman, J., & Rose, E. (2011). Constant connectivity: Rethinking interruptions at work. *Organization Studies, 32*(7), 941–961.

47. Byron, K. (2008). Carrying too heavy a load? The communication and miscommunication of emotion by email. *Academy of Management Review, 33*(2), 309–327.

48. Cellular Telecommunications & Internet Association. (2018, July 10). New CTIA annual survey shows beginning of evolution to next-generation networks. Retrieved from https://www.ctia.org/news/new-ctia-annual-survey-shows-beginning-of-evolution-to-next-generation-networks

49. Herbsleb, J. D., Atkins, D. L., Boyer, D. G., Handel, M., & Finholt, T. A. (2002). Introducing instant messaging and chat in the workplace. *Proceedings of the SIGCHI Conference on Human Factors in Computing Systems, 4*(1), 171–178.

50. Kim, S., & Niu, Q. (2014). *Smartphone: It can do more than you think*. Presented at the annual meeting of the Society for Industrial and Organizational Psychology, Honolulu, HI.

51. Middleton, C. A., & Cukier, W. (2006). Is mobile email functional or dysfunctional? Two perspectives on mobile email usage. *European Journal of Information Systems, 15*(3), 252–260, p. 252.

52. Crawford, K. (2005, February 14). Have a blog, lose your job? *CNN Money*, p. 15. Retrieved from https://money.cnn.com/2005/02/14/news/economy/blogging/

53. Black, T. (2010, April 26). How to handle employee blogging. *Inc.* Retrieved from http://www.inc.com/guides/2010/04/employee-blogging-policy.html

54. Van Grove, J. (2009, January 21). 40 of the best Twitter brands and the people behind them. *Mashable*. Retrieved from http://mashable.com/2009/01/21/best-twitter-brands

55. What is a public relations specialist? (n.d.). *U.S. News*. Retrieved from https://money.usnews.com/careers/best-jobs/public-relations-specialist

56. Freberg, K., Graham, K., McGaughey, K., & Freberg, L. A. (2011). Who are the social media influencers? A study of public perceptions of personality. *Public Relations Review, 37*, 90–92, p. 90.

57. Johnson, P. R., & Indvik, J. (2004). The organizational benefits of reducing cyberslacking in the workplace. *Journal of Organizational Culture, Communications, and Conflict, 8*(2), 55–62, p. 56.

58. Greenfield, D., & Davis, R. (2002). Lost in cyberspace: The Web @work. *CyberPsychology and Behavior, 5*(4), 347–353.

59. Lohr, S. (2008, July 22). As travel costs rise, more meetings go virtual. *New York Times*. Retrieved from http://www.nytimes.com/2008/07/22/technology/22meet.html?_r=0&pagewanted=print

60. Lohr (2008).

61. Driskell, J. E., Radke P. H., & Salas E. (2003). Virtual teams: Effects of technological mediation on team performance. *Group Dynamics: Theory, Research & Practice, 7*(4), 297–323.

62. Thompson, L. F., & Coovert, M. D. (2003). Teamwork online: The effects of computer conferencing on perceived confusion, satisfaction, and post-discussion accuracy. *Group Dynamics: Theory, Research, and Practice, 7*(2), 135–151.

63. Mehrabian, A. (1981). *Silent messages* (2nd ed.). Belmont, CA: Wadsworth.

64. Giri, V. N. (2009). Nonverbal communication theories. In S. W. Littlejohn, W. Stephen, & K. A. Foss (Eds.), *Encyclopedia of communication theory* (pp. 690–694). Thousand Oaks, CA: Sage.

65. Ambler, G. (2013). When it comes to leadership everything communicates. Retrieved from http://www.georgeambler.com/when-it-comes-to-leadership-everything-communicates

66. Gentry, W. A., & Kuhnert, K. W. (2007). Sending signals: Nonverbal communication can speak volumes. *Leadership in Action, 27*(5), 3–7, p. 4.

67. Macnamara, J. R. (2004). The crucial role of research in multicultural and cross-cultural communication. *Journal of Communication Management, 8*(3), 322–334.

68. Levine, T. R., Park, H. S., & Kim, R. K. (2007). Some conceptual and theoretical challenges for cross-cultural communication research in the 21st century. *Journal of Intercultural Communication Research, 36*(3), 205–221.

69. Matveev, A. V., & Nelson, P. E. (2004). Cross cultural communication competence and multicultural team performance perceptions of American and Russian managers. *International Journal of Cross Cultural Management, 4*(2), 253–270.

70. Spencer-Oatey, H., & Xing, J. (2003). Managing rapport in intercultural business interactions: A comparison of two Chinese-British welcome meetings. *Journal of Intercultural Studies, 24*(1), 33–46.

71. Wagner Consulting International. (n.d.). More about us. Retrieved from http://vip-translator.com/index.php/78-blog-1/1132-translation-issues

72. Dumenco. S. (2009, June 13). The meaning of Bing. *Business Insider*. Retrieved from https://www.businessinsider.com/the-meaning-of-bing-2009-6

73. Associated Press. (1994, June 8). Saudi flags on burger bags: A big MacStake: Marketing: Muslims complained that McDonald's World Cup packaging sent Koran verse to the trash bin. *Los Angeles Times*. Retrieved from https://www.latimes.com/archives/la-xpm-1994-06-08-fi-1752-story.html

74. Du-Babcock, B., & Babcock, R. D. (1996). Patterns of expatriate-local personnel communication in multinational corporations. *Journal of Business Communication, 33*(2), 141–164.

75. Levine, T. R., Park, H. S., & Kim, R. K. (2007). Some conceptual and theoretical challenges for cross-cultural communication research in the 21st century. *Journal of Intercultural Communication Research, 36*(3), 205–221.

76. Gudykunst, W. B., Matsumoto, Y., Ting-Toomey, S., Nishida, T., Kim, K., & Heyman, S. (1996). The influence of cultural individualism-collectivism, self construals, and individual values on communication styles across cultures. *Human Communication Research, 22*(4), 510–543; and Zhang, T., & Zhou, H. (2008). The significance of cross-cultural communication in international business negotiation. *International Journal of Business and Management, 3*(2), 103–109.

77. Tannen, D. T. (1984). The pragmatics of cross-cultural communication. *Applied Linguistics, 5*(3), 189–195.

78. Huang, L. (2010). Cross-cultural communication in business negotiations. *International Journal of Economics and Finance, 2*(2), 196–199.

79. Littrell, L. N., & Salas, E. (2005). A review of cross-cultural training: Best practices, guidelines, and research needs. *Human Resource Development Review, 4*(3), 305–334; and Nixon, J. C., & Dawson, G. A. (2002). Reason for cross-cultural communication training. *Corporate Communications: An International Journal, 7*(3), 184–191.

80. Ruben, B. D. (1977). Guidelines for cross-cultural communication effectiveness. *Group and Organization Studies, 2*, 470–479.

81. Gakuran, M. (2014, April 24). What you need to know about exchanging business cards in Japan [Blog post]. Retrieved from https://blog.gaijinpot.com/exchanging-business-cards-japan/

82. Sussman, N., & Rosenfeld, H. (1982). Influence of culture, language and sex on conversational distance. *Journal of Personality and Social Psychology, 42*(1), 67–74.

83. Rastogi, P. N. (2000). Knowledge management and intellectual capital—the new virtuous reality of competitiveness. *Human Systems Management, 19*(1), 39–49, p. 40.

84. Zheng, W., Yang, B., & McLean, G. N. (2010). Linking organizational culture, structure, strategy, and organizational effectiveness: Mediating role of knowledge management. *Journal of Business Research, 63*(7), 763–771.

85. Lunenburg, F. C., & Ornstein, A. O. (2008). *Educational administration: Concepts and practices.* Belmont, CA: Wadsworth/Cengage.

86. Canary, H. (2011). *Communication and organizational knowledge: Contemporary issues for theory and practice.* Florence, KY: Taylor & Francis.

87. Canary (2011).

88. Public Relations Society of America. (n.d.). All about public relations. Retrieved from https://www.prsa.org/all-about-pr/

89. Hutton, J. G., Goodman, M. B., Alexander, J. B., & Genest, C. M. (2001). Reputation management: The new face of corporate public relations? *Public Relations Review, 27*(3), 247–261.

90. Shaw, M. E. (1964). Communication networks. In L. Berkowitz (Ed.), *Advances in experimental social psychology* (Vol. 1, pp. 111–147). Cambridge, MA: Elsevier Academic Press Books.

91. Shaw (1964).

92. Characteristics of groups: Group structure. (n.d.). Retrieved from https://www.tankonyvtar.hu/hu/tartalom/tamop412A/2011-0023_Psychology/070500.scorml

93. Tsai, W., & Ghoshal, S. (1998). Social capital and value creation: The role of intrafirm networks. *Academy of Management Journal, 41*, 464–476.

94. Kogut, B., & Zander, U. (1992). Knowledge of the firm, combinative capacities and the replication of technology. *Organization Science, 3*, 383–397.

95. Tsai, W. (2001). Knowledge transfer in intraorganizational networks: Effects of network position and absorptive capacity on business unit innovation and performance. *Academy of Management Journal, 44*(5), 996–1004.

Chapter 8

1. Barringer, B. R., Jones, F. F., & Neubaum, D. O. (2005). A quantitative content analysis of the characteristics of rapid-growth firms and their founders. *Journal of Business Venturing, 20*(5), 663–687.

2. Townson, N. J. (2017, February 27). Tech: It's time to grow up about HR. *Medium.* Retrieved from https://medium.com/brightplusearly/tech-its-time-to-grow-up-about-hr-4c4043914729; and Weissman, C. G. (2016, May 10). The future of HR and why startups shouldn't reject it. *Fast Company.* Retrieved from https://www.fastcompany.com/3059673/the-future-of-hr-and-why-startups-shouldnt-reject-it

3. Armstrong, M. (2008). *Strategic human resource management: A guide to action* (4th ed.). London, England: Kogan Page, p. 11.

4. Lauver, K. J., & Kristof-Brown, A. (2001). Distinguishing between employees' perceptions of person–job and person–organization fit. *Journal of Vocational Behavior, 59*(3), 454–470.

5. Lauver & Kristof-Brown (2001).

6. Stone, D. L., Lukaszewski, K. M., Stone-Romero, E. F., & Johnson, T. L. (2013). Factors affecting the effectiveness and acceptance of electronic selection systems. *Human Resource Management Review, 23*(1), 50–70.

7. Judge, T. A., & Kristof-Brown, A. (2004). Personality, interactional psychology, and person–organization fit. In Schneider, B., & Smith, D. (Eds.), *Personality and organizations* (pp. 87–109). Hoboken, NJ: Taylor & Francis.

8. Myors, B., Lievens, F., Schollaert, E., Van Hoye, G., Cronshaw, S. F., Mladinic, A., . . . Schuler, H. (2008). International perspectives on the legal environment for selection. *Industrial and Organizational Psychology, 1*(2), 206–246.

9. Anthony, W. P., Perrewe, P. L., & Kacmar, K. M. (1993). *Strategic human resource management.* New York, NY: Dryden Press.

10. Miles, A., & Sadler-Smith, E. (2014). "With recruitment I always feel I need to listen to my gut": The role of intuition in employee selection. *Personnel Review, 43*(4), 606–627.

11. Snell, S. A., & Dean, J. W., Jr. (1992). Integrated manufacturing and human resource management: A human capital perspective. *Academy of Management Journal, 35*(3), 467–504.

12. Van Marrewijk, M., & Timmers, J. (2003). Human capital management: New possibilities in people management. *Journal of Business Ethics, 44*(2–3), 171–184.

13. Afiouni, F. (2013). Human capital management: A new name for HRM? *International Journal of Learning and Intellectual Capital, 10*(1), 18–34.

14. Boudreau, J. W., & Lawler, E. E., III. (2012). *How HR spends its time: It is time for a change.* Los Angeles, CA: Marshall School of Business, Center for Effective Organizations.

15. Totka, M. (2018, April 26). Benefits of HR outsourcing: How even small business can provide great HR. *Forbes.* Retrieved from https://www.forbes.com/sites/allbusiness/2018/04/26/benefits-of-hr-outsourcing-how-even-small-businesses-can-provide-great-hr/#7676c65f620f

16. Sheehan, C., & Cooper, B. K. (2011). HRM outsourcing: The impact of organisational size and HRM strategic involvement. *Personnel Review, 40*(6), 742–760.

17. Afiouni (2013).

18. Baron, A., & Armstrong, M. (2007). *Human capital management: Achieving added value through people.* London, England: Kogan Page.

19. Lundy, O. (1994). From personnel management to strategic human resource management. *International Journal of Human Resource Management, 5*(3), 687–720.

20. Gurchiek, K. (2008, May 28). Staffing issues critical to business strategies. Retrieved from https://www.shrm.org/hr-today/news/hr-news/pages/staffingissuescritical.aspx

21. Ployhart, R. E. (2006). Staffing in the 21st century: New challenges and strategic opportunities. *Journal of Management, 32*(6), 868–897, p. 868.

22. Chapman, D. S., Uggerslev, K. L., Carroll, S. A., Piasentin, K. A., & Jones, D. A. (2005). Applicant attraction to organizations and job choice: A meta-analytic review of the correlates of recruiting outcomes. *Journal of Applied Psychology, 90*, 928–944.

23. Turban, D. B., & Cable, D. M. (2003). Firm reputation and applicant pool characteristics. *Journal of Organizational Behavior, 24*, 733–751.

24. Binning, J. F., & Barrett, G. V. (1989). Validity of personnel decisions: A conceptual analysis of the inferential and evidential bases. *Journal of Applied Psychology, 74*, 478–494.

25. Aguinis, H. (Ed.). (2004). *Test-score banding in human-resource selection: Legal, technical, and societal issues.* Westport, CT: Praeger.

26. Cascio, W. F., & Aguinis, H. (2005). Test development and use: New twists on old questions. *Human Resource Management, 44*(3), 219–235.

27. McFarland, L. A., Ryan, A. M., Sacco, J. M., & Kriska, S. D. (2004). Examination of structured interview ratings across time: The effects of applicant race, rater race, and panel composition. *Journal of Management, 30*, 435–452.

28. Roth, P. L., Bobko, P., & McFarland, L. A. (2005). A meta-analysis of work sample test validity: Updating and integrating some classic literature. *Personnel Psychology, 58*, 1009–1037.

29. Ployhart, R. E. (2006).

30. Arthur, W., Jr., Day, E. A., McNelly, T. L., & Edens, P. S. (2003). A meta-analysis of the criterion-related validity of assessment center dimensions. *Personnel Psychology, 56*, 125–153.

31. Cascio, W. F., & Aguinis, H. (2008). 3 staffing twenty-first-century organizations. *Academy of Management Annals, 2*(1), 133–165.

32. Heathfield, S. M. (2019, July 16). How is compensation determined for an employee? *The Balance Careers.* Retrieved from https://www.thebalancecareers.com/compensation-definition-and-inclusions-1918085

33. Culpepper and Associates. (2010, November 24). Salary structures: Creating competitive and equitable pay levels. Retrieved from https://www.shrm.org/resourcesandtools/hr-topics/compensation/pages/salarystructures.aspx

34. Heathfield (2019).

35. Aguinis, H., Joo, H., & Gottfredson, R. K. (2013). What monetary rewards can and cannot do: How to show employees the money. *Business Horizons, 56*(2), 241–259.

36. Brown, M. P., Sturman, M. C., & Simmering, M. J. (2003). Compensation policy and organizational performance: The efficiency, operational, and financial implications of pay levels and pay structure. *Academy of Management Journal, 46*(6), 752–762.

37. Cascio, W. F., & Aguinis, H. (2010). *Applied psychology in human resource management* (7th ed.). Upper Saddle River, NJ: Prentice Hall.

38. Lawler, E. E. (2003). Reward practices and performance management system effectiveness. *Organizational Dynamics, 32*(4), 396–404.

39. Heidemeier, H., & Moser, K. (2009). Self–other agreement in job performance ratings: A meta-analytic test of a process model. *Journal of Applied Psychology, 94*(2), 353–370.

40. Atwater, L. E., Brett, J. F., & Charles, A. C. (2007). Multisource feedback: Lessons learned and implications for practice. *Human Resource Management, 46*(2), 285–307; and Brett, J. F., & Atwater, L. E. (2001). 360° feedback: Accuracy, reactions, and perceptions of usefulness. *Journal of Applied Psychology, 86*(5), 930–942.

41. Fedor, D. B., Bettenhausen, K. L., & Davis, W. (1999). Peer reviews: Employees' dual roles as raters and recipients. *Group and Organization Management, 24*(1), 92–120; and Ng, K., Koh, C., Ang, S., Kennedy, J. C., & Chan, K. (2011). Rating leniency and halo in multisource feedback ratings: Testing cultural assumptions of power distance and individualism-collectivism. *Journal of Applied Psychology, 96*(5), 1033–1044.

42. Caruso, K. N. (2011, August 29). Case study: Starwood Hotels takes 360-degree feedback to a new level. Retrieved from http://web.viapeople.com/viaPeople-blog/bid/65018/Case-Study-Starwood-Hotels-Takes-360-Degree-Feedback-to-a-New-Level

43. Locher, A. H., & Teel, K. S. (1988, September). Appraisal trends. *Personnel Journal,* pp. 139–145.

44. Kerr, S. (2009). *Reward systems: Does yours measure up?* Cambridge, MA: Harvard Business School Press.

45. Satterwhite, S. R. (2013, November 13). Here's to the death of Microsoft's rank-and-yank. *Forbes.* Retrieved from https://www.forbes.com/sites/forbesleadershipforum/2013/11/13/heres-to-the-death-of-microsofts-rank-and-yank/#1ebb0cf8777b

46. Murphy, K. R., & Balzer, W. K. (1989). Rater errors and rating accuracy. *Journal of Applied Psychology, 74*(4), 619–624.

47. Woehr, D. J., & Huffcutt, A. I. (1994). Rater training for performance appraisal: A quantitative review. *Journal of Occupational and Organizational Psychology, 67*, 189–205.

48. Culbertson, S. S., Henning, J. B., & Payne, S. C. (2013). Performance appraisal satisfaction. *Journal of Personnel Psychology, 12*(4), 189–195.

49. Berinato, S. (2018, January/February). Negative feedback rarely leads to improvement. *Harvard Business Review.* Retrieved from https://hbr.org/2018/01/negative-feedback-rarely-leads-to-improvement

50. Mount, M. K., & Scullen, S. E. (2001). Multisource feedback ratings: What do they really measure? In M. London (Ed.), *How people evaluate others in organizations* (pp. 155–176). Mahwah, NJ: Erlbaum.

51. Buckingham, M., & Goodall, A. (2015). Reinventing performance management. *Harvard Business Review, 93*(4), 40–50.

52. Aguinis, H., Gottfredson, R. K., & Joo, H. (2012). Delivering effective performance feedback: The strengths-based approach. *Business Horizons, 55*(2), 105–111.

53. Silver, E. (2016, July 12). 8 tips for successful performance management. *Canadian HR Reporter.* Retrieved from http://www.hrreporter.com/article/28069-8-tips-for-successful-performance-management

54. Deming, W. E. (1986). *Out of the crisis.* Cambridge, MA: MIT Center for Advanced Engineering Study; and Pfeffer, J. (1998). Six dangerous myths

about pay. *Harvard Business Review,* *76*(3), 108–120.

55. Cable, D. M., & Judge T. A. (1994). Pay preferences and job search decisions: A person–organization fit perspective. *Personnel Psychology, 47*(2), 317–348.

56. Trevor, C. O., Gerhart B., & Boudreau, J. W. (1997). Voluntary turnover and job performance: Curvilinearity and the moderating influences of salary growth and promotions. *Journal of Applied Psychology, 82*(1), 44–61; and Rynes, S. L., Gerhart, B., & Park, L. (2005). Personnel psychology: Performance evaluation and pay for performance. *Annual Review of Psychology, 56,* 571–600.

57. Ewenstein, B., Hancock, B., & Komm, A. (2016). Ahead of the curve: The future of performance management. Retrieved from http://www.mckinsey.com/business-functions/organization/our-insights/ahead-of-the-curve-the-future-of-performance-management

58. Romero, J. L. (2016, May). Re-examine perspective on performance appraisals: Design and rename process with a focus on helping employees grow. *Healthcare Registration,* pp. 7–8.

59. Rynes et al. (2005).

60. Kerr, S. (2009). *Reward systems: Does yours measure up?* Cambridge, MA: Harvard Business School Press.

61. Scandura, T. A., & Lankau, M. J. (1997). Relationships of gender, family responsibility and flexible work hours to organizational commitment and job satisfaction. *Journal of Organizational Behavior, 18*(4), 377–391.

62. Gallo, A. (2013, September 23). How to make a job sharing situation work. Retrieved from https://hbr.org/2013/09/how-to-make-a-job-sharing-situation-work

63. de Menezes, L. M., & Kelliher, C. (2016). Flexible working, individual performance and employee attitudes: Comparing formal and informal arrangements. *Human Resource Management.* doi:10.1002/hrm.21822.

64. Shen, L. (2016, March 7). These 19 great employers offer paid sabbaticals. *Fortune.* Retrieved from http://fortune.com/2016/03/07/best-companies-to-work-for-sabbaticals/

65. Bell, B. S., Tannenbaum, S. I., Ford, J. K., Noe, R. A., & Kraiger, K. (2017). 100 years of training and development research: What we know and where we should go. *Journal of Applied Psychology, 102*(3), 305–323.

66. Torraco, R. J. (2016). Early history of the fields of practice of training and development and organization development. *Advances in Developing Human Resources, 18*(4), 439–453.

67. Bound, J., & Turner, S. (2002). Going to war and going to college: Did World War II and the G.I. Bill increase educational attainment for returning veterans? *Journal of Labor Economics, 20,* 784–815.

68. Aguinis, H., & Kraiger, K. (2009). Benefits of training and development for individuals and teams, organizations, and society. *Annual Review of Psychology, 60,* 451–474, p. 452.

69. Aguinis & Kraiger (2009, p. 452).

70. Allen, T. D., Eby, L. T., & Lentz, E. (2006). Mentorship behaviors and mentorship quality associated with formal mentoring programs: Closing the gap between research and practice. *Journal of Applied Psychology, 91*(3), 567.

71. Marsick, V. J., & Watkins, K. E. (1990). *Informal and incidental learning in the workplace.* London, England: Routledge.

72. Staff. (2017). 2017 training industry report. *Training* magazine. Retrieved from https://trainingmag.com/trgmag-article/2017-training-industry-report/

73. Aguinis & Kraiger (2009).

74. Sung, S. Y., & Choi, J. N. (2014). Do organizations spend wisely on employees? Effects of training and development investments on learning and innovation in organizations. *Journal of Organizational Behavior, 35*(3), 393–412.

75. Salas, E., Tannenbaum, S. I., Kraiger, K., & Smith-Jentsch, K. A. (2012). The science of training and development in organizations: What matters in practice. *Psychological Science in the Public Interest, 13,* 74–101.

76. Kraiger, K. (2014). Looking back and looking forward: Trends in training and development research. *Human Resource Development Quarterly, 25*(4), 401–408.

77. Bell, B. S., & Kozlowski, S. W. J. (2010). Toward a theory of learner-centered training design: An integrative framework of active learning. In S. Kozlowski & E. Salas (Eds.), *Learning, training, and development in organizations* (pp. 263–300). New York, NY: Routledge.

78. Kirkpatrick, D., & Kirkpatrick, J. (2006). *Evaluating training programs: The four levels* (3rd ed.). New York, NY: Berrett-Koehler.

79. Kirkpatrick & Kirkpatrick (2006).

80. Cheng, E. W., & Ho, D. C. (2001). A review of transfer of training studies in the past decade. *Personnel Review, 30*(1), 102–118, p. 103.

81. Jefferson, A., Wick, C., & Pollack, R. (2009). The new finish line for learning. *TD Magazine.* Retrieved from https://www.td.org/magazines/td-magazine/the-new-finish-line-for-learning

82. Jefferson et al. (2009).

83. Wick, C. (2003, November). The course isn't the finish line: Keep them learning. Retrieved from https://www.questia.com/magazine/1G1-109940470/the-course-isn-t-the-finish-line-keep-them-learning

84. Jefferson et al. (2009).

85. Emerson. (n.d.). Training and development. Retrieved from https://www.emerson.com/en-us/careers/training-and-development

86. Littrell, L. N., & Salas, E. (2005). A review of cross-cultural training: Best practices, guidelines, and research needs. *Human Resource Development Review, 4*(3), 305–334, p. 308.

87. Bhagat, R., & Prien, K. O. (1996). Cross-cultural training in organizational contexts. In D. Landis & R. S. Bhagat (Eds.), *Handbook of intercultural training* (2nd ed., pp. 216–230). Thousand Oaks, CA: Sage.

88. Wright, P. M., & McMahan, G. C. (1992). Theoretical perspectives on strategic human resource management. *Journal of Management, 18*(2), 295–320, p. 298.

89. Society for Human Resource Management. (2015). Practicing strategic human resources. Retrieved from https://www.shrm.org/resourcesandtools/tools-and-samples/toolkits/pages/practicingstrategichumanresources.aspx

90. Devanna, M. A., Fombrun, C., & Tichy, N. (1981). Human resources management: A strategic perspective. *Organizational Dynamics, 9*(3), 51–67.

91. Martín-Alcázar, F., Romero-Fernández, P. M., & Sánchez-Gardey, G. (2008). Human resource management as a field of research. *British Journal of Management, 19*(2), 103–119.

92. Lado, A. A., & Wilson, M. C. (1994). Human resource systems and sustained competitive advantage: Competence-based perspective. *Academy of Management Review, 19*(4), 699–727.

93. Armstrong, M., & Baron, A. (2003). *Strategic HRM: The key to improved business performance.* London, England: CIPD, p. xviii.

Chapter 9

1. McCuddy, M. K., & Peery, B. L. (1996). Selected individual differences and collegians' ethical beliefs. *Journal of Business Ethics, 15*(3), 261–272.
2. McCuddy & Peery (1996).
3. Rotter, J. B. (1990). Internal versus external control of reinforcement: A case history of a variable. *American Psychologist, 45*(4), 489–493.
4. Funder, D. C., & Block, J. (1989). The role of ego-control, ego-resiliency, and IQ in delay of gratification in adolescence. *Journal of Personality and Social Psychology, 57*(6), 1041–1050.
5. McCuddy & Peery (1996).
6. Christie, R., & Geis, F. (1970). *Studies in Machiavellianism.* New York, NY: Academic Press.
7. Machiavelli, N. (1981). *The prince.* New York, NY: Bantam Books. (Original work published 1513.)
8. Den Hartog, D., & Belschak, F. (2012). Work engagement and Machiavellianism in the ethical leadership process. *Journal of Business Ethics, 107*(1), 35–47.
9. Clouse, M., Giacalone, R. A., Olsen, T. D., & Patelli, L. (2017). Individual ethical orientations and the perceived acceptability of questionable finance ethics decisions. *Journal of Business Ethics, 144*(3), 549–558.
10. Clouse et al. (2017).
11. Snyder, M., & Cantor, N. (1998). Understanding personality and social behavior: A functionalist strategy. In D. T. Gilbert, S. T. Fiske, & G. Lindzey (Eds.), *The handbook of social psychology* (4th ed., pp. 635–679). New York, NY: McGraw-Hill, p. 635.
12. Waller, N. G., Kojetin, B. A., Bouchard, T. J., Lykken, D. T., & Tellegen, A. (1990). Genetic and environmental influences on religious interests, attitudes, and values: A study of twins reared apart and together. *Psychological Science, 1*(2), 138–142.
13. Lykken, D. T., Bouchard, T. J., McGue, M., & Tellegen, A. (1993). Heritability of interests: A twin study. *Journal of Applied Psychology, 78*(4), 649–661.
14. Keller, L. M., Bouchard, T. J., Arvey, R. D., Segal, N. L., & Dawis, R. V. (1992). Work values: Genetic and environmental influences. *Journal of Applied Psychology, 77*(1), 79–88.
15. Murray, J. B. (1990). Review of the Myers-Briggs Type Indicator. *Perceptual and Motor Skills, 70,* 1187–1202.
16. Myers, I. B. (with Myers, P. B.). (1995). *Gifts differing.* Mountain View, CA: Consulting Psychologists Press.
17. Arnau, R. C., Green, B. A., Rosen, D. H., Gleaves, D. H., & Melancon, J. G. (2003). Are Jungian preferences really categorical? An empirical investigation using taxometric analysis. *Personality and Individual Differences, 34*(2), 233–251; and Pittenger, D. J. (2005). Cautionary comments regarding the Myers-Briggs Type Indicator. *Consulting Psychology Journal: Practice and Research, 57*(3), 210–221.
18. Myers, P. B., & Myers, K. D. (1998). *Introduction to type* (6th ed.). Mountain View, CA: Consulting Psychologists Press.
19. Nguyen, J. (2018, October 30). How companies use the Myers-Briggs system to evaluate employees. Retrieved from https://www.marketplace.org/2018/10/30/business/big-book/myers-briggs-system-evaluate-employees
20. Barrick, M. R., & Mount, M. K. (1990, April). *Another look at the validity of personality: A dimensional perspective.* Paper presented at the annual meeting of the Society for Industrial and Organizational Psychology, Miami Beach, FL.
21. Stajkovic, A. D., Bandura, A., Locke, E. A., Lee, D., & Sergent, K. (2018). Test of three conceptual models of influence of the big five personality traits and self-efficacy on academic performance: A meta-analytic path-analysis. *Personality and Individual Differences, 120,* 238–245.
22. Liu, D., & Campbell, W. K. (2017). The big five personality traits, big two metatraits and social media: A meta-analysis. *Journal of Research in Personality, 70,* 229–240.
23. Barrick, M. R., Mount, M. K., & Judge, T. A. (2001). The FFM personality dimensions and job performance: Meta-analysis of meta-analyses. *International Journal of Selection and Assessment, 9*(1–2), 9–30.
24. Judge, T. A., Higgins, C. A., Thoresen, C. J., & Barrick, M. R. (1999). The big five personality traits, general mental ability, and career success across the life span. *Personnel Psychology, 52*(3), 621–652.
25. Barrick, M. R., & Mount, M. K. (1993). Autonomy as a moderator of the relationships between the big five personality dimensions and job performance. *Journal of Applied Psychology, 78*(1), 111–118.
26. LePine, J. A., Colquitt, J. A., & Erez, A. (2000). Adaptability to changing task contexts: Effects of general cognitive ability, conscientiousness, and openness to experience. *Personnel Psychology, 53*(3), 563–595.
27. Friedman, M., & Rosenman, R. H. (1974). *Type A behavior and your heart.* New York, NY: Knopf.
28. McLeod, S. A. (2011). *Type A personality: Simply psychology.* Retrieved from http://www.simplypyschology.org/personality-a.html
29. Friedman & Rosenman (1974).
30. Booth-Kewley, S., & Friedman. H. S. (1987). Psychological predictors of heart disease: A quantitative review. *Psychological Bulletin, 101*(3), 343–362.
31. Riggio, R. E. (2012). Are you a Type A or B personality? Cutting edge leadership. *Psychology Today.* Retrieved from http://www.psychologytoday.com/blog/cutting-edge-leadership/201206/are-you-type-or-type-or-b-personality
32. Miller, R., & Krauskopf, C. J. (1999). The personality assessment system as a conceptual framework for the Type A coronary-prone behavior pattern. *Best of Personality Assessment System Journals,* pp. 121–132.
33. Friedman, H. S., Hall, J. A., & Harris, M. J. (1985). Type A behavior, nonverbal expressive style, and health. *Journal of Personality and Social Psychology, 48*(5), 1299–1315.
34. Kobasa, S. C. (1979). Stressful life events, personality, and health: An inquiry into hardiness. *Journal of Personality and Social Psychology, 37*(1), 1–11; and Kobasa, S. C, Maddi, S. R., & Kahn, S. (1982). Hardiness and health: A prospective study. *Journal of Personality and Social Psychology, 42*(1), 168–177.
35. Uchino, B. N., Cacioppo, J. T., & Kiecolt-Glaser, J. K. (1996). The relationship between social support and physiological processes: A review with emphasis on underlying mechanisms and implications for health. *Psychological Bulletin, 119*(3), 488–531.
36. Luthans, F., Avey, J. B., Avolio, B. J., Norman, S. M., & Combs, G. M. (2006). Psychological capital development: Toward a micro-

intervention. *Journal of Organizational Behavior, 27*(3), 387–393, p. 388.

37. Luthans, F., Avolio, B. J., Avey, J. B., & Norman, S. M. (2007). Positive psychological capital: Measurement and relationships with performance and satisfaction. *Personnel Psychology, 60*(3), 541–572.

38. Luthans et al. (2007).

39. Luthans, F., Avey, J. B., Avolio, B. J., Norman, S. M., & Combs, G. M. (2006). Psychological capital development: Toward a micro-intervention. *Journal of Organizational Behavior, 27*(3), 387–393.

40. Luthans, F., & Youssef, C. M. (2004). Investing in people for competitive advantage. *Organizational Dynamics, 33*(2), 143–160.

41. Goleman, D. (1995). *Emotional intelligence: Why it can matter more than IQ.* New York, NY: Bantam Books; and Salovey, P., & Mayer, J. D. (1990). Emotional intelligence. *Imagination, Cognition, and Personality, 9*(3), 185–211.

42. Law, K. S., Wong, C. S., & Song, L. J. (2004). The construct and criterion validity of emotional intelligence and its potential utility for management studies. *Journal of Applied Psychology, 89*(3), 483–496.

43. Law et al. (2004).

44. Côté, S., & Miners, C. T. (2006). Emotional intelligence, cognitive intelligence, and job performance. *Administrative Science Quarterly, 51*(1), 1–28.

45. Bar-On, R., Handley, R., & Fund, S. (2005). The impact of emotional intelligence on performance. In V. Druskat, F. Salas, & G. Mount (Eds.), *Linking emotional intelligence and performance at work: Current research evidence* (pp. 3–20). Malwah, NJ: Lawrence Erlbaum.

46. Cavallo, K., & Brienza, D. (2004). *Emotional competence and leadership excellence at Johnson & Johnson: The emotional intelligence and leadership study.* New Brunswick, NJ: Consortium for Research on Emotional Intelligence in Organizations, Rutgers University.

47. Farh, C. I., Seo, M., & Tesluk, P. E. (2012). Emotional intelligence, teamwork effectiveness, and job performance: The moderating role of job context. *Journal of Applied Psychology, 97*(4), 890–900.

48. TalentSmart. (n.d.). About emotional intelligence. Retrieved from http://www.talentsmart.com/about/emotional-intelligence.php

49. Kirk, B. A., Schutte, N. S., & Hine, D. W. (2011). The effect of an expressive writing intervention for employees on emotional self-efficacy, emotional intelligence, affect, and workplace incivility. *Journal of Applied Social Psychology, 41*(1), 179–195; and Slaski, M., & Cartwright, S. (2003). Emotional intelligence training and its implications for stress, health, and performance. *Stress and Health, 19*(4), 233–239.

50. Schutte, N. S., Malouff, J. M., & Thorsteinsson, E. B. (2013). Increasing emotional intelligence through training: Current status and future directions. *International Journal of Emotional Education, 5*(1), 56–72.

51. Goleman, D., Boyatzis, R., & McKee, A. (2013). *Primal leadership: Unleashing the power of emotional intelligence.* Cambridge, MA: Harvard Business School Press.

52. Davies, M., Stankov, L., & Roberts, R. D. (1998). Emotional intelligence: In search of an elusive construct. *Journal of Personality and Social Psychology, 75*(4), 989–1015; Landy, F. J. (2005). Some historical and scientific issues related to research on emotional intelligence. *Journal of Organizational Behavior, 26*(4), 411–424; and Locke, E. A. (2005). Why emotional intelligence is an invalid concept. *Journal of Organizational Behavior, 26*(4), 425–431.

53. Zeidner, M., Matthews, G., & Roberts, R. D. (2004). Emotional intelligence in the workplace: A critical review. *Applied Psychology: An International Journal, 53*(3), 371–399.

54. Van Rooy, D. L., & Viswesvaran, C. (2004). Emotional intelligence: A meta-analytic investigation of predictive validity and nomological net. *Journal of Vocational Behavior, 65*(1), 71–95.

55. Cherniss, C. (1999). *The business case for emotional intelligence.* Retrieved from http://www.eiconsortium.org/reports/business_case_for_ei.html; and Cooper, R. K. (1997). Applying emotional intelligence in the workplace. *Training and Development, 51*(12), 31–33.

56. Ashkanasy, N. M., & Daus, C. S. (2002). Emotion in the workplace: The new challenge for managers. *Academy of Management Executive, 16*(1), 76–86.

57. Harrison, D. A., Price, K. H., & Bell, M. P. (1998). Beyond relational demography: Time and the effects of surface-and deep-level diversity on work group cohesion. *Academy of Management Journal, 41*(1), 96–107.

58. Harrison et al. (1998).

59. Merriam-Webster. (n.d.). Definition of affirmative action. Retrieved from https://www.merriam-webster.com/dictionary/affirmative%20action

60. U.S. Equal Employment Opportunity Commission. (n.d.). Title VII of the Civil Rights Act of 1964. Retrieved from https://www.eeoc.gov/laws/statutes/titlevii.cfm

61. Definition of affirmative action. (n.d.). *Economic Times.* Retrieved from https://economictimes.indiatimes.com/definition/affirmative-action

62. U.S. Equal Employment Opportunity Commission (n.d.).

63. *Hopwood v. Texas*, 78 F.3d 932 (5th Cir. 1996). Retrieved from https://law.justia.com/cases/federal/appellate-courts/F3/78/932/504514/

64. Heilman, M. E., Block, C. J., & Stathatos, P. (1997). The affirmative action stigma of incompetence: Effects of performance information ambiguity. *Academy of Management Journal, 40*(3), 603–625.

65. Heilman, M. E., Block, C. J., & Lucas, J. A. (1992). Presumed incompetent? Stigmatization and affirmative action efforts. *Journal of Applied Psychology, 77*(4), 536–544.

66. Rynes, S., & Rosen, B. (1995). A field survey of factors affecting the adoption and perceived success of diversity training. *Personnel Psychology, 48*(2), 247–270.

67. Pendry, L. F., Driscoll, D. M., & Field, S. C. (2007). Diversity training: Putting theory into practice. *Journal of Occupational and Organizational Psychology, 80*(1), 27–50.

68. Menttium. (2001). Bottom-line benefits of mentoring. Retrieved from http://www.menttium.com

69. Eddy, E., Tannenbaum, S., Alliger, G., D'Abate, C., & Givens, S. (2001). *Mentoring in industry: The top 10 issues when building and supporting a mentoring program.* Technical report prepared for the Naval Air Warfare Training Systems Division (Contract No. N61339-99-D-0012).

70. Olson, D. A., & Jackson, D. (2009). Expanding leadership diversity through formal mentoring programs. *Journal of Leadership Studies, 3*(1), 47–60.

71. Allen, T. D., Eby, L. T., & Lentz, E. (2006). Mentorship behaviors and mentorship quality associated with formal mentoring

programs: Closing the gap between research and practice. *Journal of Applied Psychology, 91*(3), 567–578.

72. Douglas, P. H. (2008). Affinity groups: Catalyst for inclusive organizations. *Employment Relations Today, 34*(4), 11–18, p. 14.

73. Douglas (2008).

74. Bourke, J., Garr, S., van Berkel, A., & Wong, J. (2017, March 1). Diversity and inclusion: The reality gap. Retrieved from http://www2.deloitte.com/insights/us/en/focus/human-capital-trends/2017/diversity-and-inclusion-at-the-workplace.html

75. Cox, T. H., & Blake, S. (1991). Managing cultural diversity: Implications for organizational competitiveness. *Academy of Management Executive, 5*(3), 45–56.

76. Tinsley, C. H., & Ely, R. J. (2018). What most people get wrong about men and women: Research shows the sexes aren't so different. *Harvard Business Review, 96*(3), 114–121.

77. Arnania-Kepuladze, T. (2019). Gender stereotypes and gender feature of job motivation: Differences or similarity? *Management, 8*(2). Retrieved from https://businessperspectives.org/images/pdf/applications/publishing/templates/article/assets/3227/PPM_EN_2010_02_Kepuladze.pdf

78. Balliet, D., Li, N. P., Macfarlan, S. J., & Van Vugt, M. (2011). Sex differences in cooperation: A meta-analytic review of social dilemmas. *Psychological Bulletin, 137*(6), 881–909.

79. Byrnes, J. P., Miller, D. C., & Schafer, W. D. (1999). Gender differences in risk taking: A meta-analysis. *Psychological Bulletin, 125*(3), 367–383.

80. Dwyer, P. D., Gilkeson, J. H., & List, J. A. (2002). Gender differences in revealed risk taking: Evidence from mutual fund investors. *Economics Letters, 76*(2), 151–158.

81. Stewart, J. S., Oliver, E. G., Cravens, K. S., & Oishi, S. (2017). Managing Millennials: Embracing generational differences. *Business Horizons, 60*(1), 45–54.

82. Stewart et al. (2017).

83. Hall, A. (2016). Exploring the workplace communication preferences of Millennials. *Journal of Organizational Culture, Communication and Conflict, 20*, 35–44.

84. Pînzaru, F., Vatamanescu, E. M., Mitan, A., Savulescu, R., Vitelar, A., Noaghea, C., & Balan, M. (2016). Millennials at work: Investigating the specificity of Generation Y versus other generations. *Management Dynamics in the Knowledge Economy, 4*(2), 173–192.

85. Bencsik, A., Horváth-Csikós, G., & Juhász, T. (2016). Y and Z generations at workplaces. *Journal of Competitiveness, 8*(3), 90–106.

86. Francis, T., & Hoefel, F. (2018, November). True gen: Generation Z and its implications for companies. Retrieved from https://www.mckinsey.com/industries/consumer-packaged-goods/our-insights/true-gen-generation-z-and-its-implications-for-companies

87. AMA Staff. (2019, January 24). The myth of generational differences in the workplace [Blog post]. Retrieved from https://www.amanet.org/articles/the-myth-of-generational-differences-in-the-workplace/

88. Deal, J. (2007). *Retiring the generation gap: How employees young & old can find common ground.* Greensboro, NC: Center for Creative Leadership.

89. Deal (2007).

90. Deal (2007).

91. Page, S. E. (2007). Making the difference: Applying a logic of diversity. *Academy of Management Perspectives, 21*(4), 6–20.

92. Pepsico. (n.d.). Diversity and engagement. Retrieved from http://www.pepsico.com/About/Diversity-and-Engagement

93. Joplin, J. R. W., & Daus, C. S. (1997). Challenges of leading a diverse workforce. *Academy of Management Executive, 11*(3), 32–45.

94. Gilbert, J. A., & Ivancevich, J. (2000). Valuing diversity: A tale of two organizations. *Academy of Management Executive, 14*(1), 93–105.

Chapter 10

1. Duncker, K. (1945). On problem-solving (L. S. Lees, Trans.). *Psychological Monographs, 58*(5), i–113. doi:10.1037/h0093599

2. Deci, E. L. (1972). Intrinsic motivation, extrinsic reinforcement, and inequity. *Journal of Personality and Social Psychology, 22*(1), 113; and Deci, E. L., & Ryan, R. M. (1975). *Intrinsic motivation.* New York, NY: John Wiley.

3. Ryan, R. M., & Deci, E. L. (2000). Intrinsic and extrinsic motivations: Classic definitions and new directions. *Contemporary Educational Psychology, 25*(1), 54–67.

4. Ryan & Deci (2000).

5. Locke, E. A., & Schattke, K. (2018). Intrinsic and extrinsic motivation: Time for expansion and clarification. *Motivation Science.* doi:10.1037/mot0000116

6. Nyugen, S. (2017, January 4). Results only work environment: ROWE. *WorkplacePsychology.net.* Retrieved from https://workplacepsychology.net/2017/01/04/results-only-work-environment-rowe/

7. Weinberger, M. (2015, November 17). Microsoft had a secret, genius reason for making an encyclopedia in the nineties. *Business Insider.* Retrieved from https://www.businessinsider.com/history-of-microsoft-encarta-2015-11

8. Wikipedia. (2019). History of Wikipedia. Retrieved from https://en.wikipedia.org/wiki/History_of_Wikipedia

9. Watson, T. (1994). Linking employee motivation and satisfaction to the bottom line. *CMA Magazine, 68*, 4.

10. Kanfer, R. (1990). Motivation theory and industrial and organizational psychology. In M. D. Dunnette (Ed.), *Handbook of industrial and organizational psychology* (Vol. 1, 2nd ed., pp. 75–170). Palo Alto, CA: Consulting Psychologists Press, p. 79.

11. Campbell, J. P., & Pritchard, R. D. (1976). Motivation theory in industrial and organizational psychology. In M. Dunnette (Ed.), *Handbook of industrial and organizational psychology* (pp. 63–130). Chicago, IL: Rand McNally.

12. Cerasoli, C. P., Nicklin, J. M., & Ford, M. T. (2014). Intrinsic motivation and extrinsic incentives jointly predict performance: A 40-year meta-analysis. *Psychological Bulletin, 140*(4), 980–1008.

13. Batson, C. D. (1987). Prosocial motivation: Is it ever truly altruistic? In L. Berkowitz (Ed.), *Advances in experimental social psychology* (Vol. 20, pp. 65–122). New York, NY: Academic Press.

14. Grant, A. M. (2008). Does intrinsic motivation fuel the prosocial fire? Motivational synergy in predicting persistence, performance, and productivity. *Journal of Applied Psychology, 93*(1), 48–58.

15. Lawler, E. E., & Porter, L. W. (1967). The effect of performance on job satisfaction. *Industrial Relations, 7*(1), 20–28.

16. Kuvaas, B., Buch, R., Weibel, A., Dysvik, A., & Nerstad, C. G. (2017).

Do intrinsic and extrinsic motivation relate differently to employee outcomes? *Journal of Economic Psychology, 61*, 244–258.

17. Deci, E. L. (1971). Effects of externally mediated rewards on intrinsic motivation. *Journal of Personality and Social Psychology, 18*(1), 105–115.

18. Deci, E. L., Connell, J. P., & Ryan, R. M. (1989). Self-determination in a work organization. *Journal of Applied Psychology, 74*(4), 580–590.

19. Deci, E. L., Koestner, R., & Ryan, R. M. (1999). A meta-analytic review of experiments examining the effects of extrinsic rewards on intrinsic motivation. *Psychological Bulletin, 125*(6), 627–668.

20. Maslow, A. (1954). *Motivation and personality*. New York, NY: Harper.

21. Bridgman, T., Cummings, S., & Ballard, J. A. (2019). Who built Maslow's pyramid? A history of the creation of management studies' most famous symbol and its implications for management education. *Academy of Management Learning & Education, 18*(1), 81–98.

22. Maslow, A. H. (1943). A theory of human motivation. *Psychological Review, 50*(4), 370–396.

23. Soper, B., Milford, G., & Rosenthal, G. (1995). Belief when evidence does not support theory. *Psychology & Marketing, 12*(5), 415–422.

24. Bridgman et al. (2019).

25. Wahba, M. A., & Bridwell, L. G. (1976). Maslow reconsidered: A review of research on the need hierarchy theory. *Organizational Behavior and Human Performance, 15*, 212–240.

26. Taormina, R. J., & Gao, J. H. (2013). Maslow and the motivation hierarchy: Measuring satisfaction of the needs. *American Journal of Psychology, 126*(2), 155–177.

27. McClelland, D. (1961). *The achieving society*. Princeton, NJ: Van Nostrand.

28. Miner, J. B., Smith, N. R., & Bracker, J. S. (1994). Role of entrepreneurial task motivation in the growth of technologically innovative firms: Interpretations from follow-up data. *Journal of Applied Psychology, 79*(4), 627.

29. Nikitina, A. (2010, February 20). Motivation theory. *Goal Setting Guide*. Retrieved from http://www.goal-setting-guide.com/motivation-theory.html

30. Alderfer, C. P. (1969). An empirical test of a new theory of human needs. *Organizational Behavior and Human Performance, 4*(2), 142–175.

31. Herzberg, F. M., Mausner, B., & Snyderman, B. B. (1959). *The motivation to work*. New York, NY: John Wiley.

32. Herzberg et al. (1959).

33. Vroom, V.H. (1964). *Work and motivation*. Oxford, England: John Wiley.

34. Porter, L. W., & Lawler, E. E., III. (1968). *Managerial attitudes and performance*. Homewood, IL: Irwin.

35. Locke, E. A., & Baum, J. R. (2007). Entrepreneurial motivation. In J. R. Baum, M. Frese, & R. A. Baron (Eds.), *SIOP Organizational Frontiers Series: The psychology of entrepreneurship* (pp. 93–112). Mahwah, NJ: Erlbaum.

36. Barba-Sánchez, V., & Atienza-Sahuquillo, C. (2017). Entrepreneurial motivation and self-employment: Evidence from expectancy theory. *International Entrepreneurship and Management Journal, 13*(4), 1097–1115.

37. Gatewood, E. J., Shaver, K. G., Powers, J. B., & Gartner, W. B. (2002). Entrepreneurial expectancy, task effort, and performance. *Entrepreneurship Theory and Practice, 27*(2), 187–206.

38. Hsu, D. K., Shinnar, R. S., & Powell, B. C. (2014). Expectancy theory and entrepreneurial motivation: A longitudinal examination of the role of entrepreneurship education. *Journal of Business and Entrepreneurship, 26*(1), 121–140.

39. Heneman, H. G., & Schwab, D. P. (1972). Evaluation of research on expectancy theory predictions of employee performance. *Psychological Bulletin, 78*(1), 1–9.

40. Ambrose, M. L., & Kulik, C. T. (1999). Old friends, new faces: Motivation in the 1990s. *Journal of Management, 25*(3), 231–292, p. 240.

41. Locke, E. A., & Latham, G. P. (2002). Building a practically useful theory of goal setting and task motivation: A 35-year odyssey. *American Psychologist, 57*, 705–717.

42. Veyrat, P. (2017). Examples of SMART business goals: How to set and reach them. Retrieved from https://www.heflo.com/blog/business-management/examples-of-smart-business-goals/

43. Mitchell, T. R., & Silver, W. S. (1990). Individual and group goals when workers are interdependent: Effects on task strategies and performance. *Journal of Applied Psychology, 75*(2), 185–193.

44. Kleingeld, A., van Mierlo, H., & Arends, L. (2011). The effect of goal setting on group performance: A meta-analysis. *Journal of Applied Psychology, 96*(6), 1289–1304.

45. Schweitzer, M. E., Ordóñez, L., & Douma, B. (2004). Goal setting as a motivator of unethical behavior. *Academy of Management Journal, 47*(3), 422–432.

46. Ordóñez, L. D., Schweitzer, M. E., Galinsky, A. D., & Bazerman, M. H. (2009). Goals gone wild: The systematic side effects of overprescribing goal setting. *Academy of Management Perspectives, 23*(1), 6–16.

47. Locke, E. A., & Latham, G. P. (2009). Has goal setting gone wild, or have its attackers abandoned good scholarship? *Academy of Management Perspectives, 23*(1), 17–23, p. 22.

48. Kerr, S., & Landauer, S. (2004). Using stretch goals to promote organizational effectiveness and personal growth: General Electric and Goldman Sachs. *Academy of Management Executive, 18*(4), 134–138.

49. Shaw, K. N. (2004). Changing the goal-setting process at Microsoft. *Academy of Management Executive, 18*(4), 139–142.

50. Shaw (2004), pp. 140–141.

51. Tubbs, M. E. Goal setting: A meta-analytic examination of the empirical evidence. *Journal of Applied Psychology, 71*(3), 474–483.

52. Ivancevich, J. M. & McMahon, J. T. (1982). The effects of goal setting, external feedback and self-generated feedback on outcomes variables: A field experiment. *Academy of Management Journal, 25*(2), 359–372; and Locke, E. A. (1986). Motivation through conscious goal setting. *Applied and Preventive Psychology, 5*(2), 117–124.

53. Heathfield, S. M. (2017). How to provide feedback that helps employees improve. *The Balance Careers*. https://www.thebalance.com/provide-feedback-that-has-an-impact-1916642

54. Thorndike, E. L. (1911). *Animal intelligence*. New York, NY: Macmillan.

55. Skinner, B. F. (1971). *Contingencies of reinforcement*. East Norwalk, CT: Appleton-Century-Crofts.

56. Skinner (1971).

57. Latham, G. P., & Huber, V. L. (1991). Schedules of reinforcement: Lessons from the past and issues for the future. *Journal of Organizational Behavior Management, 12*(1), 125–149.

58. Gentile, D. (2009). Pathological video-game use among youth ages 8 to 18: A national study. *Psychological Science, 20*(5), 594–602.

59. Lee, B. Y. (2017, December 24). Do you have gaming disorder? A newly recognized mental health condition. *Forbes.* https://www.forbes.com/sites/brucelee/2017/12/24/do-you-have-video-gaming-disorder-a-newly-recognized-mental-health-condition/#25fd2492316d

60. Kapp, K. M. (2012). *The gamification of learning and instruction: Game-based methods and strategies for training and education.* San Francisco, CA: John Wiley, p. 10.

61. Buckley, P. & Doyle, E. (2016). Gamification and student motivation. *Interactive Learning Environments, 24*(6), 1162–1175.

62. Pinder, C. (2008). *Work motivation in organizational behavior.* New York, NY: Psychology Press.

63. Komacki, J. L., Coombs, T., & Schepman, S. (1996). Motivational implications of reinforcement theory. In R. M. Steers, L. W. Porter, & G. Bigley (Eds.), *Motivation and work behavior* (6th ed., pp. 87–107). New York, NY: McGraw-Hill.

64. Conard, A. L., Johnson, D. A., Morrison, J. D., & Ditzian, K. (2016). Tactics to ensure durability of behavior change following the removal of an intervention specialist: A review of temporal generality within organizational behavior management. *Journal of Organizational Behavior Management, 36*(2–3), 210–253.

65. Luthans, F. (1973). *Organizational behavior: A modern behavioral approach to management.* New York, NY: McGraw-Hill.

66. Schneier, C. E. (1974). Behavior modification in management: A review and critique. *Academy of Management Journal, 17*(3), 528–548.

67. Waird, H. (1972). Why manage behavior? A case for positive reinforcement. *Human Resource Management, 11*(2), 15–20.

68. Babb, H. W., & Kopp, D. G. (1978). Applications of behavior modification in organizations: A review and critique. *Academy of Management Review, 3*(2), 281–292.

69. Buckley, M. R., Beu, D. S., Frink, D. D., Howard, J. L., Berkson, H., Mobbs, T. A., & Ferris, G. R. (2001). Ethical issues in human resources systems. *Human Resource Management Review, 1*(11), 11–29.

70. Cropanzano, R., & Stein, J. H. (2009). Organizational justice and behavioral ethics: Promises and prospects. *Business Ethics Quarterly, 19*(2), 193–233.

71. Schminke, M., Ambrose, M. L., & Noel, T. W. (1997). The effect of ethical frameworks on perceptions of organizational justice. *Academy of Management Journal, 40*(5), 1190–1207.

72. Ambrose & Kulik (1999).

73. Greenberg, J. (1990). Employee theft as a reaction to underpayment inequity: The hidden cost of pay cuts. *Journal of Applied Psychology, 75*, 561–568.

74. Blakely, G. L., Andrews, M. C., & Moorman, R. H. (2005). The moderating effects of equity sensitivity on the relationship between organizational justice and organizational citizenship behaviors. *Journal of Business & Psychology, 20*(2), 259–273; and Moorman, R. H. (1991). Relationship between organizational justice and organizational citizenship behaviors: Do fairness perceptions influence employee citizenship? *Journal of Applied Psychology, 76*, 845–855.

75. Cosier, R. A., & Dalton, D. R. (1983). Equity theory and time: A reformulation. *Academy of Management Review, 8*(2), 311–319.

76. Lind, E. A., & Tyler, T. R. (1988). *The social psychology of procedural justice.* New York, NY: Springer.

77. Gilliland, S. W., Gross, M. A., & Hogler, R. L. (2014). Is organizational justice the new industrial relations? A debate on individual versus collective underpinnings of justice. *Negotiation and Conflict Management Research, 7*(3), 155–172.

78. Ambrose, M. L., & Schminke, M. (2009). The role of overall justice judgments in organizational justice research: A test of mediation. *Journal of Applied Psychology, 94*, 491–500.

Chapter 11

1. Aggarwal, P., & O'Brien, C. L. (2008). Social loafing on group projects: Structural antecedents and effect on student satisfaction. *Journal of Marketing Education, 30*(3), 255–264.

2. Hoyt, E. (2016). The 5 students you meet in group projects. *FastWeb.* Retrieved from https://www.fastweb.com/student-life/articles/the-5-students-you-meet-in-group-projects

3. Mohrman, S. A., Cohen, S. G. & Mohrman, A. M., Jr. (1995). *Designing team-based organizations.* San Francisco, CA: Jossey-Bass, p. 39.

4. Polzer, J. T. (2003). *Leading teams.* HBS Note No. 9-403-094. Boston, MA: Harvard Business School Publishing.

5. Larson, J. R. (2009). *In search of synergy in small group performance.* New York, NY: Psychology Press, pp. 6–7.

6. Hertel, G. (2011). Synergetic effects in working teams. *Journal of Managerial Psychology, 26*(3), 176–184.

7. Gupta, P. (2009). What makes a team work? *Management and Labour Studies, 34*(4), 596–606, p. 603.

8. Hackman, J. R., & Walton, R. E. (1986). Leading groups in organizations. In P. S. Goodman & Associates (Eds.), *Designing effective work groups* (pp. 72–119). San Francisco, CA: Jossey-Bass.

9. Riorden, C. M. (2013, July 3). We all need friends at work. *Harvard Business Review.* Retrieved from https://hbr.org/2013/07/we-all-need-friends-at-work

10. Leonard, K. (2019, February 1). Examples of informal work groups. *Chron.* Retrieved from http://smallbusiness.chron.com/examples-informal-work-groups-24287.html

11. Hollenbeck, J. R., Beersma, B., & Schouten, M. E. (2012). Beyond team types and taxonomies: A dimensional scaling conceptualization for team description. *Academy of Management Review, 37*(1), 82–106.

12. Larson C. E., & LaFasto, F. M. (1989). *Teamwork: What must go right/what can go wrong.* Newbury Park, CA: Sage.

13. Cohen, S. G., & Ledford, G. E., Jr. (1994). The effectiveness of self-managing teams: A quasi-experiment. *Human Relations, 47*(1), 13–43.

14. Weldon, E., & Weingart, L. R. (1993). Group goals and group performance. *British Journal of Social Psychology, 32*(4), 307–334.

15. DeShon, R. P., Kozlowski, S. W., Schmidt, A. M., Milner, K. R., & Wiechmann, D. (2004). A multiple-goal, multilevel model of feedback effects on the regulation of individual and team performance. *Journal of Applied Psychology, 89*(6), 1035–1056.

16. Kleingeld, A., van Mierlo, H., & Arends, L. (2011). The effect of goal setting on group performance: A meta-analysis. *Journal of Applied Psychology, 96*(6), 1289–1304.

17. Meyer, C. (1994a). How the right measures help teams excel. *Harvard Business Review, 72*(3), 95–101.

18. Heathfield, S. M. (2019, January 14). How and why to create team norms. *The Balance*. Retrieved from https://www.thebalance.com/how-and-why-to-create-team-norms-1919229

19. Mathieu, J. E., & Rapp, T. L. (2009). Laying the foundation for successful team performance trajectories: The roles of team charters and performance strategies. *Journal of Applied Psychology, 94*(1), 90–103.

20. Miller, D. (2003). The stages of group development: A retrospective study of dynamic team processes. *Canadian Journal of Administrative Sciences, 20*(2), 121–143, p. 122.

21. Bonebright, D. A. (2010). 40 years of storming: a historical review of Tuckman's model of small group development. *Human Resource Development International, 13*(1), 111–120.

22. Gersick, C. J. G. (1991). Revolutionary change theories: A multilevel exploration of the punctuated equilibrium paradigm. *Academy of Management Review, 16*(1), 10–36.

23. Seers, A., & Woodruff, S. (1997). Temporal pacing in task forces: Group development or deadline pressure? *Journal of Management, 23*(2), 169–187.

24. Puscasu, A. (2019, May 23). The punctuated equilibrium model of group development. *ApePM*. Retrieved from http://apepm.co.uk/punctuated-equilibrium/

25. Van Hooft, E. A., & van Mierlo, H. (2018). When teams fail to self-regulate: Predictors and outcomes of team procrastination among debating teams. *Frontiers in Psychology, 9*, 464–482.

26. Katzenbach, J. R., & Smith, D. K. (2015). *The wisdom of teams: Creating the high-performance organization*. Cambridge, MA: Harvard Business Review Press.

27. Mathieu, J., Maynard, M. T., Rapp, T., & Gilson, L. (2008). Team effectiveness 1997–2007: A review of recent advancements and a glimpse into the future. *Journal of Management, 34*(3), 410–476.

28. Harrison, D. A., Newman, D. A., & Roth, P. L. (2006). How important are job attitudes? Meta-analytic comparisons of integrative behavioral outcomes and time sequences. *Academy of Management Journal, 49*(2), 305–325.

29. Mathieu et al. (2008).

30. Whitehurst, J. (2015, May 11). Managing performance when it's hard to measure. *Harvard Business Review*. Retrieved from https://hbr.org/2015/05/managing-performance-when-its-hard-to-measure

31. Barrick, M. B., Bradley, B. H., Kristof-Brown, A. L., & Colbert, A. E. (2007). The moderating role of top management team interdependence: Implications for real teams and working groups. *Academy of Management Journal, 50*, 544–557.

32. Gilson, L. L., & Shalley, C. E. (2004). A little creativity goes a long way: An examination of teams' engagement in creative processes. *Journal of Management, 30*, 453–470, p. 422.

33. Argote, L., Gruenfeld, D., & Naquin, C. (2001). Group learning in organizations. *Groups at Work: Theory and Research, 614*, 369–411.

34. Lankau, M. J., & Scandura, T. A. (2002). An investigation of personal learning in mentoring relationships: Content, antecedents, and consequences. *Academy of Management Journal, 45*(4), 779–790.

35. Lankau & Scandura (2002).

36. Mathieu, J. E., Tannenbaum, S. I., Kukenberger, M. R., Donsbach, J. S., & Alliger, G. M. (2015). Team role experience and orientation: A measure and tests of construct validity. *Group & Organization Management, 40*(1), 6–34.

37. Meyer, C. (1994b). How the right measures help teams excel. *The Performance Measurement, Management and Appraisal Sourcebook*, 118–126.

38. Cardinal, R. (2015). 5 steps to building an effective team. *Huffpost*. Retrieved from https://www.huffingtonpost.com/rosalind-cardinal/5-steps-to-building-an-effective-team_b_7132406.html

39. Palfini, J. (2007). Forget what you learned in grade school: Five teamwork myths. *CBS News*. Retrieved from https://www.cbsnews.com/news/forget-what-you-learned-in-grade-school-five-teamwork-myths/

40. Wright, D. (2013). *The myths and realities of teamwork*. Retrieved from https://pdfs.semanticscholar.org/074d/138a0f218fb7e38582dd170a4b974fc09621.pdf

41. Wright (2013).

42. Wright (2013).

43. Janis, I. L. (1972). *Victims of groupthink: A psychological study of foreign-policy decisions and fiascoes*. Boston, MA: Houghton-Mifflin.

44. Goncalo, J. A., Polman, E., & Maslach, C. (2010). Can confidence come too soon? Collective efficacy, conflict and group performance over time. *Organizational Behavior and Human Decision Processes, 113*(1), 13–24.

45. Esser, J. K. (1998). Alive and well after 25 years: A review of groupthink research. *Organizational Behavior and Human Decision Processes, 73*(2), 116–141.

46. Leana, C. R. (1985). A partial test of Janis' groupthink model: Effects of group cohesiveness and leader behavior on defective decision making. *Journal of Management, 11*(1), 5–18.

47. Moorhead, G., Ference, R., & Neck, C. P. (1991). Group decision fiascoes continue: Space shuttle *Challenger* and a revised groupthink framework. *Human Relations, 44*(6), 539–550.

48. Latane, B., Williams, K., & Harkins, S. (1979). Many hands make light the work: The causes and consequences of social loafing. *Journal of Personality and Social Psychology, 37*(6), 822–832, p. 822.

49. Ringelmann, M. (1913). Recherches sur les moteurs animes: Travail de rhomme [Research on animate sources of power: The work of man]. *Annales de I'lnstitut National Agronomique, 2e serie-tome XII*, 1–40.

50. Latane et al. (1979).

51. Ringelmann (1913).

52. Kravitz, D. A., & Martin, B. (1986). Ringelmann rediscovered. *Journal of Personality and Social Psychology, 50*(5), 936–941.

53. Czyż, S. H., Szmajke, A., Kruger, A., & Kübler, M. (2016). Participation in team sports can eliminate the effect of social loafing. *Perceptual and Motor Skills, 123*(3), 754–768. p. 754.

54. Czyż et al. (2016).

55. Latane et al. (1979), p. 824.

56. Aggarwal & O'Brien (2008).

57. Karau, S. J., & Williams, K. D. (1993). Social loafing: A meta-analytic review and theoretical integration. *Journal of Personality and Social Psychology, 65*(4), 681–706.

58. Aggarwal & O'Brien (2008).

59. Aggarwal & O'Brien (2008).

60. Martins, L. L., Gilson, L. L., & Maynard, M. T. (2004). Virtual teams: What do we know and where do we go from here? *Journal of Management, 30*(6), 805–835, p. 807.

61. Maynard, M. T., & Gilson, L. L. (2014). The role of shared mental

model development in understanding virtual team effectiveness. *Group & Organization Management, 39*(1), 3–32.

62. Hollingshead, A. B., McGrath, J. E., & O'Connor, K. M. (1993). Group task performance and communication technology: A longitudinal study of computer-mediated versus face-to-face work groups. *Small Group Research, 24*(3), 307–333.

63. Hollingshead, A. B., & McGrath, J. E. (1995). Computer-assisted groups: A critical review of the empirical research. In R. A. Guzzo & E. Salas (Eds.), *Team effectiveness and decision making in organizations* (pp. 46–78). San Francisco, CA: Jossey-Bass.

64. Wilson, J. M., Straus, S. G., & McEvily, B. (2006). All in due time: The development of trust in computer-mediated and face-to-face teams. *Organizational Behavior and Human Decision Processes, 99*(1), 16–33.

65. Mesmer-Magnus, J. R., & DeChurch, L. A. (2009). Information sharing and team performance: A meta-analysis. *Journal of Applied Psychology, 94*(2), 535–546.

66. Griffith, T. L., Sawyer, J. E., & Neale, M. A. (2003). Virtualness and knowledge in teams: Managing the love triangle of organizations, individuals, and information technology. *MIS Quarterly, 27*(2), 265–287.

67. Saunders, C., Van Slyke, C., & Vogel, D. R. (2004). My time or yours? Managing time visions in global virtual teams. *Academy of Management Perspectives, 18*(1), 19–37.

68. Kirkman, B. L., & Harris, T. B. (2017). *3D team leadership: A new approach for complex teams.* Stanford, CA: Stanford University Press.

69. Jarvenpaa, S. L., & Leidner, D. E. (1999). Communication and trust in global virtual teams. *Organization Science, 10*(6), 791–815.

70. Ferrazzi, K. (2014). Getting virtual teams right. *Harvard Business Review, 92*(12), 120–123.

71. Kirkman & Harris (2017).

72. Kirkman, B. L., & Shapiro, D. L. (2001). The impact of cultural values on job satisfaction and organizational commitment in self-managing work teams: The mediating role of employee resistance. *Academy of Management Journal, 44*(3), 557–569.

73. Elenkov, D. S. (1998). Can American management concepts work in Russia? *California Management Review, 40*(4), 133–156; and Nicholls, C. E.,

Lane, H. W., & Brechu, M. B. (1999). Taking self-managed teams to Mexico. *Academy of Management Executive, 13*(3), 15–25.

74. Hackman, J. R., & C. G. Morris. (1975). Group tasks, group interaction process, and group performance effectiveness: A review and proposed integration. In L. Berkowitz (Ed.), *Advances in experimental social psychology* (pp. 45–99). San Diego, CA: Academic Press.

75. Jehn (1995, 1997).

76. Amason (1996); Hollenbeck, J. R., Ilgen, D. R., Sego, D. J., Hedlund, J., Major, D. A., & Phillips, J. (1995). Multilevel theory of team decision making: Decision performance in teams incorporating distributed expertise. *Journal of Applied Psychology, 80*(2), 292–316; and Schwenk, C. (1990). Conflict in organizational decision making: An exploratory study. *Management Science, 36*(4), 436–449.

77. Behfar, K. J., Peterson, R. S., Mannix, E. A., & Trochim, W. M. K. (2008). The critical role of conflict resolution in teams: A close look at the links between conflict type, conflict management strategies, and team outcomes. *Journal of Applied Psychology, 93*(2), 170–188, p. 170.

78. De Wit, F. R. C., Greer, L. L., & Jehn, K. A. (2012). The paradox of intragroup conflict: A meta-analysis. *Journal of Applied Psychology, 97*(2), 360–390.

79. Shaw, J. D., Zhu, J., Duffy, M. K., Scott, K. L., Shih, H. A., & Susanto, E. (2011). A contingency model of conflict and team effectiveness. *Journal of Applied Psychology, 96*(2), 391–400.

80. Shaw et al. (2011), p. 398.

81. Festinger, L. (1950). Informal social communication. *Psychological Review, 57,* 271–282, p. 274.

82. Evans, C. R., & Jarvis, P. A. (1980). Group cohesion: A review and re-evaluation. *Small Group Behavior, 11,* 359–370.

83. Cartwright, D. (1968). The nature of group cohesiveness. In D. Cartwright & A. Zander (Eds.), *Group dynamics: Research and theory* (3rd ed., pp. 91–109). New York, NY: Harper & Row.

84. Gully, S. M., Devine, D. J., & Whitney, D. J. (1995). A meta-analysis of cohesion and performance: Effects of level of analysis and task interdependence. *Small Group Research, 26*(4), 497–520; and Neal, D. J., Cohen, R. R., Burke, M. J., & McLendon, C. L.

(2003). Cohesion and performance in groups: A meta-analytic clarification of construct relations. *Journal of Applied Psychology, 88*(6), 989–1004.

85. Evans, C. R., & Dion, K. L. (1991). Group cohesion and performance: A meta-analysis. *Small Group Research, 22*(2), 175–186.

86. Hogg, M. A., & Reid, S. A. (2006). Social identity, self-categorization, and the communication of group norms. *Communication Theory, 16*(1), 7–30.

87. Zey-Ferrell, M., & Ferrell, O. C. (1982). Role-set configuration and opportunity as predictors of unethical behavior in organizations. *Human Relations, 35*(7), 587–604.

88. Prentice, R. (2014). Teaching behavioral ethics. *Journal of Legal Studies Education, 31*(2), 325–365; and Wines, W. A. (2008). Seven pillars of business ethics: Toward a comprehensive framework. *Journal of Business Ethics, 79*(4), 483–499.

89. McCabe, D. L., Butterfield, K. D., & Trevino, L. K. (2006). Academic dishonesty in graduate business programs: Prevalence, causes, and proposed action. *Academy of Management Learning & Education, 5*(3), 294–305.

90. Lencioni, P. (2005). *The five dysfunctions of a team.* New York, NY: John Wiley.

91. Kelly, A. (2009). The role of the agile coach. *Agile Connection.* Retrieved from https://www.agileconnection.com/article/role-agile-coach

92. Gurchieck, K. (2016). Does your organization use internal coaches? *Society for Human Resource Management.* Retrieved from https://www.shrm.org/resourcesandtools/hr-topics/organizational-and-employee-development/pages/does-your-organization-use-internal-coaches.aspx

93. Lencioni (2005).

94. De Dreu, C. K. W., & West, M. (2001). Minority dissent and team innovation: The importance of participation in decision making. *Journal of Applied Psychology, 86*(6), 1191–1201.

95. Schwenk, C. R. (1984). Devil's advocacy in managerial decision making. *Journal of Management Studies, 21*(2), 153–168.

96. Schweiger, D. M., & Finger, P. A. (1984). The comparative effectiveness of dialectical inquiry and devil's advocacy: The impact of task biases

on previous research findings. *Strategic Management Journal, 5*, 335–350.

97. Schweiger, D. M., Sandberg, W. R., & Ragan, J. W. (1986). Group approaches for improving strategic decision making: A comparative analysis of dialectical inquiry, devil's advocacy, and consensus. *Academy of Management Journal, 29*(1), 51–70.

98. Lunenburg, F. C. (2011). Decision making in organizations. *International Journal of Management, Business, and Administration, 15*(1), 1–9.

99. Robert, H. M. (2011). *Robert's rules of order newly revised in brief.* Boston, MA: Da Capo Press.

100. *Parliamentary procedure for meetings* (n.d.). Retrieved from https://www.afsc.noaa.gov/education/activities/PDFs/SBSS_Lesson6_roberts_rules_of_order.pdf

101. Tague, N. R. (2004). *The quality toolbox* (2nd ed.). Milwaukee, WI: American Society for Quality Press.

102. Osborn, A. F. (1979). *Applied imagination: Principles and procedures of creative thinking* (3rd ed.). New York, NY: Scribner.

103. Harnett, T. (2011). *Consensus-oriented decision-making.* Gabriola Island, BC: Canada New Society Publishers.

104. Harnett (2011).

105. Faure, C. (2004). Beyond brainstorming: Effects of different group procedures on selection of ideas and satisfaction with the process. *Journal of Creative Behavior, 38*(1), 13–34.

106. Delbecq, A. L., Van de Ven, A. H., & Gustafson, D. H. (1975). *Group techniques for program planning: A guide to nominal group and Delphi processes.* Glenview, IL: Scott, Foresman.

107. Rogelberg, S. G., Barnes-Farrell, J. L., & Lowe, C. A. (1992). The stepladder technique: An alternative group structure facilitating effective group decision making. *Journal of Applied Psychology, 77*(5), 730–737.

108. Rogelberg et al. (1992).

109. Delbecq et al. (1975).

Chapter 12

1. Harvey, P., Harris, K. J., Gillis, W. E., & Martinko, M. J. (2014). Abusive supervision and the entitled employee. *The Leadership Quarterly, 25*(2), 204–217.

2. Martinko, M. J., Mackey, J. D., Moss, S. E., Harvey, P., McAllister, C. P., & Brees, J. R. (2018).

An exploration of the role of subordinate affect in leader evaluations. *Journal of Applied Psychology, 103*(7), 738.

3. Yukl, G. (2013). *Leadership in organizations* (8th ed.). Boston, MA: Pearson, p. 7.

4. Yukl (2013).

5. Yukl (2013).

6. Yukl (2013).

7. Edmondson, R. (2017). *The mythical leader: The seven myths of leadership.* Nashville, TN: HarperCollins.

8. Edmondson (2017).

9. Algahtani, A. (2014). Are leadership and management different? A review. *Journal of Management Policies and Practices, 2*(3), 71–82.

10. Edmondson (2017).

11. Deluga, R. J. (2003). Kissing up to the boss: What it is and what to do about it. *Business Forum, 26*(3), 14–18.

12. Edmondson (2017).

13. Bennis, W. (1989). *On becoming a leader.* New York, NY: Basic Books.

14. Zaleznik, A. (2004, January). Managers and leaders: Are they different? *Harvard Business Review: Best of HBR*, 74–81.

15. Taormina, R. J. (2010). The art of leadership: An evolutionary perspective. *International Journal of Arts Management, 13*(1), 41–55.

16. Carlyle, T. (2003). *On heroes, hero-worship and the heroic in history 1897.* Whitefish, MT: Kessinger Publishing.

17. Woods, F. A. (1913). *The influence of monarchs: Steps in a new science of history.* New York, NY: Macmillan.

18. Kirkpatrick, S. A., & Locke, E. A. (1991). Leadership: Do traits matter? *The Executive, 5*(2), 48–60; and Stogdill, R. M. (1974). *Handbook of leadership: A survey of theory and research.* New York, NY: Free Press.

19. Isaacson, W. (2011). *Steve Jobs.* New York, NY: Simon & Schuster.

20. Murphy, R. M. (2011, November 3). How do great companies groom talent? *Fortune.* Retrieved from http://fortune.com/2011/11/03/how-do-great-companies-groom-talent/

21. Simonton, D. K. (2006). Presidential IQ, openness, intellectual brilliance, and leadership: Estimates and correlations for 42 US chief executives. *Political Psychology, 27*(4), 511–526.

22. Inam, H. (2018, April 15). The good news for introverted leaders. *Forbes.* Retrieved from https://www.forbes.com/sites/hennainam/2018/04/15/the-good-news-for-introverted-leaders/#37d1718f192f

23. Aluja, A., Garcia, O., & Garcia, L. F. (2004). Replicability of the three, four and five Zuckerman's personality super-factors: Exploratory and confirmatory factor analysis of the EPQ-RS, ZKPQ and NEO-PI-R. *Personality and Individual Differences, 36*(5), 1093–1108.

24. Stewart, G. L., Carson, K. P., & Cardy, R. L. (1996). The joint effects of conscientiousness and self-leadership training on employee self-directed behavior in a service setting. *Personnel Psychology, 49*(1), 143–164.

25. Rottinghaus, B., & Vaughn, J. (2015). *Measuring Obama against the great presidents.* Washington, DC: Brookings Institution.

26. Gallup. (2013). Presidential approval ratings—Gallup historical statistics and trends. Retrieved from https://news.gallup.com/poll/116677/presidential-approval-ratings-gallup-historical-statistics-trends.aspx

27. Rubenzer, S. J., & Faschingbauer, T. R. (2004). *Personality, character, and leadership in the White House: Psychologists assess the presidents.* Washington, DC: Potomac Books.

28. Colbert, A. E., Judge, T. A., Choi, D., & Wang, G. (2012). Assessing the trait theory of leadership using self and observer ratings of personality: The mediating role of contributions to group success. *Leadership Quarterly, 23*(4), 670–685.

29. Judge, T. A., Bono, J. E., Ilies, R., & Gerhardt, M. W. (2002). Personality and leadership: A qualitative and quantitative review. *Journal of Applied Psychology, 87*(4), 765–780.

30. Zaccaro, S. J. (2007). Trait-based perspectives of leadership. *American Psychologist, 62*(1), 6–16.

31. Dahling, J. J., Whitaker, B. G., & Levy, P. E. (2009). The development and validation of a new Machiavellianism scale. *Journal of Management, 35*(2), 219–257; Kilduff, G. J., & Galinsky, A. D. (2016). The spark that ignites: Mere exposure to rivals increases Machiavellianism and unethical behavior. *Journal of Experimental Social Psychology, 69*, 156–162; Machiavelli, N. (1952). *The prince* (translation). New York, NY: New American Library. Originally published in 1532; Pilch, I., & Turska, E. (2015). Relationships between Machiavellianism, organizational culture, and workplace bullying: Emotional abuse from the target's and the perpetrator's perspective. *Journal of Business*

Ethics, 128(1), 83–93; and Wisse, B., & Sleebos, E. (2016). When the dark ones gain power: Perceived position power strengthens the effect of supervisor Machiavellianism on abusive supervision in work teams. *Personality and Individual Differences, 99*, 122–126.

32. Spain, S. M., Harms, P., & LeBreton, J. M. (2014). The dark side of personality at work. *Journal of Organizational Behavior, 35*(Suppl 1), S41–S60.

33. Hare, R. D. (1985). Comparison of procedures for the assessment of psychopathy. *Journal of Consulting and Clinical Psychology, 53*, 7–16.

34. Machiavelli (1952).

35. Dahling et al. (2009).

36. Pilch & Turska (2015).

37. Wisse & Sleebos (2016).

38. Cosans, C. E., & Reina, C. S. (2018). The leadership ethics of Machiavelli's prince. *Business Ethics Quarterly, 28*(3), 275–300.

39. Morf, C. C., & Rhodewalt, F. (2001). Unraveling the paradoxes of narcissism: A dynamic self-regulatory processing model. *Psychological Inquiry, 12*, 177–196.

40. Hare (1985).

41. Hare, R. D. (1999). *Without conscience: The disturbing word of the psychopaths among us.* New York, NY: Guilford.

42. Jonason, P. K., Slomski, S., & Partyka, J. (2012). The Dark Triad at work: How toxic employees get their way. *Personality and Individual Differences, 52*(3), 449–453.

43. Spurk, D., Keller, A. C., & Hirschi, A. (2016). Do bad guys get ahead or fall behind? Relationships of the dark triad of personality with objective and subjective career success. *Social Psychological and Personality Science, 7*(2), 113–121.

44. Korman, A. K. (1966). "Consideration," "initiating structure," and organizational criteria: A review. *Personnel Psychology, 19*(4), 349–361.

45. Stogdill, R. M., & Coons, A. E. (1951). *Leader behavior in description and measurement* [Research Monograph No. 88]. Columbus, OH: Ohio State University Bureau of Business Research.

46. Judge, T. A., Piccolo, R. F., & Ilies, R. (2004). The forgotten ones? The validity of consideration and initiating structure in leadership research. *Journal of Applied Psychology, 89*(1), 36–51.

47. Holloman, C. R. (1967). The perceived leadership role of military and civilian supervisors in a military setting. *Personnel Psychology, 26*, 199–210.

48. Cable, D. M., & Judge, T. A. (2003). Managers' upward influence tactic strategies: The role of manager personality and supervisor leadership style. *Journal of Organizational Behavior, 24*(2), 197–214.

49. Blake, R. R., & Mouton, J. S. (1982). A comparative analysis of situationalism and 9, 9 management by principle. *Organizational Dynamics, 10*(4), 20–43.

50. Khan, M. L., Langove, N., Shah, F. A., & Javid, M. U. (2015). The modes of conflicts and managerial leadership styles of managers. *Global Business & Management Research, 7*(2), 44–52.

51. Blake & Mouton (1982).

52. Khan et al. (2015).

53. Blake & Mouton (1982).

54. Khan et al. (2015).

55. Schriesheim, C. A., & Neider, L. L. (1996). Path-goal leadership theory: The long and winding road. *The Leadership Quarterly, 7*(3), 317–321.

56. House, R. J. (1971). A path goal theory of leader effectiveness. *Administrative Science Quarterly, 16*(3), 321–339.

57. Kerr, S., Schriesheim, C. A., Murphy, C. J., & Stogdill, R. M. (1974). Toward a contingency theory of leadership based upon the consideration and initiating structure literature. *Organizational Behavior and Human Performance, 12*(1), 62–82.

58. House (1971).

59. House, R. J., & Mitchell, T. R. (1974). Path-goal theory of leadership. *Journal of Contemporary Business, 3*(4), 81–97.

60. House (1971).

61. House, R. J. (1996). Path-goal theory of leadership: Lessons, legacy, and a reformulated theory. *The Leadership Quarterly, 7*(3), 323–352.

62. House (1971).

63. House (1996).

64. Schriesheim & Neider (1996); and Wofford, J. C., & Liska, L. Z. (1993). Path-goal theories of leadership: A meta-analysis. *Journal of Management, 19*(4), 857–876.

65. Webster, J. R., Beehr, T. A., & Christiansen, N. D. (2010). Toward a better understanding of the effects of hindrance and challenge stressors on work behavior. *Journal of Vocational Behavior, 76*(1), 68–77.

66. Doyle, A. (2019, August 24). The most important soft skills employers seek.

The Balance Careers. Retrieved from https://www.thebalancecareers.com/top-soft-skills-2063721

67. Steinard, M. (n.d.). Top seven most important soft skills to have for both interviewing and in the workplace. *Indeed.com.* Retrieved from https://www.indeed.com/career-advice/resumes-cover-letters/soft-skills

68. Noel, K. (2015). Soft skills leaders need for success. *Business Insider.* Retrieved from https://www.businessinsider.com/soft-skills-leaders-need-for-success-2016-4

69. Doyle (2019).

70. Forray, J. M. (1995). A good relationship with the boss pays off. *The Academy of Management Executive, 9*(1), 79.

71. Martin, R., Guillaume, Y., Thomas, G., Lee, A., & Epitropaki, O. (2016). Leader–member exchange (LMX) and performance: A meta-analytic review. *Personnel Psychology, 69*(1), 67–121.

72. Graen, G. B., & Uhl-Bien, M. (1995). Relationship-based approach to leadership: Development of leader-member exchange (LMX) theory of leadership over 25 years: Applying a multi-level multi-domain perspective. *The Leadership Quarterly, 6*(2), 219–247.

73. Cropanzano, R., & Mitchell, M. S. (2005). Social exchange theory: An interdisciplinary review. *Journal of Management, 31*(6), 874–900.

74. Scandura, T. A., & Graen, G. B. (1984). Moderating effects of initial leader–member exchange status on the effects of a leadership intervention. *Journal of Applied Psychology, 69*(3), 428.

75. Graen & Uhl-Bien (1995).

76. Graen & Uhl-Bien (1995).

77. Mayer, R. C., Davis, J. H., & Schoorman, F. D. (1995). An integrative model of organizational trust. *Academy of Management Review, 20*, 709–734.

78. Colquitt, J., Scott, B. A., & LePine, J. A. (2007). Trust, trustworthiness, and trust propensity: A meta-analytic test of their unique relationships with risk taking and job performance. *Journal of Applied Psychology, 92*, 909–927.

79. Rousseau, D. M., Sitkin, S. B., Burt, R. S., & Camerer, C. (1998). Not so different after all: A cross-discipline view of trust. *Academy of Management Review, 23*(3), 393–404.

80. Dirks, K. T., & Ferrin, D. L. (2002). Trust in leadership: Meta-analytic

findings and implications for research and practice. *Journal of Applied Psychology, 87*(4), 611–628.

81. Shapiro, D., Sheppard, B. H., & Cheraskin, L. (1992). Business on a handshake. *Negotiation Journal, 8*(4), 365–377.

82. Rousseau et al. (1998).

83. Shapiro et al. (1992).

84. Bhattacharya, R., Devinney, T. M., & Pillutla, M. M. (1998). A formal model of trust based on outcomes. *Academy of Management Review, 23*(3), 459–472.

85. Lewicki, R. J., & Bunker, B. B. (1996). Developing and maintaining trust in work relationships. In R. M. Kramer & T. R. Tyler (Eds.), *Trust in organizations: Frontiers of theory and research* (pp. 114–139). Thousand Oaks, CA: Sage.

86. Lewicki, R., Tomlinson, E., & Gillespie, N. (2006). Models of interpersonal trust development: Theoretical approaches, empirical evidence, and future directions. *Journal of Management, 32*(6), 991–1022.

87. van der Werff, L., & Buckley, F. (2017). Getting to know you: A longitudinal examination of trust cues and trust development during socialization. *Journal of Management, 43*(3), 742–770.

88. Scandura, T. A., & Pellegrini, E. K. (2008). Trust and leader-member exchange: A closer look at relational vulnerability. *Journal of Leadership and Organization Studies, 15*(2), 100–101.

89. Conley, R. (2011). Five steps to repairing broken trust. Retrieved from https://leadingwithtrust .com/2011/07/24/five-steps-to-repair-trust/

90. Blanchard, K., Blanchard, K., & Olmstead, C. (2013). *TrustWorks!* London, England: HarperCollins.

91. Conley, R. (2011).

92. Avolio, B. J. (2011). *Full range leadership development* (2nd ed.). Thousand Oaks, CA: Sage; Bass, B. M. (1985). *Leadership and performance beyond expectations.* New York, NY: Free Press; and Bass, B. M., & Avolio, B. J. (1990). *Transformational leadership development: Manual for the multifactor leadership questionnaire.* Palo Alto, CA: Consulting Psychologists Press.

93. Bono, J. E., & Judge, T. A. (2004). Personality and transformational and transactional leadership: A meta-analysis. *Journal of Applied Psychology, 89*(5), 901–910.

94. Avolio (2011), p. 65.

95. Bono & Judge (2004).

96. Avolio, B. J., Waldman, D. A., & Yammarino, F. J. (1991). Leading in the 1990s: The four I's of transformational leadership. *Journal of European Industrial Training, 15*(4). doi:10.1108/03090599110143366

97. Bono & Judge (2004).

98. Qu, R., Janssen, O., & Shi, K. (2015). Transformational leadership and follower creativity: The mediating role of follower relational identification and the moderating role of leader creativity expectations. *Leadership Quarterly, 26*(2), 286–299.

99. Chughtai, A., Byrne, M., & Flood, B. (2015). Linking ethical leadership to employee well-being: The role of trust in supervisor. *Journal of Business Ethics, 128*(3), 653–663.

100. Fortune Editors. (2016, March 30). The world's 19 most disappointing leaders. *Fortune.* Retrieved from http://fortune .com/2016/03/30/most-disappointing-leaders/

101. Brown, M. E., & Treviño, L. K. (2006). Ethical leadership: A review and future directions. *Leadership Quarterly, 17*(6), 595–616.

102. Mayer, D. M., Aquino, K., Greenbaum, R., & Kuenzi, M. (2012). Who displays ethical leadership, and why does it matter? An examination of antecedents and consequences of ethical leadership. *Academy of Management Journal, 55*(1), 151–171.

103. Den Hartog, D. N. (2015). Ethical leadership. *Annual Review of Organizational Psychology & Organizational Behavior, 2*(1), 409–434, p. 428.

104. Mayer, D. M., Kuenzi, M., Greenbaum, R., Bardes, M., & Salvador, R. (2009). How low does ethical leadership flow? Test of a trickle-down model. *Organizational Behavior and Human Decision Processes, 108*(1), 1–13.

105. Russell, R. F., & Stone, A. G. (2002). A review of servant leadership attributes: Developing a practical model. *Leadership & Organization Development Journal, 23*(3), 145–157.

106. George, B., Sims, P., & McLean, A. N., & Mayer, D. (2007). Discovering your authentic leadership. *Harvard Business Review,* 129–138; and Walumbwa, F., Avolio, B., Gardner, W., Wernsing, T., & Peterson, S. (2008). Authentic leadership: Development and validation of a theory-based measure. *Journal of Management, 34*(1), 89–126.

107. Kidder, R. M. (2003). *How good people make tough choices: Resolving the dilemmas of ethical living.* New York, NY: HarperCollins, p. 13.

108. Gailey, T. (2015, Spring). The servant leader: Transforming executive style. *St. Joseph's University Haub School Review.* Retrieved from https://www.sju.edu/news-events/magazines/haub-school-review/haub-school-review-spring-2015

109. Barbuto, J. E., & Wheeler, J. W. (2006). Scale development and construct clarification of servant leadership. *Group & Organization Management, 31*(3), 300–326.

110. Liden, R. C., Wayne, S. J., Zhao, H., & Henderson, D. (2008). Servant leadership: Development of a multidimensional measure and multilevel assessment. *Leadership Quarterly, 19*(2), 161–177; and Liden, R. C., Wayne, S. J., Liao, C., & Meuser, J. D. (2014). Servant leadership and serving culture: Influence on individual and unit performance. *Academy of Management Journal, 37*(5), 1434–1452.

111. Hu, J., & Liden, R. C. (2011). Antecedents of team potency and team effectiveness: An examination of goal and process clarity and servant leadership. *Journal of Applied Psychology, 96,* 851–862.

112. Owens, B. P., & Hekman, D. R. (2012). Modeling how to grow: An inductive examination of humble leader behaviors, contingencies, and outcomes. *Academy of Management Journal, 55*(4), 787–818.

113. Chiu, C. Y. C., Owens, B. P., & Tesluk, P. E. (2016). Initiating and utilizing shared leadership in teams: The role of leader humility, team proactive personality, and team performance capability. *Journal of Applied Psychology, 101*(12), 1705–1720.

114. George et al. (2007).

115. Neider, L. L., & Schriesheim, C. A. (2011). The authentic leadership inventory (ALI): Development and empirical tests. *Leadership Quarterly, 22*(6), 1146–1164.

116. Steffens, N. K., Mols, F., Haslam, S. A., & Okimoto, T. G. (2016). True to what we stand for: Championing collective interests as a path to authentic leadership. *Leadership Quarterly, 27*(5), 726–744.

117. Hoch, J. E., Bommer, W. H., Dulebohn, J. H., & Wu, D. (2016). Do ethical, authentic, and servant leadership explain variance above and beyond transformational leadership? A meta-analysis. *Journal of Management, 44*(2), 501–529.

118. Banks, G. C., McCauley, K. D., Gardner, W. L., & Guler, C. E. (2016). A meta-analytic review of authentic and transformational leadership: A test for redundancy. *The Leadership Quarterly, 27*(4), 634–652.

119. Liden et al. (2015), p. 254.

Chapter 13

1. Amazon (2018). Alexa International Expansion. Retrieved from https://www.amazon.jobs/en/teams/alexa-international-expansion

2. Rubin, B. F. (2017, October 4). Amazon spreads Echo's global reach with expansion to Asia. *CNet*. Retrieved from https://www.cnet.com/news/amazon-echo-alexa-expansion-india-japan-asia/

3. Amazon (2018).

4. Amazon (2018).

5. Rubin (2017).

6. Amazon. (2019). Alexa International Expansion. Retrieved from https://www.amazon.jobs/en/teams/alexa-international-expansion

7. Kinsella, B. (2017). Bezos says more than 20 million Amazon Alexa devices sold. Retrieved from https://voicebot.ai/2017/10/27/bezos-says-20-million-amazon-alexa-devices-sold/

8. Rubin (2017).

9. Adler, N. J. (1997). *International dimensions of organizational behavior* (3rd ed.). Cincinnati, OH: South-Western, p. 19.

10. Gelfand, M. J., Erez, M., & Aycan, Z. (2007). Cross-cultural organizational behavior. *Annual Review of Psychology, 58*, 479–514.

11. Hall, E. T. (1977). *Beyond culture*. New York, NY: Random House.

12. Language and Culture Worldwide. (2015). The cultural iceberg. Retrieved from https://www.languageandculture.com/cultural-iceberg

13. Curry, K. W. (2018, January 25). Easily confused words: Prototypical vs. stereotypical. Retrieved from https://kathleenwcurry.wordpress.com/2018/01/25/easily-confused-words-proto typical-vs-stereotypical/

14. Bryant, S. (2018). What is the difference between cultural stereotypes vs. prototypes? *Country Navigator*. Retrieved from https://countrynavigator.com/blog/cultural-intelligence/stereotypes-vs-prototypes/

15. Al Hamid, A. (2013). Retrieved from https://image.slidesharecdn.com/unit9-sensepropertiesandstereotypes-130505131838-phpapp02/95/unit-9-sense-properties-and-stereotypes-27-638.jpg?cb=1367759981

16. Bryant (2018).

17. Würtz, E. (2005). A cross-cultural analysis of websites from high-context cultures and low-context cultures. *Journal of Computer-Mediated Communication, 11*(1), article 13.

18. Shao, A. T., Bao, Y., & Gray, E. (2004). Comparative advertising effectiveness: A cross-cultural study. *Journal of Current Issues & Research in Advertising, 26*(2), 67–80.

19. Würtz (2005).

20. Würtz (2005).

21. Choi, S. M., Wei-Na, L., & Hee-Jung, K. (2005). Lessons from the rich and famous: A cross-cultural comparison of celebrity endorsement in advertising. *Journal of Advertising, 34*(2), 85–98.

22. Würtz (2005).

23. Hall, E. T. (2000). Context and meaning. *Intercultural Communication: A Reader, 9*, 34–43; and Hall, E. T., & Hall, M. R. (1990). *Understanding cultural differences*. Boston, MA: Intercultural Press.

24. Gelfand, M. J., Nishii, L. H., & Raver, J. L. (2006). On the nature and importance of cultural tightness-looseness. *Journal of Applied Psychology, 91*(6), 1225–1244.

25. Gelfand, M. J., Raver, J. L., Nishii, L., Leslie, L. M., Lun, J., Lim, B. C., . . . & Yamaguchi, S. (2011). Differences between tight and loose cultures: A 33-nation study. *Science, 332*, 1100–1104.

26. Gelfand et al. (2011), p. 1104.

27. Hofstede, G. (2011). Dimensionalizing cultures: The Hofstede model in context. *Online Readings in Psychology and Culture, 2*(1), 8, p. 3.

28. Hofstede, G., & Bond, M. H. (1988). The Confucius connection: From cultural roots to economic growth. *Organizational Dynamics, 16*(4), 5–21.

29. Hofstede & Bond (1988).

30. Hofstede, G. (1980). *Culture's consequences: International differences in work-related values*. Beverly Hills, CA: Sage.

31. Hofstede (1980).

32. Hofstede (1980).

33. Gelfand et al. (2007); and Oyserman, D., Coon, H. M., & Kemmelmeier, M. (2002). Rethinking individualism and collectivism: Evaluation of theoretical assumptions and meta-analyses. *Psychological Bulletin, 128*(1), 3–72.

34. Markus, H. R., & Kitayama, S. (1991). Culture and the self: Implications for cognition, emotion, and motivation. *Psychological Review, 98*(2), 224–253; and Triandis, H. C. (1995). *Individualism and collectivism*. Boulder, CO: Westview Press.

35. Eby, L. T., & Dobbins, G. H. (1997). Collectivistic orientation in teams: an individual and group-level analysis. *Journal of Organizational Behavior, 18*(3), 275–295; Erez, M., & Somech, A. (1996). Is group productivity loss the rule or the exception? Effects of culture and group-based motivation. *Academy of Management Journal, 39*(6), 1513–1537; and Gibson, C. B. (1999). Do they do what they believe they can? Group efficacy and group effectiveness across tasks and cultures. *Academy of Management Journal, 42*(2), 138–152.

36. Triandis, H. C., & Gelfand, M. J. (1998). Converging measurement of horizontal and vertical individualism and collectivism. *Journal of Personality and Social Psychology, 74*(1), 118–128.

37. Marcus, J., & Le, H. (2013). Interactive effects of levels of individualism-collectivism on cooperation: A meta-analysis. *Journal of Organizational Behavior, 34*(6), 813–834.

38. Chen, Y., Friedman, R., Yu, E., Fang, W., & Lu, X. (2009). Supervisor-subordinate guanxi: Developing a three dimensional model and scale. *Management and Organization Review, 5*(3), 375–399.

39. Fischer, R., & Mansell, A. (2009). Commitment across cultures: A meta-analytical approach. *Journal of International Business Studies, 40*(8), 1339–1358.

40. Michael, J. (1997). A conceptual framework for aligning managerial behaviors with cultural work values. *International Journal of Commerce and Management, 7*(3), 81–101; and Smith, P. (1998). *The new American cultural sociology*. New York, NY: Cambridge University Press.

41. Jones, M. (2007, June 24–26). *Hofstede—Culturally questionable?* Presented at the Oxford Business & Economics Conference, Oxford, England.

42. Dorfman, P. W., & Howell, J. P. (1988). Dimensions of national culture and effective leadership patterns: Hofstede revisited. *Advances in International Comparative Management, 3*, 127–150.

43. Taras, V., Kirkman, B. L., & Steel, P. (2010). Examining the impact of culture's consequences: A three-decade, multilevel, meta-analytic review of

Hofstede's cultural value dimensions. *Journal of Applied Psychology, 95*(3), 405–439.

44. Green, E. (2016). What are the most-cited publications in the social sciences according to Google Scholar? *LSE Impact Blog.* Retrieved from http://blogs.lse.ac.uk/impactofsocialsciences/2016/05/12/what-are-the-most-cited-publications-in-the-social-sciences-according-to-google-scholar/

45. Michael (1997) and Smith (1998).

46. House, R., Javidan, M., Hanges, P., & Dorfman, P. (2002). Understanding cultures and implicit leadership theories across the globe: An introduction to project GLOBE. *Journal of World Business, 37*(1), 3–10.

47. Tung, R. L., & Verbeke, A. (2010). Beyond Hofstede and GLOBE: Improving the quality of cross-cultural research. *Journal of International Business Studies, 41*(8), 1259–1274.

48. House et al. (2002).

49. Hollenbeck, G. P., & McCall, M. W. (2003). Competence, not competencies: Making global executive development work. In W. Mobley & P. Dorfman (Eds.), *Advances in global leadership* (Vol. 3). Oxford, England: JAI Press.

50. Gregersen, H. B., Morrison, A., & Black, J. S. (1998). Developing leaders for the global frontier. *Sloan Management Review, 40*, 21–32.

51. Chen, J. (2019, April 4). Multinational corporation. *Investopedia.* Retrieved from https://www.investopedia.com/terms/m/multinationalcorporation.asp

52. Bird, A., & Mendenhall, M. E. (2016). From cross-cultural management to global leadership: Evolution and adaptation. *Journal of World Business, 51*(1), 115–126, p. 117.

53. Killingsworth, B., Xue, Y., & Liu, Y. (2016). Factors influencing knowledge sharing among global virtual teams. *Team Performance Management, 22*(5/6), 284–300; O'Donnell, K., & O'Donnell, M. L. (2016). Global mental health: Sharing and synthesizing knowledge for sustainable development. *Global Mental Health (Cambridge, England), 3*, E27; and Van Loggerenberg, F., Clarke, M., Furtado, T., Boggs, L., McHugh, N., Franzen, S., & Lang, T. (2013). Introducing 'global health methodology research': A knowledge sharing platform open to all. *Trials, 14*(1), P35.

54. Bird & Mendenhall (2016).

55. Lane, H. W., Maznevski, M. L., & Mendenhall, M. E. (2004). Hercules meets Buddha. In H. W. Lane, M. L. Maznevski, M. E. Mendenhall, & J. McNett (Eds.), *The handbook of global management: A guide to managing complexity* (pp. 3–25). Oxford, England: Blackwell.

56. Stahl, G., & Brannen, M. Y. (2013). Building cross-cultural leadership competence: An interview with Carlos Ghosn. *Academy of Management Learning & Education, 12*(3), 494–502, p. 495.

57. Smith, A., Caver, K., Saslow, S., & Thomas, N. (2009). *Developing the global executive: Challenges and opportunities in a changing world.* Pittsburgh, PA: Development Dimensions International, Inc.

58. Gregersen, H., & Morrison, A. (1998). Developing leaders for the global frontier. *Sloan Management Review, 40*(1), 21–32.

59. Beechler, S., & Javidan, M. (2007). Leading with a global mindset. In M. Javidan, R. M. Steers, & M. A. Hitt (Eds.), *The global mindset (advances in international management)* (Vol. 19, pp. 131–169). New York, NY: Emerald Group Publishing.

60. Thunderbird Graduate School of Management. (2017). Measuring global mindset. Retrieved from https://thunderbird.asu.edu/knowledge-network/measuring-global-mindset-article

61. Kuada, J. (2016). *Global mindsets: Exploration and perspectives.* New York, NY: Routledge, p. 64.

62. Thunderbird Graduate School of Management (2017).

63. Parish, P. (2016). A coaching framework for developing the psychological capital of a global mindset. *International Journal of Evidence Based Coaching and Mentoring,* (S10), 172–184.

64. Thunderbird Graduate School of Management (2017).

65. Mäkelä, K., & Suutari, V. (2009). Global careers: A social capital paradox. *The International Journal of Human Resource Management, 20*(5), 992–1008.

66. Thunderbird Graduate School of Management (2017).

67. Badrinarayanan, V., Madhavaram, S. & Granot, E. (2011). Global virtual sales teams (GVSTs): A conceptual framework of the influence of intellectual and social capital on effectiveness. *Journal of Personal Selling & Sales Management, 31*(3), 311–324.

68. Earley, P. C., & Ang, S. A. (2003). *Cultural intelligence: Individual interactions across cultures.* Stanford, CA: Stanford University Press.

69. Earley, P. C., & Mosakowski, E. (2004). Cultural intelligence. *Harvard Business Review, 82*(10), 139–146.

70. Earley & Ang (2003).

71. Ang, S., Van Dyne, L., Kohl, C., Ng, K. Y., Templer, K. J., Tayl, C., & Chandrasekar, N. A. (2007). Cultural intelligence: Its measurement and effects on cultural judgment and decision making, cultural adaptation and task performance. *Management and Organization Review, 3*(3), 335–371.

72. Alexandra, V. (2018). Predicting CQ development in the context of experiential cross-cultural training: The role of social dominance orientation and the propensity to change stereotypes. *Academy of Management Learning & Education, 17*(1), 62–78.

73. Eisenberg, J., Lee, H., Bruck, F., Brenner, B., Claes, M., Mironski, J., & Bell, R. (2013). Can business schools make students culturally competent? Effects of cross-cultural management courses on cultural intelligence. *Academy of Management Learning & Education, 12*(4), 603–621.

74. Earley, P. C., & Peterson, R. S. (2004). The elusive cultural chameleon: Cultural intelligence as a new approach to training for the global manager. *Academy of Management Learning & Education, 3*(1), 100–115.

75. Patel, T., & Salih, A. (2018). Cultural intelligence: A dynamic and interactional framework. *International Studies of Management & Organization, 48*(4), 358–385.

76. Earley & Peterson (2004).

77. Patel & Salih (2018).

78. Earley & Peterson (2004).

79. Patel & Salih (2018).

80. Oberg, K. (1960). Culture shock adjustment to new cultural environments. *Practical Anthropology, 7,* 177–182.

81. Mitchell, L., & Myles, W. (2010). *Risk sense: Developing and managing international education activities with risk in mind.* Ontario, Canada: University of Guelph.

82. Archer, C. M. (1986). Culture bump and beyond. In J. M. Valdes (Ed.), *Culture bound: Bridging the cultural gap in language teaching.* Cambridge, England: Cambridge University Press.

83. Business Dictionary. (n.d.) Expatriate. Retrieved from http://www.businessdictionary.com/definition/expatriate.html

84. Kraimer, M. L., Wayne, S. J., & Jaworski, R. A. (2001). Sources of support and expatriate performance: The mediating role of expatriate adjustment. *Personnel Psychology, 54*(1), 71–99; and Shaffer, M. A., & Harrison, D. A. (1998). Expatriates' psychological withdrawal from international assignments: Work, nonwork, and family influences. *Personnel Psychology, 51*(1), 87–118.

85. Daniels, J. D., & Insch, G. (1998). Why are early departure rates from foreign assignments lower than historically reported? *Multinational Business Review, 6*(1), 13–23; Forster, N. (1997). The persistent myth of high expatriate failure rates: A reappraisal. *International Journal of Human Resource Management, 8*(4), 414–433; and Harzing, A. W. K. (1995). The persistent myth of high expatriate failure rates. *International Journal of Human Resource Management, 6*(2), 457–474.

86. Right Management. (2013). Many managers found to fail in overseas assignments. Retrieved from http://www.right.com/news-and-events/press-releases/2013-press-releases/item25142.aspx

87. Shannonhouse, R. (1996). Overseas-assignment failures. *USA Today/International Edition*, p. 8; and Torbiörn, I. (1994). Operative and strategic use of expatriates in new organizations and market structures. *International Studies of Management & Organization, 24*(3), 5–17.

88. Harrison, J. (1994). Developing successful expatriate managers: A framework for the structural design and strategic alignment of cross-cultural training programs. *Human Resource Planning, 17*, 17–35; and Kotabe, M., & Helsen, K. (1998). *Global marketing management* (2nd ed.). New York, NY: John Wiley.

89. Nowak, C., & Linder, C. (2016). Do you know how much your expatriate costs? An activity-based cost analysis of expatriation. *Journal of Global Mobility, 4*(1), 88–107.

90. Forster (1997).

91. Andresen, M., Biemann, T., & Pattie, M. W. (2015). What makes them move abroad? Reviewing and exploring differences between self-initiated and assigned expatriation. *The International Journal of Human Resource Management, 26*(7), 932–947.

92. Presbitero, A., & Quita, C. (2017). Expatriate career intentions: Links to career adaptability and cultural intelligence. *Journal of Vocational Behavior, 98*, 118–126.

93. Zhang, Y., & Oczkowski, E. (2016). Exploring the potential effects of expatriate adjustment direction. *Cross Cultural & Strategic Management, 23*(1), 158–183.

94. Ramaswami, A., Carter, N. M., & Dreher, G. F. (2016). Expatriation and career success: A human capital perspective. *Human Relations, 69*(10), 1959–1987.

95. Kraimer et al. (2001).

96. Van Vianen, A. E., De Pater, I. E., Kristof-Brown, A. L., & Johnson, E. C. (2004). Fitting in: Surface-and deep-level cultural differences and expatriates' adjustment. *Academy of Management Journal, 47*(5), 697–709.

97. Grobbel, M. (2015). Managers on the move: An exclusive look at expat executives. *Experteer.com*. Retrieved from https://us.experteer.com/magazine/managers-on-the-move-an-exclusive-look-at-expat-executives/

98. Linton, I. (2017, September 26). The importance of expatriates in organizations. *Bizfluent*. Retrieved from https://bizfluent.com/info-12072421-importance-expatriates-organizations.html

99. Grobbel (2015).

100. Worldwide ERC. (n.d.). Intercultural tools. Retrieved from https://www.worldwideerc.org/intercultural-tools/

101. Grobbel (2015).

102. Mendenhall, M., & Oddou, G. (1986). Acculturation profiles of expatriate managers: Implications for cross-cultural training programs. *Columbia Journal of World Business, 21*(4), 73–79.

103. Black, J. S. & Gregerson, H. (1999, March/April). The right way to manage expatriates. *Harvard Business Review*, 52–60.

104. Black & Gregerson (1999).

105. Böhm, C. (2013). Cultural flexibility in ICT projects: A new perspective on managing diversity in project teams. *Global Journal of Flexible Systems Management, 14*(2), 115–122.

106. Black & Gregerson, (1999).

107. Känsälä, J. (2016). Expatriate families as expat performance facilitators. OSUVA Open Archives, University of Vaasa.

108. Gregersen & Black (1990).

109. Feldman, D. C., & Thomas, D. C. (1992). Career issues facing expatriate managers. *Journal of International Business Studies, 23*(2), 271–294.

110. Mezias, J. M., & Scandura, T. A. (2005). A needs-driven approach to expatriate adjustment and career development: A multiple mentoring perspective. *Journal of International Business Studies, 36*(5), 519–538.

111. Black, J. S., & Mendenhall, M. (1990). Cross-cultural training effectiveness: A review and theoretical framework for future research. *Academy of Management Review, 15*(1), 113–136.

112. Adler, N. J. (1981). Re-entry: Managing cross-cultural transitions. *Group & Organization Studies, 6*(3), 341–356.

113. Dolins, I. L. (1999). 1998 global relocation survey: Current trends regarding expatriate activity. *Employment Relations Today, 25*(4), 1–11.

114. Gaw, K. F. (2000). Reverse culture shock in students returning from overseas. *International Journal of Intercultural Relations, 24*(1), 83–104; and Hsiaoying, T. (1995). Sojourner adjustment: The case of foreigners in Japan. *Journal of Cross-Cultural Psychology, 26*(5), 523–536.

115. Feldman, D. C., & Tompson, H. B. (1992). Entry shock, culture shock: Socializing the new breed of global managers. *Human Resource Management, 31*(4), 345–362.

116. Black, J. S., & Gregersen, H. B. (1992). When Yankee comes home: Factors related to expatriate and spouse repatriation adjustment. *Journal of International Business Studies, 22*(4), 671–695; and Black, J. S., Gregersen, H. B., & Mendenhall, M. E. (1992). *Global assignments: Successfully expatriating and repatriating international managers*. San Francisco, CA: Jossey-Bass.

117. Gregersen, H. B., & Black, J. S. (1990). A multifaceted approach to expatriate retention in international assignments. *Group & Organization Management, 15*(4), 461–485.

118. Black, J. S., & Stephens, G. K. (1989). The influence of the spouses on American expatriate adjustment in overseas assignments. *Journal of Management, 15*(4), 529–544.

119. Adler, N. J. (2008). *International dimensions of organizational behavior* (5th ed.). Mason, OH: Thomson.

120. Gregersen, H. B., & Black, J. S. (1992). Antecedents to commitment to a parent company and a foreign operation. *Academy of Management Journal, 35*(1), 65–90.

121. Javidan, M., Dorfman, P. W., De Luque, M. S., & House, R. J. (2006). In the eye of the beholder: Cross cultural lessons in leadership from project GLOBE. *Academy of Management Perspectives*, *20*(1), 67–90.

122. Conner, J. (2000, Summer–Fall). Developing the global leaders of tomorrow. *Human Resource Management*, *39*(2–3), 146–157.

123. Black, J. S., Gregersen, H. B., Mendenhall, M., & Stroh, L. K. (1999). *Globalizing people through international assignments*. New York, NY: Addison-Wesley, p. 1.

124. KPMG. (2006). Status quo und Perspektiven im deutschen Lebensmitteleinzelhandel. Retrieved from http://www.kpmg.de/library/pdf/060904_Status_quo_und_Perspektiven_im_deutschen_Lebensmitteleinzelhandel_2006_de.pdf

125. Rundschau, F. (2007). Ende einer Expansion. Retrieved from http://www.lexisnexis.de/e-solutions/academic/de/index.html

126. DW Business. (2006). World's biggest retailer Walmart closes up shop in Germany. Retrieved from http://www.dw-world.de/dw/article/0,2144,2112746,00.html

127. Lebensmittel Zeitung. (2006). Walmart in Deutschland – ein Überblick. Retrieved from http://www.lznet.de/links/hotlinks/pages/protected/show53679.html

128. Senge, K. (2004). Der Fall Walmart: Institutionelle Grenzen ökonomischer Globalisierung. Retrieved from http://www.wiso.unidortmund.de/is/dienst/de/textonly/content/V4/V42/pdf/ap-soz04.pdf

129. Senge (2004).

130. Verdi (2008). Retrieved from http://international.verdi.de/ver.di_fremdsprachig/was_ist_ver.di_-_eine_einfuehrung_auf_englisch

131. ShareAlike 4.0 International, (2015). Case, example of product failure: Walmart in Germany, 1997 to 2006. CC BY-SA 4.0. Retrieved from http://www.opentextbooks.org.hk/ditatopic/7191

132. ShareAlike 4.0 International (2015).

133. Thunderbird Graduate School of Management (2017).

Chapter 14

1. My Accounting Course. (n.d.). Budgetary control. Retrieved from https://www.myaccountingcourse.com/accounting-dictionary/budgetary-control

2. WSJ Opinion. (2019, April 23). What your college isn't teaching you. *Wall Street Journal*. Retrieved from https://www.wsj.com/articles/what-your-college-isnt-teaching-11556057975

3. Garrison, R. H., Noreen, E., & Brewer, P. (2000). *Managerial accounting* (12th ed.). New York, NY: McGraw-Hill.

4. Institute of Management and Administration. (2001). 20 best-practice budgeting insights: How controllers promote faster, better decisions. *The Controller's Report*, *11*, 1–1, 17.

5. Bragg, S. (2018a, February 8). The advantages of budgeting? *Accounting Tools*. Retrieved from https://www.accountingtools.com/articles/what-are-the-advantages-of-budgeting.html

6. Bragg (2018a).

7. Accountingverse.com (n.d. a). What is responsibility accounting? Retrieved from https://www.accountingverse.com/managerial-accounting/responsibility-accounting/what-is-responsibility-accounting.html

8. Bragg (2018a).

9. Accountingverse.com (n.d. a).

10. Zimmerman, J. L. (2003). *Accounting for decision making and control* (4th ed.). New York, NY: McGraw-Hill.

11. Merriam-Webster.com. (n.d.). Bottom line. Retrieved from https://www.merriam-webster.com/dictionary/bottom-line

12. Shim, J. K., Siegel, J. G., & Shim, A. I. (2012). The what and why of budgeting: An introduction. In *Budgeting basics and beyond* (pp. 1–27). Hoboken, NJ: John Wiley.

13. Shim et al. (2012).

14. Shim et al. (2012).

15. Kagan, J. (2019). Cash budget. *Investopedia*. Retrieved from https://www.investopedia.com/terms/c/cashbudget.asp

16. Boundless.com (n.d.). The forecasting budget. Retrieved from http://oer2go.org/mods/en-boundless/www.boundless.com/finance/textbooks/boundless-finance-textbook/forecasting-financial-statements-4/building-a-cash-budget-52/the-forecast-budget-249-3817/index.html

17. Accounting Coach (n.d.). What is a fixed budget? Retrieved from https://www.accountingcoach.com/blog/what-is-a-fixed-budget

18. Shim et al. (2012).

19. Woodruff, J., & Thompson, J. (2019, March 4). The advantages of a flexible budget. *Chron*. Retrieved from https://smallbusiness.chron.com/advantages-flexible-budget-57105.html

20. Woodruff & Thompson (2019).

21. Bragg, S. (2018b, April 2). Capital expenditure budget. *Accounting Tools*. Retrieved from https://www.accountingtools.com/articles/capital-expenditure-budget.html

22. Shim et al. (2012).

23. VanBaren, J. (2017, September 26). Definition of a program budget. *Bizfluent*. Retrieved from https://bizfluent.com/facts-7639427-definition-program-budget.html

24. Shim et al. (2012).

25. Simplestudies. (n.d.). What are the budget types in accounting? Retrieved from http://simplestudies.com/what-are-budget-types-in-accounting.html/page/2

26. Shim et al. (2012).

27. Simplestudies (n.d.).

28. Shim et al. (2012).

29. Simplestudies (n.d.).

30. Shim et al. (2012).

31. Raye, K. (n.d.). What is the difference between a budget and a rolling budget? *Chron*. Retrieved from https://smallbusiness.chron.com/difference-between-budget-rolling-budget-65435.html

32. Shim et al. (2012).

33. Raye (n.d.).

34. Lee, F., Stroud, N., Laster, J., & Yakhou, M. (2005). Budget practices case studies. *Managerial Auditing Journal*, *20*(2), 171–178.

35. Colville, I. (1989). Scenes from a budget: Helping the police with their accounting enquiries. *Financial Accountability & Management*, *5*(2), 89.

36. Marshall, D. (n.d.). Lesson 6: Financial statements. *Bean Counter*. Retrieved from http://www.dwmbeancounter.com/tutorial/lesson06.html

37. Marshall (n.d.).

38. Business Dictionary. (n.d.). Income statement. Retrieved from http://www.businessdictionary.com/definition/income-statement.html

39. Marshall (n.d.).

40. Marshall (n.d.).

41. Marshall (n.d.).

42. Murray, J. (2019, January 3). Understanding cost of goods sold (cost of sales). *The Balance Small Business*. Retrieved from https://www.thebalancesmb.com/cost-of-goods-sold-398161

43. Marshall (n.d.).

44. Intuit. (n.d.). The true cost of paying an employee. *QuickBooks Resource Center*.

Retrieved from https://quickbooks. intuit.com/r/hr-laws-and-regulation/ the-true-cost-of-paying-an-employee/

45. Shelton, C. (2019). The true costs of hiring a new employee. *FitSmallBusiness*. Retrieved from https:// fitsmallbusiness.com/employer-payroll-taxes/

46. Intuit. (n.d.).

47. Pant, P. (2019, March 12). What's the difference between fixed and variable expenses? *The Balance*. Retrieved from https://www.thebalance.com/what-s-the-difference-between-fixed-and-variable-expenses-453774

48. Corporate Finance Institute. (n.d.). Budget and forecasting course: Types of budgets. Retrieved from https:// corporatefinanceinstitute.com/ resources/knowledge/accounting/types-of-budgets-budgeting-methods/

49. Corporate Finance Institute (n.d.).

50. Webb Pressler, M. (2011, September 8). What was 9/11? *Washington Post*. Retrieved from https://www.washingtonpost.com/lifestyle/style/what-was-911/2011/08/31/gIQAQL5RDK_story.html?noredirect=on&utm_term=.0110a35c6b22

51. Davis, M. (2017, September 11). How September 11 affected the U.S. stock market. *Investopedia*. Retrieved from https://www.investopedia.com/financial-edge/0911/how-september-11-affected-the-u.s.-stock-market.aspx

52. Davis, M. (2019, June 25). The impact of 9/11 on business. *Investopedia*. Retrieved from https://www.investopedia.com/financial-edge/0911/the-impact-of-september-11-on-business.aspx

53. Corporate Finance Institute (n.d.).

54. Santosuosso, P. (2013). Integration of ethical values into activity-based budgeting. *Journal of Business and Management*, 8(20), 1–13.

55. Corporate Finance Institute (n.d.).

56. Corporate Finance Institute (n.d.). C BY-SA

57. Taylor, A. (2011, November 4). Zero-based budgeting on steroids. *The Artful Manager*. Retrieved from https://www.artsjournal.com/artfulmanager/main/zero-based_budgeting_on_steroi.php

58. Taylor (2011).

59. Williams, P. (n.d. a). Zero-based vs. incremental budgeting. *Lumen Learning*. Retrieved from https:// courses.lumenlearning.com/wm-retailmanagement/chapter/zero-based-vs-incremental-budgeting/

60. Williams, P. (n.d. b). The ongoing budget process. *Lumen Learning*. Retrieved from https:// courses.lumenlearning.com/wm-retailmanagement/chapter/ongoing-budgeting-process/

61. Parayitam, S., & Papenhausen, C. (2018). Strategic decision-making. *Management Research Review*, 41(1), 2–28.

62. Bettner, M. S. (2014). *Using accounting and financial information: Analyzing, forecasting & decision-making*. New York, NY: Business Expert Press.

63. Accountingverse.com. (n.d. b). Add or drop a product line (or segment). Retrieved from https://www.accountingverse.com/managerial-accounting/relevant-costing/add-or-drop.html

64. Library of Economics and Liberty. (n.d.). Opportunity cost. *EconLib*. Retrieved from https://www.econlib.org/library/Topics/College/opportunitycost.html

65. Hutchinson, E. (2016). Exercise 1.2 in Module 1.2: Opportunity costs and sunk costs. In *Principles of microeconomics*. OpenStax Economics, Principles of Economics. OpenStax CNX. Retrieved from https:// pressbooks.bccampus.ca/uvicecon103/chapter/1-2-opportunity-costs-sunk-costs/

66. Boyd, K. (n.d.). Special orders in cost accounting. *Dummies.com*. Retrieved from https://www.dummies.com/business/accounting/a-collection-of-mastering-australian-payroll-with-xero-in-a-day-images/

67. Freedom Learning Group. (n.d. a). Special order decisions. *Lumen Learning*. Retrieved from https:// courses.lumenlearning.com/wm-accountingformanagers/chapter/special-order-decisions/

68. Freedom Learning Group. (n.d. b). Constrained resource. *Lumen Learning*. Retrieved from https:// courses.lumenlearning.com/wm-accountingformanagers/chapter/constrained-resources-in-retail/

69. Jarris, P., Leider, J., Resnick, B., Sellers, K., & Young, J. (2012). Budgetary decision making during times of scarcity. *Journal of Public Health Management and Practice*, 18(4), 390–392.

70. Partnoy, F. (2012, July 21). The cost of a human life, statistically speaking. Adapted from *Wait: The art and science of delay* (Public Affairs).

Retrieved from http://www.theglobalist.com/the-cost-of-a-human-life-statistically-speaking/; and Wikipedia. (n.d.). Professionalism/valuing of human life in risk analysis. Retrieved from https://en.wikibooks.org/wiki/Professionalism/Valuing_of_Human_Life_in_Risk_Analysis

71. Luthra, S. (2019, April 29). Is insulin's high cost keeping diabetes patients from taking their medicine? *Kaiser Health News*. Retrieved from https://khn.org/news/is-insulins-high-cost-keeping-diabetes-patients-from-taking-their-medicine/

72. CNN. (2019). Transcript from "CNN Hosts a Town Hall with Sen. Kamala Harris (D-CA) Presidential Candidate (Aired April 22, 2019, 10-11p ET)." *CNN*. Retrieved from http://www.cnn.com/TRANSCRIPTS/1904/22/se.04.html

73. American Diabetes Association. (2018a). Statistics about diabetes. Retrieved from https://www.diabetes.org/resources/statistics/statistics-about-diabetes

74. Luthra (2019).

75. American Diabetes Association. (2018b). Insulin affordability survey. Retrieved from http://main.diabetes.org/dorg/PDFs/2018-insulin-affordability-survey.pdf

76. T1 International. (2019). The USA insulin price crisis. Retrieved from https://www.t1international.com

77. Luthra (2019).

78. Luthra (2019).

79. Luthra (2019).

80. Sharma, R. (2019, July 6). Adam Smith: The father of economics. *Investopedia*. Retrieved from https://www.investopedia.com/updates/adam-smith-economics/.

81. Partnoy (2012).

82. Santosuosso (2013).

83. Google. (n.d.). Careers in budget control search terms. Retrieved from https://www.google.com/search?q=careers+in+budget+control&oq=careers+in+budget+control&aqs=chrome..69i57j33l2.5099j0j7&sourceid=chrome&ie=UTF-8&ibp=htl;jobs&sa=X&ved=2a-hUKEwiFq-bc9IzlAhVNq1kKHYxvBTMQiYsCKAF6BAgGEBA#fpstate=tldetail&htidocid=cwuJFHsIAcBhtxMsAAAAAA%3D%3D&htivrt=jobs

84. O*NET OnLine. (2019). Summary report for: 11-3031.01 - Treasurers and Controllers. Retrieved from https://www.onetonline.org/link/summary/11-3031.01

85. O*NET OnLine (2019).

86. Rice University. (2018). Ethical decision-making and prioritizing stakeholders. In *Business ethics* (module 3.3). Retrieved from https://openstax.org/details/books/business-ethics

87. Walker, K. B., & Fleischman, G. M. (2013). Toeing the line: The ethics of manipulating budgets and earnings. *Management Accounting Quarterly, 14*(3), 18–24.

88. Patricia, C. D., & Wier, B. (2005). Cultural and ethical effects in budgeting systems: A comparison of U.S. and Chinese managers. *Journal of Business Ethics, 60*(2), 159–174.

89. Bragg, S. (2019, July 15). Budgetary slack. *Accounting Tools.* Retrieved from https://www.accountingtools.com/articles/what-is-budgetary-slack.html

90. Harvey, M. E. (2015). The effect of employee ethical ideology on organizational budget slack: An empirical examination and practical discussion. *Journal of Business & Economics Research, 13*(1), 83.

91. Ashe-Edmunds, S. (n.d.). Disadvantages of manager bonuses in companies. *Chron.* Retrieved from https://smallbusiness.chron.com/disadvantages-manager-bonuses-companies-64960.html

92. Stevens, D. E. (2002). The effects of reputation and ethics on budgetary slack. *Journal of Management Accounting Research, 14*, 153–171.

93. Stevens (2002).

94. Walker & Fleischman (2013).

95. Walker & Fleischman (2013).

96. Santosuosso (2013).

97. Shim et al. (2012).

98. Kesselheim, A. S., Avorn, J., & Sarpatwari, A. (2016). The high cost of prescription drugs in the United States: Origins and prospects for reform. *JAMA, 316*(8), 858–871.

99. Gosk, S. (2013). The high cost of prescription drugs. *YouTube.* Retrieved from https://www.youtube.com/watch?v=DheVxefnbD4

100. Editors of AARP. (2017, April). Why drugs cost so much. *AARP Bulletin.* Retrieved from https://www.aarp.org/content/dam/aarp/health/healthy-living/2017/04/drug-prices-download-final.pdf

101. Kesselheim et al. (2016).

102. Chua, K. P., & Conti, R. M. (2017). Out-of-pocket spending among commercially insured patients for epinephrine autoinjectors between 2007 and 2014. *JAMA Internal Medicine, 177*(5), 736–739; and Rapaport, L.

(2017). Another look at the surge in EpiPen costs. *Reuters Health News.* Retrieved from https://www.reuters.com/article/us-health-epipen-costs-idUSKBN16Y24O

103. Bose, S. (2017, August 29). The high cost of prescription drugs in the United States. *HuffPost.* Retrieved from https://www.huffpost.com/entry/the-high-cost-of-prescription-drugs-in-the-united-states_b_59a606aae4b0d81379a81c1f

104. Hub Staff Report. (2017, April 3). Examining the rising costs of prescription drugs in the U.S. and possible alternatives. *Johns Hopkins Magazine.* Retrieved from https://hub.jhu.edu/2017/04/03/drug-pricing-health-policy-expert-gerard-anderson/

105. Bose (2017).

106. WebMD. (n.d.). What conditions does isoproterenol Hcl solution treat? Retrieved from https://www.webmd.com/drugs/2/drug-13986/isoproterenol-injection/details/list-conditions

107. Bose (2017); and Fox, E. (2017, April 6). How pharma companies game the system to keep drugs expensive. *Harvard Business Review.* Retrieved from https://hbr.org/2017/04/how-pharma-companies-game-the-system-to-keep-drugs-expensive

108. O*NET OnLine. (2019). Budget analysts. Retrieved from https://www.onetonline.org/link/summary/13-2031.00

Chapter 15

1. Ashe-Edmunds, S. (2019, March 5). How organizational control is important to organizational performance. *Chron Small Business.* Retrieved from http://smallbusiness.chron.com/organizational-control-important-organizational-performance-76209.html

2. Kyriazoglou, J. (n.d.). A new business controls framework for the 21st century. Retrieved from https://www.managementexchange.com/sites/default/files/media/posts/documents/jk-business_controls_framework.pdf

3. Vărzaru, A. A. (2015). Design and implementation of a management control system. *Finanţe: Provocările Viitorului, 1*(17), 195–200.

4. Ladislav, S. (2015). The concept of management control system and its relation to performance measurement. *Procedia Economics and Finance, 25*, 141–147.

5. Malmi, T., & Brown, D.A. (2008). Management control systems as a package—Opportunities, challenges and research directions, *Management Accounting Research, 19*(4), 287–300.

6. Grabner, I., Posch, A., & Wabnegg, M. (2018). Materializing innovation capability: A management control perspective. *Journal of Management Accounting Research, 30*(2), 163–185.

7. Lambarki, T. (n.d. a). The control process. *Lumen Learning.* Retrieved from https://courses.lumenlearning.com/wm-principlesofmanagement/chapter/the-control-process/

8. Lambarki (n.d. a).

9. Lambarki (n.d. a).

10. Gartenstein, D., & Thompson, J. (2019). The importance of strategic evaluation. *Chron.* Retrieved from https://smallbusiness.chron.com/importance-strategic-evaluation-13127.html

11. Lambarki, T. (n.d. b). Introduction to levels and types of control. *Lumen Learning.* Retrieved from https://courses.lumenlearning.com/wm-principlesofmanagement/chapter/introduction-to-levels-and-types-of-control/

12. Wright, C. (2008). The IT regulatory and standards handbook. *Science Direct.* Retrieved from https://www.sciencedirect.com/topics/computer-science/operational-control

13. Lambarki (n.d. b).

14. Boundless.com (n.d.). Strategic, tactical, and operations control. Retrieved from http://oer2go.org/mods/en-boundless/www.boundless.com/management/textbooks/boundless-management-textbook/control-8/types-of-control-62/strategic-tactical-and-operational-control-313-3960/index.html

15. Lambarki (n.d. b).

16. Lambarki (n.d. b).

17. Lambarki (n.d. b).

18. Lambarki, T. (n.d. c). Introduction to the need for a balanced scorecard. *Lumen Learning.* Retrieved from https://courses.lumenlearning.com/wm-principlesofmanagement/chapter/introduction-to-the-balanced-scorecard/

19. Balanced Scorecard Institute (n.d.). What is the balanced scorecard? Retrieved from https://www.balancedscorecard.org/BSC-Basics/About-the-Balanced-Scorecard

20. Balanced Scorecard Institute (n.d.).

21. Bain & Company. (2017, updated). Top 10 management tools. Retrieved from

http://www2.bain.com/management_tools/BainTopTenTools/2017/default.asp

22. Gallo, A. (2014, October 29). The value of keeping the right customers. *Harvard Business Review*. Retrieved from https://hbr.org/2014/10/the-value-of-keeping-the-right-customers

23. Associated Press. (2006). Fannie Mae manipulated accounting. Corporate scandals. *NBC News*. Retrieved from http://www.nbcnews.com/id/12923225/ns/business-corporate_scandals/t/report-fannie-mae-manipulated-accounting/#.XRqCgpNKhVI

24. Balanced Scorecard Institute (n.d.).

25. Bain (2017).

26. Acharjya, D. P., & Kauser, A. P. (2016). A survey on big data analytics: Challenges, open research issues and tools. *International Journal of Advanced Computer Science and Applications*, *7*(2). Retrieved from http://dx.doi.org/10.14569/IJACSA.2016.070267

27. Red Hat, Inc. (2019). What is big data? *Opensource.com*. Retrieved from https://opensource.com/resources/big-data

28. Red Hat, Inc. (2019).

29. Rossi, R. L., & Grifantini, R. M. (2018). Big data: Challenge and opportunity for translational and industrial research in healthcare. *Frontiers in Digital Humanities*, *5*, 13. Retrieved from https://www.frontiersin.org/articles/10.3389/fdigh.2018.00013/full

30. Big Data Framework. (n.d. a) The 4 characteristics of big data. *BigDataFramework.org*. Retrieved from https://www.bigdataframework.org/four-vs-of-big-data/

31. Rossi & Grifantini (2018).

32. Rossi & Grifantini (2018).

33. Big Data Framework (n.d. a).

34. Rossi & Grifantini (2018).

35. Big Data Framework (n.d. a).

36. Roberts, L. (n.d.). The history of video surveillance: From VCR's to eyes in the sky. *WE-C-U Surveillance-History of Video Surveillance and CCTV*. Retrieved from http://www.wecusurveillance.com/cctvhistory

37. Big Data Framework. (n.d. b). Data types: Structured vs. unstructured data. *BigDataFramework.org*. Retrieved from https://www.bigdataframework.org/data-types-structured-vs-unstructured-data/

38. Big Data Framework (n.d. b).

39. Big Data Framework (n.d. b).

40. Steele, H. (2018). 10 highest paying data science careers. *BusinessStudent.com*. Retrieved from https://www.businessstudent.com/careers/highest-paying-data-science-careers/

41. Red Hat, Inc. (2019).

42. Rossi & Grifantini (2018).

43. Redwood Algorithms. (2017, January 27). Big data simplified. Retrieved from https://www.redwoodalgorithms.com/ra-perspectives/2017/8/30/big-data-simplified

44. Red Hat, Inc. (2019).

45. Red Hat, Inc. (2019).

46. Redwood Algorithms (2017); and Cloudera. (2016). Apache Spark Market Survey 2016. Retrieved from https://www.cloudera.com/content/dam/www/marketing/resources/presentations/cloudera_infographic_taneja-spark.pdf.landing.html

47. Red Hat, Inc. (2019).

48. Red Hat, Inc. (2019).

49. CreativeCommons.org. (n.d.). CC BY 4.0. Retrieved from https://creativecommons.org/licenses/by/4.0/

50. Google. (n.d.). CC license search. Retrieved from https://www.google.com/search?as_rights=(cc_publicdomain|cc_attribute|cc_sharealike|cc_nonderived).-(cc_noncommercial)&q=fair%20use&hl=

51. Open Source Initiative. (2018). History of the OSI. Retrieved from https://opensource.org/history

52. Kilimci, Z. H., Akyuz, A. O., Uysal, M., Akyokus, S., Uysal, M. O., Atak Bulbul, B., & Ekmis, M. A. (2019). An improved demand forecasting model using deep learning approach and proposed decision integration strategy for supply chain. *Complexity*, 2019, 9067367. Retrieved from https://doi.org/10.1155/2019/9067367

53. Kilimci et al. (2019).

54. Kilimci et al. (2019).

55. Principles for Digital Development. (n.d.). Be data driven. Retrieved from https://digitalprinciples.org

56. Brynjolfsson, E., Hitt L. M., & Kim H. H. (2011). Strength in numbers: How does data-driven decisionmaking affect firm performance? *SSRN Working Paper*. Retrieved from https://papers.ssrn.com/sol3/papers.cfm?abstract_id=1819486

57. Brynjolfsson et al. (2011).

58. Kwon, O., Lee, N. & Shin, B. (2014). Data quality management, data usage experience and acquisition intention of big data analytics. *International Journal of Information Management*, *34*(3), 387–394. Retrieved from https://doi.org/10.1016/j.ijinfomgt.2014.02.002

59. Krasadakis, G. (2017). The data-driven corporation. *The Innovation Machine*. Retrieved from https://medium.com/innovation-machine/the-data-driven-corporation-259b5b84f9c9

60. Klatt, T., Schlaefke, M., & Moeller, K. (2011) Integrating business analytics into strategic planning for better performance. *Journal of Business Strategy*, *32*(6), 30–39. Retrieved from https://doi.org/10.1108/02756661111180113

61. LaValle, S., Lesser, E., Shockley, R., Hopkins, M. S., & Kruschwitz, N. (2011). Big data, analytics and the path from insights to value. *MIT Sloan Management Review*, *52*(2), 21. Retrieved from http://tarjomefa.com/wp-content/uploads/2017/08/7446-English-TarjomeFa.pdf

62. LaValle et al. (2011).

63. Davenport, T. (2013). Telling a story with data. Communicating effectively with analytics. *Deloitte Insights*. Retrieved from https://www2.deloitte.com/insights/us/en/deloitte-review/issue-12/telling-a-story-with-data.html

64. Davenport (2013).

65. Principles for Digital Development (n.d.).

66. Securities and Exchange Commission. (2018a). Report of investigation pursuant to Section 21(a) of the Securities Exchange Act of 1934 regarding certain cyber-related frauds perpetrated against public companies and related internal accounting controls requirements. Retrieved from https://www.sec.gov/litigation/investreport/34-84429.pdf

67. FBI. (2018, May 7). 2017 Internet Crime Report, at 12 and 21. Retrieved from https://pdf.ic3.gov/2017_IC3Report.pdf ("FBI Internet Crime Report"). The FBI defines business email compromise as "a sophisticated scam targeting businesses that often work with foreign suppliers and/or businesses and regularly perform wire transfer payments," and includes frauds impacting both private and public companies; FBI. (2017, May 4). Public service announcement: E-mail account compromise the 5 billion dollar scam. Retrieved from https://www.ic3.gov/media/2017/170504.aspx ("FBI PSA"); see also Proofpoint. (2018, February 12). 2017 email fraud threat report, at 3. Retrieved from https://www.proofpoint.com/sites/default/files/pfpt-us-tr-email-fraud-yir-180212.pdf (finding that by the fourth quarter of 2017, nearly 89%

of all organizations were targeted by at least one attack, over a 13% increase from the fourth quarter of 2016).

68. Securities and Exchange Commission (2018a).

69. FBI (2018), at 12, 21.

70. 2 15 U.S.C. § 78m(b)(2)(B)(i) & (iii).

71. The issuers with these Section 13(b)(2) obligations are those that have a class of securities registered with the Commission under Section 12 of the Exchange Act or that must file reports with the Commission under Section 15(d) of the Exchange Act. 15 U.S.C. § 78m(b)(6). Also the level of reasonable assurances required under these provisions is defined as such "degree of assurance as would satisfy prudent officials in the conduct of their own affairs." 15 U.S.C. § 78m(b)(7).

72. U.S. Senate. (1977). S. Rep. No. 95–114, at 8 ("1977 Senate Report"); see also Promotion of the Reliability of Financial Information and Prevention of the Concealment of Questionable or Illegal Corporate Payments and Practices, Exchange Act Release No. 15570, at 6 (February 15, 1979) (adopting release) ("An equally important objective of the new law . . . is the goal of corporate accountability.").

73. Securities and Exchange Commission (2018a).

74. Council of Economic Advisers (2018, February). The cost of malicious cyber activity to the U.S. economy, at 6. Retrieved from https://www.whitehouse.gov/wp-content/uploads/2018/03/The-Cost-of-Malicious-Cyber-Activity-to-the-U.S.-Economy.pdf ("Council of Economic Advisers Report") ("That said, every firm is a potential target, independent of its age, size, sector, location, or employee composition.").

75. Securities and Exchange Commission (2018a).

76. FBI (2018), at 12, 21.

77. Securities and Exchange Commission (2018a).

78. FBI (2018), at 12, 21.

79. Securities and Exchange Commission (2018a).

80. FBI (2018), at 12, 21.

81. FBI (2018), at 12, 21.

82. Securities and Exchange Commission. (2018b). Commission Statement and Guidance on Public Company Cybersecurity Disclosures, at 2 (Feb. 21, 2018). Retrieved from https://www.sec.gov/rules/interp/2018/33-10459 .pdf ("Commission Statement on Cybersecurity Disclosures"); see also World Economic Forum. (2018, January 17). The Global Risks Report 2018, at 6. Retrieved from http://www3.weforum.org/docs/WEF_GRR18_Report.pdf ("World Economic Forum Report") (identifying cyberattacks as one of the top five global risks in terms of likelihood).

83. Securities and Exchange Commission (2018b), at 18. 5.

84. 15 U.S.C. § 78m(b)(2)(B)(i) & (iii).

85. U.S. Senate (1977), at 8.

86. World Economic Forum (2018), at 14 ("Attacks are increasing, both in prevalence and disruptive potential.").

87. FBI (2018), at 12 ("In 2017, the IC3 received 15,690 BEC/EAC complaints with adjusted losses of over $675 million"); and FBI (2017). PSA ("The BEC/EAC scam continues to grow, evolve, and target small, medium, and large businesses. Between January 2015 and December 2016, there was a 2,370% increase in identified exposed losses."). These figures include losses sustained by private or public companies, and so are not limited to those with securities registered under Section 12 of the Exchange Act or those that must file reports under Section 15(d) of the Exchange Act.

88. See, e.g., Statement of Policy Regarding the Foreign Corrupt Practices Act of 1977, 46 *Federal Register* 11544, at 11547 (January 29, 1981) ("[W]hen discovery and correction expeditiously follow, no failing in the company's internal accounting system would have existed. To the contrary, routine discovery and correction would evidence its effectiveness.").

89. See U.S. Senate (1977), at 8 (". . . management must exercise judgment in determining the steps to be taken, and the cost incurred, in giving assurance that the objectives expressed, will be achieved."); Council of Economic Advisers (2018), at 45 ("Private firms are ultimately in the best position to figure out the most appropriate sector- and firm-specific cybersecurity practices.").

90. Ciullo, F., Mocanu, D., Baronchelli, A., Gonçalves, B., Perra, N., & Vespignani, A. (2012a). Beating the news using social media: The case study of *American Idol. EPJ Data Science, 1,* 8; and Reuben. (2016). Idol analytics: *American Idol* predictions, statistics, and analysis. Retrieved from http://idolanalytics.com/

91. Ciulla, F., Mocanu, D., Baronchelli, A., Gonçalves, B., Perra, N., & Vespignani, A. (2012b). Beating the news using social media: The case study of *American Idol. arXiv,* 1205.4467. Retrieved from https://arxiv.org/abs/1205.4467

92. Ciulla et al. (2012a).

93. Ciulla et al. (2012a).

Appendix

1. Katzell, R. A., & Austin, J. T. (1992). From then to now: The development of industrial-organizational psychology in the United States. *Journal of Applied Psychology, 77,* 803.

2. Derksen, M. (2014). Turning men into machines? Scientific management, industrial psychology, and the "human factor". *Journal of the History of the Behavioral Sciences, 50*(2), 148–165.

3. Gilbreth, F. B. (1911). *Motion study: A method for increasing the efficiency of the workman.* New York, NY: D. Van Nostrand Company.

4. Mayer, J. D. (2016). *The elements of mental tests.* New York, NY: Momentum Press.

5. Derksen (2014).

6. Barquet, N., & Domingo, P. (1997). Smallpox: The triumph over the most terrible of the ministers of death. *Annals of Internal Medicine, 127*(8_Part_1), 635–642; and Gauch, H. G. (2003). *Scientific method in practice.* Cambridge, England: Cambridge University Press.

7. Viaene, S., & Van den Bunder, A. (2011). The secrets to managing business analytics projects. *MIT Sloan Management Review, 53*(1), 65.

8. Carpini, J., Parker, S., & Griffin, M. (2017). A Look back and a leap forward: A review and synthesis of the individual work performance literature. *Academy of Management Annals, 11*(2), 825–885.

9. Palmer, D., Dick, B., & Freiburger, N. (2009). Rigor and relevance in organization studies. *Journal of Management Inquiry, 18*(4), 265–272.

10. Rindfleisch, A., Malter, A. J., Ganesan, S., & Moorman, C. (2008). Cross-sectional versus longitudinal survey research: Concepts, findings, and guidelines. *Journal of Marketing Research, 45*(3), 261–279.

11. Spector, P. E., & Meier, L. L. (2014). Methodologies for the study of organizational behavior processes: How to find your keys in the dark. *Journal*

of Organizational Behavior, 35(8), 1109–1119.

12. Spector & Meier (2014).

13. Chan, D. (2009). So why ask me? Are self-report data really that bad? In C. E. Lance & R. J. Vandenberg (Eds.), *Statistical and methodological myths and urban legends: Doctrine, verity and fable in the organizational and social sciences* (pp. 309–336). New York, NY: Routledge/ Taylor & Francis Group.

14. Akinola, M. (2010). Measuring the pulse of an organization: Integrating physiological measures into the organizational scholar's toolbox. *Research in Organizational Behavior, 30,* 203–223.

15. Akinola (2010).

16. Chittaranjan, G., Blom, J., & Gatica-Perez, D. (2013). Mining large-scale smartphone data for personality studies. *Personal and Ubiquitous Computing, 17*(3), 433–450.

17. Moore, J., Mountford-Zimdars, A., & Wiggans, J. (2013). *Contextualized admissions: Examining the evidence.* Cheltenham, England: Supporting Professionalism in Admissions Programme.

18. Boliver, V., Gorard, S., & Siddiqui, N. (2015). Will the use of contextual indicators make UK higher education admissions fairer? *Education Sciences, 5*(4), 306–322.

19. Shermis, M. D., & Burstein, J. (Eds.). (2013). *Handbook of automated essay evaluation: Current applications and new directions.* London, England: Routledge.

20. Douglas, S. P., & Samuel Craig, C. (2011). The role of context in assessing international marketing opportunities. *International Marketing Review, 28*(2), 150–162; and Rutz, O. J., & Trusov, M. (2011). Zooming in on paid search ads—A consumer-level model calibrated on aggregated data. *Marketing Science, 30*(5), 789–800.

INDEX

Google, 53, 110
  flexible organization structure at, 165
  Hangouts, 415
  Home devices by, 396
  mission and vision statement at, 134–135
  team coaches at, 347
Gore, Al, 15
Graphic rating scale, 241
"Great man" theory of leadership, 370
Groups versus teams, *329*, 329–330
Groupthink, 340–341
Growth mindset, 271
Growth-need strength, 185
"Gut feelings," 42

Halo error, 242
"Hard Side of Change Management, The," 112
Hard strategic human resource management
  (HRM), 252
Harris, Kamala, 453–454
Harvard Business Review, 14, 112, 271, 369
Hawthorne effect, 8
Hawthorne studies, 8–9
Headlee, Celeste, 195
Head movements, 210
Health and personality, 270, 272
Heredity and personality, 267–268
Hershatter, Andrea, 166
Herzberg, Frederick, 304
Hesse, Hermann, 385
Heuristics, 43, *44*
Hierarchy of authority, 166
Hierarchy of needs, 9, 300–301, *301*
High-context cultures, *399*, 399–400
High-performance teams, 335, *335*
Hindsight bias, 44–45
Hiring decisions, 35
Hofstede, Geert, 401, 402–404, *403*
Honesty, *24*
Horizontal communication, *211*, 213–214
Horizontal loading, 186
How Good People Make Tough Choices, 85
Hoyt, Elizabeth, 327
Hsieh, Tony, 103, 104
Hubris, 45
Human capital, 234
Human capital analytics, *50*
Human capital management (HCM), 234
Human life, cost of, 452–454
Human relations in competing values
  framework, 101–102, *102*
Human resource management (HRM)
  artificial intelligence in, 229–230
  automated systems for, 232
  compensation function of, 239–246, *241,
    242, 244, 245*
  defined, 231
  formerly known as personnel
    management, 236
  functions of, 231, 236–237
  versus management, *232*, 232–233
  managerial implications of, 254–255
  myths about, 235–236
  outsourcing of, 236
  performance management and
    (*see* performance management)
  staffing function of, 237–239, *238*
  strategic, 251–254, *253*
  time spent on legal and compliance issues in,
    234, *234*, 236
  training and (*see* Training and development)
Human Side of Enterprise, The, 9, 10
Humble leadership, 386

Hutchinson, Emma, 448
Hygienes, 304–306, *305, 306*

Idealized influence, 384
Identification-based trust (IBT), 381, *381*
IKEA, 207
I-knew-it-all-along effect, 44
*Imagine It Forward: Courage, Creativity, and the
  Power of Change,* 115–116
Imitate the majority heuristic, 43, *44*
Imitate the successful heuristic, 43, *44*
Immelt, Jeffrey, 416, *416*
Impoverished management, *374*, 376
Impression management, 106
Inattention to results in teams, *346*, 348
Incentive myth of creativity, *49*
Income statements, 439, *439*
  understanding, 440–442, *442*
Inconvenient Truth, An, 15
Incremental budgeting, *435*, 437, *443*,
  443–444, 445–446
Independence ethical climate, 77, *77*
Individuality, 274–275
Individualized consideration, 384
Individuals
  decision-making by, 265–266
  emotional intelligence (EI) in, 273–274
  personality in, 267–272, *268, 270*
  on team projects, 327–328
Informal teams, 330, *330*
Information function of managers, 4
Information managerial roles, *16*, 17
In-group, 380
Innovation and risk taking, 100
Innovative organization, *173*, 174–175
Innovator's Dilemma, The, 14
*In Search of Excellence: Lessons from America's
  Best Run Companies,* 11
Inspirational motivation, 384
Instagram, 205
Instrumental ethical climate, 77, *77*
Instrumentality in expectancy theory, 306
Insulin, 453–454
Integration, 176
Intellectual capital, global, 408
Intellectual stimulation, 384
Intelligence gap, 149
Interactional justice, 318, *318*
Internalized moral perspective, 386
Internal processes in competing values
  framework, 101–102, *102*
InterNations, 413
Interpersonal managerial roles, *16*, 16–17
Intrinsic motivation, *48*, 48–49, 298
  increasing prosocial motivation, 300
Intrinsic rewards, 300–301
Intuit, 285
Intuition, 39, 40–41, *41*
  benefits of, 42
  versus common sense, *42*
Invisible students, 327
IQ, *370*, 370–371
Isaacson, Walter, 70, 370

Jargon, 200
Javidan, Mansour, 407–408
Job characteristics theory (JCT),
  184–185, *185*
Job-crafting, 186–188
Job design, 184–185, *185*
  redesign and, 186, *186*
Job enrichment, 186
Job redesign, 186, *186*

Job rotation, 186
Jobs, Steve, 69–70, *169*, 370
Job(s)
  characteristics of, 185, *185*
  definition of, 184
Job sharing, 245
Journey to the East, 385
Judgment, *24*
Jung, Carl, 268

Kahneman, Daniel, 39
Kaiser Health News, 452
Kaiser Permanente, 285
Kawasaki, Guy, 135, 137
Kidder, Rushworth M., 85
Kilimci, Z. H., 485–486
Kirkpatrick model, 248, *249*
Knowledge, skills, and abilities (KSAs), 231
Knowledge-based trust (KBT), 381, *381*
Knowledge management, 147
  communication networks in, 214, 216,
    216, 217
  defined, 211
  downward communication in, *211*, 212
  external communication in, 214
  horizontal communication in, *211*,
    213–214
  knowledge transfer within organizations and,
    216–217
  upward communication in, *211*, 212–213
Knowledge transfer, 13, 216–217
Kohlberg, Lawrence, 73–76
Kübler-Ross, Elizabeth, 119
Kuhlman, Tom, 15

Lack of commitment in teams, *346*, 347–348
Laissez-faire attitude, 467
Language, culture-specific, 109–110
Language barriers to effective communication,
  200–201, *201*
Law and code ethical climate, 77, *77*
Law of effect, 311–312
Leader managerial role, *16*, 17
Leader-member exchange (LMX), 379–380, *380*
  trust in, *381*, 382
Leadership
  authentic, 386–387
  contemporary approaches to, 384–387, *386*
  contingency, 376–377, *377*
  defined, 366–367
  effective, 365
  ethical, 77–79, 385
  full-range model of, 15, 383
  humble, 386
  managerial implications of, 387
  myths about, 367
  role of relationships in, 378–380, *380*
  servant, 385–386, *386*
  traits of, 369–373
  transactional, 383–384, *385*
  transformational, 15, 383–384, *384*
  trust and, 380–383, *381, 382*
Leadership, 15
Leadership and the New Science, 151–152
Leadership behaviors, *374*, 374–376
Leaders versus managers, 367–369, *368*
Leading in the management process, 6, 6–7
Learning
  about diversity, 277–278
  from others, 13
  from past experience, 12
  team, *336*, 336–337
Learning organization, *11*, 11–13